W0010045

THE LIFE AND TIMES OF THE GREAT COMPOSERS

1,000 YEARS OF CLASSICAL MUSIC

The Life and Times of the Great Composers

1,000 Years of Classical Music

FOREWORD
VLADIMIR ASHKENAZY

INTRODUCTION
Dr DOROTTYA FABIAN

MILLENNIUM HOUSE

First published in 2009 as *Musica* by
Millennium House Pty Ltd
52 Bolwarra Road, Elanora Heights
NSW, 2101, Australia

ISBN: 978-1-921209-49-9
ISBN: 978-1-921209-76-5 (Cased)

This publication and arrangement
© Millennium House Pty Ltd
Text © Millennium House Pty Ltd 2009
Maps © Millennium House Pty Ltd 2009

Reprinted 2010

All rights reserved. Without limiting the rights under
copyright reserved above, no part of this publication
may be reproduced, stored in or introduced into a
retrieval system, or transmitted, in any form or by
any means (electronic, mechanical, photocopying,
recording or otherwise), without the prior written
permission of the copyright owner and publisher
of this book.

The moral rights of all contributors have
been asserted.

Every effort has been made to ensure that the information presented in this volume is accurate and correct at
the time of printing, however, the publisher cannot be
held responsible for errors and omissions.

SALES
For all sales, please contact:
Millennium House Pty Ltd
52 Bolwarra Road, Elanora Heights
NSW, 2101, Australia
Ph: (612) 9970 6850 Fax: (612) 9913 3500
Email: info@millenniumhouse.com.au
Website: www.millenniumhouse.com.au

Printed in China by Sing Cheong Printing Co Ltd
Color Separation by Pica Digital Pte Ltd, Singapore

AUTHORS
Millennium House would be happy to receive submissions from authors. Please send brief submissions to:
editor@millenniumhouse.com.au

PHOTOGRAPHERS and ILLUSTRATORS
Millennium House would be happy to receive
submissions from photographers or illustrators.
Please send submissions to:
editor@millenniumhouse.com.au

FRONT COVER: A conductor interprets an orchestral
work and directs the musical performance.

BACK COVER: A nineteenth-century painting by Josef
Danhauser (1805–1845) depicting Franz Liszt at the
piano. With him are George Sand, Alexandre Dumas,
Victor Hugo, Nicolò Paganini, Gioachino Rossini,
and Marie d'Agoult.

ENDPAPERS: One of Johann Sebastian Bach's earliest
handwritten manuscripts, dated c. 1700. The notes
were found in the Herzogin Anna Amalia Bibliothek
in Weimar, Germany.

PAGE 1: A nineteenth-century cartoon of Norwegian
composer Edvard Grieg on the conductor's podium.

PAGES 2–3: *Adagio appassionato*, painted in 1904 by
French artist Albert Maignan (1845–1908).

PAGES 4–5: A nineteenth-century engraving of the
French violinist and conductor Edouard Colonne
(1838–1910) conducting a choir.

PAGES 10–11: Leo Baker, Jake Alder-Falconer, and
Milo Harries (as the boys) with Jonathan Lemalu
(as Papageno) in the 2004 Glyndebourne Opera
production of Mozart's opera *The Magic Flute*.

PAGES 12–13: A painting entitled *Ravel's "Bolero"*
by Australian artist Arnold Shore (1897–1963).

PUBLISHER
Gordon Cheers

ASSOCIATE PUBLISHER
Janet Parker

ART DIRECTOR
Stan Lamond

PROJECT MANAGER
Loretta Barnard

SPECIAL ADVISOR
Dr Dorottya Fabian

CONTRIBUTORS
Vladimir Ashkenazy, Dr Jennifer Butler,
Dr David Brennan, Dr Denis Collins,
Dr Prudence Dunstone, Dr Patrick Fairfield,
Beau Golden, Dr Rachel Hocking, Dr Robert
Hoskins, Denise Imwold, Megan Lang,
Dr Peter McCallum, Dr Edward Maclary,
Dr Nancy November, Simon Parkin, Dr John
Peterson, Dr Michael Remson, Christine
Ryder, Christopher Sears, Richard Toop,
Dr Richard Witts, Dr Massimo Zicari

DESIGNERS
Stan Lamond
Lena Lowe

COVER DESIGN
Stan Lamond

EDITORS
Loretta Barnard
Denise Imwold
Heather Jackson

PICTURE RESEARCH
Loretta Barnard
Kathy Lamond

CARTOGRAPHER
Warwick Jacobson

MAP EDITORS
Heather Jackson
Jan Watson

INDEX
Tricia Waters

PRODUCTION
Simone Russell
Bernard Roberts

PRODUCTION ASSISTANT
Michelle Di Stefano

EARTH is an epic publishing feat never to be repeated, proudly created by Millennium House

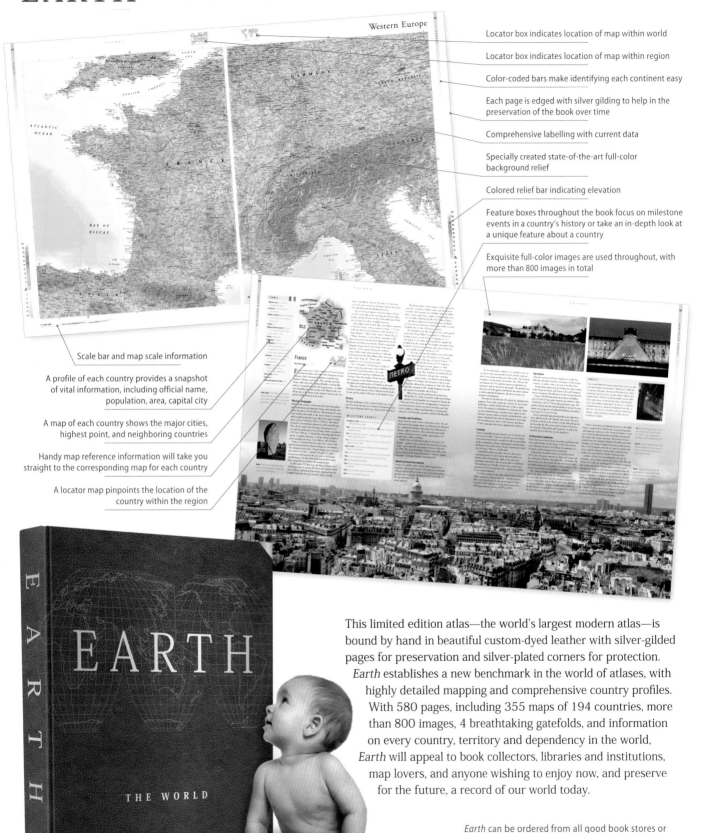

Locator box indicates location of map within world

Locator box indicates location of map within region

Color-coded bars make identifying each continent easy

Each page is edged with silver gilding to help in the preservation of the book over time

Comprehensive labelling with current data

Specially created state-of-the-art full-color background relief

Colored relief bar indicating elevation

Feature boxes throughout the book focus on milestone events in a country's history or take an in-depth look at a unique feature about a country

Exquisite full-color images are used throughout, with more than 800 images in total

Scale bar and map scale information

A profile of each country provides a snapshot of vital information, including official name, population, area, capital city

A map of each country shows the major cities, highest point, and neighboring countries

Handy map reference information will take you straight to the corresponding map for each country

A locator map pinpoints the location of the country within the region

This limited edition atlas—the world's largest modern atlas—is bound by hand in beautiful custom-dyed leather with silver-gilded pages for preservation and silver-plated corners for protection. *Earth* establishes a new benchmark in the world of atlases, with highly detailed mapping and comprehensive country profiles. With 580 pages, including 355 maps of 194 countries, more than 800 images, 4 breathtaking gatefolds, and information on every country, territory and dependency in the world, *Earth* will appeal to book collectors, libraries and institutions, map lovers, and anyone wishing to enjoy now, and preserve for the future, a record of our world today.

Earth can be ordered from all good book stores or contact Millennium House for your nearest supplier

www.millenniumhouse.com.au

Special Advisor

Associate Professor Dorottya Fabian holds a BMus (Hon) in musicology from the Liszt Academy of Music, Budapest, and an MMus and PhD from the University of New South Wales, Sydney. After a brief period working in music journalism in her native Hungary, and on various research projects in Australia, she took up a position at the University of New South Wales where she has been lecturing in musicology and musicianship. Her main research interest is European music history and performance styles on sound recordings. Her approach combines historical–analytical investigations with experimental examination of listeners' perceptions. Dr Fabian's recent book on twentieth-century Bach performance and the early music movement was published by Ashgate. Dr Fabian has been national secretary of the Musicological Society of Australia and is currently associate editor of its flagship journal. Apart from academic work, she enjoys writing CD liner notes and giving public lectures at music festivals.

Contributors

Vladimir Ashkenazy is one of the most renowned and revered pianists of our times and has a comprehensive recording catalog, with releases including the 1999 Grammy-award winning Shostakovich *24 Preludes and Fugues*, Rautavaara's *Piano Concerto No. 3* (which he commissioned), and Rachmaninov transcriptions. His latest releases include Bach's *Wohltemperierte Klavier* and Beethoven's *Diabelli Variations*. He has been conducting for the past two decades. Vladimir Ashkenazy was Chief Conductor of the Czech Philharmonic from 1998 to 2003, Music Director of the NHK Symphony Orchestra in Tokyo 2004–2007, and is Conductor Laureate of the Philharmonia Orchestra, Music Director of the European Union Youth Orchestra, and Conductor Laureate of the Iceland Symphony Orchestra. He maintains strong links with other major orchestras including the Cleveland Orchestra (where he was formerly Principal Conductor), San Francisco Orchestra, Deutsches Symphonie Orchester (Chief Conductor and Music Director 1988–1996), and the Berlin Philharmonic. He is currently Principal Conductor and Artistic Advisor to the Sydney Symphony.

Dr David Brennan has appeared for Australian national and state opera companies in major roles including Don Giovanni, Don Alfonso (*Cosi Fan Tutte*), Count Almaviva (*Le Nozze di Figaro*), Escamillo (*Carmen*), Sharpless (*Madama Butterfly*), and more than 50 other principal roles, as well as numerous concert appearances. He has appeared in several stage works that feature the music of Henry Purcell, including *King Arthur* and *Don Quixote*. He has also been a voice teacher and opera director. In 2006 he obtained his doctorate from the University of Newcastle, Australia, for his thesis on performing and acting in opera.

Dr Jennifer Butler completed her undergraduate degree at the Queensland Conservatorium and her PhD on nineteenth-century Russian opera and literature at the University of New South Wales. Her study inspired her to live in various parts of Russia for two years. She has written liner notes for Decca and Deutsche Grammophon, and reviews of Mariinsky Theater productions for *The Moscow Times*. Her hobbies include languages, literature, and slowly sightreading her way through the piano repertoire— Bach is a particular favorite. From time to time she plays badminton. She currently lives in Melbourne, where she teaches English.

Dr Denis Collins is a musicologist with interests in early music, especially Italian and English composition and music theory of the sixteenth and seventeenth centuries. He has published around two dozen articles in Australian, North American, and European journals, and his critical edition of Elway Bevin's music treatise, originally printed in 1631, was published by Ashgate in 2007. He is a senior lecturer at the University of Queensland in Brisbane where he teaches courses in music history and theory as well as occasional electives in Irish music.

Singer and teacher **Dr Prudence Dunstone** studied at the Elder Conservatorium in Adelaide, and later in London and New York. She has a PhD in musical research from the University of Newcastle, Australia. She has performed many principal roles with opera companies including the State Opera of South Australia and the Australian Opera. Highlights have included the title role in Handel's *Ariodante*, Katisha in *The Mikado*, and Ulrica in *Un Ballo in Maschera*. She has made recital broadcasts for the Australian Broadcasting Corporation, and sung as a soloist with ABC orchestras, the Sydney Philharmonia Choirs, the Adelaide Chamber Orchestra, and the Christchurch Symphony Orchestra, among many others.

Dr Patrick Fairfield holds degrees in music history, music theory, and women's studies from the University of Ottawa (BMus), the Eastman School of Music (MA), and Brandeis University (MFA, PhD). He has served on the faculties of the Eastman School of Music, Brandeis University, the Longy School of Music, the University of Miami, and the University of Toledo. He has presented conference papers for the Society for American Music and the American Musicological Society. His research interests include music history pedagogy and the intersection of contemporary critical theory, musicology, and gender studies.

Beau Golden is a music educator, performer, and composer. He earned a Bachelor of Music Bachelor of Education, majoring in jazz piano, from the University of New South Wales, Australia. A multi-instrumentalist, he teaches piano and lower brass, and regularly performs with a range of musicians in a range of musical genres. Beau is an avid collector of musical instruments, among them an assortment of early model electronic keyboards.

Dr Rachel Hocking is a pianist, pipe organist, and musicologist. She works with the Music Council of Australia assisting in research, advocacy, and the promotion and dissemination of music within the Australian music community and industry. Rachel regularly contributes to the *Music Forum*, a publication of the MCA. Her research areas have included music training and education, church music, and Australian compositions for dance; she has presented and published her research in academic and industry forums. Rachel also lectures in music at the University of New South Wales and has served as National Secretary for the Musicological Society of Australia.

Dr Robert Hoskins is an Associate Professor of Music at Massey University, New Zealand. He is the series editor of a number of musical projects that aim to promote New Zealand music, and has written three books on colonial balladry. A specialist in eighteenth-century English music, he has contributed to *Grove, New Grove, New Grove Opera, The Blackwell History of Music in Britain, Die Musik in Geschichte und Gegenwart,* and two volumes for *Music for London Entertainment 1600–1800.* Other publications include a book on Samuel Arnold (1740–1802), an edition of the 1777 score of *Polly,* sequel to *The Beggar's Opera,* and a collection of the Pacific writings of Robert Louis Stevenson.

Denise Imwold is a writer and editor from Sydney, Australia, who also worked for many years as a bookseller. She earned a BA in English literature and a Postgraduate Diploma in Editing and Publishing from Macquarie University, Sydney. Denise has contributed to a wide range of publications in fields such as arts and entertainment, history, travel, sport, gardening, health, and spirituality. Recent titles include *Cut!—Hollywood Murders, Accidents, and Other Tragedies* (2005); *501 Must-Read Books* (2006); *Historica* (2006); and *Historica's Women* (2007). She enjoys reading, walking, swimming, traveling, and animals.

Born in Tasmania, **Megan Lang** completed a Bachelor of Music in flute at the University of Adelaide in 1993. Subsequently moving to Frankfurt a.M., Germany to continue her studies, she enjoyed many years of playing in professional orchestras, as well as teaching flute, chamber music, and English. Megan returned to Australia in 2005 and began focusing on period flutes and academic research into performing practices. She completed her Masters degree in Baroque flute at the Sydney Conservatorium of Music, where she also teaches music history. She currently divides her time between performing, teaching, research, translating, and writing.

Dr Peter McCallum is an Associate Professor in musicology at the Sydney Conservatorium of Music, and the chief music critic for the *Sydney Morning Herald*. His research areas include the music of the Classical era, the music of Boulez, and Australian music criticism. His PhD research examined the analytical significance of the sketches for Beethoven's last string quartet in F major, Op. 135, and he is currently preparing an annotated transcription of Beethoven's *Kullak* sketchbook. As a byproduct of that research, he discovered what is believed to be Beethoven's last piano piece, a small bagatelle in F minor, recently recorded by his wife, pianist Stephanie McCallum.

Dr Edward Maclary is Professor of Music and Director of Choral Activities at the University of Maryland–College Park. Choirs under his direction have performed to great acclaim throughout Europe and North America, and the University of Maryland Concert Choir collaborates regularly with the National Symphony Orchestra at Washington's Kennedy Center for the Performing Arts. Edward Maclary has served as the chorus master for conductors such as Helmuth Rilling, Robert Shaw, and Ivan Fischer. Known as an outstanding teacher, he maintains a very busy schedule as a guest conductor and lecturer throughout the United States.

Dr Nancy November received her PhD from Cornell University in 2003 and is currently senior lecturer in musicology at the University of Auckland, New Zealand. Her research and teaching interests center on the music of the late eighteenth century: esthetics, analysis, and performance history and practices. Recent publications include essays on visual ideologies of the string quartet, Haydn and musical melancholy, Haydn's use of register in the strings quartets, and on "voice" in Haydn's early string quartets. In 2006–2007 she was Edison Fellow at the British Library, where she investigated the performance history of Beethoven's string quartets.

Simon Parkin was born in Manchester, England and trained as a pianist and composer at the Yehudi Menuhin School, the Royal Northern College of Music, and Manchester University. Simon has an active career as pianist, composer, and arranger, as well as a teaching position at RNCM, where he is in charge of aural training, improvisation, and practical harmony courses.

Dr John Peterson studied composition at the University of Sydney with Eric Gross, Peter Sculthorpe, and Ross Edwards. His music has been regularly performed throughout Australia and in the United States and, in general, reflects his interest in tonal idioms, as well as the energy and rhythmic propulsion inherent in many popular music styles. John graduated from the University of Sydney with a Doctorate in Composition in 2003, and has been lecturer in composition (within Music and Music Education) at the University of New South Wales since 2004. In 2005, John was the winner of the prestigious Albert H. Maggs Composition Award.

Dr Michael Remson is a composer/librettist, author, educator, and Executive and Artistic Director of the American Festival for the Arts Summer Music Conservatory in Houston, Texas. He is on the faculty of the Houston Ballet Academy and the University of Houston Moores School of Music where he teaches various music history topics. He is the author of two books on nineteenth-century composer Septimus Winner (also known as Alice Hawthorne), *Septimus Winner: Two Lives in Music* (Lanham, Md: Scarecrow, 2002), and its companion volume *The Songs of Septimus Winner* (Lanham, Md: Scarecrow, 2003). He has presented at the College Music Society and the Society for American Music. Dr Remson's compositions have been performed in the USA and Europe.

For over 20 years, **Christine Ryder** has worked in various roles in the public and private sectors in both large and small organizations including Andersen Consulting (now Accenture), the Australian Broadcasting Corporation, and the not-for-profit organization Girl Guides. Christine's early keen interest in music has always remained, though simmered in the background for many years. The opportunity to connect her main passions—music and research—in writing for *Musica* was too good to miss. Christine has a Bachelor of Commerce (Marketing) from the University of New South Wales, a Diploma of Music (Music Technology) from the Queensland Conservatorium of Music, and is an Associate in Music Australia (pianoforte performance).

Christopher Sears studied chemistry at the University of Durham and music at Trinity College of Music, London. After teaching science in the UK and east Africa, he pursued a varied career in music. Besides being a teacher, music advisor, conductor, arranger, tubist, and editor of contemporary orchestral music, he was Director of Studies of the Libyan School of Military Music. Christopher was music librarian of the Philharmonia Orchestra in London for 15 years and latterly of the Western Australian Symphony. Self-educated in musicology, he has written seven books of music analysis for teachers and many essays and program notes. He lectured at the University of Western Australia. He now lives in France.

Richard Toop is Reader in Musicology at the Sydney Conservatorium of Music. Born in England in 1945, he was Stockhausen's teaching assistant at the Cologne Musikhochschule in the early 1970s. He emigrated to Australia in 1975. In recent years he has written a book on György Ligeti, written *Revised New Grove* entries on Karlheinz Stockhausen, Brian Ferneyhough, and many other composers, and contributed a chapter to the *Cambridge History of Twentieth-Century Music*. Since 2002, Richard has lectured annually at the Stockhausen Summer Courses in Kürten, Germany.

Dr Richard Witts lectures at the University of Edinburgh in the sociology of music, especially the study of music and institutions, broadcasting, and music policy. He has written various essays on the social history of British music, and contributed to the *Cambridge Companion to Recorded Music* (2009) and *The Grove Dictionary of Music*. Concerned with radical music, his first and third books (1993, 2007) are studies of The Velvet Underground and Nico, while his second is a cultural history of the British Arts Council (1999). He has made numerous radio programs interviewing composers. He is currently developing the Donald Francis Tovey Archive in Edinburgh.

Dr Massimo Zicari, flutist and musicologist, studied at the University of Bologna, Italy, where he graduated *cum laude* with a doctoral dissertation on the dramaturgy of veristic operatic theater. Based in Lugano, Switzerland, where he teaches music history at the Conservatorio della Svizzera italiana, he has been conducting extensive research on the phenomenon of Italian opera. In particular, opera production, reception, and consumption in the late 1880s are at the core of his interests. Among his publications, of particular significance is the recently published essay on *The Land of Song, La terra del Belcanto sulla stampa londinese nel decennio 1890–1900* (Bern, Peter Lang Verlag, 2008).

CONTENTS

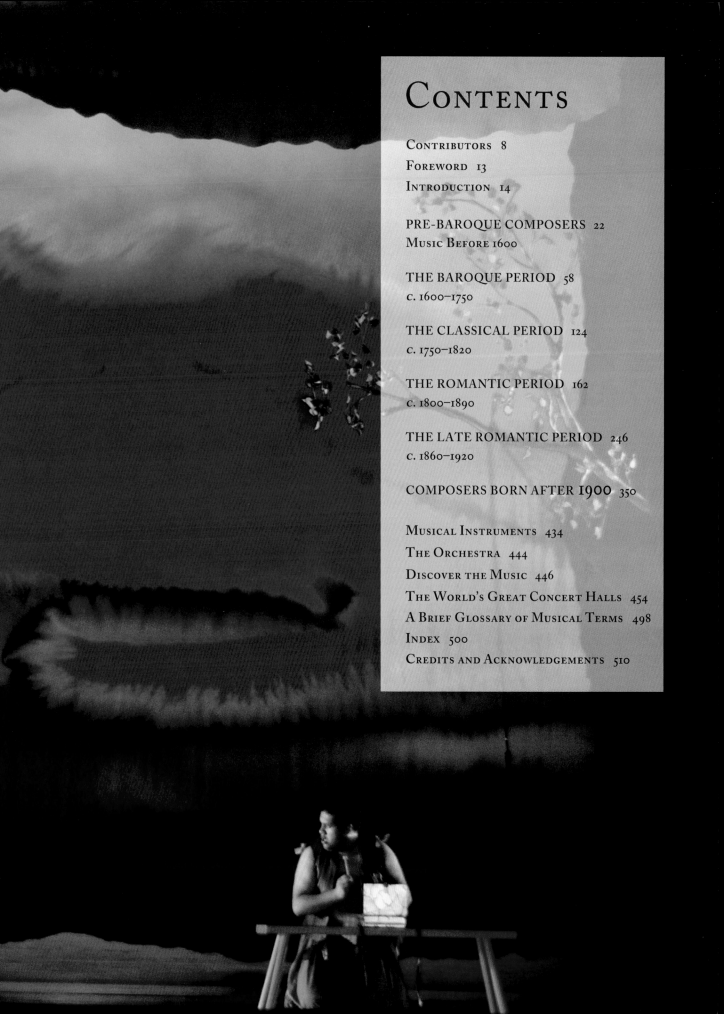

FOREWORD

When people ask me about classical music, I tell them that I prefer the term "serious music" or simply "music." I remember, some years ago, hearing a story about a teacher who offered his class a lesson in music appreciation for one hour each week. Half the class came to the lesson; the other half did not. Significantly, the children who attended the music lesson each week did better in all the other subjects they studied than the children who did not attend. They excelled in science, mathematics, and languages, and they also grew up to become music lovers. This linking of music with heightened perceptions and increased aptitudes is not peculiar to one country—countless examples can be found from all parts of the globe. This is because music has the power to sharpen our senses, to enlighten us, to uplift us.

Composers such as Bach, Beethoven, Mozart, Tchaikovsky, Sibelius, and others uplift us through their music—they bring us to that higher plane, that conscious level of perspicacity.

All of this is in sharp contrast to the mind-boggling nonsense of noise that comes under the umbrella of "pop" music, of so-called music that cannot exist without countless special effects, often including amplification, and that displays the most primitive musical elements. There are, of course, a few exceptions to this, but this kind of communication can never hope to achieve the transcendence of serious music, the joy and insights it gives us.

Likewise, Shakespeare wrote about various elements of the human condition—love, hate, despair, envy— elements and emotions with which we can all identify, yet Shakespeare has that rare power to move us, to heighten our awareness. Comic strips don't.

I regard *Musica* as a very important publication, as it attempts to draw many people into the wonderful world of serious music. Once people open their minds and hearts to music they never regret it. It becomes a lifelong passion. We cannot change the world, but we can help people enrich their lives through music.

VLADIMIR ASHKENAZY

INTRODUCTION

Introduction

AT A TIME WHEN OUR AURAL WORLD TEEMS WITH A DIVERSE VARIETY OF MUSIC—JAZZ, ROCK, POP, FOLK, AFRICAN, CARIBBEAN, INDONESIAN, WESTERN, TO NAME BUT A FEW—IT MIGHT SEEM ODD TO FOCUS ON JUST ONE TYPE. BUT *MUSICA* IS UNASHAMEDLY A BOOK ABOUT THE GREAT CLASSICAL EUROPEAN TRADITION OF COMPOSERS AND THEIR CRAFT. IT BRINGS THIS UNIQUE TRADITION TO LIFE NOT JUST THROUGH THE LAVISH ILLUSTRATIONS BUT, MOST IMPORTANTLY, BY PLACING IT IN ITS HISTORICAL, POLITICAL, SOCIAL, AND ARTISTIC CONTEXT.

We have all heard the famous names, like Bach, Handel, Beethoven, and Mozart, and we might occasionally whistle tunes from Verdi's popular operas or Brahms's folk music-inspired songs, but do we know how these people lived and why they composed the kind of music they did? And what of those who came before the best known ones of the last 200–300 years?

Previous pages *The Concert* by seventeenth-century Dutch artist Theo van Thulden. People have been making music since humanity's earliest days.

How did people make music in the early Christian era? Who were the Mozarts of the fifteenth and sixteenth centuries? How did composers make a living? Who listened to their music? Who performed it? How was it disseminated before the invention of the printing press? What influence did other technologies, such as recording, have on music-making and composing?

Left Autograph sketch for "Va Pensiero" (the chorus of Hebrew slaves) from Verdi's opera *Nabucco*. The chorus came to symbolize Italy's long fight for independence.

Musica answers these and many other questions … and not just about composers. Most of us have seen and heard common musical instruments such as the piano or the violin. But here we can also learn about many more—about their constructions, origins, and heyday, and the composers who particularly liked composing for them. Because these special feature boxes are embedded in the chronological history of Western art music, we can immediately see the link between composers and the media for which they composed.

The feature boxes cover not only musical instruments, but also common terms and other special interests as well. Thus we learn how and why the symphony developed so rapidly in the second half of the eighteenth century as aristocratic patronage was waning, and composers tried to earn money by composing attention-grabbing yet easy-to-listen-to pieces to entertain audiences at public concerts. While we might think the conductor to be an essential part of every concert, *Musica* informs us that this profession is, in fact, less than 200 years old. Early in the nineteenth century, through a variety of coinciding events, the need for a conductor came about—while small private court orchestras were being dismissed, new, publicly funded philharmonic societies started mushrooming in the bigger cities. Cheaper publishing disseminated music far beyond the immediate circle of composers who then often had to travel to hear their work performed. Because of the bigger concert halls, the size of orchestras grew and the music they were to play became more difficult, requiring more rehearsals and a central figure to help keep the ensemble together. For the first time in documented

Above Russian-born Vladimir Ashkenazy (b. 1937) is one of the twentieth century's finest pianists. He has spent the last two decades conducting some of the world's great orchestras.

history, composers were often not also instrumental or vocal virtuosos. And so it happened that Berlioz, Mendelssohn, and Wagner, in particular, pioneered the distinguished twentieth-century tradition of conducting.

Musica also lets us ponder how national and political sentiments influenced composers and how they, in turn, captured the spirit of their time in music. Verdi, for instance, composed operas the storylines of which paralleled events in contemporary Italy. The audience readily understood his message, and so in *Nabucco*, the chorus of Jewish slaves longing for their homeland while in Babylonian captivity immediately became a symbol for the liberation and unification of Italy, a struggle led by Giuseppe Garibaldi and others between the late 1840s and 1860s. So many of his works served to stir the spirit of his countrymen that Verdi's name eventually became a secret acronym for a slogan of the *Risorgimento*: *Viva Emmanuel Rè d'Italia.*

Composers of other nationalities were also politically vocal through their music. Hungarian composer Béla Bartók is well known for his struggles to bring about the sentiment of united brotherhood in his native region torn by ethnic hatred fueled by demagogue politicians. He not only collected and transcribed thousands of traditional songs and instrumental music of Croatia, Slovakia, Romania, Bulgaria, Hungary, and even Turkey and the north African Arab world, but infused his compositions with their musical characteristics, often finishing off his works with movements where the various tunes of these nations come together in an apotheosis. *Musica* tells of many more stories and gives us insights into the cultural milieu and motivations of several famous composers.

Left A concert at the La Salle Pleyel concert hall in Paris, France. One of the only auditoriums in the world specifically built for symphonic music, it seats some 1,900 people.

Right Composers Béla Bartók (seated left) and Zoltan Kodály (seated right) with the members of the Hungarian Quartet, a string quartet formed in 1935 in Budapest.

The impact of political events on composers and their work was not unique to the nineteenth and twentieth centuries. Back in the Middle Ages, at the time troubadours and trouvères were singing about courtly love, the Western world was waging its Crusades to liberate Jerusalem from Muslim rule. The knights' heroic adventures were preserved in the epic tales recounted in the songs of traveling musicians and bards.

A few hundred years later the discovery of new worlds brought a fascination with the exotic "other;" a fascination that perhaps reached its climax in Puccini's early twentieth-century operas *Madame Butterfly* and *Turandot*. But it was Rameau, the French Baroque composer who first put other races on the operatic stage in his *Les Indes Galantes* (1735). In German-speaking lands, where instead of the colonization of distant worlds there was an ongoing fight with the Ottoman Empire, Turkish music came to represent the exotic. By the time the Hapsburgs and their allies pushed the Ottomans back to the eastern parts of the Balkans in the later eighteenth century, "Alla Turca" music had become a favorite piece with its imitation of tambourines and pseudo-military bands, as Mozart's and Beethoven's popular pieces exemplify. The defeat of the Ottomans was such a sensation in the Hapsburg capital of Vienna, that anything vaguely Turkish became instantly fashionable. Mozart seized on this craze when he moved to Vienna in 1781 and composed *The Abduction from the Seraglio* to impress both the emperor and the influential nobility. That he was only half successful we know from Joseph II's oft-quoted remark after the première: "Too many notes, my dear Mozart."

Politics have affected other composers more severely. Early in the seventeenth century Heinrich Schütz complained bitterly about lack of funds and impoverished conditions as the 30-year religious war—fought primarily in German-speaking territories—depleted the country not only of food and money, but of people, including musicians. And of course, most famously, totalitarian regimes have always profoundly shaped music-making. Apart from the influence of Nazi politics on developments in European music (especially the forced migration

Right *The Concert* by nineteenth-century French artist Joseph Frederic Charles Soulacroix depicts a well-to-do family enjoying music in the intimate surrounds of the drawing room.

Above A group of players performs songs of chivalrous deeds and courtly love. Troubadours' songs were monophonic, that is, there were no accompanying harmonies.

Below A Jewish refugee family walks through the town of Memel, Germany in 1939. Displaced from their homeland, many Jews sought a haven in the United States.

of leading composers and performers to the United States) and Stalinist terrorism on composition in the Soviet Union, *Musica* tells us about earlier instances as well. The output of English Renaissance composers, such as Tallis and Byrd, clearly reflect the ruler's religious inclinations and level of tolerance. The amount of music for Catholic worship declined sharply in favor of music for Anglican services during times of religious persecution. Less bloody but not less limiting for composers' creative output was the French Sun King. The favoritism of Louis XIV allowed unique opportunities to a chosen few composers, especially Lully, whose operas often blatantly served the king's personality cult.

Social changes have impacted even more on composers' output and the style of their music than did political change. As we learn in Chapter 1, notated music was primarily vocal prior to around 1600. This was due to the influence of the Church. As the main patron of musicians, the Church

"*Music is a higher revelation than all wisdom and philosophy.*"

LUDWIG VAN BEETHOVEN

fostered the development of sacred music; vocal, because both instruments (with the exception of the organ) and music without text were regarded frivolous and flimsy as well as meaningless. With the growth of secular power and a ruling class wishing to demonstrate wealth and power through lavish entertainment, composers and musicians started to be employed by kings, dukes, and the lesser aristocracy. The steady rise, from the seventeenth century onward, of instrumental music and with it the instrumental virtuoso, heralded a new era. New genres such as the concerto, the solo sonata, and opera were developed in order to serve people's seemingly insatiable appetite for dazzling musical entertainment.

Page after page, this book shows that social arrangements and employment conditions left their indelible mark on composers' output. Take the case of Johann Sebastian Bach, for instance. When he was employed by Prince Leopold of Anhalt-Cöthen, he composed mostly instrumental pieces—chamber sonatas of

Right A detail from a fourteenth-century Italian fresco showing monks at prayer. Monks' daily duties included singing the various liturgical services, such as Prime, Matins, and Vespers.

various sorts. As Music Director of Leipzig and Cantor of its main churches, he busied himself with music for the Lutheran service—passions, cantatas, and oratorios. But as he took on some other commitments, such as directing the Collegium Musicum of the town's university, he again turned to secular music—instrumental concertos and secular cantatas.

Or think of Liszt in the nineteenth century. By his time, musicians rarely worked in secure employment. Instead they earned a living from publishing, performing, and private teaching. The bourgeoisie, or rather its civic representatives, commissioned pieces for special occasions, but it was more common to simply attend public concerts by buying a ticket or subscription. Such an audience at large is rarely sophisticated, so musicians had to ensure their success and livelihood by dazzling them with virtuosity and/or emotionally highly charged compositions. When he was young, and especially during the 1830s and 1840s, Liszt lived as a traveling virtuoso, performing everywhere from Madrid to St Petersburg to Edinburgh and Naples. But when he wanted to dedicate himself to composing, he took up a conducting (music director) post in Weimar, and later accepted prestigious teaching commitments dividing his time between Weimar, Budapest, and Rome.

Social change and its impact on music-making also manifest in the recent "democratization" of music. The confluence of high- and low-brow styles we experience in contemporary composed music with its mix of jazz, rock, folk, urban, classical, and world music traditions is a typical late twentieth-century development, perhaps the grandchild of the 1960s–1970s liberalism and the intellectual revolution. It's not that music of the past was less diverse, but modern telecommunications and sound reproduction technologies have made this diversity much more obvious, accessible to all, and clearly documented. That is why it is useful that *Musica* also includes ample information on regional developments and recent trends.

Above Franz Liszt was a virtuoso of the piano during the nineteenth century. His influence was wide-ranging—as a performer, teacher, and especially as a composer.

Below The Minnesota Ladies Symphony Orchestra c. 1895. Female musicians, especially in America, formed amateur musical societies so they had an opportunity to perform.

Apart from showing how jazz influenced American and European classical composers, it also discusses crossovers between popular and classical genres. Nor does it neglect important other regions and developments in earlier times. Thus we learn about Spanish and Latin American composers, and those English ones who are less familiar in countries where the German mainstream canon rules. There is a section on American women composers at the turn of the twentieth century as well and their struggle for recognition in an all too exclusively male world. Italian, French, and Russian musicians are also covered and we gain an insight into the Australasian scene as well. To make the coverage of musical genres complete, the worlds of ballet and opera are also discussed.

Composers were also in tune with the work of other artists and thinkers—not just those of their own time but also those who came before. The link between literary and musical works is most obvious in opera and songs, but poetry and philosophy can be seen to inspiring purely instrumental music as well. Thus we learn about Berlioz's fascination with Shakespeare;

Liszt's readings of Lamartine and Victor Hugo; Scho-penhauer's influence on Wagner, and that Nietzsche's enthusiasm for Wagner soured after *Parsifal*; Schubert's and Beethoven's regard for Goethe; Schumann's songs based on Heine's poetry; and Tchaikovsky's and Mussorgsky's inspiration from Pushkin and Gogol. Such links were obviously not limited to artists living in the nineteenth century. Lully and Molière collaborated closely on many theatrical works in praise of Louis XIV, and the artistic surrounds of composers such as Palestrina, who regularly performed at St Peter's Basilica and the Sistine Chapel decorated by Michelangelo's frescos, or Victoria—who served the Spanish court at the same time as El Greco did—must have been as significant as more global political and cultural matters. Briefly and succinctly, *Musica* draws attention to and explains these connections, making the composers and their times come to life.

Although the language is not specialist, *Musica* does not shy away from discussing some of the technical aspects of Western compositions. We can learn about the difference between polyphonic and homophonic music, between modal, tonal and atonal organizations

Right Pierluigi Palestrina, an important composer during the Renaissance, wrote mostly sacred music. He was, for a time, choirmaster at St Peter's in Rome.

Below Simon Keenlyside (Don Giovanni), Joyce DiDonato (Donna Elvira), Marina Poplavskaya (Donna Anna), Ramón Vargas (Don Ottavio), Miah Persson (Zerlina), and Robert Gleadow (Mesetto) in the Royal Opera's 2008 production of Mozart's opera *Don Giovanni* at London's Royal Opera House.

of sound, the use of computers and electronically generated sounds, serialism, minimalism, and much more. And meanwhile it becomes apparent that things we may take for granted about music have not been like that all the time. Performing music of past eras was almost unheard of prior to about the 1780s; most of our instruments did not gain their current form, material, and tuning until as late as the middle of the nineteenth century; composers have not always striven for originality and were, for a long time, regarded as craftsmen or tradesmen rather than artists.

Musica helps us to see music's role in Western society: How people thought about it and how composers realized those ideals. Because it places music-making firmly in its cultural context, it enables each epoch's thinking about music to drive the discussion. Through the historical chronology, we can see how the ancient notion of assigning divine powers to music through its seeming links with the laws of the natural world re-emerges time and again; first as music of the spheres, then as music for worship, and much later again in the notion of composer as artist–priest, as communication from soul to soul, and as the ultimate self-expression. In between these periods, music is seen in contrasting lights—as trivial entertainment, as something frivolous and lowly, as a purely intellectual pursuit, or as a means to manipulate the masses. Ultimately the question is asked anew by Cage and other mid-twentieth-century composers—what is music, what differentiates it from noise? Reading *Musica* is indispensable in assisting us to answer this question for ourselves.

DOROTTYA FABIAN

PRE-BAROQUE COMPOSERS
MUSIC BEFORE 1600

Introduction

UNTIL THE TWELFTH CENTURY MOST COMPOSED MUSIC WAS INTENDED FOR RELIGIOUS PURPOSES. INDEED, MOST NOTATED MUSICAL MANUSCRIPTS—BOTH BEFORE AND AFTER THE TWELFTH CENTURY—CAME FROM MONASTERIES AND OTHER PLACES OF LEARNING ASSOCIATED WITH THE CHURCH. GREGORIAN CHANT, OR PLAINSONG, NAMED FOR POPE GREGORY I (540–604), AND MADE UP OF A SINGLE LINE OF VOCAL MELODY, WAS AN INTEGRAL PART OF CHURCH WORSHIP FOR CENTURIES. PLAINSONG SLOWLY BROADENED INTO ORGANUM, WHERE SIMPLE HARMONIES WERE INTRODUCED. THIS LED ULTIMATELY TO POLYPHONY, WHERE MULTIPLE HARMONIES WERE EMPLOYED. WITH POLYPHONY CAME THE MOTET—MUSIC WHERE VOICES MOVED IN COUNTERPOINT WITH THE MAIN MELODY.

B ut it wasn't until the advent of the poet–troubadours, their songs dealing with courtly love and chivalry, that music took on a more secular role. This heralded the beginning of a gradual acceptance of composed music outside the Church's requirements, and music became something that could be enjoyed on a number of levels.

By the fourteenth century, composers such as Guillaume de Machaut were being more adventurous in their workings of melody and rhythms. This was the age of Ars Nova (new art). All this paved the way for the Renaissance.

The era of the High Renaissance was formed by the confluence of a number of simultaneous developments in European art music in the middle and late sixteenth century. The language of Netherlands polyphony that was inherited from Ockeghem and Josquin continued to be the most important mode of discourse in sacred music, and sacred music remained the most highly regarded means of musical expression. But other forces were also at work.

In Venice, another composer from the Netherlands, Adrian Willaert, served as master of music at San Marco, where he fostered the development of poly-choral music as well as purely instrumental music, and exploited sonority as a means of musical expression divorced from the intellectual rigors of counterpoint. This had huge implications for the music that followed in the next century. At the same time, Willaert and others in Italy—Festa, Arcadelt, and Verdelot—also began to produce the incredibly prolific secular song form that became known as the madrigal.

The madrigal had very humble beginnings as a descendant of small, simple song forms such as the

Above A Gregorian chant, used here as an introit for Christmas Day services. It comes from a volume published in Rome in 1614.

Right A winged putto (cherub) playing a lute, by Giovanni Battista di Jacopo (1494–1540). Putti were commonly depicted in Renaissance painting and sculpture.

Previous pages A detail from Italian artist Vittorio Carpaccio's *The Presentation of Jesus in the Temple* (1510) shows angelic musicians accompanying the ceremony.

"frottola," but it came to occupy a central place in the compositional mainstream. Eventually it made its way to England where, long after the Italian madrigal had become a part of continental musical history, the English madrigal had a tremendous flowering in the early to mid-seventeenth century. When considered with its other offshoots—the French chanson, exemplified by Passereau, Sermisy, and Jannequin, the German Lied of Isaac and Senfl and the works of Morley, Weelkes, and Wilbye—the madrigal comprises a body of vocal literature unmatched in quantity and variety from any other era. Remarkably, one composer, Orlando di Lasso, produced masterpieces in all these styles—madrigal, chanson, Lied—as well as much of the most important sacred polyphony of the era.

Along with Giovanni Palestrina, Tomás Luis de Victoria from Spain, and William Byrd in England, Lasso helped to perfect the language of Renaissance counterpoint. Though each of these masters' music can

Right An orchestra and choir, from a fifteenth-century French illuminated manuscript. Ensembles such as this performed for weddings, funerals, and other important events.

be identified by close attention to particular style traits, the unanimity of language and expression among them is remarkable. All produced a huge quantity of music for the Church—Masses, motets, psalms, antiphons—that represents the high watermark of sacred vocal art in European history. This style was venerated and imitated throughout the remainder of the sixteenth century and through the seventeenth century. It became the "prima prattica" prized by Claudio Monteverdi and Heinrich Schütz. Even well into the eighteenth century composers learned from this style and some continued to imitate it, notably J.S. Bach, who in the *Kyrie* of his great *Mass in B minor* pays his homage with a remarkable imitation of the Palestrinian model. While the Catholic Church was the primary beneficiary of this great sacred tradition, the music of the Protestant Church became increasingly important. The liturgies of the Church of England and the Lutheran Church in northern Germany also fostered masterpieces composed in the vernacular of their worshipers.

Alongside the twin streams of the sacred polyphony and the secular song of the later Renaissance, two other important currents of musical life must be considered. Instrumental music, for both solo and ensemble, became increasingly important in the daily life of the aristocracy and with the development of the organ, in the Church. The lute, viol, recorder, shawm, cornett, sackbut, and all manner of keyboard instruments took on a greater role in compositional thinking as the

Below right This sixteenth-century illustration shows a woman playing a bass shawm, a woodwind instrument with a double reed. Its piercing tone made it suitable for playing outdoors.

sixteenth century drew to a close. Music publishing gave wider distribution than ever before to popular music of the day and gave composers an incentive to compose to the tastes of their potential consumers, not just their specific patrons. The beginnings of musical commerce outside the realm of court or church patronage began to stir, with enormous consequences for the next 500 years of Western music.

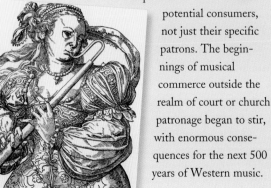

Hildegard of Bingen

1098–SEPTEMBER 17, 1179

HILDEGARD IS ONE OF THE FEW MEDIEVAL COMPOSERS WHOSE BIOGRAPHY IS KNOWN TO US. SHE WAS ACTIVE NOT ONLY AS A COMPOSER OF LITURGICAL MUSIC BUT ALSO AS THE AUTHOR OF SEVERAL THEOLOGICAL, MEDICINAL, AND POETIC TEXTS. SHE MAINTAINED CORRESPONDENCE WITH THE MOST PROMINENT FIGURES OF HER DAY, INCLUDING EMPERORS, STATESMEN, POPES, AND SENIOR CLERGY, AND HER FAME AS A VISIONARY AND COUNSELOR LASTED FOR SEVERAL CENTURIES AFTER HER DEATH.

LIFE AND WORKS

As a girl Hildegard entered the community of nuns at the monastery of Disibodenberg and became prioress in 1136. In 1150 she received permission to move her community of about 20 nuns to a new cloister at Bingen on the banks of the Rhine, and in 1165 she founded a second convent nearby at Eibingen. Her entire life was colored by numerous visionary experiences, which she described at various places in her writings. Her fame as a visionary spread throughout German lands and many people visited her in the hope of benefiting from a miracle or her supposed healing powers.

Above right Hildegard's erudition brought her to the attention of kings and religious leaders throughout Europe, many of whom wrote to her for advice and guidance on a range of issues.

HILDEGARD AS VISIONARY

Throughout the medieval period it was fairly common for members of religious communities to report experiences of visionary revelations of God's will. Some of these were taken very seriously by the Church, including the revelations of Hildegard of Bingen. In the preface to the *Scivias,* she describes one of these experiences: "In the year 1141 of the Incarnation of Jesus Christ, the Word of God, when I was forty-two years and seven months old, a burning light coming from heaven poured into my mind. Like a flame which does not burn but rather enkindles, it enflamed my heart and my breast, just as the sun warms something with its rays." Hildegard was careful to seek the approval of the Church before disclosing her visions, and received the endorsement of Pope Eugenius before completing her *Scivias.* Modern commentators have suggested that Hildegard's visions may have been the result of acute migraine. In particular, the visual hallucinations known as "scintillating scotoma" that may arise from this condition appear to match Hildegard's vivid descriptions of the physical sensations accompanying her visionary experiences.

Hildegard's principal writings survive in a series of works that form a trilogy—the *Scivias,* which deals with issues of doctrine; the *Liber Vitae Meritorum,* which deals with ethical questions; and *De Operatione Dei,* a complex collection of allegories. Each of these works includes descriptions of Hildegard's visions, which are then interpreted through biblical exegesis. Hildegard also wrote about the natural sciences and curative treatments. She invented an alternative alphabet which she used for a modified form of medieval Latin in her writings. The manuscripts in which her works survive show meticulous attention to narrative detail and have beautiful illuminations. Approximately 300 letters survive from her correspondence with important figures of her day.

HILDEGARD AS COMPOSER

Many of Hildegard's melodies are longer and more ornate than we find in the music of her contemporaries. Her beautifully melismatic melodies, use of relatively wide skips between notes, and the frequently high range of the vocal parts have given her music an ethereal quality that still has great appeal to listeners today. Hildegard wrote monophonic music (a single part with no accompaniment). Her music was performed by the nuns of her community.

Her compositions include hymns and songs for the Divine Office (the daily ritual of prayer in the monasteries and convents) and the Holy Mass, and a liturgical drama called *Ordo virtutem.* The chronology of her compositions is not known, but she gathered her works in a collection known as the *Symphonia*. The exact liturgical function of her music is not entirely clear, although she stated elsewhere that she regarded music (singing) as the audible manifestation of the Holy Spirit. Hildegard tried to convey her "belief in the universe as an ordered whole whose harmoniousness is revealed to the world through song."

ORDO VIRTUTEM

Hildegard's *Ordo virtutum* is the only medieval music drama whose composer is known to us. The occasion for which it was written is unknown. In this play, 18 female singers portray the Virtues and their queen, Humility. The subject matter of *Ordo virtutum* involves the struggle between Good, which is exemplified by the Virtues, and Evil, which is represented by the Devil—an unsinging male role (unsinging because according to Neoplatonism, evil can only be portrayed through inharmonious howls, growls, and animal noises).

Below "Man as the center of the universe," the frontispiece of *Scivias* by Hildegard of Bingen. Hildegard believed that her visions explained the meaning of religious texts, and inspired her to compose music dedicated to the glory of God.

Discover the music

Symphonia—the collection of Hildegard's music for the Divine Office, Mass, saints days, and other ceremonial occasions; between 70–80 pieces in total.

Ordo virtutem

Left Hildegard receives divine inspiration and passes it on to a scribe, from the Rupertsberger Codex of the *Scivias*. *Scivias* means "know the way."

Europe in the eleventh and twelfth centuries

THE ELEVENTH AND TWELFTH CENTURIES MARKED AN UPTURN IN THE COURSE OF EUROPEAN HISTORY. AN INCREASE IN POPULATION ACCOMPANIED IMPROVING ECONOMIC CONDITIONS, WHICH LED TO THE GROWTH OF MODERN CITIES AND THE ESTABLISHMENT OF THE FIRST UNIVERSITIES IN BOLOGNA AND PARIS. A GREATER AWARENESS OF PAST ACHIEVEMENTS WAS REFLECTED IN THE FIRST LATIN TRANSLATIONS OF CLASSICAL GREEK TEXTS, SOME OF WHICH CAME THROUGH INTERMEDIATE ARABIC TRANSLATIONS.

This period also witnessed the rise of Romanesque and Gothic architecture and the strengthening of the great traditions of courtly poetry. However, these centuries also saw the Great Schism of 1054 in which the eastern and western branches of Christianity separated, and also the launch of the Holy Crusades toward the end of the eleventh century and into the twelfth.

Musical developments during these centuries include the emergence of polyphonic performance and composition in addition to monophonic (single line) music-making, the beginning of musical notation, and a great interest in pedagogical principles and theories of music. In this last regard, Guido d'Arezzo (c. 991–c. 1033)

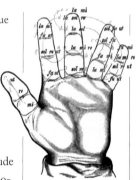

Left What is known as the Guidonian hand, a mnemonic device used to assist singers in learning to sight sing, may have been used by Guido d'Arezzo.

devised a system of singing similar in many respects to the modern solfeggio method. Many of these musical activities are known to us through surviving church records, although such evidence is, unfortunately, scant.

TROUBADORS

Aristocratic interest in poetry and music was reflected in the output of a group of musicians and poets known as the troubadours and trouvères that flourished in French-speaking regions from about 1100 until the turn of the thirteenth century. Their subject matter was courtly love, chivalry, and political or moral topics. Their love songs worshipped an adored lady from afar with discretion, respect, and humility. The lady herself, generally unaware of her devoted admirer, may have been more abstract than real

Europe in the eleventh and twelfth centuries
★ Death place of Hildegard
☆ Birthplace of Guido d'Arezzo

Left A battle during the First Crusade (1095–1099). In the background, reinforcements are streaming out of the city gates. The image is from a fifteenth-century manuscript.

THE GREAT SCHISM

The eastern branch of Christianity, centered in Constantinople (also known as Byzantium), and the western branch, centered in Rome, had a long history of disagreements stretching over several centuries. Matters came to a head in 1054 when each side excommunicated senior officials on the other side. This breach reflected an already existing division of the Christian Church along geographic, linguistic, and cultural boundaries. Culturally more advanced than their western counterparts during the Dark Ages, the fortunes of the Byzantine Empire went into gradual decline in the face of aggressive advances by Ottoman forces. The Crusades provided limited assistance and often a fair amount of hindrance, and the fate of Constantinople was sealed with the victory of the Ottoman Empire in 1453 and the imposition of Islamic rule over Byzantine territories.

Despite several attempts at reunification over the centuries, the western church evolved into what is now the Roman Catholic Church headed by the pope in Rome, while the Eastern Orthodox Church comprises many regional churches (such as the Russian Orthodox or Greek Orthodox) that are theologically unified and each administered by a synod of bishops.

and was usually well beyond the reach of the poet or musician (especially when she was married to a powerful figure of the nobility).

THE HOLY CRUSADES

A series of military expeditions by Western Christian armies against the Islamic occupation of the Holy Lands around Palestine arose out of support for harassed pilgrims, a burgeoning of fundamentalist Christianity in the eleventh century, and growing confidence in Europe about its prosperity and abilities to conquer the eastern "infidels."

The first Crusade was launched by Pope Urban II in 1095 and was the most militarily successful of all the crusades. Four independent Latin kingdoms were established in the conquered territories and the military orders of Templars, Hospitallers, and Teutonic Knights came into existence.

Left A representation of King David playing the lyre, or possibly a rebec, from an eleventh-century manuscript of St Martial de Limoges.

A further eight crusades were undertaken during the following two centuries, although most were hampered by poor military planning, squabbling between the crusaders and the eastern Byzantine Christians, and among the crusaders themselves. By 1291 the last of the crusader possessions were recaptured by Muslim forces and almost all traces of the crusader presence in the Holy Land were obliterated.

The overall significance of the crusades in European history is debatable. At the very least, they contributed to the growth of the European impulse for conquest and colonization, and they also strengthened the role of the papacy in the continent's temporal affairs. The crusades were also responsible for a hardening of relations and high level of mistrust between Islamic and Christian cultures, and they also did little to halt the slide of the Byzantine Empire toward its ultimate defeat and disintegration.

Guillaume de Machaut

c. 1300–April 1377

GUILLAUME DE MACHAUT (SOMETIMES SPELLED MACHAULT) WAS THE MOST CELEBRATED COMPOSER AND POET OF FOURTEENTH-CENTURY FRANCE. HE COMPOSED IN A WIDE RANGE OF MUSICAL STYLES AND WAS THE PRE-EMINENT REPRESENTATIVE OF THE MOVEMENT IN MUSIC KNOWN AS THE ARS NOVA (NEW ART) WHICH BROUGHT ABOUT ADVANCES IN MUSICAL NOTATION, GREATER COMPLEXITY OF RHYTHM, AND INCREASED SOPHISTICATION IN SECULAR MUSIC MAKING.

Above right A manuscript by Guillaume de Machaut, one of the most important and influential composers of the fourteenth century.

LIFE AND TIMES

Machaut was born in the region around Rheims in northern France c. 1300, and died in Rheims in 1377. He was educated as a cleric and took minor holy orders without actually becoming a priest. At the age of 23 he was employed by King John of Bohemia as a secretary and traveled throughout Europe in the service of the king. After King John's death at the battle of Crécy in 1346, Machaut was employed by other aristocrats and rulers, including those from the French court. He received several benefices including one as canon at Rheims where he took up residence in c. 1340. His connections with influential members of the upper classes provided him with creature comforts, opportunities to travel, and the patronage of his artistic inclinations. Many details of his life are known from his poetry where Machaut refers to his day-to-day life, events connected with the Hundred Years' War, the Black Death, and his interests in falconry and horse riding. One interesting aspect of Machaut's career is that in contrast to earlier generations of composers he composed much more secular than sacred music.

His compositional output comprises a setting of the Mass, 23 motets, and over 100 secular works in the courtly "formes fixes" (fixed forms) tradition of medieval poetry. These subtly complex poetic forms (known as lais, virelais, rondeaux, and ballades) were set to music by Machaut both monophonically (lais and virelais) and polyphonically (virelais, rondeaux, and ballades). Of the several manuscript sources containing his works, the most complete is a collection of poetry and music now housed at the Bibliothèque Nationale in Paris (BN f. fr. 1584). This manuscript was apparently compiled under the supervision of Machaut.

Settings of his sophisticated poetic texts unite the poetic and compositional aspects of Machaut's personality and they provide not only a continuation of the monophonic trouvère tradition but also high points in the development of polyphonic chansons. Altogether

Left Machaut was a central figure in the Ars Nova movement, marked, among other things, by more rhythmic variety. He was one of the first composers to write polyphonic settings for poetry in fixed forms.

Right A banquet scene showing a group of musicians playing violin, viol, harp, and zither, from a French edition c. 1300 of the New Testament.

Discover the music

"Qui es promesses—Ha! For-
     tune—Et non est qui adjuvat"
"Ma fin est ma commence-
     ment" (musical palindrome)
"Rose, liz, printemps, verdure"
Messe de Notre Dame

about 40 to 50 monophonic lais and virelais survive along with about 90 polyphonic rondeaux, virelaix, and ballades (known collectively as chansons). The poetic texts favored by Machaut explore themes of courtly love, chivalry, and other noble pursuits. Instrumental accompaniment may occur in some pieces, while others have two different texts among the parts.

THE MOTETS

Machaut's motets follow the notational procedures developed in the Ars Nova movement including the different ways of dividing long notes into either two or three shorter ones, a process whose codification was innovative for its time. Generally, the motets were written for three or four voices, the lower one or two

Below right Poetry and music were highly valued in Machaut's time, as shown in this image of a minstrel reciting a poem for a noblewoman. Fortunately, many of Machaut's secular works have survived to this day.

of which move in long notes relative to the upper voices. Many subtleties such as melodic inversion and retrograde are found in the motets as well as great rhythmic complexity in the ordering of repeating segments in melodic designs. The earlier tradition of different texts for each of the upper two voices in a motet persisted in Machaut's works. The result is one of incredible artistry whose beauty repays repeated listening and attention to the diverse elements of musical construction.

MESSE DE NOTRE DAME

Machaut's great work is one of the earliest settings of the sections of the Mass Ordinary conceived as one artistic unit. The Ordinary comprises the texts for the Kyrie, Gloria, Credo, Sanctus, Agnus Dei, and Ite Missa est. The wonderful variety of sonorities and balance struck between the contrasting lengths and liturgical functions of these texts mark this Mass as a worthy start to the tradition of polyphonic settings of the Mass Ordinary that flourished in the two centuries following Machaut's death and that has lasted to the present day. The text phrases of the Gloria and Credo of Machaut's Mass are clearly articulated using briskly moving melodies, with long melismas ending each movement. The more expansively set other sections contain many intricacies of rhythmic detail and design that offer a high point in the medieval approach to the composition of sacred music.

Europe in the fourteenth century

THE ECONOMIC AND SOCIAL PROGRESS OF EUROPE WAS SEVERELY
DISRUPTED BY MAJOR EVENTS OF THE FOURTEENTH CENTURY INCLUDING
THE BLACK DEATH (1348–1350), THE HUNDRED YEARS' WAR (1338–1453),
AND THE LOCATION OF THE PAPACY IN AVIGNON INSTEAD OF ROME FOR
MOST OF THE CENTURY.

Notions of a politically unified Europe that may
have existed in earlier times gave way to the
development of distinct political entities such as the
Kingdom of France or the small Italian city–states.

In the arts, the fourteenth century saw some of
the greatest literary works of all time, including
Dante's *Divine Comedy*, Chaucer's *Canterbury Tales,*
and Boccaccio's *Decameron*. The greatest painter of
the period, Giotto, is famous for his emphasis on
the natural representation of people and objects. The
fourteenth century also saw the beginning of human-
ism in intellectual thought—a movement that placed
the achievements and activities of humans foremost
instead of interpretations centered on the divinity.

Below A scene from
Dante's *Divine Comedy*.
The work is divided into
three books describing
the poet's epic journey
through the three lands
of death—the *Inferno*,
Purgatorio, and *Paradiso*.

CHURCH AND STATE

The growing distinction between sacred and secular
domains of human activity in the fourteenth century
was evident in the idea that the state looked after
people's earthly concerns while the Church concerned
itself with the welfare of their souls. The Church's
ability to counter these tendencies was hampered by
its internal problems with corruption and decadence.
Rival claimants to the papacy at this period led to the
pope's removal to the southern French city of Avignon.
The existence of these problems and their widespread
criticism from individuals in many fields led to the
foundation of movements that foreshadowed the
Protestant Reformation of the next century.

Musical developments were
centered on the emergence of
the Ars Nova (new art). Novelties
associated with this artistic movement were mainly in the realm of
musical notation and the codification of musical rhythm. Many of
the principles established by musicians of this period have lasted to
the present time (such as the consolidation of the practice of binary
division of notes—that is, one
long note can divide into two equal
shorter ones). Composers delighted
in exploring new possibilities with
rhythmic intricacy, which led to
some of the most complex compositional activity and difficulties for
performers that can be found in
European musical history.

CHANSONS AND MOTETS

During the fourteenth and fifteenth centuries, chanson was a general term for any polyphonic setting of a French secular poem. Following traditions developed by late medieval composers and poets, a chanson text was built upon one of the "formes fixes" (fixed form) structures applied in poems known as rondeaux, virelais, and ballades. Each of these forms has its own rhyming scheme, line numbers, and recurrent refrains. On the whole, composers of this period showed great sensitivity to poetic nuances when they set poetic texts to music. Earlier composers often wrote monophonic settings but as the fourteenth century progressed polyphonic settings became the norm.

As a genre, the motet is quite difficult to define as it has appeared in many different guises throughout the history of music. Perhaps the easiest way to think of the motet is as any vocal setting of a sacred text that does not have a specific place in the celebration of the Christian liturgy. Of course, many compositions such as hymns and Magnificats do have specific places in the liturgy and share many features in common with motets. Given its flexibility, it is not very surprising that motet writing grew enormously in popularity among fourteenth-century composers and retained its popularity over the course of the following two centuries. Composers wrote examples in this genre for varied occasions, from church ceremonies on a grand scale to devotional or smaller scale activities.

Above A woodcut depicting scenes from the *Decameron* by Boccaccio. This masterpiece of Italian literature was written in the 1350s, and inspired writers for generations.

THE TREATY OF CALAIS (1360)

The Treaty of Calais marked a brief truce in the so-called Hundred Years' War between England and France that started in 1337 and finally finished in 1453. The war began when Edward III of England laid claim to the French throne. His initial military successes included gaining control over much of France and capturing King John II of France. The provisions negotiated for the Treaty included a huge ransom for John, and formalizing Edward's rule over about half the French kingdom. In exchange, John was to be released and the English agreed to renounce their claims to the French throne. However, the details about John's claim to the French throne and his receipt of the French lands did not enter the final treaty. Fighting resumed shortly afterwards between the two sides and hostilities did not conclude until the English defeat in 1453.

Right A page from a chansonnier, containing poems, lyrics, and chansons of the troubadour tradition. Chansonniers, or songbooks, usually included both sacred and secular songs.

FIFTEENTH-CENTURY MASTERS: DUFAY, BINCHOIS, AND OCKEGHEM

The music of the fifteenth and sixteenth centuries is often termed Renaissance music. Composers cultivated polyphonic writing in the favored genres of Mass settings, sacred motets, and secular chansons. Renaissance musical style rooted itself in the so-called "Low" countries—parts of present-day northern France, Belgium, The Netherlands, and Luxembourg.

Almost all of the important composers from about 1420 to about 1520 were from this region, and their careers were spent in almost all European areas. The music of this region has also been called "Franco-Flemish" in recognition of the important contribution of this part of Europe to musical history.

GUILLAUME DUFAY (1397–1474)

Dufay was born near Brussels in 1397 and was educated at the cathedral of Notre Dame in Cambrai. In 1420 he moved to Italy where he lived until 1439 when

Above Guillaume Dufay's will stipulated that while he was receiving the last rites, eight singers were to sing his motet "Ave regina caelorum."

Opposite right A section of a painting by Hans Memling of five angel musicians, c. 1480. From the left, the instruments are the psaltery, tromba marina, lute, sackbut, and shawm.

he returned to Cambrai. Dufay was greatly admired and respected not only for his musical accomplishments but also for his erudition—he was a Doctor of Canon Law from the University of Bologna, and held numerous senior positions in the church.

Dufay reflected the musical spirit of his age through his cultivation of settings of the Mass Ordinary, motet composition, and his rigorous manipulation of the formes fixes structures underpinning chanson writing. A good example of a chanson is Dufay's ballade *Resvellies vous et faites chiere lye* composed in 1423 for the marriage of a niece of Pope Martin V, Victoire Colonne, to Prince Carlo Malatesta. This ballade demonstrates many features that were typical of the time, such as lyrical and ornate writing for the top voice, musical articulation of the two principal sections of the poem and its refrain, and contrasts in musical meter at different points carefully chosen by the composer.

GILLES BINCHOIS (c. 1400–1460)

Binchois was another master of the French chanson. He combined military and musical careers in addition to being a sub-deacon. For much of his career, Binchois was employed at the Burgundian court where strict courtly conventions were reflected in his approach to writing chansons. Binchois was widely revered by his contemporaries and his music was copied very frequently into music manuscripts of the time. His death was mourned in laments by his two greatest musical contemporaries, Dufay and Ockeghem.

Above Gilles Binchois is remembered for his melodic lines. His chansons of love and chivalry were greatly admired by the dukes of Burgundy, where he was employed for much of his life.

JOHANNES OCKEGHEM (c. 1410–1497)

The exact date of Ockeghem's birth is still unknown; inconclusive evidence indicates some time between 1410 and 1425. Highly regarded by his contemporaries, Ockeghem's reputation as a composer relies on his considerable intellectual rigor as well as the almost seamless blending of melodic phrases that is characteristic of his output. Born in present-day Belgium, he

OCKEGHEM'S *MISSA PROLATIONUM*

This work has long intrigued both specialists and performers of early music. It is built as a series of complex compositional challenges; the sections comprising the Mass Ordinary are treated musically as a series of canons. This means that one part begins a little later than another part and very strictly imitates the melody and rhythm of the first part. The following part may begin on the same note as the first part or it may begin on another note, higher or lower, in which case it must likewise shift all of the notes that it imitates from the first part. Obviously, this is a very difficult exercise depending upon which note the composer chooses to start the second part. Ockeghem provides solutions for all intervals of imitation from unison to octave. In another technical tour de force, some canons employ different musical meters so that some notes in one part are a little longer than in another part. This means that one part will pull ahead of its companion even though they have both started together and sing the same notes.

was employed at the Church of Our Lady in Antwerp, later by the Duke of Bourbon, and from about 1450 to his death he was employed at the French royal chapel.

Like Dufay and other composers of the mid- and late fifteenth century, Ockeghem unified his settings of the Mass through the reworking of melodies taken from music composed earlier. Unlike Dufay, whose most memorable melodies appear in the upper part of his works, Ockeghem's bass lines are more lyrical and traverse a lower vocal range than found in music by the earlier composer.

Ockeghem contributed many works to the three principal genres of Mass, motet, and chanson. His interest in compositional challenges and the far stricter forms of counterpoint have generated considerable interest in this composer from his own lifetime to the present day.

Below A page from the Chigi Codex, which contains most of the Masses written by Ockeghem, including his *Missa Ecce Ancilla Domine*. The Annunciation of the Virgin Mary is featured on the cantus part.

Josquin Desprez

c. 1450–AUGUST 27, 1521

DESPITE BEING ONE OF THE MOST REVERED COMPOSERS OF THE RENAISSANCE
PERIOD, SURPRISINGLY LITTLE IS KNOWN ABOUT THE LIFE OF JOSQUIN DESPREZ.
HE WAS BORN SOMEWHERE IN NORTHERN FRANCE AND SPENT MUCH OF HIS
LIFE IN ITALY BEFORE RETURNING TO FRANCE IN HIS LATER YEARS.

MISERERE MEI, DEUS

One of the most moving compositions from this
period, *Miserere mei, Deus* is a setting of Psalm 50
composed around 1503–1504 while Josquin Desprez
was employed at the court of Ferrara. This beautiful
motet, which was probably written at the behest of
Ercole d'Este, stands at the beginning of a sixteenth-
century musical tradition of elaborate settings of
psalm texts. It was most likely performed during Holy
Week. The composer introduces a plaintive musical
idea or motif based on the word "Miserere" at the
start of the work and repeats it at regular intervals
in the tenor voice for a total of 21 times during the
course of the setting. This helps to mark off each
verse of the psalm.

Each repetition of the motif is on a different note,
descending and ascending through the notes of the
octave. This leads, overall, to an intensely supplica-
tory effect in the music.

The situation with Josquin's known compositional
output is even murkier and has generated enormous controversy and uncertainty over what exactly he
composed, and when and where he worked. The likely
existence of at least one other composer with a similar
name has only complicated matters for modern lovers
of Renaissance music.

Above Theologian and
church reformer Martin
Luther famously said of
Josquin, "He is master
of the notes ... other
composers must do
what the notes decide."

What is certain about Josquin (he is always referred
to by his first name) is that he exerted an enormous
influence on the course of Western music by changing
how composers regarded the melodic and textural
relationships among the different parts in a composition. Specifically, Josquin is credited with establishing
the principle of imitation among the voice parts as a
compositional norm. Josquin built his works on a
succession of overlapping musical phrases each of
which is built on a musical motif passed around the
voices in imitation. This is called "pervading imitation"
by devotees of early music, and a wonderful example
by Josquin is his motet *Ave Maria virgo serena*. Pervading imitation is often freer than the strict canons of
Ockeghem, although Josquin was a master of canonic
writing and included it in every genre he cultivated.

Lute

Entering medieval Europe from Arabic culture, the lute is a descendant of the oud, and related to the Romanian cobza and the mandolin. The lute developed its classic form by about 1500. It is extremely lightweight and has a pear-shaped body. It typically has six strings, and a neck with seven to ten frets. Josquin Desprez's sacred and secular music and numerous vocal works were later transcribed for solo lute in the sixteenth century. This transcription is known as intabulation, and Josquin's lute settings represent the majority of the lute repertoire. As instrument-making progressed, the lute lost favor among composers.

JOSQUIN AND CONTEMPORARY FAME

Few musicians until Josquin received critical praise in the writings of their contemporaries. Josquin is unusual in that his contemporary fame is well documented along with some records of his attractive salary packages and teaching practices. One writer, Heinrich Glarean, wrote a treatise on music in 1547 called *Dodecachordon*, in which he generously illustrates his points under discussion with musical examples drawn from Josquin. Glarean commented that Josquin's "genius was so versatile in all things, so equipped with natural acumen and mental power, that there was nothing in this field [of music] that he could not do."

Discover the music

Missa Hercules Dux Ferrariae
Missa de beata virgine
Missa La sol fa re mi
Miserere mei, Deus
Faulte d'argent
Une musque de Biscaye
O virgo prudentissima
Ave Maria virgo serena

Below The opening of Josquin's *Missa de beata virgine*, one of the composer's later works, and widely considered a masterpiece. About 20 of Josquin's Masses have survived.

CAREER AND WORKS

Josquin's early career was spent in the service of the chapel of the Duke of Milan. He held later appointments in other Italian cities including Rome and Ferrara but many details of his middle years are unclear. He spent his last years in France. A similarly unclear picture exists in relation to his compositional output, and many pieces that were once thought to have been written by him have come under intense scrutiny by devotees, with many works called into question. Nevertheless, there remains a substantial body of music of the highest quality by Josquin that will ensure his status as the finest representative of mid-Renaissance composers.

Among the many masterpieces that are attributed to Josquin we can find a great variety of approach, from the fanfare-like chanson *Vive le roy* to the somber motet *Miserere mei, Deus*, and the inventive adaptation and elaboration of a pre-existing sacred melody such as in one of his last compositions, the "Pange lingua" Mass. We are still uncertain about the correct authorship of several works; for example, the motet *Absalon fili mi* was once thought to be by Josquin but more recently its attribution to Josquin's contemporary Pierre de la Rue has been suggested and is currently being debated by musicologists. Even among those works fairly securely assigned to Josquin, it is still difficult in many cases to establish their dates and the circumstances surrounding their composition.

An adventurous century

JOSQUIN LIVED THROUGH SOME OF THE MOST TUMULTUOUS AND FAR-REACHING EVENTS IN EUROPEAN HISTORY. FROM THE CONTINUING DEVELOPMENTS IN PRINTING, TO COLUMBUS'S VOYAGES TO THE NEW WORLD, TO THE UPHEAVALS OF THE PROTESTANT REFORMATION, JOSQUIN'S EPOCH WAS RICH IN ADVENTURE, TRAGEDY, AND OPPORTUNITY.

The great social and political upheavals of the decades on either side of the turn of the sixteenth century were matched by some of the most remarkable outpourings of artistic activity, expressed superlatively through the works of Michelangelo and Leonardo da Vinci, contemporaries based mainly in Florence and Rome, and each very deserving of the grand title of Renaissance Man.

MUSIC AND THE PRINTING PRESS

Although printing from movable type quickly gained in popularity after Gutenberg's printing of the Bible in 1450, musical works just occasionally found their way into print form. Only with the arrival of Ottaviano Petrucci's first volume of printed music in 1501, known as the *Odhecaton*, did the market potential for printed

Right Italian explorer Christopher Columbus sets off to find the New World. Funded by Spain's Queen Isabella, his voyages led to an exciting era of adventure and colonization.

Below Martin Luther (1483–1546) rejected some of the teachings of the Catholic Church thus spearheading the Protestant Reformation.

music establish itself in the minds of businessmen and musicians. Petrucci received a 20-year monopoly on printing music from the Republic of Venice in 1498 and embarked on a series of 61 collections of printed music, all of which attained a very high level of typographical elegance. Other music printing businesses quickly sprang up throughout Europe and their trade ensured rapid dissemination of music to a far greater audience than was possible in the earlier era of manuscript copies.

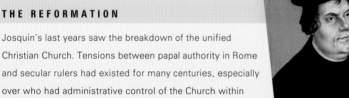

THE YEAR 1492

A number of events that occurred in the year 1492 may truly be said to reflect the end of an earlier era and the beginning of new and different directions in European history. The most famous event associated with 1492 is the voyage of Christopher Columbus to the New World of the Americas.

Columbus's undertaking was followed by many others—by Spanish, Portuguese, and English voyages that established colonies in parts of Asia as well as in North and South America. The new settlers included professional musicians and musically capable individuals. Music often served as a missionary tool for conversion purposes, and the interactions between European and indigenous musical cultures resulted in especially rich local traditions in which Gregorian chant, polyphony, and European instruments blended with native instruments, singers, and customs.

THE REFORMATION

Josquin's last years saw the breakdown of the unified Christian Church. Tensions between papal authority in Rome and secular rulers had existed for many centuries, especially over who had administrative control of the Church within national boundaries. During the fifteenth century the papacy conceded much ground to the Spanish and French monarchs, but resentment in Germany burst in 1517 when Martin Luther posted his famous "Disputation for the Clarification of the Power of Indulgences" onto the door of the Castle Church of Wittenberg. Luther's fundamental disagreement with several tenets of contemporary Christianity led quickly to the establishment of the Reformed churches, many of which had political support from local German rulers eager to lessen the influence of Rome in their affairs. Efforts at reconciliation were unsuccessful and differences between the older and newer versions of the Christian faith led to great upheavals and warfare throughout Europe over the next two centuries. Religious and geographic boundaries came into general alignment with much of northern Europe converting to Protestantism and southern Europe generally adhering to Catholicism.

The year 1492 in Spain was a particularly significant one because of the defeat by the Spanish monarchs Isabel and Ferdinand of the last stronghold of Muslim resistance in Spain. In the same year, the monarchs ordered the conversion of all members of the Jewish community to Christianity, an action that resulted in the exodus of about 165,000 Jews to other parts of Europe and northern Africa. In 1501 a similar decree was ordered against the Muslim community, thus ending the centuries-long multicultural dimension to medieval and early modern Spanish culture.

The year 1492 also marked the death of Lorenzo de Medici, the "Magnificent," ruler of Florence. Lorenzo was a gifted statesman, diplomat, and patron of the arts. His rule represented the high point of the Florentine Renaissance and his death was soon followed by the collapse of the fragile peace that he had negotiated among neighboring Italian states. Another prominent passing in this year was that of the great Italian painter Piero della Francesca on Friday, October 12 (the same day that Columbus set foot on the Bahamas). Piero's paintings are especially admired today for their use of perspective and their often enigmatic qualities.

The Franco–Flemish composers

☆ Birthplace of Guillaume de Machaut

★ Birthplace of Guillaume Dufay

☆ Possible birthplace of Johannes Ockeghem

☆ Possible birthplace of Gilles Binchois

★ Possible birthplace of Josquin Desprez

–· Modern country borders

Above *The Birth of Christ* by Piero della Francesca (c. 1415–1492). A mathematician as well as an artist, Piero's works exhibit a wonderful sense of perspective.

John Taverner

c. 1490–OCTOBER 18, 1545

ONE OF THE GREAT MASTERS OF RENAISSANCE ENGLISH MUSIC, JOHN TAVERNER WAS BORN IN LINCOLNSHIRE WHERE HE SPENT MUCH OF HIS LIFE APART FROM A BRIEF SPELL AS THE FIRST INSTRUCTOR OF THE CHOIR OF CARDINAL COLLEGE (NOW CHRIST CHURCH COLLEGE), OXFORD. HIS CAREER WAS PRIMARILY AS A CHURCH MUSICIAN, IN WHICH ROLE HE APPEARS TO HAVE PROSPERED—HE RETIRED IN 1537.

Taverner unwittingly achieved an extraordinary influence on the course of English music right up to the time of Purcell through a short melody of his composed at the words "In nomine Domini" in the Benedictus movement of his Mass "Gloria tibi Trinitas." He made some instrumental arrangements of this material and referred to them as "In nomine" pieces. This caught the imagination of some other composers who also wrote instrumental pieces taking the "In nomine" melody as their starting point, leading to a cherished tradition in English music that was honored by almost all composers of the sixteenth and seventeenth centuries.

LIFE AND WORKS

Little is known about Taverner's early career until he became a lay clerk of the choir of the collegiate church in Tattershall, Lincolnshire, in 1524. He became choir instructor at Cardinal College, Oxford in 1526. This college was associated with Cardinal Wolsey, Henry VIII's chief minister. Taverner became embroiled briefly in an outbreak of Lutheran heresy in 1528 but was cleared of serious involvement. However, by 1530 Taverner found it wise to seek employment elsewhere due to Wolsey's fall from grace from Henry's court. He returned to Lincolnshire and found a position in the choir of St Boltoph parish church in Boston.

Due to the vagaries of English legislation in the 1530s, the revenues supporting the generous musical establishment at this church were severely curtailed, a development that more than probably led to Taverner's retirement from full-time employment as a church musician. There is no justification to the claims made by some later commentators that he was a paid agent

Below Thomas Cromwell (c. 1485–1540), Henry VIII's chief minister, oversaw the dissolution of the monasteries. Suggestions that Taverner worked for Cromwell have never been substantiated.

Right Some important figures of Taverner's time—Henry VIII, Anne Boleyn (with lute), and Cardinal Wolsey. After's Wolsey's fall from grace, Taverner found work in Lincolnshire, well away from the political machinations at court.

of Thomas Cromwell, Wolsey's successor in the 1530s and the leading figure in the dissolution and persecution of the religious houses at this time. Taverner's comfortable financial position in his later years was due in the main to the large salary he enjoyed while employed at St Boltoph's.

As a composer Taverner was at the height of his powers during 1520–1530 when he was employed at Tattershall and Cardinal College. It is at this time that the bulk of his known music was composed. Taverner's church music represents one of the crowning achievements of cultural life during England's Tudor monarchy. His music is florid with expansive melodic writing and complex development of his musical motifs. In common with his contemporary English composers, his music does not share the detailed attention to word setting that may be found in continental repertoires.

His most famous works are two Masses, "Western wind" and "Gloria tibi Trinitas". He also wrote a number of motets as well as other ritual music for church settings. His secular

Discover the music

Mass "Western wind"

Missa "Gloria tibi Trinitas"

The Mean Mass

Ave Dei Patris filia

Settings of the *Magnificat*

Left Christ Church College, Oxford, formerly Cardinal College, in an engraving from 1673. Taverner worked at the college, founded by Cardinal Wolsey, as a choir master.

output is more modest in quantity, although there are some songs in addition to the "In nomine" instrumental arrangements. The Masses contain several features that had long been established in English compositional practice—frequent and long melismas, greater attention to writing for the higher and lower voices than for middle ones, and conflicting musical meters at points of interest or climax in a composition.

"WESTERN WIND" MASS

A beautiful secular song known as "Western wind" (or "Westron wynde") caught Taverner's imagination and that of two of his contemporaries, Christopher Tye (c. 1505–c. 1572) and John Sheppard (c. 1515–c. 1558). Each of these composers used this melody as the basis for a Mass setting, with Taverner's setting most likely serving as the inspiration for the other two.

Taverner employs the "Western wind" melody as a cantus firmus that is repeated with little or no alteration in each movement of the Mass. Variety is achieved through placing the melody in a different voice at different times and by constantly changing the musical textures in the surrounding voices. This variety among the musical voices means that no two successive statements of the melody sound the same.

The "Western wind" Mass is one of the final cantus firmus Mass settings in England. Stretching back over 100 years, this tradition is distinct from continental practice, especially that of early sixteenth-century composers such as Josquin. The English Reformation drew a curtain over the liturgical and political relevance of any further settings of the Mass.

Thomas Tallis

c. 1505–NOVEMBER 23, 1585

THE POLITICAL AND SOCIAL TURBULENCE OF SIXTEENTH-CENTURY
ENGLAND IS REFLECTED IN THE CAREER OF THOMAS TALLIS WHO
SERVED UNDER FOUR MONARCHS—HENRY VIII, EDWARD VI,
MARY I, AND ELIZABETH I.

The different political and artistic conditions associated with each of these rulers had a profound effect on the artistic output of Thomas Tallis and his contemporaries; some musical styles and genres were abandoned and others were invented to suit the liturgical needs of the moment.

LIFE AND MUSIC

Tallis is remembered for his large and diverse output of church music. His musical writing varied tremendously throughout his career, due not only to the changing political outlook but also to his friendship with young William Byrd and his absorption of certain features of continental compositional practice.

Tallis's early music reflects the Catholic tradition and comprises many settings of Latin texts, often on

Above An organist and composer, Tallis was also a music publisher. His co-publication with Byrd, the *Cantiones sacrae*, was dedicated to Elizabeth I, praising, among other things, her musical talents.

Left *The Byble in Englyshe*, the first authorized English edition of the Bible, printed in 1541. The empty space on the right once held a portrait of Thomas Cromwell, who had lost favor with Henry VIII.

a grand scale. With the English Reformation, Tallis was pragmatic and adaptable enough to write English-texted anthems and canticles for the Protestant liturgy. During the century's middle years, especially during Queen Mary's brief reign, Tallis was forced to move rapidly back and forth between the musical requirements of either a Protestant or Catholic monarchy.

After early appointments as organist or singer in several ecclesiastical institutions, Tallis's skills were recognized with his appointment as Gentleman of the Chapel Royal in 1540. This institution, serving the royal household, carried great prestige and salary; its membership is a roll call of some of the most eminent musicians of the time. Under Elizabeth I, the music performed by the Chapel Royal ranged from items suitable to the English Protestant liturgy to large-scale Latin-texted works in which continental (and Catholic) musical practice was evident.

THE MOTETS

A master of compositional ingenuity and technical dexterity, Tallis's formidable skills are most brilliantly displayed in his motet *Spem in alium* written for 40 parts. In the opening section, 20 voices enter with the theme in imitation. The following section has new material for the other 20 voices, and all 40 parts combine for the ending. Other compositional "tours de force" include his seven-part motet, *Miserere nostri*, in which three canons are presented simultaneously.

In 1575 Tallis and Byrd received a patent from Elizabeth I granting them a 21-year monopoly over printing music and music paper. That year they jointly published a volume of 34 Latin-texted motets, 17 from each, called the *Cantiones sacrae*. Although groundbreaking in terms of musical accomplishments, it was a commercial flop and marked the end of Latin sacred

Above Mary I (1516–1558) reigned from 1553 until her death, during which time Catholicism was re-established as the official religion. When she ordered the deaths of some 300 dissenters, she earned the nickname "Bloody Mary."

Discover the music

Spem in alium

Miserere nostri

Lamentations

Salvator mundi

Mass "Puer natus est nobis"

"God grant we grace"
  (*Tallis canon*)

Dorian Service

music as a major compositional outlet in England. Tallis was quite at home writing English-texted music that was suitable for the Protestant liturgy. Several of these compositions, such as the *Tallis canon*, the *Dorian Service*, and the anthem "If ye love me" remain in the Anglican repertoire to this day. The "Third tune," which was originally a contribution to Archbishop Parker's collection of church music, *Whole Psalter*, published in 1567, became the basis of a popular work by the twentieth-century composer Ralph Vaughan Williams, *Fantasia on a Theme by Thomas Tallis*.

Organ

One of the oldest instruments in the western musical tradition, the organ produces sound as wind vibrates through pipes of various materials (metal or wood), and with the timbre and volume altered by the keys, the handstops, and combination pistons. An accomplished organist, Thomas Tallis composed some well-regarded music of the early organ music repertoire. Unlike later keyboard instruments such as the piano, the organ's keyboard touch is not expressive (meaning every note sounds with the same velocity or force).

SALVATOR MUNDI

One of Thomas Tallis's 17 contributions to the volume of 34 motets published in the *Cantiones sacrae*, *Salvator mundi* is a brilliant exercise in large-scale polyphonic writing. It survives in two versions. The first is a demonstration of regularly balanced part-writing in which imitatively treated motifs are handled by five voices with subtle craftsmanship. *Salvator mundi* (1) likely represents Tallis's final stage of development as a composer. By contrast, *Salvator mundi* (2) may have started out originally as a two-part instrumental canon with an added bass part. A version for five voices set to an English text, "When Jesus went into Simon the Pharisee's House," found its way into the Protestant liturgy. A later revision with Latin text appeared in the *Cantiones sacrae*. This last version is also for five parts and maintains the canonic imitation between the soprano and tenor; the other parts, however, were revised considerably by Tallis. Frequent revision of earlier pieces was characteristic of Tallis, sometimes only of small details, but at other times to completely new purpose as we see with *Salvator mundi* (2).

Sixteenth-century England —100 years of adjustment

THE SIXTEENTH CENTURY BEGAN PROMISINGLY FOR ENGLAND UNDER THE SHREWDLY EFFECTIVE HENRY VII (R. 1485–1509) WHO HAD PACIFIED SQUABBLING POLITICAL FACTIONS AND SECURED A HEALTHY SURPLUS IN THE ROYAL COFFERS. HENRY'S SUCCESSORS IN THE TUDOR DYNASTY MAINTAINED A SIMILAR IRON GRIP ON POWER BUT PURSUED TUMULTUOUS POLICIES IN STATE CONTROL OVER RELIGION AND FOREIGN RELATIONS.

These had enormous consequences in England for the development of the arts, which flourished as never before and resulted in the works of the towering giants of literature: Shakespeare, Marlowe, Spenser; and music: Tallis, Byrd, Dowland, and Bull.

Below Henry VIII was a man of considerable achievements, and was an able performer and composer of music.

HENRY VIII AND THE REFORMED CHURCH

Henry VII was succeeded by his son Henry VIII. An autocratic monarch, Henry burned through the healthy state finances inherited from his father through extravagant undertakings, including his penchant for sparring

with the French—a short war in 1512, and a pompous display of wealth at a meeting with his French counterpart at the Field of the Cloth of Gold in 1520.

Henry's principal undertaking during his reign was a decisive break with papal authority. Henry's first wife, Catherine of Aragon, was unable to bear him a son. So he needed to legalize his divorce in order to marry Anne Boleyn. The pope refused to accede to Henry's demands for a dissolution of his marriage to Catherine, niece of Charles V of Spain, who had captured Rome and controlled the pope's movements. The result of these intrigues was the establishment of the Church of England headed by Henry. Initially not especially different from Catholicism in issues of doctrine, its influence on musical activity was immense due to the closure of monastic establishments, a traditional avenue of employment for musicians, and the revision of musical requirements for the emerging secular liturgy.

Left Elizabeth I (1533–1603) was the greatest of the Tudor monarchs. Her vast influence and achievements led to the period becoming known as the Elizabethan Age.

Sixteenth-century England
★ Death place of Thomas Tallis
☆ Death place of John Taverner
★ Birthplace of William Byrd

Above A 1570 work showing Catholics fleeing an English church (top), and a church service with an unrailed altar (bottom right).

AFTER HENRY

In 1547, Henry was succeeded by his nine-year-old son Edward VI, whose short rule was rendered chaotic by the maneuverings of his regents. English Protestantism strengthened during these years but suffered a big setback during Mary I's rule. Mary wanted to reinstate Catholicism and papal authority as well as strengthen relations with Spain, a development that alarmed many. Her brutal suppression of opposition to her policies led her to be reviled by the general populace and damaged the cause of Catholicism in England.

ELIZABETH I: GLORIES IN POLITICS AND THE ARTS

A prudent and wise ruler, Elizabeth's many successes are due in part to the longevity of her reign (1558–1603) and the follies of her opponents. She reinstated the reformed church throughout her kingdom and apparently did not object too much to Catholicism as long as it was discreetly practiced and was not associated with any treasonous plots. The greatest single threat she faced was arguably the Spanish Armada, a massive military force that set sail with a view to conquering England but was itself destroyed by storms off the English coast in 1588.

Elizabeth counted music among her accomplishments. She could play the lute and virginal. During her reign the Chapel Royal became the pre-eminent employer of the greatest English musicians of the period. Music for the Anglican church flourished, as did the cultivation of secular songs including the English madrigal, a genre of Italian origin that made headway into late sixteenth-century English cultural life due to interest in Italian culture and music at the time.

Elizabeth may be viewed as the greatest of the Tudor monarchs, but also the most singlehanded—she controlled every aspect of government. Upon her death in 1603, Elizabeth left an economically thriving nation with an artistic profile that could equal the accomplishments of any continental region.

THE "QUEEN'S MUSICK"

Elizabeth's interest in the arts led to many professional opportunities for musicians. Native English talent was well represented in the Chapel Royal but its high salaries were exceeded by an organization dedicated to instrumental music known as the Queen's Musick that performed at court. Unlike the Chapel Royal, this group was open to foreign employees and attracted many from Italy, especially from around Venice. Several emigrants established musical dynasties that lasted several generations, such as the Lupo and Bassano families. At an average salary of about £46 pounds a year (compared with a typical blacksmith's annual wage of about £6), musical life in England attracted Europe's best musicians. Elizabeth was not afraid to extend very competitive salaries to those she considered the finest musicians of her age—she offered Alfonso Ferrabosco £100 pounds to return to England from the continent in 1567. Ferrabosco made a deep impression on his contemporaries, including William Byrd, and is credited with influencing the course of English music for several decades.

Orlando di Lasso

1532–JUNE 14, 1594

ORLANDO DI LASSO WAS THE MOST VERSATILE COMPOSER OF HIS
GENERATION, EQUALLY AT HOME WITH MASS SETTINGS AND CHANSONS.
HE WAS BORN IN MONS IN PRESENT-DAY BELGIUM AND HELD A NUMBER
OF SHORT-TERM POSITIONS IN VARIOUS ITALIAN LOCATIONS AS WELL AS
ANTWERP BEFORE MOVING TO MUNICH TO TAKE ON THE POST OF
SINGER AT THE CHAPEL OF DUKE ALBRECHT V OF BAVARIA.

He was promoted to the post of chapel master in 1563 and remained in Munich until his death. Lasso traveled widely as ducal representative and was highly influential on younger generations of composers. In 1604, ten years after his death, his sons Ferdinand and Rudolph published the *Magnum opus musicum*, a collection of 516 of Orlando's motets—a fitting tribute to one of the finest composers of the late sixteenth century.

LASSO AND THE MUSICAL EXPRESSION OF TEXTS

Musicians of the sixteenth century were particularly concerned with proper expression of the meaning of a text. Nowhere is this more carefully demonstrated than in Lasso's large corpus of motets where meaning, emotion, and imagery are conveyed with an intensity that greatly impressed his contemporaries. In his setting of the *Penitential Psalms* as a cycle of 12 motets, Lasso captures the somber quality of the texts and often sets particular words or phrases with a musical idea that is frequently quite literal in its application, for example, a "descent" in the text receives an appropriately descending musical figure. This motet cycle was composed in 1559 at the request of Lasso's employer Duke Albrecht who spared no expense in having them copied and beautifully illuminated by his personal artist.

Lasso was equally at home with secular texts and demonstrated his sensitivity to textual nuance in a chanson such as *La nuit est froide et sombre* (*The night*

Above A master of polyphony, Orlando di Lasso wrote some 2,000 works, including motets, chansons, madrigals, psalms, and Masses.

Right A sibyl, from a work by Raphael (1483–1520). The *Prophetiae sibyllarum*, Lasso's cycle of 12 motets, takes the prophesies of the sibyls as their subject.

is cold and somber). Here the contrast between heaven and earth described in the text is captured by contrasting high and low sonorities, while the change to brighter sounding harmonies matches the approach of day that is mentioned later in the text.

RENAISSANCE COMPOSERS AND CLASSICAL GREEK THEORIES

A great interest in the theories of music by ancient Greek writers prompted many musicians and composers of the mid-sixteenth century to frequently experiment with novel sonorities that expanded the range and intensity of harmonies in contemporary music. This resulted in increased use of what is called chromaticism in musical harmonies—interspersing chords built on notes that do not normally occur in the scale or mode in which a piece of music is written.

The increased use of chromatic music, with its supposed link to the music of ancient Greece, also occupied the attention of many commentators on music, with theoretical tracts appearing on the nature of Greek modes and how they could be applied in contemporary composition and musical instrument building. One such writer, Nicola Vicentino (1511–c. 1576), proposed, and later constructed, a keyboard with 31 notes in each octave (as opposed to our usual 12 notes). This instrument was able to accommodate the very small distances between adjacent notes that Vicentino (and others) thought were characteristic of ancient Greek musical practice.

ORLANDE.

Above A manuscript of a madrigal by Orlando di Lasso. Among his prolific compositional output, he wrote over 170 madrigals, some intended for spiritual purposes.

Discover the music

In me transierunt

Cum essem parvulus

Missa Pro defunctis

Missa Locutus sum

Veni creator spiritus

Susanne un jour

Un advocate dit à sa femme

Prophetiae sibyllarum

PROPHETIAE SIBYLLARUM

Although Lasso shared the interest of his fellow composers in probing the limits of contemporary musical sonorities, he did not go to the extremes advocated by some contemporary writers. Yet his *Prophetiae sibyllarum*, a cycle of 12 motets, explores the full range of tonal intensity possible within traditional compositional means. This cycle was composed around 1560, and each of the 12 motets represents one of the Sibylline prophets. These mythological figures would have been familiar to Lasso's contemporaries not only through their education in the Classics but also because Michelangelo depicted them in his work on the ceiling of the Sistine Chapel.

The first motet in the collection particularly demonstrates the predilection for chromatic harmonies and sense of tonal disorientation that arose from mid-sixteenth-century interests in Greek music and its apparently greater range of sonorities. Lasso moves his music briskly through all 12 notes of the chromatic scale and he builds chords on many of them that lie outside the normal modal scale used in contemporary composition. The remaining motets, though perhaps less intense in their musical excursions, demonstrate Lasso's keen sense of text expression and his sensitivity to balance between the words and the notes.

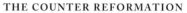

LIFE & TIMES

Religion and the arts in the sixteenth century

DURING THE COURSE OF LASSO'S CAREER, THE PROTESTANT REFORMATION HAD ESTABLISHED ITSELF AS AN ALTERNATIVE RELIGIOUS FORCE TO THE ROMAN CATHOLIC CHURCH. THE PAPACY DID NOT ADOPT A PASSIVE ROLE IN RESISTING THE MARCH OF PROTESTANTISM; IT INSTEAD EMBARKED ON A MOVEMENT TO WIN BACK ADHERENTS AND STRENGTHEN THE FAITH.

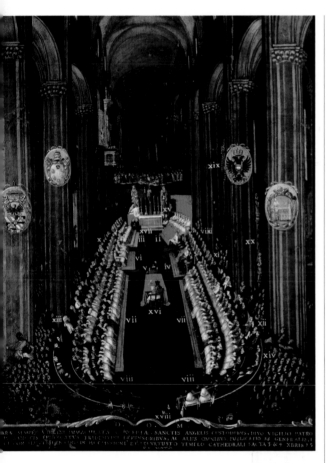

Opposite right Palladio's grand vision for the Rialto Bridge in Venice. One of history's most influential architects, Palladio wrote an important treatise on architecture in 1570.

Left The concluding session of the Council of Trent. The Council was convened in an attempt to stem the flow of Catholics to Protestantism.

Below Widely admired in his lifetime and even today, Palestrina wrote more than 100 Masses, over 300 motets, and many other works, both sacred and secular.

THE COUNTER REFORMATION

To stem the spread of Protestant churches in sixteenth-century Europe, the Catholic Church convened the Council of Trent (1545–1563). The Council's mission was to consider how the Catholic Church, with the pope as its head, could reinvigorate itself and reverse the gains made by Protestantism. Although the results of these deliberations were largely rejected by Protestant churchmen, the Council succeeded in clarifying many aspects of the Catholic faith and devising strategies to reconvert Protestants to Catholicism.

The Council only got around to considering the role of music in liturgical contexts in two sessions in 1563. The so-called Tridentine reforms in music centered on purging elements of secular music that had crept into liturgical music over the preceding centuries and also ensuring that sacred texts were clearly projected in musical settings so that worshippers were not distracted from their meaning. In general, the Council was more tolerant of musical creativity and performance than some of the reformed churches where simple congregational singing only was permitted. The late sixteenth-century composers who were associated with the Catholic Church produced many of the finest polyphonic works ever created for Christian liturgies.

PALESTRINA (1525–1594)

Giovanni Pierluigi da Palestrina was a prominent composer of the period who adapted his compositional style to suit the Tridentine reforms. Enormously popular in his lifetime, Palestrina spent

The religious upheavals of the sixteenth century affected all aspects of social and cultural life at the time. In music, the Tridentine reforms provided a stimulus toward greater transparency in sacred settings and a review of past musical practices. Elsewhere in the arts, notable advances were made particularly in painting and architecture, with new approaches in the latter field spreading rapidly across Europe and parts of the New World.

most of his career in the service of Roman Catholicism. He wrote 104 settings of the Mass, 94 madrigals and approximately 500 other works that can be loosely classified as motets. Features of his compositional style are graceful and elegant melodic lines, careful control of dissonances in the musical texture, and varied voice groupings and spacings. In accordance with Tridentine requirements, Palestrina paid careful attention to texts by setting successive phrases of text to clear melodic phrases. Palestrina's style can be most clearly heard in his *Missa Papae Marcelli* and in motets such as *Dum complerentur* and *Nigra sum*.

Palestrina is one of the few Western composers active before 1600 whose music has been performed continuously since his lifetime. His output has been studied in great depth and has served as a pedagogical model for students of Renaissance music from his time right up to the present day. Palestrina has sometimes been called "the savior of music" because of how he reconciled the sophistication of Renaissance polyphony with the demands of the Council of Trent. Yet he was only one among a generation of Catholic musicians who flourished in the aftermath of the Council. His contemporaries Jacob de Kerle and Vincenzo Ruffo, for instance, dedicated their professional compositional

PALLADIAN ARCHITECTURE

Andrea Palladio (1508–1580) was inspired by the architecture of classical antiquity to create buildings that are famous for their balance, proportion, and grandeur. He spent almost his entire life in the Veneto region where he designed churches, country villas, and urban palaces. In his book *Quattro libri dell'architectura* (1570), he emphasized that the proportions of the various parts of a building should be in esthetic balance with each other and should be in a systematic relationship to a central focal point.

Palladio's designs were studied by architects and adapted to different regions throughout Europe. Many buildings designed by Palladio himself can be seen in Venice and the Veneto region, with a rich group of palaces in Vicenza. Especially famous is the great domed church known as Il Redentore in Giudecca, one of the islands of Venice. Palladian architecture was spectacularly successful—in England Inigo Jones designed the Queen's house in Greenwich (1616), the first of many Palladian buildings in England and Ireland. In the United States, southern plantation owners, including George Washington and Thomas Jefferson, were keen adherents of the Palladian esthetic.

activities toward the recommendations of the Council. However, Palestrina's work served as a direct model for composing new religious works for use in contemporary liturgical celebrations well into the seventeenth and eighteenth centuries.

William Byrd

c. 1543–JULY 4, 1623

BYRD'S CHILDHOOD AND EARLY CAREER WERE CENTERED AROUND LINCOLN WHERE HE WAS APPOINTED ORGANIST AND MASTER OF CHORISTERS AT THE CATHEDRAL IN 1563. IN 1570 HE WAS SWORN IN AS A GENTLEMAN OF THE CHAPEL ROYAL, A PRESTIGIOUS POST IN THE SERVICE OF ELIZABETH I, WHERE HE JOINED THOMAS TALLIS AS A CHAPEL ORGANIST.

Byrd enjoyed a successful career despite being a Catholic at a time when recusancy was a criminal offence in England. The tensions between his Catholicism and his outward life in the service of a Protestant establishment are often reflected in the inner workings of Byrd's music and the circumstances of their genesis and contemporary performance.

BYRD AND ANGLICAN MUSIC

The Anglican liturgy had no direct counterpart among the Protestant denominations active in Europe. Two major musical genres—the service and the anthem—dominated composers' interactions with it. The anthem was a counterpart to the continental motet with wide-ranging texts in English drawn from Scripture or other liturgical texts. The service was a setting of any or all the components of the daily prayers of Matins, Communion, and Evensong. Byrd cultivated both genres; a fine example of an anthem is *Christ rising again*, while his Great Service demonstrates imaginative and varied textures in this genre. Byrd contributed a number of items to the Anglican liturgy during his career, but the bulk of it appears to have been written while he was employed at Lincoln Cathedral.

Right A manuscript of Byrd's "Sing joyfully unto God our strength," written for the Protestant liturgy. Another of his Anglican anthems is "O Lord make thy servant."

BROWNING

William Byrd also composed songs and instrumental works. For many of these he drew upon long-established traditions in English music, for instance, variations on a popular ballad, *Browning my dear*, that was commonly undertaken by seventeenth-century English composers. Byrd wrote his *Browning* variations for the viol consort, a set of five stringed instruments of various sizes. Viol consorts were immensely popular in sixteenth- and seventeenth-century England, with many middle and upper class families possessing a set of them for use in domestic music-making.

Byrd wrote 20 variations on the eight-bar *Browning* melody. They fall into three broad sections (variations 1–10, 11–15, and 16–20). The increasingly imitative textures of the first section are offset by the chordal progressions of variation 11, while variations 16–20 are unified by remaining in the home key only. Byrd also often pairs variations; for instance, variations 1–2 are for three parts only, and variations 5–6 are linked by the inversion of a melody. Byrd's *Browning* demonstrates his capability of controlling large-scale musical structures in both instrumental and choral works.

Discover the music

Emendemus in melius (1575)

Miserere mihi Domine (1575)

Walsingham variations

My Ladye Nevells Booke (1591)

Mass settings for three, four and five voices (1593–1595)

"Save me, O God, for thy Name's sake"

Crowned with flowers and lilies (1611)

Left English writer Henry Peacham (1576–1643) said of the composer, "For motets and music of piety and devotion, as well for the honor of our nation as the merit of the man, I prefer above all our Phoenix, Master William Byrd."

Virginal

In *Tractatus de musica* (c. 1460), Paulus Paulirinus of Prague wrote that, "... [it] is called a virginal because, like a virgin, it sounds with a gentle and undisturbed voice." Part of the harpsichord family, the virginal is a keyboard instrument that was used mainly during the late medieval and Renaissance periods. Like the harpsichord, the strings are plucked to create sounds. Most early models were played resting on the musician's lap; later models came in many different sizes, often richly decorated with ivory, mother of pearl, and marble. Byrd wrote numerous pieces for the instrument, compiled in *My Ladye Nevells Booke* of keyboard music.

BYRD AND LATIN CHURCH MUSIC

Byrd's contribution to the volume of 34 motets, the *Cantiones sacrae*, co-published with Tallis in 1575, show a greater affinity to continental compositional practice than his Anglican music. The musical textures employ frequent imitation among the voices and the declamation of the texts takes on rhetorical dimensions. Events in the 1580s forced Byrd to consider his Catholicism.

Below Lincoln Cathedral, where Byrd was employed as an organist and choirmaster, a post he held for about ten years. He continued to write for the choir even after he left.

In 1581, Father Thomas Campion and two other Jesuits were executed on charges of conspiring against the state. Subsequent anti-Catholic sentiment ran high with fines and punishments for attending Mass or being absent from Anglican services. Byrd often found himself at the receiving end of fines for his Catholic activities, and in 1593 he moved to Essex where he mixed with Sir John Petrie, a leader in the Catholic community. Much of his Catholic music was likely composed for, and sung by, Petrie's friends during celebrations of the Mass discreetly held at Petrie's home.

Byrd wrote three settings of the Mass in the 1590s, and embarked on an enormous project of musical settings for all the texts associated with the major Catholic feast days. The result was the two-volume *Gradualia*, which appeared at a sensitive political time. Volume 1 was published in 1605 but was withdrawn after the Gunpowder Plot to assassinate King James I led by Guy Fawkes, a Catholic, was uncovered. Volume 2 was published in 1607; the two volumes were reissued in calmer times in 1610. The *Gradualia* is a monumental cycle of music by a single composer for the entire liturgical year.

LIFE & TIMES

England's glory days

THE LATE SIXTEENTH AND EARLY SEVENTEENTH CENTURIES WERE A PROSPEROUS TIME FOR THE ARTS IN ENGLAND. SUPPORTED BY THE STABILITY OF ELIZABETH I'S REIGN AND BY IMPROVING ECONOMIC CONDITIONS, MUSIC, DRAMA, AND POETRY FLOURISHED. MANY OF THE OUTSTANDING NAMES IN ENGLISH CULTURE COME FROM THIS TIME, SUCH AS WILLIAM SHAKESPEARE, CHRISTOPHER MARLOWE, AND EDMUND SPENSER IN LITERATURE, AND THE COMPOSERS JOHN BULL, JOHN DOWLAND, AND THOMAS TOMKINS. IT IS WORTH-WHILE TO CONSIDER THE CAREERS OF A REPRESENTATIVE OF EACH OF THESE FIELDS TO APPRECIATE THE ACHIEVEMENTS OF THE SO-CALLED GOLDEN AGE.

CHRISTOPHER MARLOWE (1564–1593)

Born in Canterbury, Marlowe's intellectual abilities were recognized with a scholarship to the prestigious King's School in his native town before his enrolment at Corpus Christi College, Cambridge where he received his BA in 1584 and MA in 1587.

During his short but brilliant career, Marlowe wrote seven plays, several of which paved the way for Shakespeare's mature stage works. His *Dr Faustus* is perhaps the first tragi-comedy that helped Shakespeare to develop the character of Shylock in *The Merchant of Venice*, while Marlowe's *Edward II* is a history play that may have influenced Shakespeare's *Richard II* and *Henry IV*. Marlowe also made excellent verse translations of Ovid's *Elegies* and Lucan's *First Book of the Civil War*.

Involvement in Elizabethan espionage may have resulted in Marlowe's untimely death at the age of 29. The chancellor of Cambridge University, Sir Francis Walsingham, served as Secretary of State to Elizabeth I. He built up one of the most effective intelligence services in Europe and successfully uncovered the ceaseless Catholic plots to assassinate the queen. His position at Cambridge enabled him to recruit the finest minds into the espionage service,

Above right The so-called Chandos portrait of William Shakespeare (1564–1616), regarded as England's greatest poet and playwright.

Above This portrait hanging in Corpus Christi College is thought to be of Christopher Marlowe. One of his most famous plays is *Tamburlaine*, performed in 1587.

among whom was Marlowe. An early assignment during his student days saw Marlowe take a period of leave in order to visit the Catholic seminary in Rheims, possibly as a fake convert, where he would have investigated matters pertaining to the Babington plot to assassinate the queen and her chief ministers. Marlowe's activities were apparently successful and he was assigned further cases.

On May 30, 1593 Marlowe met his death in a house in Deptford while he was in the company of several characters well versed in the arts of intrigue: Richard Poley, a trusted agent who carried papers on behalf of the queen throughout Europe; Ingram Frizer, personal assistant to Thomas Walsingham, an accomplished spy-master and cousin of the recently deceased Sir Francis Walsingham; and Nicholas Skeres, an assistant to Poley with a long history of shady activities. The exact circumstances of Marlowe's death remain unclear, with rumors and speculations from that date to our own time about a drunken brawl, a murder to prevent disclosure of certain knowledge in Marlowe's possession, or a faked death after which Marlowe was possibly sent to the Continent to continue in Her Majesty's service.

JOHN BULL (c. 1563–1628)

Bull was the leading keyboard virtuoso of his day and was also a composer and organ builder. He was born in Radnorshire and became a member of the Children of the Chapel Royal by 1574, where he was a pupil of

Above Elizabeth I is reported to have once said, "I have joined myself in marriage to a husband, namely the kingdom of England."

Byrd. He held appointments at Hereford Cathedral from 1582 and was a member of the (adult) Chapel Royal from 1586. He was granted a Bachelor of Music degree from Oxford University in 1586 and received a doctorate from Cambridge University in 1592. Finding himself regularly in straitened financial circumstances, Bull devoted much of his energy to petitioning the queen for supplements to his wages and applying for positions to augment his income. He had the misfortune to encounter highway robbers in 1592 and pirates in 1610 during a voyage home from Spain. Bull joined the musical establishment of Prince Henry and in 1612 was appointed music teacher to young Princess Elizabeth, daughter of James I.

In 1613 Bull fled to the Netherlands to escape arrest and possible imprisonment on charges of adultery, although he claimed to his continental hosts that his abrupt departure was due to persecution because of his Catholicism. He made many powerful enemies in this episode—the Archbishop of Canterbury, George Abbott, wrote to the English envoy in Brussels, Sir William Trumbull, condemning Bull in detail and concluding "the man hath more music than honesty and is as famous for marring of virginity as he is for fingering of organs and virginals." Bull's employment in Brussels by Archduke Albert was terminated, for diplomatic reasons, due to the severity of King James I's wrath upon learning of his organist's flight from England. Bull spent the remainder of his life in near poverty as organist in Antwerp.

Left The composer and organist John Bull has been credited with writing *God Save the King,* which later became the British national anthem.

Tomás Luis de Victoria

1548–AUGUST 20, 1611

VICTORIA'S MUSIC HAS A DARK AND SOMBER QUALITY THAT IS VERY EXPRESSIVE AND
HIGHLY APPROPRIATE TO THE INTENSELY RELIGIOUS AND DEVOTIONAL NATURE OF HIS
COMPOSITIONAL OUTPUT. HE LIVED AT A TIME WHEN SPAIN EXPERIENCED INCREASED
RELIGIOUS FERVOR DURING THE REIGN OF PHILIP II (R. 1556–1598), A MONARCH WHO
ZEALOUSLY DEFENDED THE ROMAN CATHOLIC FAITH.

Victoria—the greatest Spanish composer of the sixteenth century—had no interest in composing secular music and all his surviving compositions were intended for religious purposes.

A RICH LIFE

Victoria was born in Avila, the hometown of St Teresa. He was a student at the Jesuit Collegio Germanico in Rome, after which he held a series of appointments in various Roman establishments that were connected with the Church, including his former school. Victoria returned to Spain in the mid-1580s and was appointed personal chaplain to the sister of King Philip II, the Dowager Empress Maria, widow of Emperor Maximilian II. In 1581 Maria had retired to the Convent of St Clare in Madrid, which housed 33 cloistered nuns. Mass and other services were performed in an exquisitely decorated small chapel and the priests there were required to be accomplished singers of sacred polyphony and Gregorian chant.

As a financially well-endowed institution, the convent was in a position to offer attractive benefits to its chaplains, including a personal servant, meals served in their private quarters adjacent to the convent, and annual leave of one month. Due in large part to these comforts, Victoria declined invitations to take up prestigious posts elsewhere in Spain. He took an extended period of leave in 1592 to travel to Rome where he supervised the printing of his second book of Mass settings. His music was performed in his presence by members of the Collegio Germanico as part of the celebrations over the Turkish defeat at the Battle of Sisak in 1593; and in February 1594 he was in the cortège at Palestrina's funeral. Victoria returned to Spain in 1595 where he resumed his duties serving the Dowager Empress as chaplain and as chapel

master until her death in 1603. He remained at the convent as organist until his death in 1611.

VICTORIA'S MUSIC

Victoria's music was immensely popular during his time. A collection of 200 settings of Masses, Magnificats, and motets was published in 1600 and included Philip II among its admirers. The collection was also circulated in Spain's colonies and enjoyed enormous popularity especially in Mexico throughout the seventeenth century. Although Victoria's most popular works today are serious in tone, it would be unfair to characterize all his compositional output this way. His many exultant and cheerful passages were noted by his

Below A twenty-first-century view of the city and famous medieval walls of Avila, the city in Spain where Victoria was born.

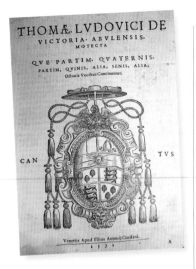

THOMÆ LVDOVICI DE
VICTORIA · ABVLENSIS.
MOTECTA
QVE PARTIM QVATERNIS.
PARTIM, QVINIS, ALIA, SENIS, ALIA,
Octonis Vocibus Concinuntur.

CAN   TVS

Venetijs Apud Filios Antonij Gardani.
1 5 7 2

Below Like his father and grandfather before him, Philip IV (1605–1665) continued to champion Victoria's music after the composer's death. Victoria had dedicated his *Missa pro victoria* (*Mass for victory*) to Philip's father, Philip III.

contemporaries, including John IV of Portugal, who remarked that Victoria "never stays downcast for long."

Victoria's greatest work was the *Officium defunctorum* (*Office for the Dead*), which is a setting of prayers for the Requiem service. This work, written to commemorate the death of his patron, Dowager Empress Maria, was published in 1605. It contains polyphonic settings of the chant melodies associated with the Requiem Mass, as well as a motet, a setting of the prayer for absolution, *Libera me*, and of one of the lessons from the Book of Job. The settings of the various pieces are superbly balanced, with moments of great poignancy such as the music for the text "Versa est in luctum" from the Book of Job.

Above The title page of a book of compositions by Victoria, dated 1572. A perfectionist, the composer monitored the publication of his works, checking the proofs at every stage of the printing process.

O MAGNUM MYSTERIUM

O magnum mysterium, written for the feast of the Circumcision on January 1, is justifiably one of Victoria's best loved works today because of its controlled delivery of the text in a melancholy and introspective musical setting. The motet exploits a variety of textures including imitative entries among the parts that alternate with block chordal passages, contrasting long and short phrases that frequently overlap, and different combinations of vocal registers. Especially vivid passages occur at settings of the words "sacramentum" and "in praesepio."

Victoria used this motet as the basis of a setting of the *Missa O magnum mysterium*. He preserved many aspects of the motet, such as the tendency to pair the voices together for short passages, and reworked the motet's opening into a large-scale fugal section. It was common for Renaissance composers to take a pre-existing model and use it as the basis for their own inspiration. The models could be from earlier works by the same composer or earlier composers (thereby paying homage to earlier masters) or they could be drawn from melodies in popular currency at the time.

Spain's golden century

SPAIN IN THE LATE SIXTEENTH AND EARLY SEVENTEENTH CENTURIES WAS AT THE HEIGHT OF ITS POWER—THE SPANISH GOLDEN AGE—WITH CONTROL OVER SEVERAL EUROPEAN REGIONS AND A GROWING OVERSEAS EMPIRE ENCOMPASSING NEWLY CONQUERED LANDS IN THE AMERICAS AND ASIA.

The political developments of this period were matched by great intensity in the arts: Victoria's close contemporaries included many of the most outstanding literary and artistic figures in Spain's history. It is worth looking at a sample of these extraordinary individuals to get a taste of the cultural environment that was inhabited by Victoria.

EL GRECO (1541–1614)

The most famous contemporary artist in Spain was an immigrant from Crete, known as El Greco (his real name was Domenikos Theotokopoulos). He settled in the city of Toledo in 1577 where he lived and worked until his death. El Greco's highly individual works cannot be conventionally classified into any school of art. He combined elements of Byzantine art that he learned in his native Crete with Western traditions, and he had a fondness for expressionistic depictions in which distorted figures and vivid landscapes grip the attention of the viewer. His *View of Toledo* is one of the most haunting visions of an urban landscape ever produced. El Greco received a great deal of

Below El Greco's *View of Toledo,* with its evocative treatment of light, reflects the artist's deep spirituality.

favorable attention in the twentieth century from both artists and audiences alike. His *Opening of the Fifth Seal*, from the last decade of his life, is considered to be the direct source of inspiration for Picasso's *Les demoiselles d'Avignon.*

Spain, sixteenth century
★ Birthplace of Tomás Luis de Victoria
☆ Birthplace of Francisco Guerrero
-·- Modern country borders

MIGUEL DE CERVANTES (1547–1616)

Nicknamed "el Principe de los Ingenios" (the Prince of Wits), Cervantes's influence on Spanish language and literature has been profound. His novel *Don Quixote* is considered the first modern novel and one of the best examples in the history of this genre. Its many colorful episodes may reflect the adventurous life that Cervantes himself had led as secretary to a cardinal, infantryman in the Spanish army, purveyor to the Spanish Armada, and later a tax collector. His irregular accounts in the last of these positions led to a short term in prison.

Don Quixote received acclaim upon its publication in two parts in 1605 and 1615. The escapades of its principal character and his servant Sancho Panza have entertained generations of readers worldwide up to the present time. The novel ridiculed many aspects of the tradition of chivalry, a code of behavior that had persisted since the Middle Ages. Cervantes also wrote a series of short stories on social and political aspects of contemporary Spain as well as volumes of verse and drama.

FRANCISCO GUERRERO (c. 1528–1599)

Second only to Victoria among Spanish composers of the sixteenth century, Guerrero's music was published widely outside Spain during his lifetime. Unlike Victoria, he was a keen composer of secular song, and he set poems by a range of Spanish poets including Lope de Vega, the greatest Spanish dramatist of the age. Guerrero, who was born and died in Seville, remained a popular composer for more than two centuries after his death, in Spanish and Spanish–American cathedrals, and his music was frequently recopied for church use throughout the New World after 1700.

Guerrero's music retained its popularity due to its attractive melodic lines that are interwoven

Above Miguel de Cervantes Saavedra, died on the same day as Shakespeare. That day—April 23—is celebrated today as UNESCO's International Day of the Book.

Below Don Quixote and his faithful servant Sancho Panza are among literature's most loved characters. This is a nineteenth-century illustration of the pair.

into harmonies that bring to mind the classical simplicity of music from the eighteenth century. Guerrero was also a master of canonic writing, and yet the technical complexities associated with this procedure never detract from the clear sense of melodic direction in his music. This trait is demonstrated admirably in his *Ave virgo sanctissima*, a motet published in 1566 that became immensely popular in Spanish-speaking lands.

THE SPANISH DECLINE

After the great prosperity and expansion of the Spanish empire in the first part of the sixteenth century, increasing tensions and strains encroached and began to have negative effects. Spain was often at war in various parts of Europe, and its naval power was under threat from pirates associated with the Ottoman Empire. As well, the failure of the Spanish Armada against English forces in 1588 greatly hindered the expansion and security of Spanish naval power.

The Protestant Reformation was perceived as a big threat to Spanish interests and a great deal of effort was expended on defending the Roman Catholic faith, including participation in costly religious wars. The combination of war, plague, and the separation of Portugal led to the decline of Spain as a European imperial power in the seventeenth century. However, Spain retained most of its overseas colonies and gradually began a process of internal improvements so that a revival of its fortunes occurred in the eighteenth century.

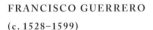

THE BAROQUE PERIOD

c. 1600–1750

Introduction

THE EMERGENCE OF THE BAROQUE PERIOD IN MUSIC HISTORY HAS OFTEN BEEN CONVENIENTLY DATED AT AROUND THE YEAR 1600. CERTAINLY MANY OF THE OUTWARD MANIFESTATIONS OF WHAT DEFINE BAROQUE STYLE—A DESIRE BY COMPOSERS FOR INCREASED EXPRESSIVENESS, A RISE IN THE IMPORTANCE OF INSTRUMENTAL MUSIC AND SECULAR DANCE AND POETIC FORMS, AND A GREATER AWARENESS OF FUNCTIONAL HARMONY AS AN ORGANIZING PRINCIPLE IN MUSIC—BEGAN TO ASSERT THEMSELVES AROUND THIS TIME.

The more or less accidental "invention" of opera by the esthetes known as the Florentine Camerata, along with the larger scale instrumental writing of Giovanni Gabrieli in Venice, and the experimental and expressive late madrigals of Claudio Monteverdi all occurred within several years around the turn of the century and within a relatively short geographic distance from one another. That the Italian peninsula was the center of this new musical world, this world of the "seconda prattica," there was little doubt. Just as in the previous era of the Renaissance, the ruling compositional style had come from France and then the Netherlands to spread down and across all of Europe, so too in the Baroque era the music of the Italians dominated and spread northward to spawn a new grammar and syntax of expression and a new set of genres—opera, cantata, concerto, and oratorio—that became the common language of art music for the next century and beyond. Composers from all Europe were directly influenced, such as Gabrieli's greatest pupil Heinrich Schütz, or, as in the case of George Frideric Handel a hundred years later, had their musical language enriched by a brief Italian sojourn.

The actual term "Baroque" as applied to music was borrowed by musicologists from art historians, who themselves had appropriated it from literary and cultural history. It generally refers to a style or an object that is elaborate, ornate, ostentatious, or at its most specific level of meaning, irregularly shaped. It is quite

Left *The Ecstasy of Saint Theresa*, by Gian Lorenzo Bernini (1598–1680), is considered one of the defining artworks of the Baroque period.

Previous pages Among the musical elements in *The Sense of Hearing* by Jan Brueghel is a range of Baroque instruments and a painting of Orpheus playing the lyre. Musicians play in the room at the back, and the sheet music is a madrigal.

Above Dancers in costume for a ballet, 1644. Men dominated the ballet in its early years—King Louis XIV was an accomplished dancer himself.

obvious to even the untrained eye how the art and architecture of the late sixteenth and early seventeenth centuries began to rely more and more on themes of emotion, aspiration, mysticism, ecstasy, and struggle, than those of proportion, purity, balance, clarity, and unity that were the hallmark of the Renaissance. Likewise, the listener can perceive in the music of the early Baroque period a similar shedding of old forms and means of expression and the emergence of a new emotional language. Characteristic of this language was an increased interest in the sonorities, colors, dynamics, range and articulations of instruments; a new preoccupation with pictorialism and direct emotional appeal; and a renewed importance for secular music as expressed in dance and song.

As we observe the history of western Europe during the seventeenth century we see a strengthening of the large nation state, centered around a large metropolitan capital—London, Paris, Vienna—with royal courts that required entertainment on a grand scale. A concentration of artists, composers, poets, actors, dancers, instrument makers, craftsmen of all sorts, were drawn together in these centers to provide the ruling class with the new forms, many of which (especially opera and oratorio) brought various skills and performing arts into partnership.

The Catholic Church, still the dominant religious force in southern Europe, continued to have influence in the arts and particularly in music. Given the fact

that the Counter Reformation of the previous century had drawn the Church more deeply into a conservative and reactionary mode, the intellectual and scientific inquiries of the day came to be more the domain of the northern Protestant countries. The Church chose to become an even stronger patron in those non-scientific areas of intellectual endeavor—art, and music.

The new musical genres of the concerto, the cantata, opera, and oratorio were all founded on the principles of expression and emotion. Music's overriding goal became to move the listener—to create an *affeckt*. The concerto sprang from the possibilities of opposing

Above A grand festival of music and dance in a Baroque palace. Note the ornamentation of the internal archictecture, and the highly decorative painting style.

musical forces—solo versus tutti—of the polychoral music of the late sixteenth century. The solo cantata, whether secular or sacred, was also built on the principle of opposing forces and variety of emotional states and direct declamatory expression. The oratorio is a later sacred offshoot of the opera—the telling of Biblical stories with solo recitatives and arias, accompanied by colorful orchestral forces and dramatic choruses. Opera was the fullest realization of the Baroque desire for differentiated expression, with the fullest variety of emotions and opposing forces dramatically, musically, and visually available to it.

Claudio Monteverdi

MAY 15, 1567–NOVEMBER 29, 1643

MONTEVERDI WAS A PROLIFIC COMPOSER AND A MASTER OF NEARLY ALL MUSICAL GENRES, INCLUDING BOTH COMPLEX COUNTERPOINT, AND DRAMATIC MONOPHONIC VOCAL MUSIC FOR A SINGLE VOICE WITH INSTRUMENTAL ACCOMPANIMENT. HIS DEVELOPMENT OF NEW COMPOSITIONAL IDEAS THAT PLACED EMPHASIS ON EXPRESSION AND DECLAMATION ATTRACTED BOTH CRITICISM AND ADMIRATION. HIS DRAMATIC WORKS, INCLUDING *L'INCORONAZIONE DI POPPEA*, ARE THE EARLIEST IN THE CANON OF REGULARLY PERFORMED OPERAS TODAY.

Monteverdi was born in Cremona to Baldassare Monteverdi and Maddalena Zignani, and studied with Marc'Antonio Ingegneri at Cremona Cathedral. At the age of 15, he published his first collection of three-voiced compositions, *Sacrae cantiunculae*. Three books of madrigals followed, in 1587, 1590, and 1592, all of them published in Venice.

MANTUA

In 1590 or 1591, Monteverdi was appointed as a musician to Vincenzo Gonzaga's court in Mantua. In 1599, he married the soprano Claudia Cattaneo and they had three children. At first Monteverdi held quite a junior position in Mantua, but then in 1601 he was appointed "maestro della musica." In 1603 and 1605, he published another two books of madrigals.

Monteverdi was famously criticized by Giovanni Maria Artusi (1540–1613), who objected to Monteverdi's use of dissonances and to some of his melodic lines. He finally answered his critic in the preface to his fifth book of madrigals (1605), explaining that his

Above Monteverdi once wrote that, "the end of all good music is to affect the soul."

Below The family of Vincenzo Gonzaga at prayer. Gonzaga employed Monteverdi as a musician in Mantua.

compositional style was part of a "second practice" as opposed to "first practice," the strict style of older composers. Claudio's brother, Cesare (also a musician), further clarifies a very important point—in the first practice, the harmony is "mistress of the words," but in the second practice, the words are "mistress of the harmony."

Monteverdi's first opera, *L'Orfeo*, was performed in 1607. The following year, 1608, his opera *Arianna* was performed. Unfortunately, the only part of this opera that survives today is Arianna's Lament, "Lasciatemi morire" ("Let me die"). Monteverdi later reworked this touching lament for five voices and included it in his sixth book of madrigals (1614).

VENICE

In 1613, Monteverdi was appointed maestro at San Marco in Venice. Here, he wrote music for the Church, but this did not preclude him from accepting commissions from elsewhere (including Mantua) and for the theater. His sixth and seventh books of madrigals were published in 1614 and 1619.

Discover the music

Cruda Amarilli (Fifth Book of Madrigals) (1605)

L'Orfeo (1607)

Lasciatemi morire (*Arianna*) (1608)

Vespro della Beata Vergine (1610)

Lasciatemi morire (Sixth Book of Madrigals) (1614)

Il Combattimento di Tancredi e Clorinda (Eighth Book of Madrigals) (1638)

Il Ritorno d'Ulisse in Patria (1640)

L'Incoronazione di Poppea (1643)

Recorder

The recorder is an end-blown vertical flute featuring a "fipple" or whistle mouthpiece which produces its airy tone. With seven finger holes and a thumbhole, the recorder is related to the ocarina and acquired its present form by around 1500. In contrast to the Renaissance recorder, the Baroque version of the instrument was normally referred to as a flute (with the transverse flute referred to as *traverso*). Monteverdi included the recorder in the score for his opera *L'Orfeo*. Today, the recorder is a popular instrument in schools and is often used in early music education.

In 1624, he wrote *Il Combattimento di Tancredi e Clorinda*, with a text from Torquato Tasso's *Gerusalemme Liberata* (*Jerusalem Delivered*). It was published in 1638 in his eighth book of madrigals. This dramatic cantata featured new string techniques including tremolo and pizzicato. In 1631, Monteverdi wrote a Mass, celebrating the end of the plague that had destroyed nearly one-third of the population of Venice.

Perhaps his greatest works were composed in the last years of his life. His opera *Il Ritorno d'Ulisse in Patria* premièred in 1640 and *L'Incoronazione di Poppea*, his last work, in 1643.

L'INCORONAZIONE DI POPPEA (1643)

The Coronation of Poppea, with a libretto by Giovanni Francesco Busenello, is the story of the Emperor Nero's obsessive love for the beautiful and scheming Poppea. The action is overseen by the three competing goddesses of Fortune, Virtue, and Love. Nero determines to banish his wife Ottavia and take Poppea as his wife. Seneca tries to dissuade Nero from doing this, but is ordered to kill himself. In a moving madrigal, Seneca's friends implore him not to die, but he accepts his fate.

Ottavia tries to have Poppea murdered by Poppea's former lover Ottone, but the scheme backfires, and Ottone and his new lover, Drusilla, are exiled. Ottavia is sent into exile and sings a magnificent farewell to Rome. Arnulta, Poppea's nurse, rejoices that her mistress will become empress, and contemplates her own social elevation. Poppea is crowned in great pomp, and the opera ends with a ravishingly beautiful love duet.

Below Roman emperor Nero's second wife is the heroine of Monteverdi's opera *The Coronation of Poppea*. The three-act work is based on the historical writings of Roman senator and chronicler, Tacitus (c. 56–c. 117 CE).

The city–states of Italy

IN MONTEVERDI'S TIME, ITALY WAS NOT A UNIFIED COUNTRY (THIS DID NOT HAPPEN
UNTIL THE NINETEENTH CENTURY), BUT RATHER A COLLECTION OF SMALL CITY-STATES.
DURING THE SIXTEENTH CENTURY, FRANCE AND SPAIN SOUGHT TO DOMINATE THE
LAND. FOLLOWING THE PEACE OF CATEAU–CAMBRÉSIS (1559), MUCH OF THE COUNTRY
CAME UNDER SPANISH RULE, ESPECIALLY THE SOUTH, BUT ALSO MILAN.

Musically, the most important cities were in the north: Mantua, Florence, Ferrara, and Venice. Musicians found financial, personal, and job security in the patronage of the heads of these cities, or else within the Catholic Church.

MANTUA

In Mantua, Monteverdi worked under the patronage of Vincenzo I Gonzaga, Duke of Mantua (1562–1612). His son, Francesco IV (1586–1612), lived for only a short time after his succession, and was followed by his brothers Ferdinando I (1587–1626) and Vincenzo II (1594–1627). None of the three brothers produced an heir, and Vincenzo II's death in 1627 led to the War of the Mantuan Succession (1628–1631) between France and Spain. A French cousin, Charles III of Nevers (1580–1637), was finally granted rule over Mantua and Montferrat in the Treaty of Cherasco (1631). Unfortunately, the war brought bubonic plague to Mantua, which spread to Milan, Venice, and Florence.

Below Francesco I de' Medici, Grand Duke of Tuscany from 1574 until his death in 1587, was a great patron of the arts, and supported a number of leading musicians, including Jacopo Peri.

FLORENCE

At the court of the Grand Dukes of Tuscany, Francesco I de' Medici (1541–1587) and his brother Ferdinando I (1549–1609), composers such as Jacopo Peri (1561–1633) and Giulio Caccini (1551–1618) enjoyed patronage.

Cosimo II de' Medici (1590–1621), son of Ferdinando, was for a short time patron to the astronomer, mathematician, and physicist Galileo Galilei (1564–1642). Galileo created the first fully functioning telescope in 1609, and this enabled him to confirm the Copernican theory of heliocentricity. Unfortunately, this was considered a heresy by the Church. Following

Right Mythological tales have long been subjects of art and music. Andromeda was the heroine of the first public opera, which was performed in Venice in1637.

THE BIRTH OF OPERA

Composers including Caccini, Vincenzo Galilei (father of Galileo) and Piero Strozzi (c. 1550–1609) were part of a Florentine academy called the Camerata, who met at the home of Giovanni de' Bardi. It is this group, with its interest in ancient Greek music, that is often said to have led to the birth of opera. These composers sought to express the natural tone and accents of the language through the use of monody in a continuously sung work. This resulted in the composition of the first opera—*Dafne* (1598) by Jacopo Peri with a libretto by Ottavio Rinuccini.

A new era of opera was launched in 1637 with the opening of a public theater, the Teatro San Cassiano in Venice. Whereas operas had previously been performed under the patronage of a nobleman for guests, now ordinary people could attend such an entertainment. The first opera to be presented to the paying public was *Andromeda* by Francesco Manelli with a libretto by Benedetto Ferrari. Manelli and his wife, Maddalena, both performed roles in the opera. Other roles and the chorus were filled by members of the choir of San Marco.

the publication of his book *Dialogue Concerning the Two Chief World Systems* in 1632, Galileo was brought before the Roman Inquisition. His book was banned, and he was under house arrest for the remainder of his life. Claudio Monteverdi's son, Massimiliano, a doctor, also ran foul of the Inquisition in 1627; his crime was reading banned books.

FERRARA

Alfonso II d'Este (1533–1597) was the last Duke of Ferrara, Modena, and Reggio in the direct line. He had an active interest in the arts and was patron of the great poet Torquato Tasso (1544–1595), whose epic poem *Gerusalemme Liberata* (*Jerusalem Delivered*, 1580) remains an important landmark in European literature. Alfonso II also began a group of women singers called the "Concerto delle Donne," which allowed women to be employed as paid musicians at the court for the first

Above The Battle of Lepanto in 1571 was a decisive naval victory over the Ottoman Empire, returning control of the Mediterranean to Venice, the Papacy, and Spain.

time. Following the rule of Alfonso, the Duchy was claimed by his cousin Cesare d'Este (1561–1628), but the Pope did not recognize his rights and Ferrara became incorporated into the Papal States.

VENICE

The Republic of Venice had been involved in a long struggle with the Ottoman Empire for supremacy in the Mediterranean. In 1570, the Turks attacked Limassol in Cyprus. The following year, John of Austria successfully led Venetian, Spanish, and Papal ships against the Turks off Lepanto, on the coast of Greece.

Venice had a strong focus on sacred music, led by the San Marco Basilica and the composer and theorist Geoseffe Zarlino (1517–1590), whose many students included Vincenzo Galilei (c. 1520–1591) and Monteverdi's nemesis, Artusi. Monteverdi was appointed maestro at San Marco in 1613.

Barbara (Valle) Strozzi

AUGUST 6, 1619–NOVEMBER 11, 1677

THE SINGER AND COMPOSER BARBARA STROZZI PUBLISHED EIGHT VOLUMES OF MUSIC
DURING HER LIFETIME, SEVEN OF WHICH HAVE SURVIVED. HER FATHER WAS INFLUENTIAL
IN LITERARY AND MUSICAL CIRCLES, ENABLING HIM TO GIVE HIS DAUGHTER AN EDUCATION
AND A MUSICAL CAREER. BARBARA IS REMARKABLE FOR BOTH THE AMOUNT AND THE
QUALITY OF THE MUSIC SHE PUBLISHED.

Barbara was born in Venice and lived in the home of Giulio Strozzi (1583–1652). Her mother, Isabella Garzoni, was his servant. Giulio Strozzi appears to have adopted Barbara, who may have been his illegitimate daughter. At first she was known as Barbara Valle, but later used the name Strozzi. Giulio Strozzi was a poet and librettist to some of the period's greatest Italian composers, including Monteverdi and his younger associate, Francesco Cavalli (1602–1676).

Below The only likeness we have of Barbara Strozzi is this painting by Bernardo Strozzi (1581–1644), possibly a relative of her father's. She is holding a viola da gamba.

From around 1634, Barbara began singing in her father's home for his friends. In 1635 and 1636, Venetian composer Nicolò Fontei wrote two books of songs, *Bizzarrie poetiche poste in musica* for Barbara, with texts mostly written by her father. Recognizing her talent, Barbara's father arranged for her to study with Cavalli.

ACCADEMIA DEGLI UNISONI

Giulio Strozzi was a member and founder of several academies, where intellectual, literary, and musical interests could be discussed. In 1637, he founded the Accademia degli Unisoni, apparently for Barbara, which met at his home. She acted as hostess and performed her own compositions.

Some academics have suggested that Barbara may have been a courtesan. Her position as the only woman at the meetings of the Accademia degli Unisoni must have appeared compromising, and anonymous satires circulated questioning her virtue. It would not have helped that around 1641, an unmarried Barbara gave birth to the first of four children. Some researchers have suggested that the father of her children was probably Giovanni Paolo Vidman, a friend of her father's, and already married.

STROZZI'S COMPOSITIONS

Barbara's first publication, a book of madrigals, with texts by her father, was issued in 1644. Her second book of cantatas, ariettas, and duets (1651) drew on a greater variety of poets. This book includes the cantata "Donna di maestà, di valor tanto," which was

Above A seventeenth-century painting of a singer accompanied by a theorbo player. Most of Strozzi's songs were written for soprano.

CANTATE, ARIETTA E DUETTI, OP. 2 (1651)

This book includes songs in many styles and forms. As well as a cantata to celebrate Ferdinand III's marriage that year, the book also includes "Gite, giorni dolenti" ("Pass, sad days") for his wedding to his previous wife, Maria Leopoldine (1648). The "sad days" were no doubt those of the Thirty Years' War (1618–1648). Cantatas are extended songs with several different sections in different styles. Some word painting emphasizes the important words; for instance, the war trumpets of Mars are imitated in a jaunty dotted rhythm, but then the god of marriage descends from the heavens and the entire vocal line descends to a low note.

Some songs are simple strophic numbers, like "Non mi dite" (Don't tell me). The singer here says not to tell her to sing of love, the scourge of musicians and lovers, because her lover is far away. This melancholy song has two verses to the same music. "Amor, non dormir più" ("Love, sleep no more") takes a different form again. It is in "da capo" (literally "from the head") form. The first section, a rousing bid to awaken love, is followed by a steadier contrasting section, as the singer voices disappointment at love's cowardliness. The song then returns to the beginning and repeats the first section.

Right Maria Leopoldine, wife of Ferdinand III, the Holy Roman Emperor. She died at the age of 17, giving birth to her only son.

written to celebrate the marriage of Ferdinand III of Austria and Eleanor of Mantua in the same year.

In 1652, Barbara's father died, but she continued to compose and publish songs. Her third publication, of cantatas and ariettas for one, two, and three voices, was published in 1654. A fourth book is lost. In 1655, she published her only book of sacred music. Three more books followed in 1657, 1659, and 1664.

Many of Strozzi's compositions are love songs in the Marinist tradition (a movement characterized by exaggerated word-play, named after the poet Giambattista Marino, 1569–1625) and intended as chamber music. While she may not have written an opera like her older contemporary Francesca Caccini, she is a remarkable woman for having maintained an independent career as a composer without the patronage of a court.

Discover the music

Donna di maestà, di valor tanto, Op. 2 (1651)
Gite, o giorni dolenti, Op. 2 (1651)
Amor, non dormir più, Op. 2 (1651)
Non mi dite, Op. 2 (1651)
Questa è la nova, Op. 3 (1654)
Amor è bandito, Op. 6 (1657)
Lagrime mie, Op. 7 (1659)

Italian women in the arts in the seventeenth century

SUCCESSFUL INTELLECTUAL AND ARTISTIC WOMEN OF THIS PERIOD WERE OFTEN EDUCATED AND ENCOURAGED BY THEIR ENLIGHTENED FATHERS, WHO RECOGNIZED THE TALENT IN THEIR DAUGHTERS. ANOTHER ENVIRONMENT THAT ALLOWED FOR THE DEVELOPMENT OF MUSICAL TALENT WAS THE CONVENT. DESPITE THE RESTRICTIONS IMPOSED BY THE COUNCIL OF TRENT, SUPPOSEDLY LIMITING MUSICAL EDUCATION AND PRACTICE IN THE CONVENTS, MUSIC STILL MANAGED TO FLOURISH.

ELENA LUCREZIA (CORNARO) PISCOPIA (1646–1684)

Elena Lucrezia Piscopia was the first woman to receive a Doctor of Philosophy, and she did so in a blaze of international publicity. Piscopia's early life sounds not unlike that of Barbara Strozzi. Her father, Gian Battista Cornaro, was a wealthy intellectual and not married to her lower-class mother, Zanetta Boni. Cornaro, recognizing her talent, arranged for her to be tutored in Greek and Latin from the age of seven, and she eventually mastered seven languages. Although her father would have preferred that she marry, she decided to take on the celibate role of a Benedictine oblate, although she never entered a convent.

Piscopia studied at Padua, and graduated with a doctorate in 1678. Her examination was held in public at the Basilica of San Antonio, and her degree was conferred by Carlo Rinaldini, her professor in philosophy. The doors of a number of academies were opened to her. After her early death, the University of Padua struck a medal in her honor.

FRANCESCA CACCINI (1587–c.1641)

Francesca Caccini's father was the composer Giulio Caccini (1551–1618) and her mother the singer, Lucia di Filippo Gagnolanti. Giulio Caccini was a member of the Florentine Camerata, and his opera *Euridice* (1600) was the first ever to be published.

In 1604–1605, the Caccini family traveled to France, where Francesca sang at the French court of Maria de' Medici to great acclaim. After returning to Florence, Francesca entered the service of the Medici Court in 1607, and she later married a court singer, Giovanni Battista Signorini.

ISABELLA LEONARDA (1620-1704)

The Council of Trent (1545–1563) recommended the enclosure of nuns, making it virtually impossible for them to leave the convent, or for outsiders to enter. Future decrees restricted music making in the convents. In spite of this, there were a number of nuns who managed to compose and publish music at this time. In Novara, Isabella Leonarda published an astonishing 20 books of music. She came from a noble family, and entered the Ursuline convent, the Collegio di San Orsola, at 16 years of age. By 1676, Leonara was the mother superior.

Her music first appeared in 1640, when two of her motets appeared in a compilation of sacred music by Gasparo Casati. In 1665, she published a book of motets for three voices (sadly, now lost). After this, her publications were issued frequently, up to and including 1700. Leonarda wrote instrumental music as well as vocal, and she was the first woman to publish an instrumental sonata (1693).

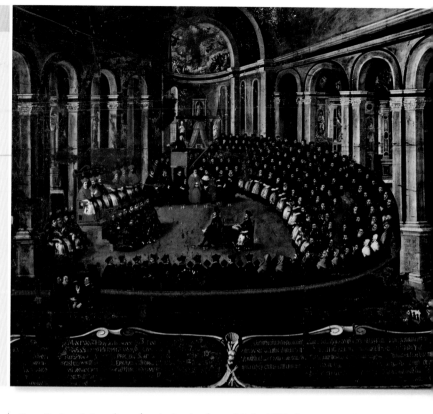

Francesca composed and sang for many entertainments at the Medici court and she also taught music. She published a book of solo songs, *Il primo libro delle musiche* (1618) and is the first woman to have composed and published an opera, *La Liberazione di Ruggiero dall'isola d'Alcina* (1625). Francesca's husband died in 1626, and the following year she left the court to marry Tomaso Raffaelli. After his death in 1630, she returned to the Medici court, where she served until 1641. Little is known about her after this time.

ARTEMESIA GENTILESCHI (1593–c. 1653)

Artemisia Gentileschi was born in Rome. Her father, the painter Orazio Gentileschi (c. 1563–1639) was a disciple of Caravaggio (1571–1610). Her mother, Prudentia Montone, died in childbirth when Artemisia was 12 years old. Artemisia studied painting at first with her father, and later with his colleague, Agostino Tassi, who raped her. The ensuing trial lasted seven months, during which Artemisia's hands were tortured with thumbscrews, to ensure that her testimony was truthful. Soon after the trial, she married Pierantonio Stiattesi and moved to Florence. She returned to Rome about 1621, and some years later moved first to Venice, then Naples. Artemisia visited England in 1638, where she collaborated with her father, who was by then court painter to Charles I.

Above The Council of Trent at the Santa Maria Maggiore church. This ecumenical council issued various decrees aimed at strengthening the Church's teachings.

Right *Judith Slaying Holofernes* by Artemisia Gentileschi is a dramatic and violent depiction of the Biblical story. Many see it as a cathartic response to the sexual abuse that the artist suffered herself.

Left Many girls from well-to-do families received a good musical education, and were often encouraged to hone their talents.

A painting by Artemisia in 1610, *Susanna and The Elders*, although it must predate the rape, perhaps shows that she feared such an event. After the trial, Artemisia painted *Judith Slaying Holofernes*, showing the first of many strong female subjects. Other subjects included Mary Magdalene, Cleopatra, and Lucretia. Artemisia Gentileschi's work is known for its use of "chiaroscuro," meaning the use of light and shade.

Marc-Antoine Charpentier

1643–FEBRUARY 24, 1704

ECLIPSED BY JEAN-BAPTISTE LULLY IN HIS DAY AND THEREAFTER, MARC-ANTOINE
CHARPENTIER HAS FINALLY BEEN RECOGNIZED AS ONE OF THE MOST HIGHLY TALENTED
FRENCH COMPOSERS OF SACRED MUSIC IN THE LATE SEVENTEENTH CENTURY. ALTHOUGH HE
NEVER OBTAINED A ROYAL APPOINTMENT, HE HELD SOME OF THE MOST SIGNIFICANT POSTS
FOR A COMPOSER OF SACRED MUSIC OUTSIDE THE ROYAL CHAPEL AT VERSAILLES.

There is scant evidence of Charpentier's early life;
even his year of birth was uncertain until the late
1980s. He was born in or near Paris, and seems to have
traveled to Rome around 1666–1667, possibly with the
intention of studying painting. He might have studied
with the composer Giacomo Carissimi (1605–1674),
and certainly copied out music by mid-century Roman
composers. In 1724 the lexicographer Sébastien de
Brossard noted that Charpentier possessed an amazing
memory and that he had brought back to Paris copies
of Italian motets and oratorios by Carissimi.

Returning to Paris around 1670, Charpentier served
the devout Marie de Lorraine ("Mademoiselle de
Guise") as a composer and singer until 1688.
Mademoiselle de Guise was an important
patron of the arts, maintaining one of the
largest musical establishments in late
seventeenth-century France. With her
considerable musical forces at his disposal,
Charpentier wrote dramatic motets, pas-
torales, and psalm settings. The secular
theatrical works that he composed at
this time may have been written for his
patron's less pious daughter-in-law.

THEATER, CHURCH, AND COURT

In 1672 Charpentier began to collaborate with
Molière's Troupe de Roy (later Comédie-Française),
composing overtures and setting to music prologues
and scenes in plays by Molière and other writers.
He continued in this post for around 20 years after
Molière's death in 1673, composing within the various
restrictions imposed on theatrical music by Lully and
Louis XIV. He was also in demand as a composer of
sacred music. For example, the *Mercure galant* of April
1680 reported that crowds of people had gone to hear
his Tenebrae compositions at the convent of the
Abbaye-aux-Bois during Holy Week. He composed
music for the chapel of the dauphin, and his motets

Discover the music

Le Malade Imaginaire (1672)

Tenebrae compositions (1680)

David et Jonathas (1688)

Te Deum (1690)

Messe de minuit pour Noël (c. 1690)

Medée (1693)

Missa Assumpta est Maria (1698–1702)

Left A receipt handwritten by Charpentier, acknowledging payment for his musical score to Molière's tragic ballet *Psyché*.

Right The biblical story of the friendship between David and Jonathan and Jonathan's tragic death was the subject of an opera by Charpentier, first performed in 1688.

were reportedly well liked by the king. Yet he never succeeded in gaining a court appointment, although in 1683 Louis XIV provided him with a pension, which may have been a gesture of thanks for Charpentier's music for the dauphin. He also became music teacher to Philippe d'Orléans, Duke of Chartres.

Despite the lack of a royal appointment, the composer gained what were some of the chief ecclesiastical musical posts in France at the time—he served as *maître de chapelle* at the Jesuit Collège de Clermont and then master of music at the principal Jesuit church in Paris, St Louis. He composed full-scale dramatic works in these posts, which were not subject to the increasingly restrictive terms laid down in Louis XIV's ordinances. In 1698 Charpentier became the master of music at Sainte-Chapelle, which was the second most important appointment for a composer of sacred music after the directorship of the royal chapel. He held this position for the rest of his life and composed some of his most outstanding works for this magnificent venue.

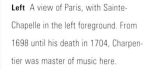

Left A view of Paris, with Sainte-Chapelle in the left foreground. From 1698 until his death in 1704, Charpentier was master of music here.

CONTINUITY AND INNOVATION IN CHARPENTIER'S SACRED MUSIC

Charpentier's earliest sacred music shows strong links to the style of seventeenth-century Roman composers such as Carissimi, while his later music bears traits of the French style, that of Lully in particular. Frequently his later works combine the two styles. An example is the Christmas Oratorio *Frigidae noctis umbra*, H. 414, which, like Carissimi's oratorio *Jephte*, is scored for six vocal parts—three sopranos, alto, tenor, and bass. The work begins with an instrumental *praeludium*, and then divides into distinct sections. There are two narrative sections, containing biblical recitative; these are set in a restrained declamatory style, reminiscent of passages in Carissimi's oratorios. The main part of the work comprises two airs, which, true to the French style of the time, are strongly linked to the dance.

Among Charpentier's most innovative works are his Tenebrae compositions for Holy Week. In their highly elaborate style, they bear witness to the seventeenth-century *airs de cour* (court airs) of his forebears. In this respect, too, they bear witness to the inspiration of a composer who was himself a highly proficient singer: Charpentier was an *haute-contre* (high tenor voice), who was able to take leading roles in his own small-scale dramatic works.

The arts in seventeenth-century France

WITH THE DEATH OF CARDINAL MAZARIN IN 1661, THE RULE OF LOUIS XIV (1638–1715) BEGAN. IN CHARPENTIER'S FRANCE, PARIS AND VERSAILLES ENTERED A GLITTERING PERIOD OF ROYAL POWER AND PRESTIGE, ALBEIT ONE SHORT-LIVED.

The arts flourished, and French developments in music at this time were to have far-reaching effects, especially in terms of the codification and institutionalization of music. The dominant force in French musical life in the late seventeenth century was Jean-Baptiste Lully (1632–1687).

During Mazarin's rule, five years of civil war (the Fronde, 1648–1653) had led to widespread devastation in France and a yearning for peace. In terms of foreign affairs, plans for peace were well in place. The signing of the peace of Westphalia in 1648 brought an end to both the Thirty Years' War in Germany and the Eighty Years' War between Spain and the Netherlands; and the Treaty of the Pyrenees, which was signed in 1659, ended the war between France and Spain. Within France, Mazarin's opponents were too disparate to effectively oppose the accession of Louis XIV; thus, thanks to new king's exceptionally close-handed politics, France entered a unique period in which the absolute rule was extreme.

THE *MUSIQUE DU ROI*
In the arts, a brilliant if short-lived school of writers emerged, including Boileau, La Fontaine, Madame de Sévigné, Mademoiselle de Scudéry, Molière, and Racine. Molière's *Les Précieuses Ridicules* was published in 1660; this was performed in the presence of the young Louis XIV, who was to make Versailles the epicenter of cultural life. Musical life centered on the *musique du roi* (the king's music). This included lavish operas, opera–ballets, and large-scale vocal works, designed expressly to represent and reinforce the power and glory of the king. In composition, Lully reigned

Right Music-making was an important part of life in seventeenth-century France, at all levels of society. As well as works meant for small audiences, the aristocracy also enjoyed the latest operas and ballets.

Above Marie de Rabutin-Chantal, better known as Madame de Sévigné, (1626–1696) is remembered for the witty and insightful letters she wrote to her daughter.

supreme thanks to royal favor and the decision to ban foreign musicians. Lully himself contributed to this time of comparative isolation in French musical culture, discouraging French court musicians from traveling abroad.

The *musique du roi* lost prominence during the regency and under Louis XV (r. 1715–1774). By this time, though, concert life was becoming well established in Paris. One of the key organizations in this development was the Concert Spirituel, founded in 1725. Music printing was also flourishing. Paris had become the European center for music publishing, owing to the high quality of the numerous Parisian engravers and the fact that their prints could be effectively advertised to the concert-going public through the burgeoning concert-giving institutions.

MUSICAL LIFE IN THE PROVINCES
The best French musicians of the late seventeenth century flocked to Paris and Versailles; or, if not, Louis XIV would take them there. He upheld the right of his representatives to "take from churches, cathedrals and elsewhere, in those places through which they pass, the finest voices and the best singers they may find and make them part of their company." Even when talented singers remained in the provinces, few musicians were prepared to try to obtain license rights from Lully in order to mount an opera. Yet provincial musical institutions were still established and maintained, including a famous oboe band in Toulouse. A decisive change for the better, in terms of the breadth of France's musical life, is witnessed by the founding of numerous musical *académies* in the provinces in the early eighteenth century.

JEAN-BAPTISTE LULLY

Given the xenophobic outlook in late seventeenth-century France, it is ironic that the man who wielded most of the power in the musical sphere was Italian born. Lully arrived in Paris in 1646 from Florence, and entered court musical life in the early 1650s. A decade later he was appointed leader of the court musicians. In 1669 Louis XIV established the Académie Royale de Musique, which he subsequently placed under Lully's guidance, and which would perform Lully's operas exclusively; the patronage and protection of French opera continued until 1791. Lully collaborated with poet Philippe Quinault in *Cadmus et Hermione*, which premièred in 1673. This was the first of eleven *tragédies en musique* (musical tragedies) created by the pair. Lully produced operas at the rate of about one per year until his death. He also monopolized the composition of court ballets from the late 1650s. He collaborated with notable writers of the day, including Molière. Their most famous work is their last, *Le Bourgeois Gentilhomme* (1670).

THE MUSIC OF SPAIN

Both Spain and Portugal remained somewhat isolated from foreign influences during the Baroque period, which meant that distinctive local musical traditions developed and flourished. The passion for novelty, artifice, and spectacle that we find in Spanish dance is also reflected in the music.

Contrasts are bold, and yet subtle nuances and inflections are plentiful, especially in the setting of texts. Forms are often dependent on earlier models, especially the imitation and variations techniques of the Renaissance; these are used with characteristic flexibility.

Right This embroidered panel showing a woman playing a guitar is from the seventeenth century.

Left The guitar was one of the favored instruments of Baroque Spanish composers. The lute, viol, and harpsichord were also widely used in instrumental music of the time.

VILLANCICOS

Sacred songs survive in large quantities and in a great variety of forms. There is a substantial repertory of Latin-texted sacred music, including Masses, deploying one or more choirs and imitative counterpoint. Of all types of sacred music, villancicos are the most prominent. These vocal works are settings of vernacular sacred texts, which celebrate the various religious occasions. They are usually strophic (where the same music is used for each successive stanza) with elaborate refrains, and were performed with or without instruments. Villancicos were cultivated by virtually all

Below The large cathedrals, such as Salamanca Cathedral built in the twelfth century, were important to cultural development, as they employed many singers and musicians.

Spanish composers of the Baroque era; sources of these works survive in cathedral archives such as those of Burgos, Salamanca, Segovia, Valencia, and Valladolid.

SECULAR SONGS

A fire in the Alcázar palace in Madrid in 1734 led to the loss of an important body of Spanish Baroque secular and theatrical songs—*tonos humanos* and *tonadas*. This repertoire contained settings of some of the best Spanish poetry of the era. Many of these songs were written to accompany musical plays, and were first performed at court in Madrid. Harp and guitar were the preferred accompanying instruments.

OPERA

Opera in Spain developed quite independently of opera in the rest of Europe. The first operatic work in Spain, *La selva sin amor*, was staged in 1627; it had a poetic text by Lope de Vega and the music was by the favorite composer of Philip IV's court, the Bolognese Filippo Piccinini. Thereafter operas were composed to celebrate important political events such as the 1659 Treaty of the Pyrenees and the marriage, in 1660, of the Spanish Infanta Marie Teresa to Louis XIV. The dramatist Pedro Calderón de la Barca, who worked at the Madrid court, devised a new theatrical genre known as the zarzuela—a light genre of semi-opera made up of songs and recitatives. In the zarzuela, women sang the roles of both classical gods and goddesses, while men took specific elderly male roles, such as Morpheus and Father Time.

INSTRUMENTAL MUSIC

The fact that there are relatively few notated sources of instrumental music surviving from seventeenth-century Spain should not surprise us: In this sphere of musical activity, improvisational practices were particularly

strong, so that the extant music represents only a part of a much larger performed repertory. Instrumental performers often came from a lower stratum of society to that of singers and composers of sacred and theatrical music. Thus when instrumental performers were also composers—as was often the case in the Baroque era—they would often have lacked the skills or monetary means to transcribe or publish their works.

The surviving sources indicate that organ music flourished in particular. This music shows the development of an independent instrumental virtuoso style. The works of the Valencian composer Juan Bautista José Cabanilles (1644–1712) epitomize the bravura style, as well as the free treatment of form that is typical of late Spanish Baroque instrumental music.

As well as comprising song accompaniments, the repertoire for guitar and harp included numerous variations on popular dances, songs, and harmonic patterns. Modern-day performers who wish to perform

Above This painting by Laurentius de Neter captures the ambience of Baroque music making. Note the range of string instruments.

this music can consult instruction books such as *Luz y norte musical par caminar por las cifras de la guitarra española y arpa*, published by Luca Ruiz de Ribayaz in Madrid in 1677; this treatise contains advice on harp and guitar technique, and the practice of improvising and realizing the chords of a bass line.

ITALIAN INFLUENCES IN SPAIN

The music of Lully and Corelli was clearly known in eighteenth-century Spain. Earlier, too, there had been a number of points of contact between Spain and Italy in particular. Records show that from around 1680 many Italian and French musicians arrived at the royal court in Madrid, and Domenico Scarlatti was employed there from about 1728 until 1757. The famous Italian castrato Farinelli (1705–1782) also found favor at the Spanish royal court in the early eighteenth century. He was appointed by Philip V as "my servant, who answers only to me or to the queen, my very beloved wife, for his unique talent and skill in the art of singing."

Arcangelo Corelli

FEBRUARY 17, 1653–JANUARY 8, 1713

ARCANGELO CORELLI WAS ONE OF THE FOREMOST VIOLINIST–COMPOSERS OF THE LATE BAROQUE PERIOD. HIS WORKS—MOSTLY SOLO SONATAS, TRIO SONATAS, AND CONCERTOS—WERE WIDELY EMULATED IN THE EIGHTEENTH CENTURY. HIS ENDURING INFLUENCE LAY NOT ONLY IN THE DEVELOPMENT AND STANDARDIZATION OF THESE THREE MAIN INSTRUMENTAL FORMS, BUT IN THE CONSOLIDATION OF HARMONY AND INSTRUMENTAL TECHNIQUE. AS A VIOLINIST HE WAS ADMIRED BOTH FOR PASSION AND REFINED SOPHISTICATION.

Corelli was born in 1653 in the small town of Fusignano, near Bologna. He spent most of his career in Rome, where, from 1675 onwards, he established his reputation as a leading violinist. He was supported by such important patrons as Cardinal Pietro Ottoboni and Queen Christina of Sweden, and contributed to Roman musical life not only through his personal performances and compositions but also by directing performances of major works.

The fact that he focused narrowly on only three main instrumental genres meant that he was able to bring these to new levels of perfection. Corelli wrote 12 solo sonatas, 48 trio sonatas (sonatas for one or two melody instruments and continuo), and 12 concerti grossi (concertos for a group of solo instruments with orchestral accompaniment). His publications appeared in a very orderly fashion, in six collections with twelve works in each. These works were reprinted in numerous editions throughout the eighteenth century.

BAROQUE SONATAS

Corelli's sonatas can be divided into the two main types of Baroque sonata. The *sonate da chiesa*, "church sonatas," are made up of movements with abstract tempo titles, such as "Allegro" or "Adagio" in the sequence slow–fast–slow–fast. While a four-movement sequence was the norm for *sonate da chiesa* at the time, the first six sonatas of his Op. 5 in fact contain five movements. Each sonata opens with a slow prelude and fugue, and concludes with a fast movement. The *sonate da camera*, "chamber sonatas," comprise mostly dance movements, such as the allemande, sarabande, gavotte, and gigue. Each dance type has a characteristic

Above Portraits of Corelli emphasize his "archangel-like" nature. An eighteenth-century description states that he was "remarkable for the mildness of his temper and the modesty of his deportment."

tempo, as well as melodic and rhythmic character. The sarabande, for example, is in slow triple time, with a weighty second beat; the gigue is fast and lively, with a compound meter.

CORELLI'S INFLUENCE

Bach and Handel were among the many eighteenth-century composers who modeled their instrumental works on those of Corelli. His music is exemplary of refinement and restraint. Melodic hallmarks and clear tonal progressions give the listener a satisfying sense of familiarity, onward drive, and resolution. His compositions have been prized for their pedagogical value, as well as their adaptability.

Subsequent generations of violinists have continued to produce editions of his Op. 5 sonatas in which they have contributed progressively more complex layers of ornamentation (decorative additions to Corelli's melodies). More generally, Corelli's works have been arranged for the keyboard as well as various other combinations of instruments.

Discover the music

12 Trio Sonatas, Op. 1 (1681)

12 Trio Sonatas, Op. 2 (1685)

12 Trio Sonatas, Op. 3 (1689)

12 Trio Sonatas, Op. 4 (1694)

12 Solo Sonatas, Op. 5 (1700)

12 Concerti Grossi, Op. 6 (1714)

THE OP. 5 VIOLIN SONATAS

The twelve solo sonatas that make up Corelli's Op. 5 (1700) comprise six *sonate da chiesa* and six *sonate da camera*. In Corelli's day it was understood that the slow movements of the *sonate da chiesa*, in particular, would be ornamented by the violinist. The degree of decoration would depend on the skill of the performer. One guide as to the kind of elaboration that he would have expected is found in a set of ornamented versions of these works, which were published in 1710 by the Dutch publisher Estienne Roger. Roger went so far as to claim these as "the ornaments for the adagios … composed by Corelli as he plays them." Regardless of the veracity of this statement, which was perhaps a rather bold sales ploy, it should be noted that the best violinists of the Baroque era would have improvised their ornaments anew each time they performed a work, rather like today's jazz musicians.

Left Queen Christina of Sweden (1626–1689) moved to Italy in 1655, following her abdication. She was one of Corelli's early influential patrons.

Below Harpsichords were made of fine woods such as walnut, and were usually beautifully decorated with paintings of birds, flowers, foliage, or pastoral scenes. Gold paneling was also common. This harpsichord from the eighteenth century was made in Italy.

Harpsichord

The harpsichord (or continuo) is a keyboard instrument that produces sound by a mechanical action that plucks each string with a plectrum rather than striking it with a hammer (like the piano). The result is a crisp tonal quality and clarity, heightened by the fact that notes cannot be sustained. (A harpsichord has no dynamics, that is, there is no loud and soft—all notes are played with the same intensity.) Corelli's twelve violin and continuo sonatas proved ideal practice material for students. The harpsichord was the primary harmonic accompaniment instrument of Baroque music, featuring in many famous works, such as Bach's *Goldberg Variations*.

Alessandro Scarlatti

MAY 2, 1660–OCTOBER 22, 1725

ALESSANDRO SCARLATTI IS WIDELY CONSIDERED TO HAVE FOUNDED THE NEAPOLITAN SCHOOL OF
EIGHTEENTH-CENTURY OPERA. THIS IS PARTIALLY CORRECT. CERTAINLY IT IS TRUE THAT HE PLAYED
A MAJOR ROLE IN THE FIELD OF OPERA IN THE LATE SEVENTEENTH AND EARLY EIGHTEENTH CENTURIES.
YET HIS WORKS ARE MORE SIGNIFICANT AS CULMINATION POINTS—HIGH POINTS IN THE DEVELOPMENT
OF OPERA SERIA—THAN AS HARBINGERS OF THE VARIOUS NEW DEVELOPMENTS THAT WERE TO HAVE A
DIRECT INFLUENCE ON LATE EIGHTEENTH-CENTURY CLASSICAL STYLE.

Scarlatti was born into a musical family in Palermo, Sicily. In 1672 he left for Rome, where he completed his musical training and soon attracted the attention of influential patrons. He married in 1678, lived in rooms in the palace of Gian Lorenzo Bernini (son of the famous architect), and served as *maestro di cappella* (musical director) at San Giacomo degli Incurabili. In 1682 Queen Christina of Sweden appointed him *maestro di cappella* at San Girolama della Carità.

It was early in his career that Scarlatti enjoyed his greatest popularity. His operas were received with increasing acclaim, starting with *Gli equivoci nel sembiante*. This small-scale pastoral comedy is designed to be performed with a single outdoor set, a small cast, and a small group of musicians. Opera in Rome at this time had to be performed in private, owing to Pope Innocent XI's disapproval of the genre.

Above It is said that Scarlatti composed over 200 Masses, but this is doubtful as few have survived. His *Mass for St Cecilia*, however, is still performed to this day.

Fortunately for Scarlatti, Queen Christina and other enlightened aristocrats were keen to patronize this art form.

SCARLATTI IN NAPLES

The Dukes of Maddaloni persuaded Scarlatti to move to Naples, where he was appointed *maestro* in the royal chapel. His operas now received their first performances at court, and were then staged at the Teatro San Bartolomeo. Scarlatti's reputation was now so great that he received various important commissions from influential patrons. In 1688 the great patron of the arts Ferdinando de' Medici sent Scarlatti a libretto to set. Ferdinando continued to commission operas from the composer into the eighteenth century.

RETURN TO ROME, THEN NAPLES

Returning to Rome at the turn of the century, Scarlatti found the social and political climate unreceptive to opera. He was appointed *maestro di cappella* of the Chiesa Nuova di San Maria, a post that allowed him to devote time to the composition of oratorios and

Bassoon

A double-reed woodwind instrument with a conical bore air column, the bassoon is the bass member of the oboe family. The player's right hand is responsible for 17 different keys, nine controlled by the thumb. The left hand controls 12 keys, four with the thumb. Domenico Scarlatti's *Il prigionero fortunato* (1698) was one of many works to feature the instrument, which he often paired with the oboe. Along with numerous bassoon concertos by Vivaldi, Domenico Scarlatti's *Three Sonatas For Two Flutes and Viola/Cello/Bassoon* has become a primary piece of repertoire for the instrument.

Discover the Music

Gli equivoci nel sembiante (1679)

Del Tirreno sul Lido (1697)

Il Mitridate Eupatore (1707)

Cantata pastorale (1716)

Il trionfo dell'onore (1718)

Messa di Santa Cecilia (1720)

12 *Sinfonie di concerto grosso* (1720)

cantatas. This was a productive time for him, but in this post, and in his next appointment as assistant director of the Cappella Liberianon in San Maria Maggiore, he showed a lack of willingness toward his teaching and directing duties.

Venice, epicenter of opera, was calling; yet Alessandro's style did not suit the taste of its opera-going public. His *Il Mitridate Eupatore* was strongly criticized by the Venetians, despite his masterful setting, which was to influence Handel. Nearing the age of 50, Scarlatti returned to Naples, where he spent most of his remaining years. Despite his reputation as a leader in eighteenth-century Neapolitan opera, he resisted many elements of the new Neapolitan comic operas. His *Il trionfo dell'onore* of 1718, for example, the most nearly Neapolitan of all his operas, does not contain any of the features that were most popular with contemporary audiences in Naples, such as the tarantella.

Below The bustling city of Naples on market day. Alessandro Scarlatti returned to Naples around 1710 and remained there until his death 15 years later.

DOMENICO SCARLATTI (1685–1757)

Domenico Scarlatti was Alessandro's sixth child. By the age of 15 his father had secured him the position of organist and composer at the Cappella Reale in Naples. His considerable talent as a harpsichordist was already evident.

His most significant position was as *maestro di cappella* to Maria Casimira, the former Queen of Poland, exiled in Rome. In that role he had the opportunity to compose several operas. But Domenico's main talent as a composer lay in the composition of some 555 sonatas for keyboard. The main sources for these works come from Lisbon, where he moved in 1719 to lead the royal chapel, and from Madrid, where he was employed at the royal court from around 1728 until the end of his life.

The Schools of Venice and Bologna

THE SEVENTEENTH AND EIGHTEENTH CENTURIES—THE PERIOD WHEN CORELLI AND SCARLATTI FLOURISHED—SAW A NORTHWARD MIGRATORY PATTERN IN EUROPE: ITALIAN MUSICIANS AND ARTISTS TENDED TO TRAVEL NORTH, TO ENGLAND, FRANCE, AND GERMANY, WHILE FRENCH ARTISTS ALSO BECAME PROMINENT IN ENGLAND AND GERMANY.

Italy remained a popular destination for foreign composers seeking to enrich their musical experiences. During the Thirty Years' War in Germany, for example, the composer Heinrich Schütz traveled to Italy and brought back to Germany a highly expressive vocal and instrumental style that was influenced by the Venetian school in particular.

Right A view of Venice showing the square of San Marco. Venice was a popular destination for Italian and foreign composers and musicians because of the wealth of opportunities the city could offer.

VENICE

In the seventeenth and eighteenth centuries, Venice was a Mecca for musicians, due to the varied educational, performing, and employment opportunities on offer there. There was, too, an accumulating history of publication and prestigious patronage, which doubtless acted as a drawcard for the most talented musicians. A focal point in the Venetian musical scene was the splendid Basilica of San Marco, where musicians were not subject to Roman injunctions and were thus free to develop their own styles, which were, like the venue itself, dramatic, ornate, and magnificent. Foreign visitors flocked to San Marco, which until the end of the seventeenth century enjoyed a succession of talented maestri to provide new music and able performers to render it.

Many of the composers who were associated with San Marco also wrote for the Venetian theaters. In this area of musical life, too, there were specifically Venetian practices to follow and develop. There was an emphasis on solo singing in Venetian opera, and choruses were rare. Mechanical scenery complemented the instrumental accompaniments, which were provided by small orchestras of around five string instruments

Below Giovanni Battista Torelli (1658–1709) was employed at San Petronio, Bologna, in 1701. He is remembered today for his concerti grossi.

and two harpsichords. A sense of resolution, conclusion, or at least punctuation in the operatic plot was provided by dances or staged battles, or, in the eighteenth century, comic intermezzi or violin solos.

The musical education provided by the city's four *ospedali* (orphanages, which were essentially conservatories) ensured that its high standard of instrumental and vocal virtuosity was maintained. Students learned not only the more typical instruments of the day, such as organ and violin, but also some that were heard less often, such as the viola d'amore. This fact helps to explain Antonio Vivaldi's varied and sometimes unusual choices of instrumentation.

BOLOGNA

San Petronio was the most famous landmark on the Bolognese sacred musical map. Thirty-three musicians were employed there by 1661; the succession of gifted composers at San Petronio included such talents as Maurizio Cazzati and Giovanni Battista Torelli, who cultivated instrumental forms including the trio sonata,

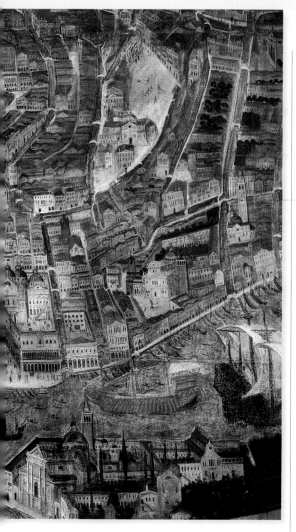

Italy, seventeenth century
★ Birthplace of Barbara Strozzi
☆ Birthplace of Arcangelo Corelli
★ Birthplace of Alessandro Scarlatti
–··– Modern country borders

THE CHANGING FACE OF STRINGED INSTRUMENTS

Late seventeenth-century Bologna was the site for a development in musical instrument design and construction that would have immediate and far-reaching effects. Makers of string instruments started to use wirewound gut stringing (winding fine wire around a gut-string core) in such a way that they could reduce the size of the bass instrument that was previously named the violone. By increasing the mass of the strings they used they could reduce the length of string required to produce the same pitch. This meant that instruments of around 29 inches (75 cm) in length could be built, rather than 31 inches (80 cm), which would now become the standard size for the so-called violincello (cello).

These smaller bass instruments were more manageable for performers, facilitating a more virtuoso style of playing. The development of the cello had immediate implications for the instrumentation and composition of bass lines in all musical genres, but perhaps most noticeably in trio sonatas and orchestral music.

concerto grosso, and violin concerto in particular. A school of string playing flourished there and became known abroad as musicians and publications traveled.

Bolognese musical life was supported by a series of academies, controlled by professional musicians. These institutions provided theoretical and practical training for their members, who at first comprised mainly young noblemen. Most significant among these academies was the Academia Filarmonica di Bologne, founded in 1661. Members would meet to discuss theoretical works, and to hear and analyze new music.

The city was also developing a reputation for practical musical instruction, in singing in particular. The main Italian and European theaters were, for a time, dominated by singers who received their training in Bologna; this was, after all, a city that boasted an uninterrupted operatic life from 1634 to 1792. Bologna was also the place of publication for one of the most important treatises on singing of the eighteenth century: Pierre Francesco Tosi's *Opinioni de' cantori antichi e moderni* (*Observations on ancient and modern singing*) which appeared in 1723.

Right This seventeenth-century painting shows a girl receiving a lesson in playing the bass viol.

Henry Purcell

SEPTEMBER 10(?), 1659–NOVEMBER 21, 1695

HENRY PURCELL IS AMONG THE GREATEST OF ENGLISH COMPOSERS. HIS LIFE, LIKE MOZART'S, WAS BRIEF BUT EXTRAORDINARILY PRODUCTIVE. HIS OPERA *DIDO AND AENEAS* IS ONE OF THE EARLIEST AND BEST LOVED WORKS IN THE REPERTOIRE; HIS SACRED MUSIC IS STILL PERFORMED AND REVERED IN CHURCHES AND CONCERTS; AND HIS SKILL AT SETTING WORDS WAS FAMOUS AMONG HIS CONTEMPORARIES AND INSPIRED COMPOSERS AS RECENT AS BENJAMIN BRITTEN AND MICHAEL TIPPETT.

There is little direct evidence about Purcell's early life. His father (almost certainly another Henry Purcell) was a respected musician, as were his uncle Thomas and his brother Daniel. Young Henry was trained in the choir of the Chapel Royal, perhaps from the age of about six, and seems to have shown early signs of extraordinary talent.

COMPOSING FOR CHURCH AND COURT

By the time he was 18, Purcell had been appointed composer for the king's violins. His works were being performed in Westminster Abbey, where he was organist from his early 20s until he died. At about 21, he commenced a career as a court composer, writing odes and anthems praising the king (then Charles II) and other noble personages. He married Frances Peters in 1680; of their children, two—Frances and Edward—lived to adulthood.

Charles II was succeeded in 1685 by James II, and for the coronation Purcell wrote the famous anthems

Right Although he died over 300 years ago, Purcell's place as possibly England's finest composer has never been usurped.

Below The classic tale of Dido and Aeneas was adapted by librettist Nahum Tate to accompany Purcell's music. The opera is rightly considered a masterpiece.

Discover the music

"Thou Knowest, Lord" (1674)

"Rejoice in the Lord Always" (the "Bell Anthem") (1683–1684)

"An Evening Hymn" (1688)

Dido and Aeneas (1689)

King Arthur (1691)

"The Blessed Virgin's Expostulation" (1693?)

"Lord, What is Man?" (1693)

Come Ye Sons of Art, Away (includes the duet "Sound the Trumpet") (1694)

The Indian Queen (1695)

> *"Here lyes Henry Purcell Esq, who left this life and is gone to that blessed place where only his harmony can be exceeded."*

EPITAPH IN WESTMINSTER ABBEY

"I Was Glad" and "My Heart is Inditing." As work from the court diminished, however, he turned more to other music, including, in the 1680s, the odes for the feast of St Cecilia, the patron saint of music.

WRITING FOR THE THEATER

Purcell's theater music became a very important part of his work. He supplied music for plays by many prominent dramatists of the time; later, he composed "semi-operas" or "dramatic operas." These include *King Arthur* (1691), by the dramatist and great poet John Dryden; *Dioclesian* (1690); *The Fairy Queen* (1692, an adaptation of Shakespeare's *Midsummer Night's Dream*); and *The Indian Queen* (1695, completed after Purcell's

Below A glimpse of Purcell's London can be seen in this seventeenth-century engraving of part of the waterfront at Westminster.

death by his brother Daniel). Today we might call these pieces musical theater—spoken plays with many songs and spectacular extended scenes that include some of Purcell's finest music.

Purcell continued to write both sacred and secular compositions; the music he wrote for the funeral of Queen Mary is justly famous. The songs he wrote throughout his career are among the finest ever composed, with haunting melodies and demonstrating an extraordinary mastery of form.

In 1695, at the age of 36, Henry Purcell died very suddenly. He was still composing on his deathbed—the published version of his great song "From Rosy Bowers" carries the note: "The last song the Author set, he being in his sickness." He was buried at the foot of the organ of Westminster Abbey.

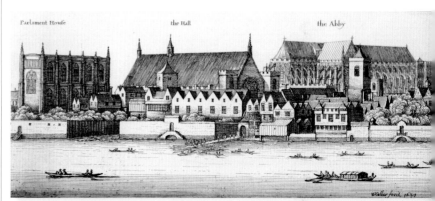

DIDO AND AENEAS AND THE GROUND BASS

The only work by Purcell that we would call a true opera is *Dido and Aeneas*, performed in 1689 at a girls' school. The libretto, by poet and dramatist Nahum Tate, is based on an episode from the *Aeneid*, the Latin epic by Virgil (70–19 BCE). Dido, queen of Carthage, falls in love with the Trojan hero Aeneas, wandering the world after his home has been destroyed by war. A jealous enchantress sends a spirit to remind Aeneas of the gods' command to leave Carthage and found the city of Rome. He departs reluctantly, and Dido, abandoned, goes to her death singing one of the most moving and sustained laments in music ("When I am laid in earth"). The opera hardly lasts an hour and uses the simplest effects, but presents varied evocative music and vivid characters, including the half-comic, half-terrifying witches and the noble Dido.

Dido's famous lament takes a form that Purcell often used with brilliant effect—the ground bass. In this technique, a tune is constantly repeated in the bass while the upper part weaves in and out, sometimes letting the bass be heard and sometimes seeming independent of it. Some of Purcell's most celebrated songs employ this technique, evoking emotions ranging from enchantment ("Music For a While") and devout meditation ("An Evening Hymn") to sprightly joy (the duet "Sound the Trumpet").

England in the late seventeenth century

LIFE IN PURCELL'S LONDON WAS INSECURE, AS HIS SUDDEN
FATAL ILLNESS SHOWS. IN 1665–1666, NEARLY A FIFTH OF
LONDON'S POPULATION DIED IN THE GREAT PLAGUE. IN THE
PURCELLS' PARISH, 3,000 PEOPLE DIED, THOUGH YOUNG HENRY
AND HIS FIVE SIBLINGS WERE UNSCATHED.

As the plague faded, it was followed by another
catastrophe, the Great Fire of London (September 2–5, 1666), which destroyed four-fifths of the city.
In its reconstruction, Sir Christopher Wren (1632–1723) and Nicholas Hawksmoor (1661–1736)
created some of London's greatest buildings.

Right Along with the destruction of many important buildings, the Great Fire of London in 1666 is estimated to have razed to the ground around 70,000 homes.

MUSIC

Political and religious turmoil had serious effects on
social, intellectual, and artistic life in the 1600s. Music,
especially church music, was severely restricted under
the Commonwealth; many church choirs were disbanded and their libraries and organs destroyed.

MONARCHY AND REVOLUTION

England in the 1600s had suffered decades of bloodshed over political and
religious conflict. After the execution of Charles I in 1649, England was not
a monarchy but a Commonwealth ruled by Parliament and the Lord Protector,
Oliver Cromwell (1599–1658). In 1660, Charles Stuart returned from exile as
King Charles II in what we know as the Restoration. Charles was succeeded
by his brother, James II, in 1685. But James's arrogance and his Catholicism
made him unacceptable to many people and in 1688 the so-called "Glorious
Revolution" took place. An influential group approached James II's daughter,
Mary, who was married to the Dutch Protestant Prince William of Orange, to
take the English throne under a constitutional monarchy. James fled into exile.
The Jacobites (the word comes from Jacobus, the Latin form of James) waged
a tragic and bloody campaign to restore the Stuart monarchy until 1746.

The constitutional restraints on the monarchy are part of the basis of the
modern democratic British state, but at the time there were also many restrictions on Roman Catholics and non-Anglican Protestants. Catholics could not
vote nor stand for Parliament nor hold commissions in the British Army, and
to this day the monarch cannot be a Catholic nor marry one.

During Purcell's boyhood this tradition was being
rebuilt and his training ground, the Chapel Royal,
nurtured many important composers, including his
mentors John Blow (1648–1708), Matthew Locke
(1630–1677), and Pelham Humfrey (1647–1674).
Blow and Locke became close friends of Purcell.

The court was an important source of employment
for musicians, though less so under William and Mary.

LITERATURE AND THEATER

Perhaps the greatest English poet after Shakespeare
was John Milton (1608–1674), most famous for his
epic *Paradise Lost*. The so-called metaphysical poets
also flourished in the 1600s—their work was characterized by dense, complex metaphors and frequent
classical, scientific, and poetic allusions. The finest
were John Donne (1572–1631) and Andrew Marvell
(1621–1678), who wrote passionate love poetry and
deeply committed religious poems and prose. Purcell
set texts by two metaphysicals, George Herbert (1593–1633) and Abraham Cowley (1618–1667). Later in
the century came poets like John Dryden (1631–1700),
who valued clarity, wit, and elegance.

Dryden was also a prominent dramatist: Purcell
provided music for his *King Arthur* and *The Indian*

Below An illustration, by Gustave Doré, of Satan summoning other fallen angels in Hell, from a nineteenth-century edition of *Paradise Lost* by John Milton.

Queen. Theater had also been suppressed during the Commonwealth but enthusiastically revived after the Restoration. William Davenant (1606–1668) founded a theater and wrote poetry and plays, including what may be the first English opera, *The Siege of Rhodes*, with music (now lost) by Matthew Locke. Restoration comedy, by playwrights like William Congreve (1670–1729), Sir John Vanbrugh (1664–1726), and George Farquhar (1678–1707), was witty, elegant, and often bawdy. The plays of more serious dramatists such as Nahum Tate (1652–1715), Thomas Shadwell (1642?–1692), and even Dryden, are mostly neglected today. Concepts of drama were very different from ours; it was accepted, for example, that Shakespeare's *Romeo and Juliet* could be rewritten with a happy ending.

Other important writing came from two famous diarists, Samuel Pepys (1633–1703) and John Evelyn (1620–1706). Pepys, a great administrator and arts patron, is especially noted for his observations of the times—for instance, he vividly describes the Great Fire—and his intimate portrait of his own life.

SCIENCE AND PHILOSOPHY

In 1660, the Royal Society was established to promote scientific discussion. One of its early presidents was Sir

Right Isaac Newton discovers the refraction of light. One of the greatest scientific minds in history, his theories on light were published in his book *Opticks* in 1704.

Isaac Newton (1642–1727), who established his theories of gravitation and light and developed calculus between 1664 and 1666.

John Locke (1632–1704) was a physician and seminal philosopher, a pioneer of a rationalist view of the world who argued for religious and political freedom. Astronomer and mathematician Edmund Halley (1656–1742), for whom Halley's Comet is named, is another great figure of the age.

INSTRUMENTS OF THE BAROQUE PERIOD

In the Baroque period, instrumental pieces such as suites were popular, and compositions for individual instruments became much more common than they had been earlier. Interestingly, the ornamentation that is associated with music in the Baroque period was often improvised by individual musicians with some of these parts and cadenzas accidentally being written into printed versions of the works.

New playing techniques such as *tremolo* (a shaking effect created by rapid repetition of a note) and *pizzicato* (where stringed instruments are plucked rather than bowed) also came to the fore during this time, as did the development of functional tonality. Keyboard instruments such as the harpsichord and organ were heavily used; and the invention of figured bass (a way of notating harmony) opened up a new way of reading and composing music.

Baroque music forms such a large part of the classical music canon, and some of history's most famous composers—including Vivaldi, Handel, Bach, and Corelli—set the pace for the music of the time. Opera, developed in the late Renaissance, became an important compositional form in the Baroque period, and the oratorio (musical drama with a religious setting) reached its peak in the compositions of Handel and Bach.

Most performances of music during the Baroque period were held in wealthy

Right A trio of music-makers, two of whom are playing chamuleaux. These recorder-like instruments came in four sizes: soprano, alto, tenor, and bass.

Above A copy of a 1670 Hieronimus Starck alto sackbut, with a modern water-key. This precursor to the modern trombone is tuned in E flat.

Above The clavichord is one of the defining instruments of the Baroque era. When a key is struck, a small metal blade called the tangent hits the appropriate string, creating the clavichord's distinctive sound.

homes, at court, or in churches, and the instruments generally were not loud. Instruments such as the sackbut (a precursor to the trombone) entered into the concert repertoire, as did the oboe da caccia and Baroque trumpet.

CHALUMEAU

This instrument, popular in many Baroque works, looks like a recorder, and has a mouthpiece and single reed, similar to a clarinet. The chalumeau is in fact the link between the two instruments. With eight tone holes, and no register key, the instrument had a small range of a little more than an octave.

RACKETT

Dating back to the 1570s, this precursor to the bassoon is a double reed wind instrument and comes in a few sizes—from soprano to bass. A wooden chamber with cylinders drilled into the sides means the fingering pattern is somewhat awkward for the musician to play. Although the rackett is a relatively small instrument (the tenor model being under 5 inches (12 cm) long), it has a range similar to a bassoon, and is a versatile instrument tonally—depending on the reed and the musician. The tone of the rackett is said to be similar to the bassoon, and it blends well with harpsichord, cornetti, and the Baroque recorder, among others.

THEORBO

A close relative of the lute, the theorbo, sometimes also known as the chitarrone, came into prominence in sixteenth-century Italy, and there are written references to the instrument dating to the 1540s. Longer than the lute, the theorbo became popular as an accompanying instrument for singers, because its open, bass strings (called diapasons) gave the instrument more resonance and volume than a traditional lute. Before too long, composers were writing pieces specifically for the instrument, and it soon featured in quite a number of Baroque compositions. The theorbo has one pegbox at the top of the fingerboard, and another at the end of the neck. A typical theorbo has 14 strings.

CORNETT

The cornett—not to be confused with the cornet, a brass, valved instrument similar to a trumpet—is a slender, curved, tube-like wind instrument that in its early days was often made of bone, horn, or ivory. By about the sixteenth century, cornetts were being carved from wood. The cornett resembles a recorder in that the shaft of the instrument has a number of holes punched into it. The player blows into a mouthpiece that is the same sort of mouthpiece that is used for

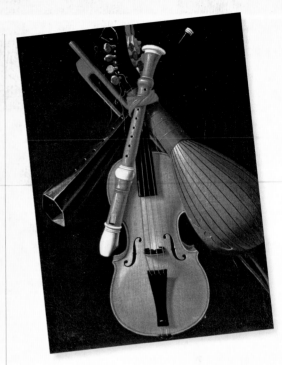

Right The long, dark brown instrument in the left of this montage of musical instruments is a cornett. It gradually fell out of favor, and by the eighteenth century was all but forgotten.

Below The theorbo, part of the lute family, was a popular accompanying instrument for singers. Good quality wood, such as maple, was used in theorbo construction.

brass instruments; the fingers of the left hand play the upper holes, while the fingers of the right hand play the lower holes.

Rarely played today, even in ensembles featuring early instruments, the cornett was commonly used for ceremonial purposes, and many paintings of the period show musicians playing this unusual instrument.

VIOL

The viol is one of the numerous bowed, stringed, or fretted instruments developed from about the late fifteenth century and commonly used before and during the Baroque period. Similar in appearance to the modern cello, it is played between the legs, and its alternative name—viola da gamba—means "leg-viol." As with other stringed instruments, it can be plucked or bowed. The viol is tuned in fourths and commonly has six strings. These are made of gut, giving the instrument a softer tone than that produced by steel strings.

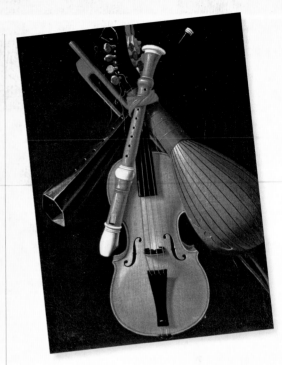

Right The viol has a gentle, mellow tone. It was usually played in a consort—a small ensemble of players. Viol consorts were popular in the Baroque period.

Elisabeth-Claude Jacquet de la Guerre

MARCH 17, 1665–JUNE 27, 1729

ELISABETH-CLAUDE JACQUET DE LA GUERRE WAS A CHILD PRODIGY, WHO WAS PATRONIZED BY KING LOUIS XIV. SHE WAS A HARPSICHORDIST AND COMPOSER, AND WAS THE FIRST FRENCH WOMAN TO PUBLISH AN ENTIRE OPERA, *CÉPHALE ET PROCRIS*, IN 1694. ALTHOUGH SHE NEVER GAINED A PROFESSIONAL POSITION IN MUSIC, SHE PUBLISHED, GAVE PRIVATE CONCERTS, AND EARNED A CONSIDERABLE REPUTATION AS A KEYBOARD PLAYER.

Of all countries in late seventeenth-century Europe, France provided one of the best social and cultural environments for a talented female musician. Teaching and publishing were considered very acceptable activities for such women, and the role of salon hostess (including that of musical hostess) was considered a culturally and politically important one in society. Jacquet de la Guerre was fortunate in having been born into a French musical family who valued and nurtured her skills.

DRAMATIC MUSIC AND OTHER WORKS

Jacquet de la Guerre began her compositional career with dramatic music. Unfortunately her first such work, the ballet *Les jeux à l'honneur de la victoire*, is lost. As is the case for many other Baroque dramatic works, the surviving libretto is the only trace that we have of

Below Upper- and middle-class women in seventeenth-century France were often well educated and also competent musicians, mainly playing harpsichord, lute, and viol.

the composition. Her *Céphale et Procris* was performed at the Académie Royale de Musique in 1694, but with little success. Two years later it was revived in Strasbourg, thanks to the efforts of French lexicographer and composer Sébastien de Brossard, who founded a musical academy there. Brossard took a keen interest in Jacquet de la Guerre, making copies of her early trio sonatas and sonatas for violin and continuo. She published a first book of harpsichord pieces in 1687, a copy of which has only recently been discovered; a second book appeared in 1707. In that year, too, she published her *Pièces de clavecin qui peuvent se jouer sur le viollon*, whose title, suggesting performance on the violin as well as the keyboard, is an example of the typically flexible practices of performance of this time.

Jacquet de la Guerre composed music in Italian genres such as the sonata and cantata, even though such works had not been entirely accepted by French composers, performers, and listeners in her time. She produced innovative works, which were some of the earliest French examples in these genres. Rhythmic vitality and adventurous harmony are among the hallmarks of her sonatas, while the cantatas, especially the secular works, show a good deal of freedom of form.

Discover the music

Pièces de clavessin (1687)

Les jeux à l'honneur de la victoire (c. 1691; lost)

Céphale et Procris (1694)

Vocal music including three books of French cantatas (1708, 1711, c. 1715)

Pièces de clavecin qui peuvent se jouer sur le viollon (1707)

Te Deum (1721; lost)

The sacred cantatas are much more restrained and balanced in terms of style and form. This composure was entirely in keeping with contemporary notions of "church style" in music, which was to be more decorous than music destined for the chamber or theater.

Most of Jacquet de la Guerre's music was dedicated to Louis XIV, excluding one set of secular cantatas, which was written for the Elector of Bavaria, Maximillian II Emmanuel. What was probably her final work, a *Te Deum* (hymn of praise), was sung in the chapel of the Louvre in 1721 to give thanks for Louis XV's recovery from smallpox. Sadly this work, too, is lost.

Right France's Louis XV (1710–1774), the son of Louis XIV, for whom Elisabeth-Claude Jacquet de la Guerre wrote her *Te Deum* in 1721.

THE *PRÉLUDES NON MESURÉS* FROM *LES PIÈCES DE CLAVESSIN*

The *Pièces de clavessin* of 1687 contain five suites (collections of dances, usually intended to be performed at one sitting). One of the striking features of these works is the presence of so-called *préludes non mesurés* (unmeasured preludes). These works can be understood as an attempt to capture on paper the spontaneous act of improvisation. Indeed the *préludes non mesurés* are one of the best indications we have of the kind of melodic and harmonic content a performer would produce when freely improvising at the keyboard. In the earliest *préludes non mesurés* the music is notated solely in whole notes, thus the performer has a good deal of room for interpretation. Modern attempts to "realize" this music, by fixing on rhythms and inserting bar lines, represent only one of many different possible readings.

As Shakespeare's Polonius observes, "Though this be madness, yet there is method in't." This applies to the realized *préludes non mesurés*, which might look complex and chaotic on the page. In fact, a logical sequence of chord progressions underlies each piece. The genre can be understood as a "composing out," or large-scale embellishment, of this progression.

François Couperin

NOVEMBER 10, 1668–SEPTEMBER 11, 1733

A COMPOSER, HARPSICHORDIST, AND ORGANIST, FRANÇOIS
COUPERIN BELONGED TO ONE OF THE GREAT DYNASTIES
OF FRENCH MUSIC. THE COUPERINS WERE A FAMILY OF
MUSICIANS ACTIVE FROM THE LATE SIXTEENTH THROUGH
TO THE EARLY NINETEENTH CENTURIES. THE APPELLATION
"LE GRAND" DISTINGUISHES THIS FRANÇOIS COUPERIN
FROM HIS LIKE-NAMED RELATIVES; IT ALSO SIGNIFIES HIS
SIZEABLE STATUS AS A MUSICIAN, NOT ONLY IN HIS FAMILY
BUT IN HIS ERA IN GENERAL.

In 1685 Couperin took over the post occupied by his uncle, Louis Couperin (c. 1626–1661), and then his father Charles Couperin (1638–1779) as organist to the king at the church of St Gervais, Paris. His career portfolio subsequently diversified—he took up the positions of organist and harpsichordist at the royal court, taught keyboard to members of the aristocracy, and also enjoyed success in publishing his own music.

COUPERIN'S WORKS

Couperin wrote sacred and secular vocal music, chamber music, and works for organ and harpsichord. He is primarily known for four books of harpsichord music, containing some 220 pieces. Among these, program music (works of a descriptive, narrative, or pictorial

Above right Couperin's influence was immense. In the early twentieth century, Maurice Ravel wrote *Le Tombeau de Couperin*, in part a tribute to the Baroque composer.

Below A nineteenth-century engraving of the church of St Gervais in Paris, where Couperin was an organist early in his career.

nature) is a particular speciality. Couperin wrote two distinct types of program music. One includes his musical portraits, depictions of his friends, pupils, or patrons. Notable in these works is the composer's keen critical sense—he was not content to represent his sitters in the best possible light, but rather to reveal both positive and negative aspects of their characters in his music. The other type comprises descriptive pieces that imitate natural phenomena. These pieces can be more or less literal in their imitation. *Les petits moulins à vent* nicely captures the windmill with a flurry of rapid notes; *Les baricades mistérieuses* is rather more metaphorical, depicting masks and masking through subtly shifting harmonies.

FEATURES AND STYLE

Couperin was a great admirer of the best Italian composers of his day. An anecdote that appears in the preface to his chamber music collection *Les nations* explains the inspiration for his incorporation of Italian style into his works, and reveals something of his own slightly mischievous personality: "Charmed by the sonatas of Signor Corelli, whose works I shall love as long as I live, just as I do the French works of Monsieur de Lully, I attempted to compose one myself which I [then] had performed in the concert series where I had heard those of Corelli … I composed others, and my Italianized name brought me, in disguise, considerable applause."

Another feature of Couperin's music, which is typically French, is his specification of ornaments. French

LE PARNASSE, OU L'APOTHÉOSE DE CORELLI AND L'APOTHÉOSE DE LULLI

Le Parnasse, ou L'apothéose de Corelli (*Parnassus, or The Apotheosis of Corelli*) is a trio sonata for two violins and continuo, which was published in Paris in 1724 in the collection *Les goûts-réünis* (*The Reunited Styles*). This was the one of two collections of suites in which Couperin was intending to make a particular point of combining French and Italian musical styles, whose differences and relative merits were a topic of considerable interest at this time. The most notable Italian element in *The Apotheosis of Corelli* is the employment of singing melodies in the slow movements; however French traits arguably predominate, including the emphasis on dances, the detailed notation of ornaments, and the entire programmatic framing of the composition.

In 1725 Couperin published *L'apothéose de Lulli* (*The Apotheosis of Lully*), in which Lully joins Corelli on Mount Parnassus and they perform a French overture followed by a trio sonata. The two musicians are represented as graciously accepting of each other's differences—and they take turns at playing *premier dessus* (the uppermost part).

Discover the music

Recueils d'airs sérieux et à boire (1697–1712)

Leçons de ténèbres (1713–1717)

Le Parnasse, ou L'apothéose de Corelli, in *Les goûts-réünis* (1724)

L'apothéose de Lulli and *Les nations: Sonades et suites de simphonies en trio* (1725)

Pièces de clavecin (1713, 1716–1717, 1722, 1730)

keyboard composers of this time used an increasing array of symbols to indicate to the performer exactly what and where to decorate their works. These decorations included the trill or *tremblement*, the appoggiatura or *port de voix*, and the mordent or *pincé*. In his major keyboard treatise of 1716, *L'art de toucher le clavecin*, Couperin provided the performer with some general rules on the application of ornamentation. The treatise also covers such topics as touch and demeanor at the instrument, fingering, and comments on the harpsichord's special capabilities as an instrument.

Above This organ in the Chapel Royal, Château de Versailles, France, was built in 1708 by Robert Cliquot, and decorated to designs by Cotte. François Couperin is believed to have played this organ.

France's Music under the Sun King

THE CENTER OF FRENCH MUSICAL DEVELOPMENTS AROUND 1700 WAS THE
COURT OF LOUIS XIV. OF THE MUSICIANS WHO HELD FAVOR WITH THE KING,
FEW WERE WOMEN AND MOST WERE FRENCH. ELISABETH-CLAUDE JACQUET DE
LA GUERRE WAS FORTUNATE ENOUGH TO BE PATRONIZED BY THE KING AND HIS
MISTRESS, AS A SINGER FOR PRIVATE MUSIC-MAKING ACTIVITIES.

Talented French instrumental performers, such as François Couperin (keyboard) and Marin Marais (bass viol), owed no small part of their success in teaching, performance, and composition to their court appointments.

The royal court had been the center of French musical life since the sixteenth century, and Italian music had flourished there. Italian operas by composers such as Luigi Rossi and Francesco Cavalli were staged in Paris, and Italian musicians such as Lully himself could enter into court musical life. With the ascendance of Louis XIV, political absolute rule was to be reflected

Right Louis XIV in a ballet costume that inspired his nickname the "Sun King." A great lover of dance, Louis is credited with the establishment of the world's first ballet school.

in musical terms. He fully appreciated the power that could be represented, enacted, and wielded through music and musical institutions. Most aspects of musical life in France were subject to controls from the central administration, where French music and musicians were privileged above all.

FRENCH MUSICAL GENRES: AIRS DE COUR
A national style of composition, and a particularly French set of musical genres, had been developed by sixteenth- and early seventeenth-century French composers. The *air de cour* (court air) generally comprised a strophic setting (with several verses set to the same tune) of a single vocal line, with lute accompaniment. Characteristically, these songs had no regular time signature, but rather shifted between meters, according to the theory of long and short syllables in the poetic text. The result was a somewhat restrained declamatory style, very different from the ornate arias found in Italy at the time. Couperin, Charpentier, and Lully set songs in a similar fashion to their French predecessors; the titles they chose—*airs sérieux* (serious songs) and *airs à boire* (drinking songs)—do not necessarily reflect two different musical styles.

FRENCH MUSICAL GENRES: DANCE
Dance music, much like French vocal music, followed particular rhythmic patterns that were associated with the various steps. Thus for each type of dance—the courante, sarabande, minuet, and gigue—there were

ENGLAND

English Channel

FLANDERS

Seine

NORMANDY

Paris ☆
Versailles CHAMPAGNE

Strasbourg

BRITTANY

MAINE
ANJOU BLOIS
Loire
TOURAINE BURGUNDY

FRANCE

AQUITAINE

Geneva

Bay of
Biscay

Bordeaux

GASCONY

Rhône

TOULOUSE

Toulouse

Marseille

Mediterranean Sea

France in the late seventeenth century
☆ Birthplace of Elisabeth-Claude Jacquet de la Guerre, François Couperin and Marin Marais

0   250 kilometers
0   125 miles

Right The viol player in this painting is playing from a score by Marin Marais. Well known in his day, Marais spent his whole life working in Paris.

particular meters, rhythmic patterns, and melodic shapes that had become conventional. These dances were central to the *ballet de cour* (court ballet), which also contained much vocal music and were often elaborately staged. The dance styles impinged on almost all areas of French music-making, including sacred music and instrumental music. The French suite comprised collections of stylized instrumental dance movements, while sacred music frequently drew on dance rhythms.

MARIN MARAIS (1656–1728)

The French viol player Marin Marais became associated with court musical life in 1676, thanks to Lully, from whom he learned composition. From 1679 he was a member of the king's chamber music. His first collection of viol music (*Pièces de viol*) was published in 1686, and was well received. He was also highly gifted as a composer of dramatic music. He composed four operas for Paris, *tragedies en musique* in the style of Lully. As a viol virtuoso he was matched only by his contemporary, Antoine Forqueray.

MUSICAL LIFE AT VERSAILLES

In 1682 Versailles became the official court residence. Music was performed both indoors and outdoors, in private and in public. It was required at all important ceremonies, as well as on a daily basis to accompany rising, Mass, meals, and going to bed. The pavilions of the Maison des Italiens and the Trianon served as alternative venues for indoor music-making. There was no opera house until 1748.

Louis XIV's title Roi Soleil ("Sun King") derives from his role as Apollo in Benserade's 1651 *Ballet du roy festes de Bacchus*. Although musically illiterate, the king was a competent dancer, well able to perform such a role. He also played lute and guitar.

PERFORMANCE PRACTICES

Under Lully's direction, the court violin band, the Twenty-Four Violins of the King, became renowned for the precision of their playing. Lully would beat time, and devised a system of bowing string instruments such that all players were synchronized. Tempi for dance music were governed by the performance conventions of the dances—sarabandes were slow and stately, gigues fast and lively, and so forth.

While French musicians did not share the same penchant for elaborate improvised ornamentation as their Italian contemporaries, they did develop a predilection for adding dotted rhythms where "straight" rhythmic values were written. This technique of "over-dotting" or "double dotting" is similar to the syncopated rhythms heard in jazz music.

Left Part of the sumptuous gardens at the palace of Versailles, where Louis XIV had his court. The château had large rooms devoted to specific functions, including a ballroom and a music room.

Tomaso Albinoni

JUNE 8, 1671–JANUARY 17, 1751

TOGETHER WITH ANTONIO VIVALDI, TOMASO ALBINONI WAS A KEY COMPOSER OF THE ITALIAN LATE BAROQUE. HE IS KNOWN FOR HIS CONCERTOS, AMONG WHICH THOSE FOR ONE OR TWO OBOES AND THOSE FOR VIOLIN ARE ESPECIALLY FINE. UNUSUALLY FOR HIS TIME, ALBINONI CHOSE NOT TO FIND A POSITION IN THE SERVICE OF A PARTICULAR PATRON OR INSTITUTION; RATHER, HE FLOURISHED AS A WEALTHY MUSICIAN OF INDEPENDENT MEANS.

Biographical details for Albinoni remain sketchy. At the close of the seventeenth century he might have served briefly as a chamber musician at the court of Mantua, under the patron of the arts, Ferdinando Carlo di Gonzaga. In the early eighteenth century he is reported to have run a singing school. In between times, he visited Florence to direct performances and lead the orchestra for his new opera, *Griselda*. Starting with the performance of his *Rodrigo in Algeri* in Naples in 1702, his theatrical works were becoming known throughout Italy. So it is perhaps not surprising that on the death of his father in 1705, Albinoni, the eldest son, did not inherit the main share of the family stationery business in Venice. By this stage he had fully committed himself to music, proudly signing himself "musico di violino."

Above right The frontispiece of Albinoni's *Balletti for Trio* (Op. 3), written in 1701 and dedicated to Ferdinand III, Grand Duke of Tuscany. It was published in Venice.

Right The ducal palace in Mantua. Musicologists believe that Albinoni worked for a short time at Mantua. Indeed, his Op. 2 concertos (1700) are dedicated to the Duke of Mantua.

Oboe

Called a "hautbois" or "hoboy" prior to 1770, the Baroque oboe is a three-keyed double reed instrument. With a clear and often piercing tone, the oboe was the main melody instrument in early military bands. Telemann, Handel, and later Mozart, all wrote concertos for the instrument. Albinoni is said to be the first of the Italian composers to write for the oboe, his Op. 7 concerto a fine example. Most professional oboists make their own reeds, carving them to fit the unique embouchure, oboe angle and the air support of the individual musician. The way the reed is made affects the pitch of the instrument.

ALBINONI'S WORKS

Albinoni enjoyed success in the composition of both secular vocal music (including solo cantatas as well as operas) and instrumental ensemble music (especially sonatas and concertos). By the 1720s his fame as an instrumental composer was becoming widespread. One index of the influence of his works is seen in Bach's use of themes drawn from Albinoni's Op. 1 trio sonatas as subjects for several of his own fugues. Albinoni's cantatas, too, were well liked, if lesser known in his day. However, he seems to have had less success in, or enthusiasm for, the composition of sacred music—the only work in this field that survives and

that can be definitely attributed to Albinoni is a Mass for three unaccompanied male voices. In his comparatively long life he produced a vast amount of music. There are about 50 extant operas (known mainly from their librettos); nearly 50 solo cantatas; 100 pieces of chamber music for between one and six instruments; 59 concertos; and eight independent orchestral works (sinfonias). Still more works are attributed to him, but these are doubtful. For example, the *Adagio in G minor*, often attributed to him, was in fact written by the twentieth-century composer and Albinoni scholar Remo Giazotto. Giazotto claimed that this work was based on fragments from the slow movement of a trio sonata by Albinoni.

THE OP. 5 *CONCERTI A CINQUE*

The violin concerto first developed in Bologna and Venice around 1700. Giuseppe Torelli (1658–1709) was one of the first to publish such works—his Op. 5 *Concerti a cinque* appeared in 1692. A vital development for the genre is found in Albinoni's own Op. 5 of 1707, which is also a set of solo violin concertos. The writing is notable because the violin part is more easily distinguishable from that of the orchestral players than was formerly the case in this genre; so too, the accompanying role of the orchestra is more clearly marked than in previous works in this genre. These musical features mean that the listener can clearly hear these concertos as a pitting of the soloist against the orchestra—the music becomes more dialogic, even competitive in nature. The works of Op. 5 had a significant impact on the northern European musical world, and were reprinted in Amsterdam in 1708, 1709, *c.* 1716, and *c.* 1722.

Discover the Music

Mass for three unaccompanied male
  voices (c. 1694?)
Cantatas for voice and basso continuo
100 pieces of chamber music for
  between one and six instruments
12 *Concerti a cinque* Op. 5 (1707)
12 *Concerti a cinque* Op. 7 (1715)
12 *Concerti a cinque* Op. 9 (1722)

Music in Italy in the eighteenth century

THE SIGNING OF THE PEACE OF WESTPHALIA IN 1648 WAS TO HAVE A NEGATIVE EFFECT ON ITALY IN THE SHORT TERM. WHEREAS THE COUNTRY HAD BEEN KEY TO THE CATHOLIC COUNTER-REFORMATION AND SPANISH IMPERIALISM, IT NOW MOVED TO THE MARGINS IN TERMS OF EUROPEAN RELIGIOUS AND POLITICAL EVENTS. HOWEVER, IN THE MUSICAL SPHERE, AND IN OPERA IN PARTICULAR, ITALY WAS CENTER STAGE IN THE EIGHTEENTH CENTURY.

Above right The church and the theater employed many composers and musicians, but private homes were also thriving as popular venues for musical performances.

Italy's Spanish and Catholic interests were linked to economic interests, especially for merchants in the major cities. With the end of the Counter-Reformation, and the blow delivered to Spanish imperialism by the Peace of Westphalia, Italy's power and European integration declined. Nonetheless, the eighteenth century saw demographic and economic advances, brought about in part by the Spanish, Polish, and Austrian Wars of Succession. There was an increase in the Italian population, from 13 million to around 18 million by the end of the century. There was also an upward movement in commerce and industry, and new developments were seen in cities such as Naples, Rome, Turin, and Florence. In the early eighteenth century, Spanish control of Italy was succeeded by Austrian hegemony. Lombardy was under absolute Austrian rule, and Tuscany was acquired by Austria following the death of the last of the Medicis in 1737.

OPERA BUFFA

Opera buffa (comic opera) was a significant develop-ment in the early eighteenth century. Venice was the site of a seminal collaboration between the librettist Pietro Pariati, the composers Francesco Gasparini and Albinoni, and the comic bass Giovanni Battista Cavana. Operas in the comic genre shared some of the reforms instituted by the Accademia dell'Arcadia, at least those concerning plot simplification, but these plots were based on charac-ters drawn from real life (rather than gods and heroes), and the vocal music was simple and largely unornamented (in comparison to the elaborate arias of *opera seria*). A crucial moment in the history of comic opera was the production of Giovanni Battista Pergolesi's *La Serva Padrona* in 1733, which exemplifies the simple plot and music of the genre, as well as *opera buffa's* believable, fallible characters.

Above Giovanni Battista Pergolesi (1710–1736) was an early composer of *opera buffa*. Among his works are *La Serva Padrona* (1733) and *Il flaminio* (1735).

PLACING MUSIC

Despite these political and religious upheavals, musical life flourished in eighteenth-century Italy in three main locales—the church, theater, and chamber. Particular styles and genres were associated with the music for each of these locations—liturgical music and the seri-ous style for the church; opera and the grand and florid style for the theater; and chamber music (including cantatas) in an intimate style for the private sphere. This tripartite scheme was by no means absolute. Often one and the same musician served in the church and performed in the theater. This intermixing of personnel was one factor that led to a blending of musical styles; specifically, music for the ecclesiastical context became more similar to opera. So too there was a gray area between the "public" and "private" spheres of music-making. Concerts of instrumental music, in which works of various genres and sizes were performed, were usually given in private homes.

Around 1800, with the rise of the concept of the "musical work" as an object for silent contemplation, came the corresponding rise of an attentive listening public. During the late Baroque period, the notion of the "musical work" as a concrete, score-based, and definable product of a single author was just about inconceivable for one important reason: The performer often was the composer, and the "work" was either created or completed (for example by adding ornamentation) in the very act of performance.

DEVELOPMENTS IN OPERA

The number of opera houses grew steadily in the late seventeenth and early eighteenth centuries, and these buildings became social and cultural focal points in the cities. Increasingly, these were run by independent impressarios (musical entrepreneurs), rather than being under court control. This was a time of new articulacy

Below In the late Baroque era, more opera houses and concert halls were being constructed in Italy, including Rome's magnificent Teatro Argentina, which opened in the early 1730s.

on the part of music theorists, writers who would give opera a fresh intellectual and philosophical basis. Of these theorists, two of the most important were Apostolo Zeno (1668–1750) and Pietro Metastasio (1698–1782). Both writers recognized the crucial social function of opera, as a purveyor of "high" culture, a means by which to offer social critique and thus a means by which to instil moral and civil education. These men were members of the Accademia dell'Arcadia, which propagated the classical ideal of unity in terms of time, place, and action; so too, they decided that there must be no comic or magical elements in the plot, and that the music must take second place, as "servant" to the text. These ideals dominated *opera seria* until the late eighteenth century; Albinoni and Vivaldi were among the new generation of composers to take them up.

Antonio Vivaldi

MARCH 4, 1678–JULY 8, 1741

ANTONIO VIVALDI WAS ONE OF THE MOST SIGNIFICANT AND INFLUENTIAL
COMPOSERS OF THE LATE BAROQUE. HIS CONTRIBUTIONS TO ORCHESTRATION
AND TO THE CONCERTO GENRE IN PARTICULAR, AND TO MUSICAL STYLE IN
GENERAL, WERE FUNDAMENTAL TO THE DEVELOPMENT OF INSTRUMENTAL MUSIC
IN THE EIGHTEENTH CENTURY. HIS ORIGINALITY IS SEEN ESPECIALLY IN HIS
DEVELOPMENT OF ORCHESTRAL PROGRAM MUSIC.

Vivaldi probably received his early musical education from his father, who was a violinist at San
Marco, Venice, one the foremost musical institutions
in that city. He became a violin teacher at the Pio
Ospedale della Pietà, an orphanage for women. This
remained his main workplace for most of his career.
His students provided frequent concerts for Venetian
nobility and visiting foreign nobles, for which Vivaldi
regularly supplied new music.

Below Renata Pokupic
(as Statira), Nicolas
Watts (as Oronte), and
Katherine Manley (as
Arpago) on stage in the
Garsington Opera's 2008
production of Vivaldi's
opera *L'Incoronazione
Di Dario* (1717).

CONCERTOS AND INFLUENCE

Vivaldi sought to establish his reputation further afield
than the Ospedale, in part through the dedication of
his music. His Op. 1 trio sonatas, for example, are
dedicated to the Bescian nobleman Count Annibale
Gambara; Op. 2 was dedicated to Frederik IV of Denmark during his visit to Venice in 1709. At this time
the composer was at work on his first concertos, works
that would travel to Germany in manuscript copies

Left This is possibly the most recognizable likeness we have of Vivaldi. In 1703, the composer was ordained as a priest and was given the nickname "The Red Priest," because of the color of his hair.

LE QUATTRO STAGIONE (THE FOUR SEASONS)

Vivaldi's Op. 8 of 1725 includes several programmatic works. Among these, the four solo violin concertos known as *Le quattro stagione* (*The Four Seasons*) are doubtless the most popular today. These works, among numerous others, completely disprove the notion that he merely "composed the same concerto 500 times." Here one is treated to the wealth of the composer's pictorial and musical imagination: The four seasons, described in four accompanying poems, are represented through a vast range of violinistic and orchestral techniques. In "Winter" for example, staccato (detached) notes in a high register suggest wintry rain, and rapidly descending passages depict treacherously slippery conditions. In "Summer" a thunderstorm is heard in the final movement.

Below A London reprint of Vivaldi's Op. 4 *La Stravaganza* dating from around 1740. The concertos in this set are scored for violin, strings, and basso continuo.

made by the musician Franz Horneck who was staying in Venice in 1708–1709. Vivaldi taught or received visits from such influential German musicians as theorist and composer Johann David Heinichen, violinist Johann Georg Pisendel, and theorist and flautist Johann Joachim Quantz. These musicians took Vivaldi's works to Dresden, an important musical center at the time. They disseminated his music in manuscript copies and through their efforts to imitate his style in their own works. Bach, too, copied out Vivaldi's music, assimilating his vividly dramatic writing.

Few of Vivaldi's many works were published during his lifetime. Of these, arguably the most influential were three sets that contain 12 concertos in each: *L'estro armonico* (*Harmonic inspiration*), Op. 3; *La stravaganza* (*Extravagance*), Op. 4; and *Il cimento dell'armonia e dell'inventione* (*The contest of harmony and invention*), Op. 8. He composed more than 500 concertos, 230 of which are for solo violin. He also wrote 50 operas, 40 cantatas, 90 solo and trio sonatas, and 50 sacred works.

RITORNELLO FORM
Vivaldi has been accused of lack of originality, a criticism that seems to be based less on a careful examination of his musical style, and more on a merely cursory acquaintance with his overwhelming output. In his *L'estro armonico*, for example, the range of different scorings and the formal innovations are striking. Particularly notable is his use of the ritornello (refrain) form in fast movements— varied restatements of this refrain, scored for the full ensemble, appear in various keys, in alternation with solo sections of a freer melodic character. Vivaldi's model was taken up by subsequent generations of composers, and it became the norm for the outer movements of the three-movement concerto (fast–slow–fast). The ritornello form also served as an important basis for the development of the symphony as the eighteenth century progressed.

VOCAL MUSIC
The influence of the concerto can be traced in Vivaldi's vocal works, in terms of their style and form. The motets, in particular, have been described as "concertos for voice." This relates to the florid vocal writing that they contain, which is designed to show off the voice as an instrument. This vocal exhibitionism, integral to opera, was becoming increasingly common in sacred music, although it was deemed unacceptable by several church authorities. Notable in the choral music is Vivaldi's allocation of the main melodic interest to the violins while the choir declaims in the background. This technique looks forward to the symphonic mass of the later eighteenth century.

Discover the Music

Gloria in D, RV 589
Nulla in mundo pax sincera, RV 630
Concerto for Mandolin in C, RV 425
L'estro armonico, Op. 3 (1711)
La stravaganza, Op. 4 (1714)
Il cimento dell'armonia e dell'inventione, Op. 8 (1725)

Music education in Italy in the eighteenth century

ALTHOUGH OPERA DOMINATED THE MUSICAL SCENE IN EIGHTEENTH-CENTURY ITALY, INSTRUMENTAL MUSIC WAS ALSO FLOURISHING AS NEVER BEFORE. THE VIOLIN CONCERTO, FOR EXAMPLE, ENJOYED TREMENDOUS POPULARITY IN NORTHERN EUROPE. THIS, AND OTHER DEVELOPMENTS IN INSTRUMENTAL MUSIC, CAN BE LINKED TO SOCIAL AND CULTURAL CHANGES OF THE TIME, WHICH AFFECTED THE LIVES OF PERFORMERS, COMPOSERS, AND LISTENERS.

Right A great deal of music was written for dance and members of the upper classes were expected to be competent dancers.

MUSIC PUBLISHING

The boom in music publishing in Amsterdam, Paris, and London at this time points to a new musical market. Whereas previously the nobility were the main purchasers of musical publications, there was now a new middle class with the musical hardware (instruments), skills (gleaned from teachers and published instruction books), and talent (mostly amateur) for these works.

Baroque violin

Violinist–composers of the Venetian and Roman schools worked with similar instruments and similar violin techniques to one another. However, their violins were slightly different to those played today. Compared with modern instruments, Baroque violins have shorter necks, which project straight out from the body rather than being angled backwards. This means that the gut (rather than metal) strings are held at lower tension, which corresponds to a softer tone and lower performance pitch. The internal bass bar and sound post, which help transmit the vibrations, are generally less massive. Bows, crucial to the tone quality and playing style of the violinist, are convex rather than concave; the bow hair, which lacks the metal ferrule at the base, was often held more loosely.

All these features facilitate a playing style that is delicately nuanced in slow movements, and clear and articulate in fast passages. Vivaldi, Albinoni, Bach, and others exploited these elements in their works for solo violin. The developments in the violin in the late eighteenth century can be linked to a quest for increased power in the face of larger audiences and performing venues.

Musical publications also functioned as commemorations of performances (opera, concerto, or another genre), which were increasingly open to broader sectors of society; and printed music could function as a memento or souvenir of a place, person, or country that one had visited and associated with a certain work—a visitor to Venice, for example, who had met Vivaldi, or been to a concerto concert in the Pio Ospedale della Pietà, or had perhaps heard his rousing *Gloria* RV 589 in a service in one of the city's churches, might purchase his music to recall the occasion, if not to actually perform the work.

MUSICAL EDUCATION IN ITALY

Venice was a likely destination for the tourist with an interest in music, as well as for the traveling foreign musician seeking musical education. Although the city shared in the country's decline in economic and political importance, it remained one of the most thriving and influential cultural centers in Europe. Together with the churches and theaters, the *ospedali* were crucial contributors to Venetian musical life. They were

Right Composer and violinist Giuseppe Tartini (1692–1770) established a very successful violin school in Padua in the 1720s. His students came from all over Europe.

also crucial to the livelihood of the female musicians that they housed. These women were fortunate enough to receive musical instruction at an advanced level (from the likes of Vivaldi, for example), and to receive the public performance experience that was afforded by the institutions' concerts. Such experience was rarely had by other female musicians of the day.

Many Italian composers received their educations in Naples, which had four music conservatories. Composers were expected to learn counterpoint and figured bass, and to imitate fine examples of opera and instrumental music. Other musicians were trained within their families, in the cathedrals, or through private lessons. Different regions boasted different musical specialties—a contemporary observer reported that, "For voices the best school is in Bologna; Lombardy excels in instrumental music."

ITALIAN SCHOOLS OF INSTRUMENTAL MUSIC

The late seventeenth century witnessed a fundamental change in the status of instrumental music. Formerly often considered as a functional and somewhat suspect addition to any musical occasion, this music could now be appraised

and enjoyed as an independent art form. The violin music of this time, especially that produced in Italy and in Austro–German lands, was both an impetus behind and product of this shift in status. The schools of Rome and Venice were understood as leading the way. In the opinion of one eighteenth-century music commentator, the Venetian school (comprised of Vivaldi, Albinoni, Giuseppe Matteo Alberti, and Carlo Tessarini) were "a light and irregular troop," whereas the Roman school (made up of Corelli, Pietro Antonio Locatelli, Francesco Geminiani, and Giuseppe Valentini) were "the greatest performers and composers for the violin which Italy could boast during the first 50 years of the present century."

Right A young woman at her music lesson. Italian women received a general education, and girls who sang or played an instrument were instructed in musical theory and instrumental technique.

Georg Philipp Telemann

MARCH 14, 1681–JUNE 25, 1767

INNOVATIVE, TALENTED, AND EXTRAORDINARILY PROLIFIC, GEORG PHILIPP TELEMANN LEFT AN INDELIBLE MARK ON THE FIRST HALF OF THE EIGHTEENTH CENTURY. IN ADDITION TO PRODUCING OVER 3,000 COMPOSITIONS SPANNING ALL THE MAJOR GENRES AND STYLES OF HIS TIME, TELEMANN CREATED CONCERT SERIES, DIRECTED OPERAS, TAUGHT STUDENTS, THEORIZED ABOUT MUSIC, AND EMBARKED ON MUSIC PUBLICATION IN A FLEDGLING MARKET.

Telemann's family were upper-middle class, well educated, and often drawn to a career in the clergy; there had not been a musician in the family for over 100 years. So it is perhaps not surprising that Telemann's youthful musical talent provoked his mother to confiscate his instruments. Telemann continued to be drawn to music, however, playing and composing in secret with the support of his teachers. At 20, he loyally resolved to study law and departed for Leipzig. Passing through Halle, he met Handel, who so delightfully infected him with the "poison" of music that he had to tear himself away. In Leipzig, his talent as a composer was quickly discovered and works commissioned, leading him into one of the longest and most widely respected musical careers of the century.

LEIPZIG AND BEYOND

Much is known of Telemann's life, not least from his autobiographies and letters to composers such as Handel and Quantz. As a newcomer in Leipzig, he became actively involved, founding a *Collegium musicum* of students and producing operas to rival those of other

Above Telemann's astonishing compositional output includes more than 50 operas, among them *Der geduldige Sokrates* (1721) and *Pimpinone* (1725).

local composers, which provoked some ill feeling. Telemann continued to compose operas throughout his life, becoming particularly well known for comic opera, for which he had a special talent.

From 1705 onward, Telemann became a court musician, appointed respectively to the courts of Sorau and Eisenach. Discovering Polish and Moravian folk music during this time, he enthusiastically described it as possessing a "true barbaric beauty." Although his compositional style was highly adaptable, folk dances and melodies remained fundamental to Telemann's music from this time onward. It was also during these years, probably around 1708 in Eisenach, that he met Johann Sebastian Bach. The two men shared great respect for one another, and Telemann later became Carl Philipp Emanuel Bach's godfather. Tiring of courtly duties, which were demanding and often involved uninterested listeners, Telemann successfully applied for a position as city director of music in Frankfurt and from 1712 began an independent life. He earned extremely well through the engraving and publication of his own music, much aimed at an amateur market, and his popularity steadily increased.

At the age of 40, Telemann became cantor of the Johanneum Lateinschule as well as musical director of the five main churches of Hamburg. This was the most productive part of his life. As well as composing and teaching, he founded a new *Collegium musicum*, continued publishing, and went abroad to market himself, most notably in Paris. He was productive right into the last years of his life, and reveled in lively discussions about music even when he was in his eighties.

Discover the music

Suite in A major for recorder and strings, TWV55:a2

Pastorelle en Musique (1712–1721)

Musique de Table (1723)

12 "Paris" quartets (1730–1738)

Symphony No. 1 in G major "Cricket", TWV50:1

Suite Burlesque de Quixotte in G major, TWV55:G10

Left Young musicians give a concert in Leipzig in 1723. Telemann spent some years in Leipzig; it was where he commenced, and abandoned, his studies of law, and where he later established a college of music.

Flute

The flute's origins go back some 30,000 years. Unlike other woodwind instruments, the flute is a reedless wind instrument; it produces its sound from the flow of air against an edge. Telemann wrote a number of works for flute. Among the most notable are *Concerto for Five in D major for transverse flute, strings and basso continuo* and *Suite in A minor for flute and piano*.

Below A musical manuscript for one of Telemann's cantatas. His *Cantata Cycle* of 1716–1717 was written while he was city director of music in Frankfurt.

MUSIQUE DE TABLE (1723)

The *Music for the Table* is a large collection of pieces compiled in three parts. Music intended for performance during feasts and banquets had a very long tradition. In Hamburg, where Telemann was employed, it was customary to alternate fully orchestrated pieces with works for small groups. In *Musique de Table*, each part begins with an overture and suite for orchestra, followed by a quartet, a concerto, a trio, a solo, and a conclusion. Various combinations of instruments are used for each piece, involving flutes, oboes, violins, trumpet, and continuo instruments such as cello, bassoon, and harpsichord. The instruments are used together to create unusual tone colors and to intensify the contrast between different voices. Often, it seems as if the instruments are speaking to one another, asking questions, raising doubts, and arriving joyously at a common goal. Telemann has shown his formidable compositional talent in the way in which he has taken the form of the suite, with its series of movements based on dances, and combined it with concerto form, exposing individual instruments suddenly in a solo part.

The Enlightenment

THE EIGHTEENTH CENTURY SAW A GROWING APPETITE AMONG ALL LAYERS
OF SOCIETY FOR UNDERSTANDING, LEARNING, AND A BETTER LIFE FOR ALL.
AN EXPLOSION OF SCIENTIFIC ADVANCES AND PHILOSOPHICAL IDEAS WAS
FORMING THE BASIS FOR A NEW AGE: THE AGE OF ENLIGHTENMENT.

Enlightenment thought affected everything. The discoveries and inventions of Newton, Kepler, Leibniz, and Descartes had largely occurred years earlier, yet were still exciting. Most importantly, it was not only their ideas that were infectious, but their methods and approaches. People wrote Newtonian poems, and theories of government. Elemental models were contrived to break down any subject, from political economy to mind and passions. More and more consistently, rational observation and experience were taken as a basis for reasoning. Blind belief and the occult were considered increasingly suspect, even evil.

Above right German philosopher Immanuel Kant (1724–1804) was one of the Enlightenment's greatest thinkers.

Below A class of boys being taught by priests, c. 1750. Education at this time was influenced by realism and naturalism.

CHALLENGES

The quest for universal answers threw everything into question and fed a new faith in human power over nature. The Church, challenged on every level, experienced a shift of emphasis as the institution itself lost credibility and gradually became less important than individual faith and practical morality.

Even social behavior was affected, with "naturalness" favored over artifice and formality. When engaged in conversation, business, music, or various other everyday pursuits, the successful citizen always tried to show a natural style, and easy confidence. Accompanying this

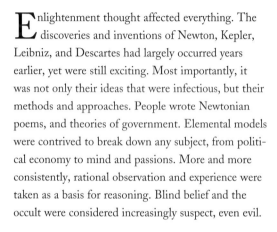

Right The effect of Enlightenment thought on music was less obvious than in other areas, but formal study of music at this time embraced broader perspectives than it had before.

was a growing interest in equality, education, and individual rights, as well as the belief that social and practical problems could be overcome by reason and knowledge.

Although enlightenment thought affected different countries in different ways, common trends emerged, not least due to increased possibilities for communication and travel around Europe. Scientific academies were founded by European rulers in centers such as Paris, St Petersburg, and Berlin. In addition, scientific societies were springing up everywhere, producing magazines covering science, moral and social philosophy, and the arts. These enjoyed wide dissemination and were discussed by all kinds of people in social centers as diverse as coffee houses, salons, and clubs. One such academy devoted to music was the Society of Musical Sciences by Correspondence, which included members such as Telemann, Handel, and J.S. Bach.

EDUCATION IN GERMANY

In Germany, where religious feeling was very strong, enlightenment thought was not absorbed into the fabric of society as quickly as it was in countries such as France or England. This was especially apparent in the education system. Universities in particular were essentially designed to train students for a career in the clergy, although it was common for families of sufficient wealth to send their offspring to study law in order to train important generic skills, such as the art of rhetoric. In the schools, such as those known as *Lateinschulen*, traditional, lecture-style classes were given in theology, history, Greek New Testament, Latin, catechism, geography, and choral singing. Telemann held a position in such a school in Hamburg, although he was exposed to criticism since he allowed his classes to be taught by someone else and rarely made an appearance. Since these institutions were not often open to change or radical thought, many great minds of the eighteenth century turned their backs on academic careers in favor of accepting state-funded employment in courts, often in highly valued and practical roles, supported by aristocratic leaders eager to gain advantage through knowledge.

"Nature and nature's laws lay hid in night; God said 'Let Newton be' and all was light."

ALEXANDER POPE

CHRISTIAN WOLFF (1679–1754)

Between Leibniz and Kant, Christian Wolff was perhaps the most important philosopher in Germany, not least for his outspoken nature. Early in his career, Wolff was not only expelled from the University of Halle for giving an address that attempted to show that human happiness was possible without the aid of religion, but was exiled when military advisors to Frederick I presented Wolff as a believer in determinism, a theory that defended army deserters who were "determined" to desert. Asked back to Prussia when Frederick II assumed the throne, Wolff went on to write volumes on philosophy, mathematics, science, and history. He was also an influential teacher and gathered a large group of followers. His principal objective was to achieve certainty in every discipline by establishing an order of truths, culminating in a system for human knowledge as a whole, which would function as a reliable foundation for human affairs and the development of knowledge.

This systematic approach was characteristic of the eighteenth century, a period that saw huge enthusiasm for categorizing, classifying, and developing systems for manipulating knowledge.

Jean-Philippe Rameau

SEPTEMBER 25, 1683–SEPTEMBER 12, 1764

IN HIS OLD AGE, JEAN-PHILIPPE RAMEAU BECAME A MAN OBSESSED. HIS BELIEF IN THE EXISTENCE OF A SINGLE PRINCIPLE FROM WHICH ALL THE RULES OF MUSIC WOULD BE FOUND TO SPRING WAS UNSHAKEABLE, AND HIS PURSUIT OF IT HAD BECOME SOMEWHAT HYSTERICAL. HOWEVER, ONLY THE MOST NAÏVE WERE HEARD TO LAUGH. RAMEAU'S CONTRIBUTIONS TO MUSIC NOT ONLY REVOLUTIONIZED THE WAY PEOPLE THOUGHT ABOUT THE SCIENTIFIC PRECEPTS OF MUSIC, HIS COMPOSITIONS, SPANNING SEVERAL GENRES, WERE WORKS OF GENIUS.

Rameau's musical career can be comforting to those who are intimidated by child prodigies such as Mozart and Mendelssohn. In fact, Rameau didn't compose anything of significance (and what he wrote was certainly significant) until the age of 50. Despite this late start, Rameau, along with his siblings, had a thorough musical grounding. Their father, an organist in Dijon, apparently taught them music even before they had learnt to read. Indeed, reading was a problem for Rameau—his difficulty with it caused him problems in school, and even by the time he was a published and respected author his French was decidedly cloudy. Rameau's early career took him to Italy, where he "refined his tastes." He then spent 20 years traveling and occupying musical positions throughout France, finally settling in 1722 in Paris, which remained his home for the rest of his life.

Above A theorist as well as a composer, Rameau once said, "Emphasis on the common emotive or affective origins of music and words in the first cries of humankind undermines words."

SCANDAL IN PARIS

For some time before his arrival in Paris, Rameau had been working on what he considered to be his most important work—the *Traité de l'harmonie*, or *Treatise on Harmony*. Before its publication, Rameau was unknown in Paris; afterwards, he was regarded as an eminent theorist, and launched a career of publishing and revising theoretical materials which lasted, almost unabated, until his death. However, Rameau's greatest success in the capital was in opera. In 1733 his first opera, *Hippolyte et Aricie*, caused an unprecedented

sensation—and scandal. The work singlehandedly split the Paris musical establishment: Rameau's detractors, the *lullistes* (after the great French composer Lully), thought his music was vile, over-complex, and worst of all, Italian. Equally vehement were his supporters, who were dubbed *ramistes*. The debate raged on through the next four operas Rameau wrote; he was alternately lionized and satirized, and one derogatory poem was the cause of a fist-fight between the composer and the author. The debate subsided over the next decade, only to be raised again in the *Querelle des Bouffons* (*Quarrel of the Buffoons*: Comic actors), which divided Paris in the early 1750s. Rameau was again center-stage in the debate, which pitted "serious" French drama and Italian comic opera against each other.

Rameau's fame and fortune were secured when his earlier operas began to be revived in new productions. His death came in his home ten comfortable years later, after contracting a fever. The tall, scraggy composer, with "more the air of a ghost than a man" was the last great exponent of French opera in the eighteenth century. His legacy would not be taken up for another century after his death, with the rise of Italian opera in Paris, and it would take until the twentieth century for the genius of his instrumental, and especially his beautiful keyboard music, to be recognized.

Discover the music

Hippolyte et Aricie (1733)

Dardanus (1739)

Pièces de Clavecin en Concerts (1741)

Zoroastre (1749, rev. 1756)

Les Paladins (1760)

ZOROASTRE (1749)

One of Rameau's operas that has received comparatively little attention is *Zoroastre*. Composed in 1749, and subsequently revised and revived in 1756, the work is a masterpiece of the *tragédie en musique* style. First fostered by Lully, the *tragédie en musique* had a very strong influence on the development of opera throughout the eighteenth century. Rameau was quite fond of the form and wrote five such works. The typical *tragédie en musique* does not necessarily contain great tragedy, but rather deals with elevated and serious dramatic material, usually based on classical myth. *Zoroastre* breaks somewhat from this tradition, being based not on Greek or Roman myth, but having its roots in Persian religion, Zoroastrianism. Essentially, it is a tale of good pitted against evil, in this case between the prophet and religious poet Zoroastre and the greedy, ambitious sorcerer, Abramane. The librettist for *Zoroastre* was Louis de Cahusac, librettist for seven of Rameau's operas. Most other collaborators worked with Rameau only once, or at most, twice. Cahusac and Rameau appear have been very close friends, and they conceived *Zoroastre* together during a summer retreat in Passy in Paris.

"Rhythm and sounds are born with syllables."

Above An eighteenth-century engraving of a concert of Rameau's music, performed especially to celebrate the marriage of the Dauphin to a Spanish princess.

Above right A portrait of the ancient Persian philosopher and spiritual poet Zoroaster, after whom the religion is named. He was the subject of an opera by Rameau.

Right Notre Dame Cathedral in Paris around the time that Rameau lived in the city. When he died in 1764, thousands of mourners paid their respects at his funeral in Paris.

French culture in the Age of Enlightenment

In the early eighteenth century, France was a nation of immense influence. A significant colonial power, a major source of Enlightenment thought, a political giant—even its language was elevated and used as a *lingua franca* throughout Europe. Streaming from the twin centers of Paris and Versailles, French culture represented the height of refinement.

The "Sun King," Louis XIV, realized that true domination lay not just in political and military spheres, but also in the culture of the nation. It was his wish for French culture to prove so powerful, so seductive, that all the nations of Europe would not be able to resist emulating it. To this end Louis became perhaps the greatest ever patron–king, fueling art, science, literature, and of course, music, with indefatigable fervor.

Right The government minister Jean-Baptiste Colbert presents the Members of the Royal Academy of Science to Louis XIV, c. 1670.

SCIENCE AND CULTURE UNDER LOUIS XIV

Louis took the *Académie française* (French Academy) under his wing, becoming its "protector," and thus ensuring that the writings of geniuses such as Molière flourished while at the same time suppressing "scandalous" material such as pornography, and any political writings with anti-royalist leanings. The *Académie des sciences* was given its first rules by Louis, who also provided them with a home at the Louvre. Treasures of antiquity were bought or plundered from sites in Egypt and the Middle East, filling the king's palaces and assuring his equality by association with leaders such as Alexander or Julius Caesar. The fashionable obsession with antiquity also led to a flourishing theatrical and operatic scene in Paris; all the successful opera composers and dramatists wrote on classical, Greco–Roman themes.

But the Sun King's true crowning achievement was doubtless the magnificent palace of Versailles.

Above This painting entitled *Allegory of the Arts* shows something of the union of art and science. An astrolabe and compass are given the same prominence as the musical score, the violin, and the sculpture.

Originally a country house for the king, albeit with beautiful gardens and fountains, Louis XIV expanded it into one of the largest—and most magnificent—buildings in the world. From Versailles he could cement his power over nobles, who were required to stay there for part of the year. From his new palace Louis had a "bird's-eye view" of the political machinations of Paris, and could more easily manipulate his underlings. In fact, Louis held France in an iron fist, albeit clothed in an embroidered glove. The king was a pedant for etiquette and routine, as illustrated by the *Levée* (raising) ceremony, which took place every day at Versailles. It was designed not so much to worship the king, but to humble, even humiliate, the nobles who attended, and paid in some cases, to watch the king getting out of bed and preparing for the day ahead. Strict etiquette and carefully chosen words were to be observed when in the king's presence.

THE ADVENT OF LOUIS XV

Musical life was vibrant and an integral part of courtly entertainment, with many works being dedicated to the king. Codified through treatises and other publications (allowed by royal privilege), the French style was transported throughout Europe. This continued for a time

under Louis XIV's successor, Louis XV, although the latter unwisely allowed his grip over the nation to loosen. A "counter-cultural" revolution under his reign began to wear away at the institutions his predecessor had nurtured. Louis XV, though a highly intelligent man, was not an effective ruler, and under his reign the country hastened toward the Revolution, which would prove disastrous for the monarchy, and profoundly changing for the arts.

Right Voltaire, key figure in the French Enlightenment, wrote essays, poetry, philosophical pamphlets, and novels. He was not afraid to voice his opinion on religious or political matters.

VOLTAIRE (1694–1778)

One could fill volumes with the ascerbic wit of Voltaire, probably France's most beloved writer. With quotes such as "It is dangerous to be right in matters on which the established authorities are wrong," Voltaire (his real name was François-Marie Arouet) had his share of enemies, along with legions of admirers. In his illustrious career, he was exiled from France for insulting the nobility, repeatedly censored, and befriended and given a salary by Frederick the Great of Prussia, whom he would later deride in an essay, resulting in his arrest and the burning of his publications. All this while almost compulsively writing, producing tens of thousands of documents, letters, books, pamphlets, essays, as well as poetry, plays, libretti, and novels. Far from being a mere troublemaker, Voltaire was always a voice of reason in what he perceived to be an insane world, and was seemingly fearless in his defense of the downtrodden, especially at the hands of the Church or monarchy. When Voltaire was finally permitted back into Paris, he received a hero's welcome, and died shortly after. After the Revolution, his was one of the first bodies placed in the Pantheon, the resting place of French national heroes.

George Frideric Handel

FEBRUARY 23, 1685–APRIL 14, 1759

ENGLISH MUSIC HISTORIAN CHARLES BURNEY (1726–1814) ONCE WROTE OF HANDEL, "... HIS HAND WAS THEN SO FAT, THAT THE KNUCKLES, WHICH USUALLY APPEAR CONVEX, WERE LIKE THOSE OF A CHILD, DINTED OR DIMPLED IN, SO AS TO BE RENDERED CONCAVE; HOWEVER HIS TOUCH WAS SO SMOOTH, AND THE TONE OF THE INSTRUMENT SO MUCH CHERISHED, THAT HIS FINGERS SEEMED TO GROW TO THE KEYS."

Chubby hands aside, George Frideric Handel grew to be one of the most highly acclaimed composers of his time. He was known as a rough, impetuous man, prone to moments of anger and impatience often made comical by his broken English, and tempered by his original humor and deep intelligence. These traits seem to shine through even in early events of Handel's life. His father found it impossible to focus his son's attention on anything other than music and grudgingly allowed the seven-year-old to take lessons in organ, harpsichord, violin, oboe, and composition. This solid preparation for a career as cantor eventually led to the 18-year-old Handel becoming cathedral organist in Halle, the town in Germany where he grew up. Handel, however, left almost immediately and traveled to Hamburg where he indulged his growing passion for opera.

Above Handel as a young man. Mozart once said that, "Handel understands effect better than any of us; when he chooses, he strikes like a thunderbolt."

Left An eighteenth-century engraving of the city square of Halle, the city where Handel was born. Bach and Scarlatti were born in the same year as Handel.

THE ITALIAN YEARS

Admiration for the beautiful melodies and clear structures of Italian music was sweeping through Europe. Wishing to succeed in this idiom, Handel undertook the arduous journey over the Alps and spent the next four years associating with rich patrons and leading musicians, including Corelli, and both Alessandro and Domenico Scarlatti. After producing a plethora of vocal works imbued with the Italian style, Handel returned to Germany, where his reputation bought him a position as court music director in Hanover. However, it seems that Handel was not suited to life in the role of court musician and he soon asked for leave of absence in order to travel to London.

LONDON

Arriving there in 1710, Handel found a vibrant center teeming with educated and opinionated writers, musicians, artists, and scientists. It was the scene in which he was to become a mature composer, producing instrumental suites and sonatas, concertos and overtures, as well as his many vocal works. Briefly visiting Germany in 1712, Handel immediately asked for permission to return to London. This was granted by the elector on the proviso that the visit be of "reasonable duration." Two years later, Handel was still in London and his truancy cornered when his master arrived and was crowned King George I of England. Legend has it that the famous *Water Music* was composed by Handel to regain favor with the new king.

Handel continued to enjoy great success in London, especially following his realization that the mediocre reception of his pastoral-style opera *Il pastor fido* (1712)

"[Handel] is the greatest composer that ever lived. I would uncover my head and kneel before his tomb."

LUDWIG VAN BEETHOVEN

Above Handel presents his *Water Music* to George I at its first performance in 1717 on the Thames River. The king is reported to have enjoyed the concert so much that he ordered it be replayed three times.

Discover the Music

Rinaldo (1711)

The Water Music (1715–1717)

The Harmonious Blacksmith,
   from *Suite No. 5 in E* (1720)

Giulio Cesare (1724)

Rodelinde (1725)

Coronation Anthems (1727)

Concerti grossi, Op. 6 (1739)

The Messiah (1742)

Music for the Royal Fireworks
   (1749)

Left Handel loved music from the earliest age, as shown in this charming nineteenth-century painting of Handel as a boy being discovered by his parents playing music instead of sleeping.

Left A scene from the English National Opera's 2005 production of Handel's *Xerxes* at the London Coliseum. The opera is in three acts and was first performed in 1738.

Right Michael Chance in the title role takes center stage during a dress rehearsal of Handel's *Rinaldo* at the Sydney Opera House, Australia, in 2005. The opera is set in the time of the First Crusade.

stemmed from a thirst for the spectacular on the part of London audiences. Returning to the heroic style with *Teseo*, which told the tale of Greek hero Theseus, Handel successfully secured his future in England.

With the decline in popularity of Italian opera in London, Handel then turned seriously to the genre of oratorios, composed in English and directed at a developing middle class that was not entirely comfortable with the aristocratic taste for Italian opera. *The Messiah* is easily the most well-known work in this style and remains immensely popular today.

It is an indication of Handel's fame and his status in England that he became the first living composer to have a statue erected to him; it was very prominently positioned in Vauxhall Gardens.

When he died, an estimated 3,000 people attended his funeral. Handel was buried in Westminster Abbey on April 20, 1759.

Below The monument to Handel in the south transept of Westminster Abbey, London. It was designed and carved by French sculptor Louis-François Roubillac (1695–1762) in 1740.

RINALDO (1711)

Handel's opera *Rinaldo*, first produced in London in 1711, caused a sensation. It was the first Italian opera composed specifically for the London stage, bursting onto an unlikely scene in which some operas were still produced with a combination of Italian and English singers, each performing in their own language. According to contemporary satirists, it was not uncommon for a hero to sing Italian, and be answered by his lover in English, or vice versa. *Rinaldo* won over audiences with its unified structure, elaborate scenic effects, and heroic story of the crusading knight, Rinaldo. The three acts, with the castrato Nicolini in the title role, were swollen with depictions of war, seduction, monsters, revenge, and enchantment, intensified to such an extent by Handel's music that he immediately became a household name. The opera opens with a French-style overture of three parts, and two stately slow sections framing a fast middle section. This leads into the common operatic format of recitatives relating the story interspersed with arias in which the characters could express the intensity of their feelings.

"Grand tours," music, and the arts in the eighteenth century

LAURENCE STERNE'S *A SENTIMENTAL JOURNEY THROUGH FRANCE AND ITALY* (1768) WAS A EUROPEAN BESTSELLER. THE NARRATOR IS MR YORICK, WHO DESCRIBES HIS PERSONAL EXPERIENCES. BURSTING WITH SEXUAL INNUENDO, THE NOVEL WAS TRANSLATED INTO SEVERAL LANGUAGES AND ENJOYED ENORMOUS SUCCESS. THE SECRET OF ITS POPULARITY WAS ITS CLEVER PERSPECTIVE ON THAT MOST RESPECTED OF GENTLEMANLY UNDERTAKINGS, THE GRAND TOUR OF THE CONTINENT.

Following a standard route leading from Dover to Calais, then usually with a hired guide to Paris, Switzerland, across the Alps to Italy, then back to Germany and Holland before returning home, the young gentleman would expect to be exposed to the unexpected, testing and deepening his intellect and knowledge, as well as his ethical and social

Below Carlo Boschi (1705–1782), known to the world as Farinelli, enjoyed a long and feted career as a castrato. He also played harpsichord.

judgment. Many books were written relaying the adventures of this or that traveler, most of them in a strictly non-personal style based on classical learning. Breaking away, the success of *A Sentimental Journey* ushered in a new style of writing which foreshadowed the romantic genres of the nineteenth century.

THE CASTRATI

Castrati singers have always inspired a kind of morbid fascination. Men such as Farinelli or Senesino were renowned for their vocal flexibility, and their full, genuine soprano voices. Almost exclusively an Italian tradition, it seems unbelievable that castration was often—but not always—performed with the boy's consent, sometimes even paid for himself. This becomes more understandable in light of the poverty rampant in Italy. In a religiously ascetic world where sexual fulfillment was often not an important consideration, the idea of emigration as a famous castrato singer was tempting. Indeed, those few who were lucky enough to be left with a beautiful voice—by no means guaranteed—were able to carve out impressive careers. The others generally followed a calling in the clergy, still a better option than many other forms of employment. A high, boyish voice was not the only physical effect of castration before puberty. Reports ranged from claims of extraordinary height, weak vision, a lack of fortitude and strength of mind, to difficulty pronouncing the letter "R". Certain is that a general obsession with "high" voices led to higher wages and continuing temptation into a practice which much of Europe already considered barbaric.

DR CHARLES BURNEY (1726–1814)

Charles Burney was a refined gentleman who worked as an organist and teacher of harpsichord to young ladies. He was known and respected as a composer, and Oxford University recognized his musicianship with the honorary title of Doctor of Music. In keeping with the diverse interests typical of educated men, and since he required only a small amount of sleep, Burney also spent his nights studying and writing so that he was able to publish a couple of works on astronomy, and in his botanical pursuits, he was even convinced that he had discovered the origin of the gooseberry.

But it was Burney's passion for historical research and writing about music that was to earn him a place in the history books. Having decided to gather material for a "General History of Music," Burney embarked on the Grand Tour several times in the 1770s. He carried with him many letters of introduction, and these—combined with his penchant for witty, intelligent conversation and his impeccable manners—gained him access to the most famous musical personages of his time. He published volumes of writings detailing his personal experience of composers

Above A 1731 production from *The Beggar's Opera* by English dramatist John Gay (1685–1732). The work was intended as a satire on Italian opera, using popular and familiar melodies instead of the structured arias of opera.

including Handel, C.P.E. Bach, Haydn, Mozart, and Gluck, as well as many others. He heard many of the most famous singers of the time, among them Farinelli. He met with librettist and poet Metastasio in Vienna, and with Diderot and Rousseau in Paris.

Left Charles Burney's musical writings were published over a 12-year period from 1776. Very well regarded, they were soon translated into German and Dutch.

TRAVELING VIRTUOSOS

Aristocrats and the wealthy were not the only people who were taking advantage of improved transport throughout Europe. Singers and virtuoso musicians were also becoming a familiar sight as they sought their fortune in various European centers. Italian singers in particular were in vogue, and London producers of opera encouraged them with high salaries and good conditions. They were even actively recruited. Handel, for example, was commissioned on behalf of the Royal Academy of Music in London to visit the Continent and engage singers for the English stage. Senesino, the famed Italian castrato, was probably the most acclaimed of those who accepted Handel's overtures. Instrumentalists also journeyed, sometimes settling in a new country, as in Handel's case, and child prodigies were marketed in all the major courts of Europe, including the young Mozart.

Johann Sebastian Bach

MARCH 31, 1685–JULY 28, 1750

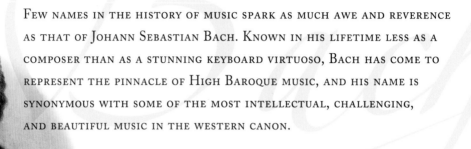

FEW NAMES IN THE HISTORY OF MUSIC SPARK AS MUCH AWE AND REVERENCE AS THAT OF JOHANN SEBASTIAN BACH. KNOWN IN HIS LIFETIME LESS AS A COMPOSER THAN AS A STUNNING KEYBOARD VIRTUOSO, BACH HAS COME TO REPRESENT THE PINNACLE OF HIGH BAROQUE MUSIC, AND HIS NAME IS SYNONYMOUS WITH SOME OF THE MOST INTELLECTUAL, CHALLENGING, AND BEAUTIFUL MUSIC IN THE WESTERN CANON.

Left Johann Sebastian Bach, possibly the greatest composer who ever lived, was a deeply religious man. He once said, "The aim and final end of all music should be none other than the glory of God and the refreshment of the soul."

Bach was born in 1685 in Eisenach, birthplace of Martin Luther, to an already highly musical family. His father and all his uncles were musicians, and Johann and his siblings were steadily nurtured along a musical path. At school, Johann was not a star student, but drew attention to himself as a particularly good boy soprano. He was just nine when his mother died. His father remarried before the end of the year, but shortly after he also succumbed to a fatal illness. Johann's new stepmother tried to hold the family together, but failed in the face of an unsympathetic legal system, and the Bach children were orphaned.

Johann and his brother Jacob were taken to live with their older sibling, Johann Christoph, an organist in a nearby town. Bach stayed there for another five years, undertaking serious musical studies with his brother, who instilled in him a lifelong passion for the organ, as well as introducing him to the music of Baroque masters from Germany and abroad. At 14 Bach was given a scholarship to study in the northern town of Lüneburg. He was a prized member of the choir until his angelic voice broke, after which he was probably relegated to the role of accompanist.

Below One of Bach's earliest handwritten manuscripts, dated c. 1700. The notes were found in the Herzogin Anna Amalia Bibliothek in Weimar.

ARNSTADT AND WEIMAR

Upon completion of his studies, Bach worked for some months in Weimar, before winning a position as the organist at a church in nearby Arnstadt in 1703. Here he was well paid for his young age, and had a relatively light workload, freeing him to spend time on composition. It was in Arnstadt that Bach was involved in a brawl with a student bassoonist, who hit Bach with a stick after the former had reputedly insulted his instrument, causing Bach to draw his sword on the man. Dissatisfaction with the inquiry into the scuffle still gnawing at his belly, Bach set out, on foot, to hear the great organist and composer Buxtehude in Lübeck, over 250 miles (400 km) away. Presumably, Bach had the ulterior motive of investigating whether he might succeed the ageing Buxtehude. A rival in this cause was Handel who, like Bach, was put off pursuing the position by the requirement of marrying Buxehude's 30-year-old daughter.

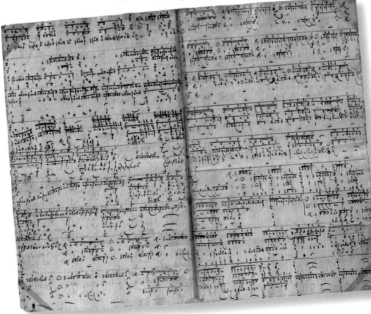

"I worked hard. Anyone who works as hard as I did can achieve the same results."

Bach returned to Arnstadt intent on finding another position, which he found in Mühlhausen. There he married his sweetheart (and second cousin) Anna Barbara, and wrote a great deal of music, perfecting his own personal brand of cantata. The couple had seven children in the following years. Among the four who survived to adulthood were Wilhelm Friedemann and Carl Philipp Emanuel, who later proved to be talented and significant composers in their own right. During Anna Barbara's first pregnancy, Bach was offered a lucrative position back in Weimar. They settled for some time, and while there Bach made the acquaintance of Telemann. The two composers evidently got on well; Telemann was chosen as young

Above A nineteenth-century painting of family music-making in the Bach household. Bach fathered a total of 20 children, of whom 10 died in infancy.

Discover the music

Brandenburg Concertos (1701–1728)

Cantata Wachet auf, BWV 140

Coffee Cantata, BWV 211

Cello Suites

St Matthew Passion, BWV 244 (1727)

The Well-Tempered Clavier, Books 1 and 2 (1722; 1738–1742)

Mass in B minor, BWV 232

Goldberg Variations, BWV 988 (1741–1742)

Partita No. 2 in D minor, BWV 1004

Art of the Fugue, BWV 1080 (1745–1750)

Bach's specialties, was less in demand in Cöthen, and much of his most beautiful and well-known secular music derives from this period, such as some of the glorious Brandenburg concertos, and the suites for cello and violin. The influence of Italian secular music is evident, particularly the Brandenburg concertos, arising in part from Bach's spending time transcribing some of Vivaldi's violin concertos. At Cöthen, as well as a handsome wage, Bach also had the opportunity to travel throughout much of Germany with Prince Leopold. One such journey in 1720 took him to a health spa in Bohemia. Bach left Anna at home with the children, and returned some weeks later refreshed and rejuvenated, only to find that his beloved wife of 13 years had suddenly died and been buried in his absence. Shattered by grief, Bach was sustained by his devout belief in God and his unshakeable faith in paradise, just as he had been after the deaths of his parents and three of his children.

Within a year Bach had married again, to Anna Magdelena, a singer and competent musician 16 years his junior. Together they had 13 more children, only six of whom survived to adulthood.

Bach stayed at Cöthen for another couple of years, but Leopold's new wife was unsympathetic to music and culture in general, and musical life at the court began to dwindle. Bach sought employment in one of the most prestigious positions in Germany: The Cantorship at the St Thomas's School in Leipzig. His

C.P.E. Bach's godfather. Bach eventually tired of life in Weimar and pressured his employers to release him to such an extent that he was jailed for a month by the county judge in 1717. Only briefly deflected, two days after his release from prison Bach commenced work as *Kapellmeister* to Prince Leopold of Cöthen.

THE CÖTHEN YEARS

Bach flourished in Cöthen: Prince Leopold was a cultured and well-traveled young man as well as being an accomplished musician, and gave Bach considerable freedom in his composition. Religious music, one of

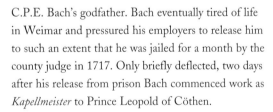

Above The Bach Window in St Thomas Church, Leipzig. The composer lived and worked in Leipzig from 1723 until his death.

application was successful, however not without a good deal of luck; he was third in line after Telemann and another applicant, both of whom were unable to leave their employers to take up the position in Leipzig. According to one of the council members: "As the best men could not be got, we must make do with the mediocre." Bach's new job had two main duties. He was teacher and choir director to the boys of the school, and he was also to provide music for civic occasions, and to supervise music in the city as a whole. In spite of almost continual tensions with the ruling council of the city, Bach stayed in Leipzig for the rest of his life. In 1729, he even took over the directorship of the *Collegium Musicum*, a secular group of musicians started by Telemann some years before, which performed twice a week at the city's most popular coffeehouse, Zimmermann's.

THE FINAL YEARS

In his final years Bach's health, and especially his eyesight, began to fail. He made a trip to the court of King Frederick II of Prussia, where his son Emanuel was employed. Frederick had heard of Bach's incredible ability to improvise a fugue on any given theme, and contrived to baffle the composer with a theme of his own. Bach rose to the challenge, improvising a three-part fugue, and upon his return to Leipzig he expanded the theme into *The Musical Offering*, a collection of canons, fugues, and a trio on the "royal" theme. It stands alongside the *Goldberg Variations* and *The Art of Fugue* as the one of the most significant contrapuntal works ever written.

In 1750, at the age of 65, Bach died of a stroke after unsuccessful eye surgery. His legacy lives not only in the influence his music exerted—and still exerts—on composers in the centuries after his death, but also in the intellectual feats he accomplished in the realm of composition, and in the sheer volume of beautiful music he produced—well over 1,000 works. It is little wonder Bach is regarded by many to be the greatest composer who ever lived.

Left An eighteenth-century engraving of the St Thomas School, where Bach was employed as cantor. The school was established in the thirteenth century.

Right Bach visited the court of Prussia's Frederick II in 1747 and dazzled the monarch with his improvisational skills. Bach was 62 at the time of this visit.

Below When Augustus II acceded to the throne of Poland in 1733, Bach began composition of the work that was eventually to become the magnificent *Mass in B minor*.

AVGVSTVS II.

50

MASS IN B MINOR

Seen by many to be the pinnacle, not only of J.S. Bach's work but of music in general, the *Mass in B minor* was never heard by the composer or even in its entirety until the mid-nineteenth century. The composition of the Mass spans almost 30 years of Bach's life. Originally intended as a small *Missa* (a fraction of a mass) to honor the accession of Augustus II, king of Poland, in 1733, parts of the Mass date back to 1724. Bach later elaborated the small *Missa* into a full-length work, and completed its final parts close to the end of his life, after he had gone blind. Taking over two hours to perform, the completed Mass is enormous, consisting of 27 pieces grouped into four sections: kyrie, gloria, credo, and sanctus. It contains beautiful arias for solo singers alternating with choruses, the orchestra both accompanying and featuring alone. One of the wonders of the Mass, despite its being drawn together from different sources, is its symmetry. Each section has a central point, and the sections as a whole revolve around the *Crucifixus* movement in the credo. Above all, it is clear that Bach poured all of his considerable energies into the Mass, creating a work of serene beauty and immense power.

The decline of the Holy Roman Empire

BACH'S GERMANY WAS POLITICALLY SHAPED DECADES BEFORE HIS BIRTH, IN THE DEVASTATING THIRTY YEARS' WAR (1618–1648), WHICH BEGAN BY PITTING PROTESTANTS AGAINST CATHOLICS, AND EXPANDED TO INVOLVE ALL THE MAJOR POWERS OF EUROPE. THE WAR LAID WASTE TO THE GERMAN COUNTRYSIDE AND RAVAGED THE POPULATION THROUGH COMBAT, FAMINE AND DISEASE, AND BY ITS END LEFT MUCH OF THE COUNTRY FRAGMENTED INTO SMALL CITY–STATES.

At the turn of the eighteenth century, the Holy Roman Empire, which had remained standing in one form or another across German-speaking lands since the mid-900s, was in the midst of a decline which would stretch over another century. Although Emperor Leopold I clung to his belief that he wielded absolute power, real control was dispersed among local dukes, electors, and kings. Many of these local rulers

Right The spectacle of soldiers marching off to war was quite a common sight during the seventeenth century in Europe.

belonged to the royal house of Hapsburg. This proud lineage had spread itself across Europe and included the leaders of Spain, Hungary, Bohemia, as well as Emperor Leopold, and its descendents still live today.

DECENTRALIZATION

This spread of power had the effect of creating decentralized points of influence and resulted in some of the most complicated politics in human history. However, it also created a large number of lavish courts as each leader tried to better those of his neighbors. The result was a land of opportunity for musicians, as well as the many other professions that relied on royal patronage—some of the crowning monuments of eighteenth-century art, science, philosophy, and music were made in service to the heads of the German states. Thus, and somewhat ironically, it was the decline of the great Holy Roman Empire that saw German Enlightenment thought blossom and flourish.

The Holy Roman Empire was beginning to feel the squeeze from both sides: Louis XIV of France had captured parts of Alsace and Lorraine, and Prussia had a new monarchy, which was to grow strong enough to rival that of the Empire. Electors were made kings and small skirmishes became wars. And yet, set against this tumultuous backdrop, life for the average person changed little. The vast majority of the population was still rural; few ever left their town of birth. Roads were

The Holy Roman Empire in Bach's time
★ Birthplace of J. S. Bach
☆ Death place of J. S. Bach
★ Birthplace of Georg Telemann

KAFFEEHÄUSER

According to legend, after the Battle of Vienna in 1683, the fleeing Ottoman troops left behind sacks of mysterious green beans. These were given as a gift to a heroic Polish soldier, and soon thereafter the first Viennese café was born. Coffee became all the rage in eighteenth-century Germany, around the same time that tobacco was gaining a foothold. Prohibitively expensive, coffee was indulged in only by the upper echelons of society, and in towns such as Leipzig, coffee houses—*Kaffeehäuser*—were the height of fashion. Unlike other European countries such as France and England, women were not banned from coffee houses in Germany, and there ensued a small social crisis wherein many young ladies were driven to extremes, and exhibited curious and disturbing behavior due to their addiction, a trend J.S. Bach commented upon in his humorous *Coffee Cantata*, BWV 211. In this secular cantata, a young bourgeois woman is berated by her father for her coffee addiction. She sings a love song to her coffee, stating: "If I can't drink my bowl of coffee three times daily, then in my torment I will shrivel up like a piece of roasted goat."

notoriously unsound in the Empire, making travel and trade even more difficult than usual. People were so isolated that local accents and dialects all but became separate languages, and travelers from two towns away might be considered foreigners.

Right Fashionable people frequented coffee houses, where they enjoyed the social scene as much as the delicious new beverage.

VILLAGE SONGS
Cultural life at this time was outlined in fairly distinct areas, just as social classes were clearly delineated. However, each level of culture exerted some degree of influence on the next. Rural culture, for example, had remained largely unchanged for centuries, and endured in the small towns of Germany. In isolated communities spinning rooms became

Right In rural areas, the task of spinning was often a community affair that was accompanied by song and dance.

important cultural centers: In the winter months when the land could no longer be worked, members of the village would congregate in large rooms, ostensibly to spin wool, but also to sing, dance, and indulge in general merriment. The songs from the villages would make their way to the coffee houses, taverns, and brothels of the cities, where the occasional composer might pick up a tune that would eventually appear in a comedy, play, or opera, accompany the Emperor's dinner in a string quartet, or even be heard in disguise in a cantata at Sunday Mass.

MUSICAL CONVENTIONS OF THE BAROQUE ERA

In homes of the Baroque era, making music was often a family affair. Paintings show contented gatherings of people holding assorted instruments, including flutes, violins, lutes, cellos or viols, as well as harpsichords in wealthier houses. Music was entertainment, a way to show flair and taste, and learning its conventions was a social necessity.

Learning how to play music during the Baroque era depended on an aural tradition just as much as a written one. Musical notation was often rather frugal in its directions, leaving questions of articulation, ornamentation, and even which notes to use to the experience of the performer. This assumed knowledge of musical rules and tastes, many of them unspoken, or subject to changing styles.

Above right The lute was one of the more popular instruments for family music-making in the Baroque period.

Below Wealthy families often had a harpsichord. Couperin wrote of the instrument, "One should have an easy manner at the harpsichord and avoid staring fixedly at any object, or looking vague."

In addition, improvisation was an integral part of eighteenth-century music. Players would add all kinds of unwritten effects, from trills and other simple additions to entire passages of their own devising. This applied not only to melodic lines, but also to accompanying instruments.

FIGURED BASS AND *BASSO CONTINUO*

Fundamental to the music of the Baroque period was the *basso continuo*, also known as through or thorough bass. It consisted of a continually present bass part,

Right A family concert featuring harpsi-chord and viol. While musical proficiency was expected of the upper classes, wealthy people also often employed musicians to perform in their homes.

which functioned as an accom-paniment for one or more upper voices. However, playing continuo was more than simply following a solo part. An accompanist was expected to keep a steady pulse, confining and supporting the rhythm. This gave melodic instrumen-talists and singers the stability they needed to "play" with the music; they might have impro-vised passages, or altered the speed of some notes (*rubato*), easily meeting up with the constant bass line a little later. Within this framework, the bass was instrumental in shaping the character of the music, striding forwards in some sections, and barely present in others.

Instruments used for continuo playing were diverse, often according to what was available. Harpsichord was a favored choice, as was lute or theorbo, often with an additional bowed bass, such as the cello or viola da gamba. Playing continuo was considered an art, needing a sure sense of rhythm and phrasing, as well as a deep understanding of harmony and voice-leading. For those instruments that could play chords, the ability to read figured bass was also necessary. This very clever device appeared as small numbers and symbols above or below the bass line, which functioned as a kind of shorthand for the harmonies being used. Reading the figures, a player could easily recognize which chord was intended, and improvise an accompaniment based upon it.

CHURCH MUSIC

The importance of music in Christian worship has a long history. During the Baroque era, religious music became highly varied, clinging to tradition in some areas and even adopting elements from such "decadent" forms as opera in others. One of the most important forms during this period was the Mass. Usually in Latin, but also in vernacular languages, the Mass followed the set format of the Ordinary of the Mass, adding new material from the Proper, according to requirements. It could be sung *a capella*, or accompanied by various instrumental ensembles, either with written-out parts, known as *obbligato*, or with a continuo bass line. Other forms also developed in response to demand for dramatic musical settings of sacred texts apart from the Eucharistic liturgy. As the Church did not approve of the kind of spectacle involved with opera, especially during Lent, a more static genre developed, without acting or dancing: The oratorio. Although it was eventually also taken up for secular subjects, the oratorio generally told a religious story. After an overture, solo arias alternated with choruses and recitatives designed to illustrate and intensify the drama. One famous oratorio is Handel's *Messiah*.

VIBRATO AND OTHER ORNAMENTS

Vibrato is heard as a fluctuation in a note, vibrating above and below the fundamental tone to produce increased volume and expression. Although it is often used almost continuously today, it was previously con-sidered an ornament to be added with discretion. A steady, singing tone was preferred, which began gently, grew in intensity, and faded away again. To this basic shape vibrato could be added, especially at the end of a long note, to express heightened emotion.

Other ornaments were also common. A trill between two notes was a simple possibility, as was the *appoggiatura*, a dissonant note tantalizingly delaying the principal note. Some ornaments became extremely complex, and apparently did not always succeed, since treatises of the time frequently lament a lack of taste and restraint in their application.

THE CLASSICAL PERIOD

c. 1750–1820

Introduction

UNLIKE THE CENTURIES BEFORE AND AFTER IT, THE EIGHTEENTH WAS
A CENTURY OF CHANGE—FROM THE STABILITY OF CENTRALIZED STATES
DOMINATED BY THE ARISTOCRACY AND ABSOLUTIST RULERS, IT
ARCHED TO THE WORLD-CHANGING UPHEAVAL OF THE AMERICAN
AND FRENCH REVOLUTIONS AND THE NAPOLEONIC WARS.

Although the Classical period is generally linked to the second half of the century, its stylistic characteristics had already started to emerge in the 1730s. Similarly, the end of the era may be marked by the 1815 peace treaty in Vienna, or by Beethoven's and Schubert's deaths in the late 1820s, even though many of their compositions display elements of Romanticism. It could be argued that the Classical period was indeed short lived, briefly reflecting the era's emphasis on classical balance and symmetry but essentially forming part of the richest 150 years of European art music.

The rapid progress of political events and change in artistic expression were ushered along by intellectual and economic developments eventually resulting in major transformations in the fabric of society. The eighteenth century, or the Age of Reason and Enlightenment, fostered reasoning from experience and observation. The applied sciences started in earnest, Pasteur making headway in chemistry, while the discovery of Pompeii in 1748 gave impetus to archaeology. The systematic scientific approach lay at the foundation

Above right A harpist plays for a soldier in this eighteenth-century painting by the French artist Leopold Boilly (1761–1845).

Previous pages Wolfgang and Nannerl Mozart at the piano. Their father, Leopold, stands beside them. The family portrait is made complete with the painting of Mozart's mother on the wall behind them.

Below An eighteenth-century depiction of a gathering of French Freemasons. Interest in Freemasonry burgeoned in the Classical era, with many noted men joining its ranks.

of Encyclopaedists' efforts (1751) and was felt in the arts as well, including music. Innumerable theoretical treatises and instrumental tutorials were published, codifying and tabulating the rules of harmony and composition as well as the know-how of playing specific instruments and performing according to "good taste." An awakening of historical interest in music of the past was also on the horizon. It spread from England where the Academy of Ancient Music was established in the 1720s and where Thomas Hawkins and Charles Burney published the very first books on the history of music.

The Enlightenment—the vibrant intellectual movement spearheaded by philosophers such as Voltaire, Rousseau, Lessing, and Kant—was instrumental in formulating and spreading the notion of egalitarianism and universal human rights. Some of its doctrines were eventually incorporated in the American Constitution and Bill of Rights. Its popular appeal also brought about the foundation of Freemasonry in London. The society gained ground quickly among intellectuals and socially aware members of the nobility, listing among its members heads of states, such as Frederick the Great of Prussia, influential thinkers such as Goethe, and artists like Mozart.

The Classical period saw marked improvements in agriculture, industry, transportation, and trade, resulting in an expanding middle class with insatiable appetites for learning and the arts. The introduction of public concerts and music-making in homes went hand in hand with the decline in aristocratic patronage and the growth of publicly funded events. While during the Baroque period most musicians held court or church appointments or served in an aristocratic households, by the end of the Classical period, freelancing became the standard; musicians had to make a living from publishing, performing, and teaching. The impact of all this on the style of music was considerable—to suit the

developing sophistication of the growing middle class, compositions had to be easy on the fingers and ears.

While distinct national styles characterized the Baroque period, by the beginning of the Classical era Italian musicians dominated all major European musical centers, establishing a common compositional language. This Italianate style suited contemporary taste, which favored vocally conceived, short, repeating and symmetrical phrases, easy to remember tunes, homophonic textures, and simple harmony.

The taste for simplicity and direct appeal felt its influence across all forms of music-making, especially opera. The popularity of pseudo-historical heroic storylines

Right Christoph Gluck (1714–1787) was an influential composer in the field of opera. One of his best-known works is *Alceste* (1767).

Above An execution by guillotine in Paris during the French Revolution. One of the seminal periods of French history, the Revolution brought changes in culture as well as everyday life.

involving royal figures sung by castrati waned. Audiences favored comic operas populated by contemporary common people singing in the vernacular. Meanwhile new instrumental genres such as the concerto and symphony gained ground through public concerts held during Advent and Lent when opera was banned. In the homes of the affluent, the new fortepiano became part of the furniture and composers busied themselves transcribing popular tunes, marches, and dances for two- or four-hand performances. Chamber music genres also developed, with string quartets written for the professionals rather than the amateurs.

By 1800 the original simplicity gave way to new complexity and emotional depth. The length of compositions doubled and the size of the orchestra grew. The sonata form, a quintessentially Classical structure with its dramatic contrast and well-balanced symmetry, gained new meaning in Beethoven's hands, providing a malleable, fluid framework for the individual expression of the emerging Romantic artist.

Carl Philipp Emanuel Bach

MARCH 8, 1714–DECEMBER 14, 1788

MENTION THE NAME BACH IN THE LATE EIGHTEENTH CENTURY AND—JUST LIKE TODAY—A MUSICAL GIANT WOULD COME TO MIND, ONE OF HISTORY'S GREATEST COMPOSERS AND PERFORMERS. BUT MENTIONING THE NAME JOHANN SEBASTIAN WOULD PROBABLY PROCURE A PUZZLED EXPRESSION: IT WAS HIS SONS, CARL PHILIPP EMANUEL, AND LATER JOHANN CHRISTIAN, WHO WERE THE REAL EUROPEAN SUPERSTARS.

Emanuel had a predictably rich musical upbringing, and could reputedly sight-read his father's most difficult works at seven years of age. He attended St Thomas School in Leipzig, where his father was the cantor. It would seem that the father and son duo were inseparable—apart from living and working together, they also often performed together in and around Leipzig. Following the example of his god-father, Telemann, Emanuel began studying law. He was, however, always destined for a musical career,

Below The main square of Leipzig, an important city for members of the Bach family. The city was the trade center for northern Europe in the eighteenth century.

and within a couple of years was already applying for musical posts around Germany. It was also around this time that he started seriously composing under the charge of his father. He quickly secured a position under the Crown Prince (soon to be king) of Prussia, Frederick. Bach was to serve Frederick the Great for the next 30 years on the modest salary of a court musician, though he hungered for recognition at court as a composer or virtuoso.

Die Boerse

Der Burg Keller Brod Baencke und Garkuche.

ACROSS THE GENRES

When a second harpsichordist was appointed to the court orchestra, Bach found himself with spare time to devote to other activities, namely teaching, composing, and attempting to secure another job. When his father died, he applied for the vacant position, and failed twice, even with Telemann's recommendation and an impressive array of works under his belt. Bach's compositions span a greater number of genres than those of his father; he was adept at the highly ornate church style, as well as chamber music, the symphony, concerto, song, and of course,

Discover the music

Sonata in E minor, Wq 59/1

Cello Concerto in A major, Wq 172

Symphony in D, Wq 183/1

Magnificat, Wq 215

Right An early eighteenth-century engraving of Hamburg, the city where Bach worked from the late 1760s, and where he died in 1788.

Left Carl Philipp Emanuel Bach was a working musician all his life. Three of his children lived to adulthood, but none followed him into the family business.

HAMBURG.

keyboard music. Pinning down C.P.E Bach's style is more problematic. He was so capricious and adaptable in his music that two works composed side by side could sound like they were written a century apart. His compositions feature a good deal of humor and quirkiness, including abrupt changes of direction and a sense of instability, balanced by whole movements featuring exquisitely lyrical melodies. Much of Bach's music is seen as belonging to the "sensitive style" (*Empfindsamer Stil*) of composition, characterized by sudden changes of emotion and unpredictability, but whose goal was, among other things, to procure "gentle tears of melancholy."

When Telemann died in Hamburg in 1767, Bach was chosen to be his successor as musical director of the principal churches there. In Hamburg Bach cultivated a group of artistic friends including poets, artists, and other musicians. Though he was criticized in his new position for being "more meticulous" (slower) than his predecessor, he produced some of eighteenth-century Germany's most important music—especially cantatas—in his late years at Hamburg. After Bach's death of a "chest ailment" in 1788, his teachings and music still exerted an enormous influence, Mozart saying of him, "He is the father, we are the children."

"What comprises good performance? The ability through singing or playing to make the ear conscious of the true content and affect of a composition."

THE *VERSUCH*

One of C.P.E. Bach's most important works is not a musical composition. The *Versuch über die wahre Art das Clavier zu spielen* (*Essay on the true art of playing keyboard*) is a monumental educational work, encompassing not only technical instruction for the keyboard, but a range of subjects pertinent to the amateur, as well as the professional, musician. The *Versuch* was written in response to demand for treatises of all kinds by the growing middle-class, who had ever-increasing desires for courtly accoutrements, including music. Modeled on a flute treatise by Bach's colleague, Quantz, the *Versuch* is in two parts. The first covers technical issues such as fingering and ornamentation, as well as the issue of how to produce a "good performance." To this end Bach composed several miniature sonatas, each a microcosm of styles and techniques designed to enhance the players' esthetic sensibilities. The second part, added some years later, consists of a thorough instruction in *continuo* playing, and reflects the expertise of a professional accompanist. The *Versuch* provides an important insight into performance practices of the eighteenth century, and is an indispensable tool for players of basso continuo, as well as keyboard in general.

Left The frontispiece of a book of keyboard pieces by C.P.E. Bach, a composer and performer whose contribution to music education in the eighteenth century was considerable.

Franz Joseph Haydn

MARCH 31, 1732–MAY 31, 1809

UNDOUBTEDLY THE MOST SUCCESSFUL, FAMOUS, AND BEST LOVED COMPOSER OF EIGHTEENTH-CENTURY EUROPE WAS HAYDN. A MAN OF SIMPLE TASTES, WHO DELIGHTED IN THE COMPANY OF FRIENDS, HAYDN IS CONSPICUOUS FOR BEING ONE OF THE HAPPIEST AND LEAST NEUROTIC ARTISTS IN HISTORY. KNOWN AFFECTIONATELY AS "PAPA HAYDN," HE DID MORE THAN ANY OTHER TO FOSTER AND PERFECT THE SYMPHONY, STRING QUARTET, AND PIANO SONATA.

Left Among Haydn's 104 symphonies is the "Farewell" where, in the last movement, the musicians leave the stage in turn until only two violinists are left.

frightened Joseph had already been rescued—ironically by another castrato. At 17, Haydn's voice broke, and soon after he applied for permission to leave, apparently to avoid being caned for cutting off another boy's ponytail. Permission was granted, but only after his punishment had been fulfilled. So he found himself on the streets of Vienna with no money, a few items of clothing, and some painfully broken skin. Haydn's charm served him well, however, for he soon found lodgings with a friend.

Haydn's parents begged him to join the clergy, a safe life that would provide him with food and board at the very least. Yet Haydn was resolute. His unwavering passion for music drove him into the precarious and ill-esteemed life of a freelance musician. Eking out an existence by teaching, performing in street bands, and selling short compositions, Haydn devoted every other hour to studying music from books, and playing C.P.E. Bach sonatas at his "worm-eaten clavichord." Much to his surprise, his pieces became quite popular on the streets and in the bars of Vienna.

Although his parents had no musical education, Haydn had an innate musical ability from a precocious age. His father had taught himself the harp, and was a lover of folk tunes. Haydn followed his example, and his playing was impressive enough to catch the attention of a relative, who was choirmaster in a nearby town. Young Joseph was soon whisked away to be educated.

THE EARLY YEARS IN VIENNA
Shortly after, eight-year-old Haydn was sent to sing and study at St Stephen's Cathedral in Vienna. Here he became proficient on most instruments of the orchestra. Haydn's high soprano voice was so charming that it was decided he would make a fine castrato, and a letter was sent to his parents asking their opinion. They rushed to Vienna to prevent any drastic action, fortunately finding that the very

Trumpet

With the highest register in the brass family, the trumpet is one of the oldest musical instruments—early trumpets date back thousands of years; for example, bronze and silver trumpets were found in Tutankhamun's tomb in Egypt. Like all brass instruments, a "buzzing" sound created from closed lips creates a vibration in the air column of the instrument to produce its sound. The chromatic trumpet emerged during the late 1700s, and Haydn's *Trumpet Concerto in E flat*—showing off the ability to play stepwise (chromatic) melodies—was one of the earliest pieces specifically written for the valved instrument.

Right The cast list for Haydn's opera buffa, *Il mondo della luna* (*The World of the Moon*, 1777), written while he was in the service of the Esterházy.

HAYDN THE KAPELLMEISTER

Haydn's long climb to fame began with his service to the Italian composer Porpora. Along with making Haydn clean his shoes (among other menial duties), Porpora filled in the many gaps in Haydn's knowledge of composition, and more importantly, introduced him into the higher circles of society. Suddenly the young composer was employed as keyboard tutor to a countess, and music master to a baron's family. Then he secured a position as Kapellmeister to Count Morzin, an Austrian aristocrat with a small orchestra. Bolstered by his new, secure income, Haydn set his sights on marriage. The young woman he had in mind was Therese Keller, one of his students. Unfortunately for Haydn, Therese became a nun, so he was obliged to marry her sister Maria instead. The union was an unmitigated disaster, and apparently the two all but hated each other, an emotional bitterness which they salved by both taking numerous lovers.

Above Haydn received his early musical education at St Stephen's Cathedral in Vienna where he was part of the choir. He was also married there in 1760.

Upon leaving the service of Count Morzin, who was in financial difficulties, Haydn quickly found new, and grander, employment as the Vice-Kapellmeister to Prince Anton von Esterházy. He remained in the employ of the Esterházy family for the rest of his career. Although his title was Vice-Kapellmeister, there was nothing secondary about his duties, and he soon replaced his elderly predecessor.

In this role, Haydn composed music at the prince's request, organized the musicians, saw to the care of the instruments, and performed regularly. He ate at the officers' table, and wore a uniform along with all the other servants. Haydn had been employed less than a year when Price Anton died and was succeeded by his brother, Niklaus. As well as being a dedicated supporter of music, Niklaus was a musician himself. He played the notoriously difficult and antiquated baryton, a kind of leg viol. Haydn composed a huge amount of music for the instrument and—much to his dismay—was requested to learn how to play it himself, so that the prince would have someone to play duets with. Though he was under enormous pressure from his master, Haydn's torrent of compositions for Prince Esterházy and the court never abated. His music was also becoming popular in the wider world, and he received a steady flow of commissions.

During the summer months the Esterházy court was resident in Eisenstadt in southern Austria, and during the winter it relocated to Vienna, along with other wealthy families. This was a joy for Haydn—most of his friends, including Mozart, were in Vienna, and he reveled in its thriving musical life. When the prince relocated his winter court to the magnificent Esterháza palace, Haydn become despondent at his isolation, and consoled himself with composition. His situation was, however, fortuitous for history. Isolated from musical civilization, Haydn wrote: "I was cut off from the world. There was no one to confuse or torment me, and I was forced to become original." Indeed, his time at Esterháza produced some of his greatest works.

THE LONDON YEARS

When Prince Niklaus died in 1790, he was succeeded by his thoroughly unmusical son, Anton. All but disbanding the court orchestra, Anton put Haydn on a pension. He was now free to publish and travel as he liked, and on the invitation of impresario Salomon, he went to London to perform new symphonies. Haydn was an enormous success in London, and it was there his fortune was made. Some of Haydn's best loved compositions date from his two visits there, such as the "Surprise," "Drumroll," and of course, "London" symphonies. On his return to Vienna, the ageing composer bought a house and settled down. His compositional output slowed considerably, and for the 10 years before his death he wrote little. Haydn died at the age of 77, while the forces of Napoleon ravaged and changed the face of Europe. Haydn's legacy is not only as a member of the great trio of the Classical era (the others being Mozart and Beethoven), but as a startlingly original and passionate composer, whose ubiquitous wit still provokes chuckles in the concert hall today.

Right Haydn attended a special performance of *The Creation* in the Great Hall of Vienna University in March 1808 held to celebrate his 76th birthday.

Below Haydn traveled to London following the death of Prince Niklaus. His "London" symphonies, inspired by his time there, are among his most popular compositions.

HAYDN'S STRING QUARTETS

Haydn has often been named the "father of the string quartet," though this is not strictly true. Music for four string instruments dates back long before Haydn's time, even to the consort music of the Renaissance, and there are many fine examples from both his predecessors and contemporaries. Haydn did, however, contribute an enormous amount to the classical form for two violins, viola, and cello. He pioneered the now standard four-movement structure of the quartet, and brought the genre to a new prominence. In his quartets, which number over 80, he achieves a balance, intimacy, and dialogue between the instruments that has served as a model for two centuries. Haydn adored playing quartets himself, and during his winters in Vienna he played in a quartet with Mozart. Also a consummate master of the form, Mozart was inspired to compose a set of "Haydn" String Quartets, a clear acknowledgement of the older man's considerable and influential achievementss.

Discover the music

String Quartets, Op. 33 "Russian" (1781)
Armida (1784)
Symphony No. 92 "Oxford" (1789)
Symphony No. 94 "Surprise" (1791)
Symphony No. 104 "London" (1795)
Trumpet Concerto in E flat (1796)
The Creation (1796–1798)
The Seasons (1801)

Above left This nineteenth-century lithograph shows Haydn conducting a string quartet. A master of this compositional form, Haydn's string quartets inspired many composers who came after him.

THE CREATION (1796-1798)

While in England, Haydn heard Handel's oratorios and was hugely impressed. Upon his return to Vienna, he began creating a massive oratorio of his own. The result is one of Haydn's best loved works: *The Creation*. The libretto was compiled from *Genesis*, the *Book of Psalms*, and curiously, John Milton's *Paradise Lost*. It depicts events in *Genesis* up to the fall of man, with music full of programmatic elements such as pastoral flutes and musical representations of animals from the lion to the worm. The work was an unprecedented success. The stunning setting of the text "Let there be light," which suddenly unleashes the full forces of the sizable orchestra as loudly as possible, won instant fame. Its dramatic effect on the first Viennese performance was described by a colleague of Haydn: "At that moment when light broke out for the first time, one would have said that rays darted from the composer's burning eyes. The enchantment of the electrified Viennese was so general that the orchestra could not proceed for some minutes."

Johann Albrechtsberger

FEBRUARY 3, 1736–MARCH 7, 1809

TOWARD THE END OF HIS LIFE, ALBRECHTSBERGER WAS HAILED AS THE BEST ORGANIST IN THE WORLD. HE COULD PLAY ENTIRE MASSES ON SIGHT AND IN ANY KEY, FLAWLESSLY PERFORMING THE MOST DIFFICULT PASSAGES. HIS PLAYING WAS ADMIRED BY MOZART AND HAYDN, AND HE BECAME ONE OF BEETHOVEN'S MOST IMPORTANT TEACHERS.

Contemporaries wrote of Albrechtsberger's organ playing in glowing terms, relating his immense mastery over the instrument. This was commonly juxtaposed with less flattering accounts of his compositional style, which was described as "dry." In fact, there are examples of Albrechtsberger's work, especially from his early years as a provincial musician, that show originality. He used a form of the concerto that was years before its time, foreshadowing the format used by J.C. Bach and Mozart. He also often asked for unusual instrumentation, including at least seven concertos for Jew's harp and orchestra, as well as a concerto for trombone and orchestra. However, at 36 years of age, after his appointment as organist in the court orchestra in Vienna, he seemed to become increasingly obsessed with that most old-fashioned of genres—the fugue.

Below An eighteenth-century representation of Vienna, showing the Old Burgtheater. Albrechtsberger lived and worked in Vienna his whole life.

A CONSERVATIVE APPROACH

Although he was only four years younger than Haydn, and showed similar early promise, Albrechtsberger never fully adopted modern genres and styles. Instead of using the three-part sonata form, he preferred two-movement church sonatas. Similarly, the popular Italian style, with its harmonically simple accompaniment under a lyrical, singing melody, was unable to keep his interest in the same way as several voices interweaving together. Perhaps it was his activity as a church organist that resulted in his conservative approach, but it proved to be fortuitous, for it was primarily his deep understanding of fugue and other kinds of counterpoint that led to his unique position as a pedagogue.

A MASTER TEACHER

Haydn held him to be the best teacher of composition in Vienna, and sent the young Beethoven to him. Beethoven was not Albrechtsberger's only student. Young musicians came in droves, seeking to enrich their understanding of composi-tional technique. In this way, Albrechtsberger had enormous influence on the development of mature Classicism in music, which was characterized by the infusion of the Italian style with the tradition of counterpoint and fugue. The era of the great masters of polyphony, with J.S. Bach at their head, may have been over. Their music was certainly seldom played. However, it was still avidly studied, imitated, and finally absorbed.

Albrechtsberger's influence was not confined to Vienna. His popular treatises on composition and figured bass earned him international recognition. Treatises for learning without a teacher, covering all manner of subjects, were in great demand at the end of the eighteenth century. Albrechtsberger's books cover subjects such as intervals, including which notes sound good together and which dissonant, and how the voices in counterpoint should move in relation to each other, all written in a language both understandable and practical. So, even though his own music was by no means progressive, his work made a unique contribution to the diversity of the music of the Classical period.

Above The only known portrait of Johann Albrechtsberger. Among his many students were the composers Johann Hummel, Josef Weigl, and Beethoven.

CONCERTO FOR JEW'S HARP, MANDORA, AND ORCHESTRA

The Jew's harp is generally more familiar as a folk instrument. Indeed, old surviving specimens as well as iconography from various continents show that it is one of the oldest and most widespread instruments of all. Yet in art music, its strange buzzing timbre has largely reduced its status to that of curiosity. That said, after 1800 there are accounts, including poetry by prominent writers, of the Jew's harp being promoted by virtuosos on the instrument and enjoying great popularity. Albrechtsberger was one of the first to compose for it. He was probably first inspired around 1765 by Father Bruno Glatzl of Melk Abbey, who could reputedly play minuets, concertos, and many other wonderful things, often in two parts simultaneously. In his performances, he was often accompanied by a mandora, a kind of small lute, hence its inclusion in the E major concerto written by Albrechtsberger almost five years later. The concerto has three movements, following the standard fast–slow–fast format, although the final movement is a minuet, and therefore a little slower and more digni-fied than the majority of final movements.

Trombone

The only brass instrument in the orchestra without valves or keys, the trombone uses a slide to extend the length of the air column, lowering the pitch. Known as the "sackbut" until the eighteenth century, the trombone (or tenor trombone) first appeared in an orchestra in Joachim Eggert's *Symphony in E flat* in 1807. Albrechtsberger's trombone concerto in B flat is still performed today. The tenor and bass trombones are now permanent fixtures in the modern symphony orchestra.

Discover the music

Concerto in B flat for Trombone and Orchestra

3 *Concertos for Jew's harp, mandora, and orchestra* (c.1770)

12 *Fugues for Organ or Harpsichord*, Op.1

Partita for Harp and Orchestra in F Major

German-speaking states in the eighteenth century

FREDERICK THE GREAT OF PRUSSIA HAS BEEN REMEMBERED VARIOUSLY AS AN ENLIGHTENED RULER, A DESPOT, A FLUTE-PLAYING WEAKLING WHO ALLOWED THE COUNTRY TO BE RUN BY HIS FLUTE-TEACHER'S WIFE'S DOG, AND ONE OF THE GREATEST MILITARY THINKERS WHO EVER LIVED. MARIA THERESA OF AUSTRIA IS RECORDED AS BEING ONE OF THE MOST CAPABLE RULERS OF HER COUNTRY, DESPITE HER GREATEST HANDICAP: HER GENDER.

As the Holy Roman Empire declined, the areas now known as Germany and Austria were in a state of flux. Rulers of varying influence worked incessantly to stay abreast of shifting alliances around them. Even the courts of more centralized countries such as France, Spain, and England were involved in a volatile set of agreements and common interests.

Above right Frederick II of Prussia (1712–1786) had a life-long passion for music and the arts. An accomplished flautist, he wrote about 100 sonatas for the instrument.

FREDERICK AND MARIA THERESA

Amid this hotbed of war and intrigue appeared the remarkable figures of Frederick and Maria Theresa, rising to the thrones of Prussia and Austria respectively.

Born only a few years apart, they were both crowned in 1740, and almost immediately became bitter opponents in a long struggle for land and power, which shaped the face of the German-speaking states.

Their backgrounds could hardly have been more disparate. Frederick had acquired an education second to none. Although his uncompromising and violent father wished him to be brought up as a simple man of the people, his French governess taught him French in addition to German, and his tutor introduced him to a secret library containing classics of poetry and philosophy. Commencing his duty in the army as an 18-year-old, he planned to desert and go to England with his closest friend, Hans Hermann von Katte. However, the attempt was betrayed and Frederick's father beheaded Katte and imprisoned Frederick, forcing him to spend over a year learning military tactics and the art of government. Afterwards, released from his schooling, he spent many happy years philosophizing and making music, inspiring in many the hope that he would become a philosopher king.

Maria Theresa was comparatively unprepared for her role as ruler. Raised under strict conditions, her views tended to be conservative and intolerant. Her father had not trained her in statecraft, and two recent wars had left her army weakened. Admittedly, her father had made every effort to secure acceptance of her ascendancy to the throne, almost 25 years previously. He had foreseen that her gender would suffice for many rulers to consider her a weak leader and it took significant influence and diplomacy to protect her. The result was an agreement called the Pragmatic Sanction, signed by most important leaders. Frederick the Great,

Map

North Sea

Baltic Sea

PRUSSIA

○ Hamburg
○ Lüneburg
○ Magdeburg

GERMANY

Antwerp ○
Aachen ○
Weimar ☆ ○ Leipzig
☆ Bonn
Frankfurt ○ ○ Gelnhausen ○ Prague
○ Bamberg
Waiblingen ○ ○ Nuremberg
○ ○ Regensburg
☆ Vienna
☆ Salzburg ○ Rohrau

AUSTRIA

Austrian and German composers, eighteenth century
★ Birthplace of C. P. E. Bach
☆ Birthplace of Franz Joseph Haydn
★ Birthplace of Johann Albrechstberger
★ Birthplace of Wolfgang Amadeus Mozart
★ Birthplace of Ludwig van Beethoven
--- Modern country borders

0   250   500 kilometers
0   125   250 miles

however, refused. He challenged Maria Theresa's right to the throne, and so began the first of many conflicts, known as the War of Austrian Succession.

THE ARTS

In her first years as ruler, Maria Theresa was so preoccupied with retaining the throne, that little thought was spared for the arts. Even the great poet Metastasio, later to collaborate so successfully with Mozart on *The Marriage of Figaro*, was idle at court. Frederick had a much more intimate relationship with the arts, and with music in particular. An accomplished flautist and composer, his concerts—in which he often performed—were legendary. He also gathered the most famous composers about him, including his flute teacher, Quantz, and as accompanist, C.P.E. Bach.

Right Mesmer trying to heal a woman using his theory of animal magnetism. He originally trained as a physician, and maintained that magnetism could heal all kinds of illnesses. His work was discredited by the medical community.

Below Maria Theresa (1717–1780) proved to be a very capable ruler. Among her civil reforms, she made elementary education compulsory, and, after a bout of smallpox, advocated inoculation against the disease.

MESMERISM

In Act I of Mozart's opera *Così fan tutte*, a magnet is used to miraculously cure two characters of a supposed poisoning. This satirical scene was clearly ridiculing an old friend of the Mozart family, Franz Anton Mesmer. Hailed variously as a miracle healer and a dangerous charlatan, Mesmer believed that he possessed concentrated levels of "animal magnetism." In combination with special magnets, he claimed to be able to cure all manner of ailments. Hostility from the medical profession reached a peak in Vienna when Mesmer claimed to have cured the blindness of pianist Maria Theresia Paradis. His claim caused a furor, and when it emerged that she could reputedly only see in his presence, her family protested. Mesmer prudently decided to leave Vienna for Paris, where he initially enjoyed great success. Clothed in lilac silk, he conducted single and group healing sessions, silent but for his playing of a glass harmonica, and earned immense profits. Much to his chagrin, medical establishments continued to deny his credibility, culminating in a royal commission which dismissed his theories outright. Mesmer was obliged to flee Paris and spent his last 20 years in obscurity.

THE AGE OF THE SYMPHONY

In a letter to his father describing the successful performance of his "Paris" symphony in 1778, Mozart wrote: "I began my Allegro with two violins only, *piano* for the first eight bars, followed instantly by a *forte*; the audience, as I expected, said 'hush' at the soft beginning, and when they heard the *forte*, began at once to clap their hands."

Composers were finding that writing symphonies could lead to fame and fortune, especially if they delighted with their originality. The orchestra provided a vastly expressive palette for composers to draw upon, both in terms of sheer volume and the different "colors" that resulted from new combinations of instruments. These factors, combined with the public nature of symphony concerts, led to an extraordinary deluge of symphonic compositions.

SYMPHONIC STRUCTURE

The genre eventually became standard concert repertoire, evolving steadily from early ensembles of various sizes and instrumentation ("symphonia" originally meaning simply to "sound together") into a common format of three or four movements for an orchestra with an increasingly consistent selection of instruments. It was not uncommon to play several symphonies in one concert, or to intersperse the movements with arias, sonatas, and even improvisations in performances which lasted for hours. As time passed, the symphony came to be regarded as the highest form of instrumental expression.

Below A nineteenth-century representation of Mozart composing a symphony. Mozart is still regarded as a master of the symphony.

Below To gain the attention of people promenading in pleasure parks, such as this one in England, symphonies usually began with a lively first movement.

The first movement was generally fast, and designed to gain the attention of an audience that was promenading, eating and drinking, or playing games such as chess or cards. Growing from the opera–overture style, its role was to be positive and uplifting, opening the heart in preparation for the sublime reverence of a slow and touching second movement. A minuet often followed, its noble elegance and poise carried over from the dance tradition. The final movement rounded off the symphony in an energetic manner, its strong pulse usually rustic and vivacious.

Within this larger form, each movement also developed a recognizable structure. In much the same way as a novelist, speaker, or playwright might construct a work using an introduction, body, and conclusion, a composer could also use familiar forms to give his music coherence. The first movement of a symphony, for example, usually presented a musical theme which would be repeated several times in the tonic, or "home" key, by way of introducing and reinforcing it. Often a second, contrasting theme would also appear, especially in later Classical symphonies. Mozart, for example, often answered his strong first theme with a softer, more lyrical second one in a new key. After "setting the scene" in the introduction, the music moves on and begins to journey through new thematic ideas. It usually becomes more dramatic, moves to farther, more dissonant keys, experiences a peak of suspense, and finally returns to the tonic, when all the main melodies are restated to provide a sense of resolution and homecoming. Audiences of the time were intimately familiar with these musical structures, and delighted in the unexpected turns or surprising rests, which abound in the music of composers such as Haydn and Mozart.

THE SONATA FORM

This kind of three-part structure was by no means restricted to symphonies. It was also extraordinarily common in sonatas, hence the name bestowed upon it—"sonata form." Sonata form has proven to be one of the most enduring and adaptable musical structures of Western culture, appearing in a steady stream of compositions even to the present day.

Above A manuscript in Beethoven's handwriting of his much-loved *Piano Sonata No. 14*, Op. 27, better known as the "Moonlight Sonata," which was composed in 1801.

Below A concert in Vienna in the presence of the royal family. As the Classical period progressed, symphonies became more popular, audiences flocking to hear the latest works by their favorite composers.

THE MANNHEIM ORCHESTRA

No orchestra of the Classical era was more renowned for its dramatic effects and astonishing precision than that of Mannheim. The orchestra offered a full complement of string, wind, and brass instruments, much as we would recognize today. Apart from the orchestra's full and brilliant sound, the listener was swept breathlessly along by its disciplined *crescendi*, beginning with the softest hint of a melody and gradually rising in both pitch and volume to the other extreme. Sometimes composers took advantage of the prodigious abilities of the musicians by writing a series of notes shooting upwards like a rocket, sighing like a lover, or fluttering like birds singing. All these effects became hallmarks of the Mannheim orchestra, and have attracted titles such as the "Mannheim Rocket," or the "Mannheim Roller." Symphonies abound containing musical elements inspired by it, including many by Mozart. Works by some composers are so full of Mannheim effects as to appear to contain nothing else. Johann Stamitz, the first important leader of the orchestra on its rise to fame, wrote some symphonies in this manner, clearly pandering to audience demand for musical thrills.

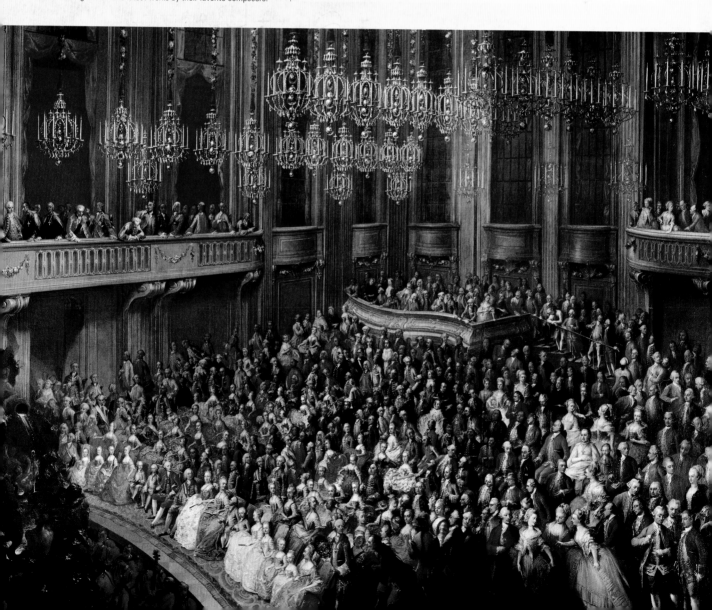

Muzio Clementi

JANUARY 23, 1752–MARCH 10, 1832

ON CHRISTMAS EVE, 1781, HOLY ROMAN EMPEROR JOSEPH II STAGED A COMPETITION FOR THE AMUSEMENT OF HIS ROYAL RUSSIAN GUESTS. THE CONTEST WAS TO PIT TWO GREAT KEYBOARD VIRTUOSI AGAINST ONE ANOTHER. THE CONTESTANTS: W.A. MOZART AND ITALIAN-BORN MUZIO CLEMENTI. THE MUSICIANS WERE TO IMPROVISE, PLAY SOME PIECES OF THEIR OWN, AND SIGHT-READ A SONATA BY OPERA COMPOSER PAISIELLO.

The skill of these two keyboard players was so impressive that the emperor declared a tie. Muzio Clementi commented of his rival, "…I had never heard anyone play with such spirit and grace." Mozart was less elegant in his assessment—"…he has not a kreuzer's worth of taste or feeling; in short he is a mere mechanicus." Mozart would later say of Clementi, "[He] is a charlatan, like all Italians." Regardless of Mozart's poor view of Clementi, it cannot be denied

Below A panoramic view of London around the time that Clementi lived there. Among his many achievements was his involvement in what eventually became the Royal Philharmonic Society.

that he was one of the great keyboard players and composers of the eighteenth and nineteenth centuries. He was also one of the longest lived, reaching the age of 80, and bore witness to some of the most radical changes in Western music that have ever occurred.

MAKING HIS MARK

Muzio Clementi was born in Rome in 1752, and began keyboard studies very early. At 13 he was organist at

Discover the music

Symphony in D major, Op. 18, No. 2 (1787)

Piano Concerto in C major (1796)

Piano Sonata in G minor, Op. 50, No. 3 (1805)

Above Clementi was a virtuosic pianist and wrote primarily for the piano, including over 100 piano sonatas. Admired also as a teacher, he counted Irish composer John Field among his illustrious students.

PIANISTIC PERFORMANCE

The expressive techniques employed by pianists during performances in the eighteenth and nineteenth centuries were highly different from what is expected of performers today. Some techniques were inherited from the long-standing tradition of continuo-playing, such as exaggerated rolling of chords, or adding more notes to thicken the texture. Others were representative of an attempt to beautify melodies; such as "dislocation"—separating two notes, that on the page are written together, for expressive effect; and right-hand *rubato*— playing the melody more freely, while the left hand accompaniment stays steady, a device composers such as Mozart and, later Chopin, were particularly fond of. The piano itself, or *fortepiano*, as Clementi would have known it, has also undergone massive changes since his day. His instruments would probably have had a wooden frame, instead of iron, and lighter hammers covered with leather as opposed to the modern felt. These factors combined to produce a more articulated, varied, and delicate sound than that of a modern concert grand, characteristics that are eminently suited to the music of the time.

his local church, and it was at this tender age that his outstanding skills caught the attention of a traveling Englishman, Peter Beckford, who was so impressed by the young prodigy that he "bought Clementi of his father for seven years," took him back to Dorset, and set about expanding his musical education. Clementi spent the next seven years in study and practice, and began to compose. After his release from Beckford's service, Clementi moved to London, and embarked on his career. Though he struggled early on, living off sporadic accompanying work, the increasing popularity of his notoriously difficult keyboard compositions saw his name rise in English esteem until he felt confident enough to embark on the first of his many European tours. It was on this first tour that Clementi played for the ill-fated Queen Marie Antoinette of France, as well as participating in the contest with Mozart under her cousin, Emperor Joseph II.

CLEMENTI & CO.

On his return to London in 1785, Clementi cemented his standing as a performer and composer, and delved into the businesses of publishing music and manufacturing instruments. The latter enterprises earned him quite a fortune, despite his piano factory being razed by fire in 1807. The success of his publishing company, Clementi & Co., was probably due to his lucrative deal with Europe's new star composer (and a great admirer of Clementi), Ludwig van Beethoven. Although the two men experienced a few personal disagreements in relation to publishing, a continuing contract was eventually secured to the benefit of both: Clementi published first editions of ten new works by Beethoven, and as a member of the Philharmonic Society was party to the commission of Beethoven's magnificent *Symphony No. 9* in D minor.

Above A manuscript in Clementi's handwriting of his Op. 10 *Sonatas for Keyboard*. This is No. 1 in A major (1782). Many of Clementi's sonatas and sonatinas are still used as teaching pieces.

On March 10, 1830, having retired from his various businesses, and having had a compositional career spanning nearly 60 years which saw the births and deaths of Mozart, Beethoven, and Schubert, Clementi died. His funeral at Westminster Abbey was filled to bursting, and was attended by England's finest, who were mourners for the Classical era's last man standing.

Luigi Boccherini

FEBRUARY 19, 1743–MAY 28, 1805

AMONG HISTORY'S LEGIONS OF COMPOSERS, RELATIVELY FEW WERE CELLISTS. FEWER STILL WERE VIRTUOSOS, OR ACHIEVED ANY SORT OF BRILLIANCE OR NOTORIETY, FACTS THAT SET LUIGI BOCCHERINI APART. BOCCHERINI ALL BUT REVOLUTIONIZED WRITING FOR THE CELLO, PENNING PARTS FOR CHAMBER MUSIC UNPRECEDENTED IN DIFFICULTY, AND ELEVATED THE CELLO CONCERTO TO EQUALITY WITH THAT OF THE VIOLIN OR KEYBOARD.

Though he became a naturalized Spaniard later in life, Boccherini was born an Italian, in the Tuscan town of Lucca at the height of the War of the Austrian Succession, in which the armies of France and Austria ravaged the Italian countryside.

Above right One of Boccherini's most recognized compositions is the minuet from the *String Quintet in E*, Op. 11, No. 5 (G 275). The piece is a triumph of Classical elegance.

Right Boccherini was born at the height of the War of the Austrian Succession when Italy was subject to many foreign invasions. The war was over Maria Theresa's right to rule.

VIENNA AND BEYOND

Taking his first cello lessons with his father, Luigi quickly rose to prominence in Lucca and by 14 was studying and performing in Vienna. By all accounts young Boccherini was a captivating and sensitive player, and for the next seven years he toured Italy with his father, returning several times to Vienna, before winning an orchestral position in his home town. During his travels Boccherini nurtured his formidable talent for composition, and developed a special affinity with chamber music, which lasted throughout his life. When he was 23, his father died. Boccherini and his friend, the violinist Manfredi, set out for Genoa, then London. Along the way, they stayed in Paris for six months, and became a musical sensation. There Boccherini came under the patronage of the immensely influential Baron de Bagge (whose real name was Charles-Ernest Ennal), and played at private chamber concerts, soon becoming a fashionable fixture in the Parisian musical *milieu*. Boccherini wrote a great deal in Paris and, for the rest of his life, Paris was the center of publication for his works.

Above Boccherini wrote a great deal of chamber music, including some much-loved string quintets. This is the frontispiece from one such work, the Op. 37, published—as all his works were— in Paris.

> ### Discover the music
>
> *Symphony in D minor*, G. 522
> *Cello Concerto No. 9 in B flat major*, G. 482
> *String Quartet in G major*, G. 223,
>   "La Tiranna"
> *String Quintet No. 60 in C Major*, G. 324

THE MOVE TO SPAIN

An offer of patronage in Spain changed the duo's plans for London, and soon they had an orchestral position in Aranjuez. Spain was Boccherini's home for the rest of his life. At 27, he entered the service of Infante Don Luis of Aranjuez as "composer and chamber virtuoso" and his compositional output rose in sympathy with his large salary increase. When his wife and Don Luis both died in 1785, Boccherini was granted a pension, and was free to seek patronage at home and abroad. This he found in foreign employers such as French consul Lucien Bonaparte (brother of Napoleon), and King Friedrich Wilhelm II of Prussia, although Boccherini serviced his new patrons from his home in Spain. The last decade of his life saw a sharp decline in his good fortune: Most of his patrons died, as did his second wife, and three daughters. Despite his possession of two Stradivari cellos, Boccherini died in poverty in 1805, the year Napoleon captured his birthplace, Lucca, turning it into what Tolstoy described in *War and Peace* as a "family estate of the Bonapartes."

NIGHT MUSIC OF THE STREETS OF MADRID

The *String Quintet No. 60 in C Major*, G. 324 was published after Luigi Boccherini's death. It is one of the few programmatic works that he wrote, and depicts night scenes familiar to Madrid residents. He went so far as to say: "The piece is absolutely useless, even ridiculous, outside Spain because the audience cannot hope to understand its significance nor the performers to play it as it should be played." The seven-movement work begins with a solemn, prayer-like *Ave Maria*. The stringed instruments are strummed, imitating the tolling of the church bell. In the next movement, the *Minuet of the Blind Beggars*, Boccherini instructs that the two cellos be placed upon the cellists' knees and strummed like guitars. Next follows the *Rosary*, a slow, hypnotic movement, not to be played in time. The composer then parodies the raucous Madrid street singers in *Los Mandolos*, before bringing in the curfew and the changing of the street guard in *Ritirata*, a piece popular in Spain ever since its composition.

Cello

Developing from the three-stringed bass violin in the 1500s, the cello (its full name is violoncello) typically provides the inner harmony parts in the string section and for the orchestra. Tuned in fifths, the cello is a member of chamber ensembles. Among the most famous works for cello are J.S. Bach's six unaccompanied suites, and Haydn's *Cello Concerto in C major*. Boccherini composed 12 much-loved cello concertos. Over time, the cello repertoire grew, with notable compositions by Schumann, Dvořák, Saint-Saëns, Elgar, and others.

Italy and France in the eighteenth century

RENAISSANCE ITALY WAS A HUB OF CULTURE AND ECONOMIC VITALITY, AS WITNESSED BY THE IMMORTALITY OF NAMES SUCH AS LEONARDO, MICHELANGELO, AND RAPHAEL. BUT BY THE EIGHTEENTH CENTURY, MUCH HAD CHANGED. THE RICH WERE RICH, BUT MOST ITALIANS LIVED IN SQUALOR. RAVAGED BY WAR AND DOMINATED BY A SUCCESSION OF FOREIGN POWERS, ITALY WAS FERTILE GROUND FOR THE IDEALISM OF REVOLUTION.

Italy could not in fact be regarded as a nation at this time. The north had long been the scene of endless power struggles between the Spanish, Austrians, and French. Southern Italy stayed largely feudal. Poverty and crime were out of control, yet Rome remained a center of the religious and artistic world and attracted cultured people from all countries. Venice was also an important city, its spectacular carnival always very well attended in spite of war. A new fervor for archaeology even drew people south to Pompeii, although the roads were dangerous and lodgings were in poor condition.

Right The Battle of Waterloo in June 1815 was Napoleon's downfall. One of Napoleon's great achievements was a civil code that stated that all French men were equal before the law.

Left Marie Antoinette, queen of France and the wife of Louis XVI, was executed by guillotine in October 1793, during the "Reign of Terror," a period in France marked by factional violence and mass executions.

WELCOMING NAPOLEON

Among the elite—including the fantastical pomp of the papacy—high art, music, and literacy were still prized. A long tradition of leaders using culture to emphasize the potency of their leadership resulted in continued production of state-supported monuments, paintings, operas, and statues, especially in northern Italy and Sicily. But overall, Italy was filled with hungry people uselessly in possession of all the traditional skills of their fathers and grandfathers. Those who could emigrate did so, among them singers and instrument makers. Those who remained dreamed of richer times, and it is perhaps not surprising that, of all the people of Europe, the Italians gave the invading French revolutionary forces of 1796 the warmest welcome. They quickly adopted French social structures for everything from the military to education and the judiciary.

France, led by Napoleon in his first major foreign campaign, was poised to challenge all of Europe. Seven years had passed since the French Revolution had begun. Louis XVI, his queen Marie Antoinette, and over 16,000 others had died beneath the guillotine, casualties of the 1793–1794 "Reign of Terror." These extraordinary events had been brewing for many years, gathering momentum from the time of a famous pamphlet by the revolutionary theorist, Sieyès, which promoted political power in the hands of the people. This pamphlet was borne of general feeling and was by no means the first of its kind. Resentment of inequality, fuelled by financial hardship and a growing belief in

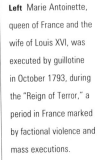

the rights of man, finally led to the moment when representatives of the common people lost patience. They openly bypassed nobles, clergy, and the king, and created a legislative body called the National Assembly, representative of all the people of France. Although invited to cooperate, the king and many nobles and clergy resisted, and the bloodshed began.

NAPOLEON'S CODE

The period from the Revolution in 1789 until the battle of Waterloo in 1815 was not only a time of fear and death. Napoleon proudly developed his Civil Code, which set down rules of law to replace the complex web of rights and privileges enjoyed according to the king's favor. A mixture of conservative and liberal concepts, the code most importantly achieved equality before the law, freedom of religion, and the abolition of feudalism.

PIERRE-AUGUSTIN BEAUMARCHAIS (1732–1799)

Beaumarchais (below) is best known as the genius behind the name Figaro. He was an intelligent and resourceful man who was able to turn his hand to almost anything. During his lifetime he became a watchmaker and inventor, a harp teacher to the daughters of Louis XV, a businessman of enough talent to buy himself into the nobility, a risk-taker who made many enemies and spent several periods in prison and in exile, and an author, most notably of three very famous plays. These plays follow the lives of two characters: Figaro and his master, Count Almaviva. The first explores the light-hearted yet traditional servant–master relationship of Figaro and the count, and is entitled *The Barber of Seville*, made famous in a Rossini opera. The second, *The Marriage of Figaro* (the basis for the opera by Mozart), has a strongly revolutionary character and was initially banned by an increasingly nervous Louis XVI. In it, Figaro and his betrothed, Suzanne, are portrayed as being intellectual and emotional equals (at least) of the count and countess. This aspect also met with resistance in Mozart's production some eight years later. The story then continues its revolutionary flavor in the third play, *The Guilty Mother*.

Johann Chrysostom Wolfgang (Amadeus) Mozart

JANUARY 27, 1756–DECEMBER 5, 1791

EVER SINCE HIS PRECOCIOUS CAREER AS A CHILD PRODIGY, MOZART'S MUSICAL ACHIEVEMENT HAS BEEN OBSCURED BY THE IMAGE OF THE NAÏVE UNREFLECTING CHILD GENIUS DISPENSING ARCADIAN DELIGHT. HIS MUSIC TODAY IS REPRESENTED AS A PANACEA FOR EVERYTHING FROM CHILD LEARNING DIFFICULTIES TO POOR LACTATION IN COWS. HOWEVER, HIS ENORMOUS MUSICAL GIFTS TRANSCEND MUSIC'S SECONDARY POSITION AS AN ART FORM IN HIS OWN DAY AND THE COMMODIFICATION OF THE MUSICAL EXPERIENCE IN MODERN CONSUMER CULTURE.

He was a peerless creator of melody, and, with J. S. Bach, among the greatest harmonists of all time. Above all, in every musical genre of his day, he wrote enduring masterpieces of unique grace and beauty.

Mozart and his sister Maria Anna (known as "Nannerl") were the only two surviving children of seven born to violinist Leopold Mozart and his wife Maria Anna, and even their survival was put at risk by their father's decision to promote and exploit their musical gifts from a tender age. Leopold took both children to Munich to play for Elector Maximillian Joseph II when Wolfgang was five, and, on a tour of Vienna and Bratislava the following year, Wolfgang contracted his first bout of rheumatic fever, the disease which was probably also the ultimate cause of his death.

Above Mozart was one of the world's greatest composers. In his short life, he wrote over 600 works, and his operas, symphonies, and chamber music are mainstays of the modern repertory.

Right A painting by French artist Michel Barthelemy Ollivier (1712–1784) showing the boy Mozart playing the clavichord at a society tea party.

pieces, chamber music, and his first symphonies in the style of Johann Christian Bach, a composer whose elegance he admired.

The most striking achievements of his early teenage years were his operas, where he revealed remarkable instincts for musical characterization, particularly in *Mitridate*, a full-length opera-seria written when he was 14 years old. During the Italian trip, Wolfgang visited St Peter's and wrote out from memory Allegri's *Miserere*, written copies of which were kept strictly secret. He was later conferred with the Order of the Golden Spur by the pope and was subject to trials and pseudo-scientific tests from musical academies and pronounced "a miracle in music, and one of those freaks Nature causes to be born."

YOUTHFUL TRAVELS

When Wolfgang was seven, the family embarked on a three-and-a-half year tour that took them through Germany, France, England, Holland, and Belgium, during which the children played before Louis XV of France, George III of England, William V of Orange, and the young Goethe. Wolfgang, with wig and sword (as Goethe remembered it) would improvise, add a bass to a given part, read music at sight and perform with a cloth covering his hands and keys. Charles Burney heard him improvise an opera to nonsense words, imitating different singers, and praised his good taste. During this tour Wolfgang wrote keyboard

---

Discover the music

The Abduction from the Seraglio, K. 384 (1782)

The Marriage of Figaro, K. 492 (1786)

String Quintet in C, K. 515 (1787)

String Quintet in G minor, K. 516 (1787)

Symphony No. 39, K. 543 (1788)

Symphony No. 40, K. 550 (1788)

Symphony No. 41 "Jupiter", K. 551 (1788)

Cosi fan tutte (1789–1790)

Clarinet Concerto in A, K. 622 (1791)

Requiem Mass in D minor, K. 626 (1791, completed
     by Süssmayr)

BACK TO SALZBURG

After these glory days, Mozart found opportunities in his hometown of Salzburg limited and the installation in 1772 of a new and somewhat less indulgent employer, Archbishop Colloredo, led to difficulties. Frustrated over their frequent absences, Colloredo dismissed both father and son in 1777 though Leopold was quickly reinstated. Wolfgang embarked on a journey with his mother, staying first in Mannheim, where he enjoyed scatological chatter with his cousin Maria Anna Thekla

Left A letter written by Mozart to his friend Haydn, in which Mozart dedicates his six sonatas for pianoforte to the older composer. The two men admired each other's works.

("the Bäsle"), and fell in love with Aloisia Weber. In Paris, Mozart composed a ballet, *Les Petits Riens*, and the "Paris" Symphony, though it is possible the trip was not as productive as suggested by Wolfgang's letters, which reveal tension between the controlling father and the brilliant son chafing for liberty. While in Paris his mother died, and Mozart soon returned to Salzburg as a salaried church composer, organist, and choir trainer under Colloredo, but remained restless.

The Salzburg years represent Mozart's first maturity, culminating in the first of his operas that are still regularly performed, *Idomeneo*. In 1781 the archbishop summoned Wolfgang to Vienna, leading to another and final quarrel, in which he was reputedly thrown from the room. "I did not know that I was a valet—and that was the last straw." Mozart moved in with the Webers who had relocated to Vienna, and fell in love with a different sister, Constanze, whom he married in 1782, obtaining the grudging approval of Leopold only just before the wedding.

Leopold's inability to resist controlling his son's career was complex—partly social, partly financial, and partly anxiety about his own split with his mother when he had married. However, Mozart's early career as an independent composer in Vienna was successful and the world can be thankful for the energy and breadth it spurred him on to. Mozart immediately turned his attention to an opera in the German *singspiel* tradition (which included spoken dialog), *Die Entführung aus dem Serail* (*The Abduction from the Seraglio*), and to the presentation of concerts for which he composed piano concertos, writing 14 between the years 1782 and 1786, and which remain the defining classics of the form. He also produced the first of his three great operas with librettist Lorenzo Da Ponte, *The Marriage of Figaro*, which opened successfully in Vienna and even more so in Prague the following year where the second Da Ponte Opera, *Don Giovanni*, was produced in 1787.

In 1788–1789, Mozart's activities lessened partly due to an economic downturn caused by war with

Opposite right A 1790 meeting of the Vienna Masonic Lodge, where Mozart is present. A practicing Mason, Mozart wrote his *Masonic Funeral March* K. 477 in 1785 especially for a Masonic service.

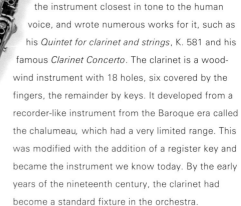

Clarinet

Mozart is said to have considered the clarinet the instrument closest in tone to the human voice, and wrote numerous works for it, such as his *Quintet for clarinet and strings*, K. 581 and his famous *Clarinet Concerto*. The clarinet is a woodwind instrument with 18 holes, six covered by the fingers, the remainder by keys. It developed from a recorder-like instrument from the Baroque era called the chalumeau, which had a very limited range. This was modified with the addition of a register key and became the instrument we know today. By the early years of the nineteenth century, the clarinet had become a standard fixture in the orchestra.

Turkey, though he still produced such masterpieces as the two quintets, K. 515 and K. 516, and his last three symphonies. Although Mozart borrowed money from, among others, his friend Michael Puchburg, a fellow Freemason, his economic problems and financial irresponsibility should not be exaggerated. He earned well and lived well in Vienna, working hard in his final years to avoid a return of financial trouble, and dying no more in debt than might be expected of an entrepreneurial person in his mid-thirties. His last years brought a third wave of operatic masterpieces, the third Da Ponte Opera, *Cosi fan tutte* (1789–1790), an old-style opera-seria, *La Clemenza di Tito*, and his enormously successful *singspiel*, *The Magic Flute*, which contained his most extended treatment of themes from Freemasonry. The facts around Mozart's death are clouded in anecdote and fantasy, yet of this we can be fairly certain. He fell ill on November 20, 1791 and died of natural causes (probably rheumatic fever) 15 days later. His funeral was modest, which was in keeping with the frugality encouraged by Joseph II, and he was widely and greatly mourned.

Below A scene from the Opera Factory's 1993 production of Mozart's *The Marriage of Figaro*. Mozart conducted the opera's first performance in May 1786.

THE MARRIAGE OF FIGARO (1786)

Beaumarchais's play *La Folle Journée ou la Marriage de Figaro* was initially banned by Louis XVI in Paris in 1784 for its representation of the aristocracy. After its eventual first performance, Beaumarchais was arrested on another trivial matter and refused to leave prison until the cabinet

had attended a performance of the play, which they did, apparently applauding appreciatively. Joseph II had also banned the play in Vienna, but as one review of the opera remarked, "What is not allowed to be said these days, is sung." The subversive aspect is the way it inverts the usual master/servant dichotomy by which the aristocratic loves are distinguished by their high ideals and the servants' by their base sensuality. In arias like "Se vuol ballare" Mozart gives the servant, Figaro, a sarcastic minuet, an aristocratic dance melody, to articulate his rage at the Count's intention to seduce his Susanna. In opera buffa, the finale traditionally involved an ensemble, which Da Ponte described as a "kind of comedy or minor drama in itself … for showing off the genius of the composer and the ability of the singers." Mozart's finale to Act II, which moves incrementally from a duet to an octet, takes the idea to a magnificent extreme.

THE *REQUIEM*

Mozart received a commission to write a requiem in July 1791, which he accepted, putting it at the bottom of a sizeable in-tray—two operas and his *Clarinet Concerto*. Constanze later said that he became obsessed with the idea that he had been poisoned, and she persuaded him to put it aside. According to Constanze, when he felt better he went back to the *Requiem* but dark thoughts returned and he took to his bed, dying 15 days later. By then he had fully orchestrated the *Requiem Aeternam*, and written vocal parts with bass for all the other movements except the *Lacrimosa* (of which he had completed only eight bars), *Sanctus*, *Benedictus*, and *Agnus Dei*. Constanze asked first Eybler and then Mozart's student Süssmayr to complete the work. There are also reports of a singing-through of various sections on the day of his death, but so many misconceptions have grown up around Mozart's death that such stories should be treated as conjectural. Constanze, who needed the money, sent the work to Count von Walsegg, who had commissioned it for the death of his wife intending to pretend it was by himself.

The age of Mozart

MUSICIANS IN MOZART'S DAY NEGOTIATED A COMPLEX SYSTEM OF PATRONAGE UNDER CHURCH, CITY, STATE, AND EMPIRE. IN AN AGE INFORMED, AT LEAST IN THEORY, BY REASON AND ENLIGHTENMENT VALUES, REFORM CAME BOTH FROM WITHIN, THROUGH ENLIGHTENED "DESPOTS" SUCH AS JOSEPH II, AND FROM WITHOUT THROUGH VIOLENT REVOLUTION.

Mozart's career can be seen to embody the independence, confidence, and aspirations of Enlightenment ideas, while his difficulties in later life and his early death ominously track its demise in the French Revolution of 1789.

Modern readers hearing the story of Mozart being kicked from the chamber by an employee of Count Hieronymus, Archbishop Colloredo may wonder how it was that the ruler of Salzburg was an archbishop. The answer relates to the rather motley systems of

Below An eighteenth-century engraving of a meeting of Freemasons, an all-male organization dedicated to fellowship. There is much symbolism and ceremony associated with lodge meetings.

FREEMASONRY

Freemasonry arose in London with the coming together of four "lodges" in 1717 to found the Grand Lodge of England. It was open to all religions and dedicated to morality, idealism, self-sacrifice, and the helping of others. Although treated with suspicion by many rulers, Joseph II encouraged it as a way of gaining support for reform. However, the movement had its own division. Some lodges, such as the Rosicrucian elements, tended toward the mystical and irrational; others, such as the Order of Illuminati (to which Mozart may have been sympathetic), pursued a rational, enlightenment, and anti-clerical agenda. In 1785, Joseph II enacted a Masonic decree that reorganized the Masonic Lodges and restricted their proliferation. Mozart had been nominated for the "Beneficence" Lodge ("Zur Wohltätigkeit") in 1784. Among the music he wrote for Masonic use is a cantata, *Die Maurerfreude* (*The Mason's Joy*), K. 471, some *Masonic Funeral Music*, K. 477 and songs, although his most detailed exploration of Masonic themes and symbolism is in *Die Zauberflöte* (*The Magic Flute*). The scene where the Queen of the Night mounts an attack on Sarastro's temple and is defeated by the forces of good may refer to an incident in 1743 when the Empress Maria Theresa was persuaded by some Jesuits to order a raid on a Masonic lodge of which her husband was a member.

government that existed under the collection of kingdoms, principalities, and independent cities known as the Holy Roman Empire. This empire had been founded in 800 by the Emperor Charlemagne on his conversion to Christianity, but, despite its name, it was, by Mozart's day, an alliance of German-speaking states north of the Alps, excluding Switzerland. Since the sixteenth century the emperors had been chosen by the Electors of the various states and principalities from the house of Hapsburg, and the archbishop was the Elector for Salzburg, ruler of the principality, and the highest ranking archbishop in the Empire. In addition to the Hapsburg states, the alliance consisted of a number of fiefs, which included the land now occupied by modern Hungary, Poland, Russia, the former Yugoslavia, northern Italy, and Romania. In Mozart's lifetime, the empire was ruled by three emperors and an empress. Maria Theresa reigned from 1740 to 1780, first with her consort Francis I (1740–1765) and then with her son and successor, Joseph II (1765–1790). Joseph then reigned alone (1780–1790) and was succeeded by his brother Leopold II. The empire was dissolved by Napoleon in 1806.

THE REFORMERS

Both Maria Theresa, and her son, Joseph II, were reformers, particularly Joseph II, who has come to represent the ultimate image of the Enlightenment ruler who rules with absolute power in the interests of his people. When ruling together, Maria and Joseph restricted the wealth, power, and abuses of the Church and curtailed frequent church holidays, which were perceived to restrict economic growth. In his own decade of rule, Joseph ended religious discrimination against Protestants, made

educational reforms, banned child labor, established poverty relief, and abolished the death penalty. Of significance for Mozart was his encouragement of free thought and Freemasonry. Enlightenment rulers are depicted several times in Mozart's opera, notably the part of the Pasha Selim (a speaking role) in *The Abduction from the Seraglio* and the character of Titus in *La Clemenza di Tito*. The character of the Count in *The Marriage of Figaro* represents an Enlightenment ruler by his opposite, a hypocrite who espouses progressive values, but retains old privileges, notably *le droit du seigneur*—the male ruler's right to the first night with a girl who married. The latter part of Joseph's rule was marked by reverses in reform, caused by a backlash from landowners, unpopular taxation, the war with Turkey in 1788–1790, and, decisively, the French Revolution.

Left An eighteenth-century engraving showing Mozart at a performance of *The Abduction from the Seraglio* in Berlin in 1789. The character of Pasha Selim represents an Enlightment ruler, possibly Joseph II.

Below During the seventeenth and eighteenth centuries, Salzburg, Mozart's birthplace, became known for its churches and palaces.

PATRONAGE AND THE RISE OF MUSIC PUBLISHING

Left The frontispiece of the *Sonata in C Minor*, Op. 3, by Beethoven. The work was dedicated to Archduke Rudolph of Austria, one of Beethoven's most important patrons.

Haydn, Mozart, and Beethoven all walked the streets of Vienna, met each other, and knew each other's music. Yet their careers were quite different. Haydn enjoyed the security of employment at court. Mozart always hoped for such a position, but was obliged to earn a living as a freelance performer, composer, and teacher. Beethoven was able to live primarily on the generosity of wealthy sponsors.

The different experience of these three composers is not coincidence. It reflects changes caused by a monumental social shift that took place from the middle of the eighteenth century.

Below A concert in a private home. As the eighteenth century progressed, concerts ceased being the privilege of the wealthy and moved much more into the public arena.

THE DECLINE OF ROYAL PATRONAGE

Gradually, aristocratic families throughout Europe were losing money and influence. Rising up to take their place were wealthy businessmen, often of modest, middle-class backgrounds. Paradoxically, although the excesses of the nobility were increasingly seen through hostile eyes, the newly rich strove to model their lifestyles on those of the upper class. As a result, demand

JOHANN PETER SALOMON (1745–1815)

As soon as news of the death of Prince Nicholas Esterházy reached London, German-born impresario Johann Peter Salomon (right) set out on the long journey from his adopted home to Vienna. The man he intended to approach was "Papa Haydn," who was now free of his demanding, music-loving master, and his goal was to tempt the famous composer to London. His gamble paid off. Among other works, the two sets of six "London" symphonies that resulted earned a fortune. In fact, Haydn was able to earn more in a two-year period than in his entire career at the court of Esterháza. Salomon himself made a living not only by bringing international artists to London audiences, of whom Haydn was doubtless his greatest success, but also through his violin playing. His leadership of the famed Salomon string quartet and his solo career soon gave him the credibility he needed to become one of the most important figures in London cultural life.

Haydn spent most of his life composing to the desires of his master, and his contract forbade him to earn through publishing or public concerts until Prince Esterházy agreed to change it. Following this, Haydn was able to capitalize on his already considerable fame and became fabulously rich. By Beethoven's time, court appointments had become the exception. Instead, wealthy middle-class patrons felt honored to support artists of genius, impresarios traveled widely in search of marketable composers and performers, and music publishing became a highly lucrative business.

MUSIC PUBLISHING

As the tides of demand and technological development worked together, musical instruments became cheaper and more accessible. Young ladies often had enough practice time to become highly accomplished pianists. Men usually played instruments such as the violin, or flute, and the sheet music market for sonatas, trios, and quartets blossomed. Professional copyists could no longer keep up with demand, and so more practical printing methods were applied to music. Engraved plates overtook moveable type, which was often unclear and difficult to read, as the principal printing technique. It became possible to produce large numbers of high quality scores, and to distribute them throughout Europe. As all these factors fell into place, music publishers sprang up everywhere. These were able to secure substantial profits, albeit not always entirely honestly.

Fledgling copyright laws made piracy inevitable, and editions produced without the knowledge of the composer abounded. There are also countless examples of lesser composers using more famous names in order to sell their music. Some of the more notable examples include over 200 works bearing Haydn's name, although he did not write them, and approximately 50 works by Giovanni Battista Pergolesi published 15 years after his own death.

for entertainments and refinements such as music lessons, public operas, and concerts increased quite dramatically. Subscription concerts and paid entry to performances became common.

Traditionally, musicians were most likely to find employment as court composers, accompanists, or orchestra members, as well as more secure but lower-paid work as church organists or cantors. They were treated as servants and expected to know their place. Now, secure employment was becoming scarce, but successful musicians were able to earn very well. Mozart, for example, taught a handful of harpsichord or piano students who generally took lessons every day, as well as some composition students. His activities as a concert pianist earned him fantastic amounts of money at the height of his popularity, and commissions for composing music appeared endlessly abundant. However, as his fortune declined, he was unable to find enough employment to support his lifestyle.

Left The cover of an 1814 edition of Mozart's opera *Don Giovanni*. As the music publishing industry grew, the design and illustrations for sheet music became more elaborate.

Ludwig van Beethoven

DECEMBER 16, 1770—MARCH 26, 1827

BEETHOVEN'S MUSIC CAPTURES THE DREAMS, FAILINGS, AND TURBULENCE OF THE
REVOLUTIONARY AGE, BRINGING OUT THE HUMAN ELEMENT IN MUSIC AT A TIME WHEN
INDIVIDUAL RIGHTS WERE EXALTED. FOR SOME, HE LIBERATED MUSIC FROM COURTLY
EIGHTEENTH-CENTURY CONVENTIONS AND OPENED IT TO THE POWER AND AWE OF THE
INFINITE AND THE SUBLIME; FOR OTHERS, HE WAS A UNIVERSAL FIGURE IN THE MOLD
OF SHAKESPEARE OR MICHELANGELO.

Beethoven stood on the cusp between the Classic and Romantic periods, expanding the genres of the former with the assertiveness and individuality of the latter. Few composers since have been unaffected by his achievements.

EARLY LIFE

Beethoven was born in Bonn, a progressive provincial center. Son of a court musician and a palace official's daughter, it was his fate to be one of the first non-operatic composers to work outside of court patronage. When he was 13, his teacher, Christian Gottlob Neefe, suggested he might become a second Mozart, a composer he apparently met in Vienna three years later with the intention of studying with him, but the visit was curtailed by his mother's death. By the time he returned to Vienna in 1792, Mozart was dead, and his patron Count Waldstein famously wrote in his farewell album, "You will receive Mozart's spirit from Haydn's hands." His relationship with Haydn was respectful but not close. Beethoven's early success in Vienna was as a pianist and a bold imaginative improviser. As a composer, Beethoven was not a prodigy like Mozart, and the body of work by which he is known today began in his twenties when he systematically turned his attention to the major genres of his day—the concerto (the first two piano concertos), the piano trio (Op. 1), the piano sonata (Opp. 2, 7, and 10), the string quartet (Op. 18), and the symphony (*Symphony No. 1*).

CRISIS, AND THE HEROIC DECADE

In 1801 Beethoven told his friend, Franz Wegeler, "For the last three years my hearing has become weaker and weaker." The next year, on his doctor's advice, he went to the town of Heiligenstadt, where on October 6 he penned an impassioned testament to his brothers revealing his despair at his deafness, saying that only "art and virtue" saved him from suicide. The music of this period, including the *Piano Sonata No. 14* "Moonlight," *Piano Sonata No. 17* "Tempest," and *Symphony No. 2*, shows innovation and deepening expressive

Below right Some of Beethoven's hearing aids. They were designed by his friend, Johann Nepomuk Maelzel, (1772–1838), inventor of the metronome.

Below A view of the town of Heiligenstadt, near Vienna, where, in October 1802, Beethoven wrote his heartfelt testament lamenting his increasing deafness.

"Music is the mediator between spiritual and sensual life."

power, but there is much music of gentle cheerfulness and subtlety that belies his personal anguish.

The year 1803 ushered in an expansive growth in scope and style that was epoch-making for music history. The works of this "heroic" period include the Third to the Eighth Symphonies, the Fourth and Fifth Piano Concertos, the "Waldstein" and "Appassionata" piano sonatas, the three so-called "Razumovsky" string quartets, the opera *Fidelio* (originally called *Leonore*), the oratorio *Christ on the Mount of Olives*, and the *Mass in C*. The undoubtedly heroic stamp of much of this music can be seen in part as an expression of the spirit of Napoleon, to whom Beethoven initially dedicated his *Symphony No. 3* "Eroica," before defacing the title page in disgust at Napoleon's self-coronation as emperor in December 1804. The heroic aspect also

Below left Beethoven in middle age. He once wrote, "Tones sound, and roar and storm about me until I have set them down in notes."

Below Beethoven conducting one of the three "Razumovsky" Quartets (Op. 59). They were commissioned by Count Andreas Razumovsky, a noted patron of the arts.

has a facet of self-identification, subconsciously representing his inner struggle. Musically, it expanded the scope, scale, and expressive domain of works to an unprecedented level.

In 1809, Napoleon's armies invaded Vienna for the second time, and Beethoven sheltered in his brother's cellar using pillows to protect his hearing. That same year Beethoven was also granted an annuity by three Viennese aristocrats to keep him in Vienna after he considered moving to Paris, and considered marriage, probably proposing (unsuccessfully) to Therese Malfatti. In 1812 he developed a passionate and traumatic attachment to a woman who is only identified as "T" or "A" and, more famously, as the Immortal Beloved in a letter discovered, apparently unsent, among his papers after his death.

Above A pastel by German artist Sigmund Walter Hampel (1868–1949) entitled *Allegory of the Genius of Beethoven*.

Below The frontispiece of Beethoven's Ninth Symphony, dedicated to Friedrich Wilhelm III, the king of Prussia.

Musicologist Maynard Solomon persuasively argued her identity was Antonie Brentano, who was married at the time. Beethoven later dedicated his serene and numinous *Piano Sonata in E*, Op. 109, which ends with a transformative set of variations, to her daughter. Whether caused by these events or not, the music from the period 1809 to 1814 has a new maturity and occasional mellowness that sets it off from the unbridled utopian optimism and assertiveness of heroic works such as the *Symphony No. 5*. Although Beethoven received universal acclaim during 1814, the year of the Congress of Vienna, his productivity eased following the completion and first performances of his Seventh and Eighth Symphonies in 1813 and 1814.

THE LAST DECADE

In 1815, Beethoven's brother Carl died of consumption, appointing his wife, Johanna, and Beethoven joint guardians of his son, Karl. This set the scene for a prolonged and distressing custody battle which revealed dysfunctionality and over-protectiveness on Beethoven's part, which reached a climax with Karl's unsuccessful suicide attempt in 1826. Beethoven's diary from this period reveals a changing sense of spirituality and resignation to fate, incorporating various ancient, Christian, Masonic, and Eastern influences.

From 1818 his creativity returned with the completion of the monumental *Piano Sonata No. 29* "Hammerklavier", Op. 106, and the first sketches for the Ninth Symphony. This ushered in an astonishingly creative final phase that included three piano sonatas (Opp. 109, 110, and 111), the Ninth Symphony, the *Missa Solemnis*, the *Diabelli Variations* for piano, the last five string quartets and several shorter works including the subtle late set of *Bagatelles* for piano, Op. 126. His final quartet ends carries the inscription, *Muß es sein?—Es muß sein!* (*Must it be?—It must be!*), creating an extreme duality in which Beethoven combined metaphysical anguish and light humor.

SYMPHONY NO. 9, OP. 125 (1824)

Beethoven seems to have first tried to set Schiller's famous poem *An die Freude* (*To Joy*) in his twenties although only sketches survive. In taking it up again in 1818, he began a six-year project interrupted by five other major works. Reports of the first performance in 1824 mix respect for Beethoven with enthusiasm and bewilderment for a work that tested some performers beyond their ability. The symphony's opening is an utterly original gesture much imitated later: A low eternal vibration swells alarmingly as soon as we become aware of it. The timpani strokes of the second movement, the *Scherzo*, brought spontaneous applause at the first performance, and at either the end of this movement, or at the end of the piece (accounts differ), the contralto, Caroline Unger, gently turned the composer around to see the applause that he could not hear. After an expanded set of variations on two themes (a form developed by Haydn) for the slow movement, the famous choral finale is a four-movement cantata in its own right. Beethoven struggled with how to achieve the change of tone from instrumental to vocal music and at one point considered two finales, eventually choosing to recall fragments of earlier movements before dismissing them theatrically: "Oh Freunde, nicht diese Töne" ("Friends, not these tones"). One report states that Beethoven collapsed when he saw how small the box office takings were.

Right This nineteenth-century engraving gives us an idea of the size of Beethoven's funeral in 1827. Thousands came to pay their respects to one of Germany's greatest composers.

STRING QUARTET IN C SHARP MINOR, OP. 131

Beethoven was initially commissioned to write three string quartets for the Russian Prince Galitzin, and after finishing the third of these, the *Quartet in B flat*, Op. 130, he continued with a further two, in an inspired flow of creative momentum just before his death. The quartets for Galitzin had grown in scale and number of movements and the *Quartet in C sharp minor*, Op. 131, composed during the first half of 1826, continues this process. On the final manuscript Beethoven numbered seven movements although the numbers may have been intended ironically. He had taken offence at his publisher who, after a throwaway line from Beethoven, "patched together from this and that," had questioned whether the work was new or just a reworking. Since Beethoven had just completed what he regarded as his greatest quartet, he did not try to conceal his annoyance. However, if the first two movements are taken as a pair, and the short third and sixth movements are seen for what they are—transitional passages—then a four-movement shape can be seen lurking behind the extended form. The deeply spiritual slow opening fugue was written immediately after the *Grosse-Fuge*, which had originally been the finale of the previous quartet in B flat, but its pained expressiveness could not be more different. Schubert asked to hear the work during his final illness, a request granted five days before his death in 1828. Beethoven's friend Karl Holz observed, "The King of Harmony has sent the King of Song a friendly bidding to the crossing."

LIFE & TIMES

The Classical Age

"WE ARE HAVING VERY HOT WEATHER HERE; AND THE VIENNESE ARE AFRAID THAT SOON THEY WILL NOT BE ABLE TO GET ANY MORE ICE CREAM. FOR, AS THE WINTER WAS SO MILD, ICE IS SCARCE. HERE VARIOUS IMPORTANT PEOPLE HAVE BEEN LOCKED UP; IT IS SAID THAT A REVOLUTION WAS ABOUT TO BREAK OUT, BUT I BELIEVE THAT SO LONG AS AN AUSTRIAN CAN GET HIS BROWN ALE AND HIS LITTLE SAUSAGES, HE IS NOT LIKELY TO REVOLT."

(Beethoven, in a 1794 letter, translated by Emily Anderson.)

Beethoven lived through revolution, war, invasion, inflation, victory, disillusion, and state-sponsored repression. His life spanned some of the most turbulent times in modern European history. When he was born, Europe comprised hundreds of small states, loosely united by the 1000-year-old Holy Roman Empire. When he died the empire had been conquered along with its conqueror, Napoleon, and power in Europe shifted increasingly to the rising middle class.

Beethoven moved to Vienna in 1792, as the era of Enlightenment reform under Emperor Joseph II, and

Right The coronation of Napoleon as emperor in the Cathedral of Notre Dame in Paris in 1804. After Napoleon's downfall in 1815, he spent the rest of his life in exile on the island of St Helena.

his brother, Leopold, was coming to a close. After the 1776 American Revolution, and the 1789 French Revolution, the new emperor, Franz, felt growing alarm about rising revolutionary activity. Following the rise of Napoleon, Austria was a central partner in anti-French coalitions and suffered a series of defeats in the Revolutionary and Napoleonic wars, notably in Marengo in 1800 and at Austerlitz in 1805 in a campaign that saw Napoleon occupy Vienna for the first time. After the second occupation in 1809, Napoleon's power reached its zenith around 1811, before his disastrous decision to invade Russia in 1812.

THE CONGRESS OF VIENNA

After Napoleon's initial capture in 1814, Vienna hosted the Congress of Vienna, an international peace conference, chaired by Metternich, the Viennese statesman, in which an estimated 10,000 foreign officials visited the city. Beethoven honored the occasion with a cantata, *Der Glorreich Augenblick* (*The Glorious Moment*), and a revised version of his "rescue" opera, *Fidelio*, depicting the triumph of freedom and love over tyranny through the idealized heroine, Leonore. Now greeted enthusiastically by Napoleon's conquerors, its first performance in 1805 had been before Napoleon's generals. The Congress continued even after Napoleon escaped from imprisonment on Elba to raise an army in the so-called Hundred Days, before his final defeat at Waterloo in June 1815. After the Congress, Vienna was left in a weakened state, politically and economically, leading to a repressive, security-conscious phase in Austrian life, closely watched by secret police from whose gaze neither Beethoven nor Schubert were immune.

A LONGING FOR THE INFINITE AND THE SUBLIME

Although Beethoven's music stands powerfully at the join between the eighteenth century's Age of Reason and the Romantic Age, it is simplistic to see his music as the step from the Enlightenment to Romanticism. A powerful stylistic thread unites the music of the period's four giants—Haydn, Mozart, Beethoven, and Schubert—creating a truly Classical Age that cuts across such style divisions. The music of all four is governed by "the Sonata Principle" in which music

Left The Congress of Vienna convened in order to settle country boundaries and various political issues that arose out of the French Revolutionary and Napoleonic wars.

of diverse genres—symphony, sonata, quartet, minuet, song, and opera—is structured around juxtaposing ideas in a home key, with contrasting ideas in a secondary key, and then working through these in a dialectical manner. Although today this is called the Classical Style, after Charles Rosen's foundational book of that title and in contrast to the ensuing Romantic period, writer E.T.A. Hoffmann characterized Haydn, Mozart, and Beethoven as Romantic composers whose essence lay in a "yearning towards the infinite."

Another key concept was the "sublime," which was introduced in Edmund Burke's *A Philosophical Enquiry into the Origin of our Ideas of the Sublime and the Beautiful* (1857). The growing appeal of the concepts of awe and the infinite in this turbulent age elevated the prestige of music, as seen in shifting views of the sonata, a piece "sounded" on instruments, as opposed to a cantata which was sung. In a famous quip from the mid-eighteenth century, "Sonate, que me veux tu?" ("Sonata, what do you want of me?"), Fontenelle

Below Jean-Jacques Rousseau (1712–1778) was one of the Enlightenment's most interesting philosophers. He wrote extensively on politics, education, and literature, and had a deep interest in, and knowledge of, music theory.

expressed chic contempt for its complexity, which philosopher Jean-Jacques Rousseau quoted approvingly when putting the case for opera and folk song as a musical ideal. In doing so he expressed the Enlightenment view that the role of art was the imitation of nature. Music's capacity to imitate is relatively feeble, and Kant, the dominant philosopher of the age, saw music as lower than the other arts, though he acknowledged its power on the emotions. By the time of Beethoven's death, the sonata, and its associated instrumental forms, had acquired unprecedented prestige on account of its capacity to express, in Hoffmann's words, "that endless longing which is the essence of Romanticism."

ALLA TURCA: ARABIC INFLUENCES ON WESTERN CLASSICAL MUSIC

Many musical parodies and references to other cultures within Classical music are sometimes completely lost on modern audiences who are removed by time and cultural differences. One of the most popular incorporations of musical references within Classical music was that of the Turkish marching band, also known as the *mehter*. This fashion reflected Western culture's preoccupation at the time with all things Turkish, a fascination that was particularly notable in Vienna.

THE MEHTER

The mehter was the band that accompanied the celebrated Janissary soldiers. The Janissary was part of the Ottoman Empire's military, and was formed from the bodyguards of the sultan's household.

Above Western society was fascinated by the exoticism of the Ottoman Empire. The clothing, furnishings, cuisine, and music of Turkey inspired artists and composers to incorporate facets of the culture into their work.

Janissary means "new soldiers," as the original corps established in the fourteenth century was made up of Christian slaves. Janissary soldiers were expected to practice celibacy and convert to Islam; they were recognizable by uniform, and as beards were forbidden, are often portrayed with lavish horizontal moustaches. In historical records, there are depictions of the mehter playing while the Janissary fought battles. During the 1600s, the Ottomans mounted an unsuccessful attack on Vienna. Following this loss, the Ottomans no longer represented a threat to Westerners; rather they were seen as "exotic others." Composers including Haydn, Mozart, and Beethoven often referred to the mehter or to aspects of Turkish culture in their works, either through musical devices, instrumentation, or operatic plots. For the audience of the day, all things Turkish were fascinating and barbaric, yet at the same time colorful and mysterious.

FEATURES OF THE MUSIC

There are many famous examples of references to Turkish music, such as Haydn's *Symphony No. 100* "Military" and the final movement of Beethoven's *Symphony No. 9*. Musical devices that define these references are related to the mehter style rather than being direct citations of Turkish melodies. One of the most notable features of the mehter was its simple duple meter (2/4), divided into an "oom-pah" pulse, with a low pitch on the first beat, and a higher pitch on the off beats. This style was just perfect for accompanying marching Janissary soldiers. Another notable feature was the texture and instrumentation of the mehter; instantly recognizable, it consisted mostly of percussive instruments such as the large bass drum or davel, and small cymbals, contrasted against high-pitched reed instruments like the zurna. The melodies were rhythmically fast, played monophonically, double octaves apart, and decorated with ornaments. These melodies often started out with three repeated notes at the pulse of the bass ostinato and regularly used the

Left A mounted mehter, a military band that accompanied the Janissary, or Ottoman soldiers, to battle. The Janissaries marched to the music of the mehter.

MOZART'S *RONDO ALLA TURCA*

The way that Turkish features were incorporated into Classical music is best seen in Mozart's *Rondo Alla Turca* (the third movement of his *Piano Sonata in A*, K. 331). The movement begins with ornamented melodic turns in a high register suggestive of a zurna-styled melody. An "oom-pah" bass throughout most of the movement refers to the mehter marching style. Rolled chords spread out over an octave punctuate the melodic line giving the impression of small percussive instruments. The tonality of the whole movement switches from A minor to A major, then down a third to the relative minor, back to A major, reminiscent of the changing modalities of mehter music.

Left A procession of musicians during celebrations given by a sultan, c. 1600. As well as percussion instruments, they played a range of stringed instruments including a baglama (left), which resembles a lute.

(1782) depicted fantasies associated by Westeners with Turkish or Arabic culture. Often the depictions incorporated the Western fascination with the harems. Such scenes or plots in operas called for suitable music to assist with these depictions. Sometimes the only reference needed to indicate the "exotic" to the listener was the tinkle of a small cymbal, or the sounding of any other Arabic instrument.

Over time, the inclusion of Arabic instruments became more common and more prevalent. Percussive instruments typical of the mehter became part of the percussion family within the orchestra—cymbals and bass drums of Arabic origin now regularly feature in symphonic works today. The modern day military marching band also incorporates instrumentation and practices that can be linked back to the mehter. One peculiar and short-lasting impact of Turkish music on Western Classical music was the development of the Turkish stop for the fortepiano. This was a stop that had allowed a percussive instrument (attached to the fortepiano) to be played. This fashion did not survive the technological developments of the piano.

The impact of the Western audiences' fascination with exotic Turkish culture has lasted to the current day. The instrumentation of orchestras, marching bands, and to a much lesser extent, mehter-styled works have continued to feature in Western Classical and community music.

interval of the third. Often tonality in these pieces seemed to jump between major and minor modalities, as well as between extremes in dynamics.

Operatic plots including Gluck's *La rencontre imprévue* (1763) and Mozart's *The Abduction from the Seraglio*

Im Auftrage Conr. Graf's

THE ROMANTIC PERIOD
c. 1800 ~ 1890

Introduction

FRAMED BY THE WORLD-CHANGING EVENTS OF THE FRENCH
REVOLUTION AND NAPOLEON'S DEFEAT AT ITS START AND
THE SEEDS OF WORLD WAR I AT ITS CLOSE, THE NINETEENTH
CENTURY WAS A TIME OF GROWTH AND PROSPERITY, THE
ESTABLISHING OF CIVIL RIGHTS AND BOURGEOIS VALUES.

With the introduction of the steam engine came a rapid industrialization of manufacturing and a revolution in transportation. The second half of the period also saw the introduction of electricity, sound recording, and the telephone, to mention but the most striking changes affecting everyday life. Rural people were lured to fast-growing cities due to increased employment, education, and entertainment opportunities. Medieval towns were redesigned to cope with the influx, their walls giving way to boulevards, their wastelands to pleasure parks. Large sums of public money were spent on better sanitation, the building of museums, concert halls and opera theaters, universities and conservatoires, and public transportation. Civil societies sprang up everywhere to preserve and disseminate cultural and artistic artefacts. Every major city established its own symphonic orchestra and historic houses trusts, publishers produced complete editions of old masters' works, and artists raised funds to help the poor or other civil causes.

The spirit of the age was like that of an adolescent, full of conflicting dualities and aborted idealism. Advances in science went hand in hand with a fascination with the irrational and morbid; the ideal of universalism did not hinder burgeoning nationalism and a delight in exoticism leading to primitivism and racism. While cities were growing and mankind was regarded the conqueror of the elements, a "back to nature" movement idealized country life—at times picturesque, simple, and protective, at times awesome, wild, and terrifying—and preached a mystical kinship between the artist's inner life and nature. Musically, dualism also manifested in the contrast of small-scale chamber or salon music for a circle of intimate friends and grandiose virtuosity displayed in ever larger halls. The lone, heroic figure of the artist-

Right The development of steam locomotives, such as this one pictured in the Hauptstrasse in Vienna in the nineteenth century, revolutionized transportation.

Below Le Sillon was an artistic movement of the late nineteenth century. The poster was created by Fernand Toussaint.

Previous pages Liszt plays piano for George Sand, Alexandre Dumas, Victor Hugo, Paganini, Rossini, and Liszt's mistress Marie d'Agoult. A portrait of Lord Byron and a bust of Beethoven complete this classic Romantic image.

composer struggling against a hostile environment was dramatized in popular concertos which tended to end triumphantly, underscoring the age's optimism. Art became a substitute for religion and the artist the high priest who, through his own suffering, showed others the deeper meaning of life.

While in its exultation of subjective feeling the first half of the period was a reaction to the eighteenth century's emphasis on reasoning based on observation, the second half moved towards naturalism and realism, capturing it in its full emotional charge rather than from a classicizing distance. There was also an extraordinary mutual fertilization of the various art forms. Composers were avid readers and often published authors (Berlioz, Liszt, Wagner), while poets and other literary figures (such as E.T.A. Hoffmann) frequently tried their hand at composing.

Romanticism was obsessed with individuality and originality, the endless pursuit of the unattainable, strangeness, and the mystical. Music was regarded the highest form of art because of its ability to express the inexpressible, to communicate feelings from soul to soul without the interference of words. Yet words and extra-musical meaning played a very important part in most Romantic compositions. Opera remained popular throughout the century. More significantly, the Lied or art song became the quintessential Romantic genre unifying poetry and music at a new level of expressive intensity. Even purely instrumental music was influenced by contemporary issues, whether it was poetry,

landscape, historic event, or a personal feeling; pieces carried titles that referred to extra-musical matters, giving new impetus to program music.

Because of the emphasis on originality, classical forms and genres were adapted to suit the expressive content so highly prized; they either shrank or became grossly enlarged. The miniature character piece or fragment was as popular early in the century as toward the end, some barely lasting a minute. At the other extreme were Berlioz's and Wagner's dramatic works or the symphonies of Bruckner and Mahler, stretching the classical type to colossal proportions. To further enhance originality and expression, harmonic vocabulary and the choice of instruments were also expanded

considerably. Orchestral color and instrumental timbre became as important as the balance of form had been during the Classical era. While music was supposed to speak in a clearly structured manner, now it was to paint in magnificent color to awaken the listener's innermost feelings.

Although a select few composers strove to uphold Classical ideals, by and large the Romantic period indulged in constantly seeking something new. Thus it steadily paved the way for the radical changes that occurred during the first two decades of the twentieth century when Western tonal music as it had been practiced since the seventeenth century came to an end.

Above left The Romantic era was known for the development of Lied, or art song, where a poem was set to music for solo voice and piano.
Below As the nineteenth century progressed, fashionable Parisians tended to meet in cafés and parks, where they could take some refreshment while listening to some of the latest musical offerings.

Nicolò Paganini

OCTOBER 27, 1782–MAY 27, 1840

AS THE LEADING VIOLINIST OF HIS TIME, PAGANINI THRILLED AUDIENCES THROUGHOUT ITALY AND THEN EUROPE WITH HIS VIOLIN WIZARDRY, BEFORE ILLNESS AND SCANDAL ENDED HIS CAREER. WHILE HIS VIOLIN COMPOSITIONS, INCLUDING THE *24 CAPRICES FOR SOLO VIOLIN*, ARE OFTEN DISCOUNTED AS MERE SHOWPIECES, THEY STRONGLY INFLUENCED THE FIRST GENERATION OF ROMANTIC COMPOSERS, INCLUDING FRANZ LISZT AND JOHANNES BRAHMS.

Paganini's rise from modest beginnings in Genoa, Italy, where his father taught him violin and composition, was fast. At 12 he was sent to distinguished violinist Alessandro Rolla (1757–1841) for lessons, but Rolla declared that there was nothing to teach him. Paganini then studied composition in Parma with Ferdinando Päer (1771–1839). He landed his first job, at 18, as the first violinist of an orchestra in the Tuscan republic of Lucca.

Paganini soon left his post there to begin a solo career, and having achieved considerable fame in Genoa and Parma, in 1813 he attracted an even wider audience with a stunning performance at Milan's La Scala opera house. But illness prevented him from leaving Italy to capitalize on his success, and he did not perform abroad until 1828, when he gave some acclaimed concerts in Vienna. He became a celebrity, not least for his unique stage presence; further triumphs followed in Germany, Paris, and London.

Above Paganini was considered a child prodigy when he quickly outpaced his early violin teachers. This portrait was painted by Giovanni Pezzotti (1839–1911).

Discover the music

24 Caprices for Solo Violin, Op. 1 (1812–1817)
Violin Concerto No. 2, Op. 7, "Little Bell" (1826)
Moto Perpetuo in C, Op. 11
Centone di Sonate, for violin and guitar, Op. 64

COMPOSITIONS AND COLLABORATIONS

Throughout his career, Paganini continued composing, adapting the works of popular composers and writing concertos and other solo works with which to dazzle his public. He met some of the foremost composers of his generation, including charismatic French composer Hector Berlioz, from whom he commissioned a viola concerto, *Harold in Italy*. But he never played it— Berlioz reported in his *Mémoires* that the virtuoso had complained, "That's no good. There's not enough for me to do there. I should be playing all the time."

SICKNESS, SCANDAL, AND DEATH

Paganini's well-known womanizing ways eventually caught up with him. He contracted syphilis, and was poisoned by the mercury used to treat the disease. He

PAGANINI IN CONCERT

Paganini had a stunning violin technique, but audiences were also fascinated by his appearance. Prone to illness from an early age, Nicolò Paganini had an emaciated look that reinforced the popular belief that his talent was demonic. According to the critic Sacheverell Sitwell, "He was so thin that he seemed tall, and so dark that even his haggard features left him ageless. His body was completely fleshless and his limbs were mere bones, everything being sacrificed, so it seemed, for his long hands and talon-like fingers." The combination of Paganini's bizarre appearance and his supernatural playing strongly affected his audiences. After a concert in London, so the story goes, 300 people were admitted to hospital with "over-enchantment." The legend of the romantic virtuoso, continued by Liszt in the 1840s, was born.

retired from the concert stage around 1834, but despite poor health, he did not rest—his late ventures included the directorship of the Teatro Ducale in Parma, and, in Paris, the building of Casino Paganini, a kind of gambler's resort, in which he lost much of the fortune he had amassed in his years of performing. In 1840, Paganini died from throat cancer.

PAGANINI'S INFLUENCE

Paganini was generous to his fellow composers—one of his last acts was to give Berlioz enough money to write *Romeo and Juliet*, one of his finest works. Paganini's compositions also inspired other composers, including Liszt, Brahms, and Rachmaninov. Paganini's influence on violin technique was also considerable. He popularized such techniques as double-stop harmonics (playing two notes together to create a high-pitched, ethereal tone) and left-hand pizzicato. (Pizzicato is plucking the string. This is normally done with the right hand, but when executed with the left hand the right hand can continue bowing.) These techniques, considered almost impossible in Paganini's time, are now commonplace in violin playing.

Violin

Immediately associated with classical music and with the virtuoso Paganini (whose violin is shown), the violin emerged in Italy in the early 1500s. It has four strings (G, D, A, E) and a range of over four octaves. Among the violin's characteristics are its singing tone and lyrical qualities. It is a pivotal member of the orchestra, which usually has around 30 violins in the string section. Construction is critical if the desired tone is to be achieved. Famous violin-makers, such as Andrea Amati (1525–1611), Giuseppe Guarneri (1666–1739), and Antonio Stradivari (c. 1644–1737) crafted violins that are still in use today.

Gioachino Rossini

FEBRUARY 27, 1792–NOVEMBER 13, 1868

GIOACHINO ROSSINI HAD A CHARMED CAREER, FROM SUCCESS AS A BOY SINGER, THROUGH TO THE TRIUMPH OF HIS COMIC OPERA *THE BARBER OF SEVILLE* IN 1816, AND PARTIAL RETIREMENT AT AGE 37. HIS GIFT FOR MELODY, COMBINED WITH A DISTINCTLY ITALIAN RHYTHMIC VIVACITY, HAS ENSURED HIS ENDURING POPULARITY, AND HIS OPERAS EXERTED ENORMOUS INFLUENCE ON HIS COMPATRIOTS BELLINI, DONIZETTI, AND VERDI.

Rossini was born into theater life, touring around Italy with his musician parents from infancy. He studied horn, keyboard, and singing, his talent for the latter gaining him admission to Bologna's prestigious Accademia Filarmonica at age 14. He started composing early—at 11, he wrote his first work, a set of violin sonatas; his first opera, the farce *The Bill of Marriage* (*La cambiale di matrimonio*), came 10 years later. This was his first commission, and many more were to follow, including the heroic opera *Tancredi*, and *The Italian Girl in Algiers* (*L'Italiana in Algeri*, both 1813).

Above right In his later years, Rossini loved to cook, and even compiled a recipe book. Not for general circulation, it was distributed among his closest friends.

SUCCESS

From 1815, Rossini found himself in an enviable, if hectic, situation, when he was appointed director of two Naples theaters, San Carlo and Fondo. Both appointments required him to compose an opera a year, and this period of enforced productivity led to one of his early masterpieces, *Othello* (1816). He also found time to fulfill two commissions from Rome, one of which was *The Barber of Seville*, based on the controversial play by Beaumarchais. The première was disrupted by angry fans of the composer Giovanni Paisiello (1740–1816), who had also set the play, but the quality of *The Barber of Seville*, originally entitled *Almaviva* after the play's naughty count, won through, and it soon received the popularity it deserved.

Rossini left his Neapolitan posts in 1822, and traveled extensively, to Vienna, Paris, and London, where he signed up for his next post, music director of Paris's Théâtre-Italien. Highlights from this period include the comic *Journey to Reims*, a minor masterpiece written to celebrate the coronation of Charles X in 1825, and his last opera, *William Tell* (1829), about

ROSSINI'S INNOVATIONS

Rossini was more than simply a popular opera composer, he was an important innovator. One of his compositional devices is known as the "Rossini crescendo." A crescendo is a gradual increase in volume, though musicians joke that it actually means "quiet," as it is difficult to increase volume if you are already playing (or singing) loudly. Rossini created his crescendos in a unique way—by starting a simple rhythmic pattern on just a few instruments, then gradually adding more instruments to build up a bustling wall of sound. Another innovation, though not Rossini's alone, was in the scoring of vocal parts. Previously, singers "ornamented" their lines by adding additional notes above and below the melody. This showed their virtuosity, and audiences loved it. Composers also liked to add some ornamentation, but performers often went overboard, and the melody—and the composer's intentions—would be lost under a pile of additional notes. Rossini, however, started to write out his own ornaments, forcing singers to respect his wishes.

Discover the music

6 String Sonatas (1804)
The Barber of Seville (1816)
Semiramide (1823)
William Tell (1829)
Stabat Mater (1842)

Left An autograph score of *The Barber of Seville*, showing the start of Figaro's first song "Largo al factotum." The repeated word "Figaro, Figaro, Figaro" is one of opera's most well-known arias.

which Donizetti gushed, "Rossini wrote the first and last acts of *William Tell*. God wrote the second act."

END OF CAREER

In 1829, Rossini returned to Bologna. His mother had died, and he wanted to spend time with his father, but in the meantime King Charles X was overthrown by the July 1830 revolution, and Rossini was forced to fight for the annuity the monarch had given him. After returning to Paris, he continued to collaborate with the Théâtre-Italien; his *Stabat Mater*, perhaps his most significant non-operatic work, premièred there in 1843.

Rossini spent the last 13 years of his life in relative seclusion in his homes in Paris and Passy, indulging his love of cooking and entertaining distinguished musicians. He died, aged 76, and was mourned at memorial services in France and Italy.

Cor anglais

Part of the oboe family, the sound of a cor anglais is produced by blowing through a double reed. French for "English horn"—although it is neither English nor a horn—it is said that at one point in its history it resembled the oboe da caccia, a Baroque instrument that was either curved or bent, thus producing the name "cor angle" (later becoming cor anglais). Similarly to the oboe d'amore, the cor anglais has a bocal—a curved, tapered tube mouthpiece with the reed attached at the end. You can hear the distinctive tone of this instrument in Rossini's *William Tell*.

Below Artists of the English National Opera bring to life the colorful characters of Rossini's *The Barber of Seville* at the London Coliseum in September 2008.

Italy under Napoleonic rule

THROUGHOUT ITS HISTORY, ITALY WAS OFTEN UNDER FOREIGN RULE, AND WHEN THE YOUNG GENERAL NAPOLEON BONAPARTE INVADED IN 1796, HE WAS OBLIGED TO EXPEL THE PRESIDING POWER, THE HAPSBURGS. WHILE AUSTRIAN RULE RESUMED UPON NAPOLEON'S ABDICATION IN 1814, THE FRENCH REVOLUTION AND THE UNIFYING LAWS IMPOSED DURING THE SUBSEQUENT OCCUPATION HAD A LASTING EFFECT ON THE ITALIAN PENINSULA—IN 1861, ITALY WAS UNITED

Italy, time of Napoleon
- Italian territory taken by Napoleon (c. 1797)
- ★ Birthplace of Nicolò Paganini
- ☆ Birthplace of Gioachino Rossini

Napoleon invaded Italy with his own Army of Italy in 1796. They made rapid progress, capturing Sardinia, Milan, and the Veneto (the region of Italy containing Venice). Reactions to Napoleon's arrival were mixed: Milan welcomed him, but the army's aggressive tactics, including the seizure of assets, enraged the populace, who staged a revolt. It was quickly put down. In 1802, Napoleon declared an Italian Republic in the lands he had conquered; then, after proclaiming himself Emperor of France in 1804, created the Kingdom of Italy. This included, among other centers, Milan and Venice, the former being made the capital. The rest of Italy became part of the French Empire. The disadvantages of French rule in Italy were many—conscription was introduced, censorship was severe, and excessive taxes resulted in mass poverty. To add insult to injury, many great Italian art

Above right Napoleon arriving, in regal style, in Venice in November 1807. Among his plans for the city were the construction of a large botanic garden.

works were removed and taken to Paris's Louvre Gallery.

BENEFITS OF FRENCH OCCUPATION

French rule did, however, provide some benefits. The French Revolution and the overthrow of King Louis XVI in 1789, both significant events in the lead-up to Napoleon's invasion, met with approval in Italy, and secret societies formed that espoused the formation of Italian republics. Napoleon himself created republics from parts of Italian lands taken from the Hapsburgs, though he did give the ancient Venetian republic to the Austrians in return for part of Belgium. Throughout Italy the Code Napoléon was adopted. The Code was not perfect—it was undeniably sexist and also disadvantaged the workers—but it was clearly written, thus more easily understood by the people, and above all, uniformly applied. The Italians now also shared a currency and an army. Not surprisingly, the idea of unity without foreign control took root.

RESTORATION

France's occupation of Italy was short-lived. After years of successful warmongering, Napoleon was forced to abdicate in 1814; the acceptance he had received in Italy had already dwindled after significant losses of Italian soldiers during his disastrous Russian campaign. In 1815, Europe was re-divided at the Congress of Vienna, and much of Italy was returned to Austrian rule. The old leaders were reinstated, and a period of restoration began. Nonetheless, certain figures and groups began agitating for Italy's unification. This

> *"Music is the voice that tells us that the human race is greater than it knows."*
>
> NAPOLEON

movement was called the Risorgimento, a term coined by the writer Vittorio Alfieri (1749–1803), who predicted that Italy would eventually be free from foreign control. The Risorgimento had two main objectives—to unite Italy, and to revive Italian culture. There were many advocates for unification, the best known of whom were the secret society, the Carbonari ("coal-burners"), which was severely repressed by the Austrian rulers; and the patriot Giuseppe Mazzini (1805–1872). In the 1820s, the Duke of Modena encouraged the Carbonari, but then turned against them, executing their leader, Ciro Menotti, in 1831. The story of the Risorgimento is continued on pages 198–199.

Below A poster from 1834 for Bellini's *Norma* at Milan's La Scala opera house.

ITALIAN OPERA UNDER NAPOLEON

Napoleon loved Italian opera, and went to the theater often. He shared this passion with many Italians; there were opera houses in even the smallest Italian towns. Accordingly, the greatest composers to emerge from nineteenth-century Italy were masters of opera, including Gioachino Rossini, who achieved unparalleled success in Paris; Vincenzo Bellini (1801–1835), whose opera *Norma* (1831) is still regularly performed; Gaetano Donizetti (1797–1848), among whose wonderful operas are *L'Elisir d'Amore* (1832) and *Lucia di Lamermoor* (1835); and Giuseppe Verdi (see pages 196–197), to name just a few. Opera was one of Italy's main artistic exports, and was especially popular in Paris, where there had been an Italian theater since the seventeenth century. Opera productions were subsidized by the government, and censorship was tough. And while the Italian public loved to monitor the performances of favorite singers, openly declaring their critiques mid-performance, the government also used the opera house for surveillance of the educated classes who gathered there.

Franz Schubert

JANUARY 31, 1797–NOVEMBER 19, 1828

FRANZ SCHUBERT WAS IN MANY WAYS THE ANTITHESIS OF A ROMANTIC COMPOSER—HE
WAS NOT A VIRTUOSO, SHUNNED THE SPOTLIGHT, AND RARELY VENTURED AWAY FROM HIS
NATIVE VIENNA. IN HIS 31 YEARS, HE QUIETLY CREATED ONE OF THE LARGEST AND MOST
VARIED OEUVRES OF ANY COMPOSER, CONCENTRATING ON CLASSICAL GENRES LIKE THE
STRING QUARTET, SYMPHONY, AND, PERHAPS MOST FAMOUSLY, THE ART SONG—LIED.

Schubert's origins were equally atypical of a great composer. Born in a Viennese suburb to a school assistant father and servant mother, he did not start serious musical tuition until 11, when he enrolled in the Imperial College, a religious seminary. He left the seminary at 16 to become a teacher, but did not give up composition, far from it—his output from 1813 to 1816 included five symphonies, four masses, three string quartets, and hundreds of Lieder, including the Goethe-inspired *Gretchen at the Spinning Wheel* (1814) and *Der Erlkönig* (*The Erl-King*) (1815), heralding a new approach to this old genre (see pages 180–181).

Above Franz Schubert's almost 1,000 works are usually listed with a "D" number. The "D" refers to Otto Deutsch, who cataloged Schubert's works chronologically by composition date.

A NEW FREEDOM

The year 1816 was a watershed year for Schubert. He had an ill-fated love affair, probably his first and last, with soprano Therese Grob, and abandoned teaching to live and compose in the center of Vienna with a friend, Franz von Schober. There he made some important contacts, including the well-known baritone Johann Michael Vogl, and in 1818 he left Austria for the first time to tutor the offspring of Count Esterházy in Zseliz, Hungary.

More great songs, including *To Music* and *Die Forelle* (*The Trout*), date from this period, as does the *Quintet in A for piano and strings*, based

Left Therese Grob was the love of Schubert's life. He entertained hopes of marriage, but his poor financial position made this an impossible dream.

on the catchy, burbling theme of *The Trout*. In contrast to the previous three years, Schubert's fortunes from 1820 to 1823 were mixed.

There were numerous failed operas—Schubert's gift for vocal settings did not translate into staged drama—and in 1822 he became sick, most likely with syphilis. This illness may have inspired one of his best known works, his eighth symphony, which is known as the "Unfinished." Symphonies usually comprise four movements, but Schubert only finished the first two, though there is a theory that the incidental music he wrote for a play formed a third.

ACHIEVING GREATNESS

Schubert's final three years produced some masterpieces, from the majesty of the *Symphony No. 9* "Great" (1825), to the intimate *Fantasy in F minor* for piano duet and the *String Quintet in C* (both 1828). Two late song cycles, *Die schöne Müllerin* (*The Beautiful Girl at the Mill*, 1823) and *Winterreise* (*Winter Journey*, 1827), based on poems by Wilhelm Müller, also rate among the composer's greatest works; they are certainly some of his most personal ones.

Schubert died in 1828, possibly from typhoid. He was buried, as he requested, next to Beethoven. But,

---

Discover the music

Der Erlkönig (1815)

Piano Quintet in A "Trout", D. 667 (1819)

Fantasie in C major "Wanderer", D. 760 (1822)

6 Musical Moments, D. 780 (1823–1828)

Die schöne Müllerin, D. 795 (1823)

Symphony No. 8 "Unfinished", D. 759 (1825)

String Quintet in C, D. 956 (1828)

"When I wished to sing of love, it turned to sorrow. And when I wished to sing of sorrow, it was transformed for me into love."

SCHUBERT'S CIRCLE

While Schubert's great musical contemporary Beethoven revolutionized the role of the artist in society, accepting commissions from nobility while turning his nose up at the notion of a regular patron, he was not a typical Viennese artist. Schubert, who died just one year after Beethoven, was more so. His friends were not nobility, but other artists of the middle class—poets, dramatists, and painters. They often gathered for readings, dancing, and performances of Schubert's works, which were known as "Schubertiades." But Schubert's companions were not completely innocuous types; many of them, despite holding comfortable public service jobs, espoused political freedom in Metternich's oppressive regime (see pages 178–179). They met in secret societies, a dangerous habit which led to Johann Senn, Schubert's schoolmate, and Schubert himself being arrested by Metternich's secret police in 1820. Schubert was later released without charge.

as musicologist Donald Tovey noted, he was scarcely known. In an 1827 English musical dictionary, Tovey found a long article on Beethoven, who died that year, but though five Schuberts were recorded in the same dictionary, Franz did not rate a mention. Schubert's friend, writer Franz Grillparzer, did the composer more honor with the epitaph: "The art of music here entombed a rich possession, but even far fairer hopes."

Below Schubert rehearses a musical serenade with his friends. These convivial gatherings came to be known as Schubertiades.

Fanny Mendelssohn-Hensel

NOVEMBER 14, 1805–MAY 14, 1847

WHEN SHE WAS 15, FANNY MENDELSSOHN'S FATHER ABRAHAM WROTE TO HER: "MUSIC … WILL ALWAYS REMAIN AN ORNAMENT, AND NEVER THE FOUNDATION OF YOUR EXISTENCE AND DAILY LIFE." THOUGH ABRAHAM HAD FOSTERED HER, AND HER BROTHER FELIX'S, PRODIGIOUS MUSICAL TALENTS IN CHILDHOOD, ONCE FANNY REACHED ADOLESCENCE SHE WAS PREPARED FOR HER TRUE ROLE IN LIFE—HOUSEWIFE—WHILE FELIX WAS ENCOURAGED TO CONTINUE HIS MUSICAL CAREER.

At the time this attitude was very much the norm. In fact, Fanny Mendelssohn was lucky to have her gifts recognized at all. Her father was a banker and son of the philosopher Moses Mendelssohn; her mother Lea was a granddaughter of a renowned entrepreneur. While her origins were Jewish, Fanny and her three siblings were brought up as Christians. In 1811 they moved from Hamburg to Berlin, where they received the best tuition available. Fanny composed from an early age, and she was an exceptionally gifted pianist; at the age of 13, she memorized the preludes from Book 1 of Bach's *Well-Tempered Clavier* as a surprise for Abraham—a stunning feat.

FANNY AND FELIX

Fanny was adored by her younger brother Felix, who respected her musical taste and sought her opinion in compositional matters. In 1828 and 1830, he allowed some of her songs to be published under his name,

Italy, which became a favorite of Queen
. Felix probably wanted to encourage his
mposition while upholding societal mores.

AGE

Fanny married Wilhelm Hensel, who was a
nter. Wilhelm encouraged Fanny's playing
ke her father and brother, even urged her
 her works. They had one child, Sebastian
Felix, named after Fanny's favorite composers.
r brother Felix traveled around Europe,
as obliged to stay home. Other than a short
ar of Switzerland when she was 17, Fanny did
not get a chance to travel until ten years
into her marriage, when she and Wilhelm
toured her dream destination, Italy. The
trip included a six-month sojourn in
Rome, and Fanny met and impressed
many luminaries, including the French
composers Hector Berlioz and Charles
Gounod. The latter described her as "a
musician beyond comparison, a remarkable
pianist, and a woman of superior mind."
Fanny's Roman holiday was perhaps the
happiest period of her life; having received
the recognition she deserved, she returned
home with renewed inspiration.

FANNY'S LEGACY

Fanny's devotion to music continued all
her life. When the Mendelssohns were
children, their mother instigated a series
of Sunday musical soirees (*Sonntagsmusik*)
where the precocious siblings performed
their own, and others' compositions with
amateur and professional musicians. In
1831, Fanny resumed this tradition, taking
on additional roles of conductor and music
arranger. While preparing one of Felix's
cantatas for such a gathering she died, at
the age of 42, of a stroke.

Discover the music

Lieder, including *Italien* (1825)

Prelude in E minor (1827)

String Quartet in E flat (1834)

Das Jahr (*The Year*) (1841)

Piano Trio, Op. 11 (1846)

Above An autograph transcription by Fanny Mendelssohn-Hensel of the "Voyages" album. The vignette was painted by her husband Wilhelm.

Left Wilhelm Hensel painted this portrait of his wife Fanny and their son Sebastian around 1832. Sebastian (1830–1898) later collected and edited the Mendelssohn family correspondence.

Far left Fanny and Felix Mendelssohn were very close. Felix, the younger by three and a half years, often sought his sister's advice and feedback in compositional matters.

While some of Fanny Mendelssohn-Hensel's works
were published during her lifetime and shortly after her
death, there was no significant revival of her oeuvre
until the 1980s. She is now best remembered for her
songs; she wrote some 300 songs. She knew many
of the poets whose works she set, including Goethe,
Heinrich Heine, and Joseph Freiherr von Eichendorff.
Her songs feature adventurous piano accompaniments,
which reflect her mastery of that instrument, and are
far more "romantic" than those of her brother.

The collection of short piano works, *Das Jahr* (written in 1841), which depicts the months of the year,
and which Fanny considered "a kind of second diary,"
is also noteworthy.

FEMALE COMPOSER–PERFORMERS IN THE NINETEENTH CENTURY

Fanny was not the only female composer and performer of note in the nineteenth century. The rise of
the piano as the domestic instrument of choice gave
rise to many female piano virtuosi, among them Clara
Schumann and Madame Camille Pleyel (1811–1875).
But while public performances by women pianists
were tolerated, composing—or at least publication
of compositions—was strictly for men. Along with
Fanny, Clara Schumann was again an exception to
this rule, and she did not just stick to salon fare,
performing her own piano concerto with the Leipzig
Gewandhaus Orchestra under Felix Mendelssohn's
directorship. Louise Reichardt (1779–1826), a prolific
and widely published songwriter, was another exception; much like Jane Austen, her failure to marry
freed her from the demands of family, and allowed
her a career as a professional composer.

Felix Mendelssohn

FEBRUARY 3, 1809–NOVEMBER 4, 1847

AT THE AGE OF 16, FELIX MENDELSSOHN, ALREADY A PIANO PRODIGY, WROTE HIS *OCTET FOR STRINGS*, A WORK OF STARTLING GENIUS THAT OVERSHADOWS EVEN MOZART'S EARLY EFFORTS. BUT THOUGH HE WAS BLESSED WITH ENORMOUS TALENT AND FAMILY WEALTH, MENDELSSOHN'S LIFE WAS NOT PLAIN SAILING; HE SUFFERED UNDER THE WEIGHT OF HIS OWN EXPECTATIONS, WAS THE VICTIM OF ANTI-SEMITISM, AND WAS CONSIDERED TOO SUPERFICIAL TO BE A TRULY GREAT COMPOSER.

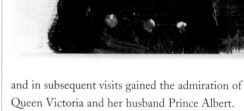

The grandson of Jewish philosopher Moses Mendelssohn, and the son of a banker, Mendelssohn had a privileged and intellectually rich upbringing in Hamburg, then Berlin. His early precocity was evident not only in his piano playing, but also in drawing, painting, and languages—he learnt English, Italian, and Latin. His sister Fanny was comparably talented, and the two shared an artistic kinship all their lives. He composed from age 13, and his 1825 *Octet*, his early masterpiece, was soon followed by another work of genius, an overture to *A Midsummer Night's Dream*.

Right An oil painting of Mendelssohn at 12 years of age. He wrote his overture to *A Midsummer Night's Dream* when he was 17; the rest of the incidental music for that work was written some 17 years later.

and in subsequent visits gained the admiration of Queen Victoria and her husband Prince Albert.

EARLY CAREER
Mendelssohn returned to Germany in 1831 and, with his father's support, officially started his music career. The most significant works of this early stage were his virtuosic first piano concerto, which he premièred, and the more intimate first volume of *Songs without Words*

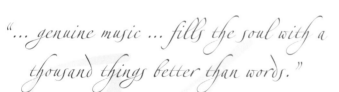

"... genuine music ... fills the soul with a thousand things better than words."

BACH REVIVAL
In 1829, Mendelssohn and a friend, Eduard Devrient, persuaded the director of the Berlin Singakademie (a type of choral society) to allow a performance of Johann Sebastian Bach's *St Matthew Passion*, which Mendelssohn had known and loved from an early age. While Bach's works were not exactly unknown at that time—the Singakademie's aims included the revival of eighteenth-century masterpieces—the two performances, with the 20-year-old Mendelssohn conducting, were a sensation. Shortly after, Mendelssohn traveled to England and was inspired to write his *Symphony No. 3* "Scottish" (1829) and the *Hebrides* overture (1830). Aided by his connections, he was well received,

MENDELSSOHN'S REPUTATION

Despite, or perhaps because of, the accessibility of Mendelssohn's works, he has been disregarded as a brilliant relic of the Classical era: Not a true Romantic, but a poor man's Mozart. It is true that compared with his contemporaries, his works lack drama; the *Hebrides* overture, for example, does not evoke a brutal landscape as well as, say, Tchaikovsky's *Tempest* symphonic fantasy. One of the most damning, and disturbing assessments of Mendelssohn came from Wagner: "Mendelssohn has shown us that a Jew may have the amplest of talents, the finest and most varied culture, the highest and most tender sense of honor, yet these qualities cannot help him even once to evoke in us the deep heart-searching effect we expect from art." These prejudices have since lifted, and Mendelssohn's music is now appreciated on its own terms.

(*Lieder ohne worte*), quite short piano works that have become mainstays of the piano literature.

SETBACKS AND SUCCESSES

In 1833 Mendelssohn endured an uncharacteristic setback—he was passed over for the job of Singakademie director. Mendelssohn's youth probably proved a disadvantage, but anti-Semitism may have also played a part. He was well compensated for this loss, however, when he was appointed director of the prestigious Leipzig Gewandhaus Orchestra in 1835. He was also able to indulge his passion for Baroque revivals with a production of Handel's *Israel in Egypt*, and composed yet another masterpiece, his popular *Symphony No. 4* "Italian". In 1837 he married Cecile Jeanrenaud, capping several years of professional success with personal fulfillment.

But Mendelssohn's happiness was soon tainted. From 1838 he was afflicted with occasional headaches and fits of exhaustion,

Above A performance of the oratorio *Elijah* at the Vienna Winter Riding School in 1890 attended by Emperor Franz Joseph.

Right A trip to Fingal's Cave in Staffa, Scotland, inspired Mendelssohn to write his evocative *Hebrides* overture.

Discover the music

String Octet in E flat major, Op. 20 (1825)
A Midsummer Night's Dream, Op. 21 (1826)
Piano Concerto in G minor, Op. 25 (1832)
Symphony No. 4 "Italian", Op. 90 (1833)
Songs without Words, Op. 30 (1835)
Violin Concerto in E minor, Op. 64 (1844)

though he still kept up a busy schedule of composing and conducting. His deep love of choral works had prompted him to write an oratorio, *St Paul*, in 1836, and ten years later he wrote another, *Elijah*. The *Violin Concerto* of 1844, lauded by famous violinist Joseph Joachim as "the heart's jewel," was another of his late masterpieces. Mendelssohn's final two years were taken up with performances of *Elijah*, and in 1847 he traveled to England for the last time. He died of a cerebral hemorrhage the same year, aged 38 years.

The arts under the Hapsburgs

AUSTRIA AND GERMANY IN THE FIRST HALF OF THE NINETEENTH CENTURY HAD LIVELY MUSICAL LIVES:
VIENNA, THE CAPITAL OF THE AUSTRIAN EMPIRE, WAS A MECCA FOR MUSICIANS, AND GERMANY
BOASTED THREE IMPORTANT MUSICAL CENTERS: BERLIN, DRESDEN, WITH ITS MAGNIFICENT OPERA
HOUSE, AND LEIPZIG, WHERE BACH, THEN MENDELSSOHN LIVED.

Music was not restricted to the talented few—amateur musicians would often gather in their homes for musical soirées, to perform songs, and piano and chamber music.

But this fervid music making was a veneer. Both Austria and Germany, the latter still waiting for unification, were under the repressive rule of the Hapsburgs. The Austrian Empire, once invincible, had been rocked by the French Revolution and the Napoleonic Wars: Vienna was twice invaded by French armies, and the Empire lost a great deal of territory, including most of the Italian peninsula. As a result, the otherwise benign Emperor Francis (r. 1792–1835), with the help of his chancellor Klemens von Metternich (1773–1859) ruled with an iron fist, discouraging political discourse of any kind. Music was considered a suitably peaceful activity for the populace, although public concert programs were still censored, and even the peaceful Franz Schubert had a brush with the law.

Above Heinrich Heine (1797–1856) was one of Germany's foremost romantic poets.
Below The Semperoper, Dresden, was built in the 1840s. It remains an important musical center.

"Experience is a good school, but the fees are high."

HEINRICH HEINE

BIEDERMEIER

A dominant esthetic in both Germany and Austria in the early nineteenth century was Biedermeier, which means, roughly, conservatism (a Biedermann is a member of the petty bourgeoisie, or, in its least charitable definition, a simpleton). Biedermeier was a result of government repression—denied public freedom, the people were obliged to cultivate a placid domestic life, where family happiness was foremost, and all leisure activities were inoffensive. The Biedermeier esthetic is perfectly exemplified in the furniture design of this period. In the Napoleonic era, furniture, often in mahogany, towered over the people it was made for. In contrast, Biedermeier furniture was simple and elegant; chairs were upholstered in light, bright colors, and floral patterns were favored.

For furniture makers, Biedermeier was all well and good; some artists, on the other hand, rebelled against Biedermeier, while others found ways to incorporate it into their works. In the theater, the plays of Ferdinand Raimund (1790–1836), often with Raimund himself in the leading role, gently satirized the dullness of Viennese society. Satirical paintings, such as *Poor Poet* by Carl Spitzweg (1808–1885), and the homely scenes depicted by Erasmus von Engert (1796–1871) and Ferdinand Georg Waldmüller (1793–1865), show a range of responses to Biedermeier.

Above *Walk at Dusk*, a typical romantic evocation of landscape by Caspar David Friedrich. His works often feature solitary individuals contemplating nature.

ROMANTICISM

There is a stark difference between von Engert's modest scenes and those of his German contemporary, Caspar David Friedrich (1774–1840), who depicted harsh landscapes and lonely wanderers, both typical romantic themes. Indeed Romanticism was alive in Austria and Germany in the first half of the century. In part inspired by contemporary English and Scottish romantics such as the adventurous poet Lord Byron and Walter Scott, Germany produced a number of romantic writers, including E.T.A. Hoffmann (1776–1822), Jean Paul Richter (1763–1825), and Novalis (1772–1801), whose work was tinged with a fast growing sense of nationalism.

WRITERS UNDER THE REGIME

Under the Hapsburg regime, writers and other public intellectuals were at particular risk of censure—and censorship. Many writers had been inspired by the French Revolution and the charismatic Napoleon Bonaparte, which put them in a difficult situation with authority. The Austrian poet and dramatist Franz Grillparzer (1791–1872), for example, ran into trouble with the censor for incorrect allusions to Napoleon in one of his plays. The German poet Heinrich Heine (1797–1856), a favorite of the art song composers, also had a difficult relationship with the authorities. After having converted from Judaism to Lutherism to obtain a university post, he left for Paris in 1831, only returning to Germany twice. In his absence, Heine was condemned for his association with the liberal movement, Young Germany, and his books were banned. Heine was an unusual Romantic in that he used an often biting irony to deal with the many travails of life and love. One of his favorite techniques was to load a poem up with romantic imagery, then destroy the illusion with an ironic comment. For example, in one poem, a man asks his friend to gallop off to find out who his bride is to be—one of two sisters—then, if she is the wrong one, to bring him back a rope.

LIEDER

While composers like Liszt and Berlioz exploited the drama and color a large orchestra could bring to their musical ideas, Lieder—accompanied songs—take the listener into a different world, more intimate but no less dramatic. In Schubert's master-piece *Der Erlkönig* for instance, a father carries his sick boy home on horseback, but before they arrive, the boy dies, taken away by the mythical Erl-King.

The direct translation of the German word Lied (pronounced "leed") is "song." In classical music a Lied—which is often referred to as "art song"—is a setting of a poem for piano and one voice (although in Schubert's setting of the *Der Erlkönig*, the one voice takes on four roles: The narrator, the boy, the father, and the Erl-King). In the nineteenth century, the piano, which had previously been assigned a mere supporting role, became a second voice, amplifying the song's message, or, occasionally, contradicting it. As only two people are needed to perform art songs, they quickly became a staple of salon gatherings.

SCHUBERT

Schubert did not invent the art song—Beethoven's collection *To the Distant Beloved* (1816) is a notable earlier example—but he was arguably the greatest ever composer of them. His songs were characterized by their sublime melodies and deceptively simple piano accompaniments. He composed over 600 art songs, so it is difficult to summarize his output, but along with *Der Erlkönig*, other Schubert songs worth exploring are *Ave Maria*, *Der Tod und das Mädchen* (*Death and the Maiden*), *Die Forelle* (*The Trout*) and the song cycles

Above The poetry that inspired composers of the Romantic period to write Lieder was often deeply contemplative and wistful—perfect for solo voice and piano.

Left The front cover of a Lieder Book, containing the sheet music for voice and piano. Collections of art songs were very popular among the elite and middle classes.

(collections of songs) *Die schöne Müllerin* (*The Beautiful Girl at the Mill*) and *Winterreise* (*Winter Journey*).

SCHUMANN

Another of the great Romantic art song composers was Robert Schumann. In his songs, the piano takes an even more active role, with scene-setting preludes and postludes, in which the piano might add an extra thought after the singer has finished. In his *Aus alten Märchen winkt es* (*From old tales someone waves*), for example, the singer enthuses about a magical land that can be seen in his dreams. The image is dispelled, like an "empty bubble," when the sun rises. The voice concludes almost at a whisper, reflecting the poet's dejection, but the piano continues, reprising the origi-nal lilting melody, which gradually slows into some soft chords, which seem to fall gently to the ground

*"If only I had a thousand arms to move ...
If I could turn all the stones!
So that the beautiful girl at the mill would
notice my faithful thoughts."*

WILHELM MÜLLER, *DIE SCHÖNE MÜLLERIN*

THE POETS

German Romantic poets revered the ability of music to express the ineffable, considering it the ultimate art. Composers, in turn, respected poetry's abstraction, which left it open to musical interpretation. Though any poetry of quality was considered good fodder for a song, a handful of German poets were favorites. Goethe, the author of *Der Erlkönig*, was one, as was Heinrich Heine (see page 179), though his irony was not necessarily reflected by the Romantic composers who set his words to music, Schumann included. Joseph von Eichendorff (1788–1857), who unlike Heine remained a true Romantic, succeeded as a poet despite working as a public servant all his life. One of his poems, *Moonlit Night*, has been set by at least eight composers. Wilhelm Müller (1794–1827) was a less significant poet than the others, but Schubert chose his works for *The Beautiful Girl at the Mill* and *Winter Journey*. Müller had long wanted to hear his poems turned into song by a "kindred spirit," and though the two never met, it is likely he would have been pleased with Schubert's efforts.

Right Johann Wolfgang von Goethe is a true giant of German literature. His works inspired composers and artists in equal measure.

like bubbles. Schumann's songs easily achieve his aim of making voice and piano equal partners in the work.

OTHER LIED COMPOSERS

Schubert and Schumann were not the only notable art song composers. Felix and Fanny Mendelssohn, and Brahms wrote many of them, and certain composers, such as Carl Loewe (1796–1869) and Robert Franz (1815–1892) dedicated their entire careers to writing art songs. Berlioz and Wagner wrote art songs with orchestral accompaniments.

Nor were German and French the only languages set. Mussorgsky, for example, wrote several important song cycles on Russian texts, *Sunless* (1874) and *Songs and Dances of Death* (1875–1877), which are as dark as even the Germans' best efforts. Mussorgsky also injected humor into his songs; in his hilarious, ultra-

realistic song *Fair Savishna* (1866), a simple man breathlessly woos his sweetheart; and in the song cycle, *Nursery* (1868–1872), the singer imitates a toddler. At the end of the nineteenth century, the undisputed master of the art song was the Austrian Hugo Wolf (1860–1903), best known for his *Mörike-Lieder*, which were published in 1888.

Hector Berlioz

DECEMBER 11, 1803–MARCH 8, 1869

HECTOR BERLIOZ WAS ONE OF THE GREATEST COMPOSERS AND MOST INFLUENTIAL CRITICS OF HIS GENERATION. HE WROTE A FAMOUS TREATISE ON ORCHESTRATION, AND DOZENS OF BRILLIANT COMPOSITIONS TO SUPPORT HIS THEORIES. HE HAD AN ACERBIC WIT, MOST EVIDENT IN HIS ENTERTAINING *MÉMOIRES*, AND A DISTINCTLY ROMANTIC TENDENCY TO TUMULTUOUS EPISODES, ONE UNREQUITED PASSION EVEN LEADING HIM TO PLOT A MURDER–SUICIDE.

Berlioz described his birth, in the small hillside town of La Côte-Saint-André, as "unheralded by any of the signs which, in poetic ages, preceded the advent of remarkable personages." Nonetheless, he had a charmed childhood, in which he learnt flute and guitar and imbibed French and Latin literature. But then Berlioz's father Louis sent him to Paris to study medicine. To his parents' dismay, Berlioz soon abandoned his studies to take up composing.

Even before his admission to the Paris Conservatoire in 1826, Berlioz was a keen student of music. He studied harmony, and during his many visits to the Paris Opéra he developed distinctive musical tastes; he praised French and some German composers, but disdained Italians, including Rossini. He survived by

Above right Berlioz once wrote, "It is not enough that the artist should be well prepared for the public. The public must be well prepared for what it is going to hear."

Below Berlioz was as famous a conductor as he was a composer and he often conducted his own works. This Berlioz caricature dates from around the mid-1830s.

Discover the music

Symphonie Fantastique, Op. 14 (1830)
Harold in Italy, Op. 16 (1834)
Requiem, Op. 5 (1837)
Romeo and Juliet, Op. 17 (1839)
Roman Carnival Overture, Op. 9 (1844)
La Damnation de Faust, Op. 24 (1845–1846)
Les Nuits d'été (*Summer Nights*), Op. 7 (with piano, 1840–1841; with orchestra 1843–1856)

---

singing in the opera chorus and giving guitar lessons. Journalism, an occupation he despised, was another income source. Berlioz's first major composition was a Mass, written in 1824. During his Conservatoire years he competed for the Prix de Rome, an artistic scholarship offering free accommodation in Rome's Mancini Palace. He won only on his fifth attempt, with a cantata, and spent almost two years in Rome.

BERLIOZ'S WRITING

In 1870, Berlioz's *Mémoires* were published. Though his contemporaries were aware of his biting sarcasm, and the accuracy of his musical judgment, through the reviews and articles he wrote as a music journalist, the *Mémoires* are a glorious testament to a life well lived. They are full of passion, crushing disappointment, and ludicrous moments, such as when Berlioz was chased around the Paris Conservatoire library by the institution's director, Luigi Cherubini. The chapter describing his new career as music critic is entitled, simply: "Fatality—I become a critic." Berlioz's humor even comes through in his influential treatises on orchestration and on conducting, where he describes the foibles of orchestral musicians and even advocates fining violinists for missing their entries, and the semi-fictional *Les Soirées de l'Orchestre* (*Nights with the Orchestra*).

SYMPHONIE FANTASTIQUE (1830)

In 1830, shortly after making the above-mentioned murderous plan, Berlioz wrote his first masterpiece, the *Symphonie Fantastique* (*Fantastic Symphony*). This passionate work was inspired not by Berlioz's homicidal fancy, but another amour, the Irish Shakespearean actress Harriet Smithson. He married her in 1833, then wrote a succession of significant works, including the symphony for viola and orchestra *Harold in Italy* (1834), the opera *Benvenuto Cellini* (1836), a requiem (1837), and the choral symphony *Romeo and Juliet* (1839).

"Love cannot express the idea of music, [yet] music may give an idea of love."

TRAVELS AND CONDUCTING

Berlioz had become frustrated with what he perceived as inadequate performances of his work, and took up conducting. From 1842, he went abroad, conducting his and others' works in Belgium, Germany, Austria, England, and even Russia. He met many of the most important composers of his generation, including Mendelssohn, Robert Schumann, Liszt, and Wagner. All were impressed but Mendelssohn, who sniped in a letter to his mother: "He [Berlioz] makes me sad, because he is really a cultured, agreeable man and yet he composes so very badly."

In 1845–1846 Berlioz wrote *The Damnation of Faust*, a cantata based on Johann Wolfgang von

Above Faust was a popular subject for the arts in nineteenth-century Europe. Around the time that Berlioz wrote his cantata, Jules Perrot had choreographed a successful ballet. It premièred in Milan.

Goethe's play *Faust*, which was well received abroad but met with complete indifference in Paris. Berlioz was deeply disappointed by the Parisian response, and from thereon he composed only intermittently. Nonetheless, in the last decade of his career he produced several significant works, including the *Te Deum* (1849), the choral trilogy *The Infancy of Christ* (1854), and the grand opera *Les Troyens* (*The Trojans*, 1856–1858), based on Virgil's epic poem the *Aeneid*.

Berlioz's final years were tainted—he developed Crohn's, a disease affecting the digestive system, and he was devastated by the death of his only son, Louis, in 1867. He died in 1869 and was interred in the Montmartre Cemetery in Paris .

France in the first half of the nineteenth century

FRANCE'S MUSICAL CULTURE IN MANY WAYS ECHOED THE DEVELOPMENTS IN FRANCE IN THE FIRST HALF OF THE NINETEENTH CENTURY, WHICH SAW SEISMIC CHANGES, INCLUDING THE NAPOLEONIC ERA, THE RESTORATION OF THE BOURBON MONARCHY, AND MORE REVOLUTION, LEADING TO THE ASCENSION OF NAPOLEON'S NEPHEW, LOUIS. DURING THIS TIME, PARIS BECAME THE UNDISPUTED CAPITAL OF EUROPE, ATTRACTING EUROPE'S BEST ARTISTS AND INTELLECTUALS.

Nonetheless, in the early 1840s, Hector Berlioz, arguably France's greatest composer, left Paris in despair, seeking recognition abroad. How could such an enlightened society be so unresponsive to Berlioz's work, which was feted throughout Europe?

Above right A page from the score of Gaspare Spontini's *Li Puntigli delle Donne*. This opera was first performed in 1796 in Rome. Napoleon was a fan of Spontini's work.

Left Louis-Philippe I was "king of the French" from 1830 until 1848, a period that was known as the July Monarchy. After his abdication, he lived the rest of his life in England.

AFTER NAPOLEON

In 1815, the Bourbon monarchy was restored, and France was led first by Louis XVII, then Charles X. The populace was unhappy—former Emperor Napoleon Bonaparte was sorely missed, and anti-royalists agitated for a republic, something they would have to wait many years to achieve. Napoleon's influence could still be seen in many aspects of life, like the continuing craze for Italian opera. Following on the success of his contemporaries Domenico Cimarosa (1749–1801) and Giovanni Paisiello (1740–1816), Napoleon's favorites, Gaspare Spontini (1774–1851), then Rossini, became all the rage. The Bourbon restoration did not last long; in 1830, Berlioz finished the *Symphonie Fantastique*, his first masterpiece, and was working on his cantata for the Prix de Rome when yet another revolution started—in July that year France became a constitutional monarchy, ruled by King Louis-Philippe.

THE JULY MONARCHY

Louis-Phillipe spent 18 years in power, a period known as the July Monarchy. The new king's reorganization of Parisian musical life reflected his priorities and insecurities. He realized that the public did not really want a monarch, and he was reluctant to antagonize those who had fought in the July revolution with signs of royal privilege and overspending. He franchised the administration of the Paris Opéra, closed the school for church musicians established during the restoration, and established a tradition of benefit concerts, the funding for which could only be obtained through direct application to himself.

SALON SOCIETY

Another feature of Parisian musical life during Berlioz's lifetime was salon society. Salons were gatherings in homes for intellectual discussion, musical performances, or literary readings. Only the elite—established through reputation—could attend, and the hosts were often women, called salonnières, sophisticated and intelligent members of the nobility or upper middle-class. As in Vienna around the same time, salon society was by no means harmless. One of the great salonnières of the late eighteenth century, the writer Madame de Staël (1766–1817), clashed with Napoleon over her forthright views and was eventually exiled from Paris. Parisian salons were also something of a tourist attraction: Visiting artists would make a point of attending a salon during their visit. Some personalities became salon favorites, like Chopin, who was called upon to entertain the other guests by improvising at the piano. The salon was also a good source of aristocratic students for budding composers, and frequently, a place where romance blossomed.

BERLIOZ LEAVES PARIS

While his more amenable colleagues such as Giacomo Meyerbeer (1791–1864) and Daniel Auber (1782–1871) flourished under the new regime, the fiesty Berlioz struggled to get his work performed under this highly regulated system. In one incident, recounted in

Above Musical soirées were integral to Parisian salon society. A network of valuable contacts could be established at these gatherings.

his *Mémoires*, he was taken to task by the Prefect of Police—who was obliged to be present at concerts—for introducing a politically sensitive chorus into a concert program. Berlioz's introduction to the conversation, highlighting the effort that went into his concerts, is more enlightening than the exchange itself: "Scarcely had Strauss and I paid off our musicians, copyists, printers, instrument makers, masons, slaters, joiners, carpenters, upholsterers, officials, and inspectors, when the Prefect of Police ... summoned us to his office."

In addition, the Parisian public's relative musical conservatism did not sit well with his desire to revolutionize the genres he composed in, a fact most evident in the indifference with which his *La Damnation de Faust* was met in Paris. In the 1840s, Berlioz left Paris on a series of tours. The once great city was no longer the intellectual, cultural, and musical capital it had once been. Berlioz was not the only person unhappy with life in Louis-Phillipe's France. In 1848, there was another revolution resulting in the suffrage of all Frenchmen, not just the rich or aristocratic, as was previously the case. The Second Empire, which was led by Louis Napoleon Bonaparte, a nephew of Napoleon I, came into existence.

CHAMBER MUSIC IN THE NINETEENTH CENTURY

Personal expression was of paramount importance to the Romantics; some, like Berlioz and Wagner, preferred to express themselves in orchestral works and operas, while others were most comfortable in the intimate surrounds of the musical salon—and with soul-searching chamber and piano music.

Chamber music, broadly defined, is music written for a small group of musicians, and in its original conception, is to be played in a small room—a chamber—whether in a palace or a modest family home. Its popularity coincided with the rise of amateur musicianship in the nineteenth century, especially in countries like Austria, where domestic music making was integral to middle-class life. Many European cities even had their own musical societies, which encouraged domestic performance of string quartets, perhaps the most popular type of chamber music.

STRING QUARTETS AND OTHER CHAMBER MUSIC

Schubert and Brahms were the nineteenth century's greatest exponents of chamber music, but chamber music's Romantic period really began with Beethoven, whose late string quartets—especially the violent *Grosse Fuge* (Op. 133)—exhibit a distinctly romantic passion. Ironically, Beethoven's string quartets also require a virtuosity—a brilliance in execution—that truly defy most amateur players. Schubert wrote some 15 string

Below Chamber music was performed in large rooms, or smaller, more intimate spaces, such as this room in Brahms's house. Most middle-class homes had a piano.

quartets, including the dramatic *Death and the Maiden* quartet, and Brahms wrote three. Not all chamber music was written in Austria and Germany: Russian Alexander Borodin wrote two wonderful quartets, as did the Czech composers Bedřich Smetana and Antonín Dvořák. Other popular chamber music genres were piano trios, string trios, and string quintets.

THE PIANO

The piano increasingly appeared in chamber works, such as in the great piano quintets (piano plus string quartet) by Schumann and Brahms. Indeed the piano, already popular in the eighteenth century, became the romantic instrument of choice. It could combine incredible effects—from big orchestral chords, to beautiful, sustained, almost voice-like melodies—satisfying the Romantics' need for both drama and intimacy. The production of pianos also increased dramatically. The Parisian manufacturer Erard, for example, went from producing approximately 160 pianos a year in the early nineteenth century to 1,500 a year by the 1850s. With increased production came affordability, and pianos soon became an essential piece of furniture in any middle-class home. A basic proficiency on the piano was expected, especially of young women, as any reader of Jane Austen would be aware. In the public domain, as well, the piano became more popular. Once, piano works were only performed as part of a concert that might also include symphonies and operatic arias, but the nineteenth century gave rise to the solo recital. Nineteenth-century audiences loved the spectacle of the lone performer, usually a pianist or violinist, pulling off wonderful feats of execution.

Above Being able to play the piano was a necessary accomplishment for young women. Renoir painted this charming portrait c. 1897.

Right Swiss composer–pianist Sigismond Thalberg had a very successful performing career. He was one of Liszt's great rivals.

PIANO COMPOSITIONS

Virtually every Romantic period composer wrote music for piano, foremost among them Chopin and Liszt. Alongside the classic works that are still popular today, there were many piano works designed merely to show off a pianist's technique and advances in piano technology, for example double-escapement, which allowed individual notes to be quickly repeated. The compositions of Sigismond Thalberg (1812–1871), a pianist who once challenged Liszt to a piano duel, and Friedrich Kalkbrenner (1785–1849) were enormously popular in the nineteenth century, but were all but forgotten after they died, and are only now being revived by adventurous pianists. Other composers, like Liszt, Chopin, Brahms, Schumann, Mendelssohn, and the little-known French composer–pianist Charles-Valentin Alkan (1813–1888), blended stunning keyboard

effects with true musicality. Yet it was not all about virtuosity: Schubert, for instance, wrote some more modest works better suited to amateurs, such as the charming *Musical Moments*, though even he could write incredible works, such as the *Wanderer Fantasy*.

BRAHMS'S *PIANO QUINTET IN F MINOR*, OP. 34

Brahms's 1864 Piano Quintet is one of the masterpieces of nineteenth-century chamber music, but, as was characteristic for Brahms's works, it had a tortuous birth. First, it was a string quintet, then a sonata for two pianos, before the highly self-critical composer decided it should be a piano quintet. It has four movements of contrasting material—a dramatic first movement; a calm, Schubert-like second movement; a menacing third movement featuring a march with exciting rhythmic syncopation; and a wandering, unpredictable, quintessentially "Romantic" last movement. Listening to this beautiful work, it is very easy to comprehend Hans Werne Henze's acute observation: "The significance of chamber music is that in dealing with the intimate it can attain to the ineffable. Chamber music conceives itself as a world of sound that has external boundaries but no internal ones."

Frédéric Chopin

MARCH 1, 1810–OCTOBER 17, 1849

AT 21, FRÉDÉRIC CHOPIN LEFT HIS NATIVE POLAND AND SETTLED IN PARIS, WHERE HE BECAME KNOWN AS A SUPERB PIANIST AND IMPROVISER. HIS WORKS, WRITTEN MAINLY FOR PIANO, ARE HIGHLY ORIGINAL, BUT SHOW BROAD INFLUENCES RANGING FROM POLISH DANCES TO JOHANN SEBASTIAN BACH. CHOPIN DEFINED ROMANTIC PIANISM, AND HIS COMPOSITIONS, FROM HIS SPIKY, POLISH MAZURKAS TO HIS PLAINTIVE NOCTURNES, ARE PERENNIAL FAVORITES.

Chopin was born in a small town not far from Warsaw. Encouraged by his parents, he soon established a reputation as a piano prodigy; at the age of 11 he performed for Tsar Alexander I. His first compositions, *Polonaises* (Polish dances), were not at all childlike, but strikingly original examples of the popular folk genre.

LEAVING WARSAW

From 1826, Chopin studied at the Warsaw Conservatory, and in 1829 performed in Vienna, cementing his reputation as a pianist. In 1830, an uprising against Russian rule in Poland stirred his nationalist pride, inspiring him to write the "Revolutionary" *Etude*, Op. 10 No. 12.

In 1831, he settled in Paris. With a concert in 1832, he quickly attracted the attention of luminaries such as Franz Liszt and Felix Mendelssohn. Robert Schumann, on hearing Chopin's variations on a Mozart aria,

Above Chopin and George Sand spent the summer of 1838 in this house in Majorca. This is where he composed his "Raindrop" prelude.

exclaimed, "Hats off, gentlemen, a genius!" An habitué of Parisian musical salons, Chopin soon attracted female interest as well, and in 1832 he was linked with the Countess Delfina Potocka.

Yet his early years in Paris were by no means easy. While he supported himself with music lessons and publications, his income was limited. In addition, the delicacy of his playing and stage fright limited his career as a concert pianist, though he still performed frequently.

GEORGE SAND

In 1836, following an ill-fated love affair in Dresden, Chopin met the novelist Aurore Dudevant, better known as George Sand. Sand (1804–1876) was an eccentric who dressed in men's clothes, smoked, and had numerous extramarital affairs that she did not bother to hide. She and Chopin soon became lovers and spent the summer of 1838 in Majorca, hoping to improve Chopin's health. (Berlioz once remarked that Chopin was "dying all his life," and he was not wrong: Chopin suffered from tuberculosis throughout his life.) Unexpectedly damp weather in Majorca exacerbated his symptoms, but the couple soon settled into a regular routine, spending summers in Nohant, south of Paris, and the rest of the year, separately, in Paris itself. The relationship lasted until 1847. It was the most productive decade of Chopin's composing career, resulting in the Bach-inspired *Preludes*, Op. 8, the imposing *Polonaise in A flat major*, Op. 53, the frothy *Minute Waltz*, Op. 64 No. 1, and the B flat minor

CHOPIN'S POLONAISES

Chopin wrote in many genres, including waltzes, nocturnes, mazurkas, ballades, scherzi, and etudes (studies). Unlike Schumann and Liszt, Chopin did not give his works descriptive titles—there were no "topics" in his music, only strong emotions. Perhaps the most stirring and nationalistic of his works are the Polonaises. He took their distinct, martial rhythmic pattern merely as a starting point, interspersing crashing chords with twisting, longing melodies of tortuous beauty, said to be inspired by bel canto singing. The most famous of his Polonaises are "Military" in A major, Op. 40, No. 1, and the virtuosic, but distinctly un-Polonaise-like "Heroic" in A flat, Op. 53.

piano sonata, Op. 35 (containing the funeral march, perhaps Chopin's greatest gift to popular culture), among numerous others.

FINAL YEARS

Chopin split with George Sand in 1847, and started traveling again. His busy schedule, including a seven-month trip to England, may have distracted him from his heartbreak, but it ruined his already fragile health. He died in Paris on October 17, 1849, in the company of his sister, Ludwika.

Discover the music

Etude "Revolutionary" Op. 10, No. 12 (1830)

Nocturne No. 2, Op. 9 (1830–1831)

Grande Valse Brillante, Op. 18 (1831)

Fantasie-Impromptu, Op. 66 (1834)

Ballade No. 1, Op. 23 (1835)

Piano Sonata, Op. 35 (1839)

Fantasy in F minor, Op. 49 (1841)

Polonaise No. 6, Op. 53 (1842)

Above Chopin preferred to perform in the intimacy of a salon setting, such as this one, the salon of Prince Radziville in Berlin in 1829.

Piano

The piano has been, and continues to be, arguably one of the most crucial instrument in the history of western classical, jazz, and popular music. It is classified as a percussion instrument—when the string is struck by the hammer it resonates, producing sound. There are two types of piano: The grand and the upright, each with 88 keys, made up of seven octaves plus a minor third. Most pianos have three pedals—the soft pedal, sostenuto, and the sustain. Chopin's name is synonymous with the piano—indeed most of his compositions are a standard part of today's piano repertoire.

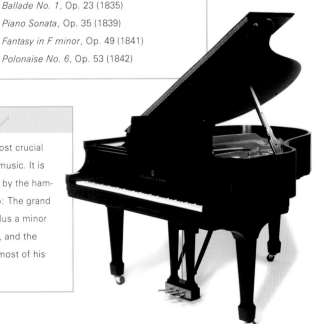

Robert Schumann and

JUNE 8, 1810–JULY 29, 1856

Clara Schumann

SEPTEMBER 13, 1819–MAY 20, 1896

ROBERT AND CLARA SCHUMANN WERE THE ROMANTIC PERIOD POWER COUPLE—HE WAS A RESPECTED COMPOSER AND INFLUENTIAL CRITIC; SHE WAS ONE OF EUROPE'S GREATEST PIANISTS. DURING THEIR LIFETIMES, THOUGH, CLARA WAS BETTER KNOWN; ONCE, ON TOUR WITH HIS WIFE IN RUSSIA, ROBERT WAS ASKED IF HE, TOO, WAS A MUSICIAN.

Robert Schumann was born in Zwickau, Saxony. His father, August, was a bookseller, publisher, and novelist, and young Schumann was brought up surrounded by literature. He read copiously—Romantic novelist Jean Paul Richter was his favorite author—and even wrote a few novels of his own. He began piano lessons at seven years of age, and showed a real talent for improvisation. All the same, after his father's death in 1826, it was decided that Schumann should pursue law, which he studied in Leipzig, and then Heidelberg, from 1828. In 1830, he started piano lessons in Leipzig with renowned pedagogue Friedrich Wieck, and met his nine-year-old daughter, piano prodigy Clara Wieck.

Above right Robert and Clara Schumann withstood fierce opposition from Clara's father, but their love prevailed and they married in 1840.

EARLY CAREERS

Clara Wieck began giving concerts from the age of 13, and she went on to establish an international reputation, but Schumann's pianistic career was not to be—two fingers on his right hand were permanently damaged, probably by a mechanical device that was used to aid piano practice. While his hopes as a performer were dashed, Schumann started to compose piano works, including the *Abegg Variations*, Op. 1, and *Papillons (Butterflies)*, Op. 2. In 1834 he embarked on another important project, his *Neue*

Discover the music

Robert Schumann
Dichterliebe, Op. 48 (1840)
Piano Concerto, Op. 54 (1841–1845)
Kreisleriana, Op. 16 (1838, rev. 1850)
Symphony No. 3, "Rhenish", Op. 97 (1850)

Clara Schumann
Piano Concerto, Op. 7 (1836)
Souvenir of Vienna, Op. 9 (1838)
Piano Trio, Op. 17 (1847)
Romance (1856)

Zeitschrift für Musik (*New Journal for Music*), which was dedicated to criticism of contemporary music.

LOVE AND MARRIAGE

In 1835, Clara turned 16, and Schumann realized that he was deeply attracted to her. Friedrich disapproved of the match, discontinued Schumann's lessons, and forbade contact between the lovers. Nonetheless, after court cases and numerous secret assignations, Robert and Clara married in 1840. His tumultuous courtship of Clara had not hindered Robert's career; he wrote

Right Schumann produced a great body of both piano music and art song. He is one of the quintessential Romantics.

several significant piano works in 1837 and 1838, and 1840, the year of their marriage, was his Liederjahr—year of song—and saw the composition of two of his greatest song cycles, *Frauenliebe und leben* (*Woman's Life and Love*) and *Dichterliebe* (*Poet's Love*). Clara's career also survived the travails of love and marriage, including having seven children; her performing and composing continued as before.

ROBERT'S MENTAL ILLNESS

In 1842, Robert exhibited the first signs of mental illness, including fits of prostration and premonitions of death, yet he continued to compose. In 1842 he concentrated on chamber music, composing the much admired *Piano Quintet*, Op. 44. He wrote his only opera, *Genoveva*, in 1848, and incidental music to Byron's *Manfred* in 1849.

The year 1850 was a significant one for both the Schumanns—they met Johannes Brahms, who had been sent to their home with a recommendation from their friend, noted violinist Joseph Joachim. They were impressed by Brahms's early works, and Robert wrote an article extolling Brahms's talent.

Brahms proved to be a loyal friend to the family during the difficult years to come, and he was also Clara's ardent admirer. In 1854, Robert's illness worsened and he began hearing voices. Shortly afterward, he attempted suicide by throwing himself into the Rhine River. He then asked to be admitted to an asylum, and remained there until his death, two years later. Clara Schumann survived her husband by 40 years. She eventually became the authoritative editor of his works, and continued her performing career until 1891. She died from a stroke, aged 77, in 1896, and was buried beside Robert.

"[There is] no pleasanter feeling than that of having satisfied a whole audience."

Above The house where Robert Schumann was born in 1810. An avid reader, Schumann wrote essays and even a novel.

CLARA'S MUSIC

While she was known better as a pianist, Clara composed from an early age. Not surprisingly, most of her works are for piano, and range from the Bach-inspired preludes and fugues to the virtuosic A minor *Piano Concerto*, which she performed with Mendelssohn and the Leipzig Gewandhaus orchestra when she was 16. While she received more encouragement than most female composers (Fanny Mendelssohn, for example), Clara often lacked confidence in her composition. In 1839, she wrote: "I once believed that I possessed creative talent, but I have given up this idea; a woman must not desire to compose—there has never yet been one able to do it. Should I expect to be the one?" Perhaps her most touching work is a piano *Romance* from 1856, the year of Robert's death, signed, "Loving Memories, Clara."

Franz Liszt

OCTOBER 22, 1811–JULY 31, 1886

FRANZ LISZT WAS A FORCE OF NATURE. LIKE PAGANINI WITH THE VIOLIN, HIS PIANO WORKS STRETCHED THE INSTRUMENT TO ITS LIMIT, AND ARE JUST AS POPULAR TODAY AS THEY WERE THEN. BUT AS WELL AS BEING THE FOREMOST PIANIST OF HIS AGE, INSPIRING "LISZTOMANIA" IN HIS LEGIONS OF FANS, HE WAS A RENOWNED COMPOSER AND TIRELESS PROMOTER OF OTHERS' WORKS.

Franz Liszt was born in the village of Raiding, a German-speaking part of Hungary, to a clerk father and chambermaid mother. While this was an unlikely beginning for such a renowned composer, his talents were recognized early and fostered. As a child, he met Beethoven, and he studied with Carl Czerny, a brilliant pedagogue known to piano students for his monotonous but highly useful piano studies. Liszt clearly benefited from Czerny's tuition, and later dedicated his considerably more exciting *Études d'exécution transcendante* (*Transcendental Studies*) to him.

In 1823, the family left Hungary and moved to Paris so that Franz could enroll in the Conservatoire there. Excluded on grounds of his nationality, Liszt nonetheless studied composition and music theory. He wrote many works for piano, and in 1825 his one-act opera *Don Sanche* premièred in Paris. His performing career also flourished, and he toured extensively.

TRAGEDY, HOPE, AND LOVE

Liszt was very shaken by his father's death in 1827, and this, coupled with a failed romance in 1828, led to

LISZT'S SYMPHONIC POEMS

Liszt wrote 13 symphonic poems, orchestral works of about 10 to 30 minutes' duration. Unlike symphonies, symphonic poems are a type of "program" music—they are not "pure" music, but tell a story, describe or depict something outside music, such as a storm or a rural landscape. Liszt's symphonic poems are often inspired by literary sources: *Tasso* (after a poem by English poet Lord Byron), for instance, and *Hamlet*. But while Liszt coined the term "symphonic poem," he was certainly not the first composer of program music—Vivaldi's *Four Seasons*, or Beethoven's *Symphony No. 6* "Pastoral" are early examples. While symphonic poems were mainly Liszt's domain, many Romantic composers wrote programmatic overtures and symphonies, as the freedom from classical forms and the wider possibilities for expression appealed to them. Other popular programmatic works from the Romantic period include Berlioz's *Fantastic Symphony*, Mendelssohn's *Hebrides* overture, and Smetana's cycle of symphonic poems, *Má vlast* (*My Country*).

Above A contemporary cartoon of Liszt's works. Among his most loved compositions are the three piano concertos and the *Mephisto Waltzes*.

Left Liszt in 1884 surrounded by some of his pupils. He wanted "to leave a work with a few useful instructions for the pianists after me."

a period of depression. Liszt removed himself from public life for a time and this led to an obituary being published in *La Corsaire*, a Parisian journal. However, his depression lifted with the July 1830 revolution. He became convinced of art's power to change society, and joined the Saint-Simonian movement, which promoted a socialist understanding of Christianity.

In 1832, Liszt began an adulterous relationship with the Countess Marie d'Agoult. Marie left her husband in 1835 and eloped with Liszt to Geneva, creating an enormous scandal in Paris. They had two children together. In their travels throughout Switzerland and Italy, Liszt began the collection *Années de Pèlerinage* (*Years of Pilgrimage*) for piano, one of his finest and best loved works. A concert by the violin virtuoso Paganini, also in 1832, was another revelation for Liszt, and he immediately worked on achieving a similar virtuosity on the piano. From 1839 to 1847

he established his reputation as one of Europe's finest pianists. As the poet Heinrich Heine observed: "One no longer thinks of difficulty overcome; the piano vanishes and music appears."

THE WEIMAR YEARS

Liszt's constant touring inevitably damaged his relationship with Marie; it also limited his composing, so in 1848 he moved to Weimar, where he had been appointed Kapellmeister (music master). His new love, Princess Carolyne zu Sayn-Wittgenstein, joined him, and he established Weimar as a progressive music capital, staging performances of Wagner's and Berlioz's works and writing symphonic poems, the *Piano Sonata in B minor*, two symphonies, and the *Totentanz* (*Dance of Death*) for piano and orchestra.

RELIGION AND DECLINE

In 1865, having moved to Rome with the intention of marrying Princess Carolyne, Liszt took minor religious orders. His new interest in religion, which was at odds with his reputation as a womanizer, was expressed in

"Inspiration is enough to give expression to the tone in singing, especially when the song is without words."

Above A consummate performer, Liszt plays here for the Viennese imperial family.

Discover the music

Années de Pèlerinage (1844–1877)
Hungarian Rhapsody No. 2 (1847)
Piano Concerto No. 1 (1849, revised 1853, 1856)
Prometheus (1850, revised 1855)
Rigoletto Paraphrase (1859)
Mephisto Waltz No. 3 (1883)

sacred compositions such as the 1867 oratorio *Christus*, and was preceded by several personal hardships, among them the deaths of two of his children. The final few decades of Liszt's life were also difficult; his works were unappreciated by critics, and he was not happy about his daughter Cosima's affair with Richard Wagner. His health gradually declined, and he died in Bayreuth, probably from pneumonia, in 1886.

LIFE & TIMES

Romanticism in the first half of the nineteenth century

ROMANTICISM IN THE FIRST HALF OF THE NINETEENTH CENTURY WAS A CORNUCOPIA OF THEMES AND PREOCCUPATIONS—NATIONALISM, THE SUPERNATURAL, THE EXOTIC, MYTHOLOGY, AND HISTORICISM. BUT THE ROMANTICS' PHILOSOPHY, WHETHER IN LITERATURE, MUSIC, OR VISUAL ART, WAS CLEAR: THE EMOTIONAL WAS VALUED OVER THE RATIONAL, AND THE IMAGINATION OVER REALITY.

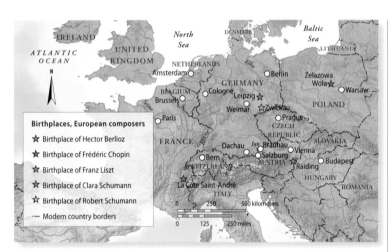

Birthplaces, European composers
★ Birthplace of Hector Berlioz
★ Birthplace of Frédéric Chopin
★ Birthplace of Franz Liszt
★ Birthplace of Clara Schumann
☆ Birthplace of Robert Schumann
·-· Modern country borders

NATIONALISM

In the years leading up to the Europe-wide revolutions of 1848, artists—including composers—became increasingly nationalistic, especially in those countries struggling under foreign rule. From Germany to Scandinavia and Russia, composers started using folk songs and dances in their works. Even composers like Chopin and Liszt, who rarely visited their home countries, took pride in their national folk dances, although they usually wrote in more cosmopolitan musical genres.

THE SUPERNATURAL

With the Romantics' interest in the imagination, it is perhaps no wonder that the supernatural was a favorite theme. One enormously popular supernatural-inspired work was Carl Maria von Weber's opera *Der Freishütz* (*The Freeshooter*, 1817–1821), based on a German folk legend, where the devil gives a marksman six shots to hit whatever he pleases, the final shot being taken by the devil himself. The fourth movement of Berlioz's *Symphonie Fantastique*, depicting a witches' Sabbath, is another fine moment in Romantic phantasmagoria. But perhaps one of the most chilling depictions of the supernatural is compacted into a song just over four minutes long: Schubert's *Der Erlkönig* (*The Erl-King*), about an evil spirit that snatches a dying boy to the afterlife.

Literary romanticism, where the movement started, had a direct effect on many composers. Robert Schumann, the bookworm, worked many literary allusions into his works, for example the collection of piano works, *Kreisleriana*, which was probably based on the main character of novels by the Romantic author E.T.A. Hoffmann. In other works, Schumann did not just make references to literature, his work is actually literary. There is a carefully coded symbolism, for example, in his early piano work *Carnaval*, Op. 9, where the four notes of the main theme partially spell out his own name. The other pieces in *Carnaval* are given names of people important to him: Clara, of course, and even Florestan and Eusebius, two imaginary characters who often featured in Schumann's reviews. Even Chopin, many of whose piano works take generic dance forms, wrote four *Ballades*, which present a distinct emotional narrative, though they are not based on any stories (ballads) as such. Liszt preferred to make his literary allusions in his symphonic poems (see pages 192–193).

Below German artist Caspar David Friedrich captured the spirit of the Romantic period in works such as *Wanderer Above the Sea of Fog*.

Above The exotic and exciting city of Cairo, in a painting by French artist Prosper Marilhat (1811–1847). Egypt and other "mysterious" lands were of intense interest to composers and writers in the nineteenth century.

> "To send light into the darkness of men's hearts — such is the duty of the artist."
>
> ROBERT SCHUMANN

THE EXOTIC

The setting of *Der Erlkönig* is a rapid journey on horseback, linking Schubert's masterpiece to another Romantic theme—travel and the exotic. This attraction to travel and adventure is most evident in Caspar David Friedrich's Romantic oil paintings, depicting a lonely wanderer in the mountains. The "mysterious" East also exerted an exotic allure. The French novelist and playwright Gustav Flaubert (1821–1880), for example, though comfortably ensconced in Paris, longed for the bustle and disorder of Egypt. This fascination for far-away places continued in the arts well past the Romantic era into the twentieth century, with Serge Diaghilev's renowned Ballets Russes.

HISTORICISM

Robert Schumann, in many ways a spokesperson for early Romanticism in music, believed the Romantic composer's main task was to be original, to constantly challenge himself, and many agreed with him. But Schumann also thought composers should understand music history, and study the works of the Classics, for example Beethoven, Mozart, and Schubert, so that they could be original in an informed way. In fact historicism was a significant trend in the Romantic generation, which was the first to conceive of what we now understand as "classical music"—in short, music that would stand the test of time. Mendelssohn revived Bach's, Handel's, and even Schubert's works; Chopin showed deep understanding of his favorite composers Mozart and Bach; Brahms so revered Beethoven that he was frightened to even attempt string quartets and symphonies, of which his predecessor had written so many iconic examples; even more overt iconoclasts like Berlioz and Liszt were extremely knowledgeable about music history. Historicism was not a harmless pursuit, though. Later, the question of how the works of the old masters should inform composition sparked one of the most divisive arguments in music history, the War of the Romantics (see pages 202–203).

Giuseppe Verdi

OCTOBER 9 OR 10, 1813–JANUARY 27, 1901

GIUSEPPE VERDI ROSE FROM MODEST BEGINNINGS TO BECOME ITALY'S MOST BELOVED OPERA COMPOSER AND A SYMBOL OF ITALY'S NATIONALIST MOVEMENT, THE RISORGIMENTO. WHILE HE WAS NOT PROLIFIC BY THE STANDARDS OF HIS TIME, VERDI LEFT US WITH DOZENS OF MEMORABLE OPERAS, RANGING FROM COMEDIES TO GRIM HISTORICAL DRAMAS.

Verdi was born in the village of Roncole, near Busseto in Parma. Proud of his heritage, he later declared, "I was, am and always will be a peasant from Roncole." He studied music in Busseto, then Milan, and in 1836 he married the daughter of his one-time mentor, merchant Antonio Barezzi. He began composing operas, and managed to get his second attempt, *Oberto*, staged at Milan's La Scala opera house.

A commission for three further operas followed, but the death of his wife in 1840 and the failure of his second opera almost derailed Verdi's career. Nonetheless, encouraged by Bartolomeo Merelli, La Scala's impresario, he achieved success in 1842 with *Nabucco*, a powerful opera about the persecution of the Jews by King Nabucco of Babylon. After that Verdi

Above right A nineteenth-century engraving of the characters in the opera *Rigoletto*.

Left Verdi, as depicted by Theobald Chartran, and published in *Vanity Fair* magazine in 1880.

Discover the music

Nabucco (1842)
Rigoletto (1850–1851)
La traviata (1852–1853)
Il trovatore (1853)
Aida (1871)
Requiem (1873–1874)

VERDI AND ITALIAN NATIONALISM

While none of Verdi's works have specifically political elements, he has long been connected with the Risorgimento. For many years it was believed that the call "Viva Verdi!", popular in 1859, simultaneously extolled the composer and called on Victor Emmanuel, then King of Sardinia, to become king of a united Italy. In addition, the Hebrew slaves' chorus "Va, pensiero" from *Nabucco*, is believed to have been encored by audiences in Milan—an extremely meaningful gesture, given that Milan was then under Austrian rule. Both stories have been discounted, but Verdi nonetheless promoted musical nationalism. In 1892, he wrote: "If the artists in the north and those in the south have different tendencies, then let them be different! They should all preserve the characteristics proper to their respective nations…"

was in demand. From 1843 to 1853 he crossed the country, supervising productions of the 14 operas he wrote in this period.

THE GREAT OPERAS

Verdi broke the mold of the Italian opera composer in many ways—he maintained unprecedented control of productions, demanded high fees, and, not content to adhere to popular formulas, he constantly experimented with operatic genres. This urge to constantly challenge himself and his audiences resulted in the composition of many great operas, including the psychological drama *Ernani* (1843), the supernatural-themed *Macbeth* (1847), *Luisa Miller* (1849), and from 1851 to 1853, three of the operas for which he is best known today: *Rigoletto*, *Il trovatore*, and *La traviata*.

After *La traviata*, Verdi slowed down, producing only six operas in the next 18 years. He married soprano Giuseppina Streponi, and worked on his farmlands outside Busseto, which he had acquired in 1848. Variety again characterized his output: *Simon Boccanegra* (1857), *The Force of Destiny* (1861), and *Don Carlos* (1867) were dark works, though this mix was leavened with the playful *Un ballo in maschera* (*A Masked Ball*) in 1859. This second period of Verdi's varied career was crowned with the French grand opera *Aida* in 1871.

THE *REQUIEM* AND FINAL OPERAS

In 1874, one of Verdi's few non-operatic works, a Requiem Mass in honor of Italian novelist and poet Alessandro Manzoni (1784–1873), was performed in Milan. It featured a large orchestra, six soloists, and a double chorus, and is instantly recognizable by its thundering "Dies Irae." This project, in addition to revisions of *Simon Boccanegra, The Force of Destiny,* and *Don Carlos,* accounted for his compositional work until *Otello* (1887), which was suggested to him by the librettist Arrigo Boito. After the success of *Otello,* Verdi followed it with another Shakespeare-inspired opera, *Falstaff.* This was his last opera, and only his second comedy. His last composition was the *Stabat Mater.* In 1901 he died of a stroke in Milan.

Bass drum

While not the most featured instrument in the orchestra by any means, the concert bass drum plays an crucial part in creating the "feel" for a piece of music. To play the instrument takes a great deal of skill as there are many variables—including the position on the drum to be hit, the type of beater, the intensity of the stroke, whether or not the stroke is muffled. All contribute to the overall texture, coloring, and shading of a piece of music. Verdi's grand march from *Aida* (using the bass drum and cymbal) is a powerful demonstration of the bass drum in an orchestral setting.

Below A rehearsal of *Aida* at Milan's La Scala opera house in late 2006. This production was directed by Franco Zefirelli.

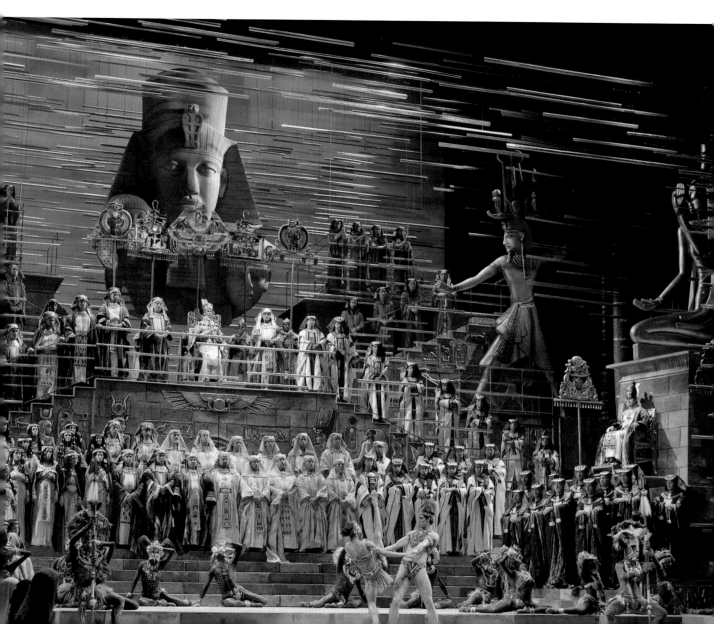

Italy in the nineteenth century

WHILE VERDI WAS MOST CLOSELY CONNECTED TO THE
RISORGIMENTO, HIS LONG LIFE TRAVERSED MANY OF THE MOST
SIGNIFICANT EVENTS IN ITALY'S HISTORY: HE WAS BORN IN THE
FINAL YEAR OF NAPOLEON BONAPARTE'S KINGDOM OF ITALY, AND
DIED LONG AFTER THE ITALIAN STATES HAD JOINED TOGETHER
INTO A NEW KINGDOM OF ITALY, BELONGING TO ITALIANS ALONE.

Throughout Verdi's youth, there was much dis-
content with Italy's rulers, who were primarily
puppets of the Hapsburg Empire who had been reinstated by the Congress of Vienna after Napoleon's
defeat in 1815. From this dissatisfaction emerged the
Risorgimento, which is discussed on pages 170–171.
Although early efforts at unification failed, the revolutionaries had more success with uprisings in places
such as Bologna and Ferrara. Local governments were
established, and the *tricolore*—the present-day Italian
flag—was adopted. Hopes for a united Italy soared,
only to be systematically crushed, once again, by the
Austrian army in the spring of 1831.

1848 REVOLUTIONS

Another round of revolutions ensued in 1848, resulting
in constitutions in the Kingdoms of Sardinia and
Naples, the ousting of the Austrian army from Milan,
and the establishment of republics in Venice, Rome,
and Tuscany. But the success of these movements
was limited by the patriots' conflicting aims and
loyalties. Should Italy be a monarchy or a republic?
And should it be a confederation of the Italian
states, or should it have a centralized government?
The Austrians once again put down the revolutions, and the old rulers regained their power.

CAVOUR AND GARIBALDI

But in the 1850s, the campaign for unification
gained focus with the help of Camillo di
Cavour (1810–1861), the prime minister of
the Kingdom of Sardinia, the only kingdom
to have kept its own constitution. Cavour was

Below Count Camillo
Benso di Cavour, a
leading figure in the
unification movement,
was prime minister of a
united Italy from March
till June 1861.

a deft diplomat. He attempted to ally Italy with France
and Britain in the Crimean War (1853–1856), and
eventually secured the support of Napoleon III, who
was also a former member of the Carbonari (covert
revolutionary societies), in the 1859 war against Austria. Napoleon consequently betrayed Cavour, secretly
seeking peace with the Austrians. Nonetheless, the
Austrians' hold on Italy was weakened, and the Kingdom of Sardinia annexed most of northern Italy.

Another very important figure of this period
was Giuseppe Garibaldi (1807–1882), who
alarmed Cavour by setting off with his army of
1,000 volunteers (the "red shirts") to take Sicily
back from France, before conquering southern
Italy and Naples. Yet Garibaldi accepted the
supremacy of Victor Emmanuel II, the king of
the Kingdom of Sardinia, who became the king
of united Italy in 1861. In the decade following
unification, Venetia and Rome were added to the
kingdom, the latter becoming its capital in 1870.
Italy was finally free of foreign rule, although its
problems were far from over.

ALESSANDRO MANZONI AND LITERARY REALISM

Writers played a key role in Italy's burgeoning self-awareness. A key figure in Risorgimento literature was Alessandro Manzoni, for whom Verdi wrote his *Requiem* (see pages 196–197). Manzoni's book, *I Promessi Sposi* (*The Betrothed*) is a classic of Italian literature. Following the story of two star-crossed lovers, Lucia and Renzo, this book has a threefold significance. First, there is its historical plot. It is set in 1626, when Italy was under Spanish control. The allusion to Austrian rule was unmistakable. Second, *The Betrothed* is highly realistic, and three chapters are devoted to a detailed description of the 1630 plague in Milan. While realism is often considered antithetic to artistic beauty, Manzoni believed that beauty in art could be achieved precisely through realism, both historical and moral. *Verismo*—realism—became an important movement in all of the arts, opera included, and is even reflected in the increasingly pragmatic efforts of Italian patriots. Finally, after having released the book written in his native Milanese dialect in 1827, in 1840 Manzoni reissued it in the Florentine dialect, which he believed should be Italy's official literary language. The idea of a national language, both for everyday and literary purposes, was vital at a time when Italians were craving unification. Manzoni's promotion of this Tuscan dialect was successful—it forms the basis of the standard Italian spoken today.

Left The revolutions of 1848 and 1849 inspired this painting entitled *A Dance Around the Tree of Liberty* by Belvederi. The Austrians roundly crushed these uprisings.

"You may have the universe if I may have Italy."

GIUSEPPE VERDI

Left The Milanese novelist and poet Alessandro Manzoni (seated, left) meets with Garibaldi. Verdi's great *Requiem* was composed to honor Manzoni's memory.

Richard Wagner

MAY 22, 1813–FEBRUARY 13, 1883

BEST KNOWN FOR HIS OPERAS, RICHARD WAGNER WAS AS MUCH A PHILOSOPHER AND WRITER AS A
MUSICIAN. IN 1876, WITH THE HELP OF KING LUDWIG II OF BAVARIA, WAGNER OPENED THE BAYREUTH
FESTSPIELHAUS AS A SHOWCASE FOR HIS AND OTHER AVANT-GARDE WORKS. HERE, AMONG OTHER WORKS,
HE PREMIÈRED HIS SEMINAL FOUR-PART OPERA CYCLE, *DER RING DES NIBELUNGEN*.

Wagner was born in Leipzig. His mother was Johanna Wagner, but it is uncertain who his father was: Friedrich Wagner, or her lover Ludwig Geyer, whom she married after Friedrich's death in 1813. The newly formed family soon moved to Dresden, where Richard Wagner started his music studies.

Wagner's musical education continued at Leipzig University in 1830, and he soon began work on his first operatic projects, including *Die Feen* (*The Fairies*, 1834), and *Das Liebesverbot* (*Forbidden Love*, 1836). He also worked as a chorus master and conductor, and broadened his range of musical influences to include French, Italian, and German composers.

Above A nineteenth-century lithograph entitled "Wagner's wild music of the future." A controversial figure even in his own lifetime, his works have engendered much debate.

Right A scene from Wagner's opera *Tristan und Isolde*. This is a detail from a mural in Ludwig II's bedroom in Neuschwanstein Castle.

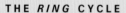

THE *RING* CYCLE

The story of the *Ring* cycle is based very loosely on the Scandinavian legend, *Niebelungenlied*. The first opera in the four-part series, *Das Rheingold* (*The Rhine Gold*) establishes the story's main characters. Alberich the dwarf (Niebelung) steals the Rhine gold from the Rhine maidens (mermaids) and forges a ring from it, making him lord of the dwarves. But Wotan, the king of the gods, also wants the ring. He takes it, plus a hoard of gold, from Alberich, who curses the ring. Wotan uses Alberich's riches to pay his creditor, Fafner (who has helped build him the castle Valhalla), but Fafner and his sidekick demand the ring in return for Wotan's love Freia, whom they had taken as a deposit on the castle. The rest of the cycle follows— with enormous digressions—the fate of those who covet the ring, which, many hours later, ends up back with the Rhine maidens.

PARIS AND DRESDEN

In 1839, after a two-year engagement as a conductor in Riga, Wagner moved to Paris with the hope of premièring his opera *Rienzi* there. This project faltered, but he made some important contacts, including Hector Berlioz, with whom he shared an unusually strong artistic kinship. He wrote the opera *Der fliegende Holländer* (*The Flying Dutchman*) in 1841, in part inspired by sailors' stories he had heard on a stormy sea voyage two years previously, and then started work on *Tannhäuser*. His next stop was Dresden, where he finally premièred *Rienzi* with great success; a production of *The Flying Dutchman* was less successful. Wagner later fled Dresden after his involvement with the failed German nationalist movement.

EXILE AND PHILOSOPHY

In exile in Zurich from 1849, the composer began a period of philosophical introspection, writing essays like *Das Kunstwerk der Zukunft* (*The Artwork of the Future*) and *Oper und Drama* (*Opera and Drama*) to explain his ideas about opera to his audience. He envisaged opera as a *gesamtkunstwerk*, a "total art work," in which music, poetry, and visual art worked together. These ideas came together in the *Ring* cycle, which he began writing in 1850, and *Tristan und Isolde* (1859). A tragic

---

Discover the music

The Flying Dutchman (1841)

Lohengrin (1846–1848)

Die Walküre (1854–1856)

Tristan und Isolde (1859)

5 Wesendonck Songs (1857–1858)

Siegfried Idyll (1870)

story about the redemptive power of love, *Tristan* features experimental harmony and lush orchestration, both of which came to epitomize Wagner's work.

SCANDAL AND KING LUDWIG II

Wagner fled Zurich too, his infatuation with the poet Mathilde Wesendonck having been discovered by his wife Minna Planer. In 1864, he was saved by a powerful admirer, the young King Ludwig II of Bavaria. Ludwig, who was also known for his predilection for extravagant castles, offered Wagner stagings of his operas, *Tristan* the first among them, as well as financial support. Wagner settled in Tibschen, near Lake Lucerne. He was soon joined by Liszt's daughter, Cosima, who was already married to Hans von Bülow,

Above Cosima Wagner directed 15 Bayreuth Festivals before retiring in favor of her son.

the conductor of *Tristan*'s première. In 1870, Cosima and Wagner married.

THE BAYREUTH FESTIVAL AND WAGNER'S FINAL YEARS

To stage his newly completed *Ring* cycle, Wagner built his Festspielhaus (Festival Theater) in the small town of Bayreuth, funded by his concert tours and Ludwig. It opened in 1876, and from thereon hosted the Bayreuth Festival, which continues to this day. Wagner wrote his last opera, *Parsifal*, in 1882, and the following year died of a heart attack in Venice. Cosima took over the directorship of the festival from the time of Wagner's death until 1906.

The War of the Romantics and rise of musical drama

WAGNER WAS AN UNUSUAL FIGURE IN MUSIC HISTORY: EVERYWHERE HE WENT, HE SEEMED TO CREATE SCANDAL, BOTH IN HIS PERSONAL LIFE AND IN HIS REFORMATION OF OPERA, WHICH HE TURNED INTO MUSICAL DRAMA. HE WAS ALSO ON ONE SIDE OF ANOTHER MUSICAL DRAMA—THE SO-CALLED WAR OF THE ROMANTICS, IN WHICH JUST ABOUT EVERY GERMAN COMPOSER OF NOTE WAS EMBROILED, WHETHER THEY LIKED IT OR NOT.

In the 1850s the War of the Romantics, a schism between the conservative and the radical musical figures, began. On the conservative side were Brahms, Clara Schumann, and the influential critic Eduard Hanslick. The radicals were led by Liszt and Wagner. The conservatives were centered in Leipzig, where the Schumanns lived and worked most of their lives, and where the legacy of Johann Sebastian Bach loomed large, thanks to another Leipzig resident, Felix Mendelssohn. The radicals were in Weimar, which Wagner set up as a center for avant-garde music.

What was the drama about? In short, the conservatives believed that the old classical forms—sonatas, symphonies, and so on—should be maintained, while the radicals thought that "new ideas need new bottles." Essentially, they wanted to create new

Above right The original caption to this cartoon of Wagner at a concert read, "Is the audience applauding or wringing their hands in despair?"

Below Winifred Wagner, the composer's daughter-in-law, welcomes Adolf Hitler to the Bayreuth Festival in August 1934.

forms for music, such as the symphonic poem. The battle became quite ugly; nasty articles were written, concerts were sabotaged, and we have been left a treasure trove of insults, not least Brahms's (reported) comment upon hearing that a musician playing in the première of Wagner's *Ring* had died: "the first corpse."

THE PROBLEM WITH OPERA

Wagner, not very surprisingly, was undeterred by the conservatives' criticism. From the late 1840s, he had started to theorize about the future of opera. In a series of articles, he challenged the supremacy of the voice in the Italian operatic tradition, the style in which his own early operas were written. He specifically objected to the use of musical "numbers"—as in a Broadway musical—as showpieces for whichever singer was in vogue, and the fact that operas could be divided up and their numbers mixed and matched without any significant damage to the drama. He also opposed the French tradition's preoccupation with elaborate scenery.

Wagner thought opera should be a *gesamtkunstwerk*—a work in which all of the arts played an equal part. One of his most important principles in achieving this was a new conception of the opera's text (libretto). Usually these were written in rhyming verse, but Wagner considered this quite unnatural, preferring to use alliteration to achieve textual unity. There was one problem with this; traditionally, the librettist—the writer of the text—had an equal share in the production process, and changes could not be made to the libretto without his permission. Wagner took care of this problem by writing his own libretti.

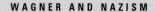

WAGNER AND NAZISM

Wagner has long been connected to the Nazis and their philosophy, and this was no accident. His opera *Die Meistersinger von Nürnberg* (*The Mastersingers of Nuremberg*), which was performed at the party's Nuremberg congress, contains a Jewish character who is a parody of Wagner's enemy, the critic Eduard Hanslick. In addition to the anti-Semitism that can be found in Wagner's works, both literary and musical, his almost unparalleled fame no doubt made him an ideal symbol of German supremacy. It is unfortunate that his work has been tainted by this association, but all the same, it gives his listeners pause for thought, and is evidence of music's associative power.

SOME OTHER CONSIDERATIONS

Wagner also endeavored to make his musical dramas "indivisible," using the orchestra to hold the threads of the drama together. His use of leitmotivs—little melodies that represent objects (like the ring), characters (like the Rhine maidens), or ideas (renunciation, for example) that recur at important moments—was a useful unifying technique. To Wagner, even the venue for performances of his operas was important. The Festspielhaus he designed for Bayreuth has an extra deep, covered orchestra pit, so that the audience can connect with the drama onstage, rather than being distracted by the orchestra.

OTHER MUSICAL DRAMAS

Wagner was not, of course, the only composer to consider how opera might be improved. His great

"The Prelude to [Wagner's] Tristan und Isolde reminds one of the old Italian painting of a martyr whose intestines are slowly unwound from his body on a reel."

EDUARD HANSLICK

Above The "radicals" were led by Wagner and Liszt, pictured here with Cosima, Liszt's daughter and Wagner's wife.

contemporary, Giuseppe Verdi, strove for greater realism in his works, as did Modest Mussorgsky, in his early experimental opera *Zhenit'ba* (*Marriage*) and later in *Boris Godunov*, and Wagner's compatriot Carl Maria von Weber (see pages 204–205).

OPERA IN THE NINETEENTH CENTURY

Most of the operas we know and love today were composed in the nineteenth century, when it was extremely popular. From the biting Italian comic operas, the bombast of French grand opera, through to the carefully calculated passion of Wagner's musical dramas, Romantic opera was the perfect vehicle for the most profound—and silliest—of Romantic ideas.

Italy was easily the most dominant force in nineteenth-century opera, and was performed in every major European city. Rossini's example (pages 168–169) was followed by Vincenzo Bellini (1801–1835), whose *Norma* is a repertoire favorite. The title role, a Druid priestess, is one of opera's most challenging soprano roles, calling for light, fluid singing in a high register called *bel canto* ("beautiful singing"). Gaetano Donizetti (1797–1848) also wrote bel canto roles. His famous opera, *Lucia di Lammermoor* (based on Walter Scott's *The Bride of Lammermoor*), is about a woman who is tricked into marrying a man she does not love,

Right One of the world's leading opera houses, the Vienna State Opera was built in the 1860s. Among its distinguished musical directors were Gustav Mahler and Richard Strauss.

Below The noted soprano Adelina Patti (1843–1919) made her operatic debut at the age of 16, when she sang the title role in Donizetti's *Lucia di Lammermoor*.

and contains one of the most haunting—or, perhaps, ridiculous—mad scenes in opera history. Verdi, with his operas of increasing realism and dramatic depth, represents the culmination of Italian opera in the nineteenth century.

FRANCE

There were many successful French composers in the nineteenth century, including Fromental Halévy (1799–1862) and Daniel Auber (1782–1871), though their works are largely unknown today. The dominant type of opera in Paris for much the first half of the century was grand opera. These operas, mostly performed at the Paris Opéra, were five acts long; they usually contained ballets, and featured elaborate scenery and stage effects. German-born Giacomo Meyerbeer (1791–1864) was an innovator in grand opera, and his *Robert the Devil* (1831) and *Les Huguenots* (1836) achieved international renown. These works are rarely performed nowadays due to their length, expense, and the sheer difficulty of their vocal parts. From around mid-century, grand opera's popularity declined, and composers such as Charles Gounod (1818–1893), with his 1859 opera *Faust* and Bizet, with *Carmen* (1874), gained prominence—and longevity.

GERMAN-SPEAKING LANDS

The most popular German-language operas near the beginning of the century were *Singspiel*s, which combined music and spoken text: Mozart's 1791 work *The Magic Flute* is perhaps the best-known example of this genre. A breakthrough in German-language opera was Carl Maria von Weber's (1786–1826) *Der Freischütz* (*The Freeshooter*), which premièred in 1821; it is renowned for its wealth of melody and unique

THE WOMEN OF NINETEENTH-CENTURY OPERA

Mozart once wrote, "I like an aria to fit a singer as perfectly as a well-tailored suit of clothes." In the nineteenth century, this situation changed. Opera roles were rarely written for particular singers, and singers had to become versatile artists, willing to take on a range of roles. Nonetheless, some singers, especially sopranos, became associated with certain composers and roles, garnering unprecedented fame. The Spanish soprano Isabella Coldran, for example, created the leads in 10 Rossini operas (she even married the composer) while Giuditta Pasta, the first *Norma*, was Bellini's favorite. The fame of another Italian soprano, Adelina Patti, was such that in Russia, Mussorgsky wrote these memorable lyrics for his satirical song, *Rayok* (*The Peepshow*), parodying a contemporary's adoration of her: "He adores Patti, he sings of Patti/O Patti, Patti, O Pa-Pa-Patti/Wonderful Patti, divine Patti."

orchestration. Wagner, of course, soon eclipsed Weber as the century's most successful composer of German-language opera. Interestingly, Weber was also a reformer of opera, and his idea that opera should be self-contained prefigured Wagner's own theories.

OTHER COUNTRIES

While other countries did not produce as many operas as Italy or France, other opera traditions emerged that blended the omnipresent western European influence with nationalist themes and local color. The Czech lands were represented by Smetana and his younger compatriot Leoš Janáček (1854–1928), who wrote a number of successful operas such as *The Cunning Little Vixen* (1823) and *Katya Kabanova* (1821). The latter

Right
A lithograph from an 1824 production of Weber's *Der Frieschütz*.

was based on a play by Alexander Ostrovsky, a realist writer in Russia, another very important non-western force in Romantic opera. Russian opera was first brought to the attention of western Europe with works by the self-taught Mikhail Glinka (1804–1857), who used Russian stories as the basis for his Italianate operas *A Life for the Tsar* (1836) and *Ruslan and Ludmilla* (1842). Glinka's example was vital to the progress of Russian opera, and by the end of the nineteenth century virtually every Russian composer of note had written at least one opera, foremost among them Tchaikovsky, Mussorgsky, Borodin, and Rimsky-Korsakov.

Anton Bruckner

SEPTEMBER 4, 1824–OCTOBER 11, 1896

ANTON BRUCKNER WAS ONE OF THE NINETEENTH-CENTURY'S LEADING CHURCH COMPOSERS AND SYMPHONISTS. LACKING CONFIDENCE IN HIS TALENT, HE OFTEN REVISED HIS WORKS; HIS MODESTY NOTWITHSTANDING, HE MADE ENEMIES OF EDUARD HANSLICK, ONE OF THE MOST POWERFUL CRITICS OF THE TIME, AND BRAHMS, WHO UNCHARITABLY DESCRIBED HIS SYMPHONIES AS "SYMPHONIC BOA-CONSTRICTORS."

Above right A contemporary silhouette of Bruckner meeting Wagner. Bruckner dedicated his third symphony to Wagner.

Left Bruckner, c. 1885, sitting beside his piano. A modest man, the composer nevertheless left all his scores to the Vienna National Library.

Bruckner was born in the Austrian town of Ansfelden. His father was a schoolmaster, and Anton seemed destined to follow his path. However Anton's early music studies at the Augustinian monastery in St Florian, where he became the organist, revealed his talent. After teaching in villages between 1841 and 1845, he settled again in St Florian, where he produced his first works of note, the *Requiem in D minor* (1849) and the *Missa Solemnis* (1854). He also gained a reputation as a fine organist, a skill that allowed him to move to Linz in 1855 as a cathedral organist.

In Linz, Bruckner began his compositional studies in earnest, working with the Viennese theoretician Simon Sechter for an astounding six years. Such devotion was typical of the humble Bruckner, who set great store by learning his craft. He wrote a succession of Masses and his first symphony, in C minor. In 1867, he suffered a nervous breakdown, after which his resolve to move to Vienna, the logical next step for a fledgling composer, was strengthened.

ARTISTIC MATURITY

Bruckner went to Vienna as a teacher of harmony and counterpoint at the Vienna Conservatory, but also worked as organist of the Hofkapelle (court chapel). Many of his students became famous, notably Gustav

---

BRUCKNER AND RELIGION

Bruckner was a devout Roman Catholic, and his religiosity informed his compositions. He was immersed in the Church's traditions for many of his formative years, working as a church composer and organist in Linz. Just like his "enemies," the musical conservatives in Leipzig, he studied old music intently, including the works of sixteenth-century composer Palestrina. Using this knowledge, he crafted his sacred works, such as

motets (polyphonic choral works), Masses, and a *Te Deum* (a chant in praise of God). Bruckner exuded religious humility—it is said he even prayed before improvising—but he was not devoid of self-esteem. He carefully managed his employees to gain better positions, for example, and speaking of Brahms, his supposed arch-enemy, he admitted that while he admired Brahms's work, he liked his own better.

Discover the music

Ave Maria (1861)

Mass No. 2 in E minor (1866)

Symphony No. 4 ("Romantic")
(Version 1, 1874)

String Quintet in
F major (1879)

Te Deum (1881–1884)

Symphony No. 8
(1884–1887)

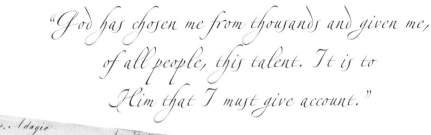

"God has chosen me from thousands and given me, of all people, this talent. It is to Him that I must give account."

Right An autograph copy of Bruckner's *Symphony No. 4* "Romantic", written in 1874. He revised this symphony a number of times.

Below After a pleasing rehearsal of his music, Bruckner tipped conductor Hans Richter (left).

THE LATER YEARS

In the 1880s and 1890s Bruckner revised many of his symphonies, which distracted him from composition. These revisions, encouraged by the composer's well-meaning supporters, are the bane of Bruckner scholars, who struggle to discover which of the many versions of his symphonies Bruckner himself preferred.

Having obtained lodgings from Emperor Franz Josef, and given up his teaching and organ playing, in the last decade of his life Bruckner focused on his *Symphony No. 9*. Upon his death, of natural causes, in 1896, he had written three movements of the work.

Mahler. In his holidays, Bruckner composed, producing in the course of his career ten symphonies. These monumental works owe much to Beethoven, and some even contained quotations from Wagner, whom Bruckner first encountered at the première of *Tristan und Isolde* in 1865. The two had great respect for each other, in contrast to the chilly reception Bruckner met from powerful contemporaries such as Hanslick and Brahms, representatives of the conservatives in the War of the Romantics (see pages 202–203).

IN THE "WAR"

Given Bruckner's sometimes excessive modesty (he is said to have tipped a conductor in gratitude for a successful rehearsal of his fourth symphony), he may have been rather bewildered to have been involved in one of the biggest musical controversies of his time. In spite of his rather academic style, Bruckner ended up in Wagner's camp, just as anyone who openly admired the German composer did. Hanslick, writing of Bruckner's *Symphony No. 3*, said it was, "A vision of Beethoven's Ninth becoming friendly with Wagner's Valkyries [warrior maidens] and finishing up trampled under their hooves." Hanslick's criticism prejudiced Vienna against Bruckner for many years.

Johann Strauss II

OCTOBER 25, 1825–JUNE 3, 1899

DEFYING HIS FATHER'S WISH THAT HE BECOME A BANKER, JOHANN STRAUSS JUNIOR
USURPED THE ELDER JOHANN'S PLACE AS VIENNA'S WALTZ KING. WITH CLASSICS SUCH AS
THE BLUE DANUBE AND *WINE, WOMEN AND SONG*, AND THE OPERETTA *DIE FLEDERMAUS*
(*THE BAT*), STRAUSS IS ONE OF THE NINETEENTH CENTURY'S MOST APPROACHABLE
COMPOSERS, AND HE REMAINS A SYMBOL OF HIS HOME TOWN.

Left Johann Strauss II, seated at center, playing cards with friends. His ubiquitous *Blue Danube* waltz is one of the most recognized tunes of the nineteenth century.

Johann Strauss II was one of three musically gifted sons of the famous conductor and composer Johann Strauss (1804–1849). Johann Junior, Eduard, and Josef all learnt to play the piano as children, but their father discouraged them from careers in music, which he considered too unreliable. Johann, destined to become a banker, pursued his music studies in secret, even learning violin with his father's concertmaster. When Johann was 17, his father left the family home to live with his mistress. Obliged to help support his family, young Johann embarked on his music career, and in 1844 he formed his first orchestra.

Johann and his orchestra struggled to find venues—Johann Senior's influence in Vienna was such that his angry threats were heeded—but managed to debut at the fashionable Dommayer's Casino. Vienna was divided between supporters of Johann Junior and his father, but the performance was a triumph. Johann's later travels within the Hapsburg Empire spread his reputation.

DEATH OF STRAUSS SENIOR

In 1848, Johann Junior sided with the revolutionaries in the bourgeois revolution, further straining his relationship with his father. In 1849, Johann Senior died from scarlet fever, and Strauss amalgamated his and his father's orchestras. Now unconditionally accepted by

Right Strauss's music is inextricably linked with Vienna. After his death, his music continued to be played at Viennese balls, such as this one held to usher in the year 1900.

Discover the music

Annen Polka, Op. 117

Perpetuum Mobile, Op. 257 (1862)

The Blue Danube, Op. 314 (1867)

Tales from the Vienna Woods, Op. 325 (1868)

Wine, Women and Song, Op. 333

Emperor Waltz, Op. 437

Die Fledermaus (1874)

DIE FLEDERMAUS

The play on which *Die Fledermaus* (*The Bat*) was based was originally intended for Parisian stages, so when Strauss set it for a Viennese audience, he had to rename it from *Le réveillon*, meaning midnight supper, to *Die Fledermaus*; and the supper, a Parisian tradition Viennese audiences would not understand, was changed into a ball. The story revolves around Rosalinde and her husband, Eistenstein, who is due to go to jail for eight nights. Eisenstein is convinced by the notary Falke to delay starting his sentence to attend a ball. It turns out that Falke, who is known as "Dr Bat" after Eistenstein played a joke on him, is getting revenge. Eistenstein is shown up as a philanderer, and even Rosalinde, who has allowed her lover, Alfred, go off to jail in Eistenstein's place, does not come out squeaky clean. In typical operetta fashion, all is forgiven in the end. The operetta, with its numerous waltzes and loose morals, has come to typify Vienna of the late 1800s.

the Viennese, Strauss struggled to fulfil their demand for his music, at night rushing between venues to lead orchestras in his "hits."

TOURS ABROAD

In 1856 Strauss took up an invitation to perform in the Russian town of Pavlovsk, to promote the newly opened rail link between Pavlovsk's park and St Petersburg, then one of the world's musical capitals. Following his success there, Russia became one of his many touring destinations. Other destinations included Britain, France, Italy, and even the United States, where he performed at the Boston Festival.

STRAUSS'S MARRIAGES

Johann married three times. His first wife was singer "Jetty" Treffz, who encouraged him to devote more time to composition. Strauss's most famous waltzes,

Above Strauss had lived with Adele Deutsch for some time before they finally married in 1882. She was his third wife.

Tales from the Vienna Woods, *Annen Polka*, and *The Blue Danube* were written during their marriage, which also saw his appointment as music director of the Royal Court balls, a great honor. Inspired by the example of Jacques Offenbach (1819–1880), Johann also started composing operettas. Jetty died in 1878. His second marriage, to the actress Angelika Dittrich, lasted only four years, in part due to her lack of enthusiasm for his work.

Strauss found great happiness with his third wife, Adele. He spent the final 17 years of his life with her, composing masterpieces such as the operetta *Die Fledermaus*, before he died from pneumonia on June 3, 1899. Perhaps the most poignant monument to Vienna's "waltz king" is the gilded bronze statue of him that stands in Vienna's Stadtpark, not one of the city's most tasteful monuments, but one of its most characteristic.

Johannes Brahms

May 7, 1833–April 3, 1897

Strongly influenced by the great German composers
Beethoven and Bach, and suspicious of his contemporaries
Liszt and Wagner, Johannes Brahms was not a typical
Romantic period composer. He was also a contradictory
personality, alienating and charming his friends and
acquaintances in equal measure.

B rahms was born in Hamburg, and was tutored in
music from an early age by his father Johann. He
became an accomplished pianist, making his debut at
16, and received composition lessons from Eduard
Marxsen. Although he played in various venues
throughout Hamburg, including taverns and dance
halls, to help support his family, stories that he played
at brothels appear unfounded.

Right Brahms once
wrote, "Without crafts-
manship, inspiration is a
mere reed shaken in the
wind." His works are
among the most loved in
the classical repertoire.

REPUTATION
While touring as an accompanist to the Hungarian
violinist Eduard Reményi (1828–1898), Brahms
embarked on his career as a composer. He had already
had his arrangements of operatic favorites published,
but in 1853, a meeting with Robert Schumann, who
extolled him as a successor to Beethoven, encouraged
him to concentrate on composing. The weight of
Schumann's judgment rested heavily on Brahms's
shoulders, and he destroyed works he considered
substandard. He also met Liszt around this time,
though he reportedly offended the Hungarian
composer by falling asleep during a

French horn
Consisting of around 12 feet (3.5m) of tubing wrapped
into a coil and a bell, the French horn is the second highest
sounding instrument in the brass family after the trumpet. It differs
from the rest of the brass family because it has rotary valves that look like flat keys.
Early horns did not have valves and were simply a coil of brass tubing with a bell. Pitch
was altered entirely by the lips. These "hunting horns" called hounds to a hunt, and the
horn was often used to invoke the idea of a hunt. Brahms's *Horn Trio*, Op. 40 (1865) is
a particularly evocative composition for French horn.

Discover the music
Serenades for Orchestra, Opp. 11 and 16
　(1857–1859)
Violin Concerto, Op. 77 (1878)
Piano Concerto No. 2, Op. 83 (1878–1881)
Two Rhapsodies, Op. 79 (1879)
Symphony No. 4, Op. 98 (1884–1885)
Clarinet Quintet, Op. 115 (1891)
Four Serious Songs, Op. 121 (1896)

BRAHMS'S PERSONALITY

Writing about Brahms in 1908, the Irish composer Charles Stanford observed: "He could look like Jupiter at one moment, and like Falstaff the next." Indeed, there are mountains of anecdotes about Brahms's contradictory personality—sometimes prickly, other times warm; patient with children, but cranky with adults; profound in his works, yet mundane and predictable in his daily habits. Understandably, people were often confused and offended by him. Composer Hugo Wolf once sent a score to Brahms for checking, but Brahms returned it without correction. "I don't want to make a cemetery of your composition," he said. But Brahms was equally tough on himself: He destroyed many of his compositions, including a reported 20 string quartets, and was so overawed by the work of his idol, Beethoven, that he worked on his first symphony for over a decade.

Above The street in Vienna where Brahms lived. Brahms first visited the city in 1862, and lived there for most of his professional life.

performance of his B minor sonata. Brahms's works from this early period include piano sonatas and scherzi, chamber music, and songs.

CLARA SCHUMANN

Brahms's meeting with Schumann was also significant as the beginning of his passionate—but platonic—relationship with Clara Schumann. Inspired by his feelings for Clara and respect for Robert, he helped the family through Robert's suicide attempt in 1854 and subsequent institutionalization. The depth of his friendship with Clara is reflected in several dedications, such as the *Serenade No. 2*, Op. 16, one of Brahms's first orchestral works.

THE VIENNA YEARS

After Robert Schumann's death in 1856, Brahms returned to Hamburg. He held positions there and continued composing, though few works were published. He then moved to Vienna where, in 1863, he accepted a position as conductor of the Vienna Sing-verein (choir). Brahms wrote some of his greatest works in Vienna and at Clara Schumann's home in Baden-Baden, including the majestic *Piano Quintet in F minor*, Op. 34 (see page 187). Having established his reputation and fulfilled Schumann's prophecy with *A German Requiem*, in 1871 Brahms settled in Vienna for good, taking up the post of conductor with the Ges-ellschaft der Musikfreunde (Society for Music Lovers).

Above A certificate of recognition of Brahms's musical works. His most loved works include his four symphonies, two piano concertos, and the *Violin Concerto*.

Despite his intention to give up composition, Brahms's final years were spent performing and composing. He was feted across Europe, and was awarded honorary doctorates from Cambridge University—which he turned down—and from the University of Breslau, which he accepted, marking the occasion with the specially composed *Academic Festival* Overture (1879). One late love was the clarinet, inspired by clarinetist Richard Mühlfeld (1856–1907). The *Clarinet Quintet*, Op. 115, composed in 1891, was one of his last masterpieces. Brahms died from cancer in Vienna, aged 63.

Germany and Austria–Hungary in the nineteenth century

DURING THE TIME OF BRUCKNER, STRAUSS II, AND BRAHMS, EUROPE CHANGED DRAMATICALLY. THE HARSH RULE OF THE HAPSBURGS IN THEIR TERRITORIES, INCLUDING AUSTRIA, BOHEMIA, THE GERMAN STATES, AND HUNGARY, FOSTERED STRONG NATIONALIST MOVEMENTS. IN 1848 A WAVE OF REVOLUTIONS BEGAN IN PARIS, BUT QUICKLY MOVED TO THE AUSTRIAN TERRITORIES AND PLACES LIKE ITALY, WHERE THERE WAS A STRONG AUSTRIAN PRESENCE.

In Italy, for example, the revolutions, although put down, prefigured the end of Austria's rule in the Italian peninsula. And in Austria itself, Klemens von Metternich was forced to resign, and Emperor Ferdinand I was replaced by his nephew Franz Josef.

FORMATION OF THE AUSTRO–HUNGARIAN EMPIRE

Hungary put up a most protracted fight for its independence. In March 1848, demonstrators demanded a Kingdom of Hungary, to be an autonomous part of the Hapsburg Empire. In response to this, the Austrians enlisted the help of minority groups in a war, which they eventually won with the help of Russia. Harsh reprisals of the revolutionaries followed. However, through several key defeats, the Hapsburg Empire was considerably weakened, and in 1867 the Austro–Hungarian Empire was founded.

UNIFICATION OF GERMANY

Another Austrian setback came in 1866, when it was defeated by Prussia and Italy in the seven-week Austro–Prussian War. Prussian prime minister, Otto von Bismarck, had aimed to exclude Austria from Germany, thus increasing Prussia's influence there, and he was successful. The Austrian-led German confederation was dissolved and in 1871, after the Franco–Prussian War, the German Second Empire was created. King Wilhelm I of Prussia was crowned its king. The empire was made up of 25 German states, and was extremely prosperous. The population surged, and industry boomed. But despite this growth, there were numerous problems. While Bismarck tried

Right The proclamation of the German Empire at the Hall of Mirrors, Versailles, in 1871, by Prussian Prime Minister Otto von Bismarck and new emperor Wilhelm I.

to keep peace with Germany's neighbors, even negotiating a triple alliance between Germany, Austro–Hungary, and Italy, he was autocratic in home affairs, battling with the Liberals, the Church, and the Social Democrat party. In a bid to unify the empire, he also enforced a policy of Germanization on minority groups such as the Poles. In 1890 he was dismissed by the new king, Wilhelm II.

Above German poet, philosopher, and dramatist Friedrich Schiller. Some of his plays and poems were set to music by Beethoven, Schubert, Brahms, and Verdi.

GERMAN CULTURE

In Germany's cultural life, nationalism had flourished since mid-century. Figures like Friedrich Schiller (1759–1805), whose poem *An die Freude* (*Ode to Joy*) was immortalized by Beethoven's *Symphony No. 9*, were embraced as symbols of German unity, and from the 1830s, statues of other great Germans sprang up across the country. This movement continued after unification. In music, Viennese composers such as Brahms and Bruckner were extremely influential on German instrumental music in the second half of the century. Opera gradually became more popular and nationalistic, culminating in the works of Wagner; orchestral and chamber concert series were established, and domestic music-making remained popular, boosted by extensive music publishing. Unfortunately, as in the political sphere, the German Empire's rise had negative elements, among them the anti-Semitism of prominent figures such as Wagner.

LIFE IN THE AUSTRO–HUNGARIAN EMPIRE

Meanwhile, in the newly formed Austro–Hungarian Empire, there were many problems. The numerous minority groups within the empire, including Romanians and Slavs, began to demand independence. Also, now that the empire was powerless in Germany and Italy, it began to focus on expanding into other areas of Europe, putting it on the path to World War I. Despite these tensions, society was much more relaxed than in the Biedermeier era that preceded the 1848 revolutions. In the capital Vienna, the waltzes of the Strausses ruled supreme, alongside operettas by Jacques Offenbach, and folk music was venerated.

Right Viennese audiences enjoyed the works of Jacques Offenbach (1819–1880), who is shown in the center of this cartoon engraving from 1825.

OTTO VON BISMARCK (1815–1898)

Otto von Bismarck, architect of the German unification, was a difficult but brilliant man. He was also capable of underhand tactics, one of which led to the Franco–Prussian War and Germany's unification. In 1870 Prince Leopold, a relative of Prussian king Wilhelm I, had accepted, then turned down an offer to be the king of Spain. The French were relieved, as they did not want Prussian influence on their southern border. But when approached by a French ambassador for confirmation that Leopold would never accept the Spanish throne, Wilhelm refused, politely, to discount Leopold's claim. He then sent a telegram about this exchange to Bismarck. Bismarck, seeing his chance to provoke war with France, shortened the telegram to read as though Wilhelm had not just refused, but insulted the French ambassador; he then had the telegram published. The French were incensed, and shortly after war broke out.

Bedřich Smetana

MARCH 2, 1824–MAY 12, 1884

BEST KNOWN FOR HIS COLLECTION OF SYMPHONIC POEMS *MÁ VLAST* AND HIS OPERA *THE BARTERED BRIDE*, BEDŘICH SMETANA WAS ONE OF BOHEMIA'S FINEST COMPOSERS. HIS LIFE WAS MARKED BY TRAGEDY, INCLUDING THE DEATHS OF MOST OF HIS YOUNG FAMILY AND, FROM THE AGE OF 50, DEAFNESS.

Right Smetana, c. 1866. Proudly patriotic, he used folk themes and rhythms in his works, aiming to imbue them with a distinct nationalist flavor.

Born in the town of Litomyšl, Bohemia, Smetana received violin lessons with his father, a brewer, and soon became known as a piano prodigy. He was sent to Prague for secondary school, but when the capital's cultural life proved too distracting, he was removed to Plzen, another Bohemian town. In 1841, he wrote what he considered to be his first real composition, *Three Impromptus* for piano.

Another important formative work of Smetana's was his *Six Characteristic Pieces* for piano. Smetana had returned to Prague in 1844 to study composition, and in 1848 sent the six pieces to Franz Liszt, hoping the older composer would accept his dedication—and alleviate his dire financial condition. While Liszt was unable to help financially, he became one of Smetana's most loyal supporters.

HAPPINESS, TRAGEDY, AND SUCCESS

After an unsuccessful attempt to establish a music school in Prague, Smetana made ends meet through teaching and playing for Emperor Ferdinand. In 1849 he married his long-time love, Katerina Kolárová. His happiness was short-lived—three of his four daughters died in close succession, and in 1859 Katerina succumbed to illness. This tragic period in his life, sadly not the last, inspired many great works, including the G minor *Piano Trio* (1855). He remarried a year later.

Smetana had been working as a conductor, teacher, and performer in the Swedish town of Göteburg from 1856, but was encouraged to return to Prague with the opening of the Provisional Theater, which was dedicated to the performance of Czech works. He wrote a number of works for the theater, including *Brandenburgers in Bohemia* (1866), and the work for which he is perhaps best known, *The Bartered Bride* (*Prodana Nevesta*, also 1866). Smetana later became the theater's director. In 1872, he started work on the symphonic poems *Má vlast* (*My Country*), completing them seven years later, after he had become completely deaf.

Far right Smetana plays the piano for friends. Among his piano works are *14 Czech Dances* (1878) and a number of lively polkas.

Below Located in the center of Prague, Czech Republic, the Smetana Museum, at front left, is dedicated to the composer's life and works.

FROM MY LIFE

Smetana wrote of his 1876 string quartet, *From my Life:* "The long insistent note in the finale … is the fateful ringing in my ears of the high-pitched tones which, in 1874, announced the beginning of my deafness. I permitted myself this little joke because it was so disastrous to me." The quick progression of his deafness, said to have been brought on by syphilis, was just one of the themes of Smetana's life expressed in *From my Life*, which also describes his happy childhood and his time with Katerina. It was not, however, Smetana's swan song; despite his unfortunate affliction, the composer wrote many other works before his death, at age 60, in a Prague asylum.

"I am not ashamed to reply to you in my mother tongue, however imperfectly, and am glad to be able to show that my fatherland means more to me than anything else."

MÁ VLAST (1872–1879)

Má vlast (*My Country*) is one of the greatest musical tributes to a country ever written. Though it comprises six symphonic poems, each work can stand alone. The second, *Vltava* (*The Moldau*), is most often performed nowadays. The Moldau River, formed from two sources, runs through much of the modern Czech Republic (then Bohemia), and merges with the Elbe. Smetana shows himself a master of tone-painting, if not as highly original, by using flutes to imitate the waves of the river's sources, to which clarinets are added to depict its broadening. This builds up to the poem's main melody,

played by strings. The origins of this melody are murky, but though it has come to represent Czech pride, it may be based on a Swedish folksong *Ack, Värmland du sköna* (*Dear Old Stockholm*). If so, this melody is another example of the broad influences nationalist composers took on, imbuing them with national flavor. The other poems in *Má vlast* also represent important Czech figures and landmarks, such as Prague's Vyšehrad castle (No. 1), a warrior from Czech folklore (No. 3), and a mountain, Blahnik, in which defenders of the fatherland are said to have slept, ready to be called into action (No. 6).

Antonín Dvořák

SEPTEMBER 8, 1841–MAY 1, 1904

BELOVED IN HIS NATIVE BOHEMIA AND CELEBRATED IN EUROPE AND ABROAD, ANTONÍN DVOŘÁK WAS ONE OF THE NINETEENTH CENTURY'S LEAST TORTURED ARTISTIC SOULS. HIS WORKS, RANGING FROM THE SIMPLE *SLAVONIC DANCES* TO THE GRAND *NEW WORLD* SYMPHONY, REFLECT HIS OPTIMISTIC PERSONALITY, AND ARE WORTHY STAPLES OF THE CLASSICAL REPERTOIRE.

Dvořák was born in the Czech village of Nelahozeves to an innkeeper father. He received his earliest musical education in the nearby town of Zlonice, then, from 1857 until 1859 attended the Prague Organ School. Proficient in the violin and viola, he found a place in the orchestra of the newly opened Provisional Theater, conducted by Bedřich Smetana. He stayed there until 1871.

Discover the music

Cypresses, song cycle (later arranged for string quartet) (1865)

Violin Concerto in A minor, Op. 53 (1879-80)

Dumka Piano Trio No. 4, Op. 90 (1890-91)

Symphony No. 9 "From the New World" (1893)

String Quartet in F major, Op. 96, "The American" (1893)

Humoresques, Op. 101 (1894)

Cello Concerto in B minor, Op. 104 (1895)

FIRST WORKS AND ONGOING SUCCESSES

While it is often said that he composed simple dances from the age of five, Dvořák wrote his earliest works of note in the 1860s, including two symphonies, chamber music, a cello concerto, and a song cycle, *Cypresses*, which was dedicated to his student Josefína Cermáková, with whom he was infatuated. Dvořák's attempts at opera met with limited success, but his 1873 patriotic cantata, *The Heirs of the White Mountain*, brought him great acclaim. He achieved economic security working

Above right The cover of the sheet music for Dvořák's *Slavonic Dances*, published by Simrock in Berlin.

Above A portrait of Dvořák in middle age. The composer had a number of students at the Prague Conservatory. Among them was Josef Suk who later married Dvořák's daughter Otilie.

Left A backdrop for the first production of Dvořák's opera *Rusalka* (1900). The opera is still regularly performed today.

as an organist and from an Austrian state stipend, and his composition flourished. It was a rewarding time personally, too. His love for Josefína was unrequited, but he married her sister, Anna, in 1873.

Helped by Brahms, who had become an admirer of his work, Dvořák established a relationship with the publisher Simrock; as a result, his *Moravian Dances* were published in 1879, and he wrote his first set of *Slavonic Dances*. He finally had some luck with an opera, *Dimitrij*, which was well received in Bohemia, and also performed extensively abroad. Dvořák was especially popular in England—he composed choral music for societies in Birmingham and Leeds, and his seventh and eighth symphonies for the Royal Philharmonic Society.

AMERICA

Following on from these triumphs, in 1891 Dvořák was invited by the American philanthropist Jeannette Thurber to head the new National Conservatory of Music in New York. The salary on offer—$15,000— was generous, and Dvořák was impressed by Thurber's intention to accept all students, regardless of color or means. The following year, after much prevaricating, he accepted. Dvořák only lasted three years in America before succumbing to homesickness, but he wrote some of his finest works there, including the *New World* Symphony and the *American* Quartet. Among the significant works he composed upon returning to Prague are his symphonic poems (1896–1897) and his finest opera, *Rusalka* (1900), which is about a water sprite who wants to become human. Dvořák died, after a short illness, on May Day, 1904.

Right Jeannette Thurber invited Dvořák to head the new National Conservatory of Music in New York. He held this position from 1892 until 1895.

Below A statue of Dvořák stands at the entrance to the Rudolfinum in Prague. Today the auditorium is the home of the Czech Philharmonic Orchestra.

THE *NEW WORLD* SYMPHONY

Dvořák was a nationalist composer, but he was also open to influences from other countries. Nowhere was this more evident than in his ninth symphony, *From the New World*. Dvořák had ample inspiration to compose his symphony. Jeannette Thurber, his employer, wanted to initiate a truly American style of composition. Dvořák, enthusiastically taking up this challenge, advocated African–American music as a source of authentic American music. In his own music, he did not usually quote folk songs and dances directly, but would identify the defining characteristics of these melodies—a distinctive rhythm, for example—and write his own, authentic-sounding melodies. There are some spiritual-like melodies in the *New World* symphony, especially the haunting English horn theme in the famous second movement (Largo). This melody so resembled a spiritual, "Goin' Home," that critics accused Dvořák of stealing it; in fact, the opposite was true—the spiritual "Goin' Home" is actually based on Dvořák's melody. There are few classical symphonies more melodic—and more approachable—than the *New World* symphony, which almost single-handedly elevated the status of American music.

"In the negro melodies of America I discover all that is needed for a great and noble school of music."

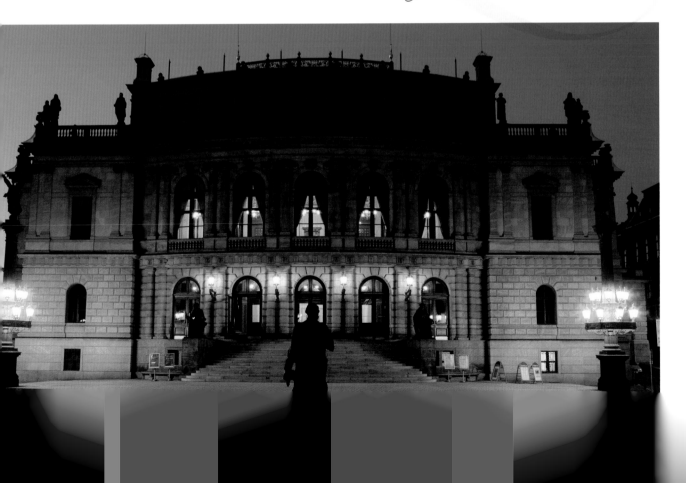

Central European music in the nineteenth century

WESTERN EUROPEAN COUNTRIES DOMINATED MUSICAL LIFE IN THE NINETEENTH CENTURY—AT LEAST IN WHAT WE CONSIDER TO BE "CLASSICAL" MUSIC. CHOPIN, FOR EXAMPLE, THOUGH POLISH, LIVED IN PARIS MOST OF HIS LIFE, AND WAS MORE STRONGLY INFLUENCED BY HIS GERMAN AND FRENCH CONTEMPORARIES THAN BY HIS COUNTRY'S MUSIC.

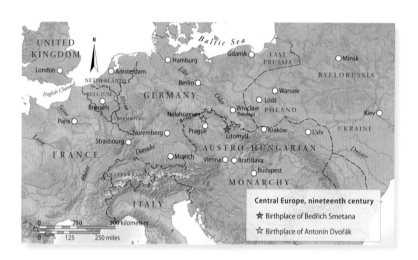

Central Europe, nineteenth century
★ Birthplace of Bedřich Smetana
☆ Birthplace of Antonín Dvořák

But living abroad did not preclude composers like Chopin and Liszt—who rarely visited his native Hungary—from being "nationalist" composers, while the most successful of those composers who spent much of their lives in their own countries were part of this Western tradition, merely coloring their works with allusions to, or quotations of, folk song and dance. This can especially be seen in central or eastern European countries such as Hungary, Poland, and Bohemia (from which a large part of the modern-day Czech Republic is comprised), where uprisings against foreign rule went hand-in-hand with musical nationalism.

HUNGARY

In Hungary there was a craze for the lively *verbunkos*, a recruiting dance for the Hungarian army. *Verbunkos* have become synonymous with Hungary, and feature in the works of one of Hungary's most important nineteenth-century composers, Ferenc Erkel (1810–1893). Erkel wrote the first Hungarian-language opera,

Below A romantic view of wandering Hungarian musicians. Music was, and remains, an integral part of Hungarian life.

Bátori Mária, in 1840. His 1861 opera *Bánk bán* is considered the Hungarian national opera, and even now is performed on Hungary's national day. The opera is based on a true story with a patriotic theme. Bánk, a duke, is forced to choose between his honor (the brother of the Hungarian queen tries to seduce Bánk's wife) and his country, parts of which the queen, Gertrude, has given away to her German relatives.

Liszt, in spite of his lack of proficiency in Hungarian and his infrequent visits to Hungary, also successfully conveyed Hungarian folk color in his compositions.

POLAND

In Poland the situation was quite different. Unlike the other central European countries, it had its own

Left The village beauty is invited to dance, in a painting by Hungarian artist Szale Ignac Janos (1833–1896). So-called "gypsy music" inspired many composers.

CSÁRDÁS

The influence of Hungarian folksong on Liszt was limited, or at best indirect, but the three examples of *csárdás* (char-dash) he wrote for piano solo are an exception. Though it is often considered gypsy music, the *csárdás* is actually a Hungarian folk dance related to *verbunkos*. A csárdás features variations in tempo—it starts out slowly, then moves into a frenzied dance. When danced, the women twirl, while the men stomp. Not surprisingly, Liszt's *csárdások*, including the *Csárdás macabre* (1881) and the *Csárdás obstinée* (1882), make the most of the almost aggressive, discordant quality of the dance's fast section. Many of Liszt's *Hungarian Rhapsodies* for piano contain less literal, but no less memorable references to csárdás. Non-Hungarian composers also made use of csárdás (and other folk dances) to color their works. In Strauss Junior's opera *Die Fledermaus*, for instance, the character Rosaline sings a csárdás to maintain her disguise as a Hungarian countess.

national opera house and its own opera repertoire from the late eighteenth century. After Napoleon's defeat in 1815, Poland's hopes of independence arising from its alliance with France were quashed, and Poland was ruled by the Prussians, the Russians, and the Austrians. Nonetheless, during the Napoleonic era a significant nationalist movement had begun, and though uprisings in 1830 and 1863 were suppressed, the Polish people found inspiration in the heroes of this movement, such as the rebellious and politically active poet Adam Mickiewicz (1798–1855).

Poland's chief musical export, Chopin, expressed his nationalist outrage from the safety of Paris, with fiery Polish mazurkas, Polonaises (see page 188), and a *Krakowiak* (folk dance from Krakow) for piano and orchestra. Stanisław Moniuszko (1819–1872), who remained in Poland, was also a nationalist. In addition to setting Mickiewicz's poems, in 1858 he wrote the opera *Halka* (*Helen*), a key work in the Polish repertoire. The opera, about a peasant girl abandoned by her

Right Hungarian dance steps are demonstrated by Herr Frappart and Fraulein Cououi, in an engraving from the nineteenth century.

noble lover, highlighted the issue of peasant emancipation, hotly debated by Poland's intellectuals at that time.

BOHEMIA

At the start of the nineteenth century, Bohemia was also part of the Austrian Empire. Even so, its capital, Prague, had already established a reputation as a musical center, with a well-established series of classical music concerts and its own music conservatory. With the works of Smetana (pages 214–215), Dvořák (pages 216–217), and their younger colleague Leoš Janáček (1854–1928), Czech music came into its own, especially in chamber and orchestral music, which gained world renown. Of the Czech folk dances, the lively, duple-time (two beats to the bar) polka was probably the most famous, and was a particular favorite of Smetana's.

THE RISE OF THE CONDUCTOR

Every classical music lover is familiar with the image of a conductor standing in front of the orchestra, frantically or calmly coaxing music from the musicians. Indeed, most people nowadays associate a conductor with classical music. However, the idea of a conductor visible to all the orchestra, baton in hand, was relatively new in the nineteenth century, when conducting as we know it originated.

In years gone by, a long stick was tapped against the floor to keep time. As legend has it, the seventeenth-century French court composer Jean-Baptiste Lully stabbed his foot with such a staff, developed gangrene, and died. Another, safer precursor to the baton, a manuscript roll, was used by the German composer Carl Maria von Weber (1786–1826) in the early nineteenth century; then, in 1820, another

Above Jean-Baptiste Lully (1632–1687) (see page 73) always beat time with a long staff. He apparently once impaled his own foot.

composer, Louis Spohr (1784–1859), used a baton to conduct a concert in London, and claimed to have been the first to do so. Felix Mendelssohn was another early baton user. From this point, the art of conducting developed quickly, and was in part necessitated by the increasing difficulty of orchestral works. Just as virtuoso soloists pushed the limits of their instruments, virtuoso conductors began to set new standards of accuracy and brilliance in orchestral playing.

THE COMPOSER-CONDUCTORS

The French opera composer Charles Gounod (1818–1893) once observed, "The conductor is nothing more than the driver of the coach engaged by the composer. He should stop at every request or quicken the pace according to the fare's orders. Otherwise the composer is entitled to get out and complete the journey on

> *"If [the conductor] uses a baton, the baton itself must be a living thing, charged with a kind of electricity, which makes it an instrument of meaning in its tiniest movement ..."*
>
> LEONARD BERNSTEIN

foot." But quite often the conductor *was* the composer, for example Hector Berlioz, one of the greatest of all nineteenth-century conductors. He took up conducting to ensure correct performances of his work, toured extensively, and even wrote a treatise on conducting, in which he outlined techniques that are still used today. His skill as a conductor was partly attributable to his enthusiasm, but his excellent understanding of orchestral instruments helped as well. Wagner was another keen conductor of his own works, and both he and Berlioz were among the first to conduct the works of others.

THE INTANGIBLES

In the introduction to his treatise on conducting, Berlioz outlines some of the qualities of a good conductor—vigor, knowledge of the composition, and familiarity with all the instruments, for example—then adds that a conductor must also possess "other indefinable gifts, without which an invisible link cannot establish itself between him and those he directs." These gifts remain indefinable, and undoubtedly add to the glamor of conducting, a glamor that has persisted to this day.

HANS VON BÜLOW

While early conductors were either primarily composers or instrumental soloists, before long professional conductors emerged. Hans von Bülow (1830–1894),

Left A modern symphony orchestra with conductor. The noted nineteenth-century conductor Hans Van Bülow once remarked that be a good conductor, "you must have the score in your head, not your head in the score."

Below The great Austrian conductor Felix Weingartner was admired by composers as different as Brahms and Stravinsky.

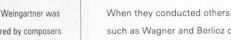

SUBJECTIVITY CHALLENGED

When they conducted others' works, conductors such as Wagner and Berlioz did not merely follow the composer's directions, but interpreted the work according to their own impressions of it. Von Bülow also believed that conducting was a subjective interpretation, rather than a precise reading of the musical score, and would often vary tempi (speeds) as he wished, without regard for the composer's instructions. However, at the end of the nineteenth century Austrian conductor and composer Felix Weingartner (1863–1942), who conducted at the Vienna State Opera and Vienna Philharmonic, wrote a pamphlet criticizing the extreme subjectivity of the Wagnerian approach. He promoted fidelity to the score and to the composer's intentions; he also objected to theatricality on the podium—the exaggerated wiping of brows, and so on. Weingartner's own approach to conducting was extremely efficient; in fact, from the audience's perspective, he looked to be standing still. Weingartner's views on interpretation, if not theatricality, have been highly influential on conductors ever since, and his recordings are testament to his beliefs.

who was also a concert pianist, could also be considered a career conductor, perhaps the nineteenth century's finest. As the director of the Munich Royal Opera, he brilliantly conducted the first performances of Wagner's *Tristan und Isolde* and *Die Meistersinger von Nürnberg*. He also established the renowned Meiningen Orchestra, which played with Liszt-like virtuosity, and toured all over Europe to great acclaim. Von Bülow was a pedant who strictly controlled his orchestra, but he also took on an educative role, introducing works to audiences before performances.

Camille Saint-Saëns

OCTOBER 9, 1835–DECEMBER 16, 1921

AN ASTONISHING PRODIGY WHO COULD PLAY ALL BEETHOVEN'S PIANO SONATAS AT THE AGE OF 10, CAMILLE SAINT-SAËNS WAS TURNED DOWN FOR THE PRIX DE ROME FOR (AS THE STORY GOES) "LACKING INEXPERIENCE." WHILE ALWAYS DISPLAYING A YOUTHFUL PRECOCITY, SAINT-SAËNS WAS A SERIOUS COMPOSER, AND WOULD HAVE BEEN MORTIFIED TO LEARN THAT HE IS NOW BEST KNOWN FOR HIS JOYFUL ROMP, *CARNIVAL OF THE ANIMALS*.

Left A portrait of Saint-Saëns at 35 by Gustave Jacquet. A prolific composer, he once said, "There is nothing more difficult than talking about music."

Above A portrait of Saint-Saëns appeared on the cover of *Musica* magazine in June 1903. The composer was also a virtuosic organist.

SAINT-SAËNS'S "ORGAN" SYMPHONY

The organ does not often feature in symphonies, though some composers, such as Saint-Saëns's contemporaries Charles-Marie Widor (1844–1937) and Louis Vierne (1870–1937) wrote organ symphonies, taking advantage of the instrument's sometimes "orchestral" sound. Saint-Saëns was known across Europe as a fine organist, but did not include it in a symphony until his third, which is properly known as a symphony "with organ." Even then, the organ is not heard until the second section, where it only plays quietly. It comes to the fore in the final section, where, with a commanding chord, it confirms the movement from foreboding C minor to a bright C major. Given Saint-Saëns's disapproval of his *Carnival of the Animals*, he may have been distressed to learn that this final section, perhaps his finest musical inspiration, is now associated with the motion picture *Babe*.

Saint-Saëns was born in Paris. His father died when he was only three months old, and he was brought up by his mother and his aunt. The latter introduced him to the piano; at the age of five, he appeared in concert, and at 10 he made his debut recital. His studies at the Paris Conservatoire resulted in many honors, and a close friendship with Liszt, and in 1853 his first symphony premièred to great acclaim.

THE EARLY SUCCESSES

Saint-Saëns was also an accomplished organist—Liszt rated him the world's best—and after graduation, he made a steady income playing for Paris churches. His organ improvisations, performed weekly, were a feature of Parisian musical life. His love for the organ also informed his composition, most notably in the finale of his *Symphony No. 3* (1886), still one of his most frequently performed works. The piano also features strongly in Saint-Saëns's compositioonal output. His first piano concerto is considered to be the first such work by a French composer.

Another source of income was piano teaching at École Niedermeyer. He ruffled feathers by including modern works by Liszt, Berlioz, and Wagner in his students' repertoire, ironically defying his reputation as a staunch classicist. He had many successful students, foremost among them Gabriel Fauré.

THE 1870s AND 1880s

After the Franco–Prussian war of 1870, during which Saint-Saëns sheltered in London, he returned to Paris and co-founded the Société Nationale de Musique, which gave fledgling composers an opportunity to perform their work. The 1870s also saw Saint-Saëns's marriage to Marie-Laure Truffot, and tragedy—his two year-old son died after falling from a window, and his other son died from illness, just weeks later. The couple separated in 1881. Two of Saint-Saëns's most popular works, the *Danse macabre* (1875) and the opera *Samson et Dalila* (1878), date from this sad time.

The next decade was scarcely less tumultuous. In 1886, controversy shook the Société Nationale. The society was devoted to French composers only, and the likes of César Franck, Jules Massenet, and Fauré took advantage of the exposure it provided. But Saint-Saëns fought for the promotion of foreign

Above An 1894 engraving of a production of Saint-Saëns's three-act opera *Samson et Dalila*. The libretto was by Ferdinand Lemaire.

Discover the music

Symphony No. 3 ("Organ") (1866)
Danse macabre, Op. 40 (1874)
Piano Concerto No. 2, Op. 22 (1875)
Samson et Dalila (1878)
Carnaval des Animaux (1886)

composers in the society. The battle resulted in his resignation. Again, his work refuted the turmoil in his life—the same year he produced *Carnival of the Animals*, which he considered too frivolous to publish during his lifetime, and his third ("Organ") symphony.

THE FINAL YEARS

Saint-Saëns's mother died two years after the Société furore, and in deep mourning he set off overseas. His travels inspired the fifth piano concerto, the 'Egyptian", and another work for piano and orchestra, *Africa*. In the final years of his life, Saint-Saëns was regarded with scorn in France. Writing in 1921, the year of Saint-Saëns's death, his compatriot Claude Debussy sniped: "Does no one care sufficiently to tell him he has written music enough?"; while Maurice Ravel commented that he would have been better off making shell-casings for the war effort. In recent times Saint-Saëns's reputation has recovered from the prejudice that "lacking inexperience" can provoke, and he is now recognized as one of France's greatest composers.

Georges Bizet

OCTOBER 25, 1838–JUNE 3, 1875

FRENCH COMPOSER GEORGES BIZET RECEIVED ONLY OCCASIONAL ACCLAIM DURING HIS 36 YEARS, WRYLY OBSERVING THAT, "IN ORDER TO SUCCEED TODAY YOU HAVE TO BE EITHER DEAD OR GERMAN." AND INDEED WHILE CONTEMPORARIES SUCH AS BERLIOZ RECOGNIZED BIZET'S TALENT, MASTERPIECES SUCH AS *CARMEN* AND *THE PEARL FISHERS*—NOW MAINSTAYS OF THE OPERA REPERTOIRE—DID NOT CAPTURE THE HEARTS OF FRENCH AUDIENCES UNTIL AFTER THE COMPOSER'S DEATH.

Georges Bizet, born Alexander Cesar Leopold Bizet, had a sound musical pedigree: His father was a singer and composer, his mother a pianist, and his uncle the well-known singing teacher François Delsarte. Bizet was born in Paris, and by the age of nine was attending its famous Conservatoire, where he won many prizes. His composition studies under the opera composer Fromental Halévy resulted in an astonishing student work, the *Symphony in C*, which was unearthed only in 1933 and has since been made into a ballet by choreographer George Balanchine.

BIZET'S OPERA PROJECTS
After winning the Prix de Rome, Bizet went to Italy for three years, and continued his opera composition there with the comic work *Don Procopio* (1858–1859). He returned to Paris in 1860.

In the 1860s, Bizet worked on a series of opera projects. One of these was the completion of an opera that his teacher Halévy had left unfinished at his death in 1862, another, a setting of the operetta *The Miracle Doctor*. In 1863, he composed another very popular opera, *The Pearl Fishers*. Best known for its haunting

Above right Bizet was another composer who did not live to old age, dying at the age of just 36. He was interred in the Père Lachaise Cemetery in Paris.

Opposite Singer Anna Caterina Antonacci as Carmen, dancing for the crowd in a 2006 production at London's Royal Opera House.

Below left A scene from the 1954 production of *The Pearl Fishers* at the Sadlers Wells Theatre in London. The opera was set in the exotic locale of Ceylon.

tenor–baritone duet dedicated to friendship, *Au fond du temple saint* (*In the depths of the temple*), it may come as a surprise to learn that the opera received a lukewarm reception. Bizet wrote other operas, but their success was equally limited. The composer made his living primarily from accompanying rehearsals, and from the publication of opera arrangements and piano works. In 1869 he married Halévy's daughter, Geneviève.

CARMEN
Bizet had spent many years battling for performances of his works, and *Carmen*, composed in 1875 on a commission from the Opéra-Comique, was no exception. The opera's tragic ending, unheard of on the Opéra-Comique's stage, was opposed, and the difficulty of its orchestration offended the musicians. The Spanish color of the work, best exemplified in the catchy *Votre toast, je peux vous le rendre* (*Song of the Toreador*), was mocked by contemporaries such as Charles Gounod, who wrote that, "Take the Spanish airs ... out of the score, and there remains nothing to Bizet's credit but the sauce that masks the fish," but, with time, it found favor with Parisian audiences, including Bizet's countrymen Claude Debussy and Saint-Saëns. Not long after *Carmen*'s première, Bizet died from a heart attack in Bougival, near Paris.

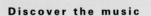

> **Discover the music**
>
> *Symphony in C* (1855)
> *The Pearl Fishers* (*Les Pêcheurs de Perles*) (1863)
> *Jeux d'Enfants* (*Children's Games*) (1871)
> *L'Arlésienne* Suites 1 (1872) and 2 (by Guiraud)
> *Carmen* (1873–1874)

"What a beautiful art, but what a wretched profession."

BIZET'S *L'ARLÉSIENNE* SUITES

In 1872, the French writer Alphonse Daudet (1840–1897) penned a rather strange play: *L'Arlésienne* (*The Maid of Arles*). The story is simple—the "hero," a peasant named Frédéri, is madly in love with a girl from Arles. The audience never sees this girl, but learns of her pre-nuptial deception of Frédéri, who goes mad and commits suicide by jumping off a balcony. The play was a failure, and Daudet went back to writing novels, but the incidental music Bizet wrote for it was more successful. The two *L'Arlésienne* Suites, each comprising four movements, are mainly derived from this incidental music: Bizet wrote the first suite shortly after the play's première, and the composer's friend Ernest Guiraud compiled the second one after Bizet's death. Both suites have become favorite orchestral showpieces, and with good reason. Bizet had a flair for melody that few of his contemporaries could match, combined with efficient but beautiful orchestration. Listen, for example, for the harp that introduces Frédéri's theme in the last part of the Prelude (Movement 1, Suite 1), and the saxophone in the Menuet (Movement 3, Suite 2). Even though the subject matter of *L'Arlésienne* is grim, the music, exemplified by the irrepressible march that pervades the suites, exudes a certain joie de vivre. Bizet himself expressed his esthetic most clearly: "Let us have fantasy, boldness, unexpectedness, enchantment—above all, tenderness, *morbidezza* (delicacy)."

Emmanuel Chabrier

JANUARY 18, 1841–SEPTEMBER 13, 1894

UNLIKE MOST SUCCESSFUL COMPOSERS, EMMANUEL CHABRIER DID NOT TAKE UP COMPOSING IN EARNEST UNTIL HALFWAY THROUGH HIS LIFE. CHABRIER MADE UP THE LOST TIME WELL, USING HIS LIMITED MUSICAL EDUCATION TO COMPOSE DELIGHTFUL, SUNNY WORKS SUCH AS THE ORCHESTRAL RHAPSODY *ESPAÑA*. HE WAS ALSO RENOWNED FOR THE COMPANY HE KEPT, INCLUDING WAGNER AND SOME OF THE FINEST POETS OF THE DAY.

The son of a barrister, Chabrier was born in the central French town of Ambert. The most important person in his childhood seems to have been his nanny, Anne, to whom he stayed close throughout his life. While he later followed his father into law, Chabrier's musical talent was encouraged; he took piano lessons, and his earliest compositions were for that instrument. His piano playing became legendary, earning this description from fellow composer André Messager: "He would attack the piano not only with his hands but also with his elbows, his forehead, his stomach, and even his feet, thereby producing the most unusual effects and a volume of sound akin to that of a

Discover the music

L'étoile (1877)

10 Pièces pittoresques (1880)

España (1883)

Gwendoline (1885)

Le roi malgré lui (1887)

Six mélodies (1890)

Below Chabrier's *España* (1883) inspired other composers, including Erik Satie and Emile Wald- teufel, who published a suite of waltzes quoting Chabrier's work.

ferocious storm; he would only relax when the unfortunate instrument was itself reeling on its legs like a drunken man."

EARLY STUDIES AND CAREER

After the family moved to Paris in 1856, Chabrier continued his musical studies, although he graduated with a law degree in 1861. He was employed by the French Ministry of the Interior, but did not give up composing. As with so many of his compatriots, Chabrier admired Wagner, even though his compositions during this early stage of his career were limited to light piano works and operettas, including *L'étoile*, a comedy about a murderous king, which premièred in 1877.

CHABRIER THE COMPOSER

Partly inspired by Wagner, this time by a performance of *Tristan und Isolde*, in 1880 Chabrier quit his public service post, and the same year produced one of his most beloved piano works, the *10 Pièces pittoresques* (*10 Picturesque Pieces*). He also took work as a secretary to the conductor Charles Lamoureux, which involved being a repetiteur—a pianist who trains singers—and a choir master, roles that provided him with vital contacts and a range of opportunities for performances of his works. As Larmoureux was active in promoting Wagner's music, Chabrier therefore also became a "Wagnerian."

A trip to Spain in 1882 inspired his most popular work, *España*, for

THE PARNASSIANS

In the 1860s, Chabrier associated with members of the literary group, the Parnassians, which included some of the foremost poets of the day. Chabrier was particularly close to Paul Verlaine and Catulle Mendès. The Parnassians rejected the Romantic interest in politics and nationalism and were more interested in craftsmanship—art for art's sake. They also had a keen sense of humor, as is evident in some of their collaborations with Chabrier. In one work, *Fisch-Ton-Kan* (which is a phonetic spelling of the French for "get lost!"), the eponymous hero saves his own life and wins his lover's hand by removing a beetle from the nose of his father's enemy. Members of the Parnassians, especially Stéphane Mallarmé (1842–1898), later developed a new style of poetry known as Symbolism, and were very influential on the new generation of French composers, among them Claude Debussy.

orchestra. Originally entitled *Jota*, which is a Spanish dance, Chabrier wrote the piece to incite in audiences the same excitement he experienced when watching Iberian dancers. He was successful—it was hugely popular with audiences, and is one of the foremost examples of the nineteenth century's craze for exotica.

OPERATIC FAILURES AND SUCCESSES

Chabrier had started work on *Gwendoline*, a serious, Wagner-inspired opera, in 1879, and in the early 1880s tried to arrange a performance. He was unlucky, though—the only company that agreed to put it on went bankrupt before *Gwendoline* made it to the stage. An opportunity to compose another comic opera, *Le roi malgré lui* (*The King, in Spite of Himself*) was also soured when, due to more machinations of fate, it had very limited seasons at the Opéra-Comique.

In his final years, Chabrier made another attempt at a serious opera, *Briséïs*, but by now his health was declining. He finally got his performance of *Gwendoline*, on December 27, 1893, but tragically he did not recognize his music. He died less than a year later.

Above Stéphane Mallarmé (1842–1898) was an important symbolist poet and a member of the Parnassians. His work inspired Chabrier, Debussy, and Ravel, among others.

Below Chabrier at the piano in a work by Henri Fantin-Latour (1836–1904). The composer knew many artists of the time, and was also painted by Degas, Manet, Tissot, and Desboutin.

France and the Second Empire

VOTED IN WITH A HUGE MAJORITY IN 1848,
LOUIS NAPOLEON BONAPARTE—NAPOLEON
III—MADE HIMSELF PRESIDENT FOR LIFE
IN 1851, THEN A YEAR LATER, EMPEROR OF
FRANCE. DESPITE HIS NUMEROUS SHORT-
COMINGS, NAPOLEON'S SECOND EMPIRE
MARKED A PERIOD OF PROSPERITY FOR
FRANCE, AND SAW THE BEGINNING OF
ITS INDUSTRIAL REVOLUTION.

Europe, mid-1860s

★ Birthplace of Camille Saint-Saëns and Georges Bizet.

☆ Birthplace of Emanuel Chabrier

Louis first proved an authoritarian, like his uncle. His 1851 seizure of the presidency, which necessitated changing the constitution, was opposed by the peasants, who had elected him in the first place. His response was to impose martial law on a number of states, which led to bloody repressions, arrests, and deportations. While he fancied himself a champion of the people, he is said to have remarked: "I am prepared to be baptized with the waters of universal suffrage, but I do not intend to live with my feet in a puddle."

SOCIAL OPPRESSION

The social atmosphere in the early years of the Second Empire was conservative; religious schools were instituted, and signs of anarchy were quickly suppressed. In 1857, the writer Gustav Flaubert (1821–1880) was

Above right The breathtaking gold-leafed foyer of the Paris Opéra, reconstructed during the reign of Napoleon III. It was designed by Charles Garnier (1825–1898).

brought to trial for his novel *Madame Bovary*. Its heroine, Emma Bovary, is bored with her provincial surroundings, and becomes an adulterer. Although Emma eventually pays for her sins, the authorities took offence at her lack of repentance. Flaubert was accused of undermining public decency and faced jail. He was acquitted, but only with help from the prominent ex-government minister to whom the book is dedicated.

ACHIEVEMENTS OF THE EMPIRE

Conservatism notwithstanding, the Second Empire flourished economically, with its extensive industrialization, cotton production, and trade. Banks were also established, offering credit and keeping the savings of the bourgeoisie. With this money, as well as Egyptian forced labor, the Suez Canal was constructed. Another achievement of Louis's reign was the revival of Paris, called "Haussmanization" after its lead architect, Baron Haussmann. Narrow streets were turned into grand boulevards, and the Paris Opéra gained a new home. However, the effects of Haussmanization were not all positive ones. Traditional class divides became much more pronounced. Now, instead of living in the upper stories of inner-city buildings while

Left Women and children working in the coal-sifting room at a mine. During this period, working class people moved further out of the city and into the suburbs.

the bourgeoisie took the first and second floors, the working class was pushed to the outer suburbs.

FAILURES AND DECLINE OF THE EMPIRE

With time, Louis's authoritarian attitudes weakened; he granted more freedom to the press, and clemency to his rivals. This led to further criticism, especially of his poor attempts at war. He had modest successes in the Crimean War, which ended in 1856, and in the 1859 war with Austria, in which France was allied with Italian state of Piedmont–Sardinia, yet failures ensued. In the 1860s, he tried, unsuccessfully, to establish an empire in Mexico, and with the Franco–Prussian War of 1868, matters came to a head. Louis, intending to get himself killed in battle, was instead captured. Radicals seized power, Paris was besieged by the Prussian army, and a provisional government was set up in Versailles and negotiated a humiliating end to the war.

Indignant at the Prussian occupation and wanting self-government, Paris elected a municipal goverment, which called itself "the Commune." Another siege, instigated by the provisional government, followed and about 30,000 people were killed. From the ashes of the war and the Commune, the Third Republic was born.

JACQUES OFFENBACH (1819–1880)

One of the most popular composers of the Second Empire was the German composer Jacques Offenbach. After enrolling as a cello student in the Paris Conservatoire in 1833, he changed his name from Jacob to Jacques, and then remained in Paris most his life. He set up the Bouffes Parisiens, for which he wrote one-act operettas, and later the works for which he is now better known, *Orphée aux enfers* (*Orpheus in the Underworld*, 1858) and *La belle Hélène* (*The Beautiful Helen*, 1864). Offenbach's operettas are often satirical, their target usually Parisian society and politics. In *La vie parisienne* (*Parisian life*), for example, a group of foreigners converge on Paris determined to have a good time; its key scene is a debauched party. While considered a minor figure in musical history (with the exception of his late masterpiece *Tales of Hoffmann*), Offenbach's influence in Paris was strong enough to attract the attention of one of the leading novelists of the time, Émile Zola (1840–1902). Zola, while recognizing Offenbach's satirical genius, took him to task for paying homage to the regime—Louis was one of the composer's biggest fans.

Alexander Borodin

NOVEMBER 12, 1833–FEBRUARY 27, 1887

MANY NINETEENTH-CENTURY RUSSIAN COMPOSERS COMBINED COMPOSITION WITH ANOTHER PROFESSION: ALEXANDER BORODIN, A CHEMIST, IS PERHAPS THE MOST DISTINGUISHED EXAMPLE OF THIS. MUSIC HISTORIAN GERALD ABRAHAM WROTE THAT BORODIN WAS "THE SUPREME JUSTIFICATION OF THE AMATEUR IN MUSIC," AND INDEED, FOR A COMPOSER WHO COULD WORK ONLY ON SUNDAYS, HIS DOUBLE CAREER WAS UNPARALLELED IN MUSIC HISTORY.

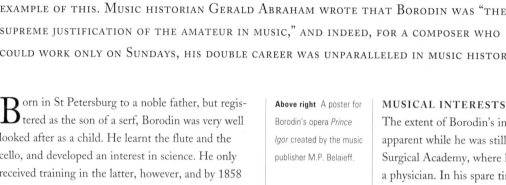

Born in St Petersburg to a noble father, but registered as the son of a serf, Borodin was very well looked after as a child. He learnt the flute and the cello, and developed an interest in science. He only received training in the latter, however, and by 1858 had a doctorate in medicine. He became a professor of chemistry and taught at his alma mater, the Medico-Surgical Academy in St Petersburg. Among other achievements, he helped organize medical courses for women, and discovered two chemical reactions, one of which is named after him.

Above right A poster for Borodin's opera *Prince Igor* created by the music publisher M.P. Belaieff.

Below St Petersburg, Borodin's birthplace, is on the Neva River. The city was the capital of the Russian empire for over 200 years.

MUSICAL INTERESTS

The extent of Borodin's interest in music became apparent while he was still a student at the Medico-Surgical Academy, where he was training to become a physician. In his spare time, Borodin played chamber music with his childhood friend, Mikhail Shchiglev, and gradually made more musical acquaintances. Accordingly, his early compositions were chamber works, which was unusual for a Romantic period composer. His mentor at the Academy admonished him for his preoccupation with "songs," but his studies

OTHER MEMBERS OF THE MIGHTY HANDFUL

The Mighty Handful, ("The Five"), the group to which Borodin and Mussorgsky belonged, is well known, however the other members of the group are still relatively obscure outside Russia. Cesar Cui (1835–1918), one of the founding members of the group, was a fortifications expert and prolific opera writer. He was also invaluable as a commentator on the group's doings and as someone who completed others' operas, including Mussorgsky's *Sorochintsy Fair*. Balakirev, now best known for his piano fantasy *Islamey*, was the only career musician, and was the Handful's founder and tireless promoter. But it is Nikolai Rimsky-Korsakov (1844–1908), known to the West primarily for his lovely *Scheherezade* orchestral suite, who is most needlessly neglected. His operas, among them the satirical *Golden Cockerel,* are permanent fixtures of Russian opera houses, but the difficulty of their vocal parts (which are also, of course, in Russian), seem to deter Western companies from trying them

Left Among Borodin's esteemed musical colleagues were Nikolai Rimsky-Korsakov (seated at right), Alexander Glazunov (standing), and Anatole Lyadov.

Prince Igor. The subject of *Prince Igor*, who protected Russia against the Polovtsy tribes in the twelfth century, was suggested by the Handful's ideologue, critic Vladimir Stasov (1824–1906). With its nationalistic theme, it fit the Mighty Handful's ideology perfectly. But although Borodin was enthusiastic about the opera, his scientific endeavors prevented him from finishing it. His friends did much of the orchestration, and Alexander Glazunov (see pages 272–273) pieced together an overture from Borodin's sketches. The resultant opera is colorful, but dramatically weak; the Polovtsian Dances in the second and third acts are quite rightly the opera's highlight. *Prince Igor* was not premièred until 1890.

progressed well, and he graduated in 1856. After gaining his doctorate in 1858, Borodin decided to go on a European study tour.

In 1861, Borodin met the pianist Ekaterina Protopopovy while she was recovering from tuberculosis in Heidelberg. They married two years later, their marriage having been deferred due to Borodin's lack of money. Despite Ekaterina's poor health, they had a very happy marriage, which was helped by their mutual passion for music.

PRINCE IGOR

In 1862, having just taken up work at the Academy, Borodin met Mily Balakirev (1837–1910), the leader of the group that became known as the "The Five" or Mighty Handful (*moguchaya kuchka*). Balakirev encouraged Borodin to write a symphony, the ultimate testing ground for a young composer, and he conducted its successful première. Borodin then started work on what was to become his most famous work, the opera

Below The set design for the Polovtsian Dances from *Prince Igor* in a 1909 Russian production of the popular opera.

RENOWN

The rest of Borodin's life was spent juggling the demands of his musical muse (and the Handful) and the difficulties of a scientist's life. In the early 1870s, he stopped doing original research, in part due to a lack of resources, and took on a supervisory role at the Academy. By the time of his sudden death at a ball in 1887, he had achieved considerable renown as a composer, especially in Belgium and France, where he had been promoted by Liszt.

Discover the music

Piano Quintet (1862)

Symphony No. 2 (1869–1876)

String Quartet No. 1 (1877–1879)

In the Steppes of Central Asia (1880)

String Quartet No. 2 (1881–1887)

Prince Igor (completed by Rimsky-Korsakov and Glazunov) (1890)

Modest Mussorgsky

MARCH 21, 1839–MARCH 28, 1881

NEAR THE END OF HIS LIFE, MODEST MUSSORGSKY WAS DEPICTED BY
THE GREAT RUSSIAN ARTIST IL'YA REPIN. WITH HIS RED FACE AND
SCRUFFY HAIR, MUSSORGSKY LOOKED LIKE THE ALCOHOLIC HE WAS.
BUT IN HIS YOUTH THE COMPOSER WAS A DEBONAIR PUBLIC SERVANT,
ENTERTAINING HIGH SOCIETY WITH HIS PIANO IMPROVISATIONS.

Mussorgsky was born into a noble family in
Karevo, Pskov district. He was taught the piano,
and while he never made a career as a pianist, his skill
on this instrument helped him both in his extensive
social life and his composition, an occupation he did
not take up seriously until many years later. From the
age of 10, he was sent to school in St Petersburg, then
to Cadet school, from which he graduated in 1856.

A CAREER IN MUSIC

Shortly after his graduation, Mussorgsky began mixing
with influential music figures, including a group of
composers called the Mighty Handful. This group
comprised himself, Alexander Borodin (whom he
had earlier met during a military posting), Cesar Cui,
Nikolai Rimsky-Korsakov, and Mily Balakirev. The
group, under the directorship of the feisty Balakirev,
was interested in promoting Russian musical nationalism through naturalistic settings of Russian speech and
the use of Russian folk songs. At this stage, none were
professional musicians, something that they considered
an advantage. Nonetheless, having resigned his commission—and living off the income from his family's
estates—Mussorgsky dedicated himself to more serious
study under Balakirev, choosing the compositional

Above right The famous
portrait of Mussorgsky by
Il'ya Repin (1844–1930).
Among the artist's many
famous Russian subjects
were Leo Tolstoy and
Dmitri Mendeleev.

Opposite Paolo Silveri
as Boris Godunov in the
opera of the same name,
in a 1949 Covent Garden,
production. The sets
are by the Russian artist,
Georges Wakhévitch.

Below left From 1989
to 2007, the famed
Mikhailovsky Theater in
St Petersburg was known
as the Mussorgsky Opera
and Ballet Theater in
honor of the composer.
The theater was built
in the 1830s.

techniques that he fancied and making up the rest in
the rather bold way that only he could get away with.

MUSICAL EXPERIMENTATION

In 1861 the Russian serfs were emancipated, and
Mussorgsky's main source of income dried up. He took
work in the public service to make ends meet. Staying
with liberal friends, and imbibing copious amounts of
alcohol and reading key philosophical works (including
Nikolai Chernishevsky's 1862 radical novel *What is to
be Done?*), Mussorgsky began an ideologically charged
stage of his career. His readings fed his nationalistic
streak, and he began setting songs with almost absolute
adherence to Russian speech patterns, in the process
revolutionizing the Russian art song.

A rarely heard Mussorgsky work from this period
is his 1868 experimental opera based on the comedy by
Nikolai Gogol, *Zhenit'ba* (*Marriage*), about a man who
permits his marriage to be arranged, only to get cold
feet and escape through the window at the last minute.
Better known is the 1867 orchestral fantasy *Night on
Bare Mountain* (*Noch' na Lisoy gore*), one of the most
captivating orchestral works of the century. He also
began work on his operatic masterpiece, *Boris Godunov*.

Boris Godunov (1872) premièred at the Mariinsky
Theater in 1874 and was a huge
success. Mussorgsky wrote more
masterpieces, including the piano
cycle *Pictures at an Exhibition*. (This
work is often heard in the orchestral
version arranged by Ravel years
later.) In 1879 he toured Russia as
an accompanist to the singer Dar'ya
Leonova. Two years later, in 1881,
at the age of 42, he died from an
alcohol-related illness.

Discover the music

Svetik Savishna (1866)

Night on the Bare Mountain (1867)

Boris Godunov (1872)

Pictures at an Exhibition (1874)

Songs and Dances of Death
　(1875–1877)

The Song of the Flea (1879)

"This deep feeling for the soul of common people; their life became the main impulse for musical improvisation before I learned the basics in piano."

BORIS GODUNOV (1872)

Mussorgsky's opera *Boris Godunov* is based on a play by Alexander Pushkin about the guilt of Tsar Boris Godunov, who was rumored to have ordered the murder of his heir, Dmitry, and later, another pretender to the throne, impersonating the dead Dmitry. The premise holds much operatic promise, and Mussorgsky's version does not disappoint. The opera's centerpiece is Boris's coronation scene: Bells clang, the chorus sings "Slava!" ("Glory!"), and the orchestra swells. Chaotically majestic, it is one of the nineteenth century's great operatic scenes. Mussorgsky had difficulty getting it performed. The

Mariinsky Theater turned down the first version, partly because it did not have a star female role. It was accepted after revisions, and the 1874 première was successful. After Mussorgsky's death, Rimsky-Korsakov, disliking Mussorgsky's orchestration and harmonies, again revised it. Until recently, this version was the most often performed, but now the original version is preferred—it is closer to the spirit of Mussorgsky, the dramatic visionary. As Anatol Lyadov mused: "It seems easy enough to correct Mussorgsky's defects; but when this is done, it is impossible not to feel the result is no longer Mussorgsky."

Pyotr Tchaikovsky

MAY 7, 1840–NOVEMBER 6, 1893

TCHAIKOVSKY ACHIEVED A POPULARITY DURING HIS LIFETIME AND BEYOND THAT FEW CLASSICAL COMPOSERS COULD RIVAL. FOR MANY, HE IS RUSSIAN MUSIC—HIS LAVISHLY ORCHESTRATED BALLET SUITES, DRAMATIC SYMPHONIES, AND DAZZLING CONCERTOS ARE PERFORMED THE WORLD OVER AND SEEM TO EXPRESS A DISTINCTLY "RUSSIAN" COMBINATION OF PASSION AND WISTFULNESS.

Tchaikovsky was born in provincial Votkinsk, and attended St Petersburg's School of Jurisprudence, a strict, often brutal, boys-only school. He also took piano lessons during his seven years there; curiously, teachers considered his musical ability only average.

Upon graduation in 1859, Tchaikovsky seemed set for a career in the civil service, but in 1862 he enrolled in the newly opened St Petersburg Conservatoire. Under the tutelage of Anton Rubinstein he made stunning progress and shortly upon graduating in 1866 was recruited to teach at the new Moscow Conservatoire.

Tchaikovsky's Moscow years were remarkably successful for a fledgling composer—his works were often performed, and earnings from his compositions supplemented his meager teaching income. He also wrote two of his many masterpieces there, the majestic first piano concerto (1875) and the ballet *Swan Lake* (1876).

MARRIAGE, PATRONAGE, AND ACCOLADES

Yet it was not all plain sailing. In 1877, despite his apparent acceptance of his homosexuality, Tchaikovsky married Antonina Ivanovna. Although they separated

Above right Tchaikovsky wrote six symphonies, of which the fifth and sixth are possibly the most popular with today's audiences. The composer conducted the first performance of his haunting *Symphony No. 6* just days before his death.

after only two months, he did not forget his estranged wife. In his opera *Eugene Onegin* (1878) the heroine, Tatyana, is cruelly rejected by the aristocratic Eugene, and her delicate portrayal seems to reflect Tchaikovsky's sympathy for Antonina. His violin concerto and fourth symphony also date from this turbulent period. It was around this same time that he received a letter from Nadezhda von Meck, a wealthy widow and admirer of his works. She offered to be his patron on the unusual proviso that the two never meet.

Von Meck's support allowed the composer to quit teaching in 1878 and indulge his wanderlust. He spent six years traveling around Russia and Europe, composing, among other works, the *1812* overture and the *Serenade for Strings*. From 1885 he settled again, and headed the Russian Musical Society's Moscow branch.

His health declining, Tchaikovsky produced some of his greatest works, including the ballets *The Sleeping Beauty* (1889) and *The Nutcracker*

Celesta

Tchaikovsky was the first major composer to use the celesta in a symphonic work for full orchestra (*The Viyevoda*), but it's the celesta in *The Nutcracker's* Dance of the Sugar Plum Fairy that everyone knows. The celesta, a keyboard instrument like a small upright piano, was patented in 1886 by harmonium builder Auguste Mustel. Instead of striking strings, the felted pads strike steel plates suspended over wooden resonators. The sound is similar to that of a glockenspiel. Although a member of the percussion section, the celesta is almost always played by a pianist.

(1892), his fifth and sixth symphonies (1888 and 1893), and the opera *The Queen of Spades* (1890). He was showered with honors: The tsar, Alexander III, awarded him a lifetime pension, and he received an honorary doctorate from Cambridge University, though his success was somewhat soured by von Meck's abrupt secession of her patronage and correspondence in 1891.

In 1893, at the height of his fame, Tchaikovsky contracted cholera and died soon after. The circumstances of his death have long been debated by music historians, but evidence suggests suicide, urged upon him by former classmates said to be concerned about his potentially scandalous relationship with a nobleman's son. It was a tragic end to a glittering career; however Tchaikovsky's music rises above the details of his life, and he remains one of music's most beloved figures.

Discover the music

Romeo and Juliet overture (1869)
String Quartet No. 2, Op. 22 (1874)
Piano Concerto No. 1, Op. 23 (1875)
Eugene Onegin (1878)
Capriccio Italien, Op. 45 (1880)
Serenade for Strings, Op. 48 (1880)
Symphony No. 6 "Pathetique", Op. 74 (1893)

Below The Royal Ballet's 2006 production of Tchaikovsky's much loved ballet *The Sleeping Beauty*, at the Royal Opera House, Covent Garden, London.

THE QUEEN OF SPADES (1890)

The Queen of Spades, loosely adapted from a work by Pushkin, is about Hermann, a poor army officer, who has two obsessions—gambling, and a young society beauty, Liza. His friends convince him that Liza's guardian, an elderly countess, knows three winning cards. On his way to a tryst with Liza, he scares the stubborn countess to death trying to discover the secret. Her ghost is more obliging, visiting him in his barracks that night with the coveted information. The tale ends in the suicides of both Liza, who forgives Hermann's crime but cannot understand his preference for gambling, and Hermann, whom the ghost has tricked. The opera has something for everyone, combining psychological realism, mysticism, and even numerology with some of Tchaikovsky's most stirring music. It is also a music history lesson, containing musical quotations from Mozart and French opera.

Politics and the arts in nineteenth-century Russia

COMPOSED OF DIFFERENT ETHNIC GROUPS, RUSSIA IN THE NINETEENTH CENTURY STRETCHED FROM WESTERN EUROPE TO ASIA, FROM THE FROZEN ARCTIC NORTH TO THE TEMPERATE BLACK SEA IN THE SOUTH. THE SEVERE CLIMATE AND HUGE DISTANCES HAMPERED COMMUNICATIONS, MAKING ADMINISTRATION SLOW AND DIFFICULT. BUT BY THE END OF THE CENTURY, RUSSIA HAD ASSEMBLED THE MIGHTY EMPIRE THAT SURVIVED AS A SINGLE STATE UNTIL THE 1990S.

Western Europe feared Russia, but Russia feared invasion from close neighbors, or revolt from conquered peoples within its shifting borders. It developed an aggressive foreign policy and a large army. In 1801 the Romanov dynasty had exerted autocratic rule over the complex Russian Empire for some 200 years. Alexander I, the grandson of Catherine the Great, came to power in 1801. Nobles and gentry peopled the bureaucracy and the officer class of the army; in the early nineteenth century, Russia had only a very tiny middle class.

While other European powers gradually liberalized their political systems, the tsars resisted. Nicholas I, whose motto was "Orthodoxy, Autocracy, Nationality,"

Above right Alexander II (1818–1881) became tsar in 1855 and set about emancipating the serfs, an action that had huge repercussions.

Below right *The Last Journey* by Vasily Perov, a founding member the artistic style Realism, where painters depicted ordinary subjects, such as peasants.

allowed little reform. Alexander II (1855–1881) freed the serfs under the Emancipation Decree of 1861. The intelligentsia responded negatively to the terms of the Emancipation Decree, leading to agitation for more change and ultimately to terrorism and revolution.

After the assassination of Alexander II, his son, Alexander III, reversed the reforms of the previous decades. He tried to strengthen the autocracy and to conquer all opposition. He promoted industrialization and constructed the Trans-Siberian railway (which was completed in 1905), but development was at the expense of agriculture. When Nicholas II, the last tsar, inherited the throne in 1894, Russia was backward compared with the other European powers— politically, socially, and economically.

The last two decades of the nineteenth century were years of intense political activity carried out in universities and secret societies by a growing middle class that questioned autocratic government. Geneva became the base for a group of Russian exiles who established Liberation of Labor, a movement aiming to educate Russian revolutionaries in the principles of Marxism. In 1895 they had a visitor: Vladmir Ilyich Ulyanov, better known as Lenin.

THE GOLDEN AGE OF LITERATURE

Russian literature flowered during the nineteenth century, partly in response to repression. Alexander Pushkin wrote his major poems between 1825 and 1836. Nikolai Gogol and Ivan Turgenev published major works between 1842 and 1852. Much intellectual life was suppressed, but poems and novels provided an outlet for the circulation of ideas. The writer and

---

Map:

```
0    50   100 kilometers
0   25   50 miles
```

ARCTIC OCEAN

Birthplaces, Russian composers
★ Birthplace of Alexander Borodin
☆ Birthplace of Modest Mussorgsky
☆ Birthplace of Pyotr Tchaikovsky
— Main Trans-Siberian Railway

Baltic Sea
SWEDEN
Barents Sea
Arctic Circle

Helsinki
Riga
Warsaw   Vilnius   ☆ St Petersburg
  Arkhangel'sk
☆ Karevo
Moscow
Minsk
RUSSIAN EMPIRE
Votkinsk ☆
Kiev
Kazan   Perm
Odessa
Volga   Tobol'sk
Don   Tyumen'   Irtysh
Black Sea   Yalta   Omsk   Tomsk
Novo-Nikolayevsk
Ob'
Yenisey

philosopher Alexander Herzen (1812–1870) suggested a union of Western ideas and Russian tradition in his published journals, and in 1863 Nikolai Chernychevsky (1828–1889) wrote *What is to be Done?* a book promoting populism, a philosophy that rejected everything, even family.

His contemporary Ivan Turgenev (1818–1883) termed this movement "nihilism" and depicted its possible effects in his famous 1862 novel *Fathers and Sons*. Under Alexander II, Turgenev continued to publish, and Leo Tolstoy and Fyodor Dostoevsky produced their masterpieces. Dostoevsky wrote about the lives of poorer sections of society, while Tolstoy wrote of the aristocracy. *War and Peace* appeared in 1869 and *Anna Karenina* in 1877. Other writers of note, including Ivan Goncharov (1812–1891) and the playwright Anton Chekhov (1860–1904), grappled with similarly serious themes such as war, crime and justice, peasant life, love, and freedom in their works. They favored different topics, yet all were dedicated to realism, which they achieved through irony (Turgenev, Chekhov) and psychology (Tolstoy, Dostoevsky).

The emancipation of serfs and calls for further social change also inspired the first truly Russian school of visual art, Realism. Following the lead of writers,

Above The Russian upper classes continued to enjoy and foster the arts, yet as the century progressed, there was a substantial growth in the size of the middle class.

painters such as Vasily Perov (1833–1882) and Il'ya Repin (1844–1930) commented on the injustices of an autocratic society—for instance the corruption and ignorance of the Russian Orthodox clergy—in their paintings. Gone were the portraits of aristocrats: The Russian countryside, artists, and haggard peasants were the Realists' preferred subjects.

THE INTELLIGENTSIA

"Intelligentsia" is a Russian term for a section of society that originated around the 1860s. Though *intelligentsi* (members of the intelligentsia) came from various levels of society, they considered themselves a separate social class. The definition of intelligentsia changed throughout history, but the intelligentsi were typically distinguished by their superior education and involvement in intellectual work. Writers, musicians, engineers, and scientists, among others, could all be named intelligentsi. Traditionally, they commented on the most pressing issues of their time, and tried to represent the will of the people. They also acted as the government's conscience, and were therefore one of the most persecuted groups in Russian society.

Edvard Grieg

JUNE 15, 1842–SEPTEMBER 4, 1907

EDVARD GRIEG WAS THE FIRST COMPOSER OF NOTE TO EMERGE FROM NORWAY. HE WAS AN UNASHAMED NATIONALIST, BUT THIS DID NOT CONDEMN HIM TO OBSCURITY—HIS *PEER GYNT* SUITE AND BRILLIANT PIANO CONCERTO ARE AMONG THE MOST LOVED CLASSICAL WORKS, WHILE HIS LYRIC PIECES ARE CHARMING GLIMPSES INTO HIS LIFE AND PASSIONS.

Grieg was born in Bergen. His talent for the piano was noted early, and in 1858 he was sent to the Leipzig Conservatory in Germany to continue his studies. He remained there until 1862, then moved to Copenhagen, where he studied with the Danish composer Niels Gade (1817–1890), who proved to be a steady sounding board for Grieg, and, perhaps most importantly, fellow Norwegian and composer of Norway's national anthem, Rikard Nordraak (1842–1866).

Above right Grieg as a young man. His epic piano concerto is one of his most loved works.

Below Bergen's fish market. Grieg once said that his music "had a taste of codfish about it.

NATIONALISM AND OTHER INFLUENCES

Nordraak, upon whose death Grieg composed his famous Funeral March, avidly promoted the revival of Norwegian folk song, imploring his contemporaries to "listen to the unclothed plaintive melodies that wander, like so many orphans, round the countryside." Grieg also became an adherent of Nordraak's nationalist philosophy; this is particularly evident in his *Lyric Pieces* for piano, many of which are transcriptions of

"Artists like Bach and Beethoven erected churches and temples on the heights. I only wanted ... to build dwellings for men in which they might feel happy and at home."

Left Peer Gynt's cottage, dating from around 1700, is located in the open air museum in Maihaugen Park on the outskirts of Lillehammer, Norway.

folk songs. Grieg did not "copy" folk songs as he found them, but was rather influenced by their style, in particular by their unusual harmonies. In 1864 Grieg composed a symphony, although he later disowned it. He was highly self-critical; he especially doubted his skills as an orchestrator, and was constantly rescoring his works. That symphony was finally revived at the 1981 Bergen Festival.

Another vital influence on Grieg's composition was his cousin, Nina Hagerup, whom he married in 1867. Nina was a well known soprano, and Grieg's output after their marriage was, understandably, dominated by songs. Their concerts of these works were rapturously received throughout Europe. In 1868 he wrote his *Piano Concerto in A minor*, Op. 16, a magnificent work whose dynamic, crashing opening shows the influence of Schumann's equally famous piano concerto in the same key.

PEER GYNT

In 1875, Grieg wrote incidental music for a play by fellow Norwegian, Henrik Ibsen (1828–1906). *Peer Gynt*, a sort of existential satire, is named after its main character, a roguish wanderer who after

many misadventures is called to account for his sins. From the incidental music Grieg made up the two suites that are very famous today, in particular the pieces *Morning* and *In the Hall of the Mountain King*. To the great surprise of both Grieg and Ibsen, the play was a huge success.

GRIEG'S LAST YEARS

Grieg's final years were marked with distinction. From 1880 to 1882, he was the director of the Bergen Philharmonic Orchestra. Later, he was provided with an annuity by the Norwegian government, drew praise from the likes of Tchaikovsky, was honored by both Cambridge and Oxford Universities, and performed extensively throughout Europe. But his touring schedule took its toll on his health, which had been poor ever since his student days, and he died in 1907. He is buried in the side of a mountain in Troldhaugen, where he and Nina had built a villa.

Discover the music

Piano Concerto in A minor,
  Op. 16 (1868)
Holberg Suite, Op. 40 (1884)
Violin Sonata No. 3 in C minor,
  Op. 45 (1887)
Peer Gynt Suites 1, Op. 46
  (1888) and 2, Op. 55 (1891)
Lyric Pieces Books 1–10
  (1867–1901)

GRIEG'S *LYRIC PIECES*

While Grieg's best-known piano work is, quite rightly, the magnificent piano concerto, his 66 *Lyric Pieces* for piano—which are much more modest—give another insight to his musical personality. In poetry, a lyric is a short poem that expresses the writer's feelings. Grieg's lyric pieces are also slight, but loaded with meaning. He composed 10 volumes of them, between 1867 and 1901. *Wedding Day at Troldhaugen* (Op. 65, No. 6), a reminiscence of Grieg's own wedding, is one of the most popular. Grieg recorded this work near the end of his life, and his rendition of it and others shows his lightness of touch and humor. Other works are masterpieces in tone-painting—the clever use of rhythm in *The Butterfly* (Op. 43, No. 1), for example, perfectly captures his subject's unpredictable trajectory. And yet others, like the *Popular Melody* and *Norwegian Melody* from the first set, Op. 12, are artful settings of folk songs.

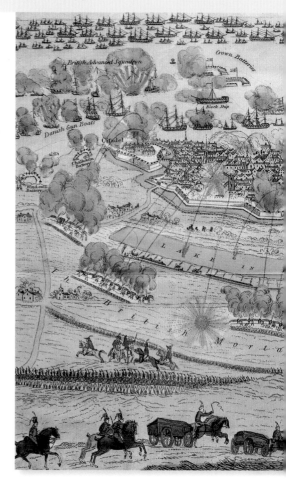

LIFE & TIMES

Romantic nationalism in Scandinavia

SCANDINAVIA'S POLITICAL MAKEUP IN THE NINETEENTH CENTURY WAS CHARACTERIZED BY ALLIANCES, NOT ALL OF THEM WILLING. BY GRIEG'S TIME, NORWAY ALREADY HAD A UNION WITH SWEDEN. THE COMPOSER LIVED LONG ENOUGH TO SEE THIS ARRANGEMENT DISSOLVED IN 1905; IN THE MEANTIME, HE GLORIFIED NORWAY'S FOLK MUSIC BY FEATURING IT IN MANY OF HIS COMPOSITIONS, BOOSTING THE COUNTRY'S CONSIDERABLE NATIONAL PRIDE.

NORWAY

Norwegian nationalism had, in fact, stirred back in the eighteenth century, partly inspired by the French Revolution. Norway was then part of Denmark–Norway, but in 1814, when Denmark was forced to cede Norway to Sweden after its defeat in the Napoleonic Wars, Norway demanded independence and its own constitution. Norwegians strongly resented the union with Sweden, although in 1838 they gained further independence by establishing self-governing districts. The Romantic nationalist movement started around the same time. One of the movement's main symbols was Norwegian farming culture, which was expressed in folk songs, stories, dances, and rosemaling (decorative flower painting).

These traditions, many of which dated back to the Vikings, were collected by Romantic nationalists such as the poet Henrik Wergeland (1808–1845), who also fought injustices faced by rural communities.

DENMARK

In the other Scandinavian countries, namely Denmark, Sweden, Iceland, and Finland, nationalism was also strong, although its motivations varied. Denmark, once prosperous, had a difficult nineteenth century. First there was the loss of territories in 1814. In 1848, Denmark became a constitutional

"Where words fail, music speaks."

HANS CHRISTIAN ANDERSEN

Below Inside a nineteenth-century Finnish home. A young girl plays folk tunes on the zither to entertain her family. The painting is by Robert-Wilhelm Ekman.

monarchy, but in 1861 it suffered a further setback when Germany took the province of Schleswig–Holstein. Danish Romantic nationalism helped counter the grim mood. One representative of this movement was the poet Adam Oehlenschläger (1779–1850), who decried Denmark's defeat by Admiral Nelson's navy in the Battle of Copenhagen, and spoke of Denmark arising again. Arise it did, but the country did not gain universal adult suffrage and parliamentary democracy until 1901.

ICELAND

Iceland, the smallest country in Scandinavia, was under Danish control in the nineteenth century, and had been since the thirteenth century. Nonetheless, under the influence of continental Europe, an independence movement began during the 1830s—a high point

GREAT DANES

The flowering of Danish culture in the nineteenth century did not stop with Oehlenschläger. In fact, the century saw many great Danes, beginning with Nicolai Frederik Severin Grundtvig (1783–1872), who originated the idea of folk high schools, egalitarian institutions that would offer adults a practical education. The first folk school opened in 1844, and they still exist today. The philosopher Søren Kierkegaard (1813–1855) was also active in the first half of the century, and his views on individualism and Christianity were influential well into the twentieth century. Danish composers also flourished. Daniel Friedrich Kuhlau (1786–1832) who used Danish folk songs in his works, gained an international reputation, as did Grieg's mentor Niels Gade (1817–1890), who became the director of the Leipzig Gewandhaus orchestra after Mendelssohn's death. And Gade's colleague Johan Peter Emilius Hartmann (1805–1900) wrote his opera *Little Kirsten* (*Liden Kirsten*) based on the work of the most universally beloved of all nineteenth-century Danes, Hans Christian Andersen (1805–1875).

of which was the publication of the first novel in the Icelandic language in 1850. In 1874, Iceland gained its own constitution.

SWEDEN

In Sweden, there was less cause for nationalistic fervor—the main problem the country faced in the nineteenth century was its difficult union with Norway. Its main nationalistic organization was the Gothic League, which was established in 1811 to revive Scandinavian sagas and mythology. Of Swedish writers, the playwright August Strindberg (1849–1912) achieved worldwide fame, while in music, Franz Berwald (1796–1868), at one stage an owner of a glass factory, proved himself as a symphonist; however, his works fell into obscurity, and have only recently been revived.

FINLAND

By the nineteenth century, Finland had been a province of Sweden for 600 years, but in 1809 it was won by the Russians, and became an autonomous grand duchy of Russia. With growing nationalistic fervor, Finns began

Left The 1807 Battle of Copenhagen led to the surrender of the Danish navy to Great Britain, and fed nationalist stirrings.

Above right Danish philosopher and theologian Søren Kierkegaard was one of the most influential thinkers of the nineteenth century.

speaking Finnish, rejecting the official Swedish language, and firmly resisting Russification. The first novel in Finnish was written in 1870, and there was an interest in and publication of orally transmitted folk songs and legends. One of the monuments in Finland's nationalist movement was Elias Lönnrot's (1802–1884) national epic *Kalevala*, on which Finland's first great composer Jean Sibelius (see pages 276–277) would later compose a famous orchestral suite. Finland finally gained independence from Russia in 1917.

Scandinavia, nineteenth century
☆ Birthplace of Edvard Grieg
- - Modern country borders

Gabriel Fauré

MAY 12, 1845–NOVEMBER 4, 1924

GABRIEL FAURÉ WAS ONE OF THE MOST INNOVATIVE COMPOSERS OF HIS GENERATION, USING UNUSUAL HARMONIES AND ESCHEWING SHOWY VIRTUOSITY. SADLY, HE BECAME DEAF DURING THE FINAL TWO DECADES OF HIS LIFE, ALTHOUGH HE CONTINUED COMPOSING. HE IS PERHAPS BEST KNOWN FOR HIS HEAVENLY, CONSOLING *REQUIEM*, ONE OF THE CHORAL MASTERPIECES OF THE NINETEENTH CENTURY.

Fauré was born in Parniers, in the south of France. As a child he enjoyed improvising on the piano, and at the age of nine was sent to the École Niedermeyer, a school for church musicians, where he studied for 11 years. One of his teachers was Camille Saint-Saëns, who, against the school's wishes, introduced his talented student to more radical contemporary composers such as Liszt and Berlioz. Saint-Saëns became Fauré's lifelong friend.

Left The imposing interior of the Church of the Madeleine in Paris, where Fauré worked as an organist and where his funeral was held.

THE CHURCH ORGANIST

After graduating, Fauré worked as an organist in a provincial town, which he hated, then, after his involvement in the lifting of the Siege of Paris in 1870, he became assistant organist at a Paris church, Saint-Sulpice. His career peaked in 1877: Saint-Saëns had retired as the organist and choirmaster of one of Paris's most famous churches, Église de la Madeleine (or La Madeleine). But this was not the boon it appeared—

PAULINE VIARDOT (1821–1910)

After he graduated, Fauré's musical education continued in the musical salon of Pauline Viardot. Viardot was a remarkable woman, one of the leading sopranos of her generation and an accomplished composer. As she was married to Louis Viardot, a republican and opponent of Louis Napoleon, she did not perform in Paris, but made up for this with numerous appearances abroad. During a tour to St Petersburg, she met novelist Ivan Turgenev (1818–1883). Turgenev was besotted with Pauline, and followed her and Louis for the rest of his life, some 40 years, where possible living near them. Viardot was not only an accomplished artist, but a valuable supporter of others. She made vocal settings of Chopin's piano mazurkas, for example, greatly expanding his popularity.

the church's repertoire was strictly "popular," leaving little room for experimentation. Fauré's own *Requiem*, generally considered a masterpiece, premièred at La Madeleine in 1888, but the vicar coldly advised Fauré to leave aside his "novelties" and make do with the existing repertoire. To add insult to injury, Fauré had to supplement his meager salary by giving private music lessons, so he had little time to compose.

Nevertheless, Fauré was in a position to marry, and he settled on Marianne Viardot, daughter of renowned soprano Pauline Viardot, whose musical salon he frequented. Originally attracted to the quiet, mysterious composer, Marianne accepted his proposal, then, after months of dithering, took his bursts of frustration as an excuse to reject him. This sent him into deep depression, and he set off traveling, including to Germany, where he was impressed by productions of Wagner's *Ring* cycle. The failed romance may also have inspired his 1880 *Élégie* for piano and cello, one of Fauré's most funereal—and passionate—works. In 1883, he married Marie Fremiet. It was an unhappy marriage, though they had two children.

Right Madame Pauline Viardot was not just an acclaimed singer, composer, and hostess, she was also a fine pianist, who had studied piano under Franz Liszt.

RECOGNITION

After many years of dissatisfaction, Fauré finally found work better suited to his temperament and composing. In 1896 he was appointed professor of composition at the Paris Conservatoire. In 1905 he was appointed director of the same institution. This position gave him financial security, and his music soon became better known. This last period in Fauré's career was very productive, and included his 1913 opera *Pénélope*, today unknown but a success at its première. Around four years after his appointment Fauré started to become deaf, and in 1920 he decided to retire. Fauré inspired a new generation of French composers and he received the Legion of Honor before dying, at the age of 79, from pneumonia. His state funeral took place at La Madeleine.

Discover the music

Élégie, Op. 24 (1880)

Dolly Suite, Op. 56 (1894–1897)

Clair de Lune, Op. 46 (1887)

Requiem in D minor, Op. 48 (1887–1890)

Pavane, Op. 50 (1887)

Masques et Bergamasques, Op. 112

Harp

The harp was prominent in many musical cultures, with different models and types found the world over, the earliest versions possibly dating back as far as 3000 BCE. The concert harp, evolving from earlier European models, is around 6 feet (1.8 m) high, and covers six and a half octaves (46 or 47 strings). The strings are plucked to create a sound. A pedal at the base of the instrument changes pitch and tuning, extending the range. The harp is featured in Fauré's expressive *Impromptu*, Op. 86.

LIFE & TIMES

France and the Third Republic

WITH THE END OF NAPOLEON III'S REIGN AND THE CREATION OF THE THIRD REPUBLIC, FRANCE ACQUIRED A STRANGE NEW POLITICAL ORDER. IT HAD NO CONSTITUTION, AND THERE WERE NUMEROUS COMPETING FACTIONS WITHIN THE GOVERNMENT. YET THE THIRD REPUBLIC SURVIVED UP UNTIL 1940, AND SAW A REMARKABLE FLOWERING OF THE ARTS AND OTHER INTELLECTUAL PURSUITS CALLED THE BELLE ÉPOQUE—THE BEAUTIFUL AGE.

Despite the numerous scandals for which the Third Republic would become known, France's development continued, with rapid industrialization, and grain and wine production. Colonial ambitions rebounded from the failures of the Second Empire, and Laos, Cambodia, Madagascar, and parts of Africa joined the empire. Some of Paris's most recognizable landmarks date from the Third Republic, including the

Below *Le déjeuner sur l'herbe,* Manet's highly controversial painting, caused a furore in 1863. The casual aspect of the subjects was unlike anything people had seen in art before.

Eiffel Tower and Sacré-Coeur, the huge basilica that overlooks Paris from the suburb of Montmartre. In science, the Polish-born Parisian Marie Curie (1867–1934) made huge advances in the study of radioactivity, while Louis Pasteur revolutionized bacteriology. But the Third Republic also suffered some notable failures, including the Panama Canal project, which was doomed by insufficient preparation and disease.

WOMEN IN THE THIRD REPUBLIC

Though equality had been prized since the Revolution, during the Third Republic French women continued to struggle against chauvinistic attitudes. In the early years of the twentieth century, this chauvinism was exemplified by the fortunes of two women—murderer Henriette Caillaux and Marie Curie. Henriette Caillaux (1874–1943) was married to the finance minister, Joseph Caillaux. In 1914, Gaston Calmette, editor of the newspaper *Le Figaro*, had defamed Joseph by publishing a letter that implicated him in misleading the public about a tax bill. Wanting to save her husband from the duel that she believed would be his only recourse, Henriette shot Calmette. But the idea of a woman solving a man's problem, with premeditation, so challenged the court's notions of female propriety that Caillaux was acquitted on the basis of temporary insanity. Marie Curie's case was quite different, but no less characteristic. Marie was fortunate in that her husband, Pierre, had encouraged her research, and after his death in 1906, she was given his position at the Sorbonne, becoming the institution's first female professor. But even after these honors—and two Nobel prizes—her gender prevented her otherwise certain election into the distinguished French Academy of Sciences.

THE ARTS

In the final years of the nineteenth century, France re-emerged as an artistic force to be reckoned with, producing world-renowned masters of music, painting, sculpture, and literature. Like any period of great artistic achievement, the Belle Époque had some notable scandals. In 1863, the painting *Le déjeuner sur l'herbe* (*The lunch on the grass*), was one of many rejected from the Paris Salon, the city's foremost art exhibition, and was exhibited instead in the newly established Salon de Refusés. The painting, by Édouard Manet (1832–1883), shocked the Salon's jury and Parisians alike. The nude in the painting's foreground was not a problem, per se, but the presence of two fully dressed men, and the nude's stare, went against conventions. Writer Émile Zola, ever ready to comment on Parisian artistic trends, defended the painting, praising its naturalism, and dryly noting, "in the Louvre there are more than 50 paintings in which are found mixes of persons clothed and nude." The staunch conservatism of the Salon later affected one of France's most famous schools of visual art, Impressionism.

THE DREYFUS AFFAIR

While artistic scandals eventually passed, others were more damaging to the fabric of French society. Among the most disturbing was the Dreyfus affair. In 1894, Alfred Dreyfus (1859–1935), a Jewish French army captain, was accused and convicted of selling French military secrets to the Germans by members of the New Right, a pro-Catholic, anti-Semitic group. The real culprit was acquitted after some high level intervention, and Parisian society was divided between those who considered Dreyfus innocent and those who believed him guilty. He was only cleared in 1906, after he had served part of his sentence on Devil's Island (a penal colony in French Guiana).

CLASS DIVIDES

Among those who took Dreyfus's side were socialists, who also worked to eliminate France's persistent class divides. Workers' conditions, though improved, still left much to be desired: 12-hour working days were the norm and disease was prevalent. Attempts were made to fix this situation, ranging from anarchic tactics such as bombings and assassinations, to the promotion of general strikes. In the early 1900s, international affairs were also predominating, with territorial disagreements with Germany leading to World War I.

Above right Marie Curie, one of the great scientific minds of all time, won the 1903 Nobel Prize for Physics. She won an unprecedented second Nobel Prize, this time in 1911 for Chemistry.

Right An engraving from the French publication *Le Petit Journal* showing Alfred Dreyfus appearing before the war council in December 1894.

LATE ROMANTIC PERIOD
c. 1860 ~ 1920

Introduction

THE SPIRIT OF THE ROMANTIC ERA IN MUSIC REMAINS, IN MANY WAYS, VERY MUCH WITH US. ESTHETICALLY, THE IDEAS OF THE ARTIST AS HERO, FIDELITY OF PERFORMERS TO THE COMPOSER'S SINGULAR VISION, AND THE PRIMACY OF CONTENT OVER FORM IN MUSICAL EXPRESSION ARE RECOGNIZABLE AS ELEMENTS OF OUR OWN PRESENT-DAY MODELS.

There has even been a return to the organizing principles of tonality in late twentieth century art music, with the application of the label "New Romanticism" to many contemporary compositions.

The basic principle of valuing originality over discipline was the essential driving force through the late nineteenth century. Like a greenhouse that cultivates rare orchids, remarkable and unique artistic triumphs resulted. Many were triumphs of individual originality without any discernible subsequent influence—the symphonic music of Berlioz; some were restricted to particular modes of expression—Verdi's operas; others bore the mark of the value placed on the fantastic and the sensational—the tone poems and early operas of Richard Strauss. But no common language would remain and no new one took its place.

The dissolution of form and the stretching of the boundaries of tonality created a new environment. In place of a unified flow of artistic development there arose a landscape where many different streams with many cross-currents flowed simultaneously. Thus composers as diverse as Bizet, Dvořák, Tchaikovsky, Grieg, Smetana, Gounod, and Mussorgsky all make important contributions to the music of the Romantic Era without leaving any important followers.

Above right An autograph manuscript by Bartók of popular Hungarian songs. The composer was a dedicated collector of folk tunes.

Below A poster by François Flameng for Jules Massenet's opera *Grisélidis* at the Théâtre de l'Opéra-Comique in Paris, c. 1900.

The two most important composers of the era, who consciously took up the challenge laid down by Beethoven, have come to represent the opposite poles of the Romantic ideal in the second half of the nineteenth century. On the one hand, Richard Wagner sensed that the dissolution of the common language of formal musical discourse—sonata, symphony, concerto—that took place during the era of Schumann, Schubert, and Mendelssohn, must be replaced by something grander, more compelling; a synthetic art that could gather up the loose strands of man's art and religion and create a universal form, a *gesammtkunstwerk*. The implications of Wagner's vision are so vast that they are still being debated today. Opposite Wagner is Johannes Brahms, who understood and addressed the problem of form in quite a different way. His solution was to harness the outpouring of lyricism and expression, the rich chromaticism of the new harmonic language, and with enormous discipline and force of will, create new symphonies, concertos, sonatas, and chamber music that are fully Romantic and yet retain the symmetry and architectural integrity of their Classical models.

Ironically, neither composer left a legacy that others were able to follow. Wagner's tremendous influence on the nineteenth-century composers who followed was less in the realm of the music drama than on the two last great symphonists of the century, Gustav Mahler and Anton Bruckner. Brahms's most direct and most lasting influence was actually on the one composer of the twentieth century held most responsible by many for the final demise of the Classical models of art music—Arnold Schoenberg.

The Romantic ideal contained the seeds of its own destruction. By placing a premium on individual expression and heroic achievement, no commonality of discourse could survive. The artist had to create expressive language at the exact moment as the idea to be

Previous pages *At the Moulin Rouge: the Dance* by Henri Toulouse-Lautrec.

expressed. At the same time, the era's desire to preserve the past had become an antiquarian pursuit. Even Brahms knew that his was an ultimately untenable situation. In 1878 he wrote, "That people in general do not understand and do not respect the greatest things, such as Mozart's concertos, helps our kind to live and acquire renown. If they would only know that they are getting from us by drops what they could drink there to their hearts' content!"

The most important composers who followed in the twentieth century took up the cause of art music surrounded by the ruins of what had preceded them. No symphony seemed possible after gargantuan efforts such as Gustav Mahler's Eighth, the "Symphony of a Thousand." Nothing in opera could

Below Schoenberg invented the controversial twelve-tone system, which influenced composers for generations.

logically succeed *Parsifal* or the *Ring* cycle. Instead, composers such as Debussy and Ravel acknowledged Wagner's legacy, but created music that was more about mood, sonority, and color and rather less about unifying themes of struggle and triumph. Folk music and dance rhythms re-emerged in the works of Bartók. And the greatest composer of the first half of the twentieth century—after shedding his youthful influences of Tchaikovsky and Rimsky-Korsakov—made his way by destroying all expectations of adherence to the old ways. In works like *The Rite of Spring*, *Les noces*, and *Petrushka*, Igor Stravinsky ushered in the new world of modern composition.

Top Tamara Rojo (as The Chosen One) in the Royal Ballet's 2005 production of Igor Stravinsky's *The Rite of Spring* at the Royal Opera House, Covent Garden. The ballet caused a riot at its first performance in 1913.

Edward Elgar

JUNE 2, 1857–FEBRUARY 23, 1934

ELGAR WAS THE FIRST MODERN BRITISH COMPOSER TO EMERGE WITH AN INTERNATIONAL REPUTATION. HE DID SO BEING SELF-TAUGHT, GAINING PLENTY OF KNOW-HOW AS AN ACTIVE MUSICIAN IN PROVINCIAL ENGLAND, AND TRAVELING FAR TO HEAR THE LATEST WORKS BY CONTINENTAL COMPOSERS. THE NATIONALIST APPEAL THAT HIS MUSIC ATTRACTED IS ONE OF THE PARADOXES SURROUNDING ELGAR'S CHARACTER AND OUTPUT.

Right Elgar (center) at a recording session in 1931 of the *Nursery Suite*. Also present were the Duke and Duchess of York (left), and the playwright George Bernard Shaw (right).

Edward Elgar was born in a village outside Worcester but the family soon moved into the city's High Street, where his father ran a music shop; he was also the organist at a Catholic church. The notion that Elgar started life in the countryside rather than a busy town is one of the myths that once clouded our understanding of the composer.

He began writing compositions from the age of 10, and used some of these tunes later for his *Wand of Youth* suites (1907) and *The Starlight Express* (1915). From the age of 16 Elgar endured an uncertain living as a deputy organist (and later replacement) to his father, as a pianist and piano teacher, violinist, and bassoonist. He conducted the local Glee Club and, from the age of 22, became "composer in ordinary" to the County Lunatic Asylum, conducting the staff band.

In 1889 Elgar married one of his piano pupils, Alice Roberts, the daughter of a major-general. From this event emerged two issues that affected Elgar throughout his life. The first was a resentful class-conscious awareness of his insecure social status; the second was

his compensatory obsession with decorations, medals, honors, rank, and ceremony (which is musically embodied in his *Pomp and Circumstance Marches* of 1901 and the *Crown of India* "imperial masque" of 1912). It is as if he wanted to outclass his military father-in-law in status and patriotism.

During the 1890s Elgar wrote choral cantatas such as *The Black Knight* (1893) and *Caractacus* (1898), while taking trips with Alice to Germany where they encountered Wagner's advanced harmonies, which strongly affected him. His previous knowledge of Romantic German music had centered on Brahms and Schumann; it was Schumann's sets of character pieces that inspired Elgar's first major success, the so-called *Enigma Variations* (1899).

Left Elgar was born in this charming cottage that is now the Elgar Birthplace Museum. It was established by the composer's daughter Carice after his death.

Discover the music

Enigma Variations, Op. 36 (1899)

Dream of Gerontius, Op. 38 (1900)

Pomp and Circumstance Marches, Op. 39 (1901)

The Apostles, Op. 49 (1903)

The Kingdom, Op. 51 (1906)

Cello Concerto, Op. 85 (1919)

Right Elgar with violin virtuoso Yehudi Menuhin (1916–1999), who was 16 years old when he recorded the composer's *Violin Concerto* in 1932.

THE ENIGMA

The exact title of Elgar's first international success is *Variations on an Original Theme*. The work is a set of 14 variations on the opening, hesitant tune. Each variation, in the style of short Schumann character pieces, relates to a friend of Edward and Alice Elgar, though the first variation is of Alice herself and the final represents the composer. Of Variations 2–13, four are of women and eight of men; Variation 9 actually describes a bulldog.

LATER WORKS

From then until 1919, Elgar gained respect as Britain's leading modern composer. Richard Strauss called him "the first English progressivist," and indeed Elgar created Strauss-like tone pictures such as *Cockaigne* (1901), *In the South* (1904), and *Falstaff* (1913). He composed oratorios with a Wagnerian use of symbolic themes—*The Dream of Gerontius* (1900) for the Catholic market, and *The Apostles* (1903) and *The Kingdom* (1906) for the Protestant.

His two symphonies (1908, 1911) and the *Violin Concerto* (1910) are considered the summit of achievement in his synthesis of Brahms-style thematic working-out and Wagnerian harmonies. His elegiac, almost

Below right Elgar's rough sketch of his *Pomp and Circumstance March No. 1*, written in 1901. The tune *Land of Hope and Glory* comes from the march's trio section.

bitter *Cello Concerto* (1919) has maintained great international esteem. It uses at its start a distinctive Elgar device of an intriguing drifting melody that seems to lack a goal, like the motto theme of his first symphony, or indeed the Enigma theme itself.

After Alice's death in 1920 he wrote no works of substance. Instead he championed the new development of gramophone recording, conducting over 50 recording sessions of his works. He died in Worcester.

LAND OF HOPE AND GLORY

The title *Pomp and Circumstance* comes from Shakespeare's *Othello*. Elgar intended to write six concert marches under this name but completed only five. The first was initially heard in London at the 1901 Proms, and such was the audience's response it was given two encores. It contains as its trio section the tune later known through the words added to it by A.C. Benson for its appearance in Elgar's *Coronation Ode* of 1902 at the crowning of Edward VII, who apparently suggested the idea of turning it into a song. Elgar's publisher thought this wouldn't work, as the tune had too great a range for general singing.

Ethel Smyth

APRIL 22, 1858–MAY 8, 1944

A PIONEERING FEMALE COMPOSER WHO WROTE LARGE-SCALE
WORKS MUCH ADMIRED IN HER TIME, SMYTH CONFRONTED
PREJUDICE IN HER ATTEMPTS TO ADVANCE HER CAREER.
ALTHOUGH MUSICALLY INFLUENCED BY BRAHMS, SMYTH
TOOK MORE INTEREST THAN HE DID IN THE STAGE, WRITING
FIVE OPERAS AND A BALLET.

Dedicated to THE WOMEN'S SOCIAL AND POLITICAL UNION.

THE MARCH OF THE WOMEN
(Popular Edition in F. To be sung in Unison)
By **ETHEL SMYTH**, Mus.Doc.
Price: One Shilling & Sixpence net.

Ethel Mary Smyth was born in
London into a high-ranking
military family. Her father had served
in the British Army during the Indian
Mutiny and returned to Kent to take
charge at the Woolwich Arsenal, later
moving the large family to Surrey
when he took command of the Aldershot barracks. Smyth grew up in highly
privileged circumstances, receiving a
private education.

SMYTH'S GERMAN TRAINING

Smyth showed an interest in music
that her father grudgingly encouraged.
Alexander Ewing, progressive composer of the popular
anthem *Jerusalem the Golden*, was stationed at Aldershot and gave Smyth her first lessons in harmony.
This stirred her interest in composition, and at 19
she entered the Leipzig Conservatory, despite family
unease. In those days a German training was thought
to be highly valuable to British composers, and the

> ### Discover the music
>
> *Serenade* (1890)
>
> *Mass in D* (1891)
>
> *Fantasio* (1898)
>
> *Der Wald* (1902)
>
> *The Wreckers* (1902–1904)
>
> *The March of the Women* (1911)
>
> *The Boatswain's Mate*
> (1913–1914)
>
> *Entente Cordiale* (1925)
>
> *Double Concerto for violin, horn,*
> *and orchestra* (1926)

Above right The cover
of the songsheet for *The
March of the Women*
(1911), Smyth's rousing
anthem for the suffra-
gette movement. The
cover illustration is by
Margaret Morris.

Opposite top right Dame
Ethel Smyth conducts
the police band during
a ceremony in 1930 to
unveil the Pankhurst
Statue in Victoria Tower
Gardens, London.

SMYTH ON MEN AND MUSIC

In her 1933 book *Female Pipings in Eden*, Smyth
wrote, "The chief difficulty women musicians have
to face is that in no walk of life do men like to see us
come barging in on their preserves. This is the deter-
mining factor in the position of Women in Music …
because the (musical) machine is cumbrous, costly,
and complicated; because it is entirely in the hands
of groups of men, not of isolated individuals … Art is
bisexual, the female element implicit with the male."

Leipzig Conservatory was considered especially useful.
However, this was not true for Smyth, who left disappointed by their standards after only a year.

Yet she stayed in Leipzig and moved in the highest
social and musical circles. Her early songs and instrumental works began to be performed and valued there,
and she met, almost as equals, the foremost composers
who visited the city—Tchaikovsky, Grieg, Dvořák,
Mahler, and above all Brahms, whom she described as
"extraordinarily kind and fatherly to me." She admitted
that she swam in the "dear old sea of German music
that surged around the feet of Brahms in the 1880s."
Her buoyant *Serenade* of 1890 is modelled on those
of Brahms. She faced the paradox that her music was
assumed to be written by a man—E.M. Smyth. But
when her *Violin Sonata* was revealed as hers, a German
critic snapped that "lack of feminine charm" made it
"unworthy of a woman."

In Britain Smyth gained the financial patronage of
the Empress Eugénie of France, widow of Napoleon
III, who, with other women in high places, helped
her to gain prestige performances. Most notable among
these was that of her expansive yet dramatic *Mass in D*,
given by the Royal Choral Society in London's Royal
Albert Hall in 1893. With this support Smyth started
to write operas—*Fantasio* (1898), *Der Wald* (1902),
The Wreckers (1902–1904), *The Boatswain's Mate*
(1913–1914), and *Entente Cordiale* (1925). The latter

two are short comic operas that represented a later shift of her style to lighter, more French-influenced forms.

SMYTH THE SUFFRAGETTE

Despite the support of influential women and conductors such as Thomas Beecham, Smyth found it difficult to get performances and commissions, complaining of a "consistent, cold trickle of neglect" from the press and that she was "born 50 years too soon and of the wrong sex." Between 1910 and 1912 Smyth became active in the Votes For Women (Suffragette) campaign and ended up in prison. To publicize the movement she wrote her choral song *The March of the Women* (1911). For this, and for her "passion" for other females, she became disapproved of in conservative circles.

It was not until the more liberated 1920s that Smyth, now in her sixties, regained favor. She was made a Dame of the British Empire in 1922. While her *Double Concerto for violin, horn, and orchestra* (1926) and symphonic poem *The Prison* (1930) reflected this newfound status, it was her 10 eloquently written books of memoirs and comments that brought her the most admiration. Author Virginia Woolf, one of Smyth's last "passions," admired in her style her "easy, large stride," and the same might be claimed for her best music. She died aged 86.

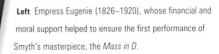

Left Empress Eugenie (1826–1920), whose financial and moral support helped to ensure the first performance of Smyth's masterpiece, the *Mass in D*.

Great Britain before the Great War

NINETEENTH-CENTURY BRITAIN WAS AN INDUSTRIAL WORLD LEADER AND COLONIAL GIANT. BY THE LATTER PART OF THE CENTURY, A QUARTER OF THE GLOBE COMPRISED BRITISH DEPENDENCIES, "PROTECTORATES," AND COLONIES— INCLUDING INDIA, AUSTRALIA, SOUTH AFRICA, NIGERIA, JAMAICA, HONG KONG, CANADA, AND EGYPT. YET THE SPEED OF GROWTH WITHIN THIS PROSPEROUS NATION HID RURAL DECLINE AND MOUNTING SOCIAL TENSIONS.

Britain had become Europe's most congested yet thriving country. Its population nearly doubled from 21 million in 1851 to 37 million by 1901. In that time the population of London alone increased from 2.4 million to nearly 6 million. Between 1860 and

Above right French playing cards showing England's Edward VII. Victoria's eldest son, he reigned from 1901 to 1910.

1900 steam railways doubled their countrywide coverage, connecting towns and ports, delivering industrial resources, and food supplies. This scale of urban population expansion, as laborers moved from farms to factories, produced acute problems in housing, hygiene, education, and democratic representation, all of which secured slow but steady action from the spreading bureaucracies of national and local government.

EDUCATION

A state elementary education system, established in 1870, was limited to children aged 5 to 10 years. "Red brick" city universities such as Bristol and Liverpool emerged in the 1880s to supply schoolteachers. It was in this context that Elgar was (unhappily) appointed Birmingham University's Music Professor (1905–1908). Similarly, London's Royal College of Music was set up in 1882 to raise teaching standards.

A CULTURAL SHIFT

Meanwhile Britain had built up its army and naval forces, which were over-stretched in colonies across the globe. Of the many skirmishes and struggles, it was the contest between Britain and Germany to garner South Africa's diamonds and gold that contributed to the infamous Boer War of 1899–1902. Britain's brutish behavior isolated it diplomatically, so its civil servants sought treaties with anti-German allies such as Japan (1902), France (1904), and Russia (1907). This created a cultural shift away from German influence. It also aggravated the rivalry between Germany and Britain that finally exploded with World War I. However,

Great Britain, turn of the nineteenth and twentieth centuries

★ Birthplace of Edward Elgar
☆ Birthplace of Ethel Smyth
🎓 University
– – Modern country borders

SCOTLAND

New Lanark
Glasgow   Edinburgh

Newcastle upon Tyne

North Sea

Irish Sea

Preston   Leeds
St Helens   Manchester
Holyhead   Liverpool
Sheffield
Stoke-on-Trent
Nottingham
Derby
Leicester   Norwich
Birmingham
Coventry
Worcester   Cambridge

IRELAND

Celtic Sea

Swansea
Oxford
Cardiff   ENGLAND
Bristol   London
Aldershot   Surrey   Kent
Southampton   Canterbury
Exeter

Falmouth   Plymouth

English Channel

0   250 kilometers
0   125 miles

style was supplanted by the gaudy flamboyance of her frivolous son Edward VII. Edward Elgar, a fan of flummery and ostentation, dedicated his *Symphony No. 2* (1911) to the king who had died the year before. It was that death that appeared to jingoists like Elgar to mark the end of a golden era.

THE SUFFRAGETTE MOVEMENT

Society was changing too. Emmeline Pankhurst (1858–1928), born to a politically radical Manchester family, created the Women's Franchise League in 1889 to press for married women to be given the vote at local elections. This was unsuccessful, but in 1903 she and her daughters Christabel and Sylvia helped start the militant Women's Social and Political Union. Its members were called "Suffragettes," from the term "suffrage," meaning the right to vote. They smashed shop windows, damaged property, and were sent in turn to prison where they went on hunger strike only to be force-fed. At the start of World War I, the Suffragette campaign changed tack and supported war work. In 1918 women over 30 were give the vote. Finally in 1928 women over the age of 21 were given the same voting rights as men.

throughout this period Britain's economic power had been quietly outstripped by the industrial rise of both the United States and Germany. In 1870 Britain accounted for 31 percent of the world's manufacturing production; by 1913 that had declined to 14 percent.

Royal events partly distracted the British from such socially disquieting occurrences as the first national rail strike held in 1911. Queen Victoria, who had reigned for 64 years, died in 1901. Her unexciting, yet practical

Above Ex-suffragette prisoners in 1908 advertising a protest meeting to be held outside Holloway Jail.

Below Stained glass window of Henry Wood conducting the Proms.

THE PROMS

Robert Newman, manager of London's new Queen's Hall, created in 1895 a nightly series of cheap Promenade Concerts during the otherwise empty late summer months. The 3,000-seat hall that had opened two years earlier was part of a wider development of theaters, built in central London during the 1880s, to entertain new suburban audiences. Stalls seating was removed to attract younger audiences to stroll—promenade—around the space. The first part of the long evening involved "serious" musical works, while the shorter second half included songs and lighter orchestral items.

From the start Newman chose as his conductor the 26-year-old Henry Wood, who introduced radical works and British premières, giving the Proms an adventurous edge that aided the public profile of living composers such as Elgar and Vaughan Williams. In 1926 Newman died unexpectedly. Henry Wood found a sponsor in BBC Radio, which broadcast the concerts. The famous BBC Proms "brand" developed through the decades. Now the Proms is the world's largest summer festival of music.

Gustav Mahler

JULY 7, 1860–MAY 18, 1911

GUSTAV MAHLER WAS BORN INTO A WORLD WITHOUT THE PHYSICAL AND
MENTAL FURNITURE OF MODERNITY—BEFORE TELEPHONES, CARS, EVEN BICYCLES,
BEFORE PASTEUR'S DISCOVERY OF GERMS AND MENDEL'S GENETIC INSIGHTS.
FREUD WAS FOUR YEARS OLD AND DARWIN'S *THE ORIGIN OF SPECIES* HAD
BEEN PUBLISHED ONLY ONE YEAR EARLIER.

Yet, such is its modernity of spirit that this introspective, questioning, often anguished music,
controversial and little understood in the composer's
lifetime, has become enormously popular since its
reclamation from obscurity in the 1960s. It is music
composed before its time.

Above right That
audiences sometimes
felt overwhelmed or
confused by Mahler's
music is demonstrated
in this 1907 caricature
by Fritz Schönpflug.

Discover the music

Lieder eines fahrenden Gesellen (1883–1885)
Symphony No. 1 "Titan" (1884)
Wunderhorn Songs (1887–1893)
Symphony No. 2 "Resurrection" (1888–1894)
Symphony No. 4 (1892–1900)
Symphony No. 5 (1901–1902)
Kindertotenlieder (1901–1904)
Symphony No. 8 "Symphony of a Thousand" (1906)
Das Lied von der Erde (1908–1909)
Symphony No. 9 (1908–1909)

EARLY YEARS AND INFLUENCES

Gustav's humble Jewish parents moved soon after his
birth to Iglau, Bohemia (now Jihlavi, Czech Republic),
a small town with a busy cultural life, where they
became brewers. With the purchase of a family piano
and lessons in piano and harmony from excellent local
musicians, the boy soon became an outstanding pianist.
He gave his first public recital at age 10 and began to
compose. No juvenile compositions survive, but musical memories of Iglau constantly color his songs and
symphonies—the trumpet calls and
marches of the local military, Czech
and German folksong, church choral
music, and the birdsong and the cow-
bells from the countryside he loved.

Tragically, eight of the Mahlers'
14 children died during Gustav's childhood. It is, therefore, hardly surprising
that funeral marches should appear in the
music that so often concerns itself with
the fragility of human life and love, and
that veers between hope, certainty, and
despair on the possibility of resurrection.

Above The exterior of
the Society of the Friends
of Music, which was the
Vienna Conservatoire in
Mahler's time.

EDUCATION AND CAREER

Mahler entered the Vienna Conservatorium in 1875,
studying piano and then composition, and gained some
experience in conducting before graduating in 1878.
Unfortunately, in championing Wagner's modernism,

he also managed to antagonize Vienna's notoriously
conservative and anti-Semitic musical establishment,
a powerful faction with a long memory.

Only a very Brahmsian movement for his *Piano
Quartet* survives from this period but in 1880 he
unveiled *Das Klagende Lied* (*The Song of Mourning*), a cantata on the grandest scale. Prophetic
of much of Mahler's later work, it employs a
large orchestra, soloists, chorus, and off-stage
band. With complete technical assurance, it
tells a tragic tale of love, loss, murder, and
magic using the composer's own poem.

In the same year, Mahler's rather sparse
conducting experience blossomed into a career
that was to bring him greater lifetime fame
than any of his controversial compositions. A succession of posts conducting opera in various corners of
the Austro–Hungarian Empire led, in just seven years,
from part-time work in tiny provincial theaters to the
pinnacle—the Vienna State Opera.

It was no easy journey. His stubborn insistence on
vocal accuracy and credible acting from singers, on

high orchestral standards, and on efficient admin-istration aroused vehement opposition but attracted immense critical acclaim. Anti-Semitism remained an issue however. Even Christian baptism, a condition of his appointment to the Vienna State Opera, failed to assuage Viennese bigotry. Unfortunately, this success made him a part-time composer, working in the meager gaps between preparation, rehearsal, and performances, an unremitting treadmill that affected his never robust health.

FINAL YEARS

Seeking distraction from 1907's traumas in work, Mahler accepted engagements in New York and throughout Europe, as well as composing three large masterpieces, *Das Lied von der Erde* (*The Song of the Earth*), and the Ninth and Tenth Symphonies. The last symphony was still unfinished when severe illness forced him to abandon the New York Philharmonic in mid-season and return to Vienna, where he died, aged 51 years, on May 18, 1911.

Double bass

Tuned in fourths, the largest and lowest-pitched bowed string instrument used in the modern symphony orchestra is the double bass. Despite its enormity, acoustically it does not project a very loud sound, due to its low range, so if the bass is being used as an ensemble instrument in the orch-estra, usually between four and eight bassists will play a part in unison to strengthen the effect. Mahler's *Symphony No. 1* features a double bass solo in the third movement, which interestingly, quotes the children's song "Frère Jacques," transposed into a minor key.

"If a composer could say what he had to say in words he would not bother trying to say it in music."

Left Mahler is reported to have once said, "My day will come." Forty years after his death, his music was revived by such eminent figures as Otto Klemperer, Bruno Walter, and others.

Following pages
Mahler's 10 symphonies are remarkable for their imaginative orchestration and range and intensity of emotions—passion, anguish, irony, rage, joy, visions of Heaven, nihilism, and resignation.

MARITAL WOES

Mahler married the 22-year-old Alma Schindler, a beautiful, intelligent, and gifted composer in 1902. The Fifth Symphony's glorious *Adagietto*, misused as a lament in *Death in Venice*, is really an eloquent love song to her. They seemed made for each other, but their undoubted love match was marred by disagree-ment and depression, reaching its lowest point in 1907. Maria, the older of their two beloved daughters died suddenly, at the age of five; Mahler resigned from the Opera in response to a long anti-Semitic press campaign and was then diagnosed with a heart condition. An informal discussion with Sigmund Freud in 1910 helped Mahler to recover, belatedly, his love for Alma but her own memoirs and numerous biographical studies suggest that their problems, not least Alma's unfaithfulness, stemmed fundamentally from Gustav's demand that she stop composing and devote herself utterly to facilitating his work.

Richard Strauss

JUNE 11, 1864–SEPTEMBER 8, 1949

STRAUSS—NOT AT ALL RELATED TO THE VIENNESE "WALTZ KING" FAMILY—EXCELLED IN A RANGE OF GENRES—15 OPERAS, 10 SYMPHONIC POEMS, OVER 200 SONGS, CHAMBER MUSIC—FROM THE PANACHE OF HIS *DON JUAN* PORTRAIT (1888) TO THE PENUMBRAL *FOUR LAST SONGS* SIX DECADES LATER.

Above Strauss was a noted conductor, and, with the Berlin Philharmonic Orchestra, made a number of recordings of the works of other composers, including Mozart and Gluck.

Discover the music

Don Juan, Op. 20 (1888)

Till Eulenspiegel's Merry Pranks, Op. 30 (1894–1895)

Also Sprach Zarathustra, Op. 30 (1895)

Salome (1905)

Der Rosenkavalier (1911)

An Alpine Symphony (1915)

Ariadne auf Naxos (1916)

Capriccio (1942)

Four Last Songs (1948)

The teenage Strauss was involved in an amateur orchestra that was run by his father, and he wrote for it a *Serenade* (1881) and two symphonies that started to circulate nationally. He rapidly developed parallel careers as a composer and orchestra conductor. At 22 he became a junior music director at the Munich Court Opera, sometimes conducting his father. From there he was appointed Kapellmeister at Weimar (1889–1894), then Munich again (1894–1898), the Berlin Royal Court Opera (1898–1913), and ultimately music director of the Vienna State Opera (1919–1924).

Richard Strauss spent his entire life within the world of music. He was the son of the celebrated principal horn player in the Munich Court Orchestra. The horn features strongly in Strauss's works, and he wrote two *Horn Concertos* (1883, 1942), but whether this is because of, or in spite of, his father, it's hard to know. His father had fixed traditional views about music, idolizing Mozart and detesting the two main rivals of the time, Brahms and Wagner. Nevertheless, young Strauss became deeply affected by both. He studied the piano from the age of four, the violin at eight, and composition from 11 years of age.

THE SONGS

Although renowned for his operas and tone poems, Strauss wrote more than 200 songs. He even married a soprano, Pauline de Ahna, with whom he undertook song recital tours. He showed early maturity at the age of 18 in a song like *Dedication* (*Zueignun*) and maintained a high standard through to his early eighties

Right John Tomlinson, Janice Watson, and Sarah Connolly in the English National Opera's production of *Der Rosenkavalier* at the London Coliseum in 2008.

when he wrote the truly glorious *Four Last Songs* (1948) that meditate on the closing days of life. Strauss wrote them after a difficult period in Nazi Germany. The elderly celebrity had been made president of the Third Reich's Music Guild in 1933 but was dismissed two years later. He did not support Nazism but continued to compose and enjoy premières during Adolf Hitler's reign. His sorrow over the war's destruction can be heard in *Metamorphosen* (1945). Strauss died, aged 85, in 1949.

STRAUSS'S OPERAS

Three of Strauss's most admired operas followed on from each other. *Salome* (1905) was a setting, in German, of Oscar Wilde's lurid play about Herod's daughter who kisses the newly decapitated head of John the Baptist. It was considered depraved— and was highly popular. He then worked with librettist Hugo von Hofmannstahl, in a partnership that was hailed as one of the greatest in opera. Hofmannstahl provided a Salome-style sensation with *Elektra* (1909). Strauss's score for that was judged to be the last word in ultra-modern dissonance. Yet he followed it with a "Mozart opera," *Der Rosenkavalier* (1911), a comic romance garnished with spicy cross-dressing erotic ambiguity. Strauss composed four more operas with Hofmannstahl, all absorbing but never quite as alluring as the first two. His last opera, *Capriccio* (1942), refers back to the world of *Rosenkavalier*, but also scrutinizes the very bond between librettist and composer.

Above Leon Bakst designed this costume for Potiphar's wife, for Strauss's ballet *Josephs-legende*, Op. 63, written in 1912 for Diaghilev's Ballets Russes.

TONE POEMS

Richard Strauss's ten tone poems are full of audaciously rich and varied orchestral invention. Yet they are marked by a consistency of subject and purpose. For the most part they portray heroes, anti-heroes, and would-be heroes. The musical source for the tone poem genre was Franz Liszt, Richard Wagner's father-in-law, who had developed the multi-section form of the tone poem to refer, through music, to the real world of things.

But for Strauss there was an intellectual source too, stemming from his interest in German philosophy, especially Nietzsche. Strauss rejected metaphysics, focusing on the material power of life and the need to overcome superstitions. The lover *Don Juan* (1889), *Macbeth* (1891), and prankster *Till Eulenspiegel* (1895) come to sticky ends, while *Zarathustra* (1895) and *Don Quixote* (1897) come to sad ones. But Strauss the atheist was never reluctant to tackle the death of his subjects. His final tone poem, *An Alpine Symphony* (1915), is written for a huge orchestra and remains the most intriguing. The mountain depicted seems also to be the whole of German music, which he ascends in sunlight and descends in a storm. It might also be Germany itself, in the savage storm of World War I.

The changing face of Germany and Austria–Hungary

FROM 1888 KAISER WILHELM II ORDERED THE EXPANSION OF GERMANY'S ARMED POWER AND GLOBAL AMBITIONS. YET FROM 1890, FOLLOWING HIS DISMISSAL OF CHANCELLOR BISMARK, GERMANY AND AUSTRIA–HUNGARY'S TACTICAL ALLIANCES AND LINKS BEGAN TO UNRAVEL, LEADING TO WORLD WAR I, THE GRINDING DEFEAT OF THE TWO NATIONS, AND FRESH—BUT TOXIC—STARTS AS DEMOCRATIC STATES.

Left Kaiser Wilhelm II, (1859–1941) was the last emperor of Germany and Prussia. After his forced abdication in November 1918, he and his family lived in Holland.

PRELUDE TO WAR

Wilhelm, among his costly ambitions, required new colonies and armaments. These aims chimed well with German business interests, as industrial growth was strong and exceeded domestic needs. There was also chauvinistic talk of *Lebensraum*—moving the borders outward for Germans to improve "living space." Some critics now feel that the gigantism and mega-tensions found in Mahler, Schoenberg, and the German Late Romantics reflect such concepts.

Germany and Austria–Hungary (still under Kaiser Franz Josef) were fixated with the prospect of a two-pronged attack from France and Russia. The *Schlieffen-plan* (1906) predicted that Russia would take longer to mobilize than France, so Germany should quickly

Kaiser Wilhelm I died in 1888. His son Frederick III replaced him, only to die soon after. In turn Frederick's son took office. Kaiser Wilhelm II, a grandson of Britain's Queen Victoria, admired the scale of Britain's industrial, naval, and colonial achievements, but he deeply desired to outclass them. He felt that old Chancellor Bismarck stood in his way and dismissed him in 1890. Between 1890 and 1918 eight chancellors succeeded Bismarck, but none of them matched his intricate political and diplomatic endeavors.

Right The assassination, by Gavrilo Princip, of Archduke Franz Ferdinand and his wife Sophie in Sarajevo, Bosnia, in June 1914, as portrayed in the Italian newspaper *La Domenica del Corriere*.

THOMAS MANN (1875–1955)

Mann, surely German's leading author of the time, was born in the northern city of Lübeck. Mann was 15 when his father died and the family moved to the Munich, where Mann trained and lived as a writer of symbolic works—such as *Buddenbrooks* (1901) and *The Magic Mountain* (1924)—until his exile in 1933 forced him to Switzerland, then to the USA (1939). During World War I he had supported the conservative Kaiser, but through the years his position became increasingly liberal. In 1930 he gave a speech denouncing the Nazis. He wrote sparingly but significantly about music, most famously in 1947's *Doctor Faustus*, which caused a rift with Schoenberg, who believed that the character, whose moral decay coincides with the rise of Nazism, was based on him.

Right Sigmund Freud, pictured in his study, c. 1935. His concept of "free association" became the basis of modern psychoanalysis.

attack France first (via Belgium) if Russia showed hostile intent.

However, they failed to take care over the delicate balances in the Balkan states. In 1908 Austria–Hungary annexed Bosnia–Herzegovina to stop Serbs having access to the Adriatic Sea. It was this that caused World War I, when on June 28, 1914, a Serb nationalist assassinated the heir to the Austria–Hungarian throne and his wife. Austria–Hungary declared war on Serbia, and the major powers took their inevitable sides.

On August 1, Germany adopted the *Schlieffenplan*. It failed grimly as Germany became bogged down in the "no-man's land" of northern France, facing British forces. Austrians saw defeat looming on the death of Kaiser Franz Josef in 1916, while Germany acknowledged demise when the USA joined the Allies in 1917, brought in by Germany's heedless use of U-boat submarines across the Atlantic Ocean.

THE WEIMAR REPUBLIC

The Armistice was signed on November 11, 1918 and the Kaiser gave way to a Reich President. Many Germans felt that the Americans were imposing "a democracy without democrats." Leftist attempts to create a communist state were confronted

Below German children in 1923 playing with money in the streets. After World War I, inflation in the Weimar Republic was so high that money simply became waste paper.

ruthlessly by the Social Democratic Party. In the ensuing national election of January 1919, the SPD gained most votes but no majority. Parliament met in the town of Weimar, which gave its name to the period of 1919–1932, the Weimar Republic. In 1921 the Allies imposed a "war guilt" fine of 132 billion marks. As John Maynard Keynes predicted, this insane penalty provoked gross inflation and a wave of turmoil that led ultimately to Nazism and World War II.

THE RISE OF PSYCHOANALYSIS

While all this was happening, in Vienna Sigmund Freud (1856–1939) was fusing together a number of psychological theories about the mind to create "psychoanalysis" as a method for investigating mental development. Beginning with studies of hysteria and repression (denial of emotions), Freud introduced "talking cures," analysis of dreams, and free association. He talked of the "unconscious" subjective mind (psyche) in terms of the id (instinct), ego (identity), and super-ego (conscience). He suggested that childhood experiences shaped personality, and that erotic desire started in infancy. These notions shocked society, but they were hugely influential to artists (Surrealism) and philosophers (Critical Theory). Although some thought Freud a fraud, Mahler sought his advice in 1910.

MUSIC AND NATIONALISM
IN THE NINETEENTH CENTURY

Music helps people to possess the idea of a nation. It does so by fortifying a nation's sense of authority through a national anthem, never mind how dreary that song might turn out to be. It also provides a potent soundworld in which national landscape, epics, folk dances, myths, and martyrs can be championed in the public spaces of concert halls, opera houses, and pageants.

The idea of a nation is a relatively new one and emerges from two "national" revolutions—the American (1776–1783) and the French (1789). Both revolutions were radical shifts away from absolute monarchies towards representative, republican democracies. In France, Napoleon rather spoiled this by declaring himself Emperor (1804), yet the main idea of this Enlightenment venture was to create a system of government where "the people" as "the nation" was the source of power, not a monarch who claimed authority thanks to "divine law."

NATION BUILDING

Nation building advanced in one of two directions during the nineteenth century—either unification or independence. First came the attempt to unify a group of historically separated but connected states, as with Germany and Italy, which were both unified in 1871. Second, were the efforts of small countries to

THE BROTHERS GRIMM'S
CHILDREN'S AND HOUSEHOLD TALES

Commissioned by Arnim and Brentano, linguists Wilhelm and Jacob Grimm collected fairy stories, including *Cinderella*, *Snow White*, and *Hansel and Gretel*. Published in 1812, the stark violence and cruelty of their renditions diminished over 17 revisions, as the stories—intended for nationalist adults—became popular with children. The tales were often turned into operas, most notably Humperdinck's *Hänsel und Gretel* (1893).

Above Artists of the Royal Opera on stage at Covent Garden, London, perform in Englebert Humperdinck's *Hansel und Gretel* in late 2008.

break away from control by others, such as the Netherlands (1815) and Belgium (1830) through to Poland, Hungary, and Czechoslovakia in 1918. Both kinds of nationalism triggered the twentieth century's two world wars.

Nations and would-be nations fed off "nationalism," a constructed set of ideas used to mark out one set of people from another. These notions usually involved assumptions about land (native soil), language (native tongue), and ancestry (native blood). Land, language, and ancestry were embodied in "folksong," a term invented by theologist Johann Gottfried Herder in his *Stimmen der Völker in Liedern* (*Voice of the People in Song*), two collections of German folksongs published in 1778–1779. Editions of songs, legends, and epic poems started to be published in countries seeking to feed nationalist outlooks.

These included the pagan *Nibelungenlied* (*Song of the Nibelungens*) adapted by Friedrich Heinrich von der Hagen between 1810 and 1842, which provided Wagner with the mythology for his operatic *Ring* cycle (1848–1874). In Finland, Elias Lönrot compiled the epic poem *Kalevala* in 1835, from which Sibelius crafted his patriotic *Kullervo* Symphony (1892). Meanwhile the Bohemian composer Smetana combined landscape and legend in the six symphonic poems of *Má vlast* (*My Fatherland*, 1874–1879).

Left This painting by Henri de Groux depicts the death of Siegfried. The story comes from the *Nibelungenlied*, the epic poem made famous by Wagner's *Ring* cycle.

Although nationalist sentiment spread and affected composers of the era in various ways, it generally gave them an opportunity to "tame" unusual sounding folk music and make it more palatable for the emerging bourgeoisie. Alternatively it gave them licence to be harmonically adventurous by engaging with indigenous styles. Dvořák's *Slavonic Dances* and Brahms's *Hungarian Dances* are examples of the former; Grieg's settings of Norwegian Hardanger fiddle music or Bartók's Hungarian peasant songs are models of the latter.

In Russia, the fact that several of its most noted composers—such as Balakirev (*Overture on Russian Themes*), Mussorgsky (*Boris Godunov*), and Rimsky-Korsakov (*The Tsar's Bride*)—were amateurs untrained in German standards, is now considered a benefit that produced highly influential "exotic" nationalist music. Elsewhere too, German stylistic influence became something to be confronted through self-conscious difference, hence the distinctive symphonic styles of Sibelius and Nielsen in Scandinavia, or the limpid classicism of Fauré and Satie in France. Overall, however, constructing and identifying a national "sound" was a way to exploit new markets, both internal (patriotism) and external (exoticism).

DES KNABEN WUNDERHORN (1805–1808)

Two writers, Achim von Arnim (1781–1831) and Clement Brentano (1788–1842), collaborated on a three-volume collection of the German words to more than 600 folksongs. At this time what we call Germany was a land of independent city–states and principalities united by language. In *Des Knaben Wunderhorn* (*The Boy's Magic Horn*), Arnim and Brentano aimed to demmonstrate a cohesive German heritage rooted in traditional verbal expression. In fact, many of these folksongs came from diverse sources and were liberally altered and adapted by the collectors. Nevertheless, a number of German and Austrian composers, including Weber, Schumann, Brahms, Mahler, and Zemlinsky, set the simple verses to their own Romantic music.

Below Village culture, including dancing and singing, were embraced by many composers who were seeking to express more nationalistic ideas in their music.

Claude Debussy

AUGUST 22, 1862–MARCH 25, 1918

POSSIBLY THE MOST INFLUENTIAL FRENCH COMPOSER WHO EVER LIVED, DEBUSSY VASTLY EXPANDED THE AVAILABLE RANGE OF MUSICAL TEXTURES AND COLORS, AS WELL AS CREATING A RICH, SUBTLE, AND ELUSIVE EMOTIONAL WORLD. HIS ORCHESTRATION WAS INNOVATIVE AND DISTINCTIVE, AND HIS WRITING FOR PIANO EXPLORED THE SONORITY OF THE INSTRUMENT IN STARTLING NEW WAYS.

He did come into contact with people with artistic connections, and showed early enthusiasm for poetry and painting, as well as talent as a pianist. It was as pianist, conductor, and music critic (under the nom de plume "Monsieur Croche"—his reviews are rather trenchant and witty) that he earned his main living.

HARMONIC INNOVATION AND ORCHESTRAL COLOR

Debussy's early influences included Wagner. (The French had a love–hate relationship with Wagner, and Debussy pokes good-natured fun at the beginning of *Tristan und Isolde* in his *Golliwog's Cakewalk*.) He soon realized that he loved Wagner's intense chromatic harmony for its color rather than its functionality, and it was in the area of harmonic innovation and orchestral color that his music made its impact. His earliest works were grandiose, and had little success, but once he had found his more subtle natural voice, his influence spread. His first major breakthrough was achieved with *Prelude à l'Après-midi d'un Faune* (1894), a work that showed his sensuous orchestration, organic sense of structure, feeling for atmosphere, and strong melodic and harmonic gifts.

The work has a programmatic structure; subsequent orchestral works, such as *Nocturnes* (1895–1899) and *La Mer* (1903–1905) are similarly atmospheric and pictorial, and use the orchestra with consummate skill to paint vivid sound-pictures.

Following his second marriage (three years after the birth of the daughter who inspired the *Children's Corner* suite) his attention turned primarily to piano music. The two volumes of *Préludes* (1910–1913) are characteristic of Debussy's mature style. All the pieces carry evocative titles ("The Girl with the Flaxen Hair," "The Submerged Cathedral," and "Footsteps in the Snow"

His music is often called "impressionist" after an artistic movement with which he had no connection, because one can hear in his music an audible analog of the work of such artists as Pierre-Auguste Renoir and Camille Pissarro.

Claude-Achille Debussy was born in St Germaine-en-Laye, just outside Paris. His early life was somewhat unsettled—his father was often away, for some of the time in prison—and he had little formal education.

Above Debussy, enjoying a picnic with his daughter Chouchou, for whom he wrote *Children's Corner*.

Top right A fan with five bars of the opera *Pelléas et Mélisande*, signed by the composer in 1894.

CELLO SONATA (1915)

This piece is less than 15 minutes long, yet it contains the contrast and range of something much longer. The stylistic variety is enormous, from the neo-classical opening, through the bizarre guitar-like sounds of the central Sérénade to the whirling, Spanish-inflected Finale. The writing for both the instruments (cello and piano) is masterful, and performance demands great rhythmic flexibility, sensitivity to color and chord-balance, and excellent ensemble between the instruments.

are three of the most well known) and show an enormous range of harmonies, styles, and piano textures.

Toward the end of his life Debussy returned to chamber music (the *String Quartet* of 1893 is an early example), and both the *Cello Sonata* (1915) and the *Violin Sonata* (1916–1917) are frequently played today. These pieces show a more integrated harmonic style, a certain neo-classicism (in French music "classical" refers to Couperin and Rameau), and a masterful compactness of form.

CHARACTERISTICS OF DEBUSSY'S MUSIC

Debussy's harmony, while mostly built up of super-imposed thirds like traditional harmony, is used mainly for its color. Chords can be used in chains of parallel harmony, preserving their voicing, color, and sonority. This gives Debussy's harmony a certain affinity with jazz. Characteristic harmonic textures include the bare, chant-like fifths of "The Submerged Cathedral" or the vaguely spooky augmented triads of "Voiles."

Regarding melody, Debussy uses a full range of modes, from the whole-tone scale to diatonic to full chromatic to pentatonic. This gives the music an enormous range of character and great flexibility.

Rhythm in Debussy's music is very flexible, and by no means always tied to a strong beat. In order to best

Discover the music

Prelude à l'Après-Midi d'un Faune (1892–1894)

La Mer (1903–1905)

Images (1905–1912)

Children's Corner (1906–1908)

Préludes (1910–1913)

Cello Sonata (1915)

PROGRAMME

7ᵐᵉ Saison des Ballets Russes

NIJINSKI, dans l'"Après-Midi d'un Faune"

"Music is the expression of the movement of the waters, the play of curves described by changing breezes."

Above An illustration by designer Leon Bakst showing Vaslav Nijinsky dancing in *L'Après-midi d'un Faune* in 1912. Choreographed by Nijinsky, it was a Ballets Russes production.

serve the musical character, the rhythm can either be languorous (as in *L'Après-Midi d'un Faune*) or spiky/jazzy (as in *Golliwog's Cakewalk*).

Debussy adds texture—the natural resonance of the piano is used expertly, and in orchestral music many novel instrumental combinations are discovered, as well as new sounds that come from writing for instruments in unusual parts of their register.

Erik Satie

MAY 17, 1866–JULY 1, 1925

A MAVERICK COMPOSER WHO WENT AGAINST THE PREVAILING ETHOS OF HIS TIME, SATIE'S CLEAN, SIMPLE, SELF-EFFACING MUSIC, TOGETHER WITH HIS ENGAGING ECCENTRICITY AND SENSE OF HUMOR, HAS MADE HIM REMARKABLY CURRENT IN THIS POST-MODERN ERA.

His pieces, being easy to assimilate and deliberately undemanding, have become enduringly popular. Their suitability as background music (as evidenced by countless advertisements and documentaries using Satie or Satie-pastiche) is something that Saties's esthetic would have embraced wholeheartedly.

SATIE THE INDIVIDUAL

Erik Alfred Leslie Satie (his mother was Scottish, hence the middle names) was born near Le Havre, and died in Paris, a city he rarely left after having moved

Above right Satie was an eccentric man, whose music was a precursor to the minimalist movement.

Below Cocteau (seated) with Les Six: Darius Milhaud, Georges Auric, Arthur Honegger, Germaine Tailleferre, Francis Poulenc, and Louis Durey.

there when he was 12 years old. His father and uncle were unconventional personalities, working as ships' brokers. When his mother died in 1872 Satie lived with his grandparents before joining his father in Paris. He showed musical talent, but was both lazy and reluctant to accept received wisdom, and was expelled from the Paris Conservatoire (which gave a rigorous and traditional musical education). Thereafter Satie lived a life of self-imposed poverty in a poor area of Paris, eschewing public transportation and eating only white-colored food. He joined the Rosicrucians, founded his own

church, the Metropolitan Church of the Art of Jesus the Conductor (it never really took off!), and later joined the Radical–Socialist party. So he was something of a figurehead and statement-maker, and achieved almost guru status, influencing composers such as Debussy and Milhaud. He was cited as a father figure by the group of French composers known as "Les Six."

The emotional detachment, the independence from conventional thought or esthetic, and the lack of pretension gave Satie's music influence over the modernist movements that followed the two world wars. His early music was a reaction to the emotional excess of the prevailing Wagnerian esthetic, and the clean, scientific ethos of early modernism could be interpreted as a reaction to the horrors of war.

Satie lived a very Spartan life, wrote music of great simplicity and purity, but drank to excess, and died, at the age of 59, of cirrhosis of the liver.

SATIE'S WORK

Satie's most famous pieces were written early in his life. *Gymnopédies* (1888) and *Gnossiennes* (1890) are both groups of short piano pieces. They are simple, repetitive and modal; the piano texture tends to consist of a single-line melody and a chordal accompaniment. The harmonies often oscillate between two chords, giving a hypnotic effect, which in some ways prefigures minimalist music.

The harmonies themselves are unresolved seventh chords, which later became the primary ingredient of light music and jazz. *Gnossiennes* is often cited because one of the pieces contains no bar-lines; although this looks modern, it is quite clearly an affectation, since the piece has a perfectly regular pulse. His rather satirical sense of humor prompted Satie, when accused of

Discover the music

3 Gymnopédies (1888)

3 Gnossiennes (1890)

Vexations (1892) [Note: do not try to listen to all of this—it is a short piece played 840 times!]

Parade (1917)

Socrate (1919)

Right Jean Cocteau (1889–1963) was a seminal figure in French drama and later film-making. He was in his twenties when he wrote the scenario for Satie's ballet *Parade*.

having no sense of form, to compose "three pieces in the form of a pear." Accusations of having poor technique clearly annoyed him, however, since he enrolled in the Schola Cantorum in order to study counterpoint; from that point on, his pieces showed some influence of these studies.

Collaboration with the influential theatrical figure Jean Cocteau led to the ballet *Parade*, an ebullient work with some unusual additions to the orchestra. Later works include the cantata *Socrate*—simple, ritualistic, modal, and somehow ancient. For an art exhibition, Satie created music that was designed to be in the background, only half listened-to. This was, clearly, a precursor to the modern, ubiquitous "Muzak" or elevator music, which has a completely flat tension-curve and is designed to relax the listener. This is a function that Satie's music is often relegated to today.

CHARACTERISTICS OF SATIE'S MUSIC

Satie has a very strong melodic gift—his tunes are simple, well shaped, and memorable, partly because they are so repetitive. Satie's harmony is somewhat static—it is a precursor to jazz harmony because of its non-functional use of seventh chords.

His rhythms are regular—repetitive to the point of being mesmerizing. The texture of his works is clear and transparent. Purity and simplicity are the hallmarks of Satie's music.

PARADE (1917)

Parade is a lively ballet score written for Serge Diaghilev's Ballets Russes (see page 319). A lightly used orchestra is augmented by a typewriter and a revolver. The music is full of little self-contained motifs and ideas, a symmetrical structure, and unpretentious good humor.

Left Gregory Milan in *Parade*, from a ballet production called *Picasso and Dance*, at the 2003 Edinburgh Festival. Picasso designed the original sets for Satie's 1917 ballet.

Symbols and impressions of late nineteenth-century France

THE LAST QUARTER OF THE NINETEENTH CENTURY IN FRANCE SAW SEVERAL SIGNIFICANT DEVELOPMENTS. IN 1871, THE TREATY OF FRANKFURT ENDED THE YEAR-LONG FRANCO–PRUSSIAN WAR, IN WHICH GERMANY ACQUIRED ALSACE–LORRAINE. THE SAME YEAR, 20,000 PEOPLE DIED IN THE PARIS COMMUNE UPRISING WHEN SOCIALISTS SEIZED THE MUNICIPAL GOVERNMENT. SUSPECTED SPY ALFRED DREYFUS WAS PARDONED IN 1899, ENDING THE HIGHLY DIVISIVE "DREYFUS AFFAIR."

In the art world, the revolutionary movements of Impressionist painting and Symbolist poetry had a profound and lasting influence on the music of Claude Debussy and his contemporaries André Caplet, Albert Roussel, and Paul Dukas.

Below Painted in 1908, Monet's *San Giorgio Maggiore at Twilight* is one of the artist's later works.

In 1874, the Artists' Cooperative Society of Painters, Sculptors, Engravers etc staged an exhibition in Paris after they were rejected by the traditionalist Paris Salon. The exhibition included works by Alfred Sisley, Berthe Morisot, Pierre-August Renoir, and Camille

PARIS WORLD'S FAIR 1889

One hundred years after the storming of the Bastille, the World's Fair (*Exposition Universelle*) was held in Paris, showcasing technology, art, entertainment, and culture from around the globe. Approximately 28,000 people visited the fair between May 6 and October 31, 1889. Debussy certainly attended, and was said to have been greatly inspired by the exotic sounds of Javanese gamelan musicians. Other attractions included Buffalo Bill's Wild West Show from the USA, and the Village Nègre, an "ethnological exhibition" of some 400 indigenous people.

World's fairs have served as an impetus for significant architectural innovations, and 1889 was no exception. The most famous landmark in Paris—the Eiffel Tower—was commissioned especially as the entrance arch to the exposition. Designed by engineer Gustav Eiffel, the tower took five years to build. It weighs 8,000 tons (8,160 tonnes), and stands at 700 ft (214 m). In 1889, it was the tallest structure in the world.

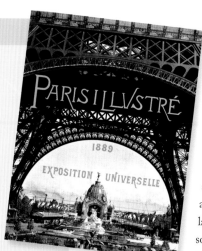

Pissarro, and met with mixed reviews. However, it was Claude Monet's misty seascape entitled *Impression, Sunrise* that attracted some of the most unfavorable criticism, and eventually earned the artists the collective name of "Impressionists."

The Impressionists broke with convention in a number of ways. Their subjects were everyday people rather than historical and political figures, depicted in outdoor settings such as cafés and seaside resorts, as opposed to the more formal studio environment. They found plenty of inspiration in Asian art. Most significantly, they experimented with a variety of techniques that enabled them to capture ephemeral qualities of nature such as sunlight and ocean waves. They painted on a white rather than a dark background, and applied their fresh, vibrant colors directly onto the canvas in short, broken strokes rather than mixing their paints beforehand, as was the norm. Overall, the effect was radiant and spontaneous.

POST-IMPRESSIONISM

Impressionism ended with the group's final exhibition in 1886, the same year as Georges Seurat's showing of *Sunday Afternoon on the Island of La Grande Jatte*, considered the genesis of what would later be termed "Post-Impressionism." Along with Seurat, the Post-Impressionists included Paul Cézanne, Paul Gauguin, and Vincent van Gogh. Unlike the Impressionists, they did not see themselves as part of a communal movement, and for the most part worked in physical and artistic isolation. Although these artists began using

Above A poster for the 1889 World's Fair, featuring one of the "star" attractions— the newly built Eiffel Tower, now Paris's most recognizable landmark.

Right Poet Arthur Rimbaud (1854– 1891) was one of the great exponents of the Symbolist movement, his poetry often shocking readers. He broke new ground in literature.

Impressionist techniques, they found its objectivity limiting and sought ways to express emotional and spiritual responses to their subjects and to elicit such responses from their viewers.

Cézanne's long career spanned both Impressionism and Post-Impressionism. His later works show a dense, somewhat architectural style.

Gauguin, influenced by the rich colors of medieval stained glass and illuminated manuscripts, is best known for his lush Tahitian scenes. Van Gogh's tormented inner life is reflected in his sometimes ecstatic and often desolate images, skillfully manipulating color for emotional effect.

SYMBOLIST POETRY

Influenced by the decadent poet Charles Baudelaire and philosopher Arthur Schopenhauer, the Symbolist movement in poetry is characterized by suggestion and fluidity, as well as emphasis on the musicality of words. The principal Symbolists were Stéphane Mallarmé, Paul Verlaine, and Arthur Rimbaud.

Mallarmé believed in the synergy of style and content, and asserted that, "the point of the poem is the beauty of the language." A friend of Debussy, his poem *L'Après-midi d'un Faune* (*The Afternoon of a Faun*) was the basis for Debussy's famous composition.

Verlaine's simple, lyrical poetry explored the themes of sexuality, city life, dreams, and other mystical states. The poems in his 1874 collection *Romances sans paroles* (*Songs without Words*) were meditations on his marriage, which ended when he left his family for his

protégé and lover, Arthur Rimbaud. Their relationship was tempestuous, fueled by hashish and absinthe. Rimbaud, best known for his poem *The Drunken Boat* (1871), became an icon in the psychedelic 1960s, and was especially revered by Jim Morrison of the band, The Doors.

Alexander Glazunov

AUGUST 10, 1865–MARCH 21, 1936

GLAZUNOV HAS A SIGNIFICANT PLACE IN RUSSIAN MUSIC. LIKE RACHMANINOV, HE IS REGARDED AS AMONG THE LATE RUSSIAN ROMANTIC COMPOSERS. HE INFLUENCED MANY YOUNG RUSSIAN COMPOSERS DURING THE EARLY TWENTIETH CENTURY. GLAZUNOV'S OWN COMPOSITIONAL STYLE WAS PRIMARILY A BLEND OF RUSSIAN NATIONALISM AND GERMANIC CLASSICAL MUSIC.

Although he was a stabilizing force during tumultuous times, Glazunov was later dismissed as old-fashioned and conservative by younger composers, including Prokofiev and Shostakovich.

Alexander Glazunov was born in St Petersburg in 1865 to a well-to-do family; his father was a book publisher, his mother a pianist. He studied piano and composition and at 15, at the recommendation of Mily Balakirev, leader of the nationalistic group of composers known as "The Five," he was introduced to Nikolai Rimsky-Korsakov who gave him weekly lessons in harmony, counterpoint, and orchestration.

By 1881, after rapid progress, he had completed his *Symphony No. 1*, Op. 5. Balakirev conducted this symphony the following year and Glazunov was hailed as

Above right Glazunov, as painted by Il'ya Repin. The composer had an incredible memory, and was able to play back entire works after only one hearing.

Below Glazunov, second row, third from left, with Rimsky-Korsakov (center) and a group of musicians, photographed in 1905.

a "rightful heir to the masters of the Russian National School." Belyayev, the influential music publisher, arranged for publication of Glazunov's works. As his reputation grew he traveled to Weimar and Paris, conducting his own music in London in the late 1890s.

AT THE ST PETERSBURG CONSERVATORY

In 1899 the St Petersburg Conservatory appointed Glazunov as instructor in composition and orchestration. When Rimsky-Korsakov was dismissed during the revolutionary restlessness in Russia in 1905, Glazunov resigned his post in protest, although he returned later that year after full independence was granted to the staff by government authorities. He was elected Director of the St Petersburg Conservatory in 1905, a post he retained until 1930. As a measure of his international esteem, Cambridge and Oxford universities conferred honorary doctorates of music on him in 1907, and cycles of entirely Glazunov concerts were given in St Petersburg and Moscow.

Following the Revolution of 1917, Glazunov soon established a sound working relationship with the new regime. Because of his reputation the Conservatory received special status among institutions of higher learning. He worked unflaggingly to develop the curriculum, raise the standards of staff and students, and shape the Conservatory's culture, prestige, and autonomy.

Within the conservatory, the teachers wanted more progressive methods and the students greater

Discover the music

Stenka Razin Op. 85 (1884)

Raymonda Op. 57 (1897)

The Seasons Op. 67 (1900)

Violin Concerto in A minor,
     Op. 82 (1904)

Right Igor Zelensky and Darcey Bussell dance in a 1998 Royal Ballet performance of *Raymonda*. The ballet was choreographed by the great ballet master Marius Petipa.

rights. Glazunov defended his post stubbornly, maintaining a conservative position. His sometimes vexed responses to some student compositions included walking out of Prokofiev's *Symphony No. 1* première and conducting Rachmaninov's *Symphony No. 1* while reportedly drunk.

A NATIONALISTIC SPIRIT

Glazunov's music shows flowing and expressive melodies, placing him in the Romantic school (although he was, for a time, swayed by Wagnerian harmonies) with Liszt's influence apparent. The national spirit of his music is considered unmistakable and his counterpoint writing is regarded as one of the most skilful of the Russian composers.

Glazunov wrote most of his works before 1906, after which he primarily wrote for special occasions. He was known to have an exceptional ear and musical memory, completing and orchestrating the overture to Alexander Borodin's *Prince Igor* from memory, having heard Borodin play it on the piano.

Like all Russians, Glazunov suffered much deprivation during World War I and the ensuing civil war years, yet he remained active—conducting concerts in factories, clubs, and Red Army posts. In 1922, in honor of his fortieth anniversary as a composer, he was named the Peoples' "Artist of the Republic." He departed for Vienna on an extended conducting tour across Europe and the USA in 1928, settling in Paris in 1932 with his wife and adopted daughter. He died in Paris in 1936, with his music having being regarded for a long period as something out of the past.

PUBLISHING RUSSIAN MUSIC

Mitrofan Belyayev (1836–1904) was a wealthy timber merchant, amateur musician, and philanthropist. He played a major role in the promotion of Russian music. In 1885 he started his own publishing house "Belaieff" in Leipzig, Germany, as international copyright did not extend to Russia at that time. At first he published music by Glazunov, Anatoly Lyadov, Rimsky-Korsakov, and Borodin. As more composers sought his assistance, Belayev asked Glazunov, Rimsky-Korsakov, and Lyadov to sit on an advisory council. The group of composers that formed the council soon became known as the "Belyayev Circle." He published over 2,000 works by Russian composers. He also organized concerts of Russian music in St Petersburg each season and provided prize money and financial assistance to budding composers. Belyayev's publishing house includes many of the great names of Russian national music.

Russian nationalism and revolution

RUSSIA WAS ONE OF THE FIRST PLACES TO DEMONSTRATE NATIONALISM IN ITS ARTISTIC OUTPUT.
BY TAKING THE UNTAMED FOLK MUSIC OF THE TIME AND PLACING IT WITHIN EXISTING
EUROPEAN MUSIC STRUCTURES, ITS COMPOSERS CREATED A UNIQUE COMBINATION.

The Romantic period in which this occurred was beginning to move toward a conclusion, form increasingly being replaced by content, and harmonic relationships becoming increasingly enigmatic. The emergence of writers such as Tolstoy, Dostoevsky, and Pushkin from the growing educated middle class also provided a cross-fertilization of creative influences.

Early nationalist composers included Mikhail Glinka who produced the first successful Russian national opera, *A Life for the Tsar* (1836). This was the first appearance of music that had grown from folk melodies. The rhythmic energy, original chromaticism, and unusual orchestration (for the times) embody a unique style that was further established by successive generations of Russian composers.

Mussorgsky was one of "The Five" (see pages 230–231), who promoted a nationalist musical style rooted in Russian folk music traditions. He was inspired to write *Pictures at an Exhibition* after the death of painter and architect Viktor Hartmann (one of the first artists to include traditional Russian motifs in his work).

Above "Welcome Comrades," a poster asking foreign workers to join the revolution.

Below Bolshevik soldiers march through Red Square, c. 1917. In the foreground is a mounted Cossack officer.

THE SOCIO-POLITICAL CONTEXT

The late nineteenth and early twentieth centuries were troubled times for Russia. In the last half of the nineteenth century Russia's economy developed more slowly than other European nations. Although there was significant industrial growth it was not widespread. In 1864 judicial reform established Western-style courts and there were reforms in education and culture. From his accession in 1855 Alexander II brought about a social restructure requiring public discussion of issues and the lifting of some censorship, yet Russia could not match Western technology in terms of warfare and was unsuccessful in using this avenue as a means of developing its industrial base.

The reforms, particularly the lifting of state censorship, prompted some significant political and social commentary. Public opinion shaped ideas opposed to tsarism and private property, ideas shared by many intellectuals, professionals, peasants, and workers. Although serfdom was abolished in 1861 the terms were unfavorable to the peasants and contributed to the increase in pressure for revolution.

As Alexander pursued his reforms, opposition to his reactionary polices grew. In 1881 he was assassinated, having just signed a decree approving the formation of a democratically elected, law-making parliament. The assassination put an end to liberal reform, and revolutionaries were hunted down by Alexander III's police.

When World War I started in 1914 Germany declared war on Russia. Despite Russia having the largest army in the world, its deployment was hindered by a lack of infrastructure and an ineffectual and corrupt administration pervading all areas of Russian life.

THE OCTOBER REVOLUTION

The introduction of bread rationing in Petrograd in March 1917 led to a chronic food shortage, the final degradation for the populace. Two hundred thousand

workers went on strike. Troops killed some strikers and the Guards regiments mutinied. Tsar Nicholas II abdicated, ending the 300-year reign of the Romanoffs; he was replaced by the Provisional Government.

Unfortunately, the Provisional Government was without firm leadership—the army soon fell apart and law and order broke down irretrievably. Lenin and Trotsky retuned from overseas and the October Revolution of 1917 took place. By November the Bolsheviks were in control of Moscow. In December Lenin asked for an armistice with Germany. In July 1918 the royal family was assassinated in Ekaterinburg.

Lenin died in 1924 and Stalin took control in 1925, leading a brutal regime. The old class structure was removed, opposition was silenced, and Russia moved toward economic self-sufficiency.

In the first years of the Soviet system the artistic avant-garde was considered the logical and necessary corollary of revolution, but as time went by this attitude changed and between 1923 and 1932 the Russian Association of Proletarian Musicians exercised a firm grip on the musical output of the Soviet Union.

Above The charismatic Lenin addressing a 1917 meeting in Petrograd. Leader of the October Revolution, he became the first leader of the newly declared Union of Soviet Socialist Republics.

Right Anton Rubinstein (1829–1894), founder of the St Petersburg Conservatory, was a noted pianist and conductor. He was also a champion of Russian nationalism.

ST PETERSBURG CONSERVATORY

Russia's first music college, the St Petersburg Conservatory, was founded in 1862 by Anton Rubenstein. Not a single Russian was appointed among the first professors at the Conservatory, musical teaching in Russian prior to 1862 apparently not being of the required standard. Most composers had studied in Germany and other parts of Europe and the Russian aristocracy imported European music. Irish composer John Field, who was living in Russia at the time, taught a number of pupils who later became leading composers and performers. Field was directly responsible for a large part of the Russian school of pianism.

The success of the St Petersburg Conservatory led to the founding of a similar faculty in Moscow in 1866.

Jean Sibelius

DECEMBER 8, 1865–SEPTEMBER 20, 1957

THE MUSIC OF JEAN SIBELIUS IS SO EVOCATIVE OF BOTH THE FINNISH
LANDSCAPE AND THE RUGGED NATIONAL CHARACTER THAT IT BECAME
A POTENT SYMBOL OF THE COUNTRY'S STRUGGLE AGAINST RUSSIAN
DOMINATION. IT WAS HIS INTERNATIONAL SUCCESS AS ONE OF THE
TWENTIETH CENTURY'S GREAT SYMPHONISTS THAT BEGAN FINLAND'S TRANSFORMATION
FROM A MUSICAL BACKWATER INTO ONE OF THE WEST'S MOST VIBRANT MUSICAL COMMUNITIES.

Above right An autograph score of the Andante movement of Sibelius's *Symphony No. 1* (1899).

Left An illustration of the story of Kullervo from the *Kalevala*, which inspired Sibelius's epic work, his Op. 7 in five movements.

Right Sibelius's best known work today is probably *Finlandia*, a short symphonic poem dedicated to the Finnish people's struggle for independence.

Discover the music

Karelia Suite, Op. 11 (1893)
Finlandia, Op. 26 (1899)
Symphony No. 2, Op. 43 (1901)
Violin Concerto, Op. 47 (1903)
String Quartet (*Voces intimae*), Op. 56 (1908–1909)
Symphony No. 4, Op. 63 (1911)
Symphony No. 7, Op. 105 (1924)
The Tempest, Op. 109 (1925)

FORMATIVE YEARS

Johan Christian Julius Sibelius—he adopted Jean later as his "music name"—displayed an early fascination with the family piano but received no serious music instruction until he began violin lessons at 15. He then made extraordinary progress—within two years he was playing string quartets and trying out his own chamber compositions. He entered Law School at Helsinki University in 1885, but simultaneously enrolled at the Conservatoire and, within a year, had abandoned law, intending to become a professional violinist.

Sibelius continued composing, however, and began taking composition lessons. By the time of his graduation in 1889, after some successful performances of his music and the publication of one of his songs, he decided to become a composer. This was also the year he met the fervently nationalist Järnefelt brothers and fell in love with their sister, Aino.

The seven centuries of Swedish rule that preceded the Russian takeover in 1809 had bequeathed Finland a Swedish-speaking governing elite that ignored the Finnish language and scorned Finland's ancient culture, an intolerable situation for nationalists. To them, pride in all things Finnish was an essential part of the path to independence from Russia. Sibelius had some Finnish, but came from a Swedish-speaking background and Aino, to whom he became secretly engaged in 1890, was firmly intent on strengthening his rather tepid commitment to the nationalist cause.

It was during an eventful nine-month visit to Vienna, where

SIBELIUS'S "NORDIC" STYLE

In his "Nordic" style, Sibelius produced, during the course of his life, a series of powerful tone poems mostly based on the *Kalevala* stories, and seven magnificent symphonies that cover a huge emotional range. These are the works, together with the *Violin Concerto*—one of the most popular, most difficult, and most truly symphonic concertos ever composed—on which his fame principally rests. But there are also numerous lighter works, like *Valse Triste* and several suites of incidental stage music that hark back to his European training and reveal the more urbane "Swedish" side of his complex character.

"Pay no attention to what the critics say; there has never been a statue set up in honor of a critic."

between studying, indulging his taste for somewhat dissolute company, and being inspired by Bruckner's music to attempt his own first orchestral compositions, that he finally made time to study the *Kalevala* which Aino had pressed upon him.

Above In the mid-1930s, virtuoso violinist Jaschsa Heifetz made the first recording of Sibelius's *Violin Concerto*.

EPIPHANY

This ancient collection of epic folk poetry and legend provided the authentic Finnish source of inspiration for which the composer had been searching. Besides being entranced by the gods, heroes, and mythical creatures that later peopled his tone poems, his musical mind was captivated by the short repetitive melodic phrases, spanning a narrow interval, to which the poetry was chanted by the old reciters.

Using similar terse phrases and his knowledge of Finnish folk music, he abruptly transformed his style. Without quoting the folk tunes, he used their strong, modal, generally melancholy contours as models for his own melodies. The result, so strangely different from the refined German tradition of his training, won from his Viennese composition teacher the affectionate title, "my Finnish barbarian."

The outcome was *Kullervo*, a huge five-movement work for soloists, chorus, and an orchestra. The triumphant Helsinki première in 1892 of this tragic tale from the *Kalevala*, quintessentially Finnish in language, subject, and melody, established Sibelius as the musical voice of Finnish nationalism.

THE FINAL YEARS

Sibelius was shy and intense, prone to self-doubt and mood swings that perhaps underlay the profligacy of his youth that undermined his health. The bouts of heavy drinking that several times landed him in serious debt, despite the generous state pension he enjoyed from 1897 onwards, also probably robbed him of his creativity later in life when, sadly, he fell silent 31 years before he died, leaving an expectant world still hungry for an eighth symphony it would never hear.

Sibelius's Scandinavia

TODAY FINLAND, DENMARK, SWEDEN, NORWAY, AND ICELAND PRESENT A PICTURE OF PEACEFUL, WELL-ORDERED COMMUNITIES, SOMEWHAT ALOOF FROM THE HURLY-BURLY OF INTERNATIONAL POWER POLITICS. BUT IN FACT, BEHIND THE CORDIAL RELATIONS THAT NOW EXIST BETWEEN THESE PROUDLY INDEPENDENT NORDIC NATIONS LIE CENTURIES OF SHIFTING ALLIANCES, NUMEROUS WARS, ETHNIC REPRESSION, FIERCE ENMITIES, AND TERRITORIAL DISPUTES, IN WHICH THE RUSSIAN BEAR LOOMING TO THEIR EAST OFTEN PLAYED A PART.

In the year of Sibelius's birth—1865—the political landscape was still very much in transition. Finland was an autonomous Grand Duchy within the Russian Empire. Until Russia annexed it in 1809, the country had belonged to Sweden for centuries and Swedish was still its official language. Norway, ruled by Denmark, had been handed to Sweden as a result of the Napoleonic wars. Denmark retained Norway's former dependencies—Iceland, Greenland, and the Faroes— but had been greatly reduced in size and wealth by Prussia's annexation of Schleswig–Holstein.

The second half of the nineteenth century was a difficult period for Scandinavia. The recent discovery of antisepsis had greatly reduced infant mortality and

Below A Norwegian popular dance of the late nineteenth century. Regional Scandinavian dances are still regularly performed today.

all the Scandinavian countries, with their essentially rural economies, were having a lot of difficulty in feeding rapidly growing populations from old-fashioned, relatively unproductive farms. The result was that between 1850 and the turn of the century a staggering one third of the Scandinavian population emigrated, mostly to America, in search of a less arduous and better-fed life, exacerbating the economic situation by reducing the rural workforce. Fortunately, the exodus slowed toward the end of the century as belated industrialization gradually brought prosperity to the Nordic communities through the exploitation of their previously untapped natural resources.

NATIONALISM, INDEPENDENCE, AND DEMOCRACY

Fundamentally, all three of these concepts rest on a single immensely powerful idea—the belief in individual worth, that "all men are created equal," as the American Declaration of Independence of 1776 so nobly states. It was this belief that ultimately brought revolution to Russia and political and cultural transformation to its Nordic neighbors.

Nineteenth-century Nordic composers began to move away from the Germanic tradition in search of a national idiom. Ole Bull's use of the Norwegian folk-fiddling tradition prepared the way for Grieg. Hugo Alfvén colored his music with Swedish folk song. Niels Gade and Carl Nielsen in Denmark and Sibelius in Finland all developed distinctive national voices.

At around the same time, Munch in Norway, the Skagen school in Denmark, Sibelius's friend Gallen-Kaliela and numerous others established national painting styles. Hans Christian Andersen, Kirkegaard, and Strindberg became important international literary

Above Swedish playwright August Strindberg (1849–1912) had a seminal influence on modern theater. *Miss Julie*, written in 1888, is one of his best-known plays.

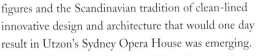

Above A painting depicting Finnish people leaving their homes as a result of the Soviet–Finnish War, a conflict that lasted from late November 1939 until mid-March 1940.

figures and the Scandinavian tradition of clean-lined innovative design and architecture that would one day result in Utzon's Sydney Opera House was emerging.

Imperialism and autocracy could not long survive this muscular national pride. By 1917, Denmark, Sweden, and Norway had quietly become independent constitutional monarchies. Finland's path was harder. Independence from Russia in 1917 was followed by a brief but bitter civil war to prevent its own Communist revolution. Some of Sibelius's relatives were killed and his letters record the dangers, severe food shortages, and mental trauma of the time. Political turmoil continued for years, even after Finland became a republic in 1919. Sibelius was deeply affected, sliding gradually deeper into alcoholism and depression until he fell silent in 1927.

Following a period of steadily rising prosperity, only Sweden escaped unscathed from World War II. Denmark and Norway, in spite of their declared neutrality, were occupied by Nazi Germany, and valiant resistance in both countries remained a thorn in the German side despite savage reprisals. Sweden remained neutral and prosperous, but Finland was attacked by Soviet Russia. Although forced to cede some territory, the hugely outnumbered Finns heroically fought their lumbering opponents to a standstill. Subsequently, when Hitler invaded Russia, Finland fought beside Germany, while specifically rejecting Nazism, to win back the ceded territory.

During the post-war boom years, Scandinavia led the world with enlightened policies of social welfare. Generous government support produced an unprecedented flowering of the arts and of Finnish music in particular—something at least to lighten the heart of Finland's reclusive grand old man, full of honors but now, sadly, musically mute, in his beautiful forest retreat at Järvenpää.

Carl Nielsen

JUNE 9, 1865–OCTOBER 3, 1931

NIELSEN IS THE UNDISPUTED MASTER OF MODERN DANISH MUSIC AND
ONE OF THE OUTSTANDING SYMPHONISTS OF THE TWENTIETH CENTURY.
HIS MUSIC EMBODIES THE IDEA THAT NOTHING IS MORE UNIVERSAL THAN
THE LOCAL PERFECTLY DESCRIBED. DENMARK ITSELF IS A PRESENCE IN HIS
SYMPHONIES, CONCERTOS, STRING QUARTETS, OPERAS, SONGS, AND CHORAL WORKS.

Above right Carl Nielsen with a group of Danish musicians. The composer could play violin and a number of brass instruments including the bugle.

Left A portrait of the composer by Danish artist Sigurd Swane (1879–1973). Nielsen's image is featured on the front of the Danish 100-kroner banknote.

conducted the orchestra). Following his marriage to sculptress Anne Marie Brodersen in 1891 (they had three children together), Nielsen soon began to establish his reputation as a composer: His first symphony (1894) broke all conventions by beginning in one key and ending in another.

In 1901 Nielsen was given an annual government stipend, which allowed him the freedom to focus on large musical projects, including the opera *Masquerade* and a symphony with singers (No. 3). Two powerful symphonies followed as well as a *Chaconne* for piano. During the 1920s, Nielsen traveled abroad, meeting fellow artists and enjoying critical acclaim. After completing his *Symphony No. 6* (1924–1925), Nielsen concentrated his efforts on composing clarinet and flute concertos, and writing his childhood memoirs. Having been appointed director of the Royal Danish Conservatory in 1931, he died later that year.

In an essay entitled "Words, Music, and Programme Music," which was published in a collection of his writings entitled *Living Music* (1925), Nielsen wrote:

"If, in common with architecture, [music] can proclaim nothing definite and cannot, like poetry, painting, and sculpture, convey information about what we call nature and reality, it can, more than any of these, illumine, emphasize, suggest, and clarify … the most elementary feelings and most heavily charged emotions … This may explain the riddle of why music, more than any other art, relentlessly reveals its origin, the composer."

Nielsen's music derives from what he called "the land that gave one its joyous force." He grew up hearing ballads sung by country people and dancing to music played on the violin by his father.

EDUCATION AND CAREER

Nielsen was born in Sortelung, near Nørre Lyndelse, a rich agricultural district south of Odense located on the island of Fyn. He learned to play the violin from his father, who taught him to play alongside him at village dances. In 1879 he joined a military band in Odense as a bugler and alto trombonist. Five years later he enrolled as a violinist at the Copenhagen Conservatory, after which he was appointed second violin in the orchestra of the Royal Theatre (he eventually

Discover the music

Helios (1903)

Masquerade (1904–1906)

String Quartet No. 4 in F, Op. 44 (1906)

Symphony No. 3, Sinfonia espansiva, Op. 27 (1910–1911)

Violin Concerto Op. 33 (1911)

Springtime on Fyn, Op. 42 (1921)

Symphony No. 5, Op. 50 (1921–1922)

Wind Quintet, Op. 43 (1922)

Flute Concerto (1926)

Clarinet Concerto, Op. 57 (1928)

"JENS THE ROADMENDER"

In 1907 Nielsen composed "Jens the Roadmender," a song that was an instant success and became a Danish classic. That this simple, strophic song, depicting an aged outcast, was so popular, may seem surprising but its achievement lies in the way the composer absorbs and uses the devices of folk song with a voice that is entirely his own. In Jens we encounter an unselfish nature, a man who undergoes years of drudgery and then dies; yet Nielsen's music affirms an enduring passion for life, inciting us to perceive connections between the roadmender's ascetic majesty and the elemental Danish landscape.

SYMPHONY NO. 5

Nielsen's six symphonies represent the heart of his creativity, transmitting something of the wonder of life, its strangeness, its goodness, and the stoicism of people everywhere. In the fifth symphony, the work that consolidated his international reputation, Nielsen speaks

SPRINGTIME ON FYN

This multi-movement choral work, set to a text by Aage Berntsen, turns to the scenes of Nielsen's childhood, to which he deeply responded. Nielsen once observed: "Everything in Fyn is different from the rest of the world ... the bees hum in a way of their own with a special Fyn accent, and when the horse whinnies and the red cows low, why, anybody can hear it's quite different from anywhere else." In this modern pastoral, the villagers wake up from their winter torpor to renewed hope, vigor, and an intimation of harmonious communion with nature. The work is a testament to the innocence of man.

Below A full dress rehearsal of Nielsen's comic opera *Masquerade,* which was part of the Bregenz Festival in Austria in July 2005.

with awesome authority—not just about the creative processes but also about the attributes of music appropriate to contemporary conditions. The first movement builds up an almost unbearable tension that explodes into one of the most harrowing passages in music; the second movement works to resolve the friction of the first, finally leaving an impression of wholeness and depth, suffused with unexpected blessing.

Denmark's golden age

CARL NIELSEN WAS BORN ON THE CUSP OF DENMARK'S "GOLDEN AGE"—A RENAISSANCE OF CULTURE, ART, AND SCIENCE FROM WHICH EMERGED STORYTELLER HANS CHRISTIAN ANDERSEN, PHILOSOPHER SØREN KIERKEGAARD, AND THE PHYSICIST HANS CHRISTIAN ØRSTED, AMONG MANY OTHERS. PARADOXICALLY, THIS GOLDEN AGE WAS ALSO A TIME OF INTENSE ECONOMIC AND POLITICAL TURMOIL.

Mounting pressure had forced King Frederick VII to concede to demands for a constitutional monarchy in 1849. This national unrest culminated in the First War of Schleswig (1848–1851) in which the duchies of Schleswig and Holstein failed in their attempt to gain independence from Denmark. A decade later, Denmark lost these duchies to Prussia in the Second War of Schleswig (1864), but was to eventually regain much of the territory as a result of the Treaty of Versailles in 1919. Denmark had remained neutral during World War I, but was not immune from the general instability that pervaded Europe.

Above right Georg Brandes (1842–1927) was a leading literary figure in the movement known as "Modern Breakthrough."

THE LABOR MOVEMENT

Rapid industrialization, the dissolution of the guild system, and growing urbanization created an atmosphere of deep unrest. The time was ripe for a labor movement in Denmark.

Despite strong opposition from business and government, an organized workers' association was formed in 1871 under the leadership of Louis Pio, a former postal employee. Strikes and demonstrations reached fever pitch in 1872, and many union members were arrested. Pio and two of his colleagues were convicted of high treason, and later emigrated to the USA.

During the 1880s the labor movement regrouped, and the Social Democratic Party was formed. It won nearly 10 percent of seats in the *Folketing* (one of the houses of Parliament) in the 1901 general elections. By the 1920s, the Social Democrats had become the largest political party in Denmark.

DANISH LITERATURE: THREE NOBEL WINNERS AND A NOMINEE

Denmark produced several significant writers during this period. Henrik Pontoppidan (1857–1943) grew up in the town of Randers, where at the age of six he experienced the invasion of the Austrian and Prussian armies. Pontoppidan was a member of the naturalistic literary movement founded by academic Georg Brandes known as the "Modern Breakthrough." His novels, which include *The Promised Land*, *Lucky Peter*, and *The Kingdom of the Dead*, sought to portray the social, spiritual, and political struggles of humankind.

Initially a disciple of Brandes's theory that literature should be a vehicle for the "great thoughts of liberty and the progress of humanity," writer Karl Gjellerup

Norwegian Sea

Arctic Circle

NORWAY

SWEDEN

FINLAND

Bergen

Tampere
Hämeenlinna ★
Turku
Vantaa

Stavanger-Sandnes

Västerås
Uppsala
Stockholm

ESTONIA

RUSSIA

Skagen
Göteborg

Aalborg

DENMARK
Copenhagen
Nørre
Lyndelse ☆
Malmö

Baltic Sea

Scandinavian composers, twentieth century
★ Birthplace of Jean Sibelius
☆ Birthplace of Carl Nielsen
— Modern country borders

POLAND

GERMANY
Bydgoszcz

0   250   500 kilometers
0   125   250 miles

Left A study of an artists' party held at Skagen in northern Denmark, painted by P.S. Krøyer (1851–1909) .

(1857–1919) moved away from naturalism toward "New Romanticism." Best known for his novels *The German Student* and *The Mill*, Gjellerup settled in Germany and aroused antipathy in Denmark for his pro-German stance. Mature works such as *The Pilgrim Kamanita* reflect a growing interest in eastern philosophies. Pontoppidan and Gjellerup shared the Nobel Prize for Literature in 1917.

Novelist, poet, playwright, and essayist, Johannes V. Jensen (1873–1950) is considered the father of Danish modernism. His historical novel based on Christian II—*The Fall of the King*—has been hailed as the greatest Danish novel of the twentieth century. Jensen reacted against French Symbolism ("Beaudelaire's poisonous hallmark"), promoting a simple poetic style, and his later writings were strongly influenced by Charles Darwin. He received the Nobel Prize in 1944.

Karen Blixen (1885–1962) has enjoyed more international popularity than any other Danish writer since Hans Christian Andersen. Her first book, entitled *Seven Gothic Tales*, was published under the pseudonym Isak Dinesen in 1934. In these richly imaginative stories, Blixen emphasized narrative over character, defying the trend for social realism. She is best remembered for *Out of Africa* (1937) which drew on her life on a coffee farm in Kenya from 1913 to 1931 and her love affair with an English game hunter. Blixen was twice nominated for the Nobel Prize, but lost out to Albert Camus in 1954 and Ernest Hemingway in 1957.

THOMAS LAUB (1852–1927)

Thomas Laub is best known for his contribution to Danish church music. He initially studied for the ministry, but abandoned his theological studies for a musical career. After traveling to Italy and Bavaria in the 1880s Laub decided that church music, which had been influenced by Romanticism, should return to the simpler styles of the Middle Ages and Renaissance. He put forward his ideas in two major works: *The Church Song* (1887) and *Danish Church Song* (1918), which included original compositions to support his theories.

Laub was approached by Carl Nielsen to help him compose secular songs, incorporating the melodic reforms he used in his hymns. The result was *A Score of Danish Songs* (1915). This was followed by a publication of 20 new songs in 1917, and the *Folk High School Melody Book* (1922).

Below Of Karen Blixen's works, possibly the most loved are her short story *Babette's Feast*, and her memoir *Out of Africa*.

THE OPERAS OF GIACOMO PUCCINI

When Giacomo Puccini first began composing, Italian opera had been in decline. Since the heady days of Rossini, Donizetti, and Bellini, numerous works had been produced, most only to run for a few nights and then disappear forever. With the notable exception of Arrigo Boito and his opera *Mefistofele*, and Verdi, who was composing into old age, there seemed to be no operatic genius left in Italy.

Puccini was born in 1858 into a family that had provided his native town, Lucca, with four generations of musicians; his father was an organist and choirmaster and director of the local music school. After his father's death in 1863, the orphaned Giacomo undertook music education with his uncle, Fortunato Magi, and Carlo Angeloni. He was granted a scholarship in 1880 to the conservatory in Milan, where he studied with Antonio Bazzini and Amilcare Ponchielli. Pietro Mascagni and Alfredo Catalani were student colleagues.

Above The original poster for *Turandot*. Puccini died in 1924, before completing this opera, which was first performed in 1926.

Below left Italian tenor Enrico Caruso (1873–1921) and American soprano Geraldine Farrar (1882–1967) star in a 1915 production of *La Bohème*.

EARLY OPERAS

Puccini's first operatic attempt was *Le Villi*, with a libretto by Ferdinando Fontana. He entered the opera into a competition in 1883, and while it received no consideration from the jury, its Milan performance, subsidized by friends, was a success. The *finale primo* was encored three times. Puccini's second opera, *Edgar*, premièred in 1889 at La Scala, but was a failure. The music was weak and the libretto, which was also by Fontana, even weaker.

It took four years for Puccini to recover from that fiasco. The preparation of *Manon Lescaut* was difficult, but its première in February 1893 was a complete success, at last redeeming the composer and setting him inexorably on his path to fame.

SUCCESSES AND FAILURES

In 1900 *Tosca* opened in Rome, and although some arias, such as *Recondita armonia*, were encored, most critics did not care for the opera. Then, later that year, Puccini attended a performance of Belasco's *Madame Butterfly* in London and fell in love with the drama even though he could not understand a single word of it. Four years later, in 1904, the première of Puccini's new opera, *Madama Butterfly*, at La Scala was a fiasco, unexpected and memorable at the same time. But a few months later, a new *Madama Butterfly*—which differed quite substantially from the first—was presented and was a great success.

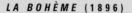

LA BOHÈME (1896)

One of Puccini's most loved operas, *La Bohème*, with libretto by Giuseppe Giacosa and Luigi Illica, was based on Henri Murger's *Scènes de la vie de Bohème* (1851). The love story between the consumptive seamstress Mimi and the poet Rodolfo contains some of opera's most beautiful melodies, including the expressive *Che gelida manina* (*Your tiny hand is frozen*). The work premièred on February 1, 1896 at Turin's Teatro Regio, and was conducted by Arturo Toscanini. It is hugely popular today, but at the time, critics were less than fulsome, one commenting: "And the music? Well, it is full of prettiness and charm without being striking in any way."

When *La fanciulla del West* (based on Belasco's play *The Girl of the Golden West*) opened in New York's Metropolitan Opera House on 10 December 1910, it featured Enrico Caruso and Emmy Destinn. It created a sensation—Puccini and Belasco, together with the performers and the conductor Arturo Toscanini, received 14 curtain calls at the end of Act I, 19 at the and of Act II, and another 14 at the end of Act III!

After Puccini's collection of three one-act operas, *Il trittico* (*The Triptych*) was completed in 1918, he commenced work on *Turandot*, based on the story by Carlo Gozzi. Renato Simoni and Giuseppe Adami prepared the libretto but it took three years to define the three-act structure of the opera. In 1924 Puccini

Discover the music

Manon Lescaut (1893)

La Bohème (1896)

Tosca (1899–1900)

Madama Butterfly (1904)

It trittico (*Il tabarro, Suor Angelica, Gianni Schicchi*) (1918)

Turandot (1926)

Below A 1986 performance of *La Bohème*, which tells of the love affair between the sickly seamstress Mimi and the struggling poet Rodolfo.

was diagnosed with a tumor in the throat and he traveled to Brussels for some X-ray treatment. He took with him sketches with which to complete the score of *Turandot*, which had been orchestrated only up to Liù's death. On November 29, 1924 Puccini died. *Turandot* was completed by Franco Alfano and premièred two years later. *Turandot* features one of the most well known and best loved arias in all opera, *Nessun dorma* (*None shall sleep*).

Giacomo Puccini achieved an almost perfect blend of melody and depth, and, furthermore, he gave full significance to the orchestra without neglecting the singers. The composer also embraced the notion of "verismo"—that is, operatic realism. Although this notion was, and remains, highly controversial, his unflinching commitment into the realization of operas that sounded realistic is well documented.

Alexander Scriabin

January 6, 1872–April 27, 1915

Scriabin was considered eccentric by some and visionary by others. One of the most important twentieth-century composers for piano, he was a pioneer of chromatic harmony in Russia. He also became intrigued with mystical philosophy, and as this interest heightened, his compositions began to shift the boundaries of both performance and harmony.

Like Debussy and Schoenberg, Scriabin initiated a new musical language—radical, advanced, and breaking with tonality. His style of writing did not continue after his death.

Scriabin's mother died when he was very young and he was raised by an aunt; his father was often overseas on diplomatic postings. Scriabin began studying theory in 1885 with Sergei Taneyev, then director of the Moscow Conservatory, and commenced piano lessons at that institution in 1888. At one point he hurt his hand and stopped performing in order to concentrate on composition. Yet, he graduated from the Conservatory in 1892 with a gold medal in performance and came to the attention of Belyayev, the publisher and philanthropist, who in 1895 financed Scriabin on a European tour performing his own music.

POEMS FOR PIANO

Scriabin married pianist Vera Isakovich in 1897 and they had four children, and from 1898 to 1903 he taught piano at the Moscow Conservatory. After Belyayev's death in 1904 he began receiving an annual grant from Morosov, a wealthy Moscow merchant. At

"I am the boundary, I am the peak!"

Above Russian-born conductor Serge Koussevitsky (1874–1951), photographed here in London in 1933, published a number of Scriabin's works.

Top After Scriabin died, Rachmaninov embarked on a Russian tour, playing an all-Scriabin program. It was the first time that Rachmaninov played another composer's works in public.

this time he also moved to Switzerland to begin work on his *Symphony No. 3* (*Divine Poem*). He also separated from his wife so he could live with a former student. During 1906 Scriabin gave recitals of his works in New York and other US cities, and commenced writing "poems" for piano. He moved to Paris in 1907, returning to Russia in 1908 to great acclaim. He visited London in 1914 for a concert of his works. His orchestral work The *Poem of Ecstasy* premièred in 1908 and was highly regarded. Serge Koussevitzky, well-known conductor and publisher, who became one of Scriabin's greatest supporters, signing him to a five-year contract in 1908.

His early works were almost exclusively written for piano and exhibit many Romantic characteristics, including some used by Chopin. Indeed, many of his

MYSTERIUM

One of Scriabin's more bizarre works was one he never completed, *Mysterium*. He spent 12 years planning it, envisaging its eventual performance in an Indian temple. The sketches he left indicate that he saw it as a seven-day-long multimedia pageant to be performed in the Himalayas as a purification ritual, leading to the rebirth of the world. He even planned a trip to India, the outbreak of World War I bringing that idea to a quick end.

piano works were written in forms used by Chopin—nocturne, mazurka, prelude, and étude. Liszt and Wagner were also early influences, although as his writing matured he evolved an original melodic and harmonic style of writing noted for its chromaticism. Scriabin's major works include ten sonatas (begun in 1892 and completed in 1913) and 85 preludes for piano. The sonatas showcase the development of his compositional style, beginning in the established mode of Chopin and Rachmaninov and verging close to atonality at their completion in 1913. His first major work for orchestra, his *Piano Concerto*, was composed in 1896. *Rêverie*, his first orchestral work, was performed in 1899 in Moscow.

THE INFLUENCE OF MYSTICAL PHILOSOPHY

In his later writing, Scriabin's interest in Madame Blavatsky's "theosophy" or mystical philosophy came to greatly influence his ideas and musical composition. The last of Scriabin's five symphonies was *Prometheus—*

Discover the music

Piano Concerto, Op. 20 (1896)
Symphony No. 3 (*Divine Poem*), Op. 43 (1905)
Poem of Ecstasy, Op. 54 (1908)
Prometheus—Poem of Fire, Op.60 (1910)
Piano Sonata No. 9 (*Black Mass*), Op. 68 (1912–1913)

Above Scriabin had a deep interest in India, seeing the country as the home of mystics and holy men. He envisioned staging his *Mysterium* in India, a goal that was never acheived.

Poem of Fire Op. 60 written in 1910. *Prometheus* was scored for large orchestra with chorus and solo piano. Some of the words he used to describe the work included: "stopped time," "sonorous silences," "white sound," and the "astral desert." Heavily imbued with symbolism, it was an early example of a multimedia performance. One part was written for a "keyboard of lights" which, according to what keys were pressed, translated the pitches into shafts of colored light.

Scriabin died at the age of 43, after developing an abscess on his lip, which led to blood poisoning. He was the Russian composer who most separated himself from the national music being written at the time. His works were original, evolving from his own tonal structures. His experimentation with a range of tonality and effects inspired the next generation of composers.

Sergei Rachmaninov

APRIL 1, 1873–MARCH 28, 1943

ONE OF THE GREAT PIANISTS OF THE TWENTIETH CENTURY, RACHMANINOV'S TECHNICAL ABILITY AND RHYTHMIC DRIVE WERE LEGENDARY. HIS LARGE HAND SPAN (HE COULD STRETCH THE INTERVAL OF A THIRTEENTH ON THE KEYBOARD, WHEREAS MOST ONLY MANAGE A NINTH) ENABLED HIM TO ACCOMPLISH VIRTUOSIC FEATS. AS A COMPOSER, RACHMANINOV IS CONSIDERED THE LAST GREAT EXAMPLE OF LATE RUSSIAN CLASSICAL ROMANTICISM.

Above right The cover of Rachmaninov's *Elegiac Trio*, Op. 9, written to mark Tchaikovsky's death.

Left An 1880 photograph of Rachmaninov with his teacher Nicolai Zverev and two other students.

Discover the music

Morceaux de Fantaisie, Op. 3 (1892)

Piano Concerto No. 2, Op. 18 (1901)

Symphony No. 2, Op. 27 (1908)

Vespers, Op. 37 (also known as *All-Night Vigil*) (1915)

Rhapsody on a Theme of Paganini in A minor, Op. 43 (1934)

EARLY INFLUENCES

Tchaikovsky, Rimsky-Korsakov, and other nineteenth-century Russian composers were early influences, yet Rachmaninov developed a personal style that included a definite lyricism, broad and sweeping melodic lines, colorful breadth, creative form, and a range of rich, distinctive orchestral colors. Chopin and Liszt also influenced his compositions; many of his works are in a mournful late Romantic style, emulating Tchaikovsky's penchant for minor keys.

While still a student Rachmaninov showed his skill for composition, writing his first piano concerto, Op. 1, in 1891, his first opera *Aleko*, Op. 24, in 1893, and a set of piano pieces, *Morceaux de Fantaisie*, Op. 3, in 1892, which includes the famous *Prelude in C sharp minor*.

Rachmaninov's *Symphony No. 1* premièred in 1897 and was severely criticized, being likened to a musical depiction of the "seven plagues of

RHAPSODY ON A THEME OF PAGANINI (1934)

Rachmaninov's concertante work, *Rhapsody on a Theme of Paganini in A minor*, Op. 43, scored for piano and orchestra, is an often-performed concert piano work, especially in piano competitions. The piece is a set of 24 variations based on the last of Nicolò Paganini's *Caprices* for solo violin, which inspired works by several composers including Schumann, Liszt, and Brahms. The work is slightly unusual in that it plays the first variation before enunciating the main theme. The slow eighteenth variation is the most well known and is often provided on disk compilations without the remainder of the work. This variation inverts (turns upside down) the main melody.

Rachmaninov was born into a noble family, and studied at the St Petersburg Conservatory. He later studied piano, harmony, and counterpoint at the Moscow Conservatory, and graduated in piano and composition in the early 1890s. He had the unusual facility of being able to replay complex compositions upon first hearing, a talent he shared with his compatriot Alexander Glazunov.

Germany, following the failed rebellion of 1905. His first tour of the USA as a pianist was in 1909, where his *Piano Concerto No. 3* was popularly acclaimed. *Vespers*, his unaccompanied choral work, is evidence of his life-long fascination with the ecclesiastical chant.

Following the Revolution in 1917, Rachmaninov moved briefly to Denmark, before finally settling in the United States in 1918. He never returned to Russia and his music was banned there for many years. One of his few later works, *Rhapsody on a Theme of Paganini*, written in Switzerland in 1934, is one of his best-known compositions.

In February 1943, the composer and his wife became American citizens. Just one month later, Rachmaninov died, only a few days before his seventieth birthday, having been diagnosed with advanced melanoma during the previous year.

Although his reputation as a composer has moved in and out of popularity over the decades, Rachmaninov's piano works and some of his orchestral output have remained part of the standard repertoire.

Egypt." However, the inadequacy of the performance was mooted as the real problem, the conductor, Alexander Glazunov, reported as having been intoxicated.

The poor reception of his symphony, together with the Eastern Orthodox Church's firm objection to his marrying his cousin, Natalie Satina, resulted in a long period of severe depression. At this time he embarked upon his career as a piano virtuoso and conductor. His 1899 London debut with the Philharmonic Society was in the capacity of pianist, conductor, and composer.

In 1901, Rachmaninov gave the first complete performance of his *Piano Concerto No. 2* in Moscow. This work was to become iconic in the piano concerto repertoire and is one of the most celebrated twentieth-century works of this genre. Rachmaninov and Natalie did eventually marry in 1902, and remained together until his death in 1943.

LEAVING RUSSIA

In 1904 Rachmaninov took a job as a conductor at the Bolshoi Theater in Moscow, resigning for political reasons two years later. In 1908 he moved to Italy and

Above A photograph of the composer taken in 1943, the year he died. Rachmaninov was one of the great piano virtuosos of the time, and his piano compositions are among the most loved works in the concert repertoire.

Bass clarinet

Part of the woodwind family, the bass clarinet resembles a saxophone. It is a straight-bodied instrument with a small unturned bell, a curved metal neck, and a distinct, rich, earthy tone. Like the rest of the clarinet family, bass clarinets use the Boehm system of keys and fingering. Although usually pitched in B flat (meaning it is a transposing instrument with B flat sounding as concert C), music has been specially written for the instrument in the key of A, such as in some of Wagner's operas, and in Rachmaninov's symphonies.

Russia and the changing world

RACHMANINOV'S LIFE COINCIDED WITH A PERIOD OF ENORMOUS ADVANCES IN TECHNOLOGY, SCIENCE, AND THE ARTS. MEDICAL ADVANCES WERE EXTRAORDINARY, POLITICIANS THRIVED, SOCIAL ORDER AND GOVERNMENTS WERE DISRUPTED, REFORMED, DISRUPTED AGAIN. CREATIVITY WAS FOSTERED AND SUPPRESSED ONLY TO RE-EMERGE MORE VIBRANTLY AND IN DIFFERENT AND UNEXPECTED FORMS.

By the second half of the nineteenth century nationalism was in full swing and few people, including composers, remained untouched by an awareness of their national culture. Some composers and artists were overtaken by the spirit of the age, which contradicted their own personal visions. On occasions a stylistic change occurred which they were unable to acquire, the age in which they were participating moving on and outgrowing them.

IMPRESSIONISM AND EXPRESSIONISM

A new style of music composition—impressionism—started in France around 1860 and followed the same ideals as those in painting which Monet, Sisley, Renoir,

Right *Café Concert at Les Ambassadeurs* by French artist Edgar Degas, one of the Impressionist painters admired by musicians and dancers across Europe and Russia.

Manet, and Pissarro, among others, had begun. Composers also aimed to create an impression in sound. Among the exponents of this musical form were Debussy, Ravel, Scriabin, and Karol Szymanowski.

Around the turn of the twentieth century, German and Austrian composers were also showing their own new idiom in a flurry of expressionism revealing their inner emotional angst (after all, this was the age of Sigmund Freud). Philosopher Friedrich Nietzsche, artists Marc Chagall, Wassily Kandinsky, Amedeo Modigliani, and Edvard Munch, and composer Alban Berg, among others, embraced this style which was appearing across the arts, in sculpture, film, literature, and, of course, the theater.

Russia before the October 1917 Revolution
★ Birthplace of Alexander Glazunov
★ Birthplace of Sergei Rachmaninov
☆ Birthplace of Alexander Scriabin

and Russia, and the "central powers": Germany, Austria–Hungary, and their associated empires. Over 8.5 million troops died during the war; another 7.5 million people disappeared or were incarcerated.

POST-REVOLUTIONARY RUSSIA

The total number of deaths during World War I is comparable to the loss of approximately 9 million people during the period of the Russian Civil War and famine from 1917 to 1922. The oppressive Stalin regime that followed, from 1924 to 1953, is responsible for anywhere between 9 and 20 million deaths; most of these occurred during the 1930s.

Following the 1917 revolution, the Soviet system became a temporary haven for experimental artists and inspired new directions. By the 1920s, however, the Communist Party was having second thoughts about its encouragement of the new and experimental in art. Terms such as "formalist" and "naturalistic" were coined by the Communist regime to apply to any composer whose music appeared to have the potential to undermine the "purity" of the Revolution, and the government, often in the name of puppet organizations such as the Russian Union of Proletarian Musicians, began stamping out originality wherever they found it.

Below An 1899 advertisement for the Edison Concert Phonograph, showing a "conductor" playing a recording in front of a large audience.

MEDICAL ADVANCES

Medical advances over the last quarter of the nineteenth century saw Louis Pasteur expound the germ theory of disease, which prompted the development of a range of vaccines—for cholera, anthrax, rabies, typhoid, and the plague—all before the end of the century. In another major medical breakthrough in 1928, the Scottish bacteriologist Alexander Fleming discovered penicillin.

WARS AND WORLD POWERS

The late nineteenth and early twentieth centuries saw new national powers appear—for instance, Germany, the United States, and Japan. The period also saw a range of wars, such as the Russo–Japanese (1904–1905) War. Consistent Japanese victories proved an embarrassment for the Russian government, exposing large-scale corruption in high places, a catalyst to the "Bloody Sunday" revolt in 1905.

The Great War is one of the major events of the early twentieth century that had a great impact on the lives of Russian composers such as Scriabin and Rachmaninov. It was fought between two major alliances, one initially consisting of France, the United Kingdom,

THE IMPACT OF CHANGING TECHNOLOGY ON MUSIC

One great Russian export was Israel Baline, who was born in Russia in 1888. In 1893, his family emigrated to the USA where he changed his name to Irving Berlin (1888–1989). He became one of the most successful composers of popular songs in history, writing more than 3,000 songs. He was one of the few popular songwriters who wrote both his own music and lyrics. His success was helped by amazing advances in technology.

Gramophone players, radios, and the talkies all played a part in the success of the Broadway musical, and music in general. The talking machine, or gramophone, was patented by American inventor Thomas Edison in 1877. In 1902 Italian tenor Enrico Caruso made his first gramophone recording. Rachmaninov was one of the first great musicians to pursue an extensive recording career, signing his first contract with Edison records in the USA before 1920. The availability of sheet music and commercial recordings soon changed the way the public thought about music.

Ralph Vaughan Williams

OCTOBER 12, 1872–AUGUST 26, 1958

HE WROTE FILM MUSIC AND HYMNBOOKS, MUSIC FOR SCHOOLS, AND NINE SYMPHONIES. IN ATTEMPTING TO GRASP WHAT IT WAS TO BE AN ENGLISH COMPOSER, HE STUDIED WITH BRUCH IN GERMANY AND RAVEL IN FRANCE. YET VAUGHAN WILLIAMS BUILT HIS STYLE OUT OF NATIVE FOLK SONG, A REVERENCE FOR BRITAIN'S TUDOR COMPOSERS, AND A NEED TO CONFRONT MODERN ANXIETIES. EARLY IN HIS CAREER A CRITIC REMARKED, "ONE IS NEVER QUITE SURE WHETHER ONE IS LISTENING TO SOMETHING VERY OLD OR VERY NEW."

Ralph (pronounced "Rayf") Vaughan Williams (an un-hyphenated surname) was a vicar's son born into a wealthy, well-connected family: His great-uncle was the famous naturalist Charles Darwin. Born in a village but raised near the market town of Dorking in Surrey, he nevertheless considered himself a Londoner, the subject of his *Symphony No. 2* (1913).

Vaughan Williams received a privileged education at Charterhouse, where he played viola in the school's orchestra. He undertook musical study at the Royal College of Music, then Cambridge University; then took lessons from Max Bruch in Berlin (1897) and—in an attempt to get out of "German thinking"—with Ravel in Paris (1908). Ravel joked that he was the only student he had who did not try to write "like Ravel." Yet Ravel's influence can be clearly heard in *Bredon Hill* from the song cycle *On Wenlock Edge* (1909) and in a lusciously meditative work for violin and orchestra, *The Lark Ascending* (1914).

Above right A true Englishman, Vaughan Williams once said, "Every composer cannot expect to have a world-wide message, but he may reasonably expect to have a special message for his own people."

Below Vaughan Williams had family connections to to the Wedgwood family, famous for pottery, and to the great naturalist Charles Darwin, pictured below with his wife.

THE TUDOR INFLUENCE

From 1904 Vaughan Williams took a keen interest in the fading tradition of English folk song, examples of which he collected. He was also inspired by modal music written four centuries earlier by Tudor composers such as Tallis and Byrd. This strand of nationalism differed from that of the senior Elgar. Influenced instead by the socialist William Morris, both Vaughan Williams and his friend Gustav Holst were concerned to elevate and enhance communally rooted material.

His first successful work, *Fantasia on a Theme of Thomas Tallis* for strings (1910), brings together in an engaged dialogue, three musical worlds—the glorious but distant past of Tallis, folk music embodied by a rhapsodic string quartet, and a third that searches for utopia through the stimulus of the other two. A highly productive composer, many of his larger works carry such ideas as these, leading in many of the symphonies to irresolute, even dark, conclusions.

HYMNS AND FILMS

Even though he was an atheist, Vaughan Williams made a living compiling two standard hymnbooks, the *English Hymnal* (1906) and *Songs of Praise* (1925). In both, he introduced folk songs and tunes by himself—*For All The Saints*, for example—and those of his friends, including Gustav Holst. These, and his radio hit the short *Fantasia on Greensleeves* (1928), aside, the general public encountered his music often through his film scores, notably the illustrative but disturbing music to *Scott of the Antarctic* (1948), which he later used for his *Symphony No. 7* (*Sinfonia Antarctica*)—surely a reflection there not of Antarctica but instead the icy landscape of the Cold War.

Above Jean Rigby (Mistress Ford), Andrew Shore (Sir John Falstaff), and Marie McLaughlin (Mistress Page) in the 2006 English National Opera Production of Vaughan Williams's *Sir John in Love*.

Discover the music

Sea Symphony (1909)

On Wenlock Edge (1909)

Fantasia on a Theme of Thomas Tallis (1910)

Symphony No. 2 (1913)

The Lark Ascending (1914)

Symphony No. 5 (1943)

Symphony No. 7 (*Sinfonia Antarctica*) (1949–1952)

MUSIC TO HEAR

Vaughan Williams wrote nine symphonies, cramming the last three into his last years (1952, 1955, 1957). They are varied in subject but reflect the development of a distinct mind undertaking 50 years of music-making in calamitous times. The first, *Sea Symphony* (1909) is the only one with singers, with settings of the American poet Walt Whitman. The intriguing *Symphony No. 3*, deceptively titled *Pastoral* (1921), uses an invisible wordless singer and, in its unsettling slow movement, a solo bugle, which gives away the work's appalling subject, World War I, in which the composer served as an officer. A long gap followed before the furious *Symphony No. 4* (1934) then the warm *Symphony No. 5* (1943). Yet it is the finale of the *Symphony No. 6* (1948) that offers up his most modernist and challenging statement ("always very quiet").

Throughout his long life Vaughan Williams was active as a teacher, a choir trainer, and also in creating organizations to assist composers—the Composers' Guild (1943)—or to promote music-making in society and education, such as the Arts Council (1945). He married twice, the second most surprisingly when he was 80 years old, to a poet half his age. This was an act considered agreeably typical of a man known to many as "Uncle Ralph."

Gustav Holst

SEPTEMBER 21, 1874–MAY 25, 1934

RARELY HAS SUCH A GAP EXISTED BETWEEN A COMPOSER'S LIFESTYLE AND HIS MUSIC. THE MENACING MARCH OF *MARS* FROM *THE PLANETS* HAS INFLUENCED MANY A FIERCE HOLLYWOOD FILM SCORE, YET ITS CREATOR WAS A MEEK AND MILD SCHOOLTEACHER WHO TAUGHT HIMSELF ANCIENT GREEK AND SANSKRIT. HIS BEST FRIEND SAID OF HIM, "HIS MUSIC REACHES INTO THE UNKNOWN, BUT IT NEVER LOSES TOUCH WITH HUMANITY."

PERFORMING, TEACHING, AND COMPOSING

To earn a living, Holst became a trombonist and rehearsal pianist for the traveling Carl Rosa Opera Company (1898–1900), then second trombonist with the Scottish Orchestra (1900–1903). Both jobs gave him a vivid practical knowledge of orchestral sounds. From then on until the end of his life he secured a salary as a director of music in London, most prominently at St Paul's Girls School in Hammersmith (1903–1934) and Morley College for Working Men and Women (1907–1924). For an ill man he traveled well, including some time in Algeria where he cycled in the desert and found material for his "oriental" suite *Beni Mora* (1912). He was a constant self-educator, fascinated by alternative spiritual practices such as Hinduism, for which he attended classes in Sanskrit in order to set five sequences of *Hymns from the Rig Veda* (1907–1912) and his minimalist opera *Savitri* (1908).

His first mature work was an unadorned *Ave Maria* for eight-part female choir (1901), the simple and clear-cut nature of which marked his lifelong style. Vaughan Williams claimed that "he was a leader in the revolt against the riot of luxurious sentiment which marked the decadence of the Romantic period." Nevertheless it was a 1913 Proms performance of Schoenberg's highly chromatic *Five Pieces for Orchestra* that inspired

Gustav Holst was born in the English spa town of Cheltenham. There was a Swedish background to the family name; both Holst's father and grandfather were music teachers; his great-grandfather once taught the harp in the Russian Imperial Court.

Holst grew up in a musically active family, but with weak eyes and a frail chest, he suffered illnesses that hindered his piano and violin training. He was given a trombone to tackle his asthma, and to improve his health Holst took long rambling walks, a habit he continued his whole life.

He started to compose from the age of 12, and by 17 he had secured local positions as a choirmaster. At 18, he went to the Royal College of Music in London to formally study composition. It was here that he met fellow student Ralph Vaughan Williams. They became lifelong friends, and would often consult each other on their latest projects and discuss their shared interest in the English folk song tradition.

Above right Holst in middle age. *The Planets* is perhaps the most popular of his many compositions, but Holst did not consider it his best work.

Above Energized by the English countryside and the writings of Thomas Hardy, Holst loved to ramble on the moors. His tone poem *Egdon Heath* was inspired by Hardy's works.

Left Holst was very interested in Hindu spirituality, and in the *Rig Veda*, the ancient Hindu scriptures, in particular. This sculpture shows Brahma holding the *Rig Veda*.

Holst to write his most famous work, *Seven Pieces for Large Orchestra*, which was ultimately known as *The Planets* (1914–1916). But perhaps his most successful work is the one that followed this, the audacious *Hymn of Jesus* for choirs and orchestra (1917).

As a socialist in the 1920s he wrote many pieces for community groups. At the same time his works followed the period's anti-Romantic trend in becoming lean and sober, such as the *Fugal Concerto* (1923) and the *Lyric Movement* for viola and orchestra, which is set in two keys simultaneously (1933). The austere and melancholy *Egdon Heath* (1927), inspired by Thomas Hardy's depiction of primitive moorland, seems to be more typical of Holst's character than the glittering *Jupiter* by which he's better known. He died in 1934, the same year as Elgar and Delius. This was considered a watershed moment in British music.

Discover the music

Savitri (1908)

Beni Mora (1912)

The Planets, Op. 32 (1914–1916)

Hymn of Jesus, Op. 37 (1917)

Fugal Concerto (1923)

Egdon Heath, Op. 47 (1927)

Below Imogen Holst (1907–1984), Gustav's only child, was also a composer and conductor. Photographed here in 1974, she compiled *A Thematic Catalogue of Gustav Holst's Music*, the definitive guide to her father's works.

THE PLANETS (1914–1916)

Holst called astrology his "vice." Here he portrays the effects of supernatural powers of seven planets on humans. The order of the movements emulates the succession of their relative psychic forces; those of *Mars* and *Venus* musically affect other movements, symbolized by a semitone in the bass for *Mars* and a whole tone in the treble for *Venus*. Holst wrote the martial *Mars* before the start of World War I, and the work's origins lie in Schoenberg's *Five Pieces for Orchestra*, where the middle movement contains a strange chord that changes color through a play of instruments. Holst emulated this in his final movement, *Neptune the Mystic*. In fact, he blithely copied many composers. Dukas's *Sorceror's Apprentice* is closely imitated in *Uranus the Magician* and represents the trombonist composer, a hapless apprentice in the worlds of music and astrology.

The end of the British Empire 1914–1940

WORLD WAR I WAS AN OBSCENE BLOODBATH KILLING 8.5 MILLION COMBATANTS AND COUNTLESS CIVILIANS. BRITISH LOSSES ALONE INCLUDED HALF A MILLION MEN UNDER 30 YEARS OF AGE. THE WAR AND ITS AFTERMATH PUT AN END TO THE BRITISH EMPIRE AND TO THE COUNTRY'S ECONOMIC HEALTH, AS CREDIT TURNED TO DEBT.

The catalyst for World War I was a petty event in the Balkan States in July 1914, which provided the pretext for a global catastrophe that persisted far longer than any country could have planned for. It introduced an advanced and gruesome technology of machine guns, poison gas, armored tanks, fighter planes, destroyers, and submarines.

INADEQUATE RESOURCES

Britain waged a war way beyond its human, industrial, or economic resources. That it was one of the 1918 Allied victors counted for little. By 1919 prices of goods were three times higher than they were before the war, in a country denuded of almost a million men. The traditional industries that had fueled Britain's pre-war rise now lost overseas markets, faced fierce competition, and fetched lower prices for their goods. Mining and shipbuilding were woefully affected, and there was a weak retraining infrastructure for the new motor trade, electrical goods, and service industries.

Britain's class poverty was critically exposed. The socialist Labour Party, founded in 1900, gained its first election victory in 1924 thanks to an alliance with the Liberal Party, which Labour replaced as the "other" main parliamentary party to the Conservatives. The Conservatives regained power a few months later.

IMPACTS ON ARTISTS

In 1926 a crisis in Welsh mining led to the exceptional though unsuccessful General Strike. The socialist call for collective ownership and a much more equal society appealed to composers like Vaughan Williams, Britten, and Tippett. This inter-war era was marked by artists who created work that expressed, in various ways, Leftist or communitarian principles, especially in the

JOHN MAYNARD KEYNES (1883–1946)

Keynes (pronounced Kaynz), below, is considered one of the great economic theorists of the century. He also created a theater in Cambridge, established a national ballet company, and nurtured a subsidy system for the arts. As the son of an economics lecturer at Cambridge University, it is not surprising that he took the same position in his mid-twenties. During World War I he advised the Treasury and became its financial representative at the 1919 Paris Peace Conference. Appalled at the short-sightedness there of penalties against Germany, he wrote *The Economic Consequences of the Peace* which predicted what came to pass. He believed in interventionist government policy to offset depression and recession, to stimulate demand through public works. This influenced policy in Britain and Roosevelt's American New Deal. He died in 1946, having negotiated American loans to aid British post-war recovery.

Top right A 1919 oil painting by Colin Gill (1892–1940), depicting heavy artillery, including a battery of camouflaged howitzers. Advanced weaponry such as this was used for the first time in World War I—at great cost to both sides.

development of documentary films which gained from the launch of sound in the late 1920s. Artists had reacted to the war by adopting leaner, anti-Romantic styles, or by compensating with "Jazz Age" joy and playfulness. Both approaches were dubbed "neo-classic."

THE BBC

One of the imposing technological advances of World War I was radio communication. Following the war, amateurs developed its potential for civilian life. The

commercial British Broadcast Company established a station in London (2LO) and other British cities from October 1922. By 1925 most people could pick up a BBC regional station on new domestic radio sets. The BBC showed its independence from political pressure during the 1926 General Strike, but in 1927 it was nationalized as the British Broadcasting Corporation. A year later it took up patronage of Henry Wood's Promenade Concerts, and in 1932 it built opposite the Queen's Hall the world's first broadcasting center, Broadcasting House, and created an Empire Service for global communication. The BBC started to experiment with television transmission in 1936.

BETWEEN THE WARS

The American-led Great Depression of 1929 hoisted up the British unemployment rate to affect a quarter of the workforce by 1932. The emergency national government set up the remedies of economist John Maynard Keynes by introducing government-backed projects to aid employment. Improved welfare schemes were also introduced, and in several ways Britain's 1930s proved to be an optimistic and creative period.

Below Unemployed workers march through London on their way to protest at Downing Street, October 1920.

However, the advance of fascism in Italy, Germany, and Spain produced heated debate. While some Britons wanted to avoid another confrontation with Germany, Hitler's invasion of Poland in September 1939 forced Britain to declare war—this time, to many, a just war.

Charles Ives

OCTOBER 20, 1874–MAY 19, 1954

LARGELY UNKNOWN FOR MOST OF HIS PROFESSIONAL LIFE, CHARLES IVES IS NOW RECOGNIZED AS THE FATHER OF AMERICAN MODERNISM. MERGING AMERICAN VERNACULAR STYLES WITH CONTEMPORARY COMPOSITIONAL TECHNIQUES OF THE EARLY TWENTIETH CENTURY, IVES CREATED A UNIQUE STYLE THAT WAS AN AMERICAN ORIGINAL.

Ives was born in Danbury, Connecticut, to the son of the youngest bandleader in the Union Army during the Civil War. In addition to his early musical training, Ives inherited from his father a love of musical experimentation and of the American musical vernacular, as exemplified by holiday parades, church hymns, military tunes, and patriotic songs. Charles and his father would also play musical games, such as humming a tune in one key while playing it on the piano in another. At age eight, Ives was a proficient musician, playing

Above right Now regarded as the father of American modernism, Ives once said, "Don't pay too much attention to the sounds, or you might miss the music."

drums in his father's bands. By age 14, Ives was the youngest salaried church organist in the state of Connecticut. Ives also began to compose, premièring some of his earliest works with his father's bands. The Ives family was also very strongly influenced by Emerson's transcendental philosophies encouraging individual expression. Taken together, these experiences would have a profound effect on the direction of America's first "homegrown" modernist.

IVES THE BUSINESSMAN

Left One important influence on Ives was American patriotic songs, such as this Union Army recruiting song "We've Got a Million in the Field," which dates from around 1861.

Ives attended Yale University, where he studied with Horatio Parker, one of America's leading composers of choral music and one of the "Boston Six." While Parker was encouraging, Ives quickly realized that his experimental ideas would not be well received in academic musical circles. At the same time, Ives's father died, leaving him without a "sounding board" for new ideas. Ives graduated from Yale (with a D+ average)

"Every great inspiration is but an experiment."

IVES'S COMPOSITIONAL "FIRSTS"

Charles Ives had a number of compositional "firsts," among them the first use of bitonality (using two simultaneous keys) in *Variations on "America"* (1891). He also first used polytonality (using three or more simultaneous keys) in *Fugue in Four Keys* (1894). In *Fourth of July* (1904–1913), Ives uses tone clusters, where the forearm plays as many notes as it can on the piano. He also first used quarter-tones (the pitches between half-steps) in *Three Quarter-Tone Piano Pieces* (1923–1924).

Discover the music

Variations on "America" (1891)

String Quartet No. 1, From the Salvation Army
  (1897–1900)

The Unanswered Question (1906, rev. 1934)

Symphony No. 3, The Camp Meeting (1908–1910)

Three Places in New England (1910–1914, rev. 1929)

Piano Sonata No. 2, Concord, Mass: 1840–1860
  (1916–1919, rev. many times)

While Ives stopped composing new works, he would revise his existing ones, endlessly tinkering with his innovations. Over time, Ives began to draw the attention of some of his musical peers. Aaron Copland and Elliott Carter were early champions, as was Henry Cowell, who published many of Ives's works in the influential magazine *New Music*.

In the 1940s, Lou Harrison conducted the première of Ives's third symphony, which would later win the Pulitzer Prize. Bernard Herrmann, the film composer best known for *Citizen Kane* and *Psycho*, was also an early admirer, conducting Ives's work with the CBS Symphony Orchestra on the radio. A few years prior to Ives's death, Leonard Bernstein conducted the world premiere of Ives's *Symphony No. 2* with the New York Philharmonic. Each of these early champions recognized the genius of Charles Ives's music and helped to build his legacy—one that continues to influence generations of young composers.

and took a position with a local insurance company. Later, he formed his own company, Ives & Myrick, where he became successful in devising policies for wealthy clients; this became the foundation of modern-day estate planning. Late in life, Ives remarked that he chose not to pursue a musical career because he didn't want his children to "starve on dissonances."

Ives composed in his spare time and on weekends, keeping almost all of his works hidden from the public. For unknown reasons, he virtually stopped composing in 1926, a successful businessman, but unknown as a musician. This is only one of the many dualities about Ives's life. He is remembered as an athlete, yet he was plagued by health problems, some of which may have been psychological. He was fond of vernacular music, frequently quoting it in his own works, yet he would consistently innovate beyond traditional harmonic technique. All of these dualities can be found in Ives's most important works, including the *Concord Sonata*, *The Unanswered Question*, and his later symphonies.

Above Walden Pond. Ives admired the transcendental writings of Emerson and Thoreau, and his *Concord Sonata* is a reflection of this.

Right One early champion of Ives's music was pianist, composer, and publisher Henry Cowell (1897–1965). Cowell published a number of Ives's works in *New Music*, and the two became close friends.

LIFE & TIMES

America finds its voice: 1840–1919

IN THE FIRST GENERATIONS OF THE NEW REPUBLIC, AMERICAN CULTURE LARGELY MIRRORED THAT OF ITS EUROPEAN FOREBEARS—ENGLISH THEATER SONGS, GERMAN SYMPHONIC MUSIC, AND ITALIAN OPERA WERE AMONG THE MOST POPULAR ENTERTAINMENTS OF THE DAY. HOWEVER, AS AMERICA MATURED, AND ESPECIALLY AFTER THE AMERICAN CIVIL WAR, THE SEEDS OF A UNIQUE AMERICAN TRADITION WERE PLANTED.

Left When "Swedish Nightingale" Jenny Lind (1820–1887) sang "Home Sweet Home" during her lengthy tour of the United States, it became the most popular song in America.

Below A caricature of Louis Moreau Gottschalk, an American composer who made his living as a virtuoso pianist. His part-Creole heritage provided inspiration for a number of his works.

In the early years of the nineteenth century, the major centers of symphonic and chamber music in America were Boston, New York, and Philadelphia, while opera initially flourished in New Orleans and gradually spread north. Many of the musicians and teachers of this time were either European-born or first-generation Americans who perpetuated the European traditions of previous generations. By 1854, some music critics, notably William Henry Fry in Philadelphia, began to question why many of the newly formed musical "societies" had yet to perform works written by American composers. Even when such works were performed, they largely imitated the music of their European counterparts.

America's musical life also tended to concentrate on European performers. Until cultured society felt that American musicians and composers could equal the Europeans, audiences were less appreciative of homegrown talent. The Norwegian violinist Ole Bull toured America in late 1843, as did the Belgian Henri

Vieuxtemps. Perhaps the most successful tour of the time was that of the "Swedish Nightingale," Jenny Lind, brought to the United States in 1850 by P.T. Barnum. The tour caused such a sensation, she ended up touring the United States for almost two years.

One of the most successful American pre-Civil War composers was also a virtuoso pianist—Louis Moreau Gottschalk (1829–1869). A native of New Orleans, Gottschalk turned down the astronomical sum of $20,000 from P.T. Barnum to undertake an American concert tour. Instead, Gottschalk managed his own career, touring the United States, the Caribbean, and Central America for almost four years, frequently playing his own compositions, many of which were based on Creole folk songs.

After the Civil War (1861–1865), musical life in the northern states grew exponentially. Groups in Boston, Providence, New York, and Philadelphia continued to prosper, while orchestras and choruses formed in many midwestern cities. At the same time, an increasing number of American-born composers became active (although many still trained in Europe). Composers such as William Mason and James Cutler Dunn Parker were among the earliest composers to build successful careers west of the Atlantic.

THE "BOSTON SIX"

As the century drew to a close, the next generation of American composers emerged, most of whom did not make the obligatory trip to study in Europe. Many of these composers were based in New England. The best known and most prolific of them were the "Boston Six"—collectively responsible for much of the important concert music written by Americans at the time—John

ITNEY PRESENTS
E COMIC OPERA

WHEN JOHNNY COMES MARCHING HOME

STANGE & EDWARDS
UTHORS OF "DOLLY VARDEN"

WHITNEY
TOR & MANAGER

KATE—"MY SOUTHERN ROSE"

Knowles Paine (1839–1906), Arthur Foote (1853–1937), Horatio Parker (1863–1919), George White-field Chadwick (1854–1931), Edward MacDowell (1860–1908), and Amy Cheney Beach (1867–1944).

Today, Amy Beach (see page 311) is arguably the best remembered of the "Boston Six"—at least partially due to her status as America's first important woman

Above One of the most recognizable songs of the Civil War, "When Johnny Comes Marching Home" was reportedly written by Irish-born American musician Louis Lambert.

composer. A concert pianist, she gave up performing when she married and focused on composing, almost always publishing under the name "Mrs. H.H.A. Beach" in deference to her husband. Her *Symphony No. 1*, inspired by the Gaelic folk themes of her own heritage, was the first symphony written by a woman to be performed by an American orchestra.

STEPHEN FOSTER (1826–1864)

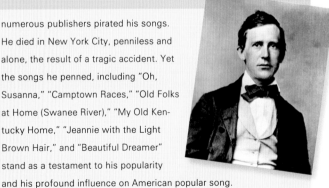

The man who can arguably be called the "Father of American Popular Song," Stephen Foster was born near Pittsburgh, Pennsylvania, the ninth of ten children. Foster was strongly influenced by the minstrel shows and popular entertainments of the time. He largely composed two types of songs: Those appropriate to American "parlor culture" and those written for the minstrel shows and so-called "black face" singers. Foster captured the spirit of America in his songs and his works are known by generations of Americans. He struggled to make a living as a songwriter and due to the lax nature of American copyright laws, Foster earned almost no royalties—mainly because numerous publishers pirated his songs. He died in New York City, penniless and alone, the result of a tragic accident. Yet the songs he penned, including "Oh, Susanna," "Camptown Races," "Old Folks at Home (Swanee River)," "My Old Kentucky Home," "Jeannie with the Light Brown Hair," and "Beautiful Dreamer" stand as a testament to his popularity and his profound influence on American popular song.

Arnold Schoenberg

SEPTEMBER 13, 1874–JULY 13, 1951

CALLED THE "FATHER OF MODERN MUSIC," ARNOLD SCHOENBERG WAS BORN TO JEWISH PARENTS IN VIENNA. ALTHOUGH HIS MOTHER WORKED AS A PIANO TEACHER, SCHOENBERG WAS LARGELY SELF-TAUGHT IN COMPOSITION AND TOOK ONLY A FEW COUNTERPOINT LESSONS WITH ALEXANDER VON ZEMLINSKY. AN ACCOMPLISHED VIOLINIST AS A YOUNG MAN, SCHOENBERG ORCHESTRATED OPERETTAS TO EARN MONEY. HE ALSO COMPOSED AT THIS TIME SEVERAL OF THE WORKS THAT WOULD GAIN HIM HIS INITIAL ADMIRERS, INCLUDING STRAUSS AND MAHLER.

Schoenberg's place in music history is a product of the times in which he lived. Romantic music, characterized by increasing chromaticism and large-scale forms, was beginning to decline. At the same time, political and social forces were impacting on artists and musicians throughout Europe: Their response resulted in new styles of art, literature, and drama. Schoenberg's earliest works were typical of the late Romantics, but in response to these changes, he rejected the musical hyperbole of the Romantic period and explored new techniques of composition.

He quickly abandoned that style in favor of smaller scale works and a harmonic language that lacked clear tonal centers. In his *Three Piano Pieces*, Op. 11, written in 1909, he left behind traditional tonal relationships and structures altogether—ultimately leading to the

Above right A portrait of the composer by the Austrian Expressionist artist Egon Schiele (1890–1918). As well as changing the course of twentieth-century music, Schoenberg was also a very capable painter.

Below left A page from Arnold Schoenberg's *Harmonielehre* (*Treatise on Harmony*), written in 1910 but not published until some 12 years later.

notion of the "emancipation of the dissonance," in which there is no need to resolve dissonances to consonant intervals.

THE TWELVE-TONE METHOD

Schoenberg began to attract talented young students, including Alban Berg and Anton von Webern (both of whom would have significant careers and, with Schoenberg, collectively came to be known as the "Second Viennese School"). Still, Schoenberg was concerned that audiences would misunderstand his atonal works. From 1916 to 1920, he devoted himself to the creation of a radically new and clearly articulated system of composing now known as the dodecaphonic, or twelve-tone, method. In it, each note of the chromatic scale is placed in a sequential "row" and no pitch in the row may be repeated before all twelve pitches

SCHOENBERG'S INFLUENCE

Schoenberg once said, " ... Whether one composes in a conventional or progressive manner, whether one tries to imitate old styles or is destined to express new ideas—one must be convinced of the infallibility of one's own fantasy and one must believe in one's own inspiration."

His position as the inventor of the twelve-tone method and his writings on compositional technique made him a leading figure in contemporary music, supplanting Stravinsky as the world's pre-eminent musical mind. Hundreds, if not thousands, of young composers were taught to compose using the twelve-tone system both in Europe and the United States. While many followed in Schoenberg's footsteps, many others resisted. Yet, even resisters like Copland and Stravinsky would come to employ Schoenberg's techniques in their works. It would not be until the 1970s that a new generation of composers would begin to break away from Schoenberg's ideology.

Left Arnold Schoenberg (right) with physicist Albert Einstein (1879–1955), center, and Polish–American pianist Leopold Godowski (1870–1938) at Carnegie Hall, New York, 1934.

"My music is not modern, it is merely badly played."

have sounded—thereby assuring that no one pitch is more prominent than any other one. Schoenberg's *Piano Suite* (1925) is generally recognized as the first twelve-tone composition.

The twelve-tone system of composition would have far-reaching implications given the social and political events of the time. Many artists, writers, and composers had begun to work in a new style—Expressionism— that reflected the inner, Freudian world of the grotesque and anxious. This was a result of the conflict and pessimism people were feeling given the earlier changes of the Industrial Revolution as well as the political tension that would result in World War I.

Schoenberg served in the army in World War I and then accepted a teaching post at the Prussian Academy of Arts in Berlin. Later, when the Nazi Party came to power, Schoenberg's music—along with jazz and swing music—was labeled degenerate. In 1933, he was dismissed and forced into exile. He moved to Paris and converted back to Judaism (having become a Lutheran

Above right On April 6, 1913, *Die Zeit* published this cartoon entitled "The upcoming Schoenberg Concert." Many of his compositions still provoke strong reactions.

as a youth). To escape persecution, Schoenberg emigrated again—this time to the United States—first to Boston where his health suffered, and ultimately to Los Angeles, where he accepted teaching positions at the University of Southern California and later UCLA. His students there included John Cage, Lou Harrison, and film composer Leonard Rosenman. Schoenberg remained in Los Angeles for the rest of his life.

Discover the music

Verklärte Nacht, Op. 4 (1899)

Gurre-Lieder, Op. 8 (1901/1911)

Three Piano Pieces, Op. 11 (1909)

Erwartung, Op. 17 (1909)

Pierrot Lunaire, Op. 12 (1912)

Variations for Orchestra, Op. 31 (1926–1928)

Moses und Aron (unfinished) (1930–1932)

String Quartet No. 4, Op. 37 (1936)

LIFE & TIMES

Vienna—European center of culture

IN 1867, THE AUSTRO-HUNGARIAN COMPROMISE WOULD CREATE ONE OF EUROPE'S LAST
REMAINING EMPIRES, ONE THAT INCLUDED PRESENT-DAY POLAND, UKRAINE, THE CZECH AND
SLOVAK REPUBLICS, SERBIA AND MONTENEGRO. UNDER THE RULE OF FRANZ JOSEF I, IT WAS
ONE OF THE MOST POLITICALLY AND ECONOMICALLY STABLE REGIONS IN EUROPE—ONE THAT
WOULD FOSTER A THRIVING ARTISTIC ENVIRONMENT.

In the early nineteenth century, the region now known as Austria, and its capital Vienna, was one of the cultural centers of Europe. Writers, artists, and especially composers flocked to Vienna due to the benevolence of the Hapsburg monarchs. Over time, Vienna had been the home of Haydn, Beethoven, Mozart, Schubert, and many others—all living and working in one of Europe's most artistically invigorating cultural environments.

Following the 1848 revolution, Vienna re-emerged as a center of commerce, business, and the arts and a new generation of composers and performers visited frequently and made their homes there. Wagner was especially popular in Vienna, visiting the city ten times over the course of his life. Brahms would also visit often, usually in conjunction with performances of his music. The noted Lieder composer Hugo Wolf and, toward the end of the century both Bruckner and Mahler, lived in Vienna. Johann Strauss brought the Viennese waltz to worldwide prominence among the cultural elite and the merchant classes.

THE EARLY TWENTIETH CENTURY

Schoenberg's presence in Vienna made the city the epicenter for the shift from late Romantic musical excess to the gradual breakdown of tonality that would characterize the composers of the Second Viennese School. But this dramatic change in the world of concert music could not have taken place without the composers who preceded it and the stable cultural and artistic environment in which these ideas could take hold. In the late nineteenth century, Wagner, Wolf,

EDUARD HANSLICK (1825–1904)

Eduard Hanslick (below) was arguably the most influential music critic in nineteenth-century Vienna. Born in Prague, Hanslick studied music and law and began his career as a music critic in his home city before moving to Vienna to become a critic for the *Wiener Musik-Zeitung* and later for Europe's most influential music magazine, *Neue Freie Presse*, where he remained until his retirement. Initially a champion of Wagner, Hanslick shifted his allegiance to the music he felt was a direct outgrowth of the traditions of Mozart and Beethoven. This shift would have significant implications for composers in Vienna, including the Second Viennese School, who championed their own work as being descended from that tradition. Hanslick's famous work *On the Musically Beautiful* attacked the Wagnerian esthetic and advocated music that could express itself purely through form—thereby laying a foundation for the innovations of the Second Viennese School in the twentieth century.

Above left A panoramic view of Vienna at the turn of the twentieth century. The city was a melting pot for artists, writers, composers, poets, philosophers, and scientists from across Europe.

Bruckner, and Mahler all stretched the idea of chromatic harmony to its limits—composing with an increasing lack of regard for the traditional harmonic progressions and relationships that characterized the music of the late Classical and early Romantic composers. Taking that as a starting point and having fully absorbed the hyper-chromaticism of the music he heard around him, it was only natural that Schoenberg and his disciples would further test the limits of the tonal system in music, resulting in atonality, the twelve-tone (dodecaphonic) method and, ultimately, leading to total serialism.

Vienna's position in the cultural world would ultimately be supplanted by geopolitical instability and the rise in ethnic nationalism that would eventually lead to the assassination of Archduke Franz Ferdinand in 1914, the outbreak of World War I, and the dissolution of the Austro–Hungarian Empire. The monarchy was officially dissolved in 1919 and Austria's parliamentary democracy was established in 1920.

Below A room in the Lower Belvedere Palace in Vienna, painted by Carl Goebel (1824–1899). The wealth of literature and art depicted here was typical of Vienna, a city that was one of Europe's artistic and intellectual hubs.

THE SECOND VIENNESE SCHOOL

The Second Viennese School is the name given to a group of composers who were the intellectual leaders of the musical world in the middle of the twentieth century. These composers believed that their work was a direct outgrowth of the Germanic Classical and Romantic traditions. It is called the "second" school to reflect the importance of the First Viennese School that included Mozart, Haydn, Beethoven, and Schubert. The most significant composers of the Second Viennese School were Arnold Schoenberg and his students, Alban Berg (see pages 322–323) and Anton von Webern (see pages 320–321).

Most musicologists also include those composers who both studied with Schoenberg and were working in Vienna at the time, including Egon Wellesz (1885–1974), Hans-Erich Apostel (1901–1972) and Hanns Jelinek (1901–1969). As a group, the Second Viennese School would profoundly influence the world of serious music for five decades.

Maurice Ravel

MARCH 7, 1875–DECEMBER 28, 1937

FOR GENERATIONS, THE WORKS OF MAURICE RAVEL HAVE DELIGHTED AUDIENCES AND CRITICS ALIKE. FROM THE DAZZLING *GASPARD DE LA NUIT* TO THE LYRIC BEAUTY OF THE *BOLÉRO*, RAVEL STANDS AS ONE OF THE TWENTIETH CENTURY'S MOST ORIGINAL AND CREATIVE MUSICAL MINDS.

Ravel was born in Ciboure, France, near the border with Spain. His mother, Marie, was Basque, and the two were very close. Ravel's many Spanish-flavored compositions were influenced and inspired by the many folk songs she sang to him as a child. After the family moved to Paris, Ravel began piano lessons, followed by lessons in harmony, counterpoint, and composition. Ravel attended the Paris Conservatoire as a pianist but was expelled in 1895 when he failed to meet their standards. In 1898, he re-enrolled as a composer and studied for 14 years under the guidance of the French master Gabriel Fauré. Fauré's influence on Ravel is unmistakable: A firm grounding in the Classics paired with an adventurous, colorful harmonic and orchestral technique.

Ravel lived most of his life in Paris. His friends and colleagues were among the most famous artists in Paris at a time when that city was the center of the cultural world. It was here that he composed the majority of his most successful works. He maintained a rigorous

Right Ravel never married and little is known about his private life. He is often quoted as saying, "The only love affair I have ever had was with music."

Below Ravel at the piano in March 1928. American composer George Gershwin is standing at right, and the Canadian mezzo-soprano Eva Gaulthier is behind Ravel.

composing schedule even during World War I, despite being a truck driver stationed at the Verdun front. In 1921, Ravel retired to the countryside but continued to go to Paris to socialize, attend performances of his work, and lead the Société Musicale Indépendante, where he promoted performances of new works by French, British, and American composers including Bax, Vaughan Williams, and Copland. He ultimately became the leading figure in French music. He undertook a four-month tour of the United States where he received standing ovations from appreciative audiences. While there, Ravel met George Gershwin who took him to a Harlem nightclub so that Ravel could deepen his appreciation of jazz—aspects of which would feature prominently in his later works.

In 1932, Ravel suffered a traumatic head injury as a result of a taxi accident. While he recovered initially, Ravel began to show signs of a brain disorder. After years of suffering, he underwent pioneering surgery, from which he came round, but then he died shortly afterwards. He was 62 years old.

Above A 1912 set design for *Daphnis and Chloé*, an engraving based on a watercolor by the ballet's designer, Leon Bakst.

Contrabassoon

This instrument is a larger version of the bassoon and sounds one octave lower. It is used in larger symphony orchestras. Most orchestras have just one contrabassoonist, although sometimes, rather than have a separate contrabassoonist, one bassoonist doubles on both bassoon and contra-bassoon. The contrabassoon had its beginnings in church music in the seventeenth century; by the eighteenth century it was appearing in military bands. Ravel used the instrument to great effect in the orchestral version of his piano piece *Ma Mère l'Oye*.

Discover the music

Rapsodie Espagnole (1907)

L'Heure Espagnole (1907–1909)

Gaspard de la Nuit (1908)

Ma Mère l'Oye (*Mother Goose*) (1908–1910)

Daphnis et Chloé (1909–1912)

Le Tombeau de Couperin (1919)

L'Enfant et les Sortilèges (1920–1925)

Boléro (1928)

RAVEL AND DEBUSSY

Music history has tended to group Ravel and Debussy together, despite their different compositional styles. While the men were friends and colleagues, admiring each other's works, they were driven apart in 1905 by feuding factions of loyal fans. While there are some similarities in their work (as with many French composers of the time), there are fundamental differences that make the two composers unmistakably different. Ravel's style is much more firmly rooted in the Classical tradition and his orchestrations are more influenced by Rimsky-Korsakov and Stravinsky than by Debussy. While both men enjoyed working with modes, exotic scales, and so-called "tall chords" (adding sevenths, ninths, and elevenths to triads), Ravel's harmonic language is more conservative than Debussy's. In addition, Ravel's emphasis on highly lyrical melodies has resulted in some of history's most memorable music.

THE *BOLÉRO* (1928)

Arguably one of Ravel's most famous works, the *Boléro* was originally conceived as a ballet, commissioned by the dancer Ida Rubinstein. The original commission was to be based on Spanish themes. When the commission fell through, Ravel kept the Spanish concept and created an original idea. He composed the famous *Boléro* melody and decided to develop it not through traditional compositional techniques—rather, he repeated it many times while shifting and building the orchestration. It was very much a compositional exercise and, as it was conceived as a ballet, Ravel was surprised that it was so successful in symphonic performances.

Originally called *Fandango*, the piece features a driving, insistent rhythm with steadily building orchestrations. The orchestra is large, featuring saxophones and almost all the auxiliary woodwinds. *Boléro* is one of the most immediately recognizable pieces of music in the repertory and is now embedded in popular culture, notably as the accompaniment to Bo Derek's famous seduction of Dudley Moore in the motion picture *10*.

Ottorino Respighi

JULY 9, 1879–APRIL 18, 1936

COMPOSER, VIOLINIST, AND MUSICOLOGIST, RESPIGHI WAS AMONG THE MOST POPULAR ITALIAN COMPOSERS OF HIS DAY. CHAMPIONED BY THE WORLD'S LEADING CONDUCTORS, INCLUDING TOSCANINI, REINER, AND KOUSSEVITSKY, RESPIGHI'S CAREER WAS AMONG THE MOST SUCCESSFUL OF THE EARLY TWENTIETH CENTURY.

Respighi was born in Bologna and received his initial musical instruction, on both piano and violin, from his father, a music teacher. His early talents were recognized when he attended the Liceo Musicale in Bologna, where he continued his violin studies and received his first instruction in composition. It was at the Liceo that Respighi studied with Luigi Torchi, an early music scholar. These musicological studies profoundly influenced Respighi's compositions.

In 1900, Respighi applied for, and was offered, a position as a violinist with the Imperial Theater in St Petersburg. It was here that he met the Russian master composer Nicolai Rimsky-Korsakov, who soon recognized Respighi's talent and worked with him on his

THE ROMAN TRILOGY

Respighi's most significant accomplishment is *The Roman Trilogy*, three multi-movement symphonic works composed between 1914 and 1928. They were composed as a tribute to the city Respighi lived in and loved and are excellent examples of the genre known as the symphonic poem.

The first work, *Fountains of Rome*, memorializes different fountains in Rome at different times of day. The *Pines of Rome*, the second, best known, and most performed of the three, portrays the pine trees of Rome at the Villa Borghese, near a catacomb, at the Janiculum and at the Appian Way. The *Roman Festival*, the last, longest, and largest of the three, depicts scenes of ancient Rome including the circuses and harvests from the heyday of the Roman Empire. Readers may recognize The *Pines of Rome* from the motion picture *Fantasia 2000*, where it was used to accompany Disney's beautiful animation of humpback whales.

LA DOMENICA DEL CORRIERE

Anno 48 - N. 8 (nuova serie)   19 Maggio 1946   L. 12,– la copia

Memorabili serate alla Scala: i concerti diretti da Toscanini

Above right The composer as a young man. Respighi's *Gli Uccelli* (*The Birds*), a Baroque-inspired composition where the instruments mimic the sounds of birds, remains one of his most popular works.

Left Arturo Toscanini (1867–1957) at La Scala, Milan, in 1946. The famed conductor made a number of recordings of Respighi's music.

orchestration techniques—techniques that can be easily heard in many of Respighi's orchestral masterpieces. Respighi also traveled throughout Europe and attended lectures by noted German composer Max Bruch.

Respighi moved to Rome in 1913 and accepted a position as a composition teacher at the Conservatorio di Santa Cecilia (he would later serve as its director from 1924 to 1926). It was there that he met Elsa Olivieri-Sangiacomo, a singer who became his pupil and later his wife. Respighi devoted the rest of his life to composing and earned accolades throughout Europe and in America, where Arturo Toscanini premièred Respighi's *Fontane di Roma* (and conducted a wildly popular recording) with the New York Philharmonic. Respighi's later years were filled with composing and conducting engagements, solidifying his position as one of Italy's preeminent composers. After his death, his wife Elsa, a composer in her own right, championed her husband's works and wrote his biography. Elsa died, at the age of 102, in 1996.

RESPIGHI'S WORKS AND LEGACY

Many are tempted to call Respighi a "neo-classical" composer, stylistically similar to many of his contemporaries. However, it was not the Classical period that inspired him. Instead, Respighi's studies with Torchi led him to the medieval, Renaissance, and Baroque periods for inspiration—combining early techniques with modern harmonic and orchestration techniques. In *Ancient Airs and Dances*, Respighi incorporated the works of many Renaissance composers including Molinaro, Galilei, Caroso, and others. He was also inspired by Gregorian chant techniques in his *Church Windows* (which he adapted from his own *Three Preludes on Gregorian Melodies*). He also published editions of works by Monteverdi, Vivaldi, and Marcello.

For many years after his death, and despite the best efforts of his wife, Respighi's music was dismissed as simplistic and contrived. However, in recent years, a resurgence of interest in Respighi's work has occurred, resulting in frequent performances of his best-known

Above An aerial view of Rome from the Villa Borghese gardens. Respighi loved Rome, and his most famous work, *The Roman Trilogy*, is a paean to that city.

Discover the music

The Roman Trilogy (1914–1928):
  Fontane di Roma (*Fountains of Rome*) (1914–1916)
  Pini di Roma (*Pines of Rome*) (1923–1924)
  Feste Romane (*Roman Festival*) (1928)
Ancient Airs and Dances, Suites 1, 2, and 3 (1917–1932)
Vetrata di Chiesa (*Church Windows*) (1925)
Gli Uccelli (*The Birds*) (1927)
Lucrezia (1935)

works and renewed interest in the lesser known ones. Of particular interest are his operas that were quite successful in their day but have since fallen out of the repertory. Respighi's last opera, *Lucrezia*, which was written while he was dying from a bacterial infection, shows him at the height of his compositional prowess, using a forceful contemporary language and rich orchestral harmonies and textures.

AMERICAN WOMEN IN MUSIC INTO THE TWENTIETH CENTURY

American women composers and performers of the nineteenth century were divided into two distinct social and cultural groups. The first was made up of the "parlor ladies" of upper-middle and upper-class American culture. Just like their European counterparts, these women received musical training as a means to make them more eligible for marriage.

The second were women who worked professionally in the theater and on stage and, due to the Victorian morals of the time, found access to upper-class society largely closed. For most women of a certain class, a career as a professional musician was not only unseemly, it was unimaginable. Even those who initially pursued careers in music often set it aside in deference to the demands of marriage and raising a family.

WOMEN IN MUSIC EDUCATION

With the growth of the middle class, especially after the Civil War, American women began to seek out better educations, in part to better raise their children, but also as a result of the burgeoning women's movement in the United States. At around the same time, professional women musicians started to bridge the gap between parlor culture and professional performers who, until very recent times, had been unwelcome in certain social circles.

Above A music lesson, c. 1925. The majority of music educators in the United States in the first quarter of the twentieth century were women.

Left Contralto Louise Homer (1871–1947) performed in Europe, and across the United States. Married to composer Sidney Homer, she was acclaimed for her roles as Amneris in Verdi's *Aida* and as the witch in Humperdinck's *Hansel und Gretel*.

Similarly, the growing field of music education would have an impact on the role of women in music in the United States. Initially taught to help young women attract a husband or to entertain family or guests, music education for women evolved to include educating the daughters of the merchant class and, after the war, as a viable career option for women. The Crane Normal Institute of Music, in Potsdam, New York, became the very first music school and teacher-training program in the country. According to writer Adrienne Fried Block, by 1910, 60 percent of the nation's music teachers were women, and although men still held the most prestigious positions, the opportunities for women increased at an exponential rate. Many of the nation's colleges offered music education programs, which became an important vehicle for women's education. Ultimately, it was these women who would open new training programs around the country, both for amateur and professional musicians.

PERFORMING TRAILBLAZERS

Professional singers may have had some of the most significant early impact on women's roles in music, largely as a result of the successful tour by the "Swedish Nightingale," Jenny Lind in 1850–1852. American

women, including Clara Louise Kellogg, Emma Abbott and, later, Louise Homer, also achieved quite considerable success as performers. Later, women pianists, including Julie Rivé-King (1854–1937) and violinists such as Maud Powell (1867–1920) began to perform publicly, sometimes featuring their own compositions while drawing appreciative audiences.

Another major factor in the growth of opportunities in music for women was the formation of amateur music clubs. The first club—formed in Portland, Maine, in 1868—spawned an influential nation-wide movement. Twenty-five years later, some 42 clubs had been organized and conventions were held to promote the sharing of information and resources. Launched for educational purposes, music clubs began to support and underwrite performances in their respective communities, both in the schools and on the stage.

From this foundation, women composers, many of whom started their careers as performers, began to emerge. Many of them published in the growing number of music magazines marketed specifically toward women. Among the composers who became known by name for their efforts were Augusta Browne (1821–1882), Carrie Jacobs Bond (1861–1946), and Margaret Ruthven Lang (1867–1971).

Above Upper- and middle-class American women usually received musical training, yet it wasn't until until the early twentieth century that female performers and composers started to come into their own.

AMY CHENEY BEACH (1867–1944)

Born to an affluent family and a musical mother, Amy Cheney (below) made her concert debut at age 16 in Boston. In addition to her skills as a pianist, she had also studied composition, both formally and on her own, studying the works of the great masters, and composing vocal and instrumental works. At 18, she performed with the Boston Symphony Orchestra and was admired by critics and the public alike. After her marriage to Dr H.H.A. Beach, 25 years her senior, she focused her attention on composing, which allowed her skills in this realm to flower. Beach wrote dozens of songs, piano miniatures, and chamber works. Among her best-received works were her *Piano Concerto*, the *Symphony No. 1 "Gaelic,"* and her many Lieder. When her husband died in 1910, she resumed her performing career and continued to compose new works. She wrote many large-scale compositions, having gained more public acceptance, and composed several excellent works for chorus. Beach's successes paved the way for generations of women composers that followed.

Béla Bartók

MARCH 25, 1881–SEPTEMBER 26, 1945

ONE OF THE SEMINAL FIGURES OF TWENTIETH-CENTURY MUSIC, BARTÓK FUSED A
VAST RANGE OF TECHNIQUES INTO AN INDIVIDUAL STYLE. HE WAS AN INNOVATOR
IN THE FIELDS OF HARMONY, MELODY, RHYTHM, AND ORCHESTRATION, MASSIVELY
DEVELOPED THE MEDIUM OF THE STRING QUARTET, AND INCORPORATED FOLK
ELEMENTS INTO HIS MUSIC IN A CONVINCING AND AUTHENTIC WAY.

Bartók was born in the town of Nagyszentmiklós (Great Saint Michael), then in Hungary, now Romania. At 13 he moved to Pozsony (then in Hungary, now Bratislava in the Czech Republic). These abrupt changes of nationality show that Hungarian borders have been historically rather fluid, subject to the whims of more powerful neighbors. It is natural that a Hungarian composer would want to affirm his national identity more strongly than most, and Bartók developed this musically in two main ways. His early, somewhat Straussian symphonic poem *Kossuth* (1903)

Above right This photograph was taken in 1902, on the occasion of Bartók's first public concert. Bartók's influence on modern composition has been far-reaching.

depicted the events of a nationalist uprising of 1848, and his research into Hungarian peasant music began as early as 1905. This was little known in mainstream European culture, which associated Hungarian music with the gypsy style popularized by Liszt.

BARTÓK AND FOLK MUSIC

Much of Bartók's early life consisted of scholarly research into folk music, collecting, arranging, and writing up, often in collaboration with Zoltan Kodály. Bartók shared with his compatriot a strong interest in

"I cannot conceive of music that expresses absolutely nothing."

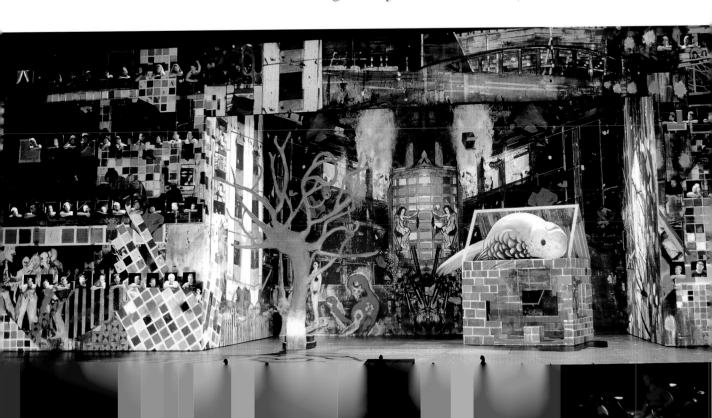

musical education (which has always been taken very seriously in Hungary). The set of 85 piano pieces *For Children*, the graded set of 153 pieces in six volumes *Mikrokosomos*, and the duos for two violins are all didactic works that are frequently played, and give an excellent entry into Bartók's style of writing.

The opera *Bluebeard's Castle* and the ballet *Wooden Prince*, both lavishly orchestrated, brought him early attention, but it was most notably in the *String Quartet No. 1* (1908–1909) that Bartók first fused folk music elements into his post-Debussy musical language. The music uses the full spectrum of modes, from intense chromaticism, through whole-tone harmonies and diatonic scales to folk-like pentatonic modes. This gives his language great variety and richness, as does his intense and innovative instrumental writing.

THREE PHASES

Bartók's music divides into three distinct phases—early, middle, and late. His middle period was the least compromising. He explored the darker side of folk music, his harmonies were often harsh and dissonant, and his instrumental writing was aggressive and percussive. Works from this period include the Quartets Nos. 3 and 4, the two violin sonatas, and the piano sonata of 1926, which he wrote for himself to play on concert tours. Bartók was another composer who also found wide fame as a pianist.

In 1940, war making life in Hungary even more unstable than usual, Bartók emigrated to America. This was not a happy time—he received relatively little attention, he had little money, and suffered from ill health. His music, though, had entered its third phase, more approachable, clearer and with a greater surface light-heartedness. Many of his most popular works come from this period; the *Piano Concerto No. 3* and the *Violin Concerto No. 2* both contain folk music elements that have been assimilated without being buried. The *Concerto for Orchestra* is shot through with humor.

Above Bartók recording folk tunes in Transylvania. The composer had a life-long interest in folk melodies and and is credited as one of the first ethnomusicologists.

Left The Vienna State Opera Chorus performs Bartók's *Cantata Profana (Die Neun Zauberhirsche)* at the 2008 Salzburg Festival. The work was written in 1930.

MUSIC FOR STRINGS, PERCUSSION, AND CELESTA (1936)

This is a highly chromatic and atmospheric piece, constructed apparently according to golden ratio proportions and featuring very novel and "spooky" writing for celesta and piano. Bartók considered the piano a percussion instrument.

The quotation from Dmitri Shostakovich's *Leningrad Symphony*, followed by an orchestral raspberry, was apparently a reaction to the constant propaganda use of the Shostakovich work on the radio.

CHARACTERISTICS OF BARTÓK'S MUSIC

Bartók generally uses a complete range of melodic styles, from wide-leaping tortuous expressionistic lines to simple folk-like tunes. Similarly, his harmonies are drawn from the widest possible range. At one level there are buzzing clusters and dissonant bitonality; at the other, clear use of fourths and fifths, as well as plain triads. Rhythm is a strong element in Bartók's music, much of the most striking patterns deriving from East European (particularly Bulgarian) folk music. This involves uneven beats at very fast tempi. The composer also used many exciting and novel colors; writing for piano, strings, and orchestra are all very individual to Bartók. Listen in particular to *Quartet No. 6*, or *Music for Strings, Percussion, and Celesta*.

Hungary— the cost of two wars

AT THE TIME OF BARTÓK'S BIRTH, HUNGARY WAS PART OF
THE DUALIST MONARCHY, THE AUSTRO–HUNGARIAN EMPIRE,
A SHARING OF POWER BETWEEN THE HUNGARIAN NOBILITY
AND THE AUSTRIAN HAPSBURGS, ESTABLISHED IN 1867.

By the turn of the twentieth century, Hungary had experienced a 20 percent growth in population, and a rapid rise in urbanization and industrialization. It was a multi-ethnic society, with large concentrations of Romanians, Slovaks, and Slavs in rural provinces, and Germans and Jews in the cities.

On June 28, 1914, Hapsburg heir Archduke Franz Ferdinand was assassinated in Sarajevo, Bosnia. This ignited a conflict between the Central Powers (Austria–Hungary and Germany) and the Triple Entente of France, Russia, and Great Britain, which eventually disintegrated into the global carnage that became known as the Great War, or World War I.

Right A poster from the 1920s showing Hungary being laid low by the Treaty of Trianon, under which the country ceded two-thirds of its territories following World War I.

THE TREATY OF TRIANON

Hungary lost approximately 1.6 million people in the Great War. As a result of the post-war Treaty of Trianon between the Allies and Hungary—held at the

Below Artillery in a Budapest street. The city was under siege in 1945 when Soviet forces tried to wrest it from German control.

Grand Trianon Palace in Versailles in June 1920—it also lost a substantial portion of its land.

Since 896, Hungary's borders had remained virtually unchanged. But after Trianon, Hungary was forced to relinquish some two-thirds of its territory. Transylvania and most of the Banat went to Romania. Northern Hungary (now Slovakia) went to the Czechs. Southern Hungary, Slavonia, and Croatia (which had been part of Hungary for 700 years) were awarded to the Serbs. Western Hungary (Burgenland) became part of Austria.

The three million indigenous ethnic Hungarians who found themselves in foreign countries were discriminated against and forced to assimilate. Because Hungary also was stripped of infrastructure and natural resources, it experienced a severe economic downturn.

THE JEWS IN HUNGARY

Before World War I, Hungarian Jews (particularly those in Budapest) enjoyed a period of prosperity and population growth, and helped contribute to the economic boom of the late nineteenth and early twentieth centuries. However, the Treaty of Trianon had unfortunate consequences for Hungary's Jewish community, who emerged as the dominant minority following the departure of other ethnic groups. The Jews became the prime scapegoats for the country's troubles. Anti-Semitic sentiments ran high, fueled by the policies of Miklós Horthy, former Austro–Hungarian admiral who served as Regent of Hungary from 1920 to 1944.

Horthy openly declared himself an anti-Semite. He was greatly disturbed that the Jews appeared to be disproportionately represented in education, business, the arts, and the professions. As soon as he took office, Horthy passed a law which allowed no more than 5 percent of university enrolment to be Jewish. (Prior to this time, Jews comprised approximately 25 percent of the student population.)

In 1938, a law was passed that restricted the number of Jews in business and the professions to 20 percent. The following year, it was decreed that anyone with two or more Jewish-born grandparents was deemed to be Jewish, and further stringent employment restrictions were put in place. In 1941, Horthy's government passed yet another law, this one banning intermarriage between Jew and gentile.

Hungary entered World War II in June 1941 as an ally of Germany, with the hope of recouping its lost territories. Horthy's wavering loyalty to Hitler resulted in the Nazi invasion and subsequent control of Hungary in 1944. During the German occupation, the Hungarian fascist Arrow Cross Party committed dreadful acts of violence against the Jews, many of whom were shot and thrown into the Danube River.

GEORGE ENESCU (1881–1955)

George Enescu was a composer, conductor, violinist, cellist, and teacher whose stature has developed over time. Born in 1881 in Liveni, Romania, he began studying violin at four, enrolled in the Vienna Conservatory at seven, and continued his education at the Paris Conservatory.

Enescu's best-loved works *Romanian Rhapsodies* (1901, 1902) were inspired by the folk tradition of his homeland, and subsequently attracted the attention of the Queen of Romania, who appointed him court violinist. Many of his compositions display a Romantic influence, while others (such as the *Piano Suite No. 2 in D major*, Op. 10) owe more to French Impressionism. In his opera *Oedipe* (1938) he experimented with quarter-tones. In 1923, Enescu made his New York debut as a composer and conductor with the Philadelphia Orchestra. He returned in 1937 to conduct the New York Philharmonic.

Above A rehearsal of Romanian composer George Enescu's opera *Oedipe* at Le Théâtre du Capitole in Toulouse, in 2008. Parts of Hungary were ceded to Romania after World War I.

In April 1944, German Colonel Adolf Eichmann made his headquarters in Budapest's Majestic Hotel and began the task of exterminating Hungary's Jews. By July, over 400,000 Jews had been transported to Auschwitz concentration camp in Poland—approximately 90 percent of those were immediately executed. When the war ended in 1945, less than one-third of Hungary's Jewish population had survived.

Igor Stravinsky

JUNE 17, 1882–APRIL 6, 1971

STRAVINSKY LIVED IN RAPIDLY CHANGING TIMES. ONE OF THE TWENTIETH CENTURY'S MOST INFLUENTIAL COMPOSERS, HIS OUTPUT CROSSED COUNTRIES, CULTURES, AND PERIODS. HE REGULARLY REINVENTED HIS COMPOSITION STYLE, EXPLORING CHANGING TASTES AND INNOVATIVE WAYS OF EXPRESSION. HIS WORKS WERE UNIQUE BUT THE IMPATIENT RHYTHMS AND THE SAME RESTLESS, SHARP, AND SPICY HARMONIES RUN THROUGH EACH OF THEM LIKE A MUSICAL FINGERPRINT.

Stravinsky's father was a bass singer; family friends included many writers and composers of the time, among them Dostoevsky and Borodin. Stravinsky was fascinated with music, and started piano lessons at the age of nine. He had access to his father's substantial music library, studying a great range of composers, including Glinka, Mussorgsky, Glazunov, Borodin, Wagner, Debussy, and Dukas. He began a law degree in 1901 at St Petersburg University, being encouraged to study for a career that would provide him with a good steady income. Nikolai Rimsky-Korsakov's son, Vladimir, was a fellow student there. Their friendship resulted in Rimsky-Korsakov Senior taking on Stravinsky as his music pupil. It was a relationship that spawned a remarkable composer.

Discover the music

The Firebird (1910)

Petrushka (1911)

The Rite of Spring (1913)

The Soldier's Tale (1918)

Pulcinella (1920)

Les Noces (*The Weddings*) (1923)

Oedipus Rex (1927)

The Rake's Progress (1951)

Requiem Canticles (1964)

Above right Stravinsky (seated) photographed with French composer Claude Debussy, c. 1911. It was around this time that Stravinsky was commissioned to write the ballet *Petrushka*.

SUCCESS WITH DIAGHILEV'S BALLETS RUSSES

Early success came in 1910 with *The Firebird*, Stravinsky's first ballet, commissioned by Russian impresario and founder of the famed Ballets Russes, Serge Diaghilev. Dancer Vaslav Nijinsky's career was also launched with this ballet, based on a Russian folk legend. This success led to two more commissions from Diaghilev—*Petrushka* (1911) and *The Rite of Spring* (1913). During this period polytonality (where music is written in two keys and played simultaneously), asymmetrical time signatures, explosive rhythms, and novel instrumentation became important to Stravinsky's musical style. The ballets mark a rapid progression of his compositions, from those, like *Petrushka*, able to be placed in the context of modern music, through to *The Rite of Spring* with its pounding rhythms and dissonant sounds.

Below The cover of the sheet music for *Petrushka*. Composed for the Ballets Russes, its first performances received very mixed reviews.

THE RITE OF SPRING

The Rite of Spring, depicting pagan rites in ancient Russia, radically transformed twentieth-century music. The first performance, staged by Diaghilev in Paris in May 1913, caused a riot. Audiences found this composition very confusing; it used radical new techniques to create restlessness, climax, and respite. It negated expected tonality and used primitive rhythms and repetition, without any metric restriction. Its morality shocked an audience used to the innocence of Romantic ballet. Stravinsky broke completely with established rules of harmony and theater-goers were intensely affronted. He became the enfant terrible of the modern age, the score bringing him wide fame. The music featured in the Walt Disney's animated film *Fantasia* in 1940.

EXILE AND BEYOND

Stravinsky moved to Switzerland in 1914 at the outbreak of World War I. The 1917 Bolshevik Revolution stripped him of his property in Russia and he became a permanent exile. In 1920 he moved to France; he became a French citizen in 1934.

Stravinsky spent the 1920s and 1930s composing, conducting, and performing. His musical style during this period changed to neo-classicism, his compositions being influenced by composers such as Bach and Mozart. *Oedipus Rex* (1927), based on the Sophocles play, is one of Stravinsky's finest neo-classical works, the words provided by the French playwright, Jean Cocteau. The work mixes opera and concert performance, with the singers in costume, though not acting. It is one of the many examples of his collaborations with other European artists, including Picasso and Gide. *The Symphony of Psalms* (1930) is another work expressing Stravinsky's growing interest in religious music and the neo-classical style.

In 1939 Stravinsky settled in the United States; he became a US citizen in 1945. At this time he wrote the neo-classical Symphony in Three Movements (1945). He was never short of commissions or conducting engagements—which ranged from compositions for dancing elephants, Broadway revues, jazz clarinettists, and musical plays.

In 1962 Stravinsky returned to Soviet Russia for celebrations surrounding his eightieth birthday. It was to great acclaim. He died at the age of 88 in 1971 and is buried in Venice near Diaghilev.

Timpani

The timpani or kettledrum consists of a skin, or head, stretched over a copper bowl, which is struck to create a sound. Unlike most drums, when struck the timpani produces a definite pitch and can be tuned during the performance with the use of a pedal. Stravinsky employed many percussion instruments in his works, with notable timpani parts in *Petrushka*, *The Rite of Spring*, and *The Firebird*, among others. A set of standard timpani consists of four drums.

Below Dancer Andris Liepa in a 1995 Kirov Ballet production of *The Firebird*. Until the 1990s, Stravinsky's ballets had not often been performed in Russia.

Spreading our wings: twentieth-century advances

BY THE TIME STRAVINSKY WAS A TEENAGER AND THE TWENTIETH CENTURY HAD COMMENCED, THERE HAD BEEN SIGNIFICANT ADVANCES MADE IN SCIENCE, ART, AND TECHNOLOGY. NEW THEORIES IN PHYSICS CONTINUED TO BE PUT FORWARD, MEDICAL DISCOVERIES WERE PROCEEDING RAPIDLY, AND LARGE AND SIGNIFICANT PROGRESS WAS BEING MADE IN WEAPONS OF WAR.

Painters and musicians were breaking from tradition at an increasing rate, and brand new ways of artistic expression—considered radical at the time—were being embraced. The political and social upheavals of the twentieth century, especially the two world wars, had a profound effect on music, as on other art forms.

Above right The first decades of the new century saw Parisian haute couture become the arbiter of styles for women of all classes.

PARIS—THE WORLD'S ARTISTIC CAPITAL

In 1920 the French music group known as "Les Six" was formed as a reaction against Wagnerism and Impressionism. It was comprised of Georges Auric, Louis Durey, Arthur Honegger, Darius Milhaud, Francis Poulenc, and Germaine Tailleferre.

In the early 1900s artists of several nationalities were working in several styles and living in Paris. Van Dongen, Matisse, Picasso, Utrillo, Sickert, Vuillard, Monet, Renoir, Rodin, and Pissarro were often in Paris and their output greatly endorsed the city as artistic capital of the world.

DEPRESSION AND WORLD WARS

One of the major events of the twentieth century was undoubtedly the Great Depression, which began in 1929. This large-scale economic downturn started in the USA and was prompted by a collapse in the stock market. Its effects continued until well into the 1930s in most countries around the world.

As a result of the impact of the economic severity, political upheaval was not uncommon. Such political uncertainty led to some countries taking their lead from certain radical fanatics, Adolf Hitler being the best-known example. The Great Depression also resulted in many job losses. Construction, farming, industry, and mining output reduced across the world, and did not recover in many countries until well after the outbreak of World War II.

Left Young girls at the piano. Painted at the end of the nineteenth century by Renoir, it evokes a time and ambience that was quickly being replaced by the harsher realities of twentieth-century life.

Left Many thousands of people lost their jobs in the Great Depression. Here, a large crowd of unemployed workers demonstrate in New York in 1930.

in 1945. The two major opposing forces were the Allies (the United Kingdom, France, and the Soviet Union) and the Axis (primarily Germany and Italy, with Japan joining later). The Allied victory resulted in the emergence of the Soviet Union and the United States as the super powers of the twentieth century, precipitating the so-called Cold War, which was to last more than 45 years.

MEDICINE AND SCIENCE

Post-World War II medical discoveries included the development of pacemakers, blood banks, and the ability to perform successful kidney transplants. New vaccines were advanced for poliomyelitis, mumps, measles, rubella, and chicken pox, and the first heart transplant was undertaken in 1967 by Dr Christaan Barnard. Many of these medical developments contributed to a dramatic increase in life expectancy.

Many of the major scientific discoveries, including the incredible advances in quantum physics, the theory of relativity, and the development of the atomic bomb, radically changed people's world view. Enhanced telecommunications, improved transport, more efficient fuels, and the beginnings of space travel were just some twentieth-century developments with wide-ranging repercussions not just for ordinary people, but for artists, philosophers, and musicians.

A noticeable influence during the 1920s and 1930s was jazz, exported to Europe from the United States. In a reverse direction, music in the USA (and Britain) was greatly enriched by the many European-based Jews forced to flee the Nazi regime.

World War II started in 1939 and involved more than 100 million military personnel until its conclusion

Below right Leon Bakst's design for *Le Dieu Bleu* (*The Blue God*), a 1912 Ballets Russes production featuring dancer Vaslav Nijinsky in the title role.

SERGE DIAGHILEV (1872–1929)

Serge Diaghilev was a leading figure in the artistic life of Russia at the turn of the twentieth century. He promoted new art and modern music, organizing grand exhibitions, concerts, opera, and ballets. He brought Western European art to Russia and Russian art to the West. In 1905 he put together a range of previously unknown Russian portrait painters in St Petersburg, the following year organizing several concerts of Russian music in Paris. Following his Paris production of the opera *Boris Godunov* in 1908, he returned there in 1909 to launch the Ballets Russes. His troupe included, among others, Anna Pavlova and Vaslav Nijinsky. The Ballets Russes had the best Russian dancers and the most imaginative designers. The energy and spirit of the dancers were in stark contrast to their French contemporaries. Stravinsky and his exciting new music became a vital part of the Ballet Russes's amazing success—a collaboration that spanned almost 20 years. Between 1909 and Diaghilev's death in 1929, the Ballets Russes was one of Europe's most important artistic groups. He commissioned works from the best composers of the day including Stravinsky, Debussy, Ravel, Satie, de Falla, Richard Strauss, and Prokofiev. Designers such as Leon Bakst, Pablo Picasso, Henri Matisse, Coco Chanel, and choreographers like Michel Fokine and George Balanchine contributed to its success. When Diaghilev died, the Ballets Russes ceased.

Anton Webern

DECEMBER 3, 1883–SEPTEMBER 15, 1945

ANTON WEBERN PUBLISHED MORE THAN 70 WORKS BUT THEY WOULD TAKE ONLY ABOUT THREE HOURS IF PLAYED WITHOUT A BREAK—THEIR AVERAGE DURATION IS LESS THAN THREE MINUTES. SOME MOVEMENTS LAST MERE SECONDS, BUT THESE EXTRAORDINARILY BRIEF COMPOSITIONS HAVE BEEN A POWERFUL INFLUENCE ON LATER TWENTIETH-CENTURY COMPOSERS.

Above right A 1924 photograph with, from left, Schoenberg, the conductor Otto Klemperer, an unknown man, Webern, and Austrian musician Erwin Stein.

Left A 1910 portrait of Webern by Max Oppenheimer. Although his output was not prolific, Webern influenced later composers such as Stockhausen and Boulez.

believing they lacked firm theoretical foundations, prescribed a rigorous program of harmonic and compositional exercises. This program bore fruit in the fluent chromaticism of a 1905 *String Quartet* movement, followed by numerous songs and, in 1908—the year in which his formal studies with Schoenberg ended—the first work Webern acknowledged with an opus number, the *Passacaglia* for large orchestra.

These compositions, like Schoenberg's own *Verklärte Nacht* and *Gurre-Lieder*, are richly harmonized in a style reminiscent of Mahler's late works but are often so highly chromatic that the tonality seems uncertain. In fact, Schoenberg, Webern, and his fellow pupil, Alban Berg, had already begun to experiment with abandoning tonality completely, feeling stifled by an idiom in which they felt everything possible had been said. Webern's *Five Songs*, Op. 3, composed in 1907, are already boldly atonal.

POST-APPRENTICESHIP

The loyalty and affection Schoenberg inspired in his pupils continued well beyond their tutelage, but Webern's attachment was neurotic. Like Schoenberg, he tried conducting operetta to earn a living, but repeatedly refused or abandoned available positions because he could not bear to be separated from his

Webern was a lonely child, shunned by his schoolmates and alienated from his teachers by his difficulty with spelling and mathematics. His cello and piano lessons and love of poetry, which led him to compose his first songs, were his consolation. His aristocratic father wanted him to study agriculture and oversee the family estates and only reluctantly allowed him to study musicology at the University of Vienna. Webern graduated in 1902 and received his doctorate in 1906.

THE SCHOENBERG YEARS

Webern became Schoenberg's first composition pupil in 1904. Schoenberg, a severe critic and demanding teacher, found Webern's compositions mediocre and,

USING THE TWELVE-TONE SCALE

Webern started using Schoenberg's twelve-tone, or serial, system of composition in 1922, before it was officially revealed to the world in 1923. He applied its rules for manipulating a chosen series of the chromatic scale's 12 notes more rigorously than Schoenberg himself and extended them to control the duration and rhythm of the notes as well. This expanded method, known as "total serialism," was seized upon by the mid-twentieth century avant-garde—Boulez, Stockhausen, and others—as their path to the future.

former teacher. Even when Schoenberg moved to Berlin in 1911, Webern followed within a few days.

This inability to detach himself from Schoenberg and hold down a job continued even after his marriage in 1911, despite a period of psychoanalysis, and it approached farce at the onset of war. He campaigned to exempt Schoenberg from service but enlisted himself. After five months he was released, but when Schoenberg was conscripted, followed him back into the ranks, where he campaigned successfully for the master's release and then his own.

This mental turmoil did not prevent him composing a sequence of exquisite miniatures—songs, chamber music, and orchestral works—that are quite unlike anything previously heard. The atonal chords are very dissonant, but, mostly quiet and brief, varied in instrumental color, spread over a wide compass and often interspersed with silence, creating a static, glittering aural kaleidoscope. Stravinsky once called the works of this period, Opp. 3–11, "Webern's dazzling diamonds."

After more doomed attempts at theater work and another house-move in pursuit of Schoenberg, Webern at last found congenial work in the 1920s. He became a respected choral and orchestral conductor, admired

Above A rather wistful watercolor of Vienna in the 1930s. The city where he was born and studied, Vienna was a place to which Webern returned often.

Discover the music

Five Songs, after Dehmel (1906–1908)

Passacaglia, Op. 1 (1908)

Six pieces for orchestra, Op. 6 (1909–1910)

Five pieces for orchestra, Op. 10 (1911–1913)

Six Bagatelles for String Quartet, Op. 9 (1913)

Concerto for Nine Instruments, Op. 24 (1934)

Cantata No. 1, Op. 29 (1938–1939)

Cantata No. 2, Op. 31 (1941–1943)

for his interpretations of Mahler, Brahms, and Bruckner, and from 1925, an equally distinguished teacher.

Sadly, the last years of Webern's life were tragic. His publisher died in 1932, Schoenberg fled Nazi anti-Semitism in 1933, Berg died an early death in 1935 and, soon after, the Nazi embargo on modernist music ended Webern's conducting career and his music was labeled "cultural Bolshevism." His soldier son was killed in February 1945. Webern survived the war only to be shot dead by a nervous American soldier four months after the hostilities ceased while innocently smoking a cigar on a veranda.

Alban Berg

FEBRUARY 9, 1885–DECEMBER 24, 1935

ALBAN BERG, ANTON WEBERN AND THEIR MASTER, ARNOLD SCHOENBERG, THE FIRST THREE IMPORTANT COMPOSERS OF ATONAL MUSIC AND PRACTITIONERS OF SERIALISM, ARE OFTEN REFERRED TO AS THE SECOND VIENNESE SCHOOL, BY VIRTUE OF THE GREAT INFLUENCE THEY HAVE HAD ON THE MUSIC OF THE TWENTIETH CENTURY AND IN DIRECT COMPARISON WITH HAYDN, MOZART, AND BEETHOVEN WHO, FROM THE SAME CITY, SO DOMINATED THE CLASSICAL ERA.

Alban Berg, born into an affluent Viennese family, was indolent and inattentive at school; literature, the piano, and girls were his consuming interests. By 1901 he was composing songs and a year later he had fathered a child on one of the family servants. Denied university education by his poor academic record, he started work as an unpaid civil service trainee. Fortunately, in 1904, his devoted sister replied on his behalf to Schoenberg's newspaper advertisement offering lessons in music theory and he began his formal music education, aged 19 years.

THE SCHOENBERG YEARS

Turn-of-the-century Vienna was awash with innovative, controversial geniuses: Klimt and Kandinsky, Freud, Kokoshka, Wedekind, Zweig, Gropius and, in music, Richard Strauss, Zemlinsky, Schoenberg, and, not least, Gustav Mahler, whose harmonic language, developed from Wagner's, was the point of departure

Above right An autograph manuscript of Berg's *Lyric Suite*, a string quartet in six movements, written in the mid-1920s.

Below A production of *Wozzeck*, Berg's first opera. The story is about a downtrodden soldier, Wozzeck, and his hapless lover Marie, whom he stabs to death.

for Schoenberg and his pupils. Berg, a gregarious, intellectually inquisitive young man, more culturally rounded than either Schoenberg or Webern, revelled in Vienna's cultural maelstrom. He knew many of the artists and compulsively attended plays, contemporary art shows, concerts, and operas.

Berg continued writing songs during the three years of theoretical study Schoenberg insisted on before beginning composition lessons, and *Seven Early Songs* already reflect a sound awareness of Schoenbergian atonality. But, by the end of his studies in 1911, he was already an assured master, progressing from the Mahlerian tonal ambiguity of the *Piano Sonata*, Op. 1, to the free atonality of the *Four Songs*, Op. 2, and the *String Quartet*, Op. 3.

WOZZECK (1914–1922)

Wozzeck is an extraordinary masterpiece. It portrays its doomed anti-hero, victim of an uncaring world, with searing dramatic power, and a political punch that is still relevant today. The opera is also a technical triumph. The hidden use of traditional formal structures, leitmotif, and reiterative rhythmic schemes give the music symphonic unity; extensive passages centered around a particular note provide pitch stability, and truly tonal passages occasionally emerge from the atonal soundscape with stunning effect. Its international success at last brought fame and financial security to the composer.

Left Berg (center), photographed in England in 1931. When Berg died in 1935, his opera *Lulu* was unfinished. Berg's widow asked Schoenberg to complete it, but he said it would take too much time and declined.

Discover the music

Piano Sonata, Op. 1 (1907–1908)
String Quartet, Op. 3 (1910)
Five Orchestral Songs, Op. 4 (1912)
Three Orchestral Pieces, Op. 6 (1914–1915)
Wozzeck, Op. 7 (1914–1922)
Lyric Suite (1925–1926)
Violin Concerto (1935)
Lulu (1925–1935, unfinished)

"The best music always results from ecstasies of logic."

AFTER SCHOENBERG

With family fortunes now reduced, Berg was scraping a living in 1911 by doing editorial work, teaching, running the family property, and answering Schoenberg's frequent peremptory demands for help, often unpaid. It was difficult to find time to compose and his first orchestral composition, *Five Songs on Picture Postcard Texts by Peter Altenberg*, was not even begun until midway through 1912.

Two of these songs, performed under Schoenberg's baton at the infamous Skandalkonzert of March 31, 1913, ignited a public brawl that actually stopped the concert. Worse still, Schoenberg was unimpressed. Berg decided to suppress the piece, but its first complete performance in 1953 revealed a masterpiece of brilliantly innovative orchestration.

Before his conscription in 1915, Berg had completed two more works, and had already begun sketching an opera, *Wozzeck*, based on a Büchner play he had seen in 1914, but his war service and the score's complexity delayed its completion until 1922.

THE LATER YEARS

In his subsequent works, Berg adopted Schoenberg's serial system but, guided always by ear rather than rigid rules, employed its twelve-note tone-rows in a characteristically free fashion, permitting a lyricism rare in atonal music, although it offended Boulez and other fundamentalist adherents to the Schoenbergian gospel.

Berg often hid coded messages in his music. The composer's annotated score of the *Lyric Suite* reveals an account of one of his adulterous affairs encoded in the music using note letter names or numerological symbolism. Berg's, Schoenberg's, and Webern's names are similarly encoded in the *Chamber Concerto* and the number 3 plays several significant roles.

A Nazi ban on his music drastically reduced Berg's income, and his desperate need of money in 1935 made him break off the orchestration of his second opera, *Lulu*, to compose the *Violin Concerto* commissioned by an American violinist. One of his greatest works, the concerto was also his last. A septic insect bite proved fatal, leaving *Lulu*, another masterpiece, incomplete.

Paul Hindemith

NOVEMBER 16, 1895–DECEMBER 28, 1963

MOST COMPOSERS SUFFER A PERIOD OF NEGLECT AFTER THEIR DEATH, BUT PAUL HINDEMITH, DESPITE HIS STATURE AS ONE OF THE LEADING TWENTIETH-CENTURY GERMAN COMPOSERS, HAS WAITED LONGER THAN MOST FOR RESURRECTION. EVEN TODAY, AFTER SEVERAL DECADES OF STEADILY GROWING INTEREST, ONLY A HANDFUL OF WORKS IS TRULY PART OF THE STANDARD CONCERT REPERTORY. THERE IS STILL MUCH GOLD HIDDEN IN THE HINDEMITHIAN HILLS.

Paul Hindemith's father was a struggling house painter and amateur zither-player. Possibly hoping to create at least one exploitable Mozartian prodigy, he forced a stringent course of musical instruction on his three children. They formed the Frankfurt Children's Trio—Paul, the eldest, on violin, sister Toni on piano, and Rudolf on cello—and played in the nearby villages to augment the family's meager income. Paul also

Above right Hindemith conducting a rehearsal of Beethoven's *Symphony No. 9*, in Bayreuth, Germany, in 1953.

played in local inns and local orchestras. This forced labor, however, never soured Paul's love of music.

Later, sympathetic teachers arranged scholarships and sponsorship so the gifted boy could study at the Frankfurt Conservatoire. He was an outstanding student, graduating in 1913 as a brilliant violinist and a composer of Mozartian facility. He joined the Frankfurt Opera orchestra in 1914, and within three years

*"People who make music together cannot be enemies,
at least while the music lasts."*

had become concertmaster, a violin concerto soloist, and the second violin in a noted professional string quartet. Even conscription into the German army, where he used his posting as a regimental drummer to learn how to play the brass and wind instruments, never stopped him composing.

POST-WAR CAREER

Hindemith resumed his playing career after the war, but composition was steadily becoming more important. Chamber music, song cycles, piano music, operas, and other works poured out of him with extraordinary facility. A publishing contract helped to publicize his music, as did the scandal surrounding the frank sexuality of his one-act operas, *Murder, Hope of Women* (1921) and *Das Nusch-Nuschi* (*Nuts*, as in testicles) (1921).

Other wide-ranging activities contributed to his rapidly increasing recognition. He was active as a viola virtuoso, he re-discovered the obsolete viola d'amore and explored the Baroque (which influenced his later music), he formed a quartet to perform contemporary music (by himself, Toch, Krenek, Weill, Stravinsky, Webern, and even Schoenberg, whose music he disliked). He became the innovative program director of the Donaueschingen Contemporary Music Festival and entered musical politics by exhorting composers, in lectures and newspaper articles, to write music for the public, especially the amateur performer, rather than purely for themselves, as in his own pieces for children and amateurs, *Sing- und Spiel-musik*.

In 1927, he began teaching at the Musikhochschule in Berlin. With typical energy and dedication, Hindemith wrote new textbooks, joined students in experimenting with the emerging technologies of recording,

Discover the music

Das Nusch-Nuschi (1921)

Kammermusik Nos. 2–7 (1924–1927)

Das Marienleben (1923, 1948)

Piano Suite 1922, Op. 26

Concerto for Orchestra, Op. 38 (1925)

Mathis der Maler (symphony) (1934)

Mathis der Maler (opera) (1938)

Nobilissima Visione (1938)

Symphonic Metamorphoses on Themes of Weber (1943)

Left Wilhelm Furt-wängler (1886–1954), c. 1935, with the Berlin Philharmonic in London's Albert Hall. The conductor was a great champion of Hindemith's music.

Below right Soprano Inga Nielsen performs in a 1995 Royal Opera production of *Mathis der Maler*. The opera was completed four years after Hindemith wrote the symphonic version.

film, radio, and electronic instruments and brought back into use the school's neglected collection of old instruments and their music. He was a demanding composition teacher, but students loved his humor and his brilliant mind.

Then in 1933, Hitler came to power. Already offended by the nude soprano in a satirical opera by Hindemith, he found the composer's left-leaning intellectualism and Jewish wife equally distasteful. Goebbels accordingly branded Hindemith "decadent," " an atonal noisemaker," and "Bolshevik." His music was banned and Hindemith left for Switzerland in 1938, moving on to the United States in 1940.

AMERICA AND AFTER

Now recognized as one of the century's greatest musical minds, Hindemith was professor of theory at Yale from 1941 to 1953, admired as a tough but brilliant teacher who could literally compose at the blackboard. He completely redesigned the music curriculum, wrote textbooks—still widely used—and initiated American interest in historically accurate performances of early music on period instruments. He composed some of his greatest orchestral works there and became an American citizen in 1946.

After World War II, Hindemith often lectured and conducted in Europe. He took a part-time teaching post in Zurich in 1951, and settled there permanently in 1953, busily composing until his death in 1963.

MATHIS DER MALER (1934)

One of Hindemith's best-known orchestral works, the *Mathis der Maler* is based on music the composer was writing for an opera of the same name. Based on the life of Renaissance painter Matthias Grünewald who railed against oppression, it was commissioned by conductor Wilhelm Furtwängler for the Berlin Philharmonic. Although audiences were receptive, the symphony was perceived by Nazi authorities as opposing party doctrine.

Carl Orff

JULY 10, 1895–MARCH 29, 1982

CARL ORFF WAS ONE OF THE MOST INNOVATIVE MUSIC EDUCATORS OF THE TWENTIETH CENTURY AND SIMULTANEOUSLY ONE OF ITS MOST PERFORMED AND MOST NEGLECTED COMPOSERS. MOST PERFORMED, BECAUSE *CARMINA BURANA* IS PERFORMED EVERY DAY SOMEWHERE IN THE WORLD; MOST NEGLECTED, BECAUSE, REGRETTABLY, IT IS ALMOST HIS ONLY WORK EVER TO SEE THE LIGHT OF DAY.

Although they were not musicians, the Orff family loved music, and Carl, infected by family enthusiasm, began studying piano, organ, and cello when he was only five. He started composing his own songs when still very young and after high school undertook two years composition study at the Munich Music Academy, graduating in 1914. The curriculum was very conservative and he had to explore the contemporary repertoire that really interested him on his own. An enthusiasm for Debussy lasted long enough to inspire an opera, *Gisei the Martyr*, before his interest moved on, rather surprisingly, to Schoenberg, Debussy's diametric opposite. In spite of these interests, neither of these composers left any noticeable trace on Orff's mature style.

EDUCATIONAL WORK

Orff's first professional post was as a composer of stage music in a Munich theater. This was interrupted by military service but a wound ended that within a year, and after a brief spell in theater work elsewhere, he

Above Orff, c. 1950. He once said, "My interest is in the expression of spiritual realities. I write for the theater to convey a spiritual attitude."

Opposite right A scene from the *Carmina Burana* Monumental Opera in Zurich in 2006. This epic for voices and orchestra was written in 1937.

returned to Munich in 1919 to become a teacher. He wanted new ways of engaging youngsters in practical music and in 1924 created, with Dorothee Günther, a special school to teach eurythmics—the combination of music, gymnastics, and dance derived from the work of Daleroze and Laban.

At the *Güntherschule*, Orff hit on the idea of asking students to accompany their own dance routines with their own music improvised on a range of small, specially designed, tuned percussion instruments that were simple to play. This motivated students to master the basic language of music. Over the years, he created a comprehensive scheme of progressive practical exercises—the *Schulwerk*—to facilitate that process. The system received the official backing of the post-war German Ministry of Education and is still in use worldwide.

COMPOSITIONS

Orff had long been dissatisfied with the composition teaching he had received at the Academy and, in 1920, he resumed his studies with the distinguished teacher, Kaminski, and began the search for a composing style of his own. He also discovered early Baroque music. Particularly inspired by the operas of Monteverdi, he composed most of his subsequent works for the stage, including *Carmina Burana*, his first great success, following a kind of Monteverdian model.

Early opera, created for seventeenth-century princes, was really about spectacle. The mythological plots concerning gods and goddesses provided a structure without any emotional involvement to trouble the

ORFF'S POLITICS

Orff remained in Germany throughout the Third Reich but never joined the Nazi Party. He wrote some theater music on request and *Carmina* gained official approval because its massive simplicity appealed strongly to Nazi megalomania, but silent acquiescence is not active support. Orff was very careful not to challenge the regime, and with good reason; he was hiding the fact that he had a Jewish grandmother. He certainly despised Nazism, but seems, like many others, to have slipped imperceptibly into a position of complicity from which it was impossible to escape without a heroism he could not command. Reprehensible, but hard to condemn from a comfortable armchair.

audience. Lavish, flamboyant sets and costumes with ingenious mechanical stage effects were as important as the music and the words—which is precisely what Orff intended in *Carmina Burana* and its two companion pieces, although the music is, of course, nothing like Monteverdi's.

Orff's music, with its broad gestures and massive climaxes is really designed to accompany visual spectacle, although it manages well enough in the concert hall without it. Obscure Latin text, simple repetitive melody, short contrasting sections, fixed tonality, simple block chords, no counterpoint, all propelled by exhuberant rhythm: It has the textural simplicity of pop music, with nothing to distract from the grand effect.

Discover the music

Carmina Burana (1937)

Der Mond (1939)

Catulli Carmina (1943)

Die Kluge (1943)

Trionfo di Afrodite (1953)

Nänie und Dithyrambe (1956)

Percussion

The percussion section plays an integral role in the overall sound of the modern symphony orchestra. Providing different textures and embellishments, percussion instruments include the glockenspiel, vibraphone, marimba, snare drum, bass drum, cymbals, mallet, triangle, chimes, gong, tam tams, shakers, castanets, cabasa, etc. Percussionists often have to play numerous instruments in each piece, jumping from one to the other as the music demands. Orff's explorations in rhythm can be seen in the lush percussion parts in his compositions.

LIFE & TIMES

Changing boundaries— Austria and Germany up to 1945

NINETEENTH-CENTURY CONTINENTAL EUROPE WAS IN POLITICAL FLUX EVEN BEFORE NAPOLEON'S MILITARY RAMPAGES RE-SHUFFLED ITS BORDERS AND ALLIANCES. GERMANY ONLY CAME INTO BEING IN 1871 WHEN A GROUP OF GERMAN-SPEAKING STATES COALESCED AROUND PRUSSIA, AFTER THE AUSTRIAN EMPIRE WAS EXPELLED FROM THE GERMAN FEDERATION. YET CULTURAL INTERACTION BETWEEN VIENNA AND BERLIN REMAINED STRONG. EVEN MOVEMENT BETWEEN THEM REQUIRED NO PASSPORT. ARTISTS EXHIBITED AND MUSICIANS PERFORMED IN BOTH. SCHOENBERG AND WEBERN LIVED AND TAUGHT IN BOTH. BERG'S *WOZZECK* WAS COMPOSED IN VIENNA AND PREMIÈRED IN BERLIN.

AROUND THE TURN OF THE CENTURY

Nineteenth-century advances in technology, education, and the dissemination of ideas, particularly from 1880 onward, created the modern world. Electric light, the train, the steamship, the telephone, the mechanization of labor, dyes, soaps, toothpaste and other modern "essentials," the internal combustion engine, the cinematograph, artificial silk, radioactivity, aspirin were all discovered or invented—many of them in Germany, before the end of the nineteenth century. Universal education spread literacy, broadening the readership of the proliferating newspapers and promoting debate

Right A scene from Fritz Lang's 1924 film *Die Nibelungen: Siegfried*, featuring Austrian actor Paul Richter as Siegfried. The film's use of special effects was revolutionary.

EXPRESSIONISM

Expressionism originated from the late nineteenth-century desire to question conventional belief, which had proved so fruitful in science. In literature and the visual arts, it meant that any subject was permissible and that the artist's emotional reaction—the psychological truth, more important than the surface reality—was most potently conveyed through stylized distortion. Kafka's and Joyce's novels, the blatantly erotic nudes of Klimt and Schiele, the savage satirical cartoons of Grosz, and the films of Fritz Lang (below) are among the most well-known examples.

The term "Expressionism" is also applied to the 1920s architecture of Gropius and his colleagues, and the music of Hindemith, Schoenberg, Webern, and Berg where, except in works that set an Expressionist text, such as Berg's operas, *Wozzeck* and *Lulu*, the idea of revealing psychological truth is hardly relevant. In this context, Expressionism implies intense self-expression in defiance of convention.

on the issues of the day—democracy, socialism, nationalism, Zionism, the psychoanalytical theories of Freud, the Bauhaus architecture of Gropius and Mies van der Rohe, and the latest scientific ideas and discoveries. Berlin and Vienna, like Paris and London, were in intellectual ferment that challenged received wisdom and practice in all areas, including the arts.

Non-realist paintings, often highly erotic, or savagely satirical, by Klimt, Kandinsky, Schiele, and Kokoschka in Vienna, and Liebermann, Grosz, and Marc in Berlin, and the sexually frank and socially radical writings of Stefan Zweig, Stefan George, and Frank Wedekind, provoked conservative opposition in both capitals. In music, the great Austro–German tradition that had dominated Western music for over a century was crumbling, stretched to its limits by the complex chromatic harmony of Wagner, Mahler, Strauss, and Schoenberg.

Left Adolf Hitler salutes a crowd of Hitler Youth. In the early 1930s, there were well over 2 million members of this branch of the Nazi Party.

all paved the way for Nazism but, before it triumphed, turbulent Berlin enjoyed its cultural heyday. Politically motivated satirical cabaret flourished in Berlin's many bars and clubs and there was an extraordinary flowering of Expressionist creativity in art, architecture, film, art photography, literature, and music. Many of the creators were Jewish.

Of course, freedom of expression was not on Hitler's agenda, but anti-Semitism certainly was. In a sad end to an era of amazing creativity, the flower of German-speaking culture either fled, mostly to America, or stayed to be murdered, to have their work suppressed, or their conscience compromised.

ATONALITY

Schoenberg and his pupils Berg and Webern responded by abandoning traditional tonality altogether. Their dissonant atonal music attracted extreme, sometimes physically violent, opposition in conservative Vienna, partly fuelled by the anti-Semitism that had made Mahler's reign at the State Opera so difficult. Hindemith's radically extended version of tonality, although often dissonant, encountered less opposition in more progressive Berlin; Orff reverted to ultra-simplicity. His punchy, primitive rhythms and short melodic phrases never strained the listeners' powers of concentration, his creativity and style were sufficiently inoffensive to escape the censure of Adolf Hitler—Austrian by birth, sometime resident of Vienna, monster of Berlin—when he eventually came to power in 1933.

PAVING THE WAY FOR NAZISM

During the 1914–1918 war, in which Germany and Austria–Hungary once more joined forces, many German and Austrian artists, writers and musicians were protected from frontline service, surviving into a world in which Germany, Austria, and Hungary became separate democratic republics.

In Austria, the Social Democrats' enlightened social policies in housing and welfare, carried out in spite of grave financial restrictions, attracted worldwide admiration. German experience of democracy proved very different. Attempted coups in successive years—by the communists in 1919 and the extreme right wing in 1920—political assassination, and runaway inflation

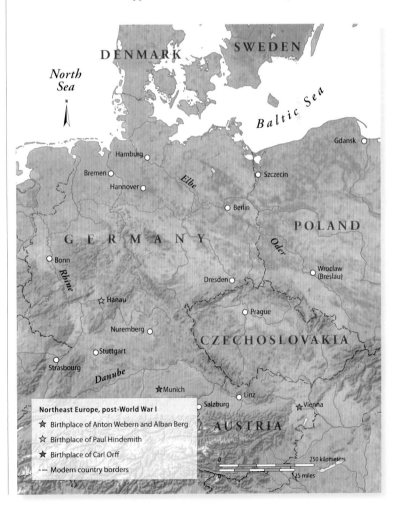

Northeast Europe, post-World War I
☆ Birthplace of Anton Webern and Alban Berg
☆ Birthplace of Paul Hindemith
★ Birthplace of Carl Orff
--- Modern country borders

THE MUSIC OF LATIN AMERICA

Latin America is a term that embraces a wealth of cultures and traditions. It is a region that has produced some of the most colorful and exciting music of the last 100 years or so. The rich sounds associated with works written by composers from Mexico and South America are the result of a unique blending of European musical traditions with local folk music and indigenous rhythms. The major Latin American composers include such greats as Mexico's Manuel Ponce (1882–1948), whose work includes chamber music and concertos, as well as the hugely popular song *Estrellita*; and Julián Carrillo (1875–1965), who devised a microtonal music system known as the Thirteenth Sound, whereby a thirteenth sound was added to the standard 12 notes that make up an octave.

Avant-garde composer Juan Carlos Paz (1899–1972) worked extensively with the twelve-tone method favored by Schoenberg. One of the most influential

Right Astor Piazzolla revolutionized traditional Argentine tango music with his new style, called "nuevo tango."

Below Manuel Ponce wrote more than 100 songs and many works for guitar, including 24 preludes.

Latin America, early twentieth century

★ Birthplace of Humberto Allende

★ Birthplace of Julián Carrillo

★ Birthplace of Juan Carlos Paz and Alberto Ginastera

★ Birthplace of Astor Piazzolla

☆ Birthplace of Manuel Ponce

★ Birthplace of Heitor Villa-Lobos

★ Birthplace of Domingo Santa Cruz Wilson

-— Modern country borders

composers and music educators in Argentina, his works include piano sonatas, *Dedalus* (1950) for piano, clarinet, flute, and orchestra, and a number of film scores. Later Argentine composers include Alberto Ginastera (1916–1983) and Astor Piazzolla (1921–1992).

HEITOR VILLA-LOBOS (1887–1959)

Heitor Villa-Lobos is Brazil's most well-known composer, and arguably the most famous composer to come out of South America. Born in Rio de Janeiro, he was largely self-taught, although he did spend some time in formal study. When he was in his twenties, he traveled around Brazil learning about its folk music traditions, elements of which he incorporated into his own works. His earliest compositions were based on guitar improvisations, such as *Suite populaire brésilienne* (1908–1912). Although his music for guitar represents only a fraction of his compositional output, these works are now a crucial part of today's guitar repertoire.

When Serge Diaghilev's Ballets Russes visited Brazil in 1917, Villa-Lobos was exposed to music by such composers as Stravinsky and Debussy. Around the same time, he met French composer Darius Milhaud, and a year later he became friends with pianist Artur Rubinstein who encouraged the Brazilian to write more works for the piano. Among these is *Carnaval das crianças* for two pianos (1920).

When Villa-Lobos visited France in 1923, he found that the French were captivated by the "Brazilianness" of his music. This reinforced his decision to focus on his own style of music, rather than incorporate European influences. His *Chôros*, based on the music of Brazilian street bands, was a new kind of composition. The first, *Chôros No. 1* (1920) was written for solo guitar; others were composed for various instruments, such as No. 2 for flute and clarinet, and No. 10 for chorus and orchestra. Among his other influential works are the nine suites of the *Bachianus Brasileiras* and his *Concerto for Guitar* (1951), which he wrote for Spanish guitarist Andrés Segovia. When he died in 1959, Villa-Lobos was given a state funeral.

MUSIC IN CHILE

Among Chile's composers, Humberto Allende (1885–1959) is known for his 1920 symphonic poem *La voz de las calles* (*The Voice of the Streets*). As a teacher at the Santiago National Conservatory in the early years of the twentieth century, he fostered a more national voice in composition. He was the first person known to have recorded the music of the Mapuche Indians.

Domingo Santa Cruz Wilson (1899–1987) studied music in Spain, and upon his return to Santiago, he lobbied for a faculty of fine arts at the University of Chile, where he became dean in 1933. He also established the Bach Society in 1917, a choral organization that became the hub of Chilean music for about 15 years. Santa Cruz's compositions include *Te Deum*, Op. 4 (1919) and *Cantata de los rios de Chile*, Op. 19 (1941) for chorus and orchestra. His works feature Spanish rhythms and strong chromaticism.

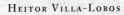

"In my music, I let the rivers and seas of this great Brazil sing. I don't put a gag on the tropical exuberance of our forests and our skies, which I intuitively transpose to everything I write."

HEITOR VILLA-LOBOS

Discover the music

Humberto Allende, *La voz de las calles* (1920)

Juan Carlos Paz, *Piano Sonata No. 2* (1925)

Juan Carlos Paz, *Dedalus* (1950)

Julián Carrillo, *First Symphony in D major* (1901)

Manuel Ponce, *Concierto del sur for guitar and orchestra* (1941)

Domingo Santa Cruz, *Cantata de los rios de Chile* Op. 19 (1941)

Villa-Lobos, *Bachianus Brasileiras*

Villa-Lobos, *Guia Prático Nos. 1 to 9*

Villa-Lobos, *Suite populaire brésilienne* (1908–1912)

Left Heitor Villa-Lobos (left) at the Ziegfeld Theater on Broadway for the 1948 première of his musical *Magdalena*. It was very well received, one critic saying it was "the most sophisticated Broadway score of our time."

Sergei Prokofiev

APRIL 27, 1891–MARCH 5, 1953

IN HIS YOUTH PROKOFIEV'S COMPOSITIONS WERE CONSIDERED DISSONANT AND
RADICAL. HIS WRITING BECAME MORE MEASURED AND LYRICAL AS HE MATURED AND,
ON HIS RETURN TO THE SOVIET UNION, MORE ORTHODOX. IN HINDSIGHT HIS WORKS
CAN BE SEEN AS REPRESENTING THE CONTINUOUS LINE OF RUSSIAN COMPOSERS,
MOVING FROM THE ADVENTUROUS AND VIBRANT FEATS OF THE NINETEENTH-
CENTURY NATIONALISTS INTO A TWENTIETH-CENTURY STYLE MARKED BY ITS
FRAGILE WIT AND ABILITY FOR STRIKING DRAMATIC REPRESENTATION.

The concert, ballet, and opera repertoires have been indisputably influenced by Prokofiev's output and he remains one of the most significant and frequently performed composers of the twentieth century.

Above right The young Prokofiev at the piano. Encouraged by his musician mother, he demonstrated his musical prowess at an early age.

EARLY STUDIES AND COMPOSITIONS

Sergei Prokofiev was an only child, born to a pianist mother and a relatively well-off agricultural engineer father. By the age of five it was clear that he possessed some extraordinary musical abilities. He also displayed an early aptitude for chess, which he continued to play throughout his life, even competing against a number of world chess champions. He started composition studies in 1902 by which time he had already written some early works. By his own initiative, he gained a

Left A portrait of the composer by Russian artist Pyotr Konchalovsky (1876–1956). Prokofiev would have been in his forties at the time the portrait was painted.

place at the St Petersburg Conservatory in 1904, being some years younger than his peers. His attitude to study was considered arrogant and he later regretted his dissatisfaction and boredom at the Conservatory, having wasted the chance to learn a great deal more from Rimsky-Korsakov, professor of composition and orchestration.

During his student years, Prokofiev performed his own works on the piano, and developed a reputation as an *enfant terrible*, his compositions considered unconventional. He graduated in composition in 1909 without distinction, but continued to study piano and conducting. When his father died in 1910, financial support ceased, but by then he was establishing a reputation as a composer, even though some of his works were very controversial. His first two piano concertos prompted angry outcries from the critics.

Prokofiev graduated from the Conservatory in 1914 winning the Rubinstein prize of a grand piano, the highest award for a piano student. Soon after his graduation, his mother took him to London where he met Sergei Balakirev, Igor Stravinsky, and importantly, impresario Serge Diaghilev, who commissioned the ballet, *The Buffoon* (1915). From the start, Stravinsky—more than any other of his contemporaries—was to have the most impact upon Prokofiev's works.

To avoid conscription during World War I, Prokofiev returned to the St

"Prokofiev has made an immense, priceless contribution to the musical culture of Russia. A composer of genius ..."

DMITRI SHOSTAKOVICH

Petersburg Conservatory to study organ. In 1917, he composed the opera, *The Gambler*, one of his most accomplished creations. During this year he also composed his *Classical Symphony* drawing upon a recreation of the formal style of the eighteenth century, and his first violin concerto. Seeing little room for his exploratory music within the Russia of the time, he decided to leave for the United States in 1918.

LEAVING RUSSIA

On arrival in America his electrifying piano playing excited audiences and he was compared with other

Below A scene from the New York City Opera's 1950 production of *The Love for Three Oranges*. The plot centers on a prince who is searching the world for three oranges, each of which conceals a princess.

Russian exiles of the time, including Rachmaninov. His opera *The Love for Three Oranges* (1919), which was commissioned by the Chicago Opera, was set for performance. Unfortunately for Prokofiev's American career, the conductor died and the première was postponed. Having expended so much time on the opera, Prokofiev found himself in financial difficulties. In 1922 he moved to France, not wanting to return to his homeland as a failure.

Prokofiev's innovative musical style appeared to fit into the Paris musical scene. He renewed his connection with Stravinsky and Diaghilev's Ballets Russes and

Discover the music

The Gambler, Op. 24 (1917)

Classical Symphony, Op. 25 (1917)

Violin Concerto No. 1, Op. 19 (1917)

The Love for Three Oranges, Op. 33 (1919)

Lieutenant Kijé, Op. 60 (1933)

Romeo and Juliet, Op.64 (1936)

Peter and the Wolf (1936)

War and Peace, Op. 91 (1943)

Below A 1965 production of *Cinderella*, with Robert Helpmann and Frederick Ashton as the Ugly Sisters.

spent much of his time concentrating on composition. At this time, he received one of many invitations to return to Russia but decided to focus on his European career.

In 1923 Prokofiev married the Spanish singer Lina Llubera. At this point reception to his works was tepid. However in 1927 things finally began to improve—the première of *The Love for Three Oranges* in Petrograd (St Petersburg/Leningrad) was received well; Diaghilev commissioned a number of works; he had a number of successful Russian tours; and two of his earlier operas were also played in Europe.

Below A scene from Sergei Eisentein's 1945 film *Ivan the Terrible*, for which Prokofiev wrote the score.

BACK TO THE USSR

From the early 1930s Prokofiev began to move many of his premières to Russia. *Lieutenant Kijé* (1933), the score for a Russian film, and *Romeo and Juliet* (1936), the ballet for the Bolshoi Theater in Moscow and one of Prokofiev's best known works, are two examples.

After 18 years abroad, Prokofiev decided to return to Russia permanently in 1936. At this time the changing authority of the Union of Soviet Composers influenced him to move toward composing some short pieces, many written for children. His symphonic fairy tale *Peter and the Wolf* (1936) constructed as music for

a child's introduction to the orchestra dates from this period. Prokofiev also attempted to write compositions to satisfy Stalinist criteria. Written for 500 performers, his colossal *Cantata for the Twentieth Anniversary of the October Revolution* composed to texts by Marx, Lenin, and Stalin, was completed in 1937. It was not performed during his lifetime. Another work, his opera *Semyon Kotko* (1939), was postponed because the producer was executed!

From 1941 the composer's health began to decline as he suffered the first of many heart attacks. World War II forced the evacuation of many artists to the south of Russia. Prokofiev's friendship with Communist party member Mira Mendelson, coupled with the decree that marriage to foreigners was illegal, resulted in his separation from his wife. He began living with Mira and remained with her till his death, separating formally from Lina Llubera in 1948 when she was arrested on charges of espionage and sentenced to a labor camp in the Soviet north.

PETER AND THE WOLF (1936)

In 1936 the Central Children's Theater in Moscow commissioned Prokofiev to write a musical symphony for children. He wrote the symphonic fairy tale, *Peter and the Wolf*, envisioned as an instructional tool to help children to learn about the different instruments of the orchestra. Each character in the story is represented by a different instrument or group of instruments: Peter by the strings, the bird by the flute, the duck by the oboe, the cat by the clarinet, the wolf by the horn section, the grandfather by the bassoon, the hunters by a woodwind theme, with gunshots on timpani and bass drum. Each character also has a particular theme, or leitmotiv. The music and text were written by Prokofiev and the story is told by a narrator accompanied by orchestra. The work has become one of the most enduring and instructive of young persons' guides to the orchestra.

In the 1940s, he wrote *War and Peace*, an opera based on the Tolstoy masterpiece, as well as more film music, including *Ivan the Terrible* (1942–1945). In 1944 Prokofiev moved to an estate outside Moscow to compose his *Symphony No. 5*, which was a great success. Soon after this, he fell and was concussed, an accident from which he never really recovered. His output greatly reduced from this time.

Above A scene from the tragic finale of the ballet *Romeo and Juliet*, one of Prokofiev's masterpieces. This 2008 production was directed by dancer and choreographer Oleg Vinogradov.

The Communist Party then decided that Prokofiev's music was dangerous to the people and his work was disparaged as bourgeois and "formalist." Performance cancellations and declining health resulted in Prokofiev passing out of the Soviet music scene. The première of his *Symphony No. 7* in 1952 was his last public performance. He died of a brain hemorrhage in 1953, on the same day as Joseph Stalin.

The Stalinist period

THE TASK OF MODERNIZING RUSSIA AND DEVELOPING A MODERN INDUSTRIAL ECONOMY
BASED ON AN EFFICIENT AGRICULTURAL SECTOR REQUIRED A COMPETENT VISIONARY
LEADER. TSAR NICHOLAS II DID NOT HAVE THE SKILLS FOR THIS TASK. AFTER THE
COLLAPSE OF THE RUSSIAN GOVERNMENT IN MARCH 1917, HE WAS FORCED FROM OFFICE
AND A PROVISIONAL GOVERNMENT WAS FORMED.

The intent was that this government would rule until a new permanent system of government was established. At the same time another body, the Soviet, was formed to advance the rights of working people. By October 1917, as a result of its inept policies, the provisional government had been discredited, and serious conflict ensued. The Russian Civil War from 1917 to 1922 was conducted on multiple fronts over a wide territory—both geographic and ideological—the White and Red Armies in bitter confrontation. The Bolsheviks eventually seized power crushing their opposition through intimidation and violence.

Right Stalin (center) frolicks with children in Gorky Park. This picture was painted in 1939 in the Socialist Realist style by Vasili Svarog (1883–1946).

From 1922 to 1928 the Communists consolidated their power. The government became more centralized, but the Communist party was more important than the government. With Lenin's death in 1924, Joseph Stalin became leader of the party.

The year 1928 marked the beginning of "Five-Year Plans," which centralized economic planning and the collectivization of agriculture. Stalin employed very brutal methods, including mass arrests, mass murder, and the deportation of hundreds of thousands of peasants to the labor camps of northern Russia and Siberia, to rapidly collectivize agriculture.

Left A political poster, c. 1930, showing Stalin opposing the capitalist factions. A "Stalin Cult" developed in the 1930s. It glorified the principles of the Soviet state as well as its leader.

In protest over these methods, peasants slaughtered their livestock and reduced their grain output. As a result there was a famine between 1932 and 1934, and millions died. Many fled the countryside for the cities, hoping both to escape the myriad difficulties of rural living and to provide resources to support the industrialization of the Soviet Union.

Stalin's Great Purges from 1936 to 1938 eliminated many of his enemies. Over 20 million people died—Stalin was the undisputed dictator.

THE CULT OF STALIN

The Cultural Revolution between 1928 and 1931 coincided with a strong push toward industrialization and collectivism. Soviet members were keen to support this revolution in education and art. From 1933 to 1939 Soviet paintings, poems, and sculptures began to promote a "Stalin Cult." Socialist Realist art of the time also glorified Stalin, and "Socialist Realism" was the guiding code for artists. Whether artists rose (like Brodsky), or fell (like Meyerhold), depended on how closely they followed the dictates of Socialist Realism.

THE COMPOSERS' BUREAU

In 1934 official Russian policy toward music changed;
a special bureau—a composers' union—was established
to keep track of artists and their doings, and regula-
tions were drawn up outlining what kind of music
was acceptable. Stalin's purge
struck fear into the lives of many
composers—their work had to be
driven by political dogma rather
than artistic innovation. With
the dissolution of the Russian
Association of Proletarian Musicians in 1932 and the subsequent
establishment of the Union of
Soviet Composers the administration of musical affairs was,
in effect, subject to government
control. Composers were advised to pay heed to the
social content of their music and its appeal to people
at large. In practice this was the start of a period of
Russia's artistic isolation from the rest of the world.

Soviet writers were subject to the same artistic restraints as other artists. In
1932, Gladkov wrote *Energy*, whose heroes are construction workers. Nikolai
Ostrovsky's 1932 book *How Steel was Tempered* became a classic work of
Socialist Realism. The hero of Ilin's *The Great Conveyor Belt* (1934) is a tractor
plant executive who resigns in despair for failing to get his factory to
achieve its Five-Year Plan production target. After attending a Stalin
lecture on how to overcome management difficulties, he is energized and
asks to be sent anywhere that the state wants him to go so that he can
use his talents to increase productivity for the well-being of the nation.

Some writers, however, would not compromise their principles. Boris
Pasternak (1890–1960), at left, author of *Dr Zhivago*, made his living translating classic works into Russian. He was removed from the execution list
during the Purges because Stalin liked his translation of Georgian classical
writings. Pasternak wrote his semi-autobiographical novel in secret during
World War II. He could not get it published in the Soviet Union, as it was
critical of the 1917–1950 period. *Dr Zhivago* was published in the West in
1957 and won Pasternak the 1958 Nobel Prize for Literature. It was not until
1987 that the novel was finally published in the Soviet Union.

PAS DE DEUX— MUSIC AND BALLET

The late nineteenth century saw ballet move out of opera and into a theatrical arena of its own. Ballet companies emerged worldwide to perform the growing balletic repertoire. Favorites such as the original balletic scores of *Swan Lake*, *The Nutcracker*, and the landmark early twentieth-century ballet *The Rite of Spring*, date from this seminal period.

Other styles of collaboration at this time involved using music in a different way, such as the borrowing of existing music (such as symphonies), creating ballets from anthologies of a composer's work (such as choreographer Michel Fokine's *Chopiniana*), or taking the music from one balletic score and using it elsewhere. Ballet continued to be featured in operas, and ballet companies also continued to employ resident composers. However, the groundbreaking scores and works now came from newly commissioned collaborations between choreographers and composers. This was particularly evident in France and Russia.

PETIPA AND THE "GRAND SPECTACLE"

Ballet's historical home of France remained influential and this influence extended to the Russian Imperial

Left A cartoon of Marius Petipa, one of the most influential choreographers in ballet history.

Below The School of American Ballet in New York opened its doors in January 1934. The American Ballet Company came into being the following year.

Ballet in St Petersburg, via its choreographic director, the Frenchman Marius Petipa (1818–1910). Petipa established the company in a permanent home, and set about commissioning new "grand spectacle" ballet works, employing well-known and proven composers for the music, rather than using resident composers who, at the time, wrote in prescriptive rhythms and melodies. Notable of these new large-scale ballets is *The Sleeping Beauty*, choreographed by Petipa with music by Tchaikovsky. The many different styles of small and large dances within Petipa's choreography allowed for an interesting score that complemented the stage action. Petipa and Tchaikovsky also collaborated on *The Nutcracker*. Tchaikovsky's other famous ballet score, *Swan Lake*, predated these works. Written for his sister around 1871, the work was revised for its theatrical debut at the Bolshoi Theater in 1877.

The music of Tchaikovsky's ballets exemplify his unique orchestral practices. The use of the celesta in *The Nutcracker* is one example; another is his incorporation of Romantic devices such as the use of leitmotiv to represent balletic characters. Tchaikovsky's expressive intentions were similar to those of the French composer Léo Delibes, whose ballet *Sylvia* (1876) utilized Delibes's practices of writing elaborate tone poems to assist with dramatic expression.

THE BALLETS RUSSES

Serge Diaghilev inherited Petipa's groundwork of full-length large-scale ballets. Diaghilev had previously toured Russian art and opera to Paris, and noted that the ballet within the operas he staged was invariably very popular with local audiences, so he seized the opportunity to stage new Russian works in France. He established the Ballet Russes and commissioned new works from composers such as Stravinsky, Ravel, Debussy, Satie, Poulenc, Milhaud, and Prokofiev.

Stravinsky's collaboration with the gifted dancer and choreographer Vaslav Nijinsky for the Ballet Russes resulted in one of the most influential musical works of the early twentieth century. *The Rite of Spring* (see pages 316–317) was a collaboration that saw the music

Following pages Ambra Vallo (as the Sugar Plum Fairy) and Dominic Antonucci (as the Prince) in the Birmingham Royal Ballet's 2006 production of *The Nutcracker*, one of the world's best loved ballets.

SPREADING DIAGHILEV'S VISION

Members of the Ballet Russes took up residency in other countries, including the United States and Britain, spreading collaborative methods. Dance companies were set up in these countries to perform what was now a large repertoire of full-scale ballets. Choreographer Ninette de Valois collaborated with composers like Vaughan Williams, Walton, and Constant Lambert in the UK. George Balanchine, who had earlier collaborated with Stravinsky, set up a ballet school in New York. This led to the establishment of ballet companies in the USA, which produced new works such as *Billy the Kid* (1939) with music by Aaron Copland. Copland's musical style incorporated Stravinsky-like rhythmic manipulations, but combined them with American folk tunes and orchestration that depicted vast American landscapes. In Russia, new works included music by Shostakovich, Prokofiev, and Khachaturian. Prokofiev's *Romeo and Juliet* (1935) left behind the rhythm-dominated style of Stravinsky, and created extended melodies, placed throughout the drama in a leitmotiv style.

faithfully fitting the synopsis to not only support, rhythmically and texturally, onstage action, but also to assist with the dramatic elements of the story. The score's impact came from the use of ostinato rhythms with irregular accents, cell-structured melodies full of discordant intervals and chords, harmony based on Russian folk modalities, polyphonic texture but with polytonality—elements pointing directly to twentieth-

Above Susan Lucas and Kevin O'Hare in the Birmingham Royal Ballet's 1990 production of *The Sleeping Beauty*. Tchaikovsky's music and Petipa's choreography went hand in hand.

century music, but also necessary to assist with the violent depiction of the pagan story. It was the combination of the dramatic choreography with the music that caused the infamous riot at the work's première in Paris. The police arrived during the interval to calm the audience, but the reception of the performance did not improve. Yet for Diaghilev, any publicity was good publicity and he continued to stage works in Paris.

George Gershwin

SEPTEMBER 26, 1898–JULY 11, 1937

BORN JACOB GERSHOWITZ IN BROOKLYN TO RUSSIAN JEWISH IMMIGRANT PARENTS, GEORGE GERSHWIN WAS ONE OF THE JAZZ AGE'S MOST SUCCESSFUL AMERICAN SONGWRITERS AND COMPOSERS. GERSHWIN TOOK AN EARLY INTEREST IN MUSIC, BEGINNING PIANO LESSONS AT AGE 10 THAT WERE ORIGINALLY INTENDED FOR HIS OLDER BROTHER, IRA. AS A TEENAGER, GERSHWIN STUDIED WITH CHARLES HAMBITZER, WHO INTRODUCED HIM TO THE GREAT CLASSICS. HIS STUDIES OF THE FRENCH MODERNISTS INFLUENCED HIS COMPOSITIONAL STYLE THROUGHOUT HIS TRAGICALLY SHORT LIFE.

Never a good student, Gershwin dropped out of school at age 15 to take a job plugging songs at the Remick and Company publishing house in New York's famed Tin Pan Alley. He also began to write his own songs, scoring his first major success in 1919 with the song "Swanee." Al Jolson's recording sold more than 2 million copies and established Gershwin as a songwriting powerhouse while gaining him entry to New York society circles. With Ira writing lyrics, the brothers conquered Broadway, writing a string of successful musicals for such stars as Fred and Adele Astaire, W.C. Fields, Ruby Keeler, Fanny Brice, Bob Hope, and many more. These early musicals had contrived plots that were only a framework for singing and dancing. But by the late 1920s, George and Ira sought to infuse their stories with satire and social commentary. This endeavor resulted in the first American musical to win a Pulitzer Prize—the political satire *Of Thee I Sing*.

Above right George (left) and Ira Gershwin, one of the most successful song-writing teams in musical history.

Right Audrey Hepburn starred in the 1956 film *Funny Face*. Among the Gershwin songs featured in the motion picture were "Let's Kiss and Make Up."

Below left Simon Estes and Grace Bumbry star in the New York City Opera's 1985 production of *Porgy and Bess*.

GERSHWIN'S SYMPHONIC STYLE

At the same time, George wanted to create a symphonic style that incorporated the African–American influences that he heard both in popular music and on the Broadway stage. Gershwin traveled to Paris, where

PORGY AND BESS (1935)

Despite confounding critics at its Broadway première, *Porgy and Bess* is considered the most important American opera ever composed. Gershwin called it a "folk opera"—combining traditional operatic elements such as recitative with an African–American musical idiom and contemporary concert music techniques including polytonality and a twelve-tone row. Based on DuBose Heyward's novel *Porgy,* and with lyrics by Heyward and George's brother Ira, *Porgy and Bess* tells the story of African–American life on Catfish Row, which was based on the real-life Cabbage Row in Charleston, South Carolina. The work features such well-known songs as "A Woman is a Sometime Thing," "Summertime," "I Got Plenty O' Nuttin," and "Bess, You Is My Woman Now."

he hoped to study with Nadia Boulanger or his idol, Maurice Ravel. In a famous piece of apocrypha, Ravel, turning Gershwin away as a student, is reported to have said "Why be a second-rate Ravel when you are a first-rate Gershwin?" Returning to New York, Gershwin composed a series of concert works that remain among the most successful merging of Classical, jazz, and popular styles: *Rhapsody in Blue*, *An American in Paris*, and his *Piano Concerto in F* are all highly successful amalgams and are still widely performed today.

Gershwin loved the music of the twentieth-century French masters and the influence of Debussy and particularly Ravel can be found in his concert works. Jazz-influenced modal styles, extended harmonic techniques (like the "tall chords" favored both in jazz and by the contemporary French composers), exciting rhythmic drive, and tuneful melodies can all be found in Gershwin's best works, both from the Broadway

Top *An American in Paris*, a Gershwin symphonic work, was made into a film in 1951, starring Gene Kelly.

Discover the music

Rhapsody in Blue (1924)
Lady Be Good (1924)
Piano Concerto in F (1925)
Oh, Kay! (1926)
Strike Up the Band (1927)
Funny Face (1927)
An American in Paris (1928)
Girl Crazy (1930)
Of Thee I Sing (1931)
Cuban Overture (1932)
Porgy and Bess (1935)

stage and the concert hall. This influence began early with his studies with Hambitzer. Later, Gershwin studied the music of, among others, Schoenberg, Berg, Stravinsky, and Shostakovich, as a means to broaden his own compositional palette.

HOLLYWOOD CALLS

After the 1935 première of *Porgy and Bess*, Gershwin answered the call of Hollywood. George and Ira wrote the Astaire and Rogers vehicle *Shall We Dance?* but Gershwin began to experience severe headaches, dizziness, and occasional blackouts. On July 9, he fell in to a coma and underwent surgery, where a brain tumor was diagnosed. Gershwin never recovered. He died just ten weeks short of his thirty-ninth birthday, but his huge legacy of songs lives on—Gershwin standards have been recorded by such diverse artists as Janis Joplin, Miles Davis, Bing Crosby, Sam Cooke, and Sting.

LIFE & TIMES

America between the wars

THE "ROARING TWENTIES" BEGAN WITH A BANG AND ENDED WITH A CRASH. THE *PROHIBITION ACT* WAS PASSED IN 1920; SO WAS THE NINETEENTH AMENDMENT GIVING AMERICAN WOMEN THE RIGHT TO VOTE. AT THE DECADE'S END, THE STOCK MARKET COLLAPSE OF OCTOBER 1929 HERALDED THE GREAT DEPRESSION, LASTING LONG AFTER PROHIBITION WAS REPEALED IN 1933.

Many feminists who fought tooth and nail to win the vote had also campaigned to ban the sale and consumption of alcoholic beverages. But a new breed of young women known as "flappers" emerged during the Prohibition era. They bobbed their hair, removed their corsets, shortened their skirts, wore heavy makeup, smoked cigarettes, and flouted the drinking laws and conventional morality. The flapper became an emblem of the change, excitement, and glamor that characterized this colorful decade.

Above A page from the magazine *Elite Style*, c. 1920, showing some of the summer fashions favored by flappers.

Left Heartthrob Rudolph Valentino in the 1926 film *The Son of the Sheik*. Valentino was the sex symbol of the day, some women even swooning in the cinema when he appeared on screen.

John W. Considine, Jr. presents

RUDOLPH VALENTINO
"The Son of the Sheik"
a Sequel to The Sheik'

with VILMA BANKY

from the novel by E.M. HULL ~ Adapted to the Screen by FRANCES MARION

A GEORGE FITZMAURICE PRODUCTION
· UNITED ARTISTS PICTURE ·

THE BIG APPLE

As hemlines rose, so did the prices on the New York Stock Exchange. The 1920s saw an unprecedented bull market that economists thought would last forever, and ordinary people shared the wealth (at least on paper) with the traditionally affluent.

If Wall Street was the center of the financial universe, Broadway was the world's entertainment hub. It was the golden age of musical theater. Highlights included George and Ira Gershwin's *Lady, Be Good* in 1924, and *Show Boat* in 1927 with music by Oscar Hammerstein II and Jerome Kern.

Even during the Great Depression of the 1930s, which left 25 percent of Americans unemployed and some 2 million homeless, audiences enthusiastically supported Broadway productions such as Cole Porter's lighthearted 1934 offering *Anything Goes* and Gershwin's groundbreaking opera *Porgy and Bess* (1935).

HOORAY FOR HOLLYWOOD!

The American motion picture industry had been established in California early in the century, but it wasn't until the 1920s that it really came of age. Two of its major stars were Clara Bow (the "It" Girl) and silent

Left New York's famous Cotton Club launched the careers of many African–American performers, including composer and bandleader Edward Kennedy "Duke" Ellington (1899–1974).

and received a number of honors at the inaugural Academy Awards presentation in 1929.

During the Depression years, movies became more popular than ever, especially musicals, comedies, and gangster films. For just 15 cents audiences could leave their troubles behind and escape into fantasy worlds populated by the likes of Fred Astaire, Shirley Temple, Will Rogers, and James Cagney.

THE JAZZ AGE

During Prohibition, drinkers obtained their alcohol illegally through mob-controlled bootleg operations. The most notorious gangsters of the day were Jack "Legs" Diamond, Dutch Schultz, and Al "Scarface" Capone, who amassed fortunes from black-market liquor. People would gather in nightclubs known as "speak-easies" to drink, dance the Charleston, shimmy, and "black bottom," and listen to a relatively new form of music from the south that had migrated to urban centers such as Chicago and New York. "Jazz" incorporated West African rhythms, ragtime, blues, and the myriad sounds of New Orleans. Some called it the "devil's music" because of its association with whore-houses and gin joints. The most illustrious speak-easy was Harlem's Cotton Club. Sumptuously decorated in plantation and jungle motifs, the club launched the careers of Duke Ellington, Cab Calloway, Lena Horne, Ethel Waters, and Bill "Bojangles" Robinson. Even though the entertainers were African–American, the club's patrons were strictly white.

screen heartthrob Rudolph Valentino. His untimely death at age 31 in 1926 sparked a national frenzy, with tens of thousands attending his memorial services in Los Angeles and New York.

If Valentino's death signaled the end of the "silent" movie period, *The Jazz Singer*, released in 1927 and starring Al Jolson, marked the birth of the "talkies." It featured the classic songs "Mammy" and "Blue Skies"

Below Scott and Zelda Fitzgerald, photographed c. 1920. Fitzgerald's writing chronicled the "Jazz Age."

F. SCOTT FITZGERALD AND THE LOST GENERATION

In the 1920s, a group of writers fled to Paris, disenchanted with American moral and material values. These included Ezra Pound, Ernest Hemingway, Gertrude Stein, John Dos Passos, and Hart Crane, but it is F. Scott Fitzgerald and his beautiful artist wife Zelda who are most closely identified with the "Jazz Age" and "Lost Generation" (terms coined by Fitzgerald and Stein respectively).

Notorious for his excessive drinking and profligate spending, Fitzgerald was nevertheless a highly disciplined writer, whose output of short stories, articles, and novels was prodigious. *This Side of Paradise* (1920) brought him fame and fortune, but

it is his allegory on the American dream—*The Great Gatsby* (1925)—that remains his most enduring work. By the 1930s, the party was drawing to a close. As Scott's alcoholism progressed, Zelda— diagnosed with schizophrenia—descended into madness. *Tender is the Night* (1934) is Fitzgerald's fictional account of his wife's mental illness. Fitzgerald died of heart disease in 1940 at age 44 before completing *The Last Tycoon*, which drew on his Hollywood screenwriting experiences. Zelda, who had become almost permanently institutionalized, died eight years later in a hospital fire.

Francis Poulenc

JANUARY 7, 1899–JANUARY 30, 1963

FRANCIS POULENC WAS A COMPOSER OF ENDURING HARMONIC AND MELODIC GIFTS, AND OF MANY CONTRADICTIONS. HIS PENCHANT FOR PARISIAN CAFÉ HARMONIES, SPARKLING INSTRUMENTAL WRITING, AND SIMPLE RHYTHMS GIVES HIS MUSIC A LIGHT-HEARTEDNESS, BUT THERE IS ALSO A SERIOUSNESS OF PURPOSE, SHOWN IN PIECES INSPIRED BY TRAGEDY OR BY HIS CATHOLIC FAITH. THESE TWO TENDENCIES CAN COEXIST WITHIN THE SAME PIECE, GIVING IT A PARTICULAR POIGNANCY—BUT ALSO MAKE IT VULNERABLE TO CRITICISMS OF BEING TOO LIGHTWEIGHT.

Francis Poulenc was born in Paris to a mother who was an amateur pianist and instigator of musical soirées. His father, a devout Roman Catholic, was one of two brothers who developed the pharmaceutical company that later became Rhône-Poulenc. There was, therefore, a heady mix of influences as well as economic security in Poulenc's early life. He showed early talent as a pianist, and spent much of his life doing concert tours with singer Pierre Bernac, for whom he wrote more than 50 songs.

MUSICAL INFLUENCES

His musical influences were two-pronged. Poulenc liked the harmonies and melodies of Parisian light music, and his harmonies are full of lush added sixth chords and sensuous piano voicings. He was also influenced by the clean lines of the neo-classical Stravinsky and the simplicity and purity of Erik Satie. It was part of Poulenc's gift that he could reconcile these quite disparate idioms into a coherent and instantly recognizable style. He came to early prominence with his *Rhapsodie Nègre* and its setting of some pseudo-African

Above Francis Poulenc (second from right) with other members of "Les Six" and Jean Cocteau at the piano, c. 1916.

nonsense poetry. He joined the circle around Erik Satie, and in 1920, he and a group of his composing friends (including Honegger and Milhaud) was collectively dubbed "Les Six" by a journalist. The ubiquitous Jean Cocteau became their spokesman. Although they were united by friendship, the group became known for a somewhat anti-Romantic, clean-cut stance in their music—modern but pleasantly so.

A GROWING EXPRESSIVE RANGE

Until this time, Poulenc had composed mostly short pieces for solo piano or small combinations of instruments. He now expanded his range. Under the guidance of Charles Koechlin, he further developed his harmony, and composed sonatas on Classical models for small groups of wind instruments, with or without

L'HISTOIRE DE BABAR (1940)

Whether in the piano solo version, or that orchestrated by Jean Françaix, this piece with narrator is a perfect, stylish setting of Jean de Brunhoff's famous children's book about an elephant. All Poulenc's styles are on display here.

Le chasseur a tué la maman
Le singe se cache, les oiseaux s'envolent
Le Babar pleure
Le chasseur court pour attraper
le pauvre Babar

piano. These culminated in his Op. 100, the *Sextet for Piano and Winds*, a sparkling combination of idiomatic wind writing, brilliant piano figurations, and natural melodies, stylishly harmonized.

The rediscovery of his Catholic faith in the 1930s gave Poulenc's music more seriousness of purpose, and a greater expressive range. Although the juxtaposition of "grave and gay" was always present in Poulenc's music, the effect of the contrast was now more often to add poignancy to the tragedy than piquancy to the humor. The *Violin Sonata* of 1942–1943, for example, took as its theme the assassination of the Spanish poet Lorca, and the *Horn Elégie* (1957) the death of horn player Dennis Brain in a car crash. Both pieces contain musical depictions of the moment of crisis.

Poulenc was comfortable in the field of liturgical music, which needs to be serious without being overly tense or dramatic. His *Gloria* and *Stabat Mater* are both admirably suited to purpose. His larger-scale

Discover the music

Sextet for piano and winds, Op. 100 (1932–1939)

Concerto in G minor for organ, strings, and timpani (1938)

Violin Sonata, Op. 119 (1942–1943)

Horn Elégie, Op. 168 (1957)

La Voix Humaine (1958)

Clarinet Sonata, Op. 184 (1962)

Below Martin Harvey and artists of London's Royal Ballet in a 2005 production of *Les Biches*. The ballet, with music by Poulenc, premièred in 1924, with Diaghilev's Ballets Russes.

vocal works include the opera based on Apollinaire's absurdist play *Les Mamelles de Tirésias*, the religious opera *Dialogues des Carmélites*, and an opera based on a phone-call, *La Voix Humaine*, in which the female protagonist talks to the lover who is abandoning her. Poulenc's most performed and popular works, the sonatas for flute, oboe, and clarinet, come from the final period of his life, and synthesize all the more popular features of his style.

CHARACTERISTICS OF POULENC'S MUSIC

Poulenc's melodies are "tuneful." They can have a folk-song-like quality, partly due to his tendency to repeat short phrases. The phrase structure is very clear-cut. He used two main harmonic "modes"—his lush, somewhat sentimental "café" chords, and his more acerbic neo-classical harmony. Both are very well heard and voiced. As to rhythm, Poulenc was not an innovator, and his rhythms are very easy to assimilate. Indeed, all aspects of his music are extremely well crafted.

Twentieth-century France— surreal, existential, and absurd

France suffered massive material losses in World War I, and experienced more casualties than any other country except Russia. The artistic movements that emerged after the war expressed the negativity and disenchantment that permeated French society. One such group was the avant-garde Dadaists, who ridiculed nationalism, capitalism, and other ideologies which they believed contributed to the outbreak of the Great War.

In 1924, the author André Breton published his first surrealist manifesto. Surrealism—a far more life-affirming philosophy than Dada but sharing similar roots—draws heavily on Freudian and Jungian psychoanalytic theory, particularly the importance of dreams as a portal to the unconscious. Surrealists developed new techniques to access the unconscious, including "automatism," whereby the artist or writer allows the hand to move freely across the canvas or page without conscious control. Salvador Dali, Paul Delvaux, and René Magritte are the most important Surrealist artists; among the principal writers are Louis Aragon, Paul Éluard, and Jean Cocteau.

Right Jean Cocteau was an important cultural figure in twentieth-century France. He was a poet, novelist, playwright, and filmmaker. This poster is for his 1946 film *Beauty and the Beast.*

COCTEAU AND THE LITTLE SPARROW

They seemed an unlikely pair of kindred spirits: Jean Cocteau, a middle-aged bisexual esthete from a privileged background, and young singer Edith Gassion, who was raised in a brothel. He was cerebral; she was passionate and earthy. However, they had in common a desire for escape (mainly through addictive substances), a craving for adulation, and a respect for each other's considerable talents.

In 1935, nightclub owner Louis Leplée discovered the petite 15-year-old singing on the streets of Paris. Her nightclub debut was a resounding success, and soon led to further engagements, a recording contract, and a new name—Piaf—meaning "sparrow" (left). She met Cocteau in 1939 and the following year starred in a play he wrote for her, *The Beautiful Indifferent*, in which Piaf and her lover at the time, actor Paul Meurisse, played themselves. Piaf's colorful but often desolate life ended on October 11, 1963 at age 47, from cancer. Cocteau paid tribute to his friend on national radio: "She died as if consumed by the fire of her fame." In a bizarre coincidence, Cocteau died of a heart attack one hour later.

Left Jean-Paul Sartre (1905–1980) was one of the leading lights of twentieth-century French philosophy. He was also a novelist, playwright, and critic.

Right Absurdist writer Albert Camus (1913–1960) once said, "You will never be happy if you continue to search for what constitutes happiness. You will never live if you are looking for the meaning of life."

LES SIX

Cocteau considered himself a poet first and foremost, but he also had an illustrious career as novelist, essayist, playwright, and filmmaker. He is best known for his experimental play *The Human Voice*; the films *The Storm Within* and *Orpheus*; and his involvement with ballet impresario Serge Diaghilev and the group of composers known as Les Six.

There has been considerable discussion as to the origins of Les Six. One argument is that the critic Henri Collet—in an article written in 1920—randomly designated a group of composers as a sort of French counterpart to the Russian "Five" (or "Mighty Handful"). He chose Georges Auric, Louis Durey, Arthur Honegger, Darius Milhaud, Francis Poulenc, and Germaine Tailleferre, musicians who had broken away from prevailing Wagnerian and Impressionist styles.

Some believe that Cocteau conceived the idea of Les Six, placing himself as a kind of de facto leader and sometimes percussionist. The 1921 recording of piano music *L'album des Six* is the only project in which all six were engaged. That year, the group (minus Durey) collaborated with Cocteau on a ballet libretto *The Wedding on the Eiffel Tower*.

SARTRE, DE BEAUVOIR, AND CAMUS

Existentialism is a philosophy that became a huge cultural phenomenon in Europe in the 1940s and 1950s, and was largely borne out of the French Resistance movement of World War II and the collective sense of post-war despair and alienation. Very basically, Existentialists saw the

Below Novelist, feminist, and philosopher, Simone de Beauvoir (1908–1986) wrote, among other works, *The Ethics of Ambiguity* (1947), an essay explaining the concepts of Existentialism.

world as inherently meaningless, and believed that there is no authority over an individual but themselves. Many of them were atheists and socialists, including three important French existentialists— Jean-Paul Sartre, Simone de Beauvoir, and Albert Camus.

Sartre was a professor, author, and activist who came to prominence with his first novel *Nausea* in 1938. His 1947 play *No Exit* contains the famous quote, "Hell is other people." His defining work is *Beingness and Nothingness* (1943), which has become the basic text of Existentialism. Sartre met his lifelong partner and colleague Simone de Beauvoir in 1928 while she was a student at the prestigious École Normale Supérieure. De Beauvoir's writings also spanned several genres, but she is best known for her seminal feminist work *The Second Sex* (1949) which asserts that women are more influenced by social conditioning than biology.

Albert Camus is identified with "absurdist" literature, its underlying premise being that the only meaning or clarity in the world is what we bring to it. His major works include the novels *The Stranger* (1942) and *The Plague* (1947); his 1957 essay *Reflections on the Guillotine* helped win him the Nobel Prize for Literature.

COMPOSERS BORN AFTER 1900

Introduction

THE HISTORY OF THE TWENTIETH CENTURY IS FULL OF
UPHEAVAL, UNCERTAINTY, UNPRECEDENTED SCIENTIFIC,
TECHNOLOGICAL, AND SOCIAL CHANGE, WITH ALL OF THE
BEST AND WORST OF HUMANITY'S VARIOUS POTENTIALS
ON FULL DISPLAY. ART MUSIC BOTH ANTICIPATES AND
REFLECTS THIS HISTORY AND ANY ATTEMPT TO IMPOSE
THEMATIC LOGIC UPON IT IS DOOMED TO FAILURE.

There are a few seminal events, however, that can be used as points of contact with the directions and trends of twentieth-century Western art music—World War I, the rise of Nazism and the European Diaspora, the rise of the technological society, and the globalization of the world's economy and telecommunications. The so-called Great War was supposed to end all wars. All it truly ended was the last vestiges of nineteenth-century Europe, but it also announced the United States as a dominant force on the world stage. One of the first important artistic exports America sent back to Europe and out to the rest of the world was jazz. This unique combination of Western harmonic language and African rhythmic complexity has had a profound effect on music and musicians of all kinds.

The political events in Germany in the 1930s also provided an important stimulus to music, again with the consequences felt most importantly in the United States. An enormous group of artists was forced to flee the Nazi regime and many of them took up residency across the Atlantic. Composers born before the turn of the century such as Stravinsky, Hindemith, Bartók, and Schoenberg all found their way to America. Even more influential were the number of teachers, musicians, and singers that soon populated the ranks of American orchestras and conservatories and swung the pendulum of artistic influence toward the United States and away from Europe.

As technology started to change society at an ever accelerating pace, composers began to explore the means of electronic and aleatoric music as a viable means of expression. And finally, as the twentieth century drew to a close, the concept of the "global village" truly began to become a reality. Music and performance from all over the world are now instantly available via the internet, and the model of art music with a strictly Eurocentric language seems no longer truly viable.

However, if we step back and examine the works of the most important Western art music composers born after the year 1900 we can still trace a line of continuity among most of them that allows us to place them in a proper context. These composers were still subject to the great historical flows of the Renaissance, Baroque, Classical, and Romantic eras. Indeed, no other century's composers have been as acutely aware of the burden of the entire legacy of the Western music tradition. While they struggled to find their own forms, styles, and modes, the composers of the mid-twentieth century laid claim to any and all of what came before them and appropriated it to their own use.

Above right The gramophone changed the way we listened to music. Now people could hear their favorite works without leaving home.

Previous pages A scene from the 2008 Sadler's Wells' production of Leonard Bernstein's *West Side Story*.

Below German refugees arrive in America in 1933. The United States was a haven for those fleeing the Nazi regime.

It was this conscious eclecticism, this historical awareness, this essentially "conservative" unifying trait that can be seen in the works of composers who are as diametrically opposed to one another in temperament as Benjamin Britten, Dmitri Shostakovich, and Aaron Copland. After World War II many of their successors proceeded to push the boundaries of art music well beyond anything recognizable as part of the legacy. Many others remained content to stay on the path already illuminated. Diversity and divergence have reigned uninterrupted since.

The latest generation of composers that has followed on the heels of these giants has yet to have its greatest practitioners identified by the perspective of time. As art music has become more eclectic and more able to subsume alternative styles and means of expression, it has also become less dominating of the cultural land-scape. Listeners and consumers of classical music are now also more likely to be consumers of all kinds of other styles and types of music. That fact alone makes judging the relative "artistic merit" of any given com-position more difficult for those who care to do so and

Above A painting by Pablo Picasso depicting the great American jazz clarinettist Sidney Bechet (1897–1959). Many African–American jazz musicians lived in Paris in the 1930s and 1940s, bringing jazz to Europe.

less important to those who do not. We can at least say that there is a large number of important composers who have emerged since the 1950s. How their work will be regarded in the coming decades is certainly not subject to any accurate prediction. But names such as Pärt, Gubaidulina, Raautavara, and Ádes may well one day become just as familiar to audiences as Messiaen, Cage, Carter, and Boulez.

Right American com-poser Elliott Carter is known for his complex rhythms. He has written chamber, orchestral, and solo instrumental music, as well as works for ballets and operas.

Aaron Copland

NOVEMBER 14, 1900–DECEMBER 2, 1990

A TALE OF TWO COPLANDS: COPLAND EMBODIED AMERICAN MUSIC, YET FACED PERSECUTION AT THE MCCARTHY HEARINGS ON UN-AMERICAN ACTIVITY; HE LIVED IN A WORLD OF MEN, YET WOMEN PROVED INSTRUMENTAL TO HIS CAREER; PIECES SUCH AS *FANFARE FOR THE COMMON MAN* MADE HIM FAMOUS, YET MANY RESPECT HIM MOST FOR LESS APPROACHABLE PIECES SUCH AS THE *PIANO VARIATIONS*; HE WAS AN INTENSELY PRIVATE PERSON, BUT HIS ROLES AS COMPOSER, TEACHER, AUTHOR, AND CONDUCTOR PLACED HIM SQUARELY IN THE LIMELIGHT.

Copland was born of Russian Jewish parents in Brooklyn, New York. His sister, Laurine, provided him with his earliest musical education, teaching him piano and introducing him to ragtime and opera. Copland formally studied piano with Wolfsohn from 1913 to 1917 and theory and composition with Goldmark beginning in 1917. Nadia Boulanger, however, became his most important teacher. At first, Copland was reluctant: "I couldn't think of a single composer in the history of music who had ever studied composition with a woman teacher …" Nonetheless, he did study with her in Paris from 1921 to 1924, joining a long list of American composers including Thomson, Piston, Carter, Diamond, Bernstein, Harris, and Glass. She arranged his first major American première—the *Organ Concerto*. This concert marked the

Discover the music

Piano Variations (1930)

El salon México (1932–1936)

Billy the Kid (1938)

Rodeo (1942)

Fanfare for the Common Man (1942)

Appalachian Spring (1943, 1957 reworking)

Piano Fantasy (1952–1957)

Connotations (1962)

Inscape (1967)

beginning of a string of honors including the Presidential Medal of Freedom, the Medal of the Arts, and the Congressional Gold Medal.

In addition to composing, Copland steadfastly championed contemporary American music, published numerous articles, and wrote several books including the classic *What to Listen for in Music*. By 1972, he had ceased to compose regularly, and from the mid-1970s, he suffered short-term memory lapses, which grew progressively worse. In spite of these lapses, he enjoyed great success as he shifted from composing to conducting. He died shortly after his ninetieth birthday.

WORKS AND STYLE

Copland's eclectic style led him to divide his music into two broad categories—"simple" and "severe." His earliest works reflect influences including jazz, Italian opera, Romantic era piano music, and numerous contemporary European composers. In the mid-1920s in particular, Copland turned to blues and jazz to capture the feel of his native New York. The unfavorable reception of his *Piano Concerto* of 1926, however, led him away from this course. From that point, he turned to jazz less overtly. What Copland dubbed his "severe style" pieces of the late 1920s and early 1930s include his *Symphonic Ode*, *Piano Variations*, and *Statements*, works that earned him much admiration.

The turbulent events of the 1930s onwards—the Great Depression and the subsequent beginnings of World War II—prompted introspection. Referring to the new audiences sprouting from broadcasting and the phonograph, Copland observed that "… composers were in danger of working in a vacuum … I felt that it

Left Aaron Copland (left) photographed in 1987 with Leonard Bernstein. Copland mentored the young Bernstein, and in turn, Bernstein became a staunch champion of the older composer's works.

"To stop the flow of music would be like the stopping of time itself, incredible and inconceivable."

was worth the effort to see if I couldn't say what I had to say in the simplest possible terms." This new phase saw some of Copland's most popular and accessible works, including film scores and the ballets *Billy the Kid*, *Rodeo*, and *Appalachian Spring*. These latter pieces, along with *Fanfare for the Common Man*, exemplified what became known as the American sound, leading some to call Copland the Dean of American Music, or

Below A 1999 production of Martha Graham's ballet *Appalachian Spring* at New York's Joyce Theater. Copland's music is regarded by many as the epitome of twentieth-century American music.

as Virgil Thomson quipped, the "Mother of Us All." Yet by the 1950s Copland had returned to his more "severe" style by composing, as so many did after the war, serial works. Even though these compositions failed to engage a broad public, his style in this idiom preserved a voice that was strictly his own. *Inscape* and *Connotations* stand as superior examples of postwar dodecaphonic composition.

APPALACHIAN SPRING (1943)

This ballet, proposed by the choreographer Martha Graham, centers on a nineteenth-century pioneer couple's relationship in Pennsylvania. It celebrates their newly constructed farmhouse and explores their feelings of hope and uncertainty. The conclusion leaves them strong and optimistic. The ballet's plot, coupled with Copland's style, cemented the notion of quint-essential American sound. While one might mistake this music as a setting of American vernacular songs, Copland composed all the melodies anew, except for the Shaker hymn "Simple Gifts." As did Bartók with Magyar melo-dies, Copland assimilated the esthetic so thoroughly that he was able to compose very convincingly in the genre. Copland reworked *Appalachian Spring* as an orchestral piece that works extraordinarily well without the support of the narrative. The variations on "Simple Gifts" have remained a favorite to this day.

Immigration and music in the United States

THE QUESTION "WHAT IS AMERICAN MUSIC?" HAS EVOKED A WIDE RANGE
OF RESPONSES, FROM "ANY AMERICAN WHO COMPOSES CREATES AMERICAN
MUSIC" TO A DISTINCT ESTHETIC AS EMBODIED BY COMPOSERS SUCH AS
IVES AND COPLAND. APART FROM THE MUSIC OF INDIGENOUS PEOPLE,
HOWEVER, ALMOST ALL MUSIC IN THE UNITED STATES BEARS
THE INFLUENCE OF IMMIGRATION.

Early colonists brought European practice with them, and much music-making in the United States continued the tradition, at least in part. The growth of urban centers led to a corresponding increased interest in music, but the cities drew overwhelmingly upon conductors and musicians who had trained in Europe.

Jazz, often described as America's only original art form, also came about through immigration—both voluntary and forced. The African Diaspora beginning in the seventeenth century contributed a distinctive rhythmic sense, a focus on percussion, and conceptions of timbre atypical of Western sensibilities. European immigrants furnished Western ideas concerning form, instrumentation, and harmony. By the late nineteenth century, a time when 40 percent of the population of New Orleans had been born in Europe, the interaction of these influences led to ragtime, blues, and ultimately,

Above Igor Stravinsky in 1956, photographed in the office of his home in Hollywood, California.

Below Darius Milhaud (right) with actors Gene Kelly and Leslie Caron. In 1940, Milhaud left France to live in the USA.

jazz. With the exception of composers like John Frederick Peter and William Billings, American music really only came into its own in the late 1800s with artists including Amy Cheney Beach and Charles Ives. Yet just as the United States was beginning to establish its own musical culture, events in Europe precipitated some significant changes.

IMMIGRATION IN THE TWENTIETH CENTURY

Edgar Varèse's arrival in 1915 marked an important turning point in the status of the United States as a cultural center. Unable to secure a permanent position in Europe, Varèse immigrated to the USA and became an ardent advocate for contemporary music. He co-founded the International Composers Guild, and later, founded the Pan-American Association of Composers. With these developments, the United States was no longer considered a cultural backwater.

A confluence of events in the 1930s made Europe and its environs increasingly inhospitable to significant populations. Adolf Hitler became chancellor in 1933, the same year that saw the first establishment of a concentration camp, and the year that Germany and Japan withdrew from the League of Nations. In 1934,

Left An immigrant family looking at the New York skyline as they arrive by boat in the early 1930s in search of a better life.

Mussolini began aggressive military action while Germany withdrew from the Treaty of Versailles and invoked compulsory military service. A 1935 letter from the Nazi Party to the Office of Culture, Ravensburg, Germany deemed a number of artists "degenerate," including George Antheil, Alban Berg, Aaron Copland, Rubin Goldmark, Otto Klemperer, Ernst Krenek, Erik Satie, and Kurt Weill. Many, but not all, composers listed were Jewish, but significantly, all held views incompatible with Nazi ideology. Events of this sort created an artistic chill that caused many musicians to consider leaving Europe.

The combination of the rising artistic prominence of the United States with deteriorating conditions in Europe led many composers to immigrate. Between 1933 and 1940, a number of extraordinarily gifted composers moved to the United States, including Arnold Schoenberg (1933), Ernst Toch (1934), Kurt Weill (1935), Ernst Krenek (1938), Igor Stravinsky (1939), Béla Bartók (1940), Paul Hindemith (1940), and Darius Milhaud (1940).

After World War II, a number of factors led to an increase in the teaching and studying of music. Soldiers returning from war usually wished to return to civilian life, and the *GI Bill* encouraged many to pursue studies at post-secondary level. As a result, music programs enjoyed much growth, not only as an art, but as a valid discipline of study. As such, composition no longer depended solely upon concert revenue, but also upon the patronage of university appointments. Many immigrant composers won positions teaching in universities, which provided not only a stable income but an artistic freedom unencumbered by the demands of the concert-going public. In addition, their new roles placed them in a position to influence generations of composition students in the following decades.

THE NEW ROLE OF AMERICA

In the aftermath of World War II, the geopolitical map underwent significant change. Many European cities suffered catastrophic damage; most saw their economies eradicated or left in disarray. As such, artistic endeavors largely halted. The United States and Russia rose to prominence, with the former playing an instrumental role in the reconstruction of Europe. Along with its new status as an economic and military superpower, the United States enjoyed its new identity as a global center of artistic endeavor. In addition to those composers who made the United States their home, many composers who did not immigrate, like Boulez and Penderecki, for example, nonetheless spent substantial parts of their careers there. The first half of the twentieth century, then, transformed the United States from a cultural desert into an international center of artistic creativity.

Below A 1962 photograph showing Austrian-born composer Ernst Toch admiring a sculpture of his head created by artist Anna Mahler (at right), the daughter of Gustav Mahler.

Joaquin Rodrigo

NOVEMBER 22, 1901–JULY 6, 1999

IN THE MIDST OF TWENTIETH-CENTURY EXPERIMENTATION AND AVANT-GARDE STYLES, RODRIGO'S MUSIC STANDS OUT AS A REVIVALIST MIX OF PAST AND LOCAL TRADITIONS. NATIONALISTIC SPANISH MELODIES AND POETRY MIX WITH FORMS AND TEXTURES BORROWED FROM THE RENAISSANCE, BAROQUE, AND CLASSICAL PERIODS, A STYLE RODRIGO DESCRIBED AS "NEOCASTICISMO"—A RETURN TO PURE OLD STRUCTURES AND TRADITIONAL WAYS.

Left Rodrigo with his wife, the pianist Victoria Kamhi. Rodrigo embraced traditional, folk, and modern forms. His style shows wide influences—from Scarlatti to the great Spanish composer Manuel de Falla.

Although Rodrigo is known for his guitar work *Concierto de Aranjuez*, he was never a virtuosic guitarist. His music education, which began very early after becoming blind from diphtheria at the age of three, incorporated violin and piano lessons as well as composition tuition from Francisco Antich in Valencia. In his early career, Rodrigo lived and studied in France while the Spanish Civil War was causing unrest at home; his friends included composers such as Ravel. His lessons with Paul Dukas in Paris were particularly influential on his compositional output, and in the year that Dukas died, Rodrigo wrote *Sonada di adios*, paying homage to his influence. Dukas, known also for his impact on composers such as Messiaen and Durufle, encouraged students to study traditional forms as used by Scarlatti, Rameau, and J.S. Bach. Certainly Rodrigo's own compositions refer to forms such as the Classical sonata, concerto, and sonatina, the Baroque suite, and Renaissance madrigals.

CONCIERTO DE ARANJUEZ (1939)

The famous *Concierto de Aranjuez* was Rodrigo's first concerto and was also the work that established him as a composer of distinction. The work's name refers to the palatial gardens built by Philip II of Spain at the Royal Palace in Aranjuez, and attempts to capture the scene, sounds, and scents of the garden. The concerto was dedicated to Spanish guitar virtuoso Regino Sainz de la Maza who also performed it at its première in 1940. Fifty years later, Spain's King Juan Carlos bestowed the hereditary title "Marquis of the Gardens of Aranjuez" on Rodrigo and his wife, a title that acknowledged the impact of Rodrigo's work and reinforced the success of Rodrigo's career. Rodrigo's *Concierto* cleverly orchestrates the guitar against orchestral forces, which could overwhelm texturally but never do. The middle movement has been used in movies, advertising, and has been quoted by many musicians, among them jazz greats Miles Davis and Chick Corea.

COMMISSIONS

In 1978, Rodrigo was commissioned by Irish flautist James Galway (below) to write a concerto for flute and orchestra. The composer said of the *Concierto pastoral* that the first movement was Classical in form, the second movement was reminiscent of the music of Valencia, and the third movement's pastoral mood gave the concerto its name. Another commission was from English cellist Julian Lloyd Webber. The *Concierto como un divertimento* (Concerto like a divertimento, 1981) for cello and orchestra is notable for its melodic sparkle and strong rhythms. The *Adagio nostalgico* movement is particularly fine.

AFTER *ARANJUEZ*

Rodrigo went on to compose another ten concertos including the dance-inspired guitar concerto *Fantasia para un gentilhombre*, as well as orchestral works for the concert hall, ballet, theater, and film. His large catalog of original songs incorporates classical Spanish poetry and often uses guitar for accompaniment.

Rodrigo's popularity, which originated in Spain, was widespread by the end of the twentieth century. Both Rodrigo and his wife toured internationally, giving recitals and lectures into the 1980s. His ninetieth birthday celebrations were held internationally over two years, but Rodrigo's success was acknowledged throughout his career—by the end of his life he had received six honorary doctorates, and held numerous prestigious positions including the suitably named Manuel de Falla Chair at the Complutense University

Above Part of the beautiful gardens at Aranjuez in Andalusia, Spain. The names Aranjuez and Rodrigo are forever linked by the composer's guitar work.

in Madrid, a position that was created specifically for Rodrigo. In 1996 he received the Award of Prince of Asturias, the most prestigious honor in Spain.

Rodrigo's personal life was also content, evident in his long marriage to the pianist, Paris Conservatoire teacher and fellow collaborator, Victoria Kamhi. Joaquin Rodrigo died in Madrid two years after his wife's death, and was buried in Aranjuez, the town that had inspired his famous concerto.

Discover the music

Concierto de Aranjuez (1939)

Fantasia para un gentilhombre (1954)

Invocación y danza (1961)

Concierto Andaluz (1967)

Concierto madrigal (1968)

Concierto pastoral (1978)

Concierto como un divertimento (1981)

Guitar

Usually associated with rock and popular music, blues or jazz, the guitar is not a standard part of the orchestra by any means, although mention Rodrigo and the guitar immediately springs to mind. The six-stringed classical guitar first appeared in Spain, probably descending from stringed instruments such as the oud and the gittern. Made of cedar or spruce, the instrument has a resonating space, which, when the strings are plucked, creates the guitar's quite distinctive sound. Over time, metal screws replaced the wooden tuning pegs. Today's guitar strings are usually made of nylon.

LIFE & TIMES

Spain's turbulent century

TWENTIETH-CENTURY SPAIN WILL BEST BE REMEMBERED FOR ONE MAJOR EVENT, THE SPANISH CIVIL WAR, AND ONE INDIVIDUAL, GENERAL FRANCISCO FRANCO. THE WAR RAGED FOR THREE YEARS AND CLAIMED APPROXIMATELY 500,000 LIVES, BUT FRANCO'S REGIME—WHICH LASTED FROM 1939 UNTIL HIS DEATH IN 1975—WAS SO DAMAGING THAT IT WAS A LONG TIME BEFORE THE COUNTRY RECOVERED FROM HIS REACTIONARY, DICTATORIAL POLICIES.

The Spanish Civil War grew out of many years of political turbulence and increasing polarization. Early in 1936, the conservative factions—backed by business, military, and Catholic Church leaders—became concerned about the social reforms that were likely to take place under the newly elected Popular Front government. The military staged a series of rebellions in July, and on October 1 General Francisco Franco appointed himself both leader of the armed forces and head of state.

Officially supported by Mexico and the Soviet Union (and unofficially by volunteers from a number of other countries, including the United States), the Republicans were no match for Franco's Nationalist forces, who had the aid of Mussolini and Hitler. The war ended on April 1, 1939.

Above right A dramatic poster from the Spanish Revolution, calling on the people to "smash Fascism." About a half a million people lost their lives during the course of the conflict.

FRANCO AND BEYOND

General Franco's 35-year regime was characterized by isolation, repression, and censorship. After the war, he set up concentration camps, executing thousands of his political opponents. Catholicism became the only legal religion and Spanish the only legal language. Divorce and contraception were banned, and women could be imprisoned for adultery. Spain was excluded from both NATO and the United Nations, and an estimated half a million citizens fled the country (including many writers, artists, and musicians).

Spain, twentieth century
- ★ Birthplace of Joaquin Rodrigo
- ★ Birthplace of Pablo Casals
- ★ Birthplace of Andrés Segovia
- –· Modern country borders

PICASSO'S PROTESTS

Spanish painter and sculptor Pablo Picasso (1881–1973) was a pacifist, socialist, and ardent Republican, but was always careful not to allow politics to intrude into his art. But in 1937, he was so outraged at the devastation wreaked by Franco's army that he created a series of illustrations entitled *The Dream and Lie of Franco*, which portray the general as a grotesque monster.

On April 27, 1937, Hitler's army (acting on Franco's instructions) bombed the Basque village of Guernica in northern Spain. About 1,600 civilians were killed or wounded. Horrified by the newspaper photographs, Picasso added four more sketches to the *Franco* series, and began painting what would become his masterpiece. *Guernica* was completed in just over three weeks and is a massive work: 11 feet (3.5 m) tall and 26 feet (7.8 m) wide. It features black-and-white nightmare images of grief-stricken mothers, dead children, and mutilated humans and animals. The painting was featured in the Spanish pavilion of the World's Fair (1937), and traveled the world until eventually it found its true home—at the Reina Sofía museum in Madrid—on the one hundredth anniversary of Picasso's birth in 1981.

Above General Franco takes the salute at a victory parade during the Spanish Civil War.

Spain finally became a member of the UN in 1955. In the 1960s Franco began to relax some of his policies, and the beleaguered economy began to improve. Upon Franco's death in 1975, Juan Carlos de Borbón was crowned King of Spain, and democracy returned.

In the 1970s and 1980s, many social reforms were initiated. Women were granted equal rights, religious freedom was restored, and contraception and abortion became legalized.

TWO EXILES: PABLO CASALS AND ANDRÉS SEGOVIA

Two of the greatest performing musicians of the twentieth century, the cellist Pablo Casals and the classical guitarist Andrés Segovia, escaped their native Spain at the outset of the war.

Born in Catalonia in 1876, Casals graduated from the Escola Municipal de Música at age 16, and by his twenties was performing for the crowned heads of Europe. In 1919, he formed and conducted the trio Orquesta Pau Casals in Barcelona, which disbanded when war erupted. Casals passionately supported the Republican government, relocating to France during the war years (which coincided with his recordings of the Bach cello suites). He swore never to return to Spain while Franco was in power, and died aged 96 in Puerto Rico—two years before Franco's death.

Andrés Segovia (1893–1987) achieved his goal to "win the guitar a respected place in the great music schools, along with the piano, violin, and other instruments." Like Casals, Segovia was a child prodigy, learning to play guitar at the age of four. He was performing publicly at 16, and was at the peak of his career when civil war broke out.

Segovia left Spain in 1936, and lived in Italy, Uruguay, England, and the United States before eventually returning home. In 1954, Joaquin Rodrigo composed his famous *Fantasia para un gentilhombre* for Segovia, a concerto for guitar and orchestra. Segovia died in 1987 in Madrid at the age of 94, six years after King Juan Carlos awarded him the title Marquess of Salobreña.

Left Andrés Segovia, photographed here in 1968, was one of Spain's great musical exports. His musicianship and virtuosity were widely admired.

Michael Tippett

JANUARY 2, 1905–JANUARY 8, 1998

TIPPETT AND BRITTEN ARE OFTEN MENTIONED IN THE SAME BREATH, YET, WHILE BRITTEN WAS CONSIDERED "CLEVER" AND SKILLED, TIPPETT WAS JUDGED CLUMSY AND NAÏVE. AND ALTHOUGH TIPPETT WAS OLDER THAN BRITTEN, HE ALWAYS SEEMED MUCH YOUNGER, WITH A ZEST FOR MODERN LIFE EMBODIED IN HIS SPIRITED SOUNDWORLD. TIPPETT'S MUSIC IS OFTEN WILD, THORNY, SPLASHY, AND OPULENT. HE TOOK MORE RISKS THAN OTHER BRITISH COMPOSERS OF HIS AGE.

Michael Tippett was born in Edwardian London, though brought up outside it, by a prosperous and politically progressive family. He remained a man of the Left all his life, and took an interest in the work of Swiss psychologist Carl Jung. Tippet said that this assisted him to work out his sexuality as a gay man, of which, like Britten, he made no secret. Learning the piano as a youth gained Tippett a place at London's Royal College of Music (1923–1928), which in 1930 he returned to solely in order to develop his ability in counterpoint—a skill he used (some say overused) in his concert and opera music. He found work as a choir trainer and teacher in a southern suburb of London where he lived (1928–1951) and composed music for community pageants and socialist plays. He also conducted the South London Orchestra for Unemployed Musicians and eventually became Director of Music at Morley College (1940–1951), where Holst once taught. Here he promoted the study and performing of English madrigal composers and of Purcell, an interest he shared with Britten, whom he met at this

Right Tippett was highly self-critical of his early works, and came into his own as a composer when he was in his thirties.

Far right A rehearsal for Tippett's opera *The Midsummer Marriage*, at London's Covent Garden, in January 1955.

Below Tippett (second from left) with conductor Sir Adrian Boult, composer Ralph Vaughan Williams, and Ursula Vaughan Williams.

time. As a composer, though, more direct influences were Hindemith and Stravinsky; the warmly life-affirming opening of Tippett's *Symphony No. 2* (1960) is borrowed from the Russian.

DEVELOPMENT OF A PERSONAL STYLE

Tippett's personal style developed slowly. It can be heard initially in his first *Piano Sonata* (1937) and then the *Concerto for Double String Orchestra* (1939) where the influence of both folk song and the madrigalists can be followed. His most noted work of this time remains his most celebrated, *A Child Of Our Time* (1941). This oratorio was written in reaction to the assassination of a Nazi soldier by a Polish youth. It was innovative in its anti-fascist response to current events, but is treasured now chiefly for the settings of "Negro" spirituals that are used, Bach-like, as chorales. When Tippett later conducted a performance in the United States, he was moved to hear the audience singing along with the spirituals.

Discover the music

Piano Sonata (1937)

Concerto for Double String Orchestra (1939)

A Child Of Our Time (1941)

Symphony No. 2 (1960)

The Vision of Augustine (1965)

The Mask of Time (1984)

His debut opera, *The Midsummer Marriage* (1955), occupied him for 12 years. Supposedly about a couple contemplating marriage, its synthesized mixture of Jungian themes and opera conventions, together with an awkward libretto by the composer, makes for an intriguing, if unruly experience, buoyed by some ecstatic music. The same might be said for his other four operas: *King Priam* (1962), *The Knot Garden* (1970), *The Ice Break* (1977), and *New Year* (1989).

In the 1960s his style became more radical, in keeping with the times. The collage form of the *Concerto for Orchestra* (1963) displays this, as does the harmonically spiky oratorio *The Vision of Augustine* (1965). Later, Tippett became more ambitious still in making comprehensive references to social concerns, not only in his later operas but also his *Symphonies No. 3* (1972) and *4* (1977), and the oratorio *The Mask of Time* (1984). He spent the second half of his life in England's West Country, and died at the age of 93.

"*Music is a performance and needs an audience.*"

Below left William Walton with Edith Sitwell (left) and an unidentifed woman at a garden party in 1953. The Sitwells introduced Walton to poets, writers, and painters.

WILLIAM WALTON (1902–1983)

Benjamin Britten called William Walton "one of the twentieth-century stars of British music." Walton, born in Lancashire, won, as a 10-year-old, a choral scholarship to Oxford University, where he spent his youth and met rich people who became his patrons. The bohemian Sitwells championed him, and Walton's setting of Edith Sitwell's surreal poems, *Façade* (1923), brought the new "jazzy" style of French modern music to Britain. His *Viola Concerto* (1929), the choral extravaganza *Belshazzar's Feast* (1931) and the *Symphony No. 1* (1935) showed a stylistic magpie mind at work that could nevertheless produce something personal. Walton's film music, modeled in symphonic style on Prokofiev's, was well used in Laurence Olivier's versions of Shakespeare's *Henry V* (1944) and *Richard III* (1955). After World War II, Walton lived on the Italian island of Ischia and produced more modest work.

Benjamin Britten

NOVEMBER 22, 1913–DECEMBER 4, 1976

IT SEEMS FITTING THAT THE WORDS "BRITAIN" AND "BRITTEN" SOUND
THE SAME. CRITICS HAVE WRITTEN OF BRITTEN AS THE FIRST "NATURAL"
COMPOSER BORN IN ENGLAND SINCE PURCELL OVER TWO CENTURIES EARLIER.
THEY MEAN BY THIS THAT HE HAD A CREATIVE EASE, FLUENCY, AND MASTERY
IN WRITING FOR INSTRUMENTS AND FOR SETTING WORDS.

Benjamin Britten was certainly the first British composer to write operas—such as *Peter Grimes* and *Billy Budd*—that have been staged internationally and that have held their place in the repertory. He was also astute in the careful way he organized his career as a full-time composer.

Britten was born in the east coast town of Lowestoft, where his father was a dentist. His mother, a pianist and singer, instilled in her son strong ambitions to succeed musically. Britten claimed that "I have always found reading music easier than reading books," and by his early teens he had written over 100 pieces, some of which he re-used, as in the *Simple Symphony* (1934).

The modernist composer Frank Bridge was certainly impressed enough to give the teenage Britten lessons for which he had to travel to London. Bridge helped Britten to hone practical skills, which school and the subsequent Royal College of Music (1930–1932) did not. Britten re-paid the debt to his teacher in his first international success, the virtuoso *Variations on a Theme of Frank Bridge* (1937).

Discover the music

Variations on a Theme of Frank Bridge (1937)
Peter Grimes (1945)
The Rape of Lucretia (1946)
The Young Person's Guide to the Orchestra (1947)
Albert Herring (1947)
Billy Budd (1951)
The Turn of the Screw (1954)
Noye's Fludde (1958)
War Requiem (1962)

Below Britten (at piano) accompanies Pears as they perform an aria from *Billy Budd* for musicians Ronald Duncan (center) and Arthur Oldham.

While living in London between 1930 and 1939, Britten created scores for a range of progressive and socialist artists working in film (the GPO Film Unit), radio (BBC), and stage (the Group Theatre), among them the poet W.H. Auden. Britten wrote, often at brisk speed, incidental music for 30 short films (among them *Coal Face* and *Night Mail*), 20 radio plays, and 18 stage plays. An early stylistic inspiration of his had been Vaughan Williams, but he soon gained more adventurous continental influences from Mahler, Stravinsky, and Berg. Mahler's impact is clear in the sonorities of *Sinfonia da requiem* (1941), while Britten's first full opera *Peter Grimes* (1945) is based on Berg's *Wozzeck*.

MOVING TO THE USA, AND BACK AGAIN

In 1939, when "Europe looked finished," Auden moved to America. Britten followed with his lover, tenor Peter Pears. Aiming to establish himself professionally in the United States, Britten gained some commissions, including one for the first and most famous of his nine operas, the tragic drama *Peter Grimes*. He also became

Above Baritone Nmon Ford dominates the stage during a rehearsal of Britten's opera *Billy Budd* at the State Opera House in Hamburg, Germany in March 2007.

WAR REQUIEM (1962)

Britten's monumental choral work, the pacifist *War Requiem* (1962), is an homage to those who died in war. A non-liturgical adaptation of the requiem Mass, and based on poems by World War I poet Wilfrid Owen, it was written for three specific soloists—German baritone Dietrich Fischer-Dieskau, British tenor Peter Pears, and the Russian soprano Galina Vishnevskaya. Its message of reconciliation and its grand scale made it a hit with British audiences.

Below Britten (left) with his lifelong partner, the tenor Peter Pears (1910–1986). Britten wrote a number of roles specifically for his lover.

friendly with Aaron Copland, who showed Britten how to operate as a music entrepreneur.

Britten and Pears returned to England in 1942, but as pacifists, gave state-sponsored concerts in place of war work. Just four weeks after the war's end, Pears starred as the unloved fisherman when Sadler's Wells Opera gave *Peter Grimes* its wildly successful première. From that moment Britten very shrewdly advanced his status as the country's leading living composer. He wrote pieces for children to listen to (*The Young Person's Guide to the Orchestra*, 1947) and to perform (*Noye's Fludde*, 1958). He also created a budget opera company to tour works that he composed for them, such as the comical *Albert Herring* (1947) and the rather creepy *Turn of the Screw* (1954).

Britten and Pears lived together in the isolated seaport of Aldeburgh, near Britten's birthplace, where they ran an annual summer festival devoted to his works. They built around them a rather sycophantic "court" where Britten's insecurities and reputed spitefulness were entertained. However, worldwide he was admired for the simplicity and ingenuity of his compositional style, which became ever more limpid through the years, especially so in the evocations of night that absorbed him (in the *Serenade for Tenor, Horn and Strings* of 1944, the *Nocturne* of 1958, and the opera *A Midsummer Night's Dream*). Yet Britten was equally judged a throwback to 1930s neo-classicism, while his fascination with boyhood "innocence" was considered by some commentators to be dubious.

LIFE & TIMES

Great Britain in the mid-twentieth century

"BRITAIN CAN TAKE IT" WAS A SLOGAN USED DURING THE BLITZ OF LATE 1940 AND EARLY 1941, WHEN THE GERMAN LUFTWAFFE BOMBED LONDON, INDUSTRIAL CITIES AND PORTS, KILLING CIVILIANS, AND DESTROYING HOMES. BUT BRITAIN DID INDEED "TAKE IT" AND SURVIVED TO BE ONE OF THE WAR'S VICTORS. THE POST-WAR PERIOD UP TO THE MID-1970S WAS ONE OF IMPROVED SOCIAL SECURITY, GROWING AFFLUENCE, RISING BIRTH RATES, AND TECHNOLOGICAL INNOVATION. BRITAIN BECAME THE STAR OF THE SWINGING SIXTIES.

Britain managed World War II (1939–1945) far better than the 1914–1918 war, assisted by the ingenuity of the defence system RADAR, by the Royal Air Force in fighting off a series of attacks by the German Luftwaffe known as the Battle of Britain (1940), and the inspirational speeches of the Prime Minister Winston Churchill (1874–1965).

Above right A World War II ration book for various foodstuffs. The British people lived with the rationing of food and essential services well into the 1950s.

Great Britain, twentieth century
- ☆ Birthplace of Benjamin Britten
- ★ Birthplace of Michael Tippett
- ★ Birthplace of William Walton
- –- Modern country borders

REBUILDING BRITAIN

A payment scheme called Lend-Lease, which became a loan, was provided by the United States and helped Britain handle the huge cost of arming and defending itself. Yet the years of food rationing and austerity continued well after the war until the mid-1950s.

During the war Britain began to plan for a post-war society. The Beveridge Plan (1942) devised a social security system that also paved the way for the National Health Service in 1948. The *Butler Act* (1944) established free secondary education for children up to the age of 15. These plans were drawn up by Conservatives, but put into operation by the first-ever majority Labour government, which came to power in 1945 and nationalized many industries including coal, rail, and electricity. But it also dampened consumer spending and promoted wage restraint.

Britain's colonial embarrassment ended with the constitution of the Commonwealth (no longer "British") in 1949 and the granting of independence to a number of its former colonies. This took place in response to freedom movements, such as Mahatma Gandhi's civil disobedience campaigns in India.

When the Conservatives regained power in the 1950s, employment levels were high and Britain embraced American-style consumerism. "Baby boom" post-war teenagers adopted or created new cultural trends that embodied a confidence and hedonism that were unlike the recent past. From 1965 on, it was Labour's turn to claim credit for Britain's seeming success. The Beatles, The Rolling Stones, The Who, and Led Zeppelin were among the British rock bands that gained global esteem.

However, Britain had been spending beyond its means. In 1967 Labour Prime Minister Harold Wilson (1916–1995) devalued the currency. In the early 1970s a global increase in oil costs created a major crisis of inflation generating the "three day week," substantial strikes, and protests. In 1979, the new Conservative government of Margaret Thatcher ditched Keynesianism for a free market ideology, and a new period of economic delusion began.

THE ARTS COUNCIL
Britain's first systematic arts subsidy scheme was set up in 1940 as CEMA, the Council for Encouragement in Music and the Arts. Swayed by Vaughan Williams, it supported unemployed artists and produced regional

Above An air raid over London's iconic Tower Bridge during the Battle of Britain in 1940. The Battle of Britain was one of the most famous battles of World War II.

tours by orchestras and singers to factories doing war work. John Maynard Keynes took over as chairman in 1942 and re-directed its work toward his pet project, a national ballet company. He changed its name in 1945 to the Arts Council of Great Britain and he bought up the Covent Garden Theatre (now the Royal Opera House, Covent Garden) to re-house the Sadler's Wells Ballet Company (now the Royal Ballet). The Arts Council became an influential example of the British "arm's-length principle" of public money being distributed for arts projects, not by government, but by a non-governmental agency staffed by bureaucrats, advised by practitioners. However, it has been rarely out of trouble for the choices it has made.

BARBARA HEPWORTH (1903–1975)

Hepworth (right) was a highly influential sculptor, who crafted objects of simple, geometric forms that produced an almost elemental, prehistoric impact. Born in Yorkshire, she trained at the Leeds School of Art where she met Henry Moore (1898–1986), with whom her style is often linked, if not confused. She married twice, the second time to artist Ben Nicholson (1894–1982). They moved with her large family to the Cornish port of St Ives at the start of World War II. The spot became an artists' colony. After the war Hepworth gained international notice at the 1950 Venice Biennale. She provided scenery and costumes for Michael Tippett's opera *The Midsummer Marriage* (1955) while her *Family of Man* (from a series) resides at Britten's Snape Concert Hall. Barbara Hepworth embodies an international modernism to which only Tippett responded. Hepworth died in a fire at her St Ives house in 1975.

Aram Khachaturian

JUNE 6, 1903–MAY 1, 1978

ARMENIA IS A SMALL COUNTRY CRAMMED BETWEEN TURKEY TO THE SOUTH, AZERBAIJAN AND IRAN TO THE EAST, WITH GEORGIA AND THE VAST SPACES OF RUSSIA TO THE NORTH. IT HAS BEEN FOUGHT OVER, CHOPPED UP, REUNITED, AND BEEN PART OF THE OTTOMAN EMPIRE, OF IMPERIAL RUSSIA, THEN THE SOVIET UNION BEFORE ACHIEVING FINALLY INDEPENDENCE IN 1991.

Each change added another cultural layer, making its folk music tradition one of the most diverse, ancient, and thanks to a unique system of notation devised in the eighth century, one of the best preserved and documented. There are songs and instrumental music designed to accompany work, dance, worship, storytelling, weddings, and other rituals, each kind of music with its own distinct melodic and rhythmic style. It was these subconsciously absorbed sounds—learned as any child learns language—that would give Khachaturian's music its strong Armenian accent.

THE STUDENT YEARS

Compared with most professional composers, Khachaturian was a late developer. He shared his family's love of folk music and dancing, played in the school band, and made up his own music on the family piano, but it was for biology that he went to Moscow to study in 1921. However, Moscow's busy cultural life ignited his musical ambitions, and by 1922 he was studying the cello and later, composition. Progress was swift and he had already had music published when he began his serious professional composition training at the Moscow Conservatoire a few years later.

Above right Such is the regard in which the composer is held that the concert hall in Yerevan, Armenia is named the Aram Khachaturian Concert Hall.

Left Andrei Zhdanov (center) with Joseph Stalin. Zhdanov was responsible for Soviet cultural policy and kept a close eye on composers, writers, and artists who could be considered "non-conformist."

Some of the many works he composed during these student years, such as the *Toccata for Piano,* show touches of Ravel, but others, like the *Dance Suite,* are based on folk tunes from Armenia or nearby regions. He was clearly working his way toward a synthesis of Western symphonic procedures with the colorful folk music absorbed in his youth. The huge success of the *Piano Concerto* signaled his arrival at this goal in 1936.

PROFESSIONAL LIFE

Khachaturian believed in the communist ideal. He became a party member in 1943, was elected to the Composers' Union even before completing his studies, and was an officer of the union for many years. His ballet *Gayaneh* is even set on a collective farm. Rather mysteriously then, given this official commitment, plus his music's clarity and clear connection to popular music, he was censured for "formalism" (that is, modernism) in 1948, together with Prokofiev and Shostakovich, by Stalin's "art tsar," the notoriously tin-eared and incompetent Andrei Zhdanov. It was a shattering experience, but he made the requisite groveling apology, took refuge in writing mostly film music, albeit in unchanged style, and remained friends with his fellow musical criminals.

After Stalin's death, Khachaturian visited the West frequently to conduct and record his works, scoring public success with his music, and winning great affection from orchestral musicians with his personal charm and technical proficiency.

Khachaturian's compositional output was large. There are symphonies, ballets, film scores, plenty of incidental theater music, piano music, a small quantity

of chamber music and, among his finest achievements, six concertos. There are also several patriotic marches for brass or wind band.

This is music dominated by melody with an unusual and characteristically Armenian melodic contour and restlessness of rhythm. The orchestral works are enlivened by colorful and inventive orchestration and the fast movements have the intoxicatingly wild energy that makes the *Sabre Dance* so popular, sadly to the exclusion of so much else of equal energy and possibly greater interest. Likewise, the dreamy extract from the ballet *Spartacus*, known popularly as the theme tune to *The Onedin Line* television series, is just one example that can be easily matched with a little exploration of Khachaturian's extensive recorded legacy.

Khachaturian was awarded numerous Soviet honors but would perhaps have taken greater pride, passionate Armenian as he was, in being the composer of his newly independent country's national anthem and appearing on an Armenian banknote in 1998. He was named UNESCO Artist of the Year in 2003 in recognition of his achievement in promoting his country's culture.

Above Marat Shemiunov (Crassus) and Anastasia Matvienko (Sabina) starred in the 2008 Mikhailovsky Theater's production of *Spartacus* at the London Coliseum.

THE "BELL" SYMPHONY (1943)

Khachaturian's dramatic *Symphony No. 2*—the "Bell"—is more somber in mood than his other two symphonies. The composer wanted to convey the sufferings and struggles of ordinary people during the Great Patriotic War, when the Soviet Union was at war with Nazi Germany. Khachaturian said that when writing the third movement, the Andante, he tried to imagine the "tragic scenes of German brutality."

Discover the music

Trio for Clarinet, Violin and Piano (1932)
Piano Concerto (1936)
Masquerade (1941)
Gayaneh (1942)
Symphony No. 2 "Bell" (1943)
Spartacus (1954)
Concerto–Rhapsody for cello and orchestra (1963)

Dmitri Shostakovich

SEPTEMBER 25, 1906–AUGUST 9, 1975

A GIANT OF TWENTIETH-CENTURY MUSIC, DMITRI SHOSTAKOVICH WAS ONE OF WHAT HAS BEEN ACCURATELY CALLED "THE CURSED GENERATION" OF SOVIET COMPOSERS, THOSE WHO LIVED THEIR ARTISTIC LIVES SUBJECT TO THE UNPREDICTABLE WHIMS OF THE STALINIST REGIME THAT COULD WITHER OR OBLITERATE THEIR CAREERS OVERNIGHT. SHOSTAKOVICH SURVIVED BY SEEMING TO SUBMIT WHILE REMAINING, THROUGH HIS MUSIC, HIS OWN SUPREMELY ELOQUENT MAN.

Shostakovich's mother was a professional pianist but Dmitri refused piano lessons until he was nine, when he revealed a prodigious talent. He could play pieces by Mozart and Haydn within a month, Bach preludes and fugues within a year and was soon composing his own music. He entered the Leningrad Conservatoire at 13, composed his Op. 1, *Scherzo for Orchestra* in the same year and by the time he graduated in 1923, was a brilliant pianist, already planning his first symphony.

RIDING THE ROLLERCOASTER

His *Symphony No. 1*, completed while he was still a 19 year-old postgraduate student, quickly won him both international fame as the first Soviet symphonist of real stature, and numerous commissions to compose music for propagandist films, plays, and ballets. These earned him party approval, but his own creative music favored the dissonant modernism of Berg, Bartók, and Prokofiev. He thus upset

officialdom with his 1930 opera, *The Nose*, based on Gogol's satirical story. Audiences loved its surreal, acid satire and appropriately spiky music, but party apparatchiks labeled it "formalist" and it was withdrawn.

Less abrasive works gradually returned him to favor but, in 1936, the cycle was repeated. His successful, long-running opera, *Lady Macbeth of the Mtsensk District*, was suddenly condemned as "muddle, not music." This was a time of purges and disappearances and, while his colleagues joined in the condemnation with hurtful alacrity, the terrified Shostakovich, with a suitcase packed in expectation of the midnight knock on the door, made a cringing apology.

CLOSE TO THE EDGE

In 1948 the party set out firm ideological guidelines and independent-minded artists in all disciplines were denounced for "formalism and anti-democratic tendencies." Even the wartime patriotism aroused by Shostakovich's

---

Discover the music

Symphony No. 1 (1923–1924)
Lady Macbeth of the Mtsensk District (1930–1932)
Piano Concerto No. 1 (1933)
Symphony No. 5 (1937)
Symphony No. 7 "Leningrad" (1941)
Violin Concerto No. 1 (1947–1948)
Piano Concerto No. 2 (1957)
String Quartet No. 8 (1960)

Left A portrait by Russian artist I.A. Serebryany (1907–1979). Shostakovich was one of the most important Russian composers of the twentieth century.

Right Shostakovich plays the piano for friends on the occasion of his fiftieth birthday in 1956.

defiant *Leningrad* symphony did not save him from censure. His music was banned, another public apology delivered, and then it was back to humiliating work on propaganda films and cantatas aggrandizing Stalin. Real music was safely hidden in the desk drawer. The requirement to attend international conferences as a Soviet representative, and read out prepared speeches was a further humiliation.

Even in the so-called "thaw" after Stalin's death in 1953, artistic freedom remained quite restricted. Some previously withheld works such as the Jewish song cycle were released in 1955, but a revival of *Lady Macbeth* was denied. Any apparent musical pessimism or frivolity was criticized.

In his last 20 years, resistance weakened by ill health, Shostakovich was increasingly manipulated or coerced into official posts and awarded honors that made him appear an establishment figure. But he could still raise party hackles. In 1962, he used Yevgeny Yevtushenko's poems—clearly critical of the regime—in his *Symphony No. 13*. Although certain lines were changed, it was probably only the composer's recent induction into the

SYMPHONY NO. 5 (1937)

Shostakovich regained official favor with the seemingly conformist *Symphony No. 5*. But is the triumphant finale really the "onward and upward" music the party demanded or a caricature? And in the slow movement that reduced its first audience to tears, do not those woodwind solos suggest voices snuffed out before their time? Solomon Volkov's book, *Testimony*, reports Shostakovich saying, "The rejoicing is forced, created under threat," and of the slow movement, "The audience understood." This view of Shostakovich as the quiet subversive inserting coded anti-Stalinist messages into his music has been challenged, but it is endorsed by many eminent Russian musicians and affords convincing insights into the music composed after this time.

Below Maria Ewing (center) with the chorus of female convicts in a scene from the 1994 Metropolitan Opera première of Shostakovich's *Lady Macbeth of the Mtsensk District.*

Communist Party, a source of intense shame to him, that prevented cancellation of the première.

Throughout his life Shostakovich believed in the ideals of communism as strongly as he fought against the perversions of Stalinism. A line from his penultimate symphony may serve as an epitaph to his hugely productive but ultimately tragic life: "What comfort is there for talent among villains and fools?"

"I always try to make myself as widely understood as possible; and if I don't succeed, I consider it my own fault."

Galina Ustvolskaya

JUNE 17, 1919–DECEMBER 22, 2006

VIRTUALLY UNKNOWN IN THE WEST UNTIL THE ADVENT OF *PERESTROIKA* IN THE 1980S, GALINA USTVOLSKAYA WAS A COMPLEX AND CONTRADICTORY HUMAN BEING: A WOMAN WHO DETESTED HEARING OTHER WOMEN PERFORM HER WORK, AND A RUSSIAN WHO DELETED ALL RUSSIAN-INSPIRED PIECES FROM HER CATALOG. THOUGH NOT RELIGIOUS, MUCH OF HER MUSIC HAD OVERTLY RELIGIOUS THEMES.

Most of Ustvolskaya's life remains a mystery. She was born in Petrograd (later Leningrad and St Petersburg) in 1919 and attended the Leningrad Conservatory between 1937 and 1947, interrupting her studies during the war to serve in a military hospital. She taught at Leningrad until she retired in 1977.

Above right Galina Ustvolskaya pictured in the 1950s. Shostakovich is reported to have labeled the composer a "phenomenon."

RELATIONSHIP WITH SHOSTAKOVICH

One of her instructors at the conservatory was Dmitri Shostakovich, with whom she had a difficult, intense relationship, both personally and professionally. The older composer had great faith in his protégée, and predicted that she would achieve "worldwide renown." He valued her critical opinion, and would often consult her about his own compositions.

During the 1950s—some time after Shostakovich allegedly proposed marriage following the death of his first wife—Ustvolskaya acrimoniously severed all ties with her mentor, and denied that he had any influence on her compositions. She later married a student who was many years her junior.

Left Russian cellist Mstislav Rostropovich (1927–2007) recorded Ustvolskaya's *Grand Duet for Cello and Piano* in the 1960s. He commented that the composer's shy demeanor belied the intensity of her music.

Discover the music

Trio for Clarinet, Violin, and Piano (1949)

Piano Sonata No. 2 (1949)

Violin Sonata (1952)

Symphonic Poem No. 1 (1958)

Grand Duet for Piano and Cello (1959)

Duet for Piano and Violin (1964)

Composition No. 1 Dona Nobis Pacem (1971)

Symphony No. 3 Jesus Messiah, Save Us (1983)

THE LADY WITH THE HAMMER

Ustvolskaya's official oeuvre consists of a total of 21 works including a piano concerto, six piano sonatas, five symphonies, and several chamber orchestrations. For most of her career, she was forced to balance her personal musical integrity with public demand and financial necessity. Some of her early works include pieces that were inspired by Russian folk tradition, as well as patriotic Soviet compositions with such titles as *Young Pioneers* (1950), *The Hero's Exploit* (1957), and *Fire on the Steppes* (1958). (She would later remove these pieces from her list of works.)

The music of Galina Ustvolskaya shares qualities of the modernist, minimalist, expressionist, and avant-garde movements, but is so individual that it is virtually impossible to categorize. The composer experimented with various instrumental combinations and came up with some highly idiosyncratic blends. For example, the 1949 *Octet* combines four violins, two oboes, piano, and timpani; and *Dies Irae* (1973) was composed for piano, eight double basses, and a homemade wooden percussion cube, which one observer has evocatively described as a "coffin box."

Above A view of St Petersburg, the beautiful city where Galina Ustvolskaya lived and worked for most of her life.

Dutch music critic Elmer Schoenberger dubbed Ustvolskaya "the lady with the hammer," possibly because of the angry, violent effect produced by her dissonant chords and insistent repetition. The piano is perhaps the instrument best suited to express her driving, forceful style.

The ultimate perfectionist, Ustvolskaya's total output was relatively small, because she could take up to eight years to complete a composition. The first time Westerners heard her music played was at the 1986 *Wiener Festwochen* (Vienna International Festival). As she grew older, Ustvolskaya became increasingly reclusive and rarely left St Petersburg, although she made an exception in 1986 to attend a performance of her work in Amsterdam. In 1999—the year of her eightieth birthday—Ustvolskaya's music was featured at the British Royal Academy of Music's annual festival.

SYMPHONY NO.5 AMEN (1989–1990)

Galina Ustvolskaya was a deeply spiritual woman, and although she didn't practice any formal creed, her later works were strongly imbued with Christian themes. She maintained that all her music sounded best when performed in a church, "without scholarly introductions and analyses." Her Symphonies 1 to 5 written between 1971 and 1990 all have religious subtitles; some of them were based on hymns written by eleventh-century German Benedictine monk Hermannus of Reichenau, also known as Hermann the Cripple because of his severe physical disabilities.

Symphony No. 5 Amen was Ustvolskaya's final composition. As in many of her symphonies, the 12-minute work was scored for what most people would class as a chamber ensemble, and features solo voice, tuba, trumpet, oboe, violin, and "coffin box" percussion. Throughout the symphony, a speaker recites the Lord's Prayer, with long intervals between phrases. Ustvolskaya instructed that the soloist "must recite the text as if he were fervently praying to God." The effect, as various music critics have noted, is stark, bleak, uncompromising, and challenging. *Amen* made such an impression on the English reviewer Peter Grahame Woolf that he admitted to "going into a degree of shock" when he first heard it.

The Soviet state

"MAY YOU LIVE IN INTERESTING TIMES" SAYS AN ANCIENT CHINESE CURSE AND FEW HAVE
LIVED IN TIMES MORE "INTERESTING" THAN TWENTIETH-CENTURY RUSSIANS. BEGINNING
THE CENTURY IN A NEAR-FEUDAL AUTOCRACY, THEY SUFFERED THROUGH WORLD WAR I,
REVOLUTION, AND BITTER CIVIL WAR TO THE BRIGHT DAWN OF IDEALISTIC COMMUNISM
ONLY TO FIND THEY HAD EXCHANGED ONE HEGEMONY FOR ANOTHER, EVEN MORE BRUTAL.

Pressure had been growing for reform of Russia's
essentially medieval society ever since the French
Revolution. Even in 1900, many serfs, the bulk of the
nation, lived in such appalling poverty that the fear-
some Russian winter carried off thousands every year.
In 1905, mutiny on the battleship *Potemkin* sparked
the first revolution in the capital St Petersburg, later
renamed Petrograd and subsequently Leningrad. It
was savagely put down but wrung some reforms from
the tsar. A parliament, the Duma, was established but,
dominated by the nobility and bourgeoisie, did little
for the ill-fed, landless, and mostly illiterate peasantry.

The privations of the Great War
proved the last straw. Armed rebellion
in February 1917 forced Tsar Nicholas's abdication and in October the
ineffectual Provisional Government
was itself overthrown, establishing
Lenin as leader of a Bolshevik government that returned the capital to
Moscow because Petrograd, swarming with heavily
armed ex-soldiers, was too dangerous. The treasury
was nearly empty, inflation was rampant, and the wide-
flung empire was in severe danger of dissolution.

Soviet Union, mid-twentieth century
☆ Birthplace of Aram Khachaturian
★ Birthplace of Dmitri Shostakovich and Galina Ustvolskaya
--- Modern country borders

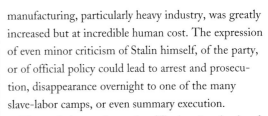

Left A work entitled *Nuvola dorata* by Russian abstract painter Wassily Kandinsky (1866–1944). Kandinsky was one of many creative artists who made a life for himself outside of Russia.

Below Britain's prime minister Sir Winston Churchill (left), American president Franklin D. Roosevelt (center), and Soviet leader Joseph Stalin met at Yalta on the Black Sea in 1945 to determine the reorganization of Europe following the end of World War II.

manufacturing, particularly heavy industry, was greatly increased but at incredible human cost. The expression of even minor criticism of Stalin himself, of the party, or of official policy could lead to arrest and prosecution, disappearance overnight to one of the many slave-labor camps, or even summary execution.

The statistics are depressing. The heroic role played by the USSR in World War II cost some 20 million Russian lives, more losses than all other combatant nations combined, but the death toll between 1918 and Stalin's death in 1956 is close to 48 million and—almost unbelievably—more than half died at the hands of their own countrymen.

Alas, such sacrifice achieved little for the ordinary Soviet citizen. Rather than improving housing and the supply of much-needed food and consumer goods, Stalin and his successors engaged in an ideological struggle between capitalism and communism. In a grotesque parody of the tsarist state which had inspired the Revolution, luxury was reserved for the elite and huge resources were poured into sustaining a massive army, a huge internal security apparatus, international subversion, competing in the arms race, the space race, supporting vassal states, and promoting the cause of world-wide communism.

As modern communications penetrated the Iron Curtain, the imbalance proved unsustainable. Internal dissatisfaction with living conditions grew steadily and the defections of Russia's great musicians, dancers, and authors told their own tale. Perhaps fortunately, neither Shostakovich nor Khachaturian lived to see communism, the noble ideal in which they had somehow retained faith through all their vicissitudes, proved impractical by human imperfection.

Worst of all, the White Russians, a coalition of the Bolsheviks' many opponents, launched a bitter Civil War that lasted until 1921, almost strangling the fragile revolution at birth.

EXODUS OF ARTISTS

Artists of all disciplines, including émigrés like Chagall, flocked to Moscow, thinking to celebrate the Revolution's heroes, create inspiring visions of the communist future and design buildings worthy of it, producing a wonderful creative flowering that was sadly short-lived. In 1918, even the relatively broad-minded Lenin censured the exuberant celebration of May Day by artists who, misreading his wishes, covered Moscow's buildings and even the Kremlin trees with brightly colored Cubist and Futurist paintings. By 1922, many creative artists, Chagall, Kandinsky, Stravinsky, Rachmaninov, and Glazunov among them, had left the country, disillusioned with restrictive officialdom, even before Lenin's premature death in 1924 disastrously opened the way for Stalin's rise to absolute power.

STALINISM AND AFTER

The USSR's achievements under Stalin in the decades leading up to World War II were enormous. Thousands of miles of railways and roads were built, communications and education dramatically improved and

ARTS AND RELIGION IN THE SOVIET STATE

In the arts, any poem, music, play, or painting that did not actively glorify the Revolution or was adjudged by the party apparatchiks to be "modernist" attracted harsh penalties. Jews and other religious believers were also targeted by the officially atheist state and most churches and synagogues were closed. With secret police and informers everywhere, no one at any level of society was safe. Composers like Khachaturian and Shostakovich attracted severe criticism and were probably only saved from a worse fate by their international fame. *Testimony by Volkov* and *Memories of Shostakovich* by writer Michael Ardov vividly evoke these terrible times.

Olivier Messiaen

DECEMBER 10, 1908–APRIL 27, 1992

LIKE THE EIFFEL TOWER, OLIVIER MESSIAEN IS UNIQUE, WITH NO
PRECURSORS, FEW SUCCESSORS, AND VERY FRENCH. HE WAS A TOWERING
FIGURE OF TWENTIETH-CENTURY MUSIC AND DEDICATED NEARLY ALL HIS COMPOSITIONS TO THE
CELEBRATION OF HIS SIMPLE, UNQUESTIONING CATHOLICISM—A PHILOSOPHICAL STANCE ALMOST
AS RARE IN MODERN TIMES AS THE SOUND OF HIS EXTRAORDINARILY INDIVIDUAL MUSIC.

Messiaen's ability to "see" sound as color made the piano irresistible. He taught himself to play and when he eventually received lessons, made such rapid progress that he was accepted into the Paris Conservatoire at 11 years of age. He won many awards, among them the Composition Prize in 1930, his graduation year, and one year later, not yet 23, he became principal organist of La Trinité, Paris, with its magnificent Cavaillé-Coll organ, a post he was to hold for 60 years.

MESSIAEN'S APPROACH TO MUSIC

The unique flavor of Messiaen's music depends largely on a deceptively simple idea he used throughout his career. Abandoning conventional scales, he devised his own by rearranging the sequence of tones and semitones within the octave. Then, by constructing both melody and harmony from these new scales—or modes—he created music in which familiar chords appear in an entirely novel context and to novel effect.

Above right Messiaen photographed in 1983. A hugely influential composer, he wrote a number of works for piano, many for his second wife, pianist Yvonne Loriod.

MESSIAEN, BIRDSONG, AND GOD

Messiaen always loved watching birds and, especially from 1950 onward, became increasingly fond of incorporating their songs, which he traveled widely to collect, into his music. This was sometimes constructed almost entirely of birdsong. *Catalogue d'oiseaux* for piano (1956–1958) and *Oiseaux exotiques* (1955–1956) for orchestra are examples. These works are still part of his religious celebratory agenda because he saw the whole of the natural world as a manifestation of the Christian God. Even in his frankly erotic texts in *Poèmes pour Mi* (1936), the song cycle written for his first wife, he is celebrating marital love as a Christian sacrament.

He also had a very personal approach to pulse and rhythm, describing himself once as "composer and rhythmacist." His fast movements are always very rhythmic, but they have a fluidity imparted by processes borrowed from Greek and Indian music. On the other hand, in slow movements, rhythm may almost completely disappear because of the extremely slow tempo. For example, *Le banquet céleste* (*The Celestial Banquet*), his first published work, is just 25 bars long but takes six minutes to perform. The effect is quite extraordinary. Western music before Messiaen moved forward in time. This is static beauty, like the stained glass windows he loved.

Most of Messiaen's early pieces are for the organ, but he gradually abandoned that instrument in favor of the orchestra, where he often used the electronic, ethereal voice of the ondes Martenot, together with various tuned percussion instruments and the piano, to create a bright, glittering, richly colored orchestral

Left Olivier Messiaen (at piano) with two of his students, the composers Michel Fano (center), and Pierre Boulez. Messiaen was considered a truly inspirational teacher.

Left Belgian baritone Jose Van Dam (right) during a dress rehearsal of Messiaen's only opera *St François d'Assise* at the 2003 Ruhr Triennale Arts Festival in Bochum, Germany.

sound with a distinctly Eastern touch. He once defined his objective in orchestration as "dazzlement."

Messiaen's only important chamber piece is *Quartet for the end of time*, composed for piano, clarinet, violin, and viola in 1940, while he was a prisoner of war. It was movingly premièred in front of 5,000 prisoners and is still one of his most performed and popular pieces.

INFLUENCES

Messiaen was a devoted and much loved teacher of composition, with Pierre Boulez, Karlheinz Stockhausen, and Iannis Xenakis among his distinguished pupils. Few chose to follow their teacher's personal compositional methods, but they profited from his lucid guidance through the thickets of serialism, the path most of them chose to pursue. Intriguingly, they in their turn influenced Messiaen into making some use of serial techniques, especially with regard to rhythm. In his later years, Messiaen largely returned to his stylistic beginnings, but in works that were conceived on a grand time scale that often required enormous forces, as in his sole opera, *St François d'Assise* (1975–1983), which lasts five hours and requires 150 singers and 120 instrumentalists.

Eclairs sur l'Au-delà, (*Revelations of the Hereafter*), completed in his final year, is a magnificent summation of his work and credo. It is a glowing orchestral tour de force, with a 128-strong orchestra sparingly and delicately used to portray the heaven in which its composer so ardently believed.

Discover the music

Le banquet céleste (1928)
L'Ascension (1933)
Quatuor pour la fin du temps (1940)
Vingt regards sur l'enfant Jésus (1944)
Turangalîla-Symphonie (1946–1948)
Catalogue d'oiseaux (1956–1958)
Et exspecto resurrectionum mortuorem (1964)
Méditations sur le mystère de la Sainte Trinité (1969)
Des canyons aux étoiles (1971–1974)

"I give bird songs to those who dwell in cities ... make rhythms for those who know only military marches or jazz, and paint colors for those who see none."

France between the wars

OLIVIER MESSIAEN WAS BORN INTO THE LAST DECADES OF LA BELLE ÉPOQUE, THE YEARS OF PEACE AND GLITTERING CULTURAL AND INTELLECTUAL ACTIVITY THAT ENLIVENED EUROPE'S CAPITALS BETWEEN THE FRANCO–PRUSSIAN WAR OF 1870 AND THE GREAT WAR OF 1914. AND NO CAPITAL GLITTERED MORE BRIGHTLY THAN PARIS WITH ITS ELEGANT BOULEVARDS, HAUTE COUTURE HOUSES, RISQUÉ CABARET SHOWS, SUPERB RESTAURANTS, ARTS NOUVEAU CAFÉS, AND THE WORLD'S TALLEST BUILDING, THE EIFFEL TOWER, STILL A NOVELTY.

Besides attracting the idle rich, the city became a magnet for the intellectually curious and radically minded whose revolutionary ideas challenged accepted practice in art, film, music, architecture, literature, theater, and philosophy.

PARIS—CITY OF EXCITEMENT

This was the Paris of the Fauvists Matisse and Dufy, Cubists Braque and Picasso, Diaghilev's Ballets Russes, writers Sartre, de Beauvoir, Proust, James Joyce, Gide, and Genet, to name but a few of those artists, French or émigré, who challenged the social and sexual mores of their time. In music, Debussy, Satie, Ravel, and their disciples had already re-asserted a French style against nineteenth-century Austro–German dominance and soon, in 1913, Stravinsky would shock Parisian sensibilities with *The Rite of Spring*.

Then, abruptly in 1914, Paris was transformed from the artistic capital of the world into an armed camp servicing 4.5 million combatants in a conflict that

Above right American entertainer Josephine Baker (1906–1975) brought the Charleston to Paris. She lived in France most of her life and was active in the French Resistance during World War II.

would consume approximately 10 million of the world's male population.

Post-war France had lost a generation of young men and was bankrupt. Much of the rich land of northern France was poisoned wasteland; fuel and food were scarce. Women who had run war-time offices, factories, and farms did not return quietly to their kitchens but continued their much more visible role in society, demanding the vote—granted only in 1946!—as well as access to the professions and property rights. Nor had the Russian Revolution of 1917 gone unnoticed. Many aristocratic Russian émigrés settled in Paris and both left- and right-wing political groups proliferated, ushering in two decades of political and social unrest.

Many demobilized conscripts from backward rural areas preferred the newly discovered comforts of the city, adding to the exodus from the land that had already begun through mechanization, placing great strain on urban resources and necessitating huge house building projects in France's cities.

WORLD WAR II AND BEYOND

When Hitler once more plunged Europe into full-scale war in 1939, France, militarily strong on paper, was rapidly overrun. Paris was taken in June 1940 and France was divided into a northern Occupied Zone and the unoccupied remainder, administered from Vichy by a collaborationist puppet government that was subservient to Berlin. Much of France's produce and manpower was sent to Germany. Food was scarce. The occupation period is still scathingly referred to in France as "Rutabagas," the despised root vegetable grown for cattle feed, which now reached the family

Left Two seminal figures of twentieth-century French culture and philosophy, writers Jean-Paul Sartre and Simone de Beauvoir.

dinner table. More seriously and shamefully, the French police participated, often enthusiastically, in the "Final Solution," rounding up thousands of Jews for the concentration camps.

The fast and humiliating defeat saved Paris from destruction and, surprisingly, the Germans actively encouraged the city's musical life. Even the avant-garde music of Messiaen and his contemporaries was performed despite Hitler's well-known aversion to "decadent" modernism. Questioned about it he said dismissively, "Let them be decadent. They're French." Avant-garde painting was suppressed, however, although Picasso and a number of other international subversives were allowed to remain, probably as a sign of Nazi tolerance.

With much of its infrastructure destroyed or crumbling through neglect, depleted in manpower, faced with almost medieval living conditions in large rural

CULTURAL LIFE BETWEEN THE WARS

Between the wars and after 1945, Parisian musical, artistic, literary, and intellectual life remained vibrant and attractive to foreign musicians, artists, and writers. The visual arts produced a bewildering succession of "movements": Constructivism, Dadaism, Surrealism, and so on. Copland and other American composers came to study; Hemingway, Gertrude Stein, and American musicians and dancers fled Prohibition, bringing jazz and the Charleston to the city's clubs (left) and bars, where it was possible to dance the night away and ignore the gathering clouds of war.

areas, post-war French reconstruction was a huge task, hampered by expensive colonial wars in Vietnam and Algeria. Governments constantly rose and fell, and stability and prosperity were only achieved with the formation of the European Community in 1957, which led to an unprecedented rise in living standards and at last brought modern facilities to the more remote areas of France.

Below Members of the New Women's Organization take to the streets in 1934 campaigning for the right to vote.

SERIALISM

Late nineteenth- and early twentieth-century composers faced a significant artistic conundrum— the perceived dissolution of common practice tonality. Wagner's prelude to *Tristan und Isolde* provides over 12 minutes of continuous music without a strong cadence to reinforce the tonic. Strauss employed chromaticism to such an extent in *Salome* and *Elektra* that the tonal system ceases to provide large-scale organization. Strauss later returned to a less chromatic language for his masterpiece *Der Rosenkavalier*.

French composers, including Debussy, turned away from the Viennese style and looked for inspiration in their own culture. Schoenberg, however, followed a very different path, one that profoundly changed music for the rest of the century.

EARLY ATONALITY

Schoenberg (pages 302–303) did not see the weakening of traditional tonality as problematic, and chose to pursue increasing chromaticism. In lieu of granting primacy to the tonic-dominant axis—the basis of common-practice tonality—he argued for the "emancipation of dissonance," effectively eradicating the distinction between consonance and dissonance. Motives or pitch cells became the new generating force. Outstanding compositions including *Die glückliche Hand* and *Pierrot Lunaire* followed. While music history considers these pieces revolutionary, Schoenberg saw them as evolutionary: The pursuit of late nineteenth-century chromatic compositional practice to its logical conclusion.

Above Rudolf Nureyev in a 1977 Royal Danish Ballet production of *Pierrot Lunaire*. Schoenberg's music is for solo vocalist and a small ensemble of instruments.

BEGINNINGS OF SERIALISM

Despite the success of *Pierrot Lunaire*, Schoenberg faced a new challenge. In the absence of the tonic-dominant axis and hierarchical key areas, how to sustain long compositions? Text in vocal music provided the needed structure to maintain interest in longer pieces. In pieces without text, however, Schoenberg needed a new technique and devised an extraordinary new process called serialism or dodecaphony.

Consider the pattern of keys on the keyboard shown in Figure 1. The black keys appear in groups of two and three, with the white keys interspersed. With two exceptions, a black key intervenes between each white key. The combination of these patterns reveals that there are only 12 pitches before the sequence begins once again. The stave in Figure 2 shows this pattern in notation (C sharp and D flat are equivalent and may be notated either way; the same holds true for other bracketed pitches). Schoenberg would commence a composition by creating a tone row—this is a particular ordering comprising all 12 pitches. He then subjected that ordering to the operations of transposition, inversion, retrograde, and retrograde inversion. An example is provided in Figure 3. The line entitled P_0 read from left to right is the Prime Form of the row. The remaining lines read from left to right show transposed versions of the Prime Form. P_1, for example, shows P_0 transposed up one step, for instance B becomes C, A sharp becomes B and so forth. Reading from right to left yields the retrograde of the row, from top to bottom the inversion, and from bottom to top the retrograde inversion.

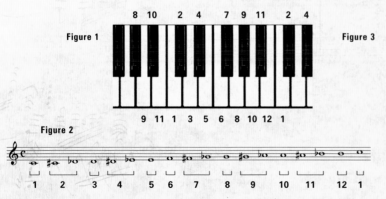

Figure 1

Figure 2

Figure 3

	I_0	I_{11}	I_3	I_4	I_8	I_7	I_9	I_5	I_6	I_1	I_2	I_{10}	
P_0	B	A#/Bb	D	D#/Eb	G	F#/Gb	G#/Ab	E	F	C	C#/Db	A	R_0
P_1	C	B	D#/Eb	E	G#/Ab	G	A	F	F#/Gb	C#/Db	D	A#/Bb	R_1
P_9	G#/Ab	G	B	C	E	D#/Eb	F	C#/Db	D	A	A#/Bb	F#/Gb	R_9
P_8	G	F#/Gb	A#/Bb	B	D#/Eb	D	E	C	C#/Db	G#/Ab	A	F	R_8
P_4	D#/Eb	D	F#/Gb	G	B	A#/Bb	C	G#/Ab	A	E	F	C#/Db	R_4
P_5	E	D#/Eb	G	G#/Ab	C	B	C#/Db	A	A#/Bb	F	F#/Gb	D	R_5
P_3	D	C#/Db	F	F#/Gb	A#/Bb	A	B	G	G#/Ab	D#/Eb	E	C	R_3
P_7	F#/Gb	F	A	A#/Bb	D	C#/Db	D#/Eb	B	C	G	G#/Ab	E	R_7
P_6	F	E	G#/Ab	A	C#/Db	C	D	A#/Bb	B	F#/Gb	G	D#/Eb	R_6
P_{11}	A#/Bb	A	C#/Db	D	F#/Gb	F	G	D#/Eb	E	B	C	G#/Ab	R_{11}
P_{10}	A	G#/Ab	C	C#/Db	F	E	F#/Gb	D	D#/Eb	A#/Bb	B	G	R_{10}
P_2	C#/Db	C	E	F	A	G#/Ab	A#/Bb	F#/Gb	G	D	D#/Eb	B	R_2
	RI_0	RI_{11}	RI_3	RI_4	RI_8	RI_7	RI_9	RI_5	RI_6	RI_1	RI_2	RI_{10}	

Above Dancers of the Rambert Dance Company perform *Pierrot Lunaire* in 2000. The music requires the vocalist to use specific rhythms and pitches in a dramatic style of singing known as "sprechstimme" ("speaking voice").

Selecting various permutations of the rows provided a structural framework and resulted in compositions that, at least in theory, favored no particular pitch over another. Moreover, Schoenberg discovered a technique called hexachordal combinatoriality, a combination of two versions of the row in such a way that the first six pitches of each row, and by extension, the last six pitches of each row, would each form an aggregate of all 12 pitches (consider P_0 and P_2—the first six pitches of P_0 do not appear in the first six of P_2).

Schoenberg and his pupils Webern and Berg came to be known as the second Viennese School (pages 320–323). Serialism and its various incarnations enjoyed a resurgence after World War II.

MILTON BABBITT (b. 1916)

American composer Milton Babbitt's *Three Compositions for Piano* is among the earliest integral serialism pieces. Babbitt (below) uses the numbers 5–1–4–2 in conjunction with a twelve-tone row as the compositional seed. The sum of the numbers equals 12, the number of pitches in the row, allowing Babbitt to separate pitch, articulation, durations, etc. He subjects this numeric series to the processes of retrograde, inversion, and retrograde inversion. The series in retrograde is simply 2–4–1–5. For inversion, he maps the series such that 5 inverts to 1, 1 to 5, 4 to 2, and 2 to 4. The retrograde inversion would then be 4–2–5–1. He then uses this sequence and its variants to determine various aspects of the composition. In some cases, the sequence indicates the number of notes articulated in a phrase. In others, the sequence defines the number of sixteenth notes for a given pitch. For example, 5–1–4–2 generates a quarter note tied to a sixteenth note, a sixteenth note, a quarter note, and an eighth note respectively. Similarly, Babbitt associates dynamics to particular versions of the row. In later works, he explored segmenting the row into tetrachords or trichords to extend hexachordal combinatoriality; he combines three to four simultaneous versions of the row as Schoenberg did with two.

Samuel Barber

MARCH 9, 1910–JANUARY 23, 1981

MUSIC PREMIÈRES FREQUENTLY SPARK CONTROVERSY. ROSSINI'S *BARBER OF SEVILLE* WAS
A FIASCO. AUBER'S *LA MUETTE DE PORTICI* SPURRED A RIOT THAT PRECIPITATED THE
BELGIAN REVOLUTION FOR INDEPENDENCE. STRAVINSKY'S *RITE OF SPRING* CAUSED SUCH
A RUCKUS THAT DIAGHILEV HAD TO DIRECT THE DANCERS FROM BACKSTAGE AS THEY WERE UNABLE TO HEAR
THE ORCHESTRA. RUSSOLO'S *NETWORK OF NOISES* RESULTED IN 11 HOSPITALIZED AUDIENCE MEMBERS.

The 1938 première of Barber's *Adagio for Strings* engendered a highly public and heated debate among composers and critics. Olin Downes of the *New York Times* called the music honest and direct. Critic Ashley Pettis countered that the *Adagio for Strings* was dull and anachronistic. He argued that championing Barber's music would have a "retarding influence" on contemporary music as it did not conform to the prevailing modern style. Barber's companion, the composer Gian Carlo Menotti, called for a plurality of musical styles and suggested that Pettis glorified the Parisian style in vogue 20 years earlier. Composer Roy Harris suggested that Pettis was resurrecting an old but fruitless argument concerning avant-garde versus traditional styles and that it would be better to leave these issues to the judgment of time.

Above right Barber was an individualist, a musical conservative at a time when everything modern was prized. Today he is considered one of the twentieth century's greatest composers.

BARBER'S STYLE IN CONTEXT

After the Franco–Prussian war, French composers sought a different path from the Austrian tradition, and Paris became a cultural center for music and the arts. Many American composers, including Copland, Bernstein, Carter, and Thomson journeyed to Paris to study composition, especially with the noted teacher Nadia Boulanger. Many wrote avant-garde music until the 1930s, turned to a more approachable style during the Great Depression, then pursued a dodecaphonic idiom after World War II.

Barber followed a different path. His contralto aunt Louise Homer and composer uncle Sydney Homer supported his musical development, instilling a deep affinity for nineteenth-century Romanticism. Barber's European travels in the 1930s reinforced this, as did

Left The 1986 film *Platoon*, directed by Oliver Stone, featured Barber's *Adagio for Strings*. The haunting music movingly conveyed some of the horror and futility of war.

ADAGIO FOR STRINGS, OP. 11 (1936)

Barber's *Adagio for Strings* stands as one of the most beloved pieces of American music. Its poignancy led to performances at the funerals of Franklin D. Roosevelt, Princess Diana, Prince Rainier of Monaco, and a 2001 commemoration of the victims of the September 11 attack on the World Trade Center. Many film scores including *Platoon*, *The Elephant Man*, *Amélie*, *El Norte*, and *Lorenzo's Oil* have incorporated it for the same reason. A lush texture of strings supports waves of melody introduced in the opening eight measures. These waves build into a climax and then gently dissipate into a restatement of the opening. Even though some have characterized this music as a rehashing of nineteenth-century Romanticism, its enduring popularity suggests that something more is at play. As Copland observed, "It's really well felt, it's believable, you see, it's not phony ... It comes straight from the heart."

conducting and voice lessons in Vienna. He composed in the tonal, if chromatic, style of Wagner, Strauss, and early Schoenberg. His work as a singer in 1934–1935 also influenced his style. He composed a significant number of songs (almost two-thirds of his output) and brought a lyrical quality to his instrumental works. Barber continued in the Viennese Romantic tradition, a style eschewed by many as outdated.

LIFE AND WORKS

Born in West Chester, Pennsylvania, Barber wrote his first operetta, *The Rose Tree*, at seven. At 14, he enrolled at Philadelphia's Curtis Institute of Music,

Right A 1999 performance of *Vanessa*, at London's Lyric Theater. Barber's opera was written in 1957. Menotti was the librettist.

Below Leontyne Price in a scene from Barber's *Antony and Cleopatra* at New York's Metropolitan Opera House in 1966.

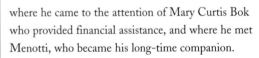

Discover the music

The School for Scandal, Op. 5 (1931)
Symphony No. 1, Op. 9 (1936)
Adagio for Strings, Op. 11 (1936)
First Essay for Orchestra, Op. 12 (1937)
Medea, Op. 23 (1947)
Hermit Songs, Op. 29 (1952–1953)
Vanessa, Op. 32 (1957)
Piano Concerto, Op. 38 (1962)

where he came to the attention of Mary Curtis Bok who provided financial assistance, and where he met Menotti, who became his long-time companion.

He won two Bearns awards in 1928 and 1931. Soon after, he won the Prix de Rome, which allowed him to pursue further studies at the American Academy. After the debut of *Adagio for Strings*, Barber seldom composed a piece that was not commissioned. Yet his work garnered a number of honors including two Pulitzer Prizes, the Henry Hadley Medal, and the Gold Medal for Music. After 1945, Barber experimented with new approaches. The *Capricorn Concerto* recalls Stravinsky's neo-classicism; *Excursions* employs jazz idioms; and *Knoxville: Summer of 1915* draws upon the folk esthetic.

Even though Barber considered it among his best works, his opera *Antony and Cleopatra* (1966) received tepid reviews. He spent much energy over the next decade with revisions, but the opera failed to earn the recognition Barber felt that it deserved. Moreover, he began to suffer from depression, creative blocks, and alcoholism. Menotti severed their relationship in the mid-1970s, and from 1978 to his death, Barber struggled with cancer. Despite this period of decline, he left a trove of extraordinary music.

John Cage

SEPTEMBER 5, 1912–AUGUST 12, 1992

JOHN CAGE'S COMPOSITIONS, LECTURES, WRITINGS, FILMS, AND "HAPPENINGS" HAVE
ENGENDERED A GREAT DEAL OF DEBATE LEADING SOME TO COUNT HIM AMONG THE
MOST INFLUENTIAL COMPOSERS OF THE SECOND HALF OF THE TWENTIETH CENTURY.
OTHERS BRAND HIM A PRACTITIONER OF MOUNTEBANKERY.

Cage attended Pomona College in Claremont, California, but soon withdrew to travel to Europe, where he explored different art forms and worked as an architect's apprentice. He returned to the United States to study music composition and was extraordinarily fortunate with his teachers—they included Henry Cowell and Arnold Schoenberg. His studies with Cowell embraced contemporary and non-Western

Above right John Cage photographed in 1987. His most famous work is possibly *4'33"* where not a single note is played. The composition, in three movements, reflects his interest in Zen Buddhism.

music. As his interests turned to chromatic counter-point, Cowell encouraged him to study with Schoenberg. Cage later said that Schoenberg inspired him so thoroughly that he decided to dedicate his life to composition. Cage explored variations of Schoenberg's dodecaphonic idiom, in particular, by using a 25-note row spanning a range of two octaves and partitioning rows into segments that he manipulated and repeated.

PERCUSSION, PIANOS, AND PALINDROMES

By the mid-1930s, Cage's attention was directed toward percussion. This may have served as a balance to his concentration on pitch during his studies with Schoenberg. The filmmaker Oskar Fischinger's notion that "Everything in the world has its own spirit which can be released by setting it into vibration," possibly led Cage to contemplate wider sonic resources. A reaction against the lush sound of strings that characterized much Romantic era music might have also been a catalyst. In any case, this new direction set Cage on a path to explore and expand sonic possibilities. His percussion concerts generated sufficient interest that CBS commissioned him to compose a soundtrack for poet Kenneth Patchen's radio play *The City Wears a Slouch Hat*. On occasion, a lack of performers or space led Cage to revisit a resource he learned under Cowell—the prepared piano. Placing various materials such as screws, bolts, and so forth between the strings transforms the piano into what Cage described as "a percussion orchestra under the control of a single player."

One of his early percussion compositions, *First Construction (in Metal)*, provided a formal blueprint that he drew upon until 1956. The sequence of numbers 4–3–2–3–4 generates the overall form. The basic building block comprises five phrases of 4, 3, 2, 3, and 4 measures, respectively. At a larger level, the piece subdivides into five sections containing 4, 3, 2, 3, and 4

Left Dancers in the ballet *Empty Moves* by choreographer Angelin Preljocaj in Montpellier in 2007. The work was inspired by Cage's 1979 book *Empty Words*.

Above Cage (left) with composer David Tudor in 1965. The male dancer behind them is Merce Cunningham who was Cage's long-term partner.

of these building blocks. This schema appealed to Cage for a number of reasons: The overall form mirrored its constituent parts; it allowed him to use time as structural element in lieu of harmony, rhythm, or pitch; and it provided a preconceived structure into which he could spontaneously fill segments, as he put it, "as one chooses shells while walking along a beach."

Discover the music

First Construction (in Metal) (1939)
Bacchanale (1940)
Living Room Music (1940)
Sonatas and Interludes (1946–1948)
4'33" (1952)
HPSCHD (1967–1969)
Two (1987)

THE POSTWAR YEARS

In the mid-1940s, Cage explored Eastern philosophy, music, and esthetics, leading to new understandings of silence, the role of the composer, and the very meaning of music. Cage began to consider silence as the absence of intended sounds. Moreover, he strove to limit the role of ego in composition and turned to aleatoric procedures. As he famously explained: "I have nothing to say and I am saying it and that is poetry as I need it." Inspired by the *I Ching* (*The Book of Changes*), Cage developed a system of composition whereby he created a series of carefully constructed charts containing pitch, rhythm, dynamics, and texture. Half the entries in each chart contained silence. He then tossed coins or used some other chance process to select the pitch, rhythm, dynamics, texture, and so forth from the charts. His 1951 *Music of Changes* stands as an important example of this. The "chance" aspect of this music stood in direct opposition to the prevailing practice of dodecaphonic composition and total serialism.

SONATAS AND INTERLUDES 1946–1948

Many consider *Sonatas and Interludes* the finest of Cage's compositions for prepared piano. The work followed his 1946 meeting with Gita Sarabhai who introduced Cage to Indian philosophy, music, and esthetics. Cage strove to express the eight "permanent emotions" or *rasa* of Indian esthetics—the darker emotions of anger, fear, sorrow, and the odious, and the lighter emotions of the erotic, the heroic, mirth, and the wondrous. Combined, they tend to a ninth *rasa*, tranquility. This 70-minute piece comprising 19 movements is quiet, static, yet astonishingly powerful.

Twentieth-century America

BARBER AND CAGE WERE BORN AT AN EXCITING PERIOD IN AMERICAN HISTORY. JUST A
FEW YEARS EARLIER, THE INTRODUCTION OF THE PHONOGRAPH AND THE FORD MODEL T
CHANGED THE WAY MANY AMERICANS LIVED. ARIZONA AND NEW MEXICO JOINED
THE UNION IN THE YEAR THAT CAGE WAS BORN, 1912. THE 1910S SAW THE EXPANSION
OF COMMERCIAL RADIO, THE BLOOMING OF THE JAZZ AGE, THE BEGINNING AND END
OF THE GREAT WAR, AND EINSTEIN'S GENERAL THEORY OF RELATIVITY.

B y the time Barber and Cage were teenagers,
the United States enjoyed economic prosperity, Congress ratified the long overdue nineteenth
amendment granting women the right to vote,
and the phonograph began to change the way
Americans listened to music.

THE GREAT DEPRESSION

The stock market crash of 1929 and subsequent
depression of the 1930s led many composers to recon-
sider their esthetics—the heady, unabashed musical
experimentalism of the 1920s seemed out of place with
the somber reality of day-to-day life. While composers
such as Ives and Cowell forged ahead along avant-garde
lines, the Federal Music Project (1935–1939) and the
subsequent Works Progress Administration (WPA)
Program (1939–1943) provided income for film scores
and other commissions for new music geared toward
the general public. For example, these funds subsidized
Virgil Thomson's superior movie score, *The Plow that
Broke the Plains.* Moreover, widespread poverty resulted

Above The first
Ford Model T was built
in 1908 and was touted
as the most affordable
motor vehicle on offer.

Below The Great
Depression of the 1930s
affected thousands of
people. Here, unemployed
lodgers from New York's
Municipal Lodging House
line up to receive a meal.

in sympathy with social-
ist ideals, and composers
wrote music expressly
socialist in nature or
turned to American folk
music in solidarity with
the suffering public.
Copland composed
*Into the Streets May
First,* a chorus for American workers, and moved
from what he called his
"severe" style to one that
was much more acces-
sible. He remarked, "I felt that it was worth the effort
to see if I couldn't say what I had to say in the simplest
possible terms," and then proceeded to compose some
of his most popular works including *Appalachian Spring*
and *Fanfare for the Common Man.*

AMERICA THE REFUGE

Events in Europe in the 1930s, particularly the rise
of Nazism, compelled many artists, writers, and composers to seek refuge elsewhere, including the United
States. Their immigration furthered America's importance as a cultural center and, through their teaching
at universities, influenced numerous composition
students in the following decades.

AFTER WORLD WAR II

Loss of life, the dawn of the atomic weapons age, and
new geopolitical structures led to a contemplative,
introspective mood after the war that inspired many
composers to seek new directions in composition. For
some, a need for order and control to balance the chaos

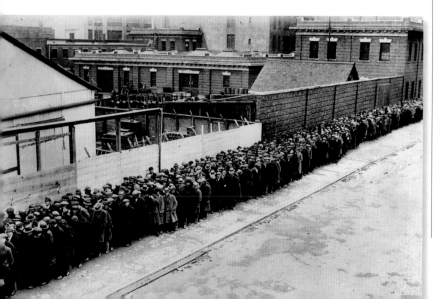

Left Big-band jazz was at its peak during the 1940s, and one of the great bands was led by Duke Ellington (at piano), pictured here with his orchestra in a scene from the 1943 motion picture *Reveille with Beverly*.

selected pitch, rhythm, dynamics, texture, and so forth from pre-prepared charts. His 1951 *Music of Changes* stands as an important example of this technique. The "chance" aspect of this music provided a compelling alternative to dodecaphonic composition and total serialism, and Cage's work influenced many composers both in the United States and in Europe.

THE AGE OF ECLECTICISM

By the mid-1950s, television had become ubiquitous, and radio programming turned increasingly to music. As the decade came to a close, the counter-culture movement had gained momentum, and musical eclecticism continued to grow. Cage found himself at home touring and presenting musical "happenings" such as his 1969 *HPSCHRD*, which featured seven harpsichords, 51 tapes of computerized sounds, thousands of slides, and the use of space to create a sensational multimedia experience. This eclectic period brought tonality back into vogue and should have been one of vindication for Barber, but he began to suffer from depression, creative blocks, and alcoholism. Although neither Barber nor Cage saw the turn of the millennium, they lived through exciting times and provided strikingly different contributions to musical culture.

of the war years led to a reexamination of serialism. In Europe, Messiaen, who had spent time in a German concentration camp, provided an important model for younger composers in his *Mode de valeurs et d'intensités*. Boulez extended Messaien's technique by separating pitch, rhythm, and dynamics into discrete serialized lists. By the 1950s, serialism had become the dominant method of composition in the United States, and to a lesser extent, in Europe. Its influence was such that composers such as David Diamond and Igor Stravinsky, who eschewed serialism earlier in their careers, began to compose in that idiom. Even Barber, who steadfastly held to the Romantic tradition, turned to serialist techniques in the first movements of his *Piano Sonata*, the *Nocturne*, and *Prayers of Kierkegaard*.

While some pursued compositional control, others favored the opposite. Maintaining that ego was a major factor in warfare, Cage propounded a direction that displaced the composer and turned to aleatoric approaches. He developed a system of composition whereby the tossing of coins, or some other chance process,

Right By the mid-1960s, most American homes had a television set. Television soon became the dominant entertainment medium and has remained as such.

Witold Lutoslawski

January 25, 1913–February 7, 1994

Like Shostakovich, Polish composer Lutoslawski underwent an early period of Soviet-style censorship; unlike Shostakovich, he emerged from these restrictions in the late 1950s to become a founding figure of the Polish avant-garde, as well as one of the most widely admired and respected composers of his generation.

Though born into Polish landed gentry, Witold Lutoslawski's early life was never comfortable. His father had political affiliations that led to him being executed in Moscow in 1918 by the Bolsheviks. Returning to Poland, his family struggled to maintain their estates, and just as his musical studies in Warsaw began to yield significant compositions (notably the *Symphonic Variations* of 1939), World War II broke out. Not unlike Wladyslaw Szpilman, as depicted in Polanski's film *The Pianist*, he and fellow composer Andrzej Panufnik eked out an existence through café and cabaret performances, though with a more radical and perilous repertoire, including Resistance songs. He escaped from Warsaw just before the 1944 uprising, but lost almost all his scores in the process. After the

Below The Warsaw Uprising in 1944 was an attempt to liberate the city from German control. Here, Polish soldiers have been captured and are prisoners of war. Lutoslawski escaped Poland just before the uprising.

war, as with Ligeti, a brief period of artistic freedom was terminated in 1947–1948 by the imposition of Stalinist "Social Realist" dictates. But with Stalin's death in 1953, a measure of creative freedom was restored to Polish artists. This is already reflected in Lutoslawski's *Concerto for Orchestra* (1954), a brilliantly crafted piece that more than holds its own against obvious antecedents like Bartók's *Concerto for Orchestra* (1943).

RADICAL CHANGE, INTERNATIONAL IMPACT

In 1956, in conjunction with Kazimierz Serocki, Lutoslawski founded the Warsaw Autumn Festival, an Eastern European festival of New Music that persists to this day. His musical style was now changing and works like *Venetian Games* (1961) and *3 Poems of Henri*

Michaux (1963), with their clusters and radical use of musical color, brought him close to young "sonorist" avant-gardists such as Gorecki and Penderecki. Unlike Serocki, Lutoslawski soon withdrew from this extreme position, but he remained an emphatic modernist, with an increasingly strong personal voice. While not shying away from the traditional genres like the symphony and the concerto, he had his own highly individual way of reshaping them.

One of the most significant and influential aspects of Lutoslawski's music from 1960 onwards is his use of "controlled chance." He heard a performance of Cage's ultra-indeterminate *Concert for Piano and Orchestra* (1958), and though he rejected Cage's "anything goes" esthetic, he was fascinated by the possibilities of letting individual musicians operate independently within a controlled harmonic framework. This became a cornerstone of his compositional method—a constant counterpoint between fixed and free that is already spelt out in the first movement of *Venetian Games*. There the

CELLO CONCERTO (1967)

The *Cello Concerto*, written for Russian cellist Mstislav Rostropovich, is not only a major work, but also embodies the way in which many composers, in the politically sensitive 1960s and early 1970s, took a fresh, contemporary look at the meaning of traditional genres like the concerto. Here, the soloist is not so much a virtuoso superstar as a rugged individual (embodied in the insistent repeated notes at the beginning), doggedly pitting himself or herself against the mass (political?) forces represented by parts of the orchestra, and not always winning. Though Rostropovich, given his Soviet background, may have exaggerated this element in his personal comments on the work, it still seems relevant. Highly originally, the single-movement work starts with a long cello solo; it is almost four minutes before it is interrupted by the first of many "antagonistic" brass interjections which, however, also gradually bring the cello into a much more sympathetic discourse with the rest of the orchestra. Although the work has no explicit extra-musical program, listeners may find it hard not to read one into it.

Right In the mid-1980s, Lutoslawski composed *Chain 2* for the German violinist Anne-Sophie Mutter, whose repertoire includes many contemporary works.

two approaches are simply juxtaposed. In later works such as the *Chain* series, they are ever more subtly intertwined; each new texture gently insinuates itself into the previous one.

LATER YEARS

In the 1970s and 1980s, Lutoslawski's international reputation grew enormously, but his decision to remain in Poland made him acutely aware, at a personal level, of continuing repressive traits in communist cultural politics, especially under the Jaruzelski regime, which led to a composer-based cancellation of the 1982 Warsaw Festival that he undoubtedly supported. But he was never an ideologue—his music was never political, but human and humanist, not overtly emotionalist, but always engaged with the sensibility of the listener. He was, in the best sense of the word, a "gentleman" among contemporary composers.

Left Much loved in his native land, Lutoslawski was awarded Poland's highest official honor in 1994, when he was presented with the Order of the White Eagle.

György Ligeti

MAY 28, 1923—JUNE 12, 2006

THANKS TO EXTENSIVE (AND UNAUTHORIZED) USE OF HIS MUSIC IN STANLEY KUBRICK'S FILM *2001: A SPACE ODYSSEY*, LIGETI BECAME THE FIRST AVANT-GARDE COMPOSER TO GAIN BROAD PUBLIC ATTENTION. INITIALLY, HIS MUSIC CONCENTRATED ON DENSE, PROVOCATIVE BUT HIGHLY ARRESTING TEXTURES.

Left Ligeti wanted his music to be understood. He once said, "I know already the music I will write. But the words? I have not yet decided."

Above right A poster from the iconic 1968 film *2001: A Space Odyssey*, which featured various pieces of Ligeti's work. Permission to use his music was not sought, but Ligeti ultimately decided not to pursue the matter in the courts.

Right Ning Liang as Mescalina (top) during a rehearsal for Ligeti's opera *Le Grand Macabre*, performed by La Fura dels Baus, at De Munt/La Monnaie, in Brussels, Belgium, in March 2009.

Later, he became fascinated with all kinds of musical paradoxes, such as how fast music can sound slow, and vice versa, as well as the music of many different cultures. Many musicologists regard him as the most significant late twentieth-century composer.

Ligeti's early life was dominated by personal and social trauma. A Transylvanian-born Jew, his father and brother were victims of the Nazi Holocaust, and Ligeti only narrowly escaped death himself. After the war, he went to Budapest, hoping to study with Bartók, but just days after Ligeti had gained entrance to the Conservatorium, Bartók died. Yet, in the following years it looked as if the younger generation's artistic dreams could be realized; but in 1947 the communist regime assumed power in Hungary, and restrictions were placed on art. Though Ligeti enjoyed the support of Zoltán Kodály, the most important Hungarian composer after Bartók, the failed Hungarian uprising of 1956 led Ligeti to flee to the West. He soon found himself in Cologne, working in the WDR Electronic Music Studio alongside Stockhausen, and a brief piece composed there—*Articulation*—gained some attention, not least because of its dry sense of humor, which remained a characteristic of his work.

TOWARD A TEXTURAL MUSIC

With the two orchestral pieces *Apparitions* and *Atmosphères* (1961–1962), Ligeti was catapulted into the limelight as a leading avant-gardist. These fascinating, densely textured pieces immediately became classics of a new "textural music" (also espoused by Xenakis and many Polish composers), and were followed up by deliberately provocative (yet strangely durable) pieces

ATMOSPHÈRES (1961)

Though a relatively early piece, and a short one (about 10 minutes), *Atmosphères*—the musical focus of the "trip" sequence in Kubrick's *2001*—remains emblematic of Ligeti's work. It was consciously conceived as music without harmony or melody, where the orchestral textures were the essential substance of the work. It's a classic "cluster" piece, where dense bands of neighboring notes expand and contract, drift upward and downward, and undergo all kinds of subtle internal changes of timbre. A key notion here is what Ligeti calls "micropolyphony"—each instrument has its own separate, intricate part, but one can't hear the individual parts, only their overall effect. While clearly influenced by electronic music, *Atmosphères* also set out to show how much more the conventional orchestra could achieve, especially in terms of timbre. Another notable aspect of the score is its size; each instrument has its own stave, and there are about 100 in all. This leads, as in *Apparitions* and the *Requiem*, to a startlingly tall, thin score. Unable to accommodate such huge scores on his desk, Ligeti had to write them kneeling on the floor.

"Yes, fractals are what I want to find in my music."

like *Volumina* for organ, whose score is entirely graphic, with no conventional notation; and the theater piece *Aventures*, whose three singers go through a bizarre range of emotions with no conventional text, just phonetics. Even the *Requiem* of 1965, at one level an ultra-imposing big statement, has an ironic side—the *Dies Irae* is conceived as a sort of musical cartoon strip.

In the later 1960s, Ligeti became more obsessed by the development of a highly refined, personal style, characterized by "Ligeti fingerprints." He also became fascinated by paradox (he admired the drawings of M.C. Escher and the writings of Lewis Carroll). An example of the latter is the harpsichord piece *Continuum*, where the notes come so fast that they seem to stand still.

Discover the music

Atmosphères (1961)

Requiem (1965)

Chamber Concerto (1970)

Le Grand Macabre (1975)

Horn Trio (1983)

Etudes for piano (three books, 1985–2001)

Hamburg Concerto (2002)

CRISIS AND RESOLUTION

The 1970s brought an artistic crisis. Ligeti felt his music was falling into predictable ruts. His opera *Le Grand Macabre*, though hugely successful, was for him a way of evading basic problems. With the *Horn Trio* of 1983, an ostensibly conservative piece, Ligeti found the breakthrough to what, for him, was not post- or anti-modernism, but a "different" modernism, which could draw on all kinds of external inspirations, especially rhythmic ones, ranging from medieval to Central African music. He became fascinated by microtones, especially as a way of blurring familiar harmonic structures. His last major work, the *Hamburg Concerto*, encapsulates many of these later preoccupations within five short movements.

The "textures" of Central Europe

AFTER STALIN'S DEATH IN 1953, THE INFLUENCE OF SOVIET CULTURAL POLICIES ON EASTERN
EUROPE REMAINED SIGNIFICANT, BUT BECAME LESS CONSISTENTLY REPRESSIVE IN SOME
COUNTRIES. POLAND ESTABLISHED THE GREATEST ARTISTIC INDEPENDENCE, AND ITS
NEIGHBOR EAST GERMANY THE LEAST. ELSEWHERE, IN HUNGARY AND THE FORMER
CZECHOSLOVAKIA AND YUGOSLAVIA, THE SITUATION WAS MORE EQUIVOCAL—
AVANT-GARDE TENDENCIES WERE TOLERATED, BUT SCARCELY ENCOURAGED.

In the nineteenth century, as nationalism became an increasingly important factor in both political and artistic life, central European music (music to the east and south of Germany) began to establish its own identity, first through Dvořák and Smetana, then Janáček, Bartók, and Kodály. But by the 1930s, this regional nationalism was a waning force in music, and was scarcely encouraged by the increasing interference coming from Stalinist Russia.

EXODUS AND RETURN

After World War II, most of Eastern Central Europe (including Czechoslovakia, Hungary, Poland, and East Germany) was under Soviet control. A number of socialist-orientated German artists who had left Europe for the safety of America in the late 1930s returned to East Germany in the late 1940s, and produced significant work, despite regular brushes with communist authorities. Notable among these were the

Above left The Polish filmmaker Andrjez Wajda displays his Alfred Bauer Prize at the 59th Berlin International Film Festival in February 2009.

playwright Bertolt Brecht (1898–1956) and the composer Hanns Eisler (1898–1962).

After Stalin's death in 1953, there was a relative easing of cultural and political dictates, but in many cases it was short-lived, as witnessed by the brutal Soviet repression of the Hungarian Revolution in 1956—which led Ligeti to flee to the West—and later, the same response to Alexander Dubček's Prague Spring in 1968. In this context Poland, while likewise under Soviet domination, proved to be a curious and vital exception, especially where music was concerned. The year of the failed Hungarian Revolution, 1956, also saw the foundation of the Warsaw Autumn, a festival that not only provided a platform for emerging older modernists like Lutoslawski, Grazyna Bacewicz, Tadeusz Baird, and Kazimierz Serocki, but also launched the careers of young radicals like Henryk Gorecki and Krzystof Penderecki. It also provided a unique opportunity for the presentation of radical Western European works, such as those of Nono, Stockhausen, and Xenakis.

AVANT-GARDE THEATER

While music may have provided the most spectacular arena for an emerging arts avant-garde in Poland, it was by no means alone. Experimental theater flourished, the most well-known exponents being Jerzy Grotowski and his "poor theater," and Tadeusz Kantor. In addition, there were some brilliant "art-house" film directors. Andrjez Wajda gained international acclaim for his *Ashes and Diamonds*, and in his wake came Roman Polanski, though he soon moved to the USA. Common to all these artistic endeavors was a hard-edged provocative "reduction of means," whether it was a matter of the abrasively juxtaposed textures of

Birthplaces, Eastern European composers
★ Birthplace of Witold Lutoslawski
☆ Birthplace of György Ligeti
★ Birthplace of Krzysztof Penderecki
★ Birthplace of Henryk Górecki
★ Birthplace of Iannis Xenakis
--- Modern country borders

the musical sonorism espoused by young composers, or experimental theater's rejection of the distinction between stage and auditorium.

Other Eastern European countries also sprouted innovative artistic movements that were opposed to the prevailing communist ideology, but more discreetly, as quasi-underground movements. This was particularly apparent in Czechoslovakia, with composers such as Rudolf Komorous, Peter Kotik, and the more "acceptable" Marek Kopelent, whose works were given limited exposure on the official state record label Supraphon. In Hungary, the process was slower, but eventually there was official recognition of some major figures, such as György Kurtag.

In current terms, the strangest situation is that of former East Germany. Since the death of Eisler in 1962, it has produced no composers with major international reputations, in stark contrast to its West German counterpart. However, in the wake of German Reunification in 1990, there seems to be an official cultural policy of "division denial" that seeks to minimize the artistic differences between the two Germanys. Seen from outside, this is hard to take seriously.

Below Two of the most famous Poles of the twentieth century: Pope John Paul II (1920–2005) with Lech Walesa (b. 1943), leader of the trade union movement Solidarity.

Above Czech youth stand atop an overturned truck as other people surround Soviet tanks during the so-called Prague Spring in former Czechoslovakia in 1968.

POLISH SYMBOLS OF LIBERATION

For Poles, there were two people who came to symbolize liberation from Soviet oppression: Lech Walesa and Pope John Paul II. Though children of the same time and place, their career paths could scarcely have been more different. Walesa led the first non-communist union in Poland (Solidarity), in constant conflict with authorities, notably the government of General Wojciech Jaruzelski. When Jaruzelski had Walesa arrested in 1981 and imposed martial law, Polish composers responded by cancelling the internationally prestigious Warsaw Autumn festival in 1982. Pope John Paul II, on the

other hand, represented Eastern Europe's ancient ties to Catholicism, and though a poet himself, his increasingly conservative outlook distanced him from avant-garde tendencies in Polish art, and may have influenced formerly radical composers like Gorecki and Penderecki to write religious works in much more conservative styles.

MUSIC AND TECHNOLOGY

Music and technology have been closely linked from the start of the twentieth century, with the emerging record industry, mechanical instruments (especially pianos) and, above all, broadcasting. After World War II came tape recorders, synthesizers, and eventually computers, all of which have had a huge effect on the way music is made and distributed. By the end of the century, music without electronic technology was almost unthinkable.

During World War II, especially in Germany, the tape recorder was developed for military communications purposes. After the war, some of the captured

Right The French composer Pierre Schaeffer (1910–1995) developed "musique concrète."

machines found their way into radio stations, where in addition to use for news and features they provided sound effects for radio plays.

MANIPULATING MUSIC

Then, in Paris around 1950, the writer–composer Pierre Schaeffer, working at French Radio, came up with the idea of "musique concrète"—music existing only on tape, and based on the manipulation of recorded sounds (speeding up, slowing down, reversing etc). These didn't have to be "musical" sounds; they could come from locomotives, saucepans, or anything else. So potentially, anything could be music. Within a few years a rival, much more "structuralist" school of thought (centered on Karlheinz Stockhausen) emerged in Cologne. Its starting point was that taped music should not be based on recorded sounds, but on completely new sounds, built from electronically generated wave forms. Logically, this became known as "electronic music." However, the distinction between the two approaches soon became fuzzy, and nowadays the term "electro-acoustic music" is widely used to describe any music that is based on technological sound production.

The mid-1950s also saw the development of multi-track recording. This immediately gave composers enormous new spatial possibilities—sounds could now be moved from one location to another, and the audience was surrounded by sound, in front, behind, or even above them. Still, in concert, the lack of live

Left RCA unveils its Electronic Music Synthesizer in 1955. It could electronically reproduce the sound of any musical instrument or voice. The synthesizer came into its own in the late 1960s, when it brought an exciting new dimension to popular music.

Right An audio engineer at a studio mixing desk uses the controls to regulate or change the dynamics and volume of the music being recorded.

THE COMPUTER AS MUSICAL INSTRUMENT

Even more than the synthesizer, the musically applied computer is esthetically neutral. When the pioneering Australian Fairlight CMI (Computer Musical Instrument) was put on the market in 1979, the first order was placed by young composers at the Sydney Conservatorium, but (money talks?) the first example was delivered to performer Stevie Wonder. At that stage, speed and storage space were primitive by modern standards, but the basic principle was clear—any newly created or imported (sampled) sound existed as digital data, and could be subjected to any kind of (digitally based)

manipulation. In both art and popular music, sampling has become particularly important—for spontaneous transformation in the former, for remixes in the latter. Initially, art music composers explored these possibilities in the studio, but they rapidly spilt out into live performance situations. Equally importantly, computer notation software such as Finale and Sibelius allows composers and arrangers not only to notate their works at professional levels, but also to hear them over home or studio computer systems with ever increasing levels of accuracy and sophistication.

performers was obviously problematic, and soon composers came up two options: First, pieces that combined taped music with live performers, and second, pieces in which the sounds produced by live performers were immediately transformed by electronic equipment into so-called "live electronic music."

BROADCASTING, COMPUTERS, AND THE INTERNET

Much new music, electronic or not, was initially disseminated through broadcasting. In the 1950s and early 1960s, most European stations used medium wave (AM); monophonic but with a range of some several hundred kilometers. When radio stations subsequently moved to the FM band, quality improved greatly (for instance, stereo became possible), but the range was much reduced, so access to different broadcasters was rather limited. It has only been in the last few years, with the advent of internet streaming, that the old international access has been restored, and indeed greatly increased.

Above An audio technician, pictured in 1991, works with audiotape on a current affairs radio program. Audiotape allowed tighter control over what went to air.

Internet streaming is a product of the computer age. Composing with computers started in the 1960s, although it only came into its own in the late 1970s. In practice, the 1960s were dominated by the development of synthesizers, which effectively package a range of different kinds of equipment (generators, filters etc) into a single unit. When valves were replaced by transformers, the units became portable, and were immediately seized on by many "progressive" rock groups for live performance. As for computer music instruments, these too started out in laboratories, but have now become household tools, expensive at a professional level, but almost free at a domestic one. They give the well-informed user complete control over the creation and processing of sound, and are equally applicable to styles ranging from the concert hall avant-garde to dance music "electronica."

Leonard Bernstein

AUGUST 25, 1918–OCTOBER 14, 1990

PROBABLY NO CLASSICAL MUSICIAN HAS MADE AS DEEP A MARK ON HIS NATIVE LAND AS LEONARD BERNSTEIN MADE ON AMERICA. BEFORE HIM, THERE WAS CONSIDERABLE PREJUDICE AGAINST HOME-GROWN TALENT, PARTICULARLY IN THE FIELD OF CONDUCTING. REAL PUBLIC ACCLAIM WAS RESERVED FOR FOREIGNERS, BUT BERNSTEIN'S UNDENIABLE BRILLIANCE SHATTERED THE GLASS CEILING, ASSURING AMERICAN MUSICIANS OF THE HONOR DUE IN THEIR OWN COUNTRY.

Bernstein's parents were Russian–Jewish immigrants. Samuel, his father, had risen from extreme poverty to become a successful businessman and feared that his son's obsession with music might divert him from a prosperous business career. Only after the 10-year-old boy raised his own fees for piano lessons did Samuel's opposition thaw. Once a family piano was purchased, Leonard spent hours practicing, improvising, and composing, and was already a brilliant pianist with rare skills of improvisation and musical parody when he entered Harvard in 1935.

THE STUDENT YEARS

At 17, Bernstein was extraordinarily handsome and already possessed his characteristic charm, wit, and generosity of character, and he soon adopted the raffish, gay lifestyle that remained his hallmark. He pursued every performing opportunity but avoided "boring" music lectures in favor of linguistics and philosophy. Even so,

Above right Bernstein in 1945. He once famously remarked, "Life without music is unthinkable. Music without life is academic. That is why my contact with music is a total embrace."

Discover the Music

Symphony No. 1 "Jeremiah" (1943)
On the Town (1944)
Suite from On the Waterfront (1954)
Candide (1956)
West Side Story (1957)
Symphony No. 3 "Kaddish" (1963)
Chichester Psalms (1965)
Mass (1971)

---

he graduated *summa cum laude* in 1939. He then studied with Fritz Reiner and later Serge Koussevitsky. Neither conductor approved of his libertine ways, but both recognized an extraordinary talent. The famously dour Reiner, apostle of minimalist podium techique, gave him the only A grade he ever awarded, and Koussevitsky recommended him for the Assistant Conductorship of the New York Philharmonic in 1943.

TRIUMPH FOR "LITTLE SNOT-NOSE"

Soon after Bernstein's appointment, Bruno Walter, the great Austrian conductor, fell ill before a concert. Bernstein had to step in at six hours' notice after an all-night party. Neither apprehensive orchestra nor disappointed audience hoped for more than a disaster-free run-through of the program, but heard instead an electrifying interpretation quite different from the one Walter had prepared.

At the end, even the orchestra's hardened professionals stood and cheered. One musician described his amazement that "this little snot-nose" turned out to be "the most extraordinary musician I ever met." A star was born, in demand all over the US as a conductor, pianist, and composer. Hollywood even offered him a screen test for the role of Tchaikovsky.

The peak of his hugely successful career was probably his long innovatory tenure as Music Director of the New York Philharmonic. He promoted modern music, particularly that of Copland and other American composers, played a major role in resurrecting Mahler's music, gave illuminating talks to the audience and—his most-applauded innovation—made a series of television programs aimed at enthusing the young.

Left A poster for the 1961 film version of *West Side Story*. A reworking of the tale of the doomed lovers, Romeo and Juliet, the musical is set in New York in the mid-1950s. Leonard Bernstein's music is a tour de force.

Tuba

One of the most recent additions to the symphony orchestra, appearing the mid-nineteenth century, the tuba is the largest and lowest pitched brass instrument. Commonly used in military, marching, and concert bands, the tuba is typically pitched in B flat, E flat or F. Vaughan Williams's *Tuba Concerto in F Minor* is a famous work for the instrument. Bernstein composed a very short piece for tuba called *Waltz for Mippy III* (1948). His famous directions for performance are "as graceful as possible under the circumstances."

compose. He wanted to write the great American opera and the great American symphony, and was never fully satisfied by the huge success of his theater works. His symphonies and other "serious" pieces are enjoyable both for their finely crafted tonal music and for their philosophical search for the God he wished he could believe in, but even his friend Copland characterized them as "conductor's music." They clearly lack the sheer genius of the theater music, especially what is possibly the greatest musical ever composed, *West Side Story*.

Bernstein died in 1990, just two months after conducting his last concert with the Boston Symphony, aged 72—or, as his friend Ned Rorem said, aged 288, because "he lived four lives in one."

THE COMPOSER

Despite his success, Bernstein was an unsatisfied and sometimes contradictory man. Avowedly homosexual, he nevertheless married Felicia Cohn in 1951. They had three children together before he left her for a male lover, only to return and care devotedly for her during her final illness.

Similarly, he was torn all his life between enjoying the ephemeral art of conducting and finding time to

Below An exuberant Leonard Bernstein conducting the New York Philharmonic in Central Park in August 1986, in front of an estimated audience of 200,000.

IMPORTANT CONNECTIONS

Two of Bernstein's romantic attachments proved to be particularly important. Aaron Copland became a life-long friend and compositional mentor and, crucially, an affair with charismatic conductor Dmitri Mitropoulos (1896–1960) influenced Bernstein to follow the same profession. Like Mitropoulos, Bernstein continued to compose throughout his life.

INSTRUMENTS OF THE TWENTIETH CENTURY

The twentieth century saw the invention of a range of new instruments, some more successful than others in making an impact on the development of music. The single greatest progression for music of that century was unquestionably the invention of electronic equipment. The electric guitar, the synthesizer, sampler, and computers have all changed the way music is created and performed.

THE THEREMIN

One of the more interesting instruments (if you can call it that) is the theremin. Invented in 1919 by Lev Theremin, this unique instrument is played with no actual physical contact. The musician controls the instrument by the closeness of the hands to two antennae. The distance from one antenna controls the pitch (frequency), and the other controls the volume (amplitude). Some theremins have only one antenna and use a volume knob. While not embraced by "classical" musical composers, the theremin found a home in film music and was used to produce a "ghostly" sound.

Above Inventor Thaddeus Cahill with his telharmonium, the forerunner of the Hammond organ and the synthesizer.

Left Lev Theremin with his amazing instrument. Vladimir Lenin is said to have been so impressed with the invention that he took lessons in playing it.

Right A Moog synthesizer, named for its inventor Dr Robert Moog (1934–2005), who once sold theremins. This electronic instrument gained acceptance with the 1968 recording *Switched-On Bach*.

Apart from such special effects, the theremin is used in avant-garde performance and composition. Composers as varied as Percy Grainger, Joseph Schillinger, and Vladimir Komarov used the instrument; Dmitri Shostakovich used it in the 1931 movie score *Odna*.

THE TELHARMONIUM

One early electronic instrument was the telharmonium, a precursor to the Hammond organ, and arguably the first synthesizer. Invented in 1897 by Thaddeus Cahill, its tone wheels generated sounds as electrical signals; this synthesis produced numerous combinations of overtones and pitches. Thirty years later, the Hammond organ emerged, with technology featuring a rotating speaker cabinet called a "Leslie" speaker that created a tremolo effect.

THE SYNTHESIZER

This electronic keyboard instrument shaped popular music to a large degree in the second half of the twentieth century. Probably the most famous type—the Moog synthesizer invented by Robert Moog—is still used today. It made a dramatic impact in 1968 when the instrument was featured on Wendy Carlos's album *Switched-On Bach*, a popular recording of classical music using the new sounds of the synthesizer.

Although it was originally created as a monophonic instrument (one note at a time) polyphonic synthesizers emerged quickly, enabling the musician to play chords. The use of the synthesizer is popular in most genres of music, including film and television scores.

Left Possibly no instrument says "rock music" more than the electric guitar. The first electric guitar appeared in the United States in the 1930s.

VIBRAPHONE

This mallet-played instrument is similar to the xylophone, marimba, and glockenspiel, but with aluminum bars; it also has a sustain pedal, like a piano. The vibraphone has resonators—thin-walled aluminum tubes underneath each tone bar, which amplify the sound of each note; a motor is attached to these resonators controlling the volume. A damper pad attached to the pedal is used to deaden the sound. Invented in the 1920s, the instrument has a three-octave range and can be played with two mallets or four mallets (two in each hand). Messiaen's *Turangalîla Symphony* and his *Saint-François d'Assise* feature the instrument. The vibraphone (vibes) was popularized by jazz virtuoso Lionel Hampton whose melodic invention and the speed at which he could play dazzled audiences and critics alike.

DRUM KIT

While combinations of various percussion instruments have been used in countless orchestral works over the centuries, the drum kit (or drum set) has gone widely unnoticed as a tool for composers. The

Above Jazz virtuoso Lionel Hampton (vibes) with clarinettist Benny Goodman at a concert at New York's Carnegie Hall in 1978.

early part of the twentieth century saw the invention of the bass drum pedal as well as the hi-hat stand, and these essentially completed the modern drum kit we know today. The exact make-up of a drum kit varies depending on genre, style, repertoire, and the individual musician playing it, but a standard set-up includes bass drum, snare drums, one to three toms, hi-hats, and cymbals.

Although there is little repertoire written for the drum kit in an orchestral setting, the drum kit is an integral part of jazz, rock, and pop music. It played an important role in the big dance bands of the 1940s and 1950s. Indeed, instruments such as the drum kit and the electric guitar helped to create the new genres of the latter part of the twentieth century. Rock music introduced new textures and timbres; the invention of dance music and hip-hop utilized such technology as the sampler and the drum machine.

Left A modern drum kit. The musician uses sticks, brushes, and mallets to create various sounds. The bass drum is controlled with a pedal.

Pierre Boulez

BORN MARCH 26, 1925

PIERRE BOULEZ WAS A LEADER OF THE TWENTIETH-CENTURY POSTWAR AVANT-GARDE,
EXPLORING THE NEW POSSIBILITIES OF SERIALISM WITH RIGOR, INTELLECT, MUSICIANSHIP, AND
IMAGINATION. AS A CONDUCTOR, HE IS NOTED FOR PERFORMANCES OF ORCHESTRAL LANDMARKS
OF THE TWENTIETH CENTURY THAT COMBINE PRECISION, CLARITY, AND ANALYTICAL INSIGHT.

Born in Montbrison, France, Boulez entered the Paris Conservatoire in 1942, against the wishes of his father who wanted him to become an engineer. He studied in Messiaen's harmony class and took private lessons with René Leibowitz, developing a distinctive approach to musical analysis (particularly of Stravinsky, Schoenberg, and Webern), which drove his own research toward a progressive musical language. This radical distinctiveness manifested itself right from his earliest works: *Notations* for piano (1945), *Flute Sonatina* (1946), *Piano Sonata No. 1* (1946), *Le soleil des eaux* (1950), and *Le visage nuptial* (1951–1952).

EXPERIMENTATION

In 1946 he became musical director of the Compagnie Renard-Barrault theater group, where he was mentored in conducting by Roger Desormière, later founding the Domaine Musical concerts devoted to new contemporary works alongside significant music from the past. The tension between genres is captured in his *Piano Sonata No. 2* (1947–1948), an iconoclastic work in the mold of Beethoven, which prompted Boulez toward a period of experimentation and polemical writing. Out of this formative period came what many regard as his most important work, *Le marteau sans maître*.

The opposite face of Boulez's serialism, in which all musical elements are rationally connected (as in *Structure I* for two pianos), was his interest in the irrational to release elements unavailable to rational processes. He had a lifelong interest in the relationship between music and poetry, and, from the second half of the 1950s, became increasingly interested in open musical form and chance, following the ideas of John Cage,

Left Boulez conducting a rehearsal with Ensemble Intercontemporain, the orchestra in residence at Paris's Cité de la Musique. This orchestra was founded by Boulez in 1976.

LE MARTEAU SANS MAÎTRE (1953–1955)

Le marteau sans maître can be seen as an avant-garde response to Schoenberg's earlier modernist masterpiece, *Pierrot Lunaire*. Like *Pierrot Lunaire* it is in three parts, and links the flute and the voice in dream-like delirium, but in a complex way, Boulez interlocks the three parts, each based on a separate poem by René Char. Boulez saw poetry and music in this way: "The poem is the *center* of the music, but it is *absent* from the music, just as volcanic lava can retain the shape of an object even though the object itself has disappeared." The sound world spans from the sustained notes of the human voice to the rapidly decaying xylophone sound, which Boulez saw as nevertheless connected. The human voice is linked to the alto flute as both rely on human breath and create a single line. The viola also creates single lines but in addition it can be plucked, connecting it to the guitar. Guitars resonate longer like the vibraphone, which is struck like the more abrupt wooden xylophone. The complex rhythm and floating evaporating textures create a timeless and glittering listening experience.

Left Pierre Boulez (at right) with pianist and conductor Daniel Barenboim. Regarded as one of the world's leading serialist composers, Boulez is also highly esteemed as a conductor.

Above right An aerial view of Montbrison, the town in central France where Boulez was born in 1925. At the age of 17, the composer went to Paris to study music.

though with a totally different result. Elements of chance appeared in *Improvisation sur Mallarmé I* and *II* (1957)—which later became part of *Pli selon Pli* (1957–1962)—and in the *Piano Sonata No. 3* (1955–1957), in which the player chooses the order of movements and elements within them, like taking a series of possible different pathways over the same terrain. *Pli selon Pli*, a portrait of the poet Stéphane Mallarmé, revolved less around the expression of individual texts, but engaged instead with the poet's overall esthetic view.

Boulez continuously reworked pieces into complex interlocking forms. Thus *Eclat* (1965) became *Eclat/multiple* (1970), and his early piano pieces *Notations* became extended orchestral works. *Rituel* (1974–1975), derived from *explosante-fixe* (1972) and composed in memory of the composer Bruno Maderna, explores a solemn, austere, dark expressive world elsewhere largely absent from his music.

Discover the music

Le soleil des eaux (1950)
Le visage nuptial (1951–1952)
Le marteau sans maître (1953–1955)
Piano Sonata No. 3 (1955–1957)
Pli selon Pli (1957–1962)
Eclat (1965)
Répons (1980–1984)

USING TECHNOLOGY

In 1976 Pierre Boulez returned to the music research institute, IRCAM. Although he had experimented with electronic music in the early 1950s, it was the potential of the new digital technology for live transformation of music sounds, and the redistribution of them in space that drew him back to the medium. The most spectacular result was *Répons* (1980–1984), in which a central orchestra is surrounded by soloists and an outside speaker array, creating a sound world in a state of continuous movement and transformation around the listener.

The aftermath of World War II

THE EUROPEAN CULTURAL ETHOS THAT EMERGED IMMEDIATELY FOLLOWING WORLD WAR II
CAN BE SEEN AS ONE SHAPED BY THREE HISTORICAL FORCES—THE AFTERMATH OF THE WAR
AND THE HOLOCAUST, THE RAPID DEVELOPMENT OF THE COLD WAR BETWEEN AMERICA AND
RUSSIA AND THEIR EUROPEAN ALLIES, AND THE ADVANCE OF NEW TECHNOLOGY WITH ITS
TWIN-EDGED PROMISE OF PROSPERITY AND ANNIHILATION.

The destruction caused by World War II created a *tabula rasa* in Europe that required much more than simply the rebuilding of cities. Music, like many other aspects of European culture, was partly tainted with Nazi associations. Tyrants and their acolytes had committed unspeakable atrocities by day and listened to Wagner and Schubert by night. Although not necessarily blaming this even on the anti-Semitic Wagner, let alone the guiltless Schubert, the rising generation, either consciously or subconsciously, channeled its post-war energy into creating not only new forms, but a new musical language that strove to avoid resonance with the immediate past.

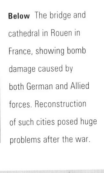

Below The bridge and cathedral in Rouen in France, showing bomb damage caused by both German and Allied forces. Reconstruction of such cities posed huge problems after the war.

CREATING A NEW ESTHETIC

The new esthetic was one of fierce rationality, imagination, and an austere form of optimism that allowed for no false veneers of decoration, sentimentality, or puffed-up feelings. The best music of this phase of bold experimentation, by composers such as Boulez, Cage, Stockhausen, Xenakis, and Berio, can be heard as the expression of an ethos of fierce purity that demanded truth, unbounded imagination, and progress away from a tainted past. Yet even as this project was pursued, the ever-present nuclear threat created by Cold War rivalry cried out against the expression of false optimism. The shadow of nuclear war in the musical thought of the avant-garde is seen most famously in Penderecki's *Tren* (*Threnody to the Victims of Hiroshima*) (1960) (the title, however, was an afterthought).

In the attempt to create a musical language removed from tainted tradition, the development of recording and tape technologies (the latter largely from 1951) and electronic music synthesis offered unlimited new possibilities, resulting in the establishment of experimental studios in Paris by Pierre Schaeffer (1948), in Cologne by Herbert Eimert (1951), and at Columbia University in New York (1951), among others. Stockhausen, who was working in Cologne, stands out as one of the enduring innovators of the experimental phase. The development of digital musical synthesis (most notably pursued at the Institut de Recherche et Coordination Acoustique/Musique [IRCAM] set up by Boulez at the invitation of President Pompidou in 1970), combined with the advent of the personal computer, brought previously unimaginable musical possibilities into the mainstream and the private studio.

Left Some of the horrors of the Belsen
concentration camp as depicted in a painting
by English artist Leslie Cole.

DEVELOPING SERIALISM

An early experiment in serialism
was Messiaen's *Mode de valeur
et d'intensité* (1949) though the
composer himself regarded it as a
failure. A more rigorous exposition
is found in Boulez's *Structure I* for
two pianos. In a polemical article of
1952, Boulez wrote "any musician
who has not experienced—I do not
say understood, but truly experienced—the necessity of dodecaphonic language is USELESS."

> *"After Auschwitz, to write poetry is barbarism."*
>
> THEODOR ADORNO

Although the purity and intensity of the post-war
avant-garde faded as eclectic and postmodern styles
developed from the late 1970s, the music of the
period remains a potent expression of a singular
and anguished historical moment.

INTO SERIALISM

The idea of composing music according to a series of
notes related not to a traditional scale but only to one
another had been started by Arnold Schoenberg in
around 1921 and pursued by his pupils Alban Berg
and Anton Webern. In the music of these composers
(the so-called "Second Viennese School"—a reference
back to a notional "First Viennese School" comprising
Haydn, Mozart, Beethoven, and Schubert), a "row" or
"series" of all twelve notes of the chromatic scale in a
certain order created a template of significant motives
that, used in continuous rotation, would give the piece
unity and coherence, while also ensuring that no one
of them started to dominate. An alternative name was
"dodecaphony." (See also pages 380–381.) In avoiding
a tonal center, the style was *atonal*, as opposed to *tonal*
music, which has a home key or chord to which other
harmonies are drawn through voice-leading.

Right The Italian
experimental composer
Luciano Berio (1925–
2003) was one of the
pioneers of electronic
music. In the 1970s,
he was director of the
electro-acoustic depart-
ment of IRCAM in France.

After World War II Schoenberg's pupil René
Leibowitz promoted Schoenberg's ideas to a younger
generation in Paris, and the serial principle was taken
up by the avant-garde as a technique for re-inventing
the musical language. The serial principle was based
on the idea that a pre-defined order could be used to
control all the elements of a musical composition—
pitch, rhythm, dynamic (loud or soft), and timbre (or
tone color). By using order to determine musical ideas,
it deliberately excluded the personal and subjective.

Karlheinz Stockhausen

AUGUST 28, 1928–DECEMBER 5, 2007

STOCKHAUSEN'S NAME IS SYNONYMOUS WITH MANY OF THE MOST RADICAL
TRENDS IN MUSIC OF THE SECOND HALF OF THE TWENTIETH CENTURY: NEW
STRUCTURAL MEANS OF ORGANIZING SOUND (SERIALISM), ELECTRONIC MUSIC,
AND OPEN FORMS ARE JUST A FEW. IN THE 1950S AND 1960S, EVERY NEW WORK
OPENED UP NEW POSSIBILITIES. YET THE SECOND HALF OF HIS CREATIVE LIFE
WAS MAINLY DEVOTED TO A SINGLE, HUGE PROJECT—A CYCLE OF SEVEN
OPERAS COLLECTIVELY ENTITLED *LICHT* (*LIGHT*).

Above right The album
cover for the Beatles'
1967 album *Sgt. Pepper's
Lonely Hearts Club Band*.
Stockhausen is pictured
in the back row, fifth
from the left.

Left Stockhausen in a
recording studio in 1965.
Always controversial, the
composer's influence on
later generations has
been considerable.

Right A seventeenth-
century painting of
the archangel Michael
defeating Lucifer. Along
with Eve, these Biblical
characters are at the
center of Stockhausen's
massive work *LICHT*.

a highly systematized compositional method—serialism—which applies arithmetic proportioning not only
to notes, but also to rhythms, dynamics, textures, and
almost every aspect of the overall form. They also seek
to make big, dramatic musical statements. Yet in the
late 1950s, Stockhausen also became intrigued by John
Cage's "indeterminate" works, while looking for different, more structured ways of integrating chance into
his own music. He developed "variable forms," and,
in conjunction with his own Stockhausen Ensemble,
"process compositions" whose scores contained no
specific materials, only transformation processes (such
as *Prozession* and *Kurzwellen*), conveyed by symbols
such as plus and minus signs.

FROM FREE TO FIXED

In the 1960s, Stockhausen became an icon of avant-
garde music, and not just in "new music" circles—
his portrait was included on the album cover of the
Beatles' *Sgt. Pepper's Lonely Hearts Club Band*. He
traveled internationally, and absorbed (or rather, integrated) all kinds of musical and other experiences
into his work, from traditional Japanese music ("Tele-
musik") to national anthems ("Hymnen"). Then, in
1970, after a decade of increasing "openness," Stockhausen made a drastic about-face, and returned to
exactly written music, usually based on a formula,
which prescribes the pitches, durations, etc of a work,
but not in abstract terms, but rather as a singable (but
still serial) melody.

In 1977, he announced that the next 25 years of his
creative life would be devoted to the realization of a
single enormous project—the *LICHT* cycle, comprising
seven operas named after the days of the week, with

B orn in Modräth (near Cologne), Stockhausen
was an orphan, and he worked as a farmhand
for relatives. He entered the Cologne Conservatory in
1947, and by the time he graduated in 1951, he had
already completed *Kreuzspiel*, the first of many revolutionary works that would eventually have a huge effect
on Western music. Shortly after, he went to study with
Messiaen in Paris, where he also met Pierre Boulez.

Returning to Cologne in 1953, he immersed himself
in the newly evolving field of electronic music, soon
producing works that remain popular. The first, *Gesang
der Jünglinge* (1956), embodies two essential and constant aspects of his work—religious belief, and a fascination with science and technology. Common to his
early pieces (and indeed to most subsequent ones) is

Discover the music

Kreuzspiel (1951)

Gruppen for 3 Orchestras (1957)

Kontakte (1960)

Stimmung (1968)

Mantra for 2 pianists (1970)

Freitag aus LICHT (1996)

Freude (second hour of *KLANG*) (2006)

STIMMUNG (1968)

A 70-minute work based on a single chord (a dominant ninth) may seem an unattractive proposition, but *Stimmung* for six vocalists is widely regarded as one of Stockhausen's most fascinating works. It introduced into Western music the idea of "overtone singing," where the singer makes the overtones of each note audible independently of the fundamental note. The piece is both spiritual and erotic, invoking the names of gods from all cultures to determine the mood of individual sections, but also inserting some fairly explicitly sexual elements.

Though the score looks very open, and each group of performers has to make their own version, it is actually highly organized—every detail of rhythms, pitches, and tempi for the 51 basic "models" is the product of a highly unified scheme.

three principal mythological figures: Eve, Michael, and Lucifer. This announcement was greeted with general disbelief, but the cycle was indeed completed in 2003. Originally intended to last 16 hours, rivaling the length of Wagner's *Ring* cycle, it eventually became far longer. Astonishingly, almost every single aspect of the cycle—melodic, harmonic, rhythmic, and formal—is extrapolated from a single page of music, a "superformula."

Few composers have been as little influenced by others as Stockhausen. From the very beginning, once he knew what others had done, he strenuously avoided it, and looked for something different.

Above right Karlheinz Stockhausen receiving the Polar Music Prize from the Swedish king, Carl XVI Gustaf, during a ceremony in the Berwald Concert Hall in Stockholm, Sweden, in 2001.

Similarly, while his general influence has been unquestionably enormous, very few composers of younger generations have sought to emulate his work directly; as with Beethoven, this seemed to be a futile task. More important was to attempt to recapture his endlessly innovative spirit.

The changing twentieth century

STOCKHAUSEN'S TIME IS OURS, OR AT LEAST, THAT OF OUR ELDER GENERATION. IT EVOLVED
AMID THE DISASTER OF WORLD WAR II, AND PASSED THROUGH PERIODS OF INTENSE
INNOVATION AND ASTONISHING DISCOVERIES, IN BOTH ART AND SCIENCE. THE 1950S
FRANTICALLY REBUILT, THE 1960S WERE REVOLUTIONARY, THE 1970S WITHDREW INTO
MORE CONSERVATIVE SOCIAL MODELS; AFTER THAT, WE ENTERED A "POST-MODERN" ERA,
WITH ENDLESS POSSIBLE PERSPECTIVES, BUT NO WIDELY SHARED AGENDAS.

Every European composer of Stockhausen's gene-ration is, in some way, a child of World War II. Both Ligeti, in a Jewish labor camp, and Stockhausen, assigned to frontline hospital duties, constantly came close to death; Iannis Xenakis, a member of the Greek resistance, was gravely wounded and lost an eye. After the war came a difficult period of reconstruction; it took decades for many German cities to be rebuilt. But rebuilding took other forms—social, political, and technological. This period saw revolutions not just

Right The Biosphère in Montreal, Canada, one of the geodesic domes designed by American architect Buckminster Fuller. Fuller's designs were an inspiration to John Cage.

in the arts, but in the sciences. The 1950s and 1960s that saw the rise of artistic avant-gardes also saw men in space, and ultimately on the moon.

Scientific theory built on classic instances such as Einstein's Theory of Relativity, Heisenberg's Uncertainty Principle, and Gödel's Theorem, and many discoveries turned previous assumptions about the nature of the universe on their head. Indeed, research into subatomic particles continues to unveil constant new labyrinths and puzzles. Scientists have also posited the existence of anti-matter and dark matter, and string theory suggests the existence of up to eleven dimensions, rather than the traditional four.

Left Albert Einstein presents an award to mathematical logician Kurt Gödel (second from right) in 1951. The mathematical physicist Julian Schwinger is on the right. Scientists such as Einstein and Gödel changed the way we perceived the world.

THE COLD WAR

The period of reconstruction in the 1950s saw the emergence of enormous tensions between the Soviet Union and the West, spearheaded both ideologically and financially by the United States. The result was the Cold War, which reached a peak in the Cuban Missile Crisis of 1962. It was probably this event, above all, that detonated cynicism in younger Western generations toward their senior political leaders. The result was a revolt against authority that took two distinct forms. One, prevalent in the USA and UK, was the soft anarchy of the flower-power generation, in which rock music played a defining role. The other, more typically European, had a strong left-wing focus, which peaked in the (failed) uprisings of 1968.

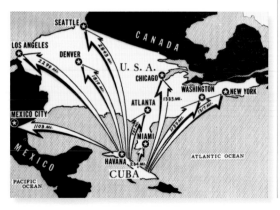

Left A 1962 newspaper map showing the distances from Cuba of various cities in North America. The Cuban Missile Crisis was a display of military brinkmanship between the United States, the Soviet Union, and Cuba.

ARCHITECTURE AND MUSIC

Goethe famously described architecture as "frozen music." Conversely, music too has its own architecture, and in the post-war period, many composers were acutely aware of this, not just as an abstract idea, but as something relating directly to radical contemporary architecture. John Cage often referred to Buckminster Fuller, but for European composers, the seminal figure was Le Corbusier, the high priest of abstract modernism in architecture. Xenakis worked with him in Paris, and even co-designed some buildings, such as La Tourette Convent. Other composers were inspired by Corbusier's book *Le Modulor*, and especially his advocacy of the Fibonacci series, in which each arithmetical term is the sum of the two preceding ones (1 2 3 5 8 13 etc), and the ratio between adjacent terms comes progressively closer to the Golden Section. This they applied to time portions in their works, and especially to the relative lengths of sections. Ligeti flirted with it, and Stockhausen made huge use of it in the 1960s, returning to it in some of his last works.

RETURN TO CONSERVATISM

In the 1970s, there was a swing away from radicalism, either toward emphatic political conservatism, which was embodied in Margaret Thatcher's England, or to a disillusioned relativism, represented by "post-modern" social theorists and philosophers in France and elsewhere. Allied to this is the notion of "post-history," which disputes the value and even possibility of previous social dynamics in a modernist, evolutionary sense. In the arts, this is mirrored on the one hand by neo-conservatism, on the other by "polystylism," where artists feel free to adopt any style, or mixture of styles, from one work to the next.

At the start of the twenty-first century, there are many striking socio–political issues, such as the overt antagonisms between cultures dominated by Christian and Islamic beliefs, the fall of communism outside China, and the latter's emergence as a major economic force, that make "post-history" look like an outdated concept.

For the arts, and especially music, it may be particularly significant that there are now many artists who are projecting Middle Eastern views within a Western context. On the other hand, it seems that, at least among young European composers, the modernist obsession with innovation is by no means a spent force.

Left British Prime Minister Margaret Thatcher with US President Ronald Reagan in 1983. The late 1970s and 1980s was a time of political conservatism.

Peter Sculthorpe

BORN APRIL 29, 1929

ONE OF AUSTRALIA'S MOST WELL-KNOWN COMPOSERS, PETER SCULTHORPE REPRESENTS A DISTINCTIVE MUSICAL VOICE EXPRESSED THROUGH A WIDE VARIETY OF MUSICAL FORMS, FROM INTIMATE STRING QUARTETS TO LARGE-SCALE SYMPHONIC AND CHORAL WORKS. HIS MUSIC HAS BECOME CLOSELY IDENTIFIED WITH THE EVOCATION OF THE AUSTRALIAN LANDSCAPE, AND DEMONSTRATES HIS INTEREST IN ABORIGINAL, TORRES STRAIT ISLAND, AND OTHER AUSTRALASIAN MUSICAL CULTURES.

Sculthorpe was born in Launceston, Tasmania. He studied music at the University of Melbourne, and later at Oxford, and taught composition at the University of Sydney from 1963 until 1999.

ABORIGINAL INFLUENCES

Sculthorpe has always shown a deep respect for the music and culture of the Australian Aboriginal people. Early works such as the *Piano Sonatina* (1954) and *The Loneliness of Bunjil* (1954) are programmatic, and based on Aboriginal legends. The *Sonatina* also provides some of the earliest examples of Sculthorpe's personal compositional style. The repetition of small melodic units, the ritualistic use of rhythm, and even the programmatic idea behind the work, are essential parts of the compositions that followed.

Above In 1998, Peter Sculthorpe was elected, by popular vote, one of Australia's 100 Living National Treasures.

In 1958, Peter Sculthorpe undertook doctoral studies at Wadham College, Oxford, where he studied composition with Egon Wellesz, a former student of Schoenberg, and with Edmund Rubbra. These composers had little impact on Sculthorpe's musical style, but it is through his rejection of their European-based methodologies, and the experience of living outside Australia for the first time, that Sculthorpe found confirmation of his desire to create a distinctly "Australian" voice in his music.

In works like *The Fifth Continent* (1963) and *Sun Music I* (1965), he sought to musically represent the stark, sun-drenched Australian landscape, a concept that remains a primary concern for him. These early evocations are especially noticeable in *Sun Music I* where instrumental texture plays a very important role and the lack of melody, the use of harsh dissonances, and extended string techniques add to the composition's descriptive nature.

EXOTIC ELEMENTS

In the mid-1960s, Sculthorpe began to incorporate elements of Balinese gamelan music into his own. A gamelan is a group of metallic and wooden pitched percussion instruments, and players use an intricate system of interlocking rhythmic patterns to create a uniquely compelling texture. *Sun Music III* (1967) and *Tabuh Tabuhan* (1968) demonstrate this new approach.

Viola

The viola is nearly identical in playing position and close in pitch range to the violin. Yet, with a deeper and more full-bodied tone than the violin, it is often limited to filling in harmony with little melodic material. There are, of course, notable exceptions—Berlioz famously featured the viola in *Harold in Italy* (1834). Peter Sculthorpe, known for his use of unusual timbre effects, featured the instrument in *Sonata for Viola and Percussion* (1960), and *Elegy* (2006) for solo viola and strings. The viola pictured dates from the seventeenth century.

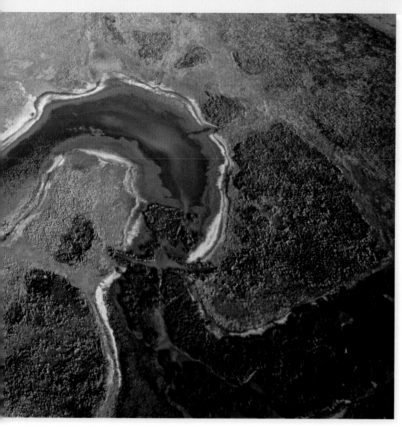

Above An aerial view of a flood plain in Kakadu National Park in northern Australia. This dramatic landscape inspired Sculthorpe's *Kakadu*.

Discover the music

Irkanda IV (1961)

Sun Music I (1965)

Mangrove (1979)

Piano Concerto (1983)

Earth Cry (1986)

Kakadu (1988)

String Quartet No. 11 (1990)

Great Sandy Island (1998)

Requiem (2004)

that are delicately woven into Sculthorpe's increasingly distinctive harmonies and instrumental textures.

Aboriginal music remained a major influence, and in *The Song of Tailitnama* (1974) he made use of Aboriginal song texts, while *Port Essington* (1977) marked the first time that he used a direct quotation from an Aboriginal melody. In works like *Earth Cry* (1986) and *Kakadu* (1988) Sculthorpe continued to evoke the landscapes of northern Australia; in *Nourlangie* (1989) and *Island Dreaming* (1996), he began to investigate the music of the Torres Strait Islands. Certainly, in acknowledging Aboriginal music, the music of Bali and other island cultures, Sculthorpe has sought to offset the influence of European musical traditions and, in doing so, has created his own unique voice.

Simultaneously, the harsh starkness of many of the earlier works began to be replaced by a more expressive sound, with simple melodies drifting over intricate but delicate accompanying textures. Later compositions, for example, *Mangrove* (1979) and the *Piano Concerto* (1983), utilize some ancient Japanese folk melodies

EARTH CRY (1986)

Sculthorpe said that in this work he wants the audience to "listen to the cry of the earth, as the Aborigines have done for many thousands of years." After a brief, solemn introduction, the main section is devoted to material taken from *The Song of Tailitnama* (1974), an earlier work originally written for high voice, six cellos, and percussion, transformed into powerfully evocative music for full orchestra. The music of this vividly orchestrated section is fast and rhythmic, with a distinctive melody that creates a thrilling effect. The original 1974 work used Aboriginal texts sung to this melody and, by using the same melody here, Sculthorpe unites his evocation of the Australian landscape with his respect for the Aboriginal people. This section gives way to slower music that builds to the climax, before becoming more subdued and returning to the solemn music of the opening section as a resolution. The didgeridoo (center, right) adds an extra dimension.

The music of Australia

When a British colony was established in Sydney in 1788, the new settlers struggled with their sense of geographical isolation from the rest of the world, especially from Britain and Europe. Britain was "home" for most settlers, and Europe was, for musicians, the "home" of Western musical composition.

During the nineteenth century, composers in Australia lacked regular contact with any new musical trends and, looking for inspiration, some took an interest in the music and culture of the local indigenous Aboriginal population—this being "Australian" music in its purest form. The interest in Aboriginal music was not widespread, however, and even in the twentieth and twenty-first centuries relatively few composers have incorporated elements of Aboriginal

Above right Although Australian, composer and pianist Percy Grainger (1882–1961) lived most of his life out of Australia. He developed an interest in English folk songs, and was the first to record them on wax cylinders.

music into their own. There were, however, attempts to create a sense of identity for Australian composed music, and some composers gave Aboriginal titles to their otherwise European-influenced musical scores.

The beautiful, often harsh landscape of Australia, and the evocation of the huge diversity of its natural features, the sounds of birds, and the uniqueness of much of its flora and fauna has provided many composers with inspiration for their music.

GEOGRAPHICAL INFLUENCES

In the twentieth century, in an attempt to give Australian music a discernible identity, and also to place it firmly in the Pacific region rather than the Atlantic region, some composers began to be influenced not only by Aboriginal music and culture but also by the music of their nearby geographical neighbors. Thus, the Asian musical influences, including those of Bali, China, and Japan, for example, have become increasingly prominent since the 1960s. Similarly, the steady influx of people emigrating to Australia from all over the world, including virtually every European country, the Americas, and most Asian countries, since the 1950s, has led to a rapid increase in the number of composers from diverse cultural backgrounds.

A DISTINCT AUSTRALIAN SOUND?

Increasingly, Australian composers are more concerned with developing their own distinctive musical style, and composing music that represents aspects of their own cultural identity and their own experience of what it is to be an Australian, and less concerned with how their music might sound "Australian."

Attempts to create a distinctly Australian "sound" or musical style in contemporary art music have, therefore, become less important to many composers. Music is being written in an ever-increasing variety of styles. The influence on some composers of popular music, including genres as diverse as jazz, heavy metal, and electronic dance music, is producing results that clearly attempt to bridge the traditional divide between low and high art forms and to bring new audiences into the concert hall. Electronic music, including the design and use of new instruments, improvised music, musical theater, opera, and chamber music of all types, are all represented in the work of Australian composers. There

Above Australian composer Malcolm Williamson (1931–2003), here rehearsing his children's opera *Knights in Shining Armour* in 1968, became England's Master of the Queen's Music from 1975 until his death.

Left Aboriginal boys making traditional music on the banks of a river in northern Australia. Aboriginal culture is increasingly a source of musical inspiration.

are composers who explore sound in innovative ways, creating music not intended for the concert hall but meant for installation into various natural or man-made environments, emphasizing wider community interaction with the music.

The exponential increase in the power of communication technologies, and the subsequent availability of, and access to, enormous amounts of information of all types at the end of the twentieth century have led many composers to write music whose influences come from an increasingly wide variety of sources. Ultimately, if Australian art music has any sense of identity at the start of the twenty-first century it is one that is marked more by its eclecticism, and the sheer multiplicity of styles and musical languages represented, rather than by any single compositional esthetic or any homogenous national Australian style.

MUSIC IN NEW ZEALAND

James Burney, sailing with Captain Cook, was the first to transcribe a Maori chant and to observe the range of indigenous instruments. The sound world of the Maori—and the wider Pacific—has since been a source of inspiration to New Zealand composers, many of whom have sought the fusion of ethnic tradition with Western art music. An early instance of this is "Waiata Poi," a song by Alfred Hill that includes chanted sections. Recent examples are Gillian Whitehead's *Puhake Ki Te Rangi*, which melds imaginative improvisation on a wide range of Maori instruments with written music for string quartet, and Jack Body's *Pulse*, a large-scale orchestral work underpinned by a Papua New Guinea fire dance. The composer dubbed the "father of New Zealand music" is Douglas Lilburn (1915–2001), whose legacy is a corpus of works, including *Aotearoa* (*Land of the Long White Cloud*) and three symphonies, which have been instrumental in establishing a genuinely vernacular voice in New Zealand art music. The fertile range of expression by subsequent generations of composers is summarized in the incisive songs of David Farquhar, the electro-acoustic narratives of John Cousins, and the neo-primitive percussive scores of Gareth Farr. (At right is a Maori flute trumpet.)

Sofia Gubaidulina

BORN OCTOBER 24, 1931

SOFIA GUBAIDULINA IS ONE OF THE MOST INNOVATIVE AND
RESPECTED MUSICIANS LIVING IN EUROPE TODAY. THE HARSH
RESTRICTIONS SHE ENDURED UNDER THE SOVIET REGIME FAILED
TO SUPPRESS HER STRONG RELIGIOUS BELIEFS AND MYSTICAL
NATURE, WHICH COLOR SO MUCH OF HER WORK. ONLY WHEN
HER MUSIC WAS BROUGHT TO THE ATTENTION OF WESTERN
AUDIENCES IN THE 1980S DID SHE RECEIVE THE BELATED
RECOGNITION SHE LONG DESERVED.

Gubaidulina was born in Chistopol in
the former Soviet Tatar republic, of
Tatar and Russian ancestry. She learned to
play piano at the age of five, and from the
time she was very small her only ambition
was to become a composer. After she
graduated from the Kazan Conservatory at
age 17, she went on to the Moscow Conservatory. As a postgraduate student at
Moscow, Gubaidulina encountered oppo-
sition from the authorities there, who felt her music
was going in the wrong direction. One of the examin-
ers, Dmitri Shostakovich, defended her compositional
skills and encouraged her to remain true to herself.

Above Latvian-born
violinist Gidon Kremer
(b. 1947) for whom
Gubaidulina wrote
Offertorium in 1980.
This work brought her
international recognition.

UNDER SOVIET RULE

Much of Sofia Gubaidulina's early compositional
output was rejected by the state-controlled cultural
bodies, who deemed its themes unacceptably religious

Left Sofia Gubaidulina
photographed in 2007
while on a trip to Britain.
The composer's works
reflect her deep sense
of spirituality.

and its style unacceptably avant-garde. To earn a living
she wrote music for Soviet films, and although she
chafed under the creative restrictions placed on her by
communism, her rich inner life sustained her during
those oppressive decades.

While the Russian Orthodox Church remains her
soul's home, as a child she absorbed influences from
the Jewish, Catholic, and Islamic faiths. For Gubaidulina, music and spirituality are inseparable. She also
found inspiration in the folk traditions of her country,
and in 1975 formed "Astraea," a trio whose repertoire
included music played on various ethnic instruments
such as the bayan (a type of accordion).

The low point in Gubaidulina's career came in 1979.
The head of the composers' union, Tikhon Khrennikov,
placed her and six of her colleagues ("Khrennikov's
Seven") under official boycott, stating their music was
"not representative of the work of Soviet composers."

INTERNATIONAL RECOGNITION

Gubaidulina's fortunes began to turn when Latvian
violinist Gidon Kremer introduced international audiences to her 1980 violin concerto *Offertorium*, a work
influenced by J. S. Bach and Anton Webern.

The Soviet government allowed Gubaidulina to visit
Europe in 1985, and in 1987 she toured the United

CANTICLE OF THE SUN (1997)

Canticle of the Sun, based on a thirteenth-century hymn by St Francis of Assisi, is one of Sofia Gubaidulina's most important compositions and a good entry point for those just beginning to discover her music. *Canticle* is a prayer of praise and gratitude. St Francis so loved the sun, moon, and all the wonders of God's creation that he personified them as "brother" and "sister."

> *Be praised, my Lord, through Sister Moon and the stars;*
> *In the heavens you have made them bright, precious, and beautiful.*

Gubaidulina's composition was written for cello, percussion, celesta, and chamber choir in honor of cellist Mstislav Rostropovich's seventieth birthday. It is divided into four sections (sun and moon; four elements; life; death). In keeping with the simplicity of the prayer, Gubaidulina intentionally subdued the choral section, giving more emphasis to the cello and percussion.

Discover the music

Offertorium (1980)
Stimmen…Verstummen…(1986)
Hommage à T. S. Eliot (1987)
Music for Flute, Strings, and Percussion (1994)
Canticle of the Sun (1997)
Two Paths: A Dedication to Mary and Martha (1998)
St John's Passion (2000)
Feast during a Plague (2006)

States, the same year she wrote *Hommage à T. S. Eliot* for Kremer, a chamber work in eight movements based on Eliot's poems *Four Quartets*.

The 1990s was an especially fruitful decade for Gubaidulina, who by this time was in her sixties. She moved to Hamburg, Germany in 1992 and composed a number of important works including *Two Paths: A Dedication to Mary and Martha*, a concerto for two violas commissioned by the New York Philharmonic. Gubaidulina's keen interest in Asian music found

Above Since the early 1990s, Sofia Gubaidulina has lived in Hamburg, Germany, where she is a central figure in the city's musical life.

expression in the 1998 orchestral composition *In the Shadow of the Tree* which features the Chinese zheng and Japanese koto (both stringed instruments).

In 2000, Gubaidulina composed *St John's Passion* as part of the commemorations to honor the two hundred and fiftieth anniversary of the death of her musical idol, Johann Sebastian Bach. The American music reviewer Philip Greenfield found its evocations of the fire and hail of Judgment Day "hair-raising."

Sofia Gubaidulina has been the recipient of a number of prestigious international awards including the Japanese Praemium Imperiale in 1998, the Polar Music Prize in Sweden (2002), and the Living Composer Prize of the Cannes Classical Awards (2003).

Russia in the late twentieth century

WHEN PRESIDENT LEONID BREZHNEV DIED IN 1982 AFTER 18 YEARS AS LEADER, THE SOVIET UNION'S ECONOMY AND LIVING STANDARDS WERE AT AN ALL-TIME LOW. THE FOLLOWING DECADE WOULD SEE AN UPHEAVAL THAT WOULD RIVAL THE OCTOBER REVOLUTION OF 1917— THE COLLAPSE OF THE SOVIET UNION, THE DEMISE OF ITS COMMUNIST PARTY, AND THE END OF THE COLD WAR.

Left Mikhail Gorbachev receiving the 1990 Nobel Peace Prize, for his role in granting East European nations autonomy from the Soviet Union.

Right A view of the Russian space station *Mir* taken from the US space shuttle *Atlantis* in September 1996.

The key architect for change at this time was Mikhail Gorbachev, who served as the General Secretary of the Communist Party from 1985 to 1991, and President of the Soviet Union from 1988 to 1991. During his term of leadership Gorbachev attempted to persuade the conservative factions of the party to yield to much-needed reforms, while at the same time containing the demands of extremists.

Gorbachev's innovative policies—*perestroika* (reconstruction) and *glasnost* (openness)—allowed for greater freedom of speech, the release of thousands of political prisoners, and some private ownership of business. He also initiated some plans to limit the power of the communist party.

Internationally, Gorbachev formed cordial relationships with western leaders including US President Ronald Reagan and British Prime Minister Margaret Thatcher. In 1988 he announced the withdrawal of troops from Afghanistan, and gave eastern bloc countries autonomy in their internal affairs. Gorbachev was awarded the Nobel Peace Prize in 1990.

THE YELTSIN YEARS

Whereas Gorbachev hoped to effect changes within the framework of communism, his successor Boris Yeltsin believed Russia's direction should be toward democracy and a market economy. A protégé and supporter of Gorbachev, Yeltsin attracted the world's attention in August 1991 when he climbed to the top of an army tank and rallied citizens against a right-wing anti-Gorbachev coup.

However, it was not long before Yeltsin turned against his former mentor and set the wheels in motion that would dismantle the Soviet Union and its republics.

Right Boris Yeltsin (left) with US President George H.W. Bush in 1992. The summit between the two leaders resulted in a new era of cooperation in space research.

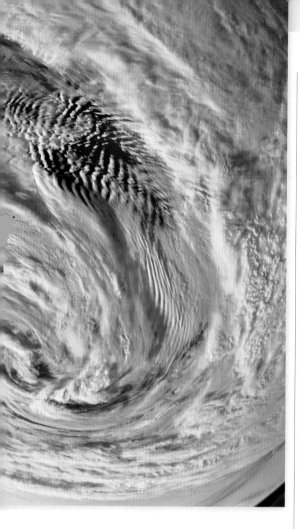

ALLA PAVLOVA

Alla Pavlova is a composer who left the Soviet Union just prior to its dissolution. Born in the Ukraine in 1952, she commenced her musical studies at the Gnessin Academy of Music when her family relocated to Moscow. Pavlova spent three years in Sofia at the Union of Bulgarian Composers, then at the Bulgarian National Opera. She then returned to Moscow, and during the last year of Soviet rule was employed by the Russian Musical Society Board. She had been composing original music since 1972, but it wasn't until her move to New York in 1990 that Pavlova's compositional career really began to flourish. Her *Symphony No. 1 Farewell Russia*, composed for 11 instruments, is a somber piece that reflects the country's mood of confusion, and her own feelings of homesickness.

From 2000 onward, Pavlova has concentrated on large orchestral compositions. Her ballet *Sulamith* is one of her most ambitious works and is based on the biblical story of Solomon.

On December 25, 1991 Mikhail Gorbachev resigned, and the following day the Soviet Union was formally dissolved. Yeltsin took over as Russian head of state.

Boris Yeltsin received almost as much criticism for his erratic public behavior as he did for the crime, corruption, and severe economic hardship that Russia endured during his time in office. And his invasion of Chechnya in 1994—which led to a 20-month war and the loss of approximately 80,000 lives—was considered a major human rights' travesty. Yeltsin resigned in 1999 and died of heart failure in 2007. Yet in spite of his many failures, he will go down in history as the person who dismantled the Russian communist party and the Soviet Union.

SHARING SPACE

During the Bush–Yeltsin summit of June 1992, Boris Yeltsin and US President George H.W. Bush agreed to cuts in nuclear warheads. In addition, they signed an agreement to implement a joint space venture.

The following year, the Russian Prime Minister Victor Chernomyrdin and US Vice President Al Gore discussed plans to build an international space station. It was decided that US space shuttles would carry

Above As part of Gorbachev's policy of *glasnost*, in 1989 Soviet soldiers and tanks withdrew from East Berlin and returned to the Soviet Union.

provisions and personnel to the Russian space station *Mir*, and the US provided funding to enable American astronauts on *Mir* to learn how to cope with extended space flights. On February 6, 1995, Eileen Collins became the first US astronaut to rendezvous with *Mir*. Colonel Collins was also the first American woman to pilot a space shuttle.

Between 1995 and 2001, a total of seven US astronauts spent just over two years on *Mir*. Although several technical difficulties occurred over the period and scientific discoveries were limited, the mission was deemed a success because it taught Russian cosmonauts and US astronauts to work together. The two countries had come a long way from the Cold War "space race" of the 1950s and 1960s.

Arvo Pärt

BORN SEPTEMBER 11, 1935

ARVO PÄRT'S POSITION AS ONE OF THE MOST PERFORMED AND
ADMIRED OF CONTEMPORARY COMPOSERS IS PERHAPS A LITTLE
SURPRISING. WHAT COULD BE MORE AT ODDS WITH OUR NOISY,
ATHEISTIC, WAR-TORN WORLD THAN THE QUIETLY CONTEM-
PLATIVE, MYSTICAL MUSIC OF HIS MATURE STYLE AND ITS
EXPRESSION OF DEEPLY SINCERE CHRISTIAN FAITH?

Yet his music has grown steadily in popularity over
the last four decades, suggesting that people find
it a refuge from the modern world, a cooling draught
in our overheated lives. But the artistic journey that
has brought Pärt to this position has been neither
easy nor conventional.

EDUCATION AND EARLY COMPOSITIONS

Estonia, where Pärt was born in 1935, was part of the
Soviet Union from 1940 until 1991. His musical studies at the Conservatoire in Tallinn, which he attended
from 1957 until 1963, were accordingly undertaken
within a system governed by Stalinist dogma that
forbade contact with the "modernist" music of the
Western avant-garde. Undeterred, Pärt secretly studied
the forbidden techniques of serialism from textbooks
and scores, while gaining the approval of his teachers
by composing music that was acceptably reminiscent

Right Arvo Pärt was awarded the Leonie Sonnig Music Prize in May 2008, during a performance with the Danish National Symphony Orchestra.

Below A still from the 2002 film *Gerry*, directed by Gus Van Sant. The movie featured Pärt's music *Für Alina*.

of Shostakovich. he was regarded as an especially gifted
student—one tutor remarked that notes seemed just to
"fall out of his sleeves." However, he attracted official
censure in 1960 for the sin of modernism when his
orchestral work *Nekrolog*, which was composed in the
twelve-tone serial manner of Arnold Schoenberg,
revealed his secret studies as well as winning him his
first recognition in the West as a composer of enormous technical accomplishment and promise.

Despite first prizes won in 1962 at the All-Union
Young Composers' Competition for a children's cantata and an oratorio in a more conventional style, he
continued to defy Soviet artistic edicts by composing
complex, stridently dissonant music that explored
almost every avant-garde technique of the period—
pointillism, aleatoric writing (instructing players to
improvise upon a specified set of pitches), and serialism
extended to include note-values and rhythm. This
period lasted until 1964, the year after his graduation
from the Conservatoire, before Pärt's restless musical
mind moved on to explore a kind of collage technique.
This alternates sections composed in his aggressive
modernist style with passages of real or imitation

Discover the music

Credo (1968)

Wenn Bach Bienen Verzüchtet Hätte (1976)

Cantus in Memoriam Benjamin Britten (1977)

Fratres (1977–c. 1992; this appears in several
    instrumentations)

Summa (several instrumentations)

Festina Lente (1988)

Magnificat (1989)

CREDO (1968)

This setting of the Latin creed for piano, chorus, and orchestra was Pärt's first overt statement of the Christian faith to which virtually all his later works would be dedicated and—obviously a direct challenge to official Soviet atheism—it was immediately banned. The collage structure pits complex serial music against the tonal clarity of Bach's *C major Prelude* from Book 1 of *The Well-Tempered Klavier*. It is a conflict that clearly reflects the composer's internal philosophical turmoil and, significantly, it is Bach's sublime tonal purity that emerges the victor.

Baroque or Classical music. This process reached its culmination in 1968 with *Credo*, the real turning point in the composer's career.

SILENCE, RESURRECTION, MATURITY, AND EXILE

After *Credo*, Pärt retreated into near silence, seeking simplicity in the study of plainsong, Gregorian chant, and the spare open-textured music of early church composers such as Machaut and Ockeghem. He emerged eight years later with a new personal style he called *tintinnabuli* (bell sounds) based on slow-moving consonant chords against which the quicker movement of a melodic line creates gentle passing dissonances, not unlike the clash of distant bells.

The new style was unveiled in its simplest form in 1976 with the tiny piano piece *Für Alina* which, set against *Credo*, must surely represent the greatest stylistic about-turn by any composer in musical history.

In the following year, the beautiful and haunting lament *Cantus in Memoriam*

Benjamin Britten brought the composer worldwide acclaim and a popularity that he has never lost.

Pärt's high-profile Christianity was embarrassing to Estonia's communist government. He was encouraged to leave and did so in 1980, moving first to Vienna and then to Berlin where he has lived ever since.

Arvo Pärt's music is that of an ascetic but serene, gentle man, much loved by his (generally irreligious) musical colleagues for his warmth and quiet wit. Listen, for example to his string piece, *If Bach Had Kept Bees,* or ponder this story of the too-insistent publicist: He persuaded the reluctant composer to agree to a lunch meeting only to find, after driving 50 miles (80 km), that Pärt's lodging was a Trappist retreat and speech was forbidden. Arvo Pärt's seventy-fifth birthday in 2010 will be celebrated with enthusiasm by musicians everywhere.

Left Pärt's music has proved a popular choice with filmmakers, among them Paul Thomas Anderson, who used *Fratres for cello and piano* in his 2007 motion picture *There Will Be Blood*.

Postmodern music

POSTMODERNISM MEANS MANY THINGS TO MANY PEOPLE, AND ONE'S DEFINITION DEPENDS
UPON A NUMBER OF FACTORS. WHAT DOES MODERNISM MEAN? DOES THE MODERN PERIOD
BEGIN IN THE LATE SIXTEENTH CENTURY OR THE TWENTIETH? DOES ONE CONSIDER
POSTMODERNISM A HISTORICAL CONTINUATION OR A REJECTION OF MODERNISM? IF THE
LATTER, WHAT FACTORS CONTRIBUTE TO THIS REJECTION—SOCIAL, POLITICAL, ESTHETIC,
INTELLECTUAL, OR SOME COMBINATION THEREOF?

In terms of music, postmodernism commonly refers to the period from 1945 onward, corresponding to the end of World War II and the consequent expansion of musical plurality. Musicologist Jann Pasler suggests that musical postmodernism may be described as falling into three main categories—reaction to the modernist movement, resistance against Western hegemony, and (re)interpretation of musical elements.

Above *In C*, a work written in 1964 by American composer Terry Riley (b. 1935) brought the minimalist ethos to wider public attention.

REACTIONS AGAINST MODERNISM
The first category of postmodernism seeks to balance excesses sometimes found in compositions of the first half of the twentieth century. Many listeners consider much twentieth-century music ugly, dissonant, and unapproachable. A common joke holds that Schoenberg's music is much better than it sounds. Some composers seem to have cared little for the general audience; Milton Babbitt, for example, argues in his "Who Cares if You Listen?" that in the same way that physicists, mathematicians, and other specialists safely assume a certain disciplinary competence, composers should as well. Of course, the first half of the twentieth century saw many compositions—dissonant or otherwise—of the highest caliber, and these works have deservedly garnered a large audience among specialists and the general public alike. Nonetheless, the notion of musical progress characterized by constant change and novelty championed by many avant-garde composers provoked a postmodernist reaction. Calling into question the notion of progress (is Brahms better than Beethoven, Beethoven better than Mozart, Mozart better than Bach?), a number of composers embraced a return to accessibility, often creating playful music that weakened the link between high and low art. However, David Del Tredici's *Final Alice* symphonies, Arvo Pärt's sacred vocal music, such as *Miserere* (1989), and Ellen Zwilich's work from the second symphony onward embrace accessibility while also maintaining high artistic standards.

CHALLENGING WESTERN HEGEMONY
A second category of postmodernism challenges the hegemony of Western art music. It undermines traditional tonal narratives in order to make room for music that fails to conform to Western tradition. An overwhelming majority of Western art music moves from stasis, to disruption, and finally to resolution. Tonal music in particular articulates that formal plan via the moving away from, and then the returning to, the tonic. Minimalist composers, including Terry Riley and Steve Reich, combined Eastern esthetics with Western

language in compositions that provided alternative formal plans. Riley's *In C* (1964) comprises 53 brief melodic segments to be played sequentially by a group of musicians. However, musicians move from one segment to the next slowly and not necessarily at the same time. This schema avoids traditional formal practice, encouraging improvisation and collaboration over hierarchy. This type of postmodernist music seeks collaboration with other cultures and replaces exploitation with exploration. Marginalized groups particularly welcome the inclusive nature of postmodern esthetics.

REINTERPRETATIONS

Collage, parody, and inclusion of non-traditional elements characterize the third category. John Cage's *HPSCHRD* draws upon music by composers such as Mozart, Beethoven, Chopin, and Schumann and uses chance processes to arrange music for seven harpsichordists. Film, photography, lighting, and taped music accompany these musicians to create what Cage referred to as "happenings." The third movement of Luciano Berio's *Sinfonia* combines Samuel Beckett's text *The Unnamable* with a reworking of the third movement of Mahler's second symphony and layers of quotations from musical works of the Baroque through to the twentieth century. As in Renaissance Masses, motivations for parody range from homage to competition. Postmodernism adds an additional aspect: Commentary on musical tradition.

Right French-born American composer Edgard Varèse (1883–1965) experimented with various electronic media to create a distinctive sound.

Left Steve Reich (see page 424) is an American minimalist composer who has been hugely influential over the last half-century or so. His work is characterized by layering of rhythmic and instrumental textures.

The exploration of non-traditional forms, genres, and instrumentation also expanded and questioned traditional norms. Varèse's *Ionization*, scored for 13 percussionists, constituted a reaction to what he considered the overly lush sound of strings that characterizes much Romantic era music. Experiments with recorded media and electronics after World War II widened sonic resources and finally allowed Varèse to pursue his vision with his *Poème électronique* in 1958. Cage's investigation into aleatoric processes called into question the very nature of what constitutes music, and many consider his *4'33"* (a three-movement piece, each movement directing silence from the performer) a provocative gesture leading to a complete reconsideration of musical esthetics.

At present, it may be far too early to settle on a definition of postmodernism. For some commentators, postmodernism entails skepticism of absolute truth and singular realities, and argues instead for multiple understandings of reality.

Postmodernism in this sense scrutinizes esthetic principles, actively discourages the marginalization of disempowered groups, makes room for alternative voices, and "de-centers" the established literary, artistic, and musical canons.

Philip Glass

BORN JANUARY 31, 1937

PHILIP GLASS STANDS AS ONE OF THE MOST IMPORTANT AND INFLUENTIAL COMPOSERS OF THE LAST 30 YEARS, SERVING AS AN INSPIRATION FOR ARTISTS AROUND THE WORLD. INITIALLY SHUNNED BY THE "SERIOUS" MUSIC COMMUNITY, HE GAINED FAME THROUGH COLLABORATIONS WITH PEERS IN THE THEATER, ART, POPULAR MUSIC, AND DANCE WORLDS.

Left The composer photographed in 1988. The Philip Glass Ensemble has been performing his works since its founding in 1968.

Right Philip Glass performs at the XXXIII Cervantes International Festival in Mexico in 2005. The didgeridoo player is Mark Atkin.

Discover the music

Music in Twelve Parts (1971–1974)

Einstein on the Beach (1976)

Satyagraha (1980)

Koyaanisqatsi (1982)

Akhnaten (1983)

Concerto for Violin and Orchestra (1987)

Symphony No. 1 "Low" (1992)

The Hours (2002)

In his remarkable career, he has collaborated with, to name only a few, poet Allen Ginsberg, novelist Doris Lessing, director Robert Wilson, choreographer Twyla Tharp, as well as Ravi Shankar, David Bowie, David Byrne, Leonard Cohen, and Woody Allen, and he has successfully bridged the bastions of serious music, theater, dance, and film.

Glass was born in Baltimore, the grandson of Lithuanian immigrants and the son of a record store owner. Interested in classical music from an early age, Glass studied flute at the Peabody Conservatory and attended an accelerated college program at the University of Chicago. Turning to the keyboard, Glass attended the Juilliard School and composed serial works, all while searching for a style of his own.

Seeking inspiration, Philip Glass went to Paris and studied with Nadia Boulanger (who taught, among others, Elliott Carter, Aaron Copland, Quincy Jones, Michel Legrand, Charlie Parker, and Astor Piazzolla). In Paris, Glass was exposed to avant-garde theater and the cinema of the French New Wave, including films by Jean-Luc Godard and François Truffaut, and he worked with Indian sitar virtuoso Ravi Shankar. All these people and experiences profoundly influenced his approach to composition.

"MUSIC WITH REPETITIVE STRUCTURES"

Glass settled in New York City and, renouncing his earlier style, began to compose using a method he called "music with repetitive structures" that incorporated what he learned on his European and Indian visits. Later dubbed "minimalism," a term Glass dislikes, the music is based on carefully controlled

Saxophone

Commonly associated with jazz and popular music, the saxophone has been used in almost every musical setting, including the modern symphony orchestra. Invented in 1841 by Adolphe Sax, the saxophone is a single reed instrument and is played using 23 keys. Although Sax originally created 14 different sizes, these days there are only four that are commonly used—soprano, alto, tenor, and baritone. Glass's *Concerto for Saxophone Quartet* is a fascinating work, involving dissonant and interesting harmony, the instruments arranged to utilize the range and tonal quality of each of the different saxophones.

"What came to me as a revelation was the use of rhythm in developing an overall structure in music."

rhythms, consonant and repetitive melodic structures, and slow harmonic changes. These early works rather bewildered audiences and Glass struggled to gain acceptance, working as a plumber and taxi driver in order to support his craft.

Over time, Glass built a devoted following that led to his early successes—the most important of which was the opera *Einstein on the Beach*. Created in collaboration with the director Robert Wilson and premièred at New York's Metropolitan Opera, *Einstein* brought Glass international recognition and, by breaking all the rules, it stands as one of the world's most important contemporary operas. From this time forward, Glass's style as a composer was maturing and becoming more accessible. While he still retained the repetitive melodic and rhythmic structures that typified his style, he began to deepen his harmonic language and broaden his melodic writing. Glass also began to write for more traditional ensembles (for example,

Below A still from Godfrey Reggio's 1982 film *Koyaanisqatsi*, for which Glass wrote the evocative score.

KOYAANISQATSI (1982)

Glass wrote the score to Godfrey Reggio's film *Koyaanisqatsi*, cited as one of the twentieth century's most important art films. Featuring no conventional plot or dialogue, the film explores the impact of modernization on the natural world through a series of visual tableaux. Contrasting natural and urban landscapes from across America, the film delivers a powerful message consistent with its title, meaning "life out of balance" in the Hopi Native American language.

string quartet, orchestra) that allowed the major performing groups to present his work. Glass's eight
symphonies (to date) are often performed worldwide.

In recent years, Philip Glass has maintained an
active performance and composing schedule. He has
embraced many of the idioms of his classical predecessors (including symphonies, concertos, and chamber
music) while composing new operas, incidental music
for theater, and a number of film scores. Glass has been
nominated for Academy Awards three times—for
Kundun (1997), *The Hours* (2002), and *Notes on a Scandal* (2006). When he is not touring, lecturing or performing, Glass, now in his seventies, divides his time
between New York City and Nova Scotia. With an
impressive body of work, Glass's influence will be felt
for decades to come.

Above The score for
The Hours (2002) won
Glass a BAFTA award for
best film music as well
as an Academy Award
nomination.

Right A 1981 perform-
ance of Glass's opera
Satyagraha, which is
based on the life of
Mahatma Gandhi and his
advocacy of non-violent
resistance to inequity.

THE PORTRAIT OPERAS

Among Glass's numerous stage works, three early
operas—collectively dubbed the Portrait Operas—are
among the best known. Each one explores the life of
a seminal historical figure who changed the world
through their ideas: Alfred Einstein (*Einstein on the
Beach*, 1976), Mahatma Gandhi (*Satyagraha*, 1980)
and one of Egypt's important pharaohs
(*Akhnaten*, 1983). These works explore the
impact of science, monotheism, and non-
violence, and how they have shaped our
world. Written in a continuously maturing
style, they are among the most important
operas in the contemporary repertory.

Right Philip Glass was nominated for a third Academy
Award for his score to the 2006 film *Notes on a Scandal*,
directed by Richard Eyre.

LIFE & TIMES

American art music

AS EUROPEAN MUSIC DID IN THE EARLY TWENTIETH CENTURY, SO HAS AMERICAN MUSIC
FROM 1960 FORWARD MIRRORED MOVEMENTS IN ART, FILM, AND LITERATURE—FROM POST-
MODERNISM TO MINIMALISM, POP ART TO ABSTRACT EXPRESSIONISM. THE WATCHWORD FOR
THE LATTER PART OF THE CENTURY AND INTO THE NEXT CENTURY IS DIVERSITY.

As social and political events moved at an ever-increasing speed, so too did the cultural response. Immediately following the events of World War II, composers turned to a postmodernist style—one that rejected all ideas of formalism in creative expression. Later, the environmental art movement would help spawn minimalism in music—favoring a simple, direct form of expression, as exemplified by the music of Philip Glass, Steve Reich, and John Adams.

BROADENING HORIZONS

Changes in transportation and communications enabled composers to explore indigenous music from around the world, including African drumming, Indian Carnatic and Hindusthani traditions, Indonesian gamelan music, and Japanese theatrical genres, and to incorporate these styles into their own work. Additionally, the popularity of rock and roll and the Broadway

Right Adrian Thompson (as Mao Zedong) in the English National Opera's 2006 production of *Nixon in China* by John Adams.

Below Performers in front of a large video screen during the 2002 première of the video opera *Three Tales* by Steve Reich and his wife Beryl Korot.

musical have had a significant impact on many younger composers. After decades of being alienated, audiences were welcomed back in the concert hall by this new generation of American composers with accessible, exciting, and powerful new works.

American composers in the latter half of the twentieth century veered from total serialism (an outgrowth of Schoenberg's twelve-tone technique that can be seen in the works of Elliott Carter, Iannis Xenakis, and Pierre Boulez) to aleatoricism (characterized by letting chance and performer discretion determine each performance, as seen in the works of John Cage). Composers like George Crumb explored hyper-virtuosity in performance and incorporated improvisational techniques similar to many indigenous performance styles, while technological advances allowed composers to experiment with synthesizers, recording loops, and music generated by computers. At the same time,

STEVE REICH (B. 1936)

Strongly influenced both by the minimalist movement in art and by indigenous musical traditions, Reich has emerged as one of the twenty-first century's great composers. Born in New York, Reich attended Juilliard, and then Mills College in California. His teachers included Darius Milhaud and Luciano Berio. Reich also studied in Ghana, absorbing influences of West African drumming. Indonesian gamelan music is another influence that would feature in his work. His unique voice has made him highly sought after; he receives commissions from major orchestras and ensembles around the world.

JOHN ADAMS (B. 1947)

The least "minimal" of the composers labeled "minimalist," Adams's work has always been infused with a strong neo-Romantic flair. Raised in New England, Adams attended Harvard University before moving to California and becoming composer-in-residence with the San Francisco Symphony. While he may be best known for his stage works, including two collaborations with poet June Jordan and director Peter Sellars, *Nixon in China* and *The Death of Klinghoffer*, his chamber music, and orchestral works are also frequently performed. Adams received the 2003 Pulitzer Prize for *On the Transmigration of Souls*, written for the anniversary of the 9/11 attacks. He is also an author, conductor, and an active advocate for American music.

Right James Horner is known for his film music. Among the many movies for which he has composed is Ron Howard's *How the Grinch Stole Christmas* (2000).

composers have been increasingly drawn to the collaborative world of performance art—merging theater, film, dance, visual art, and contemporary music to create wildly popular narrative works. As a result, American composers ranging from John Corigliano (b. 1938) to Christopher Rouse (b. 1949), to name only two, have carved out multi-faceted careers.

With the women's movement of the 1960s and 1970s, women composers have come increasingly to the forefront. As diverse and eclectic as their male counterparts, American female composers such as Joan Tower (b. 1938), Laurie Anderson (b. 1947), Barbara Kolb (b. 1939), Shulamit Ran (b. 1949), Libby Larsen (b. 1950), and Meredith Monk (b. 1942) have forged successful and diverse careers.

While the world of university music departments, the symphony hall, and the opera and ballet houses still feature prominently in the world of contemporary music, Hollywood has become increasingly significant, fostering many

Below Laurie Anderson is a composer and performance artist who, in 2003, was named NASA's first (and so far only) artist-in-residence.

American composers who have built careers in film scoring. Great masters of the genre, including John Williams (b. 1932), Bernard Herrmann (1911–1975) and Jerry Goldsmith (1929–2004), have inspired generations of younger composers to enter the field, among them Danny Elfman (b. 1953), James Newton Howard (b. 1951), and James Horner (b. 1953).

Discover the music

John Adams, *Harmonielehre* (1984–1985)
John Adams, *Nixon in China* (1985–1987)
Laurie Anderson, *O Superman* (1981)
John Corigliano, *Symphony No. 2* (2001)
George Crumb, *Ancient Voices of Children* (1970)
Meredith Monk, *Atlas* (1991)
Steve Reich, *Drumming* (1970–1971)
Steve Reich, *The Desert Music* (1984)
Joan Tower, *Fanfare for the Uncommon Woman* (1987)

"CROSSING OVER"

Most readers of this text have some conception of "classical" music. Perhaps the term brings to mind composers—Bach, Haydn, Mozart, Beethoven, Brahms, Mahler—or genres such as the sonata, symphony, or concerto. Similarly, with popular music, depending upon one's age, one might think of Glenn Miller, Elvis Presley, Led Zeppelin, Madonna, Billy Joel, or Britney Spears. It should be simple then, to define classical/popular crossover music.

Yet the issue is far more complicated than it first appears. The label "classical" itself is problematic. Strictly speaking, the term refers to the period of ancient Greece and Rome. In music, it commonly designates the period c. 1750–c. 1820. So what term does one use to denote the music described in this book? Commonly proposed alternatives such as "art music" or "concert music" suffer similar shortcomings. Most, if not all, composers of rock, folk, and other forms of popular music justifiably consider themselves artists, and their music art. Moreover, much of this music finds its way into the concert hall. Musicologist H. Wiley Hitchcock suggests "vernacular" and "cultivated" to differentiate these styles. Although the former corresponds to popular styles, and the latter to music that requires effort on behalf of the listener, these designations are also lacking. Many popular styles require effort, as does almost any style or genre of music foreign to one's cultural conditioning.

Left Bill Haley (left) and Elvis Presley in 1955. As rock and roll developed, some performers adopted "classical" conventions, such as the use of choirs and orchestral backing.

Below George Gershwin successfully crossed musical genres. He composed works that are "classical," including an opera, as well as many of the most popular songs of the twentieth century.

DISTINGUISHING THE MUSIC

Consider the distinction between popular music and the style that occupies most of this book. What characteristics separate the two? One might argue that in the case of "classical" music, artists compose music in the form of scores that are read by musicians; in contrast, popular music often arises through improvisation and spreads aurally. Many "classical" composers, however, improvised music—contests of skill between composers, cadenzas, realizing figured bass, etc—and much popular music is readily available in scores. In many cases, artists compose popular pieces for others to perform in the same way one generally thinks of "classical" music. Perhaps the answer lies in commercialism: "classical" music is art for art's sake, whereas profit drives popular music. This distinction also does not hold true. Most "classical" composers had patronage of one sort or another. Mozart rarely composed without an expectation of some form of payment. Rossini famously extracted as much money as possible by recycling major portions of his compositions for different patrons. Other distinctions such as instrumentation, complexity, or methods of dissemination fare no better under scrutiny.

CROSSING FROM ONE STYLE TO ANOTHER

In terms of crossing from one style to the other, two principal categories come to mind—composers of "classical" music quoting, emulating, or seeking inspiration from folk, blues, ragtime, jazz, or other popular styles; and popular music quotations or re-workings of "classical" compositions.

The first category has a long tradition in Western music. Composers of medieval and Renaissance Masses often used preexisting popular melodies in the tenor

Left John Gay's *The Beggar's Opera* was first performed in 1728. A satiric work, Gay took the standard operatic framework but used popular tunes of the day.

voice, frequently the tune *L'homme armé*. Martin
Luther, in a practice called *contrafactum*, added liturgical text to popular melodies in a number of his compositions for the newly formed Protestant church.
Baroque composer John Gay set the libretto for *The
Beggar's Opera* to popular tunes. Classical composers
wrote variations on common tunes, such as Mozart's
Ah vous dirai-je, maman. Similarly, Mahler used the
folk tune *Bruder Martin* (*Frère Jacques*) in the third
movement of his first symphony. Charles Ives borrowed extensively from American popular tunes,
often quoting several in a single piece of
music. The opening measures of Stravinsky's
The Rite of Spring quotes an old Lithuanian
folk melody almost verbatim. Gershwin
included ragtime and jazz in *Rhapsody in
Blue* and his masterpiece opera *Porgy and
Bess*. There are many more such examples.

Such borrowing works both ways. Electronic artists have set Barber's *Adagio
for Strings*, Orff's *Carmina Burana*, and
Albinoni's *Adagio in G minor* in dance
and ambient styles. Composer Richard

Above The Proms are
a fixture on the London
musical scene. During its
annual summer season,
the Proms feature
performances of much-
loved classical works,
as well as more modern
pieces, including music
from Bollywood films.

Souther arranges Hildegard von Bingen's music with
popular percussion backgrounds in *Vision*. Mezzo-
soprano Louise Tucker's hit *Midnight Blue* borrows
the melody from the second movement of Beethoven's
Sonata Pathetique; Walter Murphy gives a disco rendition of the opening of Beethoven's *Symphony No. 5* in
his *A Fifth of Beethoven*. Other examples abound.

Some pieces of music cross boundaries over time.
Mozart's *Piano Sonata in C major* was popular music
in every sense of the word. Many of Schubert's Lieder
were similarly popular. Opera excerpts often appeared
in arrangements for piano so that they could be enjoyed
by others in the same way that sheet music of
popular music circulates today. Over time,
much of this music has been classed "classical" rather than popular. We can reasonably expect the same might happen with
some music that we consider popular today.

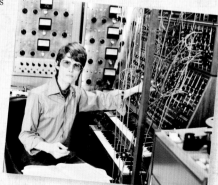

Left Wendy Carlos (b. 1939) made her famous recording
Switched-On Bach in 1968, using the Moog synthesizer. This
electronic treatment of Bach's music was hugely successful.

Kaija Saariaho

BORN OCTOBER 14, 1952

THE LAST AND YOUNGEST COMPOSER PRESENTED IN THIS BOOK, KAIJA SAARIAHO
EMBODIES MUCH OF WHAT, FORGETTING OLD CONVENTIONS, A YOUNG COMPOSER AT THE
START OF THE TWENTY-FIRST CENTURY MIGHT HOPE TO ASPIRE TO. SHE COMES FROM THE
GEOGRAPHICAL OUTER FRINGES OF EUROPE (FINLAND), AND NOW, ESTABLISHED IN PARIS,
IS ONE OF THE MOST SUCCESSFUL AND HIGHLY REGARDED COMPOSERS OF HER GENERATION.

Saariaho began as an angry radical; since then her style has softened, but she has retained a personal voice, creating music that draws both on new technology and the traditions of the concert hall.

Though Finland may not have produced a truly major, internationally influential composer since Sibelius, it has continued to attach enormous importance to cultivating music as an art form. So the environment in which Saariaho commenced composition studies at the Sibelius Academy in Helsinki (studying with the modernist Paavo Heininen) was very supportive, as it was for her slightly younger contemporary Magnus Lindberg. She was no prodigy; her first important work, the strikingly aggressive *Verblendungen* (*Dazzles*) for orchestra, was composed at the age of 32, but after that she scarcely looked back.

After studies in Freiburg with "complexist" composer Brian Ferneyhough, in 1982 she moved to Paris. At IRCAM, the music research center founded by Pierre Boulez in 1977, she immersed herself in computer music, producing many pieces for live instruments and tape. She also married Jean-Baptiste Barrière, a

GRAAL THÉÂTRE (1994)

When Saariaho composed *Graal théâtre* (*Grail theater*) for violin and orchestra, it was a new venture for her in two ways. It was her first work for some time not to involve electronics, and it was also her first engagement with a traditional genre, in this case, the concerto. The title reflects this; it comes from a book by Jacques Roubaud that seeks to reinterpret an old tradition (the legend of the Holy Grail) in modern terms. This is exactly what Saariaho sought to do in her new "concerto." Another inspiration was the extraordinary playing of the Latvian-born virtuoso violinist Gidon Kremer (left), to whom the work is dedicated.

The piece, which lasts about half an hour, is in two movements. In both movements, the solo violin is almost constantly present, and always in the foreground. Despite some "discursive" moments near the start, the orchestra functions predominantly as a luscious sonic backdrop, which the soloist mainly soars above (especially in the first movement), but sometimes also plunges down into. The violin writing is both traditional and modern—it explores the post-Paganini "extended techniques" of composers like Salvatore Sciarrino, involving the fringe regions between pitch and noise, but it also recreates many of the typical rhetorical virtuoso gestures of the Romantic era.

Left The Lincoln Center in New York. Saariaho was the conductor of the Center's 2008 Mostly Mozart season.

pioneer of computer music at IRCAM. At this time, a powerful force in Parisian music was "spectralism," a movement headed by young composers such as Gerard Grisey and Tristan Murail, which sought to derive new harmonic possibilities from the microtones that occur naturally as part of the overtone series, but also from analysis of "inharmonic" sounds such as those of cathedral bells. Though never an orthodox spectralist, Kaija Saariaho's fondness for rich, widely spaced harmonies reflects this trend. Her fascination with luminous, glistening colors seems to make her more an adopted French composer than a brooding Scandinavian.

"I'm a square peg that won't fit into a round hole."

TITLES, INSPIRATIONS, AND NEW TECHNOLOGY

Virtually all the titles of Saariaho's works have some kind of extra-musical reference. While some are merely poetic/impressionist (*Petals, Nymphéa, Six Japanese Gardens*), there are three consistent, partly related obsessions, namely with light (*Lichtbogen, Notes on Light*), the flight of birds (*Sah den Vöglen, Laconisme d'aile*), and galactic space (*Orion, Solar, Asteroid 4179*). In recent years her style has sometimes been criticized (but also praised) for becoming more immediately accessible, especially in vocal works such as the operas *L'Amour de loin* (which won the

Discover the music

Verblendungen (1984)

Lichtbogen (1986)

Noa-Noa (1992)

Graal théâtre (1994)

L'Amour de loin (2000)

Adriana Mater (2005)

La Passion de Simone (2006)

Notes on Light (2007)

prestigious Grawemeyer Award in 2003) and *Adriana Mater*. But whatever the superficial stylistic changes, she retains a very eloquent personal voice. She is also, clearly, very conscious of the possibilities of the computer age as a means of documentation as well as musical creation. Saariaho's CD-ROM album *Prisma* is, perhaps, a preliminary model for the way that twenty-first century composers will now seek to reach and address new, computer-orientated generations.

Below Pia Freund (left) and Michael Schumacher rehearse Saariaho's opera *La Passion de Simone*, in Vienna's Jugendstiltheater in 2006.

Composing in the twenty-first century

WHAT DOES IT MEAN TO BE A TWENTY-FIRST CENTURY COMPOSER OF "ART MUSIC"? IT INVOLVES ENDLESS CHOICES—ESTHETIC, TECHNOLOGICAL, AND SOCIAL. IT CAN MEAN ANYTHING FROM SITTING ALONE WITH PEN AND PAPER, JUST AS BACH OR BRAHMS DID, TO SQUATTING ON THE FLOOR WITH A LAPTOP.

Stylistically, it can involve anything from reinventing the past to trying to plot the future. And in an increasingly technological age, the means of communicating the results are in a state of constant flux.

YOUTUBE

Even amid the spiraling growth of media distribution in the first decade of the twenty-first century, the meteoric rise of YouTube was a startling phenomenon. Created in 2005, within eighteen months it had grown to the point where it was acquired by Google for US$1.65 billion. Though primarily designed as a means of sharing video files, it has also made music of every kind accessible. Like purely audio predecessors such as Napster, it is fraught with copyright infringement problems; it seems fair to assume that a huge amount of the material available on YouTube has no copyright clearance. On the other hand, where contemporary art music is concerned, much of this material is not pirated from commercially available sources, but comprises material one would never have access to otherwise—rehearsals, interviews, archival performance footage, and so forth. Typing in names like John Cage or Karlheinz Stockhausen, one can be astonished by what becomes instantly available. The dilemma of balancing the rival claims of ethics and knowledge has never been more acute. And this, clearly, is just the beginning.

"THE NEW UNSURVEYABILITY"

In the 1970s, as the notion of postmodernism took an increasing hold on cultural thinking, the philosopher Jurgen Habermas introduced the notion of "die neue Unübersichtlichkeit" (literally, though clumsily, "the new unsurveyability"). It implied that it was no longer possible to identify any significant threads driving cultural production, that we were simply swamped by diversity, by an overload of information, and we had to accept everything as more or less equal. Thirty years later, one could say that, objectively, the situation as depicted by Habermas has escalated many times over. But at the same time, one could say that this relativist approach seems as lazily defeatist now as it did then. Clear trends can indeed be identified. Where traditional "concert hall" music is concerned, one can see

Above left A laptop computer and mixing board in a recording studio. Many composers now favor working with computer-assisted composition programs.

Above right These days, home studios and recording equipment are more affordable, and composers have access to an enormous range of technical effects.

a clear polarization between Europe and the United States that is both stylistic and ideological (in the sense of what art music should be "about," and what it should strive to communicate).

In the USA, the driving force is a restoration of tonal or modal idioms, often extrapolated from 1960s minimalism; the main figures here are John Adams and Steve Reich. However, despite the affirmative surface of their music, neither composer shies away from controversial social issues, as witnessed by Reich's *City Life*, and Adams's opera *Dr Atomic*. In Europe, on the other hand, minimalism has gained little foothold, though Reich's work is often heard. The most prominent source of tonal–modal music in Europe is probably the Baltic states; the best-known figure is Arvo Pärt, whose work is primarily vocal and religious.

NEW EMPHASES

After a relative retreat from modernism in the 1970s and 1980s, younger composers seem to be returning to a situation where—however diverse their styles—the emphasis is once again on originality and innovation. Particularly striking here is the renewed interest in microtones, in both melody and harmony. Partly this stems from the French "spectral" composers who emerged in the 1970s (of whom Tristan Murail is still active), but also from an interest in the music of other (especially Arab) cultures where such intervals

Above Rather than visit a concert hall, many people listen to music using the latest technology, such as iPods, which can store vast amounts of music.

Left La La founders Bill Nguyen (left), Anselm Baird-Smith (right), and Billy Alvarado. La La is just one way to get music in the digital age, by swapping CDs on its website for US$1.

Above Michael Tilson Thomas rehearses the YouTube Symphony Orchestra. Musicians from over 30 countries auditioned via YouTube and the winners were selected by popular vote. The orchestra performed at Carnegie Hall in New York in April 2009.

occur naturally. This in turn reflects a major change in the demographics of many European cities, with their increased Middle Eastern populations.

Now, in the early years of the twenty-first century, most music is not heard in concert halls but via home audio systems. Moreover, with exception of students and professional musicians, few listeners read music, and fewer still buy scores of contemporary works—their experience of music is almost entirely auditory. In principle, most composers could distribute their music almost solely via the internet, and many do. However, most major composers still prefer to be represented by a major publisher, whose function is not so much to sell scores as to publicize works, negotiate performances, and handle performing rights issues. Beyond that, such publishers provide better prospects for the survival of authors' works after their death, and composers' dreams of immortality, in this sense, are by no mean a thing of the past.

MUSICAL INSTRUMENTS

STRINGED INSTRUMENTS

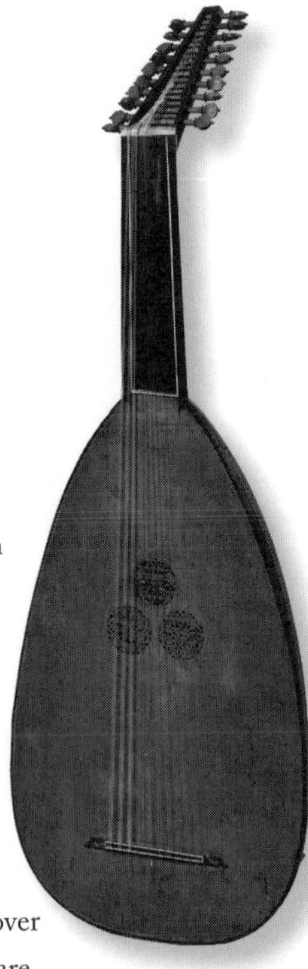

LUTE

Entering medieval Europe from Arabic culture, the lute is a descendant of the oud, and related to the Romanian cobza and the mandolin. The lute developed its classic form by about 1500. It is extremely lightweight and has a pear-shaped body. It typically has six strings, and a neck with seven to ten frets. As instrument-making progressed, the lute lost favor among composers.

VIOLIN

Immediately associated with classical music, the violin emerged in Italy in the early 1500s. It has four strings (G, D, A, E) and a range of over four octaves. Among the violin's characteristics are its singing tone and lyrical qualities. It is a pivotal member of the orchestra, which usually has about 30 violins in the string section. Construction is critical if the desired tone is to be achieved. Famous violin makers, such as Andrea Amati (1525–1611), Antonio Stradivari (c. 1644–1737), and Giuseppe Guarneri (1666–1739), crafted violins that are still in use today.

Some noted violinists
Nicolò Paganini 1782–1840
Joseph Joachim 1831–1907
Fritz Kreisler 1875–1962
Jascha Heifetz 1901–1987
David Oistrakh 1908–1974
Yehudi Menuhin 1916–1999
Isaac Stern 1920–2001
Itzhak Perlman b. 1945
Gidon Kremer b. 1947
Nigel Kennedy b. 1956
Anne-Sophie Mutter b. 1963
Joshua Bell b. 1967
Hilary Hahn b. 1979

VIOLA

The viola is nearly identical in playing position and close in pitch range to the violin. Yet, with a deeper and more full-bodied tone than the violin, it is often limited to filling in harmony with little melodic material. There are, of course, notable exceptions— Berlioz famously featured the viola in *Harold in Italy* (1834).

Some noted violists
Lionel Tertis 1876–1975
William Primrose 1904–1982
Nobuko Imai b. 1943
Yuri Bashmet b. 1953

CELLO

Developing from the three-stringed bass violin in the 1500s, the cello (its full name is violoncello) typically provides the inner harmony parts in the string section and for the orchestra. Tuned in fifths, the cello is a member of chamber ensembles.

Some noted cellists
Pablo Casals 1876–1973
Mstislav Rostropovich 1927–2007
Jacqueline du Pré 1945–1987
Ralph Kirshbaum b. 1946
Maria Kliegel b. 1952
Yo Yo Ma b. 1955
Steven Isserlis b. 1958
Alban Gerhardt b. 1969

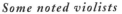

DOUBLE BASS

Tuned in fourths, the largest and lowest-pitched bowed string instrument used in the modern symphony orchestra is the double bass. Despite its enormity, acoustically it does not project a very loud sound, due to its low range, so if the bass is being used as an ensemble instrument in the orchestra, usually between four and eight bassists will play a part in unison to strengthen the effect.

Some noted bassists
Giovanni Bottesini 1821–1889
Oscar G. Zimmerman 1910–1987
François Rabbath b. 1931

HARP

The harp was prominent in many musical cultures, with different models and types found the world over, the earliest versions possibly dating back as far as 3000 BCE. The concert harp, evolving from earlier European models is around 6 feet (1.8 m) high and covers six and a half octaves (46 or 47 strings). The strings are plucked to create a sound. A pedal at the base of the instrument changes pitch and tuning, extending the range.

Some noted harpists
Turlough O'Carolan 1670–1738
Alphonse Jean Hasselmans 1845–1912
Henriette Renie 1875–1956
Carlos Salzedo 1885–1961
Marcel Grandjany 1891–1975

GUITAR

Usually associated with rock and popular music, blues or jazz, the guitar is not a standard part of the orchestra by any means, although there are pieces written for it. The six-stringed classical guitar first appeared in Spain, probably descending from stringed instruments such as the oud and the gittern. Made of cedar or spruce, the instrument has a resonating space, which, when the strings are plucked, creates the guitar's quite distinctive sound. Over time, metal screws replaced the wooden tuning pegs. Today's guitar strings are usually made of nylon.

Some noted guitarists
Fernando Sor 1778–1839
Andrés Segovia 1893–1987
Julian Bream b. 1933
John Williams b. 1941
Pepe Romero b. 1944
Aniello Desiderio b. 1971

BRASS INSTRUMENTS

TRUMPET

With the highest register in the brass family, the trumpet is one of the oldest musical instruments—early trumpets date back thousands of years; for example, bronze and silver trumpets were found in Tutankhamun's tomb in Egypt. Like all brass instruments, a "buzzing" sound created from closed lips creates a vibration in the air column of the instrument to produce its sound. The chromatic trumpet emerged during the late 1700s.

Some noted trumpet players

Adolph "Bud" Herseth b. 1921

Maurice André b. 1933

Wynton Marsalis b. 1961

TROMBONE

The only brass instrument in the orchestra without valves or keys, the trombone uses a slide to extend the length of the air column, lowering the pitch. Known as the "sackbut" until the eighteenth century, the trombone (or tenor trombone) first appeared in an orchestra in Joachim Eggert's *Symphony in E flat* in 1807. The tenor and bass trombones are now permanent fixtures in the modern symphony orchestra.

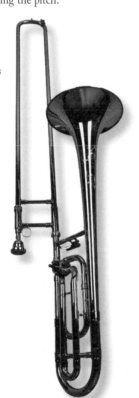

Some noted trombonists

John Kenny b. 1957

Christian Lindberg b. 1958

Alain Trudel b. 1966

FRENCH HORN

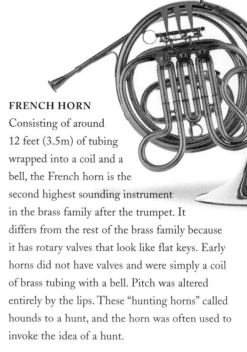

Consisting of around 12 feet (3.5m) of tubing wrapped into a coil and a bell, the French horn is the second highest sounding instrument in the brass family after the trumpet. It differs from the rest of the brass family because it has rotary valves that look like flat keys. Early horns did not have valves and were simply a coil of brass tubing with a bell. Pitch was altered entirely by the lips. These "hunting horns" called hounds to a hunt, and the horn was often used to invoke the idea of a hunt.

Some noted French horn players

Dennis Brain 1921–1957

Barry Tuckwell b. 1931

Herman Baumann b. 1934

TUBA

One of the most recent additions to the symphony orchestra, appearing the mid-nineteenth century, the tuba is the largest and lowest pitched brass instrument. Commonly used in military, marching, and concert bands, the tuba is typically pitched in B flat, E flat or F.

Some noted tuba players

Arnold Jacobs 1915–1998

Roger Bobo b. 1938

WOODWIND INSTRUMENTS

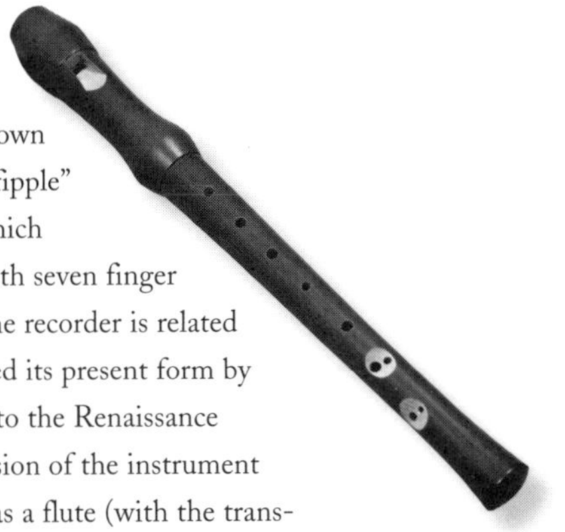

RECORDER

The recorder is an end-blown vertical flute featuring a "fipple" or whistle mouthpiece, which produces its airy tone. With seven finger holes and a thumbhole, the recorder is related to the ocarina and acquired its present form by around 1500. In contrast to the Renaissance recorder, the Baroque version of the instrument was normally referred to as a flute (with the transverse flute referred to as traverso). Today, the recorder is a popular instrument in schools and is often used in early music education.

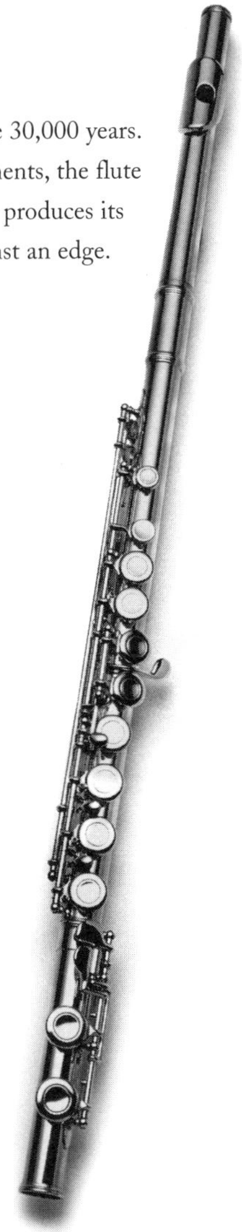

FLUTE

The flute's origins go back some 30,000 years. Unlike other woodwind instruments, the flute is a reedless wind instrument; it produces its sound from the flow of air against an edge.

Some noted flautists

Julius Baker 1915–2003
Jean-Pierre Rampal 1922–2000
Sir James Galway b. 1939
Jasmine Choi b. 1983

CLARINET

The clarinet is a woodwind instrument with 18 holes, six covered by the fingers, the remainder by keys. It developed from a recorder-like instrument from the Baroque era called the chalumeau, which had a very limited range. This was modified with the addition of a register key and became the instrument we know today. By the early years of the nineteenth century, the clarinet had become a standard fixture in the orchestra. Mozart is said to have considered the clarinet the instrument closest in tone to the human voice.

Some noted clarinettists

Anton Stadler 1753–1812
Jack Brymer 1915–2003
Alan Hacker b. 1938
Sabine Meyer b. 1959

BASS CLARINET

Part of the woodwind family, the bass clarinet resembles a saxophone. It is a straight-bodied instrument with a small unturned bell, a curved metal neck, and a distinct, rich, earthy tone. Like the rest of the clarinet family, bass clarinets use the Boehm system of keys and fingering. Although usually pitched in B flat (meaning it is a transposing instrument with B flat sounding as concert C), music has been specially written for the instrument in the key of A, such as in some of Wagner's operas, and in Rachmaninov's symphonies.

BASSOON

A double-reed woodwind instrument with a conical bore air column, the bassoon is the bass member of the oboe family. The player's right hand is responsible for 17 different keys, nine controlled by the thumb. The left hand controls 12 keys, four with the thumb.

Some noted bassoonists
Etienne Ozi 1754–1813
George Zukerman b. 1927
Klaus Thunemann b. 1937
Judith LeClair b. 1958

CONTRABASSOON

This instrument is a larger version of the bassoon and sounds one octave lower. It is used in larger symphony orchestras. Most orchestras have just one contrabassoonist, although sometimes, rather than have a separate contrabassoonist, one bassoonist doubles on both bassoon and contrabassoon. The contrabassoon had its beginnings in church music in the seventeenth century; by the eighteenth century it was appearing in military bands.

OBOE

Called a "hautbois" or "hoboy" prior to 1770, the Baroque oboe is a three-keyed double reed instrument. With a clear and often piercing tone, the oboe was the main melody instrument in early military bands. Most professional oboists make their own reeds, carving them to fit the unique embouchure, oboe angle and the air support of the individual musician. The way the reed is made affects the pitch of the instrument.

Some noted oboists
Marcel Tabuteau 1887–1966
Anthony Camden 1938–2006
Heinz Holliger b. 1939
Maurice Bourgue b. 1939

COR ANGLAIS

Part of the oboe family, the sound of a cor anglais is produced by blowing through a double reed. French for "English horn"—although it is neither English nor a horn—it is said that at one point in its history it resembled the oboe da caccia, a Baroque instrument that was either curved or bent, thus producing the name "cor angle" (later becoming cor anglais). Similarly to the oboe d'amore, the cor anglais has a bocal—a curved, tapered tube mouthpiece with the reed attached at the end.

SAXOPHONE

Commonly associated with jazz and popular music, the saxophone has been used in almost every musical setting, including the modern symphony orchestra. Invented in 1841 by Adolphe Sax, the saxophone is a single reed instrument and is played using 23 keys. Although Sax originally created 14 different sizes, these days there are only four that are commonly used—soprano, alto, tenor, and baritone.

Some noted saxophonists
Jean-Marie Londeix b. 1932
Eugene Rousseau b. 1932
Harvey Pittel b. 1943

KEYBOARD INSTRUMENTS

ORGAN

One of the oldest instruments in the Western musical tradition, the organ produces sound as wind vibrates through pipes of various materials (metal or wood), and with the timbre and volume altered by the keys, the handstops, and combination pistons. Unlike later keyboard instruments such as the piano, the organ's keyboard touch is not expressive (meaning every note sounds with the same velocity or force).

Some noted organists

Charles-Marie Widor 1844–1937
E. Power Biggs 1906–1977
Olivier Messiaen 1908–1992
Rachel Laurin b. 1961

VIRGINAL

In *Tractatus de musica* (c. 1460), Paulus Paulirinus of Prague wrote that, "… [it] is called a virginal because, like a virgin, it sounds with a gentle and undisturbed voice." Part of the harpsichord family, the virginal is a keyboard instrument that was used mainly during the late medieval and Renaissance periods. Like the harpsichord, the strings are plucked to create sounds. Most early models were played resting on the musician's lap; later models came in many different sizes, often richly decorated with ivory, mother of pearl, and marble.

HARPSICHORD

The harpsichord (or continuo) is a keyboard instrument that produces sound by a mechanical action that plucks each string with a plectrum rather than striking it with a hammer (like the piano). The result is a crisp tonal quality and clarity, heightened by the fact that notes cannot be sustained. (A harpsichord has no dynamics, that is, there is no loud and soft—all notes are played with the same intensity.) The harpsichord was the primary harmonic accompaniment instrument of Baroque music, featuring in many famous works, such as Bach's *Goldberg Variations*.

CELESTA

The celesta, a keyboard instrument like a small upright piano, was patented in 1886 by harmonium builder Auguste Mustel. Instead of striking strings, the felted pads strike steel plates suspended over wooden resonators. The sound is similar to that of a glockenspiel. Although a member of the percussion section, the celesta is almost always played by a pianist.

PIANO

The piano has been, and continues to be, arguably one of the most crucial instruments in the history of western classical, jazz, and popular music. It is classified as a percussion instrument—when the string is struck by the hammer it resonates, producing sound. There are two types of piano: The grand and the upright, each with 88 keys, made up of seven octaves plus a minor third. Most pianos have three pedals—the soft pedal, sostenuto, and the sustain.

Some noted pianists

Alfred Cortot 1877–1962

Artur Rubinstein 1887–1982

Claudio Arrau 1903–1991

Vladimir Horowitz 1903–1989

Sviatoslav Richter 1915–1997

Géza Anda 1921–1976

Glenn Gould 1932–1982

Alicia de Larrocha b. 1923

Vladimir Ashkenazy b. 1937

Stephen Hough b. 1961

PERCUSSION

PERCUSSION

The percussion section plays an integral role in the overall sound of the modern symphony orchestra. Providing different textures and embellishments, percussion instruments include the glockenspiel, vibraphone, marimba, snare drum, bass drum, cymbals, mallet, triangle, chimes, gong, tam tams, shakers, castanets, cabasa, etc. Percussionists often have to play a number of instruments in each piece, jumping from one to the other as the music demands.

Some noted percussionists
James Blades 1901–1999
Evelyn Glennie b. 1965

BASS DRUM

While not the most featured instrument in the orchestra by any means, the concert bass drum plays a crucial part in creating the "feel" for a piece of music. To play the instrument takes a great deal of skill as there are many variables—including the position on the drum to be hit, the type of beater, the intensity of the stroke, and whether or not the stroke is muffled. All contribute to the overall texture, coloring, and shading of a piece of music.

TIMPANI

The timpani or kettledrum consists of a skin, or head, stretched over a copper bowl, which is struck to create a sound. Unlike most drums, when struck the timpani produces a definite pitch and can be tuned during the performance with the use of a pedal. A set of standard timpani consists of four drums.

Some noted timpanists
Fred D. Hinger 1921–2001
Louis Charbonneau b. 1932
Richard Miller b. 1948

DRUM KIT

While combinations of various
percussion instruments have been used
in countless orchestral works over the
centuries, the drum kit (or drum set) has gone
widely unnoticed as a tool for composers. The
early part of the twentieth century saw the invention of the bass drum pedal as well as the hi-hat
stand, and these essentially completed the modern
drum kit we know today. The exact make-up of
a drum kit varies depending on genre, style, repertoire, and the individual musician playing it, but a
standard set-up includes bass drum, snare drums,
one to three toms, hi-hats, and cymbals.

VIBRAPHONE

This mallet-played instrument is similar to the xylophone, marimba,
and glockenspiel, but with aluminum bars; it also has a sustain pedal,
like a piano. The vibraphone has resonators—thin-walled aluminum
tubes underneath each tone bar, which amplify the sound of each note;
a motor is attached to these resonators controlling the volume.
A damper pad attached to the pedal is used to deaden the sound.
Invented in the 1920s, the instrument has a three-octave
range and can be played with two mallets or
four mallets (two in each hand).

Some noted conductors

Arturo Toscanini 1867–1957
Sir Henry Wood 1869–1944
Serge Koussevitzky 1874–1951
Sir Thomas Beecham 1879–1961
Leopold Stokowski 1882–1977
Otto Klemperer 1885–1973
Wilhelm Furtwängler 1886–1954
Sir Adrian Boult 1889–1983
Karl Böhm 1894–1981
Eugene Ormandy 1899–1985
Sir John Barbirolli 1899–1970
Herbert von Karajan 1908–1989
Sir Georg Solti 1912–1997

Georg Tintner 1917–1999
Sir Charles Mackerras b. 1925
Bernard Haitink b. 1929
Nicholas Harnoncourt b. 1929
Richard Bonynge b. 1930
Lorin Maazel b. 1930
Rafael Frühbeck de Burgos b. 1933
Zubin Mehta b. 1936
Edo de Waart b. 1941
James Levine b. 1943
Michael Tilson Thomas b. 1944
Marin Alsop b. 1956
Simone Young b. 1961

Clockwise from top right Sir Thomas Beecham photographed in 1945; Herbert von Karajan in 1976; Leopold Stokowski in 1950; the conductors Bruno Walter, Arturo Toscanini, Erick Kleiber, Otto Klemperer, and Wilhelm Fürtwangler photographed at a reception for Toscanini in 1929.

The Orchestra

A full-sized modern symphony orchestra consists of around 90 to 100 musicians. The stringed instruments make up the largest section of the orchestra—there are usually about 12–16 first violins, 10–14 second violins, 8–12 violas, 8–10 cellos, and eight double basses. The principal first violin is known as the concertmaster.

The 12–16-member woodwind section is made up of flutes, piccolos, oboes, cor anglais, clarinets, bass clarinets, bassoons, and contrabassoons. The brass section typically has four French horns, three or four trumpets, three trombones, and a tuba.

The percussion section is responsible for the timpani, snare and bass drums, cymbals, gongs, glockenspiels, chimes, triangle, and a range of other instruments.

The orchestra is directed by the conductor who stands on a podium in front of the musicians.

PERCUSSION   CYMBALS   BASS DRUM   TIMPANI

FRENCH HORNS   TRUMPETS   TROMBONES   TUBA

BASS CLARINET CLARINETS   BASSOONS   BASSES

PICCOLOS   FLUTES   OBOES   BASSES

PIANO
Normal position
when in use

HARP   SECOND VIOLINS   VIOLAS

FIRST VIOLINS   CELLOS

CONDUCTOR

Discover the Music

The following pages contain a collection of some of the music written by the many composers who are featured in *Musica*. This list is presented in chronological order. It is not intended to be a comprehensive listing of all the composers' works; rather it provides a small selection of compositions chosen to reflect some major works, and serves as a starting point for people wishing to discover the music for themselves.

CHAPTER 1

THE PRE-BAROQUE PERIOD: MUSIC BEFORE 1600

HILDEGARD OF BINGEN (1098–1179)

Symphonia—the collection of Hildegard's music for the Divine Office, Mass, saints days, and other ceremonial occasions; between 70–80 pieces in total.

Ordo virtutem

GUILLAUME DE MACHAUT (c. 1300–1377)

"Qui es promesses – Ha! Fortune – Et non est qui adjuvat"

"Ma fin est ma commencement" (musical palindrome)

"Rose, liz, printemps, verdure"

Messe de Notre Dame

GUILLAUME DUFAY (1397–1474)

Nuper rosarum flores

Adieu ces bons vins de Lannoys

GILLES BINCHOIS (c. 1400–1460)

De plus en plus

JOHANNES OCKEGHEM (c. 1410–1497)

In hydraulis

Plus regrets

JOSQUIN DESPREZ (c. 1440–1521)

Missa Hercules Dux Ferrariae

Missa La sol fa re mi

Miserere mei, Deus

Faulte d'argent

Une musque de Biscaye

O virgo prudentissima

Ave Maria virgo serena

Missa de beata virgine

JOHN TAVERNER (c. 1490–1545)

Mass "Western wind"

Missa Gloria tibi Trinitas

The Mean Mass

Ave Dei Patris filia

Settings of the *Magnificat*

THOMAS TALLIS (c. 1505–1585)

Spem in alium

Miserere nostri

Lamentations

Salvator mundi

Mass "Puer natus est nobis"

"God grant we grace" (*Tallis canon*)

Dorian Service

PIERLUIGI PALESTRINA (1525–1594)

Missa Papae Marcelli

Dum complerentur

Nigra sum

ORLANDO DI LASSO (1532–1594)

In me transierunt

Cum essem parvulus

Missa Pro defunctis

Missa Locutus sum

Veni creator spiritus

Susanne un jour

Un advocate dit à sa femme

Prophetiae sibyllarum

WILLIAM BYRD (c. 1543–1623)

Emendemus in melius (1575)

Miserere mihi Domine (1575)

Walsingham variations

My Ladye Nevells Booke (1591)

Mass settings for three, four and five voices (1593–1595)

Save me, O God, for thy Name's sake

Crowned with flowers and lilies (1611)

TOMÁS LUIS DE VICTORIA (1548–1611)

Vere languores

Missa pro victoria

Officium defunctorum

O magnum mysterium

Officium Hebdomadae Sanctae

O vos omnes

Missa Dum complerentur

CHAPTER 2

THE BAROQUE PERIOD
c. 1600–1750

CLAUDIO MONTEVERDI (1567–1643)

Cruda Amarilli (Fifth Book of Madrigals) (1605)

Orfeo (1607)

Lasciatemi morire (Arianna) (1608)

Vespro della Beata Vergine (1610)

Lasciatami morire (Sixth Book of Madrigals) (1614)

Il Combattimento di Tancredi e Clorinda (Eighth Book of Madrigals) (1638)

Il Ritorno d'Ulisse in Patria (1640)

L'Incoronazione di Poppea (1643)

BARBARA STROZZI (1619–1677)

Donna di maestà, di valor tanto, Op. 2 (1651)

Gite, o giorni dolenti, Op. 2 (1651)

Amor, non dormir più, Op. 2 (1651)

Non mi dite, Op. 2 (1651)

Questa è la nova, Op. 3 (1654)

Amor è bandito, Op. 6 (1657)

Lagrime mie, Op. 7 (1659)

JEAN-BAPTISTE LULLY (1642–1687)

Le Bourgeois Gentilhomme (1670)

Cadmus et Hermione (1673)

MARC-ANTOINE CHARPENTIER (1643–1704)

Le Malade Imaginaire (1672)

Tenebrae compositions (1680)

David et Jonathas (1688)

Te Deum (1690)

Messe de minuit pour Noël (c. 1690)

Medée (1693)

Missa Assumpta est Maria (1698–1702)

ARCANGELO CORELLI (1653–1713)

12 Trio Sonatas, Op. 1 (1681)

12 Trio Sonatas, Op. 2 (1685)

12 Trio Sonatas, Op. 3 (1689)

12 Trio Sonatas, Op. 4 (1694)

12 Solo Sonatas, Op. 5 (1700)

12 Concerti Grossi, Op. 6 (1714)

MARIN MARAIS (1656–1728)

Pièces de viol, Book 1 (1685)

Pièces de viol, Book 3 (1711)

ALESSANDRO SCARLATTI (1660–1725)

Gli equivoci nel sembiante (1679)

Del Tirreno sul Lido (1697)

Il Mitridate Eupatore (1707)

Cantata pastorale (1716)

Il trionfo dell'onore (1718)

Messa di Santa Cecilia (1720)

12 Sinfonie di concerto grosso (1720)

HENRY PURCELL (1659–1695)

"Thou Knowest, Lord" (1674)

"Rejoice in the Lord Alway" (the "Bell Anthem") (1683–1684)

"An Evening Hymn" (1688)

Dido and Aeneas (1689)

King Arthur (1691)

"The Blessed Virgin's Expostulation" (1693?)

"Lord, What is Man" (1693)

Come Ye Sons of Art Away (includes the duet "Sound the Trumpet") (1694)

The Indian Queen (1695)

ELISABETH-CLAUDE JACQUET DE LA GUERRE (1665–1729)

Pièces de clavessin (1687)

Les jeux à l'honneur de la victoire (c. 1691; lost)

Céphale et Procris (1694)

Vocal music including three books of French cantatas (1708, 1711, c. 1715)

Pièces de clavecin qui peuvent se jouer sur le viollon (1707)

Te Deum (1721; lost)

FRANÇOIS COUPERIN (1668–1733)

Leçons de ténèbres (1713–1717)

Airs in Recueils d'airs sérieux et à boire (1697–1712)

Le Parnasse, ou L'apothéose de Corelli, in *Les goûts-réünis* (1724)

L'apothéose de Lulli and *Les nations: sonades et suites de simphonies en trio* (1726)

Pièces de clavecin (1713, 1716–17, 1722, 1730)

TOMASO ALBINONI (1671–1751)

Mass for three unaccompanied male voices (c. 1694?)

Cantatas for voice and basso continuo

100 pieces of chamber music for between one and six instruments

12 Concerti a cinque Op. 5 (1707)

12 Concerti a cinque Op. 7 (1715)

12 Concerti a cinque Op. 9 (1722)

ANTONIO VIVALDI (1678–1741)

Gloria in D, RV 589

Nulla in mundo pax sincera, RV 630

Concerto for Mandolin in C, RV 425

L'estro armonico, Op. 3 (1711)

La stravaganza, Op. 4 (1714)

Il cimento dell'armonia e dell'inventione, Op. 8 (1725)

GEORG PHILIPP TELEMANN (1681–1767)

Suite in A Major for recorder and strings, TWV55:a2

Pastorelle en Musique (1712–1721)

Musique de Table (1723)

12 "Paris" quartets (1730–1738)

Symphony No. 1 in G major "Cricket", TWV50:1

Suite Burlesque de Quixotte in G major, TWV55:G10

JEAN-PHILIPPE RAMEAU (1683–1764)

Hippolyte et Aricie (1733)

Dardanus (1739)

Pièces de Clavecin en Concerts (1741)

Zoroastre (1749, rev. 1756)

Les Paladins (1760)

DOMENICO SCARLATTI (1685–1757)

555 keyboard sonatas

Il prigionero fortunato (1698)

GEORGE FRIDERIC HANDEL (1685–1759)

Rinaldo (1711)

The Water Music (1715–1717)

The Harmonious Blacksmith, from *Suite No. 5 in E* (1720)

Giulio Cesare (1724)

Rodelinde (1725)

Coronation Anthems (1727)

Concerti grossi, Op. 6 (1739)

The Messiah (1742)

Music for the Royal Fireworks (1749)

JOHANN SEBASTIAN BACH (1685–1750)

Brandenburg Concertos (1701–1728)

Cantata Wachet auf, BWV 140

Coffee Cantata, BWV 211

Cello Suites

St Matthew Passion, BWV 244 (1727)

The Well-Tempered Clavier Books 1 and 2 (1722; 1738–1742)

Mass in B minor, BWV 232

Goldberg Variations, BWV 988 (1741–1742)

Partita No. 2 in D minor, BWV 1004

Art of the Fugue, BWV 1080 (1745–1750)

GIOVANNI BATTISTA PERGOLESI (1710–1736)

La Serva Padrona (1733)

Polonaise No. 6, Op. 53 (1842)

Fantasy in F minor Op. 49 (1841)

ROBERT SCHUMANN (1810–1856)

Dichterliebe, Op. 48 (1840)

Piano Concerto, Op. 54 (1841–1845)

Kreisleriana, Op. 16 (1838, rev. 1850)

Symphony No. 3, "Rhenish", Op. 97 (1850)

CLARA SCHUMANN (1819–1896)

Piano Concerto, Op. 7 (1836)

Souvenir of Vienna, Op. 9 (1838)

Piano Trio, Op. 17 (1847)

Romance (1856)

FRANZ LISZT (1811–1886)

Années de Pèlerinage (1844–1877)

Hungarian Rhapsody No. 2 (1847)

Piano Concerto No. 1 (1849, revised 1853, 1856)

Prometheus, (1850, revised 1855)

Rigoletto Paraphrase (1859)

Mephisto Waltz No. 3 (1883)

GIUSEPPE VERDI (1813–1901)

Nabucco (1841)

Rigoletto (1850–1851)

La traviata (1852–1853)

Il trovatore (1853)

Aida (1871)

Requiem (1873–1874)

RICHARD WAGNER (1813–1883)

The Flying Dutchman (1841)

Lohengrin (1846–1848)

Die Walküre (1854–1856)

Tristan und Isolde (1859)

Siegfried Idyll (1870)

5 Wesendonck Songs (1857–1858)

JACQUES OFFENBACH (1819–1880)

Orpheus in the Underworld (1858)

La belle Hélène (1864)

The Tales of Hoffmann (1880)

NINETEENTH-CENTURY OPERA

Der Freischütz (*The Freeshooter*) (Carl Maria von Weber, 1786–1826)

Les Huguenots (Giacomo Meyerbeer, 1791–1864)

Lucia di Lammermoor (Gaetano Donizetti, 1797–1848)

Norma (Vincenzo Bellini, 1801–1835)

A Life for the Tsar (Mikhail Glinka, 1804–1857)

Faust (Charles Gounod, 1818–1893)

The Cunning Little Vixen (Leoš Janáček, 1854–1928)

ANTON BRUCKNER (1824–1896)

Ave Maria (1861)

Mass No. 2 in E minor (1866)

Symphony No. 4 ("Romantic") (Version 1, 1874)

String Quintet in F major (1879)

Te Deum (1881–1884)

Symphony No. 8 (1884–1887)

BEDŘICH SMETANA (1824–1884)

Six Characteristic Pieces (1848)

Piano Trio in G minor (1855, rev. 1857)

The Bartered Bride (1866)

String Quartet No. 1 in E minor, (*From My Life*) (1876)

Má vlast (1872–1879)

JOHANN STRAUSS II (1825–1899)

Annen Polka, Op. 117

Perpetuum Mobile, Op. 257 (1862)

The Blue Danube, Op. 314 (1867)

Tales from the Vienna Woods, Op. 325 (1868)

Women, Wine and Song, Op. 333

Emperor Waltz, Op. 437

Die Fledermaus (1874)

JOHANNES BRAHMS (1833–1897)

Serenades for Orchestra, Op. 11 and 16 (1857–1859)

Violin Concerto, Op. 77 (1878)

Piano Concerto No. 2, Op. 83 (1878–1881)

Two Rhapsodies, Op. 79 (1879)

Symphony No. 4, Op. 98 (1884–1885)

Clarinet Quintet, Op. 115 (1891)

Four Serious Songs, Op. 121 (1896)

ALEXANDER BORODIN (1833–1887)

Piano Quintet (1862)

Symphony No. 2 (1869–1876)

String Quartet No. 1 (1877–1879)

In the Steppes of Central Asia (1880)

String Quartet No. 2 (1881–1887)

Prince Igor (completed by Rimsky-Korsakov and Glazunov) (1890)

CAMILLE SAINT-SAËNS (1835–1921)

Symphony No. 3 ("Organ") (1866)

Danse macabre, Op. 40 (1874)

Piano Concerto No. 2, Op. 22 (1875)

Samson et Dalila (1878)

Carnaval des Animaux (1886)

GEORGES BIZET (1838–1875)

Symphony in C (1855)

The Pearl Fishers (*Les Pêcheurs de perles*) (1863)

Jeux d'Enfants (*Children's Games*) (1871)

L'Arlésienne Suites 1 (1872) and 2 (by Guiraud)

Carmen (1873–1874)

MODEST MUSSORGSKY (1839–1881)

Svetik Savishna (1866)

Night on the Bare Mountain (1867)

Boris Godunov (1872)

Pictures at an Exhibition (1874)

Songs and Dances of Death (1875–1877)

The Song of the Flea (1879)

PYOTR TCHAIKOVSKY (1840–1893)

Romeo and Juliet overture (1869)

String Quartet No. 2, Op. 22 (1874)

Piano Concerto No. 1, Op. 23 (1875)

Eugene Onegin (1879)

Capriccio Italien, Op. 45 (1880)

Serenade for Strings, Op. 48 (1880)

Symphony No. 6 "Pathetique", Op. 74 (1893)

ANTONÍN DVOŘÁK (1841–1904)

Cypresses, song cycle for tenor and piano (later arranged for string quartet) (1865)

Dumka Piano Trio No. 4, Op. 90 (1890-91)

Violin Concerto in A minor, Op. 53 (1879-80)

Symphony No. 9 "From the New World" (1893)

String Quartet in F major, Op. 96, "The American" (1893)

Humoresques, Op. 101 (1894)

Cello Concerto in B minor, Op. 104 (1895)

EMMANUEL CHABRIER (1841–1894)

L'étoile (1877)

España (1883)

Gwendoline (1885)

Le roi malgré lui (1887)

10 Pièces pittoresques (1880)

Six mélodies (1890)

EDVARD GRIEG (1842–1907)

Piano Concerto in A minor, Op. 16 (1868)

Holberg Suite, Op. 40 (1884)

Violin Sonata No. 3 in C minor, Op. 45 (1887)

Peer Gynt Suites 1, Op. 46 (1888) and 2, Op. 55 (1891)

Lyric Pieces Books 1–10 (1867–1901)

NIKOLAI RIMSKY-KORSAKOV (1844–1908)

Capriccio Espagnol, Op. 34 (1887)

Scheherazade, Op. 35 (1888)

Russian Easter Festival Overture, Op. 36 (1888)

The Golden Cockerel (1907)

GABRIEL FAURÉ (1845–1924)

Élégie, Op. 24 (1880)

Dolly Suite, Op. 56 (1894–1897)

Clair de Lune, Op. 46 (1887)

Requiem in D minor, Op. 48 (1887–1890)

Pavane, Op. 50 (1887)

Masques et Bergamasques, Op. 112

CHAPTER 5

LATE ROMANTIC PERIOD– MID-TWENTIETH CENTURY

EDWARD ELGAR (1857–1934)

Enigma Variations, Op. 36 (1899)

Dream of Gerontius, Op. 38 (1900)

Pomp and Circumstance Marches, Op. 39 (1901)

The Apostles, Op. 49 (1903)

The Kingdom, Op. 51 (1906)

Cello Concerto, Op. 85 (1919)

ETHEL SMYTH (1858–1944)

Serenade (1890)

Mass in D (1891)

Fantasio (1898)

Der Wald (1902)

The Wreckers (1902–1904)

The March of the Women (1911)

The Boatswain's Mate (1913–1914)

Entente Cordiale (1925)

Double Concerto for violin, horn and orchestra (1926)

GIACOMO PUCCINI (1858–1924)

Manon Lescaut (1893)

La Bohème (1896)

Tosca (1900)

Il trittico (Il tabarro, Suor Angelica, Gianni Schicchi) (1918)

Madama Butterfly (1904)

Turandot (1926)

GUSTAV MAHLER (1860–1911)

Wunderhorn Songs (1887–1893)

Lieder eines fahrenden Gesellen (1883–1885)

Symphony No. 1 "Titan" (1884)

Symphony No. 2 "Resurrection" (1888–1894)

Symphony No. 4 (1892–1900)

Symphony No. 5 (1901–1902)

Kindertotenlieder (1901–1904)

Symphony No. 8 (1906)

Das Lied von der Erde (1908–1909)

Symphony No. 9 (1908–1909)

RICHARD STRAUSS (1864–1949)

Don Juan, Op. 20 (1888)

Till Eulenspiegel's Merry Pranks, Op. 30 (1894–1895)

Also Sprach Zarathustra, Op. 30 (1895)

Salome (1905)

Der Rosenkavalier (1911)

An Alpine Symphony (1915)

Ariadne auf Naxos (1916)

Capriccio (1942)

Four Last Songs (1948)

CLAUDE DEBUSSY (1862–1918)

Prelude à l'Aprés-Midi d'un Faune (1892–94)

La Mer (1903–1905)

Images (1905–1912)

Children's Corner (1906–1908)

Préludes (1910–1913)

Cello Sonata (1915)

ERIK SATIE (1866–1925)

3 Gymnopédies (1888)

3 Gnossiennes (1890)

Vexations (1892)

Parade (1917)

Socrate (1919)

ALEXANDER GLAZUNOV (1865–1936)

Stenka Razin Op. 85 (1884)

Raymonda Op. 57 (1897)

The Seasons Op. 67 (1900)

Violin Concerto in A minor, Op. 82 (1904)

JEAN SIBELIUS (1865–1972)

Karelia Suite, Op. 11 (1893)

Finlandia, Op. 26 (1899)

Symphony No. 2, Op. 43 (1901)

Violin Concerto, Op. 47 (1903)

String Quartet (Voces intimae), Op. 56 (1908–1909)

Symphony No. 4, Op. 63 (1911)

Symphony No. 7, Op. 105 (1924)

The Tempest, Op. 109 (1925)

CARL NIELSEN (1865–1931)

Helios (1903)

Masquerade (1904–06)

String Quartet No. 4 in F, Op. 44 (1906)

Symphony No. 3, Sinfonia espansiva, Op. 27 (1910–11)

Violin Concerto Op. 33 (1911)

Springtime on Fyn, Op. 42 (1921)

Symphony No. 5, Op. 50 (1921–22)

Wind Quintet, Op. 43 (1922)

Flute Concerto (1926)

Clarinet Concerto, Op. 57 (1928)

AMY CHENEY BEACH (1867–1944)

Symphony No. 1 "Gaelic" (1896)

Piano Concerto in C sharp minor, Op. 45 (1899)

ALEXANDER SCRIABIN (1872–1915)

Piano Concerto, Op. 20 (1896)

Symphony No. 3 (Divine Poem), Op. 43 (1905)

Poem of Ecstasy, Op. 54 (1908)

Prometheus—Poem of Fire, Op.60 (1910)

Piano Sonata No. 9 (Black Mass), Op. 68 (1912–1913)

SERGEI RACHMANINOV (1873–1943)

Morceaux de Fantaisie, Op. 3 (1892)

Piano Concerto No.2, Op. 18 (1901)

Symphony No. 2, Op. 27 (1908)

Vespers, Op. 37 (also known as *All-Night Vigil*) (1915)

Rhapsody on a Theme of Paganini in A minor, Op. 43 (1934)

RALPH VAUGHAN WILLIAMS (1872–1958)

Sea Symphony (1909)

On Wenlock Edge (1909)

Fantasia on a Theme of Thomas Tallis (1910)

Symphony No. 2 (1913)

The Lark Ascending (1914)

Symphony No. 5 (1943)

Symphony No. 7 (Sinfonia Antarctica) (1949–1952)

GUSTAV HOLST (1874–1934)

Savitri (1908)

Beni Mora (1912)

The Planets, Op. 32 (1914–1916)

Hymn of Jesus, Op. 37 (1917)

Fugal Concerto (1923)

Egdon Heath, Op. 47 (1927)

CHARLES IVES (1874–1954)

Variations on "America" (1891)

String Quartet No. 1, From the Salvation Army (1897–1900)

The Unanswered Question (1906, rev. 1934)

Symphony No. 3, The Camp Meeting (1908–1910)

Three Places in New England (1910–1914, rev. 1929)

Piano Sonata No. 2, Concord, Mass: 1840–1860 (1916–1919, rev. many times)

ARNOLD SCHOENBERG (1874–1951)

Verklärte Nacht, Op. 4 (1899)

Gurre-Lieder, Op. 8 (1901/1911)

Three Piano Pieces, Op. 11 (1909)

Erwartung, Op. 17 (1909)

Pierrot Lunaire, Op. 12 (1912)

Variations for Orchestra, Op. 31 (1926–1928)

Moses und Aron (unfinished) (1930–1932)

String Quartet No. 4, Op. 37 (1936)

MAURICE RAVEL (1875–1937)

Rapsodie Espagnole (1907)

L'heure Espagnole (1907–1909)

Gaspard de la Nuit (1908)

Ma Mère l'Oye (Mother Goose) (1908–1910)

Daphnis et Chloé (1909–1912)

Le Tombeau de Couperin (1919)

L'enfant et les Sortilèges (1920–1925)

Boléro (1928)

OTTORINO RESPIGHI (1879–1936)

The Roman Trilogy (1914–1928)

Ancient Airs and Dances, Suites 1, 2, and 3 (1917–1932)

Vetrata di Chiesa (Church Windows) (1925)

Gli Uccelli (The Birds) (1927)

Lucrezia (1935)

BÉLA BARTÓK (1881–1945)

Allegro Barbaro (1911)

String Quartet No. 2 (1915–1917)

String Quartet No. 5 (1934)

Music for Strings, Percussion and Celesta (1936)

Violin Concerto No. 2 (1937–1938)

Concerto for Orchestra (1943)

Piano Concerto No. 3 (1945)

GEORGE ENESCU (1881–1955)

Romanian Rhapsodies (1901, 1902)

Piano Suite No. 2 in D major, Op. 10 (1903)

Oedipe (1938)

IGOR STRAVINSKY (1882–1971)

The Firebird (1910)

Petrushka (1912)

The Rite of Spring (1913)

The Soldier's Tale (1918)

Les Noces (The Weddings) (1923)

Pulcinella (1920)

Oedipus Rex (1927)

The Rake's Progress (1951)

Requiem Canticles (1964)

ANTON WEBERN (1883–1945)

Passacaglia, Op. 1 (1908)

Five Songs, after Dehmel (1906–1908)

Six Pieces for Orchestra, Op. 6 (1909–1910)

Six Bagatelles for String Quartet, Op. 9 (1913)

Five pieces for orchestra, Op. 10 (1911–1913)

Concerto for Nine Instruments, Op. 24 (1934)

Cantata No. 1, Op. 29 (1938–1939)

Cantata No. 2, Op. 31 (1941–1943)

ALBAN BERG (1885–1935)

Piano Sonata, Op. 1 (1907–1908)

String Quartet, Op. 3 (1910)

Five Orchestral Songs, Op. 4 (1912)

Three Orchestral Pieces, Op. 6 (1914–1915)

Wozzeck, Op. 7 (1914–1922)

Lyric Suite (1925–1926)

Violin Concerto (1935)

Lulu (1925–1939)

LATIN AMERICAN COMPOSERS

First Symphony in D major (1901) (Julián Carrillo, 1875–1965)

Concierto del sur for guitar and orchestra (1941) (Manuel Ponce, 1882–1948)

La voz de las calles (1920) (Humberto Allende, 1885–1959)

Piano Sonata No. 2 (1925) (Juan Carlos Paz, 1899–1972)

Dedalus (1950) (Juan Carlos Paz, 1899–1972)

Cantata de los rios de Chile Op. 19 (1941) (Domingo Santa Cruz (1899–1987)

HEITOR VILLA-LOBOS (1887–1959)

Bachianus Brasileiras

Guia Prático Nos. 1 to 9

Suite populaire brésilienne (1908–1912)

SERGEI PROKOFIEV (1891–1953)

The Gambler, Op. 24 (1917)

Classical Symphony, Op. 25 (1917)

First Violin Concerto, Op. 19 (1917)

The Love for Three Oranges, Op. 33 (1919)

Lieutenant Kijé, Op. 60 (1934)

Romeo and Juliet, Op.64 (1936)

Peter and the Wolf (1936)

War and Peace, Op. 91 (1943)

PAUL HINDEMITH (1895–1963)

Das Nusch-Nuschi (1921)

Kammermusik Nos. 2 –7 (1924–1927)

Das Marienleben (1923, 1948)

Piano Suite 1922, Op. 26

Concerto for Orchestra, Op. 38 (1925)

Mathis der Maler (symphony) (1934)

Mathis der Maler (opera) (1938)

Nobilissima Visione (1938)

Symphonic Metamorphoses on Themes of Weber (1943)

CARL ORFF (1895–1982)

Carmina Burana (1937)

Der Mond (1939)

Catulli Carmina (1943)

Die Kluge (1943)

Trionfo di Afrodite (1953)

Nänie und Dithyrambe (1956)

GEORGE GERSHWIN (1898–1937)

Rhapsody in Blue (1924)

Lady Be Good (1924)

Piano Concerto in F (1925)

Oh, Kay! (1926)

Strike Up the Band (1927)

Funny Face (1927)

An American in Paris (1928)

Girl Crazy (1930)

Of Thee I Sing (1931)

Cuban Overture (1932)

Porgy and Bess (1935)

FRANCIS POULENC (1899–1963)

Sextet for piano and winds, Op. 100 (1932–1939)

Concerto in G minor for organ, strings, and timpani (1938)

Violin Sonata, Op. 119 (1942–1943)

Horn Elégie, Op. 168 (1957)

La Voix Humaine (1958)

Clarinet Sonata, Op. 184 (1962)

CHAPTER 6

COMPOSERS BORN AFTER 1900

AARON COPLAND (1900–1990)

Piano Variations (1930)

El salon México (1932–1936)

Billy the Kid (1938)

Rodeo (1942)

Fanfare for the Common Man (1942)

Appalachian Spring (1943, 1957 reworking)

Piano Fantasy (1952–1957)

Connotations (1962)

Inscape (1967)

JOAQUIN RODRIGO (1901–1999)

Concierto de Aranjuez (1939)

Fantasia para un gentilhombre (1954)

Invocación y danza (1961)

Concierto Andaluz (1967)

Concierto madrigal (1968)

Concierto pastoral (1978)

Concierto como un divertimentio (1981)

WILLIAM WALTON (1902–1983)

Viola Concerto (1929)

Belshazzar's Feast (1931)

Symphony No. 1 (1935)

Henry V (1944)

Richard III (1955)

ARAM KHACHATURIAN (1903–1978)

Trio for Clarinet, Violin and Piano (1932)

Piano Concerto (1936)

Masquerade (1941)

Gayaneh (1942)

Symphony No. 2 ("Bell") (1943)

Spartacus (1954)

Concerto–Rhapsody for cello and orchestra (1963)

MICHAEL TIPPETT (1905–1998)

Symphony No. 2 (1957)

Piano Sonata (1937)

Concerto for Double String Orchestra (1939)

A Child Of Our Time (1941)

The Vision of Augustine (1965)

The Mask of Time (1984)

DMITRI SHOSTAKOVICH (1906–1975)

Symphony No. 1 (1923–1924)

Piano Concerto No. 1 (1933)

Symphony No. 5 (1937)

Symphony No. 7 "Leningrad" (1941)

Violin Concerto No. 1 (1947–1948)

From Jewish Folk Poetry (1948)

String Quartet No. 4 (1949)

Piano Concerto No. 2 (1957)

String Quartet No. 8 (1960)

OLIVIER MESSIAEN (1908–1992)

Le banquet célestiale (1928)

L'Ascension (1933)

Quatuor pour la fin du temps (1940)

Vingt regards sur l'enfant Jésus (1944)

Turangalila-Symphonie (1946–1948)

Catalogue d'oiseaux (1956–1958)

Et exspecto resurrectionum mortuorem (1964)

Méditations sur le mystère de la Sainte Trinité (1969)

Des canyons aux étoiles (1971–1974)

SAMUEL BARBER (1910–1981)

The School for Scandal, Op. 5 (1931)

Symphony No. 1, Op. 9 (1936)

First Essay for Orchestra, Op. 12 (1937)

Adagio for Strings, Op. 11 (1936)

Medea, Op. 23 (1947)

Hermit Songs, Op. 29 (1952–1953)

Vanessa, Op. 32 (1957)

Piano Concerto, Op. 38 (1962)

JOHN CAGE (1912–1992)

First Construction (in Metal) (1939)

Bacchanale (1940)

Living Room Music (1940)

Sonatas and Interludes (1946–1948)

4'33" (1952)

HPSCHD (1967–1969)

Two (1987)

BENJAMIN BRITTEN (1913–1976)

Variations on a Theme of Frank Bridge (1937)

Peter Grimes (1945)

The Rape of Lucretia (1946)

The Young Person's Guide to the Orchestra (1947)

Albert Herring (1947)

Billy Budd (1951)

The Turn of the Screw (1954)

Noye's Fludde (1957)

War Requiem (1962)

WITOLD LUTOSLAWSKI (1913–1994)

Concerto for Orchestra (1954)

Funeral Music in memoriam Béla Bartók
    (1956)

Venetian Games (1961)

String Quartet (1964)

Cello Concerto (1967)

Preludes and Fugue (1972)

Chain 1–3 (1983–1986)

DOUGLAS LILBURN (1915–2001)

Aotearoa (1940)

Symphony No. 3 (1961)

LEONARD BERNSTEIN (1918–1990)

Symphony No. 1 (Jeremiah) (1943)

On the Town (1944)

Suite from On the Waterfront (1954)

Candide (1956)

West Side Story (1957)

Symphony No.3 (Kaddish) (1963)

Chichester Psalms (1965)

Mass (1971)

GALINA USTVOLSKAYA (1919–2006)

Trio for Clarinet, Violin, and Piano (1949)

Piano Sonata No. 2 (1949)

Violin Sonata (1952)

Symphonic Poem No. 1 (1958)

Grand Duet for Piano and Cello (1959)

Duet for Piano and Violin (1964)

Composition No. 1 Dona Nobis Pacem (1971)

Symphony No. 3 Jesus Messiah Save Us (1983)

GYÖRGY LIGETI (1923–2006)

Atmosphères (1961)

Requiem (1965)

Chamber Concerto (1970)

Le Grand Macabre (1975)

Horn Trio (1983)

Etudes for piano (three books, 1985–2001)

Hamburg Concerto (2002)

PIERRE BOULEZ (B. 1925)

Le soleil des eaux (1950)

Le visage nuptial (1951–1952)

Le marteau sans maitre (1953–1955)

Piano Sonata No. 3 (1955–1957)

Pli selon Pli (1957–1962)

Eclat (1965)

Repons (1980–1984)

KARLHEINZ STOCKHAUSEN
    (1928–2007)

Kreuzspiel (1951)

Gruppen for 3 Orchestras (1957)

Kontakte (1960)

Stimmung for 6 vocalists (1968)

Mantra for 2 pianists (1970)

Freitag aus *Licht* (1996)

Freude (second hour of *Klang*) (2006)

PETER SCULTHORPE (b 1929)

Irkanda IV (1961)

Sun Music I (1965)

Mangrove (1979)

Piano Concerto (1983)

Earth Cry (1986)

Kakadu (1988)

String Quartet No. 11 (1990)

Great Sandy Island (1998)

Requiem (2004)

GEORGE CRUMB (b. 1929)

Ancient Voices of Children (1970)

SOFIA GUBAIDULINA (b. 1931)

Offertorium (1980)

Stimmen ... Verstummen ... (1986)

Hommage à T. S. Eliot (1987)

Music for Flute, Strings, and Percussion
    (1994)

Viola Concerto (1997)

Two Paths: A Dedication to Mary and
    Martha (1998)

St John's Passion (2000)

Feast during a Plague (2006)

ARVO PÄRT (b. 1935)

Credo (1968)

Cantus in Memoriam Benjamin Britten
    (1976)

Wenn Bach Bienen Verzüchtet Hätte (1976)

Fratres (1977–c. 1992; this appears in
    several instrumentations)

Summa (several instrumentations)

Festina Lente (1988)

Magnificat (1989)

STEVE REICH (b. 1936)

Drumming (1970–1971)

The Desert Music (1984)

PHILIP GLASS (b. 1937)

Music in Twelve Parts (1971–1974)

Einstein on the Beach (1976)

Satyagraha (1980)

Koyaanisqatsi (1982)

Akhnaten (1983)

Concerto for Violin and Orchestra (1987)

Symphony No. 1 "Low" (1992)

The Hours (2002)

JOHN CORIGLIANO (b. 1938)

Symphony No. 2 (2001)

JOAN TOWER (b. 1938)

Fanfare for the Uncommon Woman (1987)

GILLIAN WHITEHEAD (b. 1941)

Puhake Ki Te Rangi (2006)

MEREDITH MONK (b. 1942)

Atlas (1991)

JACK BODY (b. 1944)

Pulse (1995)

JOHN ADAMS (b. 1947)

Nixon in China (1985–1987)

Harmonielehre (1984–1985)

LAURIE ANDERSON (b. 1947)

O Superman (1981)

KAIJA SAARIAHO, b. 1952

Verblendungen (1984)

Lichtbogen (1986)

Noa-Noa (1992)

Graal théâtre (1994)

L'Amour de loin (2000)

Adriana mater (2005)

La Passion de Simone (2006)

Notes on Light (2007)

THE WORLD'S GREAT CONCERT HALLS

The great concert halls and opera theaters of the world are visited each year by many thousands of people. These buildings are home to symphony orchestras, opera and ballet companies, theatrical groups, and various other performing artists. Some of the most famous concert halls and opera houses, such as Milan's La Scala, have been around for hundreds of years. Others, such as the Finlandia Concert Hall in Helsinki, which opened in 1971, are much more recent.

Yet they all share certain characteristics, the most important of which is acoustics. Generally speaking, the great concert venues are designed with excellent acoustic properties, where volume is maximized without unnecessary reverberation. As well, these grand theaters can seat many people in comfort. Another consideration is the beauty of the building itself. This is why some of the major performing venues are also significant landmarks of their cities. Who does not recognize the distinctive sails of the Sydney Opera House or the irregular forms of Berlin's Philharmonic Hall?

A handful of the world's most important and impressive concert halls and opera houses is presented on the following pages.

Below and right Finlandia Concert Hall, Helsinki, Finland

Above   The Royal Opera House, London, England

Previous pages   Concertgebouw, Amsterdam, The Netherlands

Above Zurich Opera House, Zurich, Switzerland

Top The Royal Festival Hall, London, England

Following pages Vienna State Opera, Vienna, Austria

Above and right Paris Opera House, Paris, France

Above Festspielhaus, Bayreuth, Germany

Previous pages Mozarteum, Salzburg, Austria

Above Philharmonic Hall, Berlin, Germany
Following pages National Theater, Munich, Germany

Above Bolshoi Theatre, Moscow, Russia
Following pages Mariinsky Theater, St Petersburg, Russia

PATRIAE ET MUSIS

Above Hungarian State Opera House, Budapest, Hungary

Left State Opera House, Prague, Czech Republic

Below and following pages La Scala, Milan, Italy

Above and left Palau de la Musica Catalana, Barcelona, Spain

Following pages Romanian Athenaeum, Bucharest, Romania

Below Teatro Real, Madrid, Spain

Above Cairo Opera House, Cairo, Egypt

Following pages Golda's Center Opera House, Tel Aviv, Israel

Above Shanghai Grand Theater, Shanghai, China
Following pages Sydney Opera House, Sydney, Australia

Above Metropolitan Opera House, Lincoln Center for
the Performing Arts, New York, USA

Left Carnegie Hall, New York, USA

Above and following pages Walt Disney Concert Hall, Los Angeles, USA

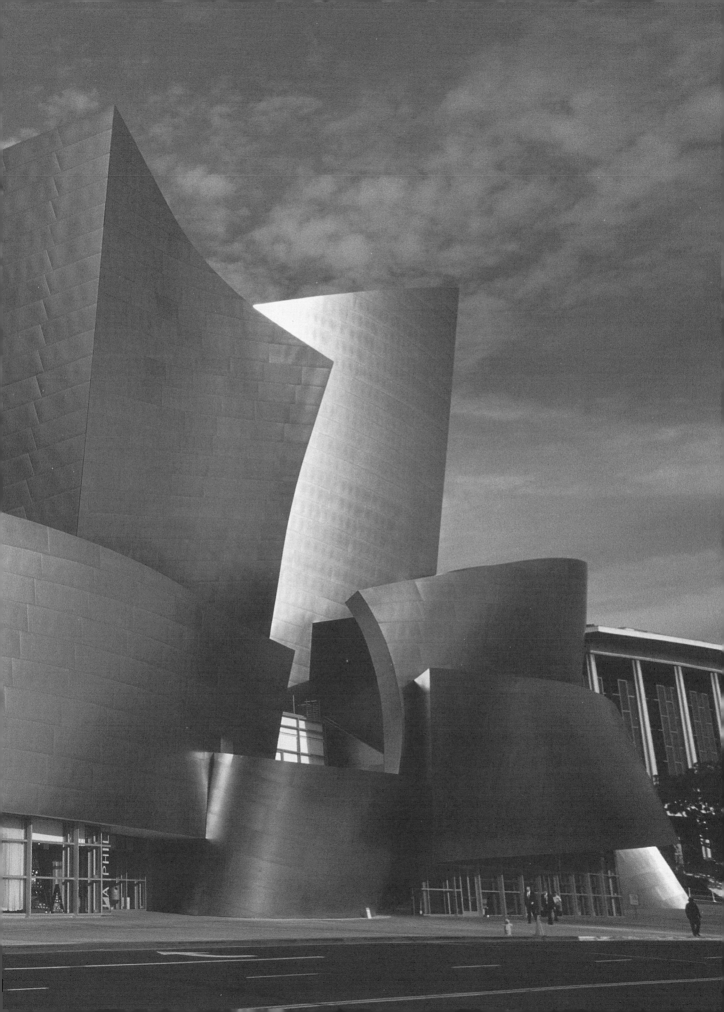

Above and right Teatro Colon, Buenos Aires, Argentina

Following pages Teatro Amazonas, Manaus, Brazil

A Brief Glossary of Musical Terms

Adagio: A term directing that the music be played slowly.

Aleatoric music: Music in which some part of a composition is established by chance elements.

Allegro: A term directing that the music be played fast and lively.

Aria: An operatic vocal solo.

Arpeggio: Where the notes of a chord are played separately, one after the other, instead of altogether.

Atonal: Not written in any key.

Andante: A term directing that the music be played at a "walking pace," that is, moderately slowly.

Cadenza: A virtuoso passage for a solo instrument. It is often, but not always, at the end of a work.

Cantata: A work for voices and instruments usually based on a sacred text, but it can also be secular.

Castrato: A male singer who had been castrated before reaching puberty, in order that he retain a high voice, most commonly soprano, but alto as well.

Chamber music: Music originally intended to be performed in a small venue or chamber. A chamber ensemble typically consists of between two to eight instrumentalists. They perform trios, quartets, quintets, etc.

Chord: A group of three or more notes played at the same time.

Chromatic scale: A scale that ascends or descends in semitones.

Clef: The symbol placed at the beginning of every line of music to indicate the pitch and register of the notes to be played.

Coda: The concluding passage of a piece of music.

Concerto: A musical work for orchestra and one or more solo instruments.

Concerto grosso: A concerto for a group of solo instruments with orchestral accompaniment.

Counterpoint: Where two or more equally important melodies are played at the same time. The adjective is "contrapuntal."

Divertimento: A piece of lighthearted music usually performed by chamber musicians.

Dodecaphony: *See* Serialism.

Forte: A term directing that the music be played loud.

Fugue: A composition in which the subject (the central melodic motif) is played first by one voice, then restated and developed contrapuntally through staggered entries of additional voices. (In this instance, "voice" means each individual part of a composition; it is not necessarily vocal.)

Gregorian chant: *See* Plainsong.

Homophony: The opposite of counterpoint, that is, music where a principle melody is accompanied by other voices in harmony or "chordally." The adjective is "homophonic."

Kapellmeister: The director or conductor of an orchestra or other musical ensemble.

Lento: A term directing that the music be played slowly.

Libretto: The text of an opera.

Lieder (plural of Lied [meaning "song"]): A type of song, typically German, performed by a solo singer accompanied by piano. Can be part of a song cycle.

Madrigal: A song for a small group of unaccompanied vocalists singing in harmony.

Melisma: A group of notes that is sung to one syllable of text. It was commonly used in Gregorian chants.

Minimalism: A compositional style characterized by simplification of rhythms and harmonies, and the use of repetition.

Minuet: A dance in three-four time.

Moderato: A term directing that the music be played at a moderate speed.

Monophony: Music with a single melodic line without any accompaniment.

Motet: Vocal polyphonic music where the parts move generally in counterpoint.

Motif, motive: A thematic element that recurs throughout the piece of music.

Neo-classicism: A musical movement during the first half of the twentieth century that aimed to return to compositional features of the Classical and Baroque periods.

Nocturne: A short expressive work, usually for piano, evoking the night.

Opera buffa: Italian comic opera popular in the eighteenth century.

Oratorio: A large-scale work for voices and instruments usually with a sacred theme, performed without costumes or scenery.

Orchestration: The manner in which a composition uses the different instruments of the orchestra. Also called "arranging" or "instrumentation."

Overture: (1) A short piece of orchestral music that comes before an opera, ballet, or oratorio and intended as an introduction to that work. (2) A one-movement, stand-alone orchestral work.

Piano: A term directing that the music be played softly. Also the common name of the instrument pianoforte.

Pizzicato: A technique whereby the strings of an instrument (violin, viola, cello, bass) are plucked rather than bowed.

Plainsong: Monophonic liturgical music for unaccompanied voices. Also called Gregorian chant and plainchant.

Polyphony: Music with two or more voices or parts that are played at the same time.

Prelude: (1) A piece of music normally played as an introduction to another piece of music such as a fugue. (2) A self-contained short work often composed for the piano.

Presto: A term directing that the piece be played very fast.

Program music: A work of a descriptive, narrative, or pictorial nature.

Recitative: A singing style that follows the rhythms of normal speech. It is used as a narrative device in opera.

Rondo: A musical form in which the main theme recurs from time to time.

Scale: The stepwise arrangement, either ascending or descending, of the notes of a given key, for example, the scale of B major.

Scherzo: A fast, light, playful piece in triple time.

Semitone: The smallest interval between notes used in the Western Classical tradition. It is equal to half a tone.

Serialism: A method of composing in which the composition is based around a tone row, which is when each note of the chromatic scale is placed in a sequential "row" or "series." No pitch in the row may be repeated before all twelve pitches have sounded—thereby assuring that no one pitch is more prominent than any other one.

Sonata: A musical work for one or more solo instruments, one of which is usually the piano. There are typically three or four movements.

Sonata form: The basic structure of the opening movement of a Classical work such as the sonata or symphony, beginning with the exposition, which presents the main subject or themes of the work. The first theme is written in the tonic or "home" key; the second theme in a different key. The exposition is followed by the development, where the themes are varied. Following this is the recapitulation, where the subjects are restated in the tonic key. The recapitulation also often contains a coda.

Song cycle: A set of songs, usually based on a poetic work, intended to form a single musical entity.

Stabat mater: A hymn whose subject is the sorrow of the Virgin Mary at the Crucifixion of Jesus Christ.

Suite: A set of musical works intended to be played in succession. (1) The classic suite of dance style pieces developed in the seventeenth century and consisted of the allemande, courante, sarabande, and gigue, played in that order. Later suites often included other dances such as the gavotte, minuet, and passepied. (2) In later centuries composers arranged "suites" of the most popular sections of their stage works, especially of ballets, for concert performance.

Symphony: A large, imposing orchestral work usually, but not always, in four movements. The first movement is often in sonata form.

Tempo: The speed at which a piece of music should be played.

Tone-poem: A large orchestral work with the scope of a symphony but freer in form. Also known as "symphonic poem," it is usually in one extended movement.

Tremolo: The rapid repetition of the same note to create a tremulous effect.

Twelve-tone method: *See* Serialism.

Vibrato: The slight variation in the pitch of a note to create a pulsating effect.

Vivace: A term directing the music to be played fast and vivaciously.

INDEX

Page numbers in **bold** indicate main entry.

CREDITS AND ACKNOWLEDGEMENTS

The Publisher would like to thank the following picture libraries and other copyright owners for permission to reproduce these images.

KEY: (t) top of page; (b) bottom of page; (l) left side of page; (r) right side of page; (c) center of page

Front cover image: Mel Curtis/Photonica/Getty Images
Back cover image: Josef Danhauser/Bridgeman Art Library/Getty Images
Endpapers: © Martin Schutt/dpa/Corbis

1 The Art Archive/Bergen Theatre Museum/Alfredo Dagli Orti; 2–3 The Art Archive/Musée des Beaux Arts Lyon/Gianni Dagli Orti; 4–5 The Art Archive/Musée Hector Berlioz (maison natale) La Côte-Saint-André/Gianni Dagli Orti; 7 © Andy Warhol Foundation/Corbis; 10–11 © Robbie Jack/Corbis; 12–13 The Art Archive/Art Gallery of New South Wales; 14–15 The Art Archive/Musée des Arts Décoratifs Paris/Alfredo Dagli Orti; 16 © Jacques Sarrat/Sygma/Corbis; 17(t) The Art Archive/Museo Teatrale alla Scala Milan/Alfredo Dagli Orti; 17(c) © David Lees/Corbis; 17(b) The Art Archive/Bela Bartok House Budapest/Alfredo Dagli Orti; 18(t) © Michael Nicholson/Corbis; 18(b) © Bettmann/Corbis; 19(t) © Christie's Images/Corbis; 19(b) The Art Archive/San Nicola Basilica Tolentino/Gianni Dagli Orti; 20(t) The Art Archive/Richard Wagner Museum Bayreuth/Alfredo Dagli Orti; 20(b) © Minnesota Historical Society/Corbis; 21(t) Photo Scala, Florence; 21(b) © Robbie Jack/Corbis; 22–23 Photo Scala, Florence, courtesy of the Ministero Beni e Att. Culturali; 24(c) unique-dimension.com-Edimedia; 24(b) uniquedimension.com-Edimedia; 25(t) uniquedimension.com-Edimedia; 25(b) uniquedimension.com-Ann Ronan Picture Library; 26, 27 uniquedimension.com-Ann Ronan Picture Library; 28(t) uniquedimension.com-Ann Ronan Picture Library; 28(br) uniquedimension.com-World History Archive; 29 uniquedimension.com-World History Archive; 30(t), (b) unique-dimension.com-Edimedia; 31(t) The Art Archive/British Library; 31(b) uniquedimension.com-World History Archive; 32(b) uniquedimension.com-The Literature Archive; 33(t) unique-dimension.com-The Literature Archive; 33(b) uniquedimension.com-Edimedia; 34, 35 uniquedimension.com-Edimedia; 36 uniquedimension.com-World History Archive; 37(t) Photo Scala, Florence; 37(b) uniquedimension.com-Edimedia; 38 © The Gallery Collection/Corbis; 39(t) The Art Archive/Palazzo Reale Milan/Gianni Dagli Orti; 39(b) uniquedimension.com-Edimedia; 40 uniquedimension.com-World History Archive; 41(t) The Art Archive; 41(b) uniquedimension.com-World History Archive; 42(c) uniquedimension.com-World History Archive; 42(b) uniquedimension.com-The Literature Archive; 43(l) Photo Scala, Florence; 43(r) bpk/Musikinstrumenten-Museum, SPK/Jürgen Liepe/Scala, Florence; 44, 45 unique-dimension.com-World History Archive; 46, 47(t) uniquedimension.com-World History Archive; 47(b) Photo Scala, Florence; 48(l) The Art Archive/Museo Tridentino Arte Sacra Trento/Alfredo Dagli Orti; 48(b) uniquedimension.com-World History Archive; 49 The Art Archive/Gulbenkian Foundation Lisbon/Gianni Dagli Orti; 50(t) uniquedimension.com-World History Archive; 50(b) uniquedimension.com-Edimedia; 51(t) bpk/Musikinstrumenten-Museum, SPK/Jürgen Liepe/Scala, Florence; 51(b) The Art Archive/Usher Art Gallery Lincoln/Eileen Tweedy; 52(t), (b) uniquedimension.com-The Literature Archive; 53(t) uniquedimension.com-World History Archive; 53(b) © Bettmann/Corbis; 54–55 © Tibor Bognar/Corbis; 55(t) uniquedimension.com-The Literature Archive; 55(r) uniquedimension.com-World History Archive; 56 Image copyright The Metropolitan Museum of Art/Art Resource/Scala, Florence; 57(t) The Art Archive/Academia de la Lengua Madrid/Laurie Platt Winfrey; 57(b) © The Gallery Collection/Corbis; 58–59 The Art Archive/Museo del Prado Madrid/Alfredo Dagli Orti; 60(t) The Art Archive/Gianni Dagli Orti; 60(c) The Art Archive/Biblioteca Nazionale Turin/Gianni Dagli Orti; 61 The Art Archive/Academia BB AA S Fernando Madrid; 62(t), (b) Photo Scala, Florence, courtesy of the Ministero Beni e Att. Culturali; 63(t) © Bob Jacobson/Corbis; 63(b) The Art Archive/Museo Civico Modena/Alfredo Dagli Orti; 64(c) Photo Scala, Florence; 64(br) Photo Scala, Florence; 65 The Art Archive/Museo Correr Venice/Alfredo Dagli Orti; 66 Photo Scala, Florence/BPK, Bildagentur fuer Kunst, Kultur und Geschichte, Berlin 67(l) The Art Archive/Musée du Louvre Paris/Gianni Dagli Orti; 67(r) Photo Austrian Archive/Scala Florence; 68 The Art Archive/Galleria Corsini Rome/Gianni Dagli Orti; 69(t) Photo Scala, Florence; 69(b) Photo Scala, Florence, courtesy of the Ministero Beni e Att. Culturali; 70 © Annebicque Bernard/Corbis Sygma; 71(l) The Art Archive/Collection Comedie Francaise Paris/Marc Charmet; 71(r) Photo Scala, Florence; 72 The Art Archive/Musée Carnavalet Paris/Gianni Dagli Orti; 73(t) The Art Archive/Musée Thomas Dobrée Nantes/Gianni Dagli Orti; 73(b) © Stefano Bianchetti/Corbis; 74(t) Photo Scala Florence/HIP; 74(c) Photo Scala, Florence; 74(b) © Michael Busselle/Corbis; 75 Laurentius de Neter, Bridgeman Art Library/Getty Images; 76 The Art Archive/San Pietro Maiella Conservatoire Naples/Gianni Dagli Orti; 77(t) The Art Archive/Gripsholm Castle Sweden/Alfredo Dagli Orti; 77(b) Photo Scala, Florence; 78(c) © The Art Archive/Corbis; 78(b) © Bob Jacobson/Corbis; 79 © The Art Archive/Corbis; 80 The Art Archive/Museo Bibliografico Musicale Bologna/Alfredo Dagli Orti; 80–81 The Art Archive/Museo Correr Venice/Gianni Dagli Orti; 81(b) The Art Archive/Musée du Louvre Paris/Alfredo Dagli Orti; 82(t) © Bettmann/Corbis; 82–83 Photo Scala, Florence, courtesy of the Ministero Beni e Att. Culturali; 83 © Historical Picture Archive/Corbis; 84–85(c) The Art Archive/London Museum/Eileen Tweedy; 85(t) © Blue Lantern Studio/Corbis; 85(b) The Art Archive/Museo Tosio Martinengo Brescia/Alfredo Dagli Orti; 86(t) Photo Scala, Florence; 86(c) © Graham Salter/Lebrecht Music & Arts/Corbis; 86(b) bpk/Musikinstrumenten-Museum, SPK/Jürgen Liepe/Photo Scala, Florence; 87(t) Photo Scala, Florence, courtesy of the Ministero Beni e Att. Culturali; 87(bl) The Art Archive/Musée des Beaux Arts Strasbourg/Gianni Dagli Orti; 87(br) bpk/Musikinstrumenten-Museum, SPK/Jürgen Liepe/Photo Scala, Florence; 88 Photo Scala, Florence, courtesy of the Ministero Beni e Att. Culturali; 89(t) © Fine Art Photographic Library/Corbis; 89(b) © Christie's Images/Corbis; 90(t) White Images/Scala, Florence; 90(b) The Art Archive/Bibliothèque des Arts Décoratifs Paris/Gianni Dagli Orti; 91 The Art Archive/Gianni Dagli Orti; 92(t) The Art Archive/Bibliothèque des Arts Décoratifs Paris/Gianni Dagli Orti; 93(t) The Art Archive/Château de Blois/Gianni Dagli Orti; 93(b) © Stefano Bianchetti/Corbis; 94 © Bob Jacobson/Corbis; 95(t) The Art Archive/Museo Bibliografico Musicale Bologna/Alfredo Dagli Orti; 95(b) The Art Archive/Museo Civico Modena/Alfredo Dagli Orti; 96(t) The Art Archive/National Portrait Gallery Scotland/Alfredo Dagli Orti; 96(c) The Art Archive/Pinacoteca Civica Iesi/Alfredo Dagli Orti; 97 Giovanni Paolo Pannini/Bridgeman Art Library/Getty Images; 98 © Robbie Jack/Corbis; 99(t) Photo Scala, Florence; 99(c) © Arne Hodalic/Corbis; 100(t) Photo Scala, Florence, courtesy of the Ministero Beni e Att. Culturali; 100(b) Photo Scala, Florence; 101(t) The Art Archive/San Pietro Maiella Conservatoire Naples/Alfredo Dagli Orti; The Art Archive/Musée de l'Ain Bourg-en-Bresse/Gianni Dagli Orti; 102 The Art Archive/Society Of The Friends Of Music Vienna/Alfredo Dagli Orti; 103(tl) The Art Archive/Bach House Leipzig/Alfredo Dagli Orti; 103(tr) © Image Source/Corbis; 103(b) The Art Archive/Society Of The Friends Of Music Vienna/Alfredo Dagli Orti; 104(t) © Bettmann/Corbis; 104(b) The Art Archive/Museum der Stadt Wien/Gianni Dagli Orti; 105 The Art Archive/Rheinischeslandesmuseum Bonn/Alfredo Dagli Orti; 106 The Art Archive/Museo Bibliografico Musicale Bologna/Alfredo Dagli Orti; 107(tl) The Art Archive/Bibliothèque des Arts Décoratifs Paris/Gianni Dagli Orti; 107(r) © Kazuyoshi Nomachi/Corbis; 107(b) © Leonard de Selva/Corbis; 108 The Art Archive/Musée du Louvre Paris/Gianni Dagli Orti; 109(t) © The Gallery Collection/Corbis; 109(b) Photo Scala, Florence; 110(c), (b) The Art Archive/Handel Museum Halle/Gianni Dagli Orti; 111(t) © Bettmann/Corbis; 111(b) Margaret Isabel Dicksee/Bridgeman Art Library/Getty Images; 112(t) © Robbie Jack/Corbis; 112(b) © Angelo Hornak/Corbis; 113 Patrick Riviere/Getty Images; 114 The Art Archive/Museo Bibliografico Musicale Bologna/Alfredo Dagli Orti; 115(t) The Art Archive/Tate Gallery London/Eileen Tweedy; 115(b) Photo Scala, Florence; 116(t) © Bettmann/Corbis; 116(b) | © Martin Schutt/dpa/Corbis; 117 © Bettmann/Corbis; 118(l) © Dave Bartruff/Corbis; 118(r) The Art Archive/Bach House Leipzig/Alfredo Dagli Orti; 119(t) © Bettmann/Corbis; 119(b) © Hulton-Deutsch Collection/Corbis; 121(t) The Art Archive/Musée du Château de Versailles/Gianni Dagli Orti; 121(c) White Images/Scala, Florence; 121(b) The Art Archive/Ca Rezzonico Museum Venice/Gianni Dagli Orti; 122(t) The Art Archive/Canova Museum Possagno/Alfredo Dagli Orti; 122(b), 123 White Images/Scala, Florence; 124–125 Photo Austrian Archive/Scala Florence; 126(t) 510004106 World History Archive/Edimedia; 126(b) White Images/Scala, Florence; 127(t), (b) World History Archive/Edimedia; 128(t) World History Archive/Edimedia; 128(b) The Art Archive/Bach House Leipzig/Alfredo Dagli Orti; 129(t) The Art Archive/Handel Museum Halle/Alfredo Dagli Orti; 129(b) World History Archive/ARPL; 130(l) Photo Austrian Archive/Scala Florence; 130(b) bpk/Musikinstrumenten-Museum, SPK/Jürgen Liepe/Scala Florence; 131(l) The Art Archive/Mozart Apartment Vienna/Gianni Dagli Orti; 131(r) The Art Archive/National Library, Budapest/Gianni Dagli Orti; 132(t), (b) The Art Archive/Museum der Stadt Wien/Alfredo Dagli Orti; 133 The Art Archive/Museum der Stadt Wien/Alfredo Dagli Orti; 134 © The Gallery

Collection/Corbis; 135(c) World History Archive/ARPL; 135(br) © Bob Jacobson/Corbis; 136(t) World History Archive/ARPL; 137(t), (b) World History Archive/ARPL; 138(t) The Art Archive/Private Collection Paris/Gianni Dagli Orti; 138(b) World History Archive/ARPL; 139(t) The Art Archive/Beethoven Museum Bonn/Gianni Dagli Orti ; 139(b) White Images/Scala, Florence; 140 Photo Scala Florence/HIP; 141(t) World History Archive/ARPL; 141(b) World History Archive/Edimedia; 142(t), (b) World History Archive/Edimedia; 143(t) World History Archive/Edimedia; 143(b) bpk/Musikinstrumenten-Museum, SPK/Antonia Weiße/Scala Archive; 144 World History Archive/Edimedia; 145(t), (b) World History Archive/Edimedia; 146 World History Archive/Edimedia; 147(t) © The Art Archive/Corbis; 147(b) World History Archive/Edimedia; 148(t) © Comstock/Corbis; 148(b) © Robbie Jack/Corbis; 149 The Art Archive/Museum der Stadt Wien/Alfredo Dagli Orti; 150 White Images/Scala, Florence; 151(t) Photo Austrian Archive/Scala Florence; 151(b) The Art Archive/Mozarteum Salzburg/Alfredo Dagli Orti; 152(t) The Art Archive/Society Of The Friends Of Music Vienna/Alfredo Dagli Orti; 152(b) The Art Archive/Casa Goldoni Museum Venice/Alfredo Dagli Orti; 153(t) The Art Archive/Society Of The Friends Of Music Vienna/Alfredo Dagli Orti; 153(b) The Art Archive/Theatre Museum London/V&A; 154(l) The Art Archive/Historisches Museum (Museen der Stadt Wien) Vienna/Gianni Dagli Orti; 154(r) © Bettmann/Corbis; 155(l) World History Archive/Edimedia; 155(r) © Bettmann/Corbis; 156(t) The Art Archive/Beethoven House Vienna/Alfredo Dagli Orti; 156(b) The Art Archive/Society Of The Friends Of Music Vienna/Gianni Dagli Orti; 157 The Art Archive/Beethoven House Bonn/Gianni Dagli Orti; 158 Photo Scala, Florence; 159(t) World History Archive/Edimedia; 159(b) Gianni Dagli Orti/Corbis; 160(t) World History Archive/Edimedia; 160(b) The Art Archive/Topkapi Museum Istanbul/Alfredo Dagli Orti; 161 The Art Archive/University Library Istanbul/Gianni Dagli Orti; 162–163 Getty Images/Bridgeman Art Library/Josef Danhauser; 164(t) The Art Archive/Museum der Stadt Wien/Alfredo Dagli Orti; 164(c) © Swim Ink 2, LLC/Corbis; 165(l) Louis Edmond Pomey/Fine Art Photographic/Getty Images; 165(b) The Art Archive/Bibliothèque des Arts Décoratifs Paris/Gianni Dagli Orti; 166 The Art Archive/Accademia Carrara Bergamo Italy/Gianni Dagli Orti; 166–167 Photo Scala, Florence; 167(b) DeAgostini Picture Library/Scala, Florence; 168(t) © Leonard de Selva/Corbis; 168(b) The Art Archive/Museo Bibliografico Musicale Bologna/Alfredo Dagli Orti; 169(t) bpk/Musik-instrumenten-Museum, SPK/Jürgen Liepe, Scala Florence; 169(b) © Robbie Jack/Corbis; 171(t) White Images/Scala, Florence; 171(b) © Bettmann/Corbis; 172(t) © Michael Nicholson/Corbis; 172(b) © The Art Archive/Corbis; 173 © The Art Archive/Corbis; 174(l) © Bettmann/Corbis; 174(r) Photo Scala, Florence/BPK, Bildagentur fuer Kunst, Kultur und Geschichte, Berlin; 175 Photo Scala, Florence/BPK, Bildagentur fuer Kunst, Kultur und Geschichte, Berlin; 176 The Art Archive/Bodleian Library Oxford; 177(t) Imagno/Austrian Archives/Getty Images; 177(b) Photo Scala Florence/HIP; 178(t) © Bettmann/Corbis; 178(b) © Aldo Pavan/Grand Tour/Corbis; 179 © Christie's Images/Corbis; 180(b) The Art Archive/Society Of The Friends Of Music Vienna/Alfredo Dagli Orti; 180–181 The Art Archive/Bibliothèque des Arts Décoratifs Paris/Gianni Dagli Orti; 181 The Gallery Collection/Corbis; 182(t) © The Art Archive/Corbis; 182(b) © Stefano Bianchetti/Corbis;

183 The Art Archive/Musée des Beaux Arts Lyon/Gianni Dagli Orti; 184(t) © The Art Archive/Corbis; 184(b) The Art Archive/Musée du Château de Versailles/Alfredo Dagli Orti; 185 The Art Archive/Musée d'Art et d'Histoire Metz/Gianni Dagli Orti; 186 The Art Archive/Museum der Stadt Wien/Alfredo Dagli Orti; 187(t) The Art Archive/Walter/Guillaume Coll L'Orangerie Paris/Alfredo Dagli Orti; 187(b) Hulton Archive/Getty Images; 188 © Dave G. Houser/Corbis; 189(t) © Fine Art Photographic Library/Corbis; 189(b) © Envision/Corbis; 190 © Bettmann/Corbis; 191 (t) The Art Archive/Schumann birthplace/Alfredo Dagli Orti; 191(b) © Michael Nicholson/Corbis; 192(t) The Art Archive/Liszt House, Weimar, Germany/Alfredo Dagli Orti; 192(b) © Bettmann/Corbis; 193 The Art Archive/Society Of The Friends Of Music Vienna/Alfredo Dagli Orti; 194(b) © The Gallery Collection/Corbis; 195 The Art Archive/Mohammed Khalil Museum Cairo/Gianni Dagli Orti; 196(l) © Hulton-Deutsch Collection/Corbis; 196(t) The Art Archive/Museo Teatrale alla Scala Milan/Gianni Dagli Orti; 197(t) Dorling Kindersley/Getty Images; 197(b) © Stringer/epa/Corbis; 198(b) The Art Archive/Museo del Risorgimento Rome/Gianni Dagli Orti; 198–199 The Art Archive/Alfredo Dagli Orti; 199(b) Photo Scala, Florence; 200 © Bettmann/Corbis; 201(t) The Art Archive/Richard Wagner Museum Bayreuth/Alfredo Dagli Orti; 201(b) The Art Archive/Neuschwanstein Castle Germany/Gianni Dagli Orti; 202(t) © Bettmann/Corbis; 202(b) © Bettmann/Corbis; 203 The Art Archive/Richard Wagner Museum Bayreuth/Alfredo Dagli Orti; 204 The Art Archive/Culver Pictures; 205(t) Fine Art Photographic/Hulton Archive/Getty Images; 205(b) The Art Archive/Sally Chappell; 206(t) The Art Archive/Museum der Stadt Wien/Alfredo Dagli Orti; 206(l) © Bettmann/Corbis; 207(t) © The Art Archive/Corbis; 207(b) The Art Archive/Museum der Stadt Wien/Alfredo Dagli Orti; 208, 209 The Art Archive/Museum der Stadt Wien/Alfredo Dagli Orti; 210(t) © The Art Archive/Corbis; 210(b) © David Arky/Corbis; 211(t) The Art Archive/Kunsthistorisches Museum Vienna/Gianni Dagli Orti; 211(b) The Art Archive/Museum der Stadt Wien/Alfredo Dagli Orti; 212 The Art Archive/Marc Charmet; 213(t) The Art Archive/Musée Carnavalet Paris/Marc Charmet; 213(b) The Art Archive/Museum der Stadt Wien/Alfredo Dagli Orti; 214(t) © Bettmann/Corbis; 214(b) Jonathan Smith, Lonely Planet/Getty Images; 215 © The Art Archive/Corbis; 216(t) The Art Archive/Conservatoire Prague/Alfredo Dagli Orti; 216(c),(b), 217(c) The Art Archive/Dvorak Museum Prague/Alfredo Dagli Orti; 217(b) © Peter Adams/Corbis; 218, 218–219 The Art Archive/National Gallery Budapest/Gianni Dagli Orti; 219(r) The Art Archive/Museum der Stadt Wien/Alfredo Dagli Orti; 220(t) © Bettmann/Corbis; 220(b) Oliver Benn/Getty Images; 221 © Bettmann/Corbis; 222(l) The Art Archive/Château-Musée de Dieppe/Alfredo Dagli Orti; 221(r) © Gianni Dagli Orti/Corbis; 223 The Art Archive/Bibliothèque des Arts Décoratifs Paris/Gianni Dagli Orti; 224(t) © The Art Archive/Corbis; 224(b) © Hulton-Deutsch Collection/Corbis; 225 © Robbie Jack/Corbis; 226 The Art Archive/Bibliothèque des Arts Décoratifs Paris/Gianni Dagli Orti; 227(t) © The Art Archive/Corbis; 227(b) The Art Archive/Musée d'Orsay Paris/Alfredo Dagli Orti; 228 The Art Archive/Conservatoire des Arts et Métiers Paris/Marc Charmet; 229(t) © Alfred/epa/Corbis; 229(cr) The Art Archive/Kharbine-Tapabor; 230(t) © The Art Archive/Corbis; 230(b) The Art Archive/Bibliothèque des Arts Décoratifs Paris/Gianni Dagli Orti; 231(t) The Art Archive; 231(b) The Art Archive/Victoria and

Albert Museum London/Eileen Tweedy; 232(t) Photo Scala, Florence; 232(b) Jonathan Smith/Lonely Planet Images/Getty Images; 233 Hulton Archive/Getty Images; 234(t) © Bettmann/Corbis; 234(b) Dorling Kindersley/Getty Images; 235 © Robbie Jack/Corbis; 236(t) The Art Archive/Miramare Museum Trieste/Alfredo Dagli Orti; 237(t) White Images/Scala, Florence; 237(b) Photo Scala, Florence; 238(t) The Art Archive/Edward Grieg House, Nordas Lake, Bergen, Norway/Alfredo Dagli Orti; 238(b) The Art Archive/Historical Museum Bergen/Alfredo Dagli Orti; 239 © Paul Almasy/Corbis; 240(b) The Art Archive/Ateneum Helsinki/Alfredo Dagli Orti; 240–241(t) The Art Archive/Maritime Museum Kronborg Castle Denmark/Alfredo Dagli Orti; 241(r) © Bettmann/Corbis; 242 The Art Archive/Bibliothèque des Arts Décoratifs Paris/Gianni Dagli Orti; 243(t) White Images/Scala, Florence; 243(b) © Bob Jacobson/Corbis; 244 The Art Archive/Musée d'Orsay Paris/Alfredo Dagli Orti; 245(t) © Hulton-Deutsch Collection/Corbis; 245(b) The Art Archive/Gianni Dagli Orti; 246–247 © Philadelphia Museum of Art/Corbis; 248(t) The Art Archive/Bela Bartok Archive Budapest/Alfredo Dagli Orti; 248(b) © Swim Ink 2, LLC/Corbis; 249(t) © Robbie Jack/Corbis; 249(b) The Art Archive/Museum der Stadt Wien/Alfredo Dagli Orti; 250 © Michael Nicholson/Corbis; 250–251(t) © Hulton-Deutsch Collection/Corbis; 251(r), (b) Photo Scala Florence/HIP; 252 Photo Scala Florence/HIP; 253(t) Hulton Archive/2007 Getty Images; 253(b) © Hulton-Deutsch Collection/Corbis; 254 The Art Archive/Private Collection/Marc Charmet; 255(t) Photo Scala Florence/HIP; 255(b) The Art Archive; 256(t) The Art Archive/Private Collection/Marc Charmet; 256(c) The Art Archive/Museum der Stadt Wien/Alfredo Dagli Orti; 257(t) Standard RM|© Chris Stock/Lebrecht Music & Arts/Corbis; 257(b) Photo Austrian Archive/Scala Florence; 258–259 Imagno/Austrian Archives/Getty Images; 260 The Art Archive/Strauss house Garmisch/Alfredo Dagli Orti; 261(t) © Robbie Jack/Corbis; 261(c) The Art Archive/Bibliothèque des Arts Décoratifs Paris/Gianni Dagli Orti; 262(l) The Art Archive/Eileen Tweedy; 262(b) The Art Archive/Domenica del Corriere/Gianni Dagli Orti; 263(c) The Art Archive/Private Collection/Marc Charmet; 263(tr) © Austrian Archives/Corbis; 263(b) © Hulton-Deutsch Collection/Corbis; 264(t) © Robbie Jack/Corbis; 264(b) © Christie's Images/Corbis; 265 The Art Archive/National Gallery Budapest/Alfredo Dagli Orti; 266(t), (l) The Art Archive/Claude Debussy Centre St Germain en Laye/Gianni Dagli Orti; 267 The Art Archive/Private Collection Paris/Gianni Dagli Orti; 268(t), (b) © Bettmann/Corbis; 269(t) © Condé Nast Archive/Corbis; 269(b) © Robbie Jack/Corbis; 270 © Francis G. Mayer/Corbis; 271(t) © Leonard de Selva/Corbis; 271(b) The Art Archive/Musée d'Orsay Paris/Gianni Dagli Orti; 272(t) Photo Scala, Florence; 272(b) The Art Archive; 273 © Robbie Jack/Corbis; 274(t) The Art Archive/Musée des 2 Guerres Mondiales Paris/Gianni Dagli Orti; 274(b) © Corbis; 275(t) © Bettmann/Corbis; 275(b) White Images/Scala, Florence; 276(t) The Art Archive/Sibelius Museum Turku Finland/Alfredo Dagli Orti; 276(l) The Art Archive/Ateneum Helsinki/Alfredo Dagli Orti; 277(t) © Condé Nast Archive/Corbis; 277(b) The Art Archive/Sibelius Museum Turku Finland/Alfredo Dagli Orti; 278 The Art Archive/Edward Grieg House, Nordas Lake, Bergen, Norway/Alfredo Dagli Orti; 279(l) The Art Archive/Alfredo Dagli Orti; 279(r) © Bettmann/Corbis; 280(t), (l) The Art Archive/Nielsen Museum Odensa Denmark/Alfredo Dagli Orti; 281 © Barbara Bindl/epa/Corbis; 282 © Corbis; 283(t) © The Gallery Collection/

Corbis; 283(b) Hulton Archive/Getty Images; 284(t) The Art Archive/Puccini Foundation Lucca/Alfredo Dagli Orti; 284(b) © Bettmann/Corbis; 285 © Vittoriano Rastelli/Corbis; 286(t) © Bettmann/Corbis; 286(c) © BBC/Corbis; 287 © Fine Art Photographic Library/Corbis; 288(t) The Art Archive/Society Of The Friends Of Music Vienna/Alfredo Dagli Orti; 288(l) The Art Archive; 289(t) © Bettmann/Corbis; 289(b) © Comstock/Corbis; 291(t) © The Gallery Collection/Corbis; 291(b) © Bettmann/Corbis; 292(t) © Hulton-Deutsch Collection/Corbis; 292(b) The Art Archive/Royal College of Surgeons/Eileen Tweedy; 293 © Robbie Jack/Corbis; 294(t) © Bettmann/Corbis; 294(c) © Robert Estall/Corbis; 294(b) © Lindsay Hebberd/Corbis; 295 Hulton Archive/Getty Images; 296 © Bettmann/Corbis; 297(t) The Art Archive/Imperial War Museum; 297(b) © Bettmann/Corbis; 298(t) © Bettmann/Corbis; 298(b) © Corbis; 299(t) © David Muench/Corbis; 299(b) © Bettmann/Corbis; 300(t) © Fine Art Photographic Library/Corbis; 300(b) © Swim Ink 2, LLC/Corbis; 301(b) © Bettmann/Corbis; 302(t) Photo Austrian Archive/Scala Florence; 302(b) © The Art Archive/Corbis; 303(l) Photo Scala, Florence/BPK, Bildagentur fuer Kunst, Kultur und Geschichte, Berlin; 303(r) Hulton Archive/Getty Images; 304(t) The Art Archive/Culver Pictures; 304(b) © Bettmann/Corbis; 305 © Ali Meyer/Corbis; 306(t) The Art Archive/Museo Teatrale alla Scala Milan/Alfredo Dagli Orti; 306(b) © Hulton-Deutsch Collection/Corbis; 307(l) The Art Archive/Bibliothèque des Arts Décoratifs Paris/Gianni Dagli Orti; 307(r) Dorling Kindersley/Getty Images; 308(t) © Bettmann/Corbis; 308(b) © David Lees/Corbis; 309 © Bob Krist/Corbis; 310(t) Hulton Archive/Getty Images; 310(b) © Bettmann/Corbis; 311(t) © Smithsonian Institution/Corbis; 311(b) © Corbis; 312(t) The Art Archive/Bela Bartok House Budapest/Alfredo Dagli Orti; 312(b) © Barbara Gindl/epa/Corbis; 313 The Art Archive/Bela Bartok House Budapest/Alfredo Dagli Orti; 314(t) The Art Archive/Private Collection/Marc Charmet; 314(b) © Yevgeny Khaldei/Corbis; 315 Pascal Pavani/AFP/Getty Images; 316(t) © Bettmann/Corbis; 316(b) The Art Archive/Conservatoire Prague/Alfredo Dagli Orti; 317(t) C Squared Studios/Getty Images; 317(b) © Robbie Jack/Corbis; 318(t) Photo Scala Florence/HIP; 318(b) The Art Archive/Walter/Guillaume Coll L'Orangerie Paris/Gianni Dagli Orti; 319(t) The Art Archive/Alfredo Dagli Orti; 319(b) The Art Archive/Private Collection Paris/Gianni Dagli Orti; 320(t), (l) Hulton Archive/Getty Images; 321 The Art Archive/Museum der Stadt Wien/Alfredo Dagli Orti; 322(t) The Art Archive/Society Of The Friends Of Music Vienna/Alfredo Dagli Orti; 322(b) © Robert Eric/Corbis Sygma; 323 The Art Archive/Alban Berg Collection Vienna/Alfredo Dagli Orti; 324(t) © Hulton-Deutsch Collection/Corbis; 324(b) © Austrian Archives/Corbis; 325 © Robbie Jack/Corbis; 326 © Condé Nast Archive/Corbis; 327(t) © Eddy Risch/epa/Corbis; 327(b) bpk/Musikinstrumenten-Museum, SPK/Jürg/Scala Archives; 328(t) © Cat's Collection/Corbis; 328(b) © Lebrecht Music & Arts/Corbis; 329(t) © Corbis; 330(tl) © Corbis; 330(tr) © William Coupon/Corbis; 331 © Bettmann/Corbis; 332(t) © Bettmann/Corbis; 332(b) Photo Scala, Florence; 333 Time & Life Pictures/Getty Images; 334(t) © Hulton-Deutsch Collection/Corbis; 334(c) Mosfilm/Kobal Collection; 334(b) © Lebrecht Music & Arts/Corbis; 335 © Shamukov Ruslan/ITAR-TASS/Corbis; 336 The Art Archive/Private Collection/Marc Charmet; 337(t) Time & Life Pictures/Getty Images; 337(b) The Art Archive/Zeller Collection Turin/Gianni Dagli Orti; 338(t) The Art Archive/Bibliothèque de l'Opéra Paris/

Eileen Tweedy; 338(b) © Condé Nast Archive/Corbis; 339 © Robbie Jack/Corbis; 340–341 © Robbie Jack/Corbis; 342(t) The Art Archive; 342(c) Paramount/Kobal Collection; 342(b) © Jacques M. Chenet/Corbis; 343 MGM/Kobal Collection; 344(t) © PoodlesRock/Corbis; 344(b) United Artists/Kobal Collection; 345(t) © Michael Ochs Archives/Corbis; 345(b) © Underwood & Underwood/Corbis; 346(t) © Bettmann/Corbis; 346(b) © Corbis Sygma; 347 © Robbie Jack/Corbis; 348(t) © Swim Ink 2, LLC/Corbis; 348(b) The Art Archive/Private Collection/Marc Charmet; 349(tl) James Andanson/Apis/Sygma/Corbis; 349(tr) The Art Archive/Zeller Collection Turin/Gianni Dagli Orti; 349(b) © Hulton-Deutsch Collection/Corbis; 350–351 © Robbie Jack/Corbis; 352(t) The Art Archive/Private Collection/Marc Charmet; 352(b) © Bettmann/Corbis; 353(t) White Images/Scala, Florence; 353(b) © Jacques M. Chenet/Corbis; 354 Photo Scala Florence/HIP; 355 © Julie Lemberger/Corbis; 356–357(t) © Bettmann/Corbis; 356(c) © Marvin Koner/Corbis; 356(b) © Bettmann/Corbis; 357(b) © Bettmann/Corbis; 358(t), (b) © Bettmann/Corbis; 359(t) © Nik Wheeler/Corbis; 359(b) bpk/Musikinstrumenten-Museum, SPK/Antonia Weiße/Scala Archives, Florence; 360(t), 361(t) World History Archive & Edimedia Archive; 361(b) © Hulton-Deutsch Collection/Corbis; 362(t) World History Archive & Edimedia Archive; 362(b), 363(t) Hulton Archive/Getty Images; 363(b), 364(b) © Hulton-Deutsch Collection/Corbis; 364–365(t) © Sebastian Widmann/dpa/Corbis; 365(b) © Condé Nast Archive/Corbis; 366(t) The Art Archive/John Meek; 367(t) The Art Archive/National Archives Washington DC; 367(b) © Lebrecht Music & Arts/Corbis; 368(t) © Dean Conger/Corbis; 368(b) © Hulton-Deutsch Collection/Corbis; 369 © Robbie Jack/Corbis; 370(bl) Photo Scala, Florence; 370(br) © Bettmann/Corbis; 371 Time & Life Pictures/Getty Images; 372(t) World History Archive & Edimedia Archive; 372(b) © Hulton-Deutsch Collection/Corbis; 373 © David Clapp/Arcaid/Corbis; 374(t) Photo Scala, Florence; 374(b) World History Archive; 376(t) © Melloul Richard/Corbis Sygma; 376(b) Roger Viollet/Getty Images; 377 Volker Hartmann/AFP/Getty Images; 378(t) © Leonard de Selva/Corbis; 378(b) © Georges Pierre/Sygma/Corbis; 379(t) © Terry Cryer/Corbis; 379(b), 380(c) © Bettmann/Corbis; 380(b) Dr Patrick Fairfield; 381(t) © Robbie Jack/Corbis; 381(b) © Brown, Jennifer/Star Ledger/Corbis; 382(t) © Bettmann/Corbis; 382(b) Orion/Kobal Collection; 383(t) © Robbie Jack/Corbis; 383(b) Michael Rougier/Time & Life Pictures/Getty Images; 384(t) © Richard Schulman/Corbis; 384(b) Anne-Christine Poujoulat/AFP/Getty Images; 385 World History Archive & Edimedia Archive; 386(t) The Art Archive/Laurie Platt Winfrey; 386(b) The Art Archive; 387(t) © Bettmann/Corbis; 387(b) © H. Armstrong Roberts/ClassicStock/Corbis; 388, 389(l) © Hulton-Deutsch Collection/Corbis; 389(r) © Uli Deck/epa/Corbis; 390(t) MGM/Kobal Collection; 390(cl) © Hulton-Deutsch Collection/Corbis; 391 © Herwig Vergult/epa/Corbis; 392(t) © Soeren Stache/epa/Corbis; 393(t) © Libor Hajsky/epa/Corbis; 393(b) © Fabian Cevallos/Corbis Sygma; 394(t) © Sophie Bassouls/Sygma/Corbis; 394(cl) © Bettmann/Corbis; 395(t) © Gideon Mendel/Corbis; 395(b) Piotr Powietrzynski/Getty Images; 396(t) World History Archive & Edimedia Archive; 396(b) Mirisch-7 ARTS/United Artists/Kobal Collection; 397(t) Coll. privée milanaise/Scala Archives; 397(b) © Patrick Chauvel/Sygma/Corbis; 398(t) bpk/Musikinstrumenten-Museum, SPK/Scala Archives, Florence; 398(bl) © Hulton-Deutsch Collection/Corbis; 398(br) © Michele Asselin/Corbis; 399(tl) © Bettmann/Corbis; 399(tr) © Comstock/Corbis;

399(b) C Squared Studios/Getty Images; 400 Mehdi Fedouach/AFP/Getty Images; 401(l) © Jacques Sarrat/Sygma/Corbis; 401(r) © Yann Arthus-Bertrand/Corbis; 402 © Hulton-Deutsch Collection/Corbis; 403(t) The Art Archive/Imperial War Museum; 403(b) © Pelletier Micheline/Corbis Sygma; 404(t) Michael Ochs Archives/Getty Images; 404(l) © Hulton-Deutsch Collection/Corbis; 405(l) © Gallery Collection/Corbis; 405(r) © Henrik Montgomery/epa/Corbis; 406(t), (b) © Bettmann/Corbis; 407(t) © Philippe Renault/Hemis/Corbis; 407(b) © Jean Louis Atlan/Sygma/Corbis; 408(t) Gaye Gerard/Getty Images; 408(b) DEA/G. Cigolini/Getty Images; 409(t) © Yann Arthus-Bertrand/Corbis; 409(b) © Penny Tweedie/Corbis; 410(t) © Bettmann/Corbis; 410(b) © Penny Tweedie/Corbis; 411(t) © Hulton-Deutsch Collection/Corbis; 411(b) © Werner Forman/Corbis; 412(t) © Gatis Diezins/epa/Corbis; 412(b) © Anne Purkiss/Lebrecht Music & Arts/Corbis; 413 © Guenter Rossenbach/zefa/Corbis; 414(l) © Pascal Le Segretain/Corbis Sygma; 414(b) Jeffrey Markowitz/Sygma/Corbis; 414–415(tl) © NASA/Roger Ressmeyer/Corbis; 415(r) © Leif Skoogfors/Corbis; 416(b) My Cactus/Kobal Collection; 416–417 Kristian Juul Pedersen/AFP/Getty Images; 417(b) Paramount/Vantage/Kobal Collection; 418(t) © Christopher Felver/Corbis; 418(b) Henrietta Butler/Redferns/Getty Images; 419(tl) © Jacques Sarrat/Sygma/Corbis; 419(r) © Condé Nast Archive/Corbis; 420(t) © Corbis; 420(b) bpk/Musikinstrumenten-Museum, SPK/Antonia Weiße/Scala Archives; 421(t) © Enrique Contla/epa/Corbis; 421(b) Institute for Regional Education/Kobal Collection; 422(t) Paramount/Miramax/Kobal Collection; 422(b) Fox Searchlight/Kobal Collection; 423 Johan Elbers/Time Life Pictures/Getty Images; 424 © Roland Schlager/epa/Corbis; 425(t) © Robbie Jack/Corbis; 425(c) Imagine Ent/Kobal Collection/Gordon, Melinda Sue; 425(b) © Corbis; 426(t) © Michael Ochs Archives/Corbis; 426(c) © Bettmann/Corbis; 426(b) Art Archive; 427(t) © Gideon Mendel/Corbis; 427(b) © Bettmann/Corbis; 428(c) © Jean Pimentel/Kipa/Corbis; 428(b) © Rudy Sulgan/Corbis; 429 © Barbara Gindl/epa/Corbis; 430(t) Thinkstock Images/Getty Images; 430(b) © Solus-Veer/Corbis; 431(t) © Stephen Chernin/epa/Corbis; 431(c) © Kimberly White/Corbis; 431(b) © Katy Raddatz/San Francisco Chronicle/Corbis; 432–433 © Lebrecht Music & Arts/Corbis; 442(b) C Squared Studios/Getty Images; 443(t) © Bettmann/Corbis; 443(cl) © Hulton-Deutsch Collection/Corbis; 443(cr), (b) © Bettmann/Corbis; 454, 455 © Adam Woolfitt/Corbis; 456–457 © Cees Van Leeuwen; Cordaiy Photo Library Ltd/Corbis; 458 © Eric Nathan/Loop Images/Corbis; 459(t) © Arcaid/Corbis; 459(b) © Atlantide Phototravel/Corbis; 460–461 © Adam Woolfitt/Corbis; 462–463 © Bob Krist/Corbis; 464(t) © Nathalie Darbellay/Sygma/Corbis; 464(b) © Hulton-Deutsch Collection/Corbis; 465 © Free Agents Limited/Corbis; 466–467 © Santos/Corbis; 468–469 © Svenja-Foto/Corbis; 470–471 © Jon Arnold/JAI/Corbis; 472–473 © Philip Gould/Corbis; 474 © Pawel Wysocki/Hemis/Corbis; 475(t) © Catherine Karnow/Corbis; 475(b) © Massimo Ripani/Grand Tour/Corbis; 476–77 © George Steinmetz/Corbis; 478 © Charles & Josette Lenars/Corbis; 479(t) © Atlan-tide Phototravel/Corbis; 479(b) © Despotovic Dusko/Corbis Sygma; 480–481 © Peter Adams/Corbis; 482–483 © Caroline Penn/Corbis; 484–485 © Hanan Isachar/Corbis; 486–487 © Justin Guariglia/Corbis; 488–489 © R. Wallace/Stock Photos/Corbis; 490 © Tom & Dee Ann McCarthy/Corbis; 491(t) © Bettmann/Corbis; 491(b) © Richard Bryant/Arcaid/Corbis; 492–493 © Kurt Krieger/Corbis; 494 Aldo Sessa/Getty Images; 495 © Bettmann/Corbis; 496–497 © Wolfgang Kaehler/Corbis